OPERATIONS STRATEGY

PRINCIPLES AND PRACTICE

OPERATIONS STRATEGY

PRINCIPLES AND PRACTICE

JAN A. VAN MIEGHEM

Harold L. Stuart Distinguished Professor of Managerial Economics
Professor of Operations Management
KELLOGG SCHOOL OF MANAGEMENT
NORTHWESTERN UNIVERSITY

Dynamic Ideas
43 Lantern Road
Belmont, Mass. 02478
U.S.A.
WWW information and orders: http://www.dynamic-ideas.com

Cover art: Maximiliaan Roger Van Mieghem (at age 3)

Library of Congress Cataloging-In-Publication Data

Van Mieghem, Jan A.
Operations Strategy: Principles and Practice
Includes bibliographical references and index
ISBN 0-9759146-6-9
1. Operations Management. 2. Strategy. 3. Business Logistics. I. Title.
HD38.5.MI 2008

Waar een wil is, is een weg
Mama en Papa

To Shannon and our future:
Maximiliaan, Katherine, Marcus and Karolien

ABOUT THE AUTHOR

Jan A. Van Mieghem

Harold L. Stuart Distinguished Professor of Managerial Economics and Professor of Operations Management at the Kellogg School of Management of Northwestern University, Dr. Van Mieghem is the chairman of the Managerial Economics and Decision Sciences department. He teaches a variety of courses in Kellogg's full-time and executive programs, including the core MBA course in operations management, an MBA elective in operations strategy, and a Ph.D. course in operations economics.

His research focuses on manufacturing, service and supply chain operations and studies both strategic questions as well as tactical execution. His articles have appeared in leading journals, including *Annals of Applied Probability, Journal of Economic Theory, Management Science, Manufacturing and Service Operations Management* and *Operations Research*. He is past editor of the operations and supply chain area of *Operations Research* and has served on the editorial board of several journals.

Professor Van Mieghem is the co-author of the MBA textbook *Managing Business Process Flows: Principles of Operations Management*. He received his Ph.D. from the Graduate School of Business at Stanford University in 1995. Born in Belgium, he currently lives in Evanston, Illinois, with his wife and four children.

PREFACE

This book explains the principles of operations strategy and describes how companies can apply these principles in practice to increase value. Designing and implementing a successful operations strategy require judgment, experience, creativity, and luck, all of which cannot be taught. What *can* be taught, however, are the concepts, principles, and tools to help you in that process—and therein lies the purpose of this book.

"Principles and practice" is my guiding motto throughout this book. Going beyond telling war-stories, my goal is thus to describe the practice of operations strategy while revealing its driving principles in a structured manner. I am writing under the assumption that *we*—which in this book means you, the reader and I, the writer—seek to build sound intuition for designing, assessing, and improving operations strategies. I believe that sound intuition results from a journey of logical analysis that culminates in a theory. Good theory gives you intuition into the familiar, and beyond.

Each chapter opens with a description of how a real company practices some aspect of operations strategy and then reviews the concepts behind that practice. Tools are provided to analyze the concepts, distill their principles, and suggest guidelines for implementation and improvement. When appropriate, state-of-the-art research findings are integrated in the discussion. Each chapter closes with a mini-case that asks you to explore how you would apply the principles and tools in practice. The last part of the book contains a set of "full-blown" cases to integrate the chapters and emphasize the relevance of our topic to practice.

To increase accessibility, most analysis is described in words and is exhibited with minimal notation and mathematics. For example, equations are stated only if they capture a relationship better than words alone can. To increase usefulness and illustrate implementation, a particular example of each analysis is worked out in a spreadsheet (all spreadsheets can be downloaded from www.vanmieghem.us). More advanced analysis or spreadsheet implementations are relegated to appendices for those who are interested.

Though we are interested in designing *good* operations strategies, strategy evaluation is as much art as it is science. We will adopt a dual perspective that combines qualitative analysis with a financial evaluation of the value created by the operations strategy. Throughout this book, value will thus be our yardstick and our guide to assess and improve operations strategy. Merging the strategic and financial perspective should be natural to the intended reader:

I have written this book with a specific focus on MBA and engineering management students, and on their instructors. I hope that the structured approach of using analysis to build intuition and reveal improvement levers within a coherent framework facilitates learning and instruction. While the book naturally follows a core course in operations and supply chain management and adopts basic financial evaluation, all concepts are explained "from scratch" to make the book accessible to every business or engineering management student. The book should also be of interest to consultants and practitioners as a reference for concepts, principles, and tools.

According to Francis Bacon, "writing makes an exact man." While a valiant goal, operations strategy is not an exact science. Nor is there an agreed-upon paradigm for its study, let alone agreement on what exactly "is part" of operations strategy. Given these constraints, this book reflects my best effort to structure concepts and principles in a unified framework for operations strategy. Like any good operation, however, this really is a process of continuous improvement. It never ends, as better ways always exist. If you have any suggestions for improvement, I welcome hearing about them.

Jan Van Mieghem (Jan@VanMieghem.us)
July 13, 2007

ACKNOWLEDGMENTS

This book results from the MBA elective course, *Operations Strategy*, that I began designing and teaching in 1998. It reflects the experience and knowledge of the colleagues, teachers, and managers that I have worked with. I have also benefited greatly from the experience, suggestions, and questions of the many MBA and executive students that I have interacted with; while I was teaching, I was learning even more.

Many people have helped me while writing this book. I would especially like to acknowledge the following people:

My students who collaborated with me or shared experiences that are described in this book: Troy Anderson, Mark Bruno, Steven Rudolf Bystriansky, Hsing-Chien (Ken) Chou, Mary Delaney (*Careerbuilder.com*), Hubert Fisher, Devika Gupta, Daisuke Kobayashi, Vikram Malhotra, Kai-Lung (Ron) Nien, Dan Nisser (*Cargill*), Thomas John O'Reilly, Chinmay Pandit, Dhruv Patel, Richard Pérez, Kitikun Prasithrathsint, Mark Price, Chris Recktenwald, Mani Sundaram, Ron Tamir, Brendan F. Tansill, Shaun Usmar, Christian Walters (*Harley-Davidson*), Stacey Watson (*Harley-Davidson*), all my OPNS454 students who provided feedback during Winter 2007 on a early version, and especially my doctoral advisee Lauren Lu (now at *Univ. of North Carolina*) for her research collaboration, careful readings, and suggestions.

All the colleagues who shared their knowledge, especially Gad Allon, Baris Ata, Sunil Chopra, and Marty Lariviere (*Northwestern University's Kellogg*) for all their encouragement during this long project. Sunil's energy and supply chain book have inspired me and Marty has been an incredibly valuable source of information on recent managerial developments. I would also like to thank: Dan Adelman (*University of Chicago*), Costis Maglaras (*Columbia University*), Serguei Netessine (*University of Pennsylvania's Wharton*), and Sharon Novak (*UCLA*) for carefully reviewing chapters and suggesting many improvements;John Birge (*University of Chicago*), Vishal Gaur (*NYU*), Steve Graves (*MIT*), Panos Kouvelis (*University of St.Louis*), Christoph Loch, Ioana Popescu and Nils Rudi (*INSEAD*), Costis Maglaras (*Columbia University*), Scott McKeon (*Northwestern University's Kellogg*), Glen Schmidt (*University of Utah*), and Serguei Netessine (*University of Pennsylvania's Wharton*) for sharing their teaching materials.

All the friends, managers, and professionals for sharing their time, knowledge and experience, especially: Eddy Dumarey (*Cortina*), Maggie and Ken Fleming (for fine culinary and carpentry provisions), Bill Fox (*Eli Lilly*), Cort Jacoby and Ruchir Nanda (*Deloitte Consulting*), Marc van Gelder and Mike Brennan (*Peapod*), Philippe Geyskens (*Digitas*), Luc Kerkhof (*Poppies*), Colin Kessinger (*Vivecon*, Jeff Pharris (*Harley-Davidson*) , Martine Van Campenhout (*Procter & Gamble*), and Dirk Wouters (*Dynaco*).

I am especially grateful to Alexandru Rus for compiling the references, glossary, and indexes, as well as for offering many suggestions; to Akhila Kolisetty for final copy-editing the entire manuscript; and to Joshua Miller for all his help during graphic design and typesetting. It is a joy having assistance of that caliber—I could not have finished this project in time without them. (They compressed time during the last week through time-shifting: Josh worked in Evanston, Alex was vacationing in Romania, and Akhila in India!) Meg Stuart and Kate Iberg edited several chapters in early format. Many thanks to Uwe Kern (author of xcolor.sty), Frank Mittelbach (author of the LaTeXCompanion), Michael Sofka, Lieven Vandenberghe, and my brother Piet for generously sharing their knowledge of LaTeX. I am grateful to my editor and colleague, Dimitris Bertsimas, for publishing my book, and to Laura Rose for her careful handling of the production.

I am particularly indebted to the organization that has graced my business card for the last 12 years—after all, this book would have never seen the light of day without the Kellogg School of Management. I am also thankful for the hospitality of the Katholieke Universiteit Leuven during my sabbatical in 2005, when half this book was written.

Finally, and most importantly, I would like to thank my lovely wife, Shannon Cahill, for her unwavering support during this project and so many others. She managed the family with a smile, even during my extensive absence during the last months of this project. It is done at last!

Jan Van Mieghem

CONTENTS

Part I

Operations Strategy: Concept and Competencies

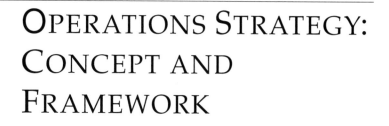

OPERATIONS STRATEGY: CONCEPT AND FRAMEWORK

There's nothing here to take by storm; to strategy we must conform.
    Johann Wolfgang von Goethe (Faust, 1808).

Learning Objectives

After reading this chapter, you will be able to:

1. Explain the concept of operations strategy and discuss its impact on an organization.
2. Adopt three complementary views to describe operations.
3. Identify the key decisions and relationships in our framework for operations strategy.
4. Use three tools to implement the principle of alignment and tailor operations strategy.

This first chapter starts by explaining the concept of operations strategy. We introduce three views to describe operations and discuss the principle of alignment or strategic fit. This naturally leads to a framework for formulating and analyzing operations strategy. The framework also identifies key decisions in operations strategy. Several tools and examples illustrate the impact of operations strategy and the technique of tailoring to increase value and alignment.

1.1 | WHAT IS OPERATIONS STRATEGY?

To explain the concept of operations strategy, we first review the meaning of strategy and operations. The word strategy originally referred to the military thought processes of the *stratégos*, meaning "the commander of the army" in Greek.[1] Nowadays, strategy simply means a specific plan of action to reach a particular objective. The essential notion of strategy is captured in the distinction

---

[1] Stratégos derives from stratos ("army") and égoume ("to lead"). Military strategy (the planning of warfare) is only one of the three "arts" of the general. The other two are tactics (the execution of plans by deployment of forces) and logistics (the organization of supplies to support an army).

Example 1.1 Zara and the Inditex Group

Zara is a designer, manufacturer, distributor and retailer of fashion clothing. The first Zara shop opened its doors in 1975 in La Coruña in north-west Spain. La Coruña also witnessed the early beginnings of Zara's corporate parent, the Inditex Group, and is now home to the group's central offices. In 2005, its 724 stores could be found in the most important shopping districts of more than 400 cities in 54 countries throughout Europe, the Americas, Asia, and Africa. Zara is only one of eight business units (and brands) of the Inditex group, but is by far the largest and most profitable. It boasted net sales of 3,320 million euros in 2003, or 70% of Inditex's total. Inditex's 2001 IPO revealed its impressive financial performance: 16 percent earnings before interest and taxes, 39 percent return on capital employed, and a 24 percent revenue growth.

Zara aims to distinguish itself in the eyes of the consumer by providing timely fashion for the masses: "Zara offers the latest trends in international fashion ... In Zara, design is conceived as a process closely related to ... the concerns and demands of the public." Zara can design more than 11,000 new styles per year and put them in stores within three weeks from concept start. *Source: Zara (2005), Tagliabue (2003).*

between ends and means. A strategy clearly articulates what to do (the ends or the goals) and how to get it done (the means). A textbook example is Toyota's strategy which leverages its famous Toyota Production System as a powerful competitive advantage and important contributor to profitability. The Spanish company Zara, introduced in Example box 1.1, is another example: its strategy of fast fashion relies on its capability of designing more than 11,000 new styles per year with a design-to-rack time that can be as short as three weeks. Let's use these companies to illustrate the goal of strategy and how to implement that goal.

The goal of strategy: value maximization

Strategy is a plan to reach a particular goal. Given that we are interested in organizations or firms, we must specify the goal of the firm's strategy. Managers often say that the goal is to provide superior and sustainable performance.[2] It seems reasonable to measure organizational performance in terms of the *value* of the organization. Organizations thrive when they create more value for their stakeholders (owners, employees, customers, and communities) than rivals do. Ultimately, the value of an organization stems from the value it is able to create for its customers over time minus the firm's cost of providing it.

Financial metrics are indicators of organizational performance. For example, Toyota's consistent profitability generated a cumulative net income of $36.3 billion from April 2004 to March 2007. In contrast, Ford and General Motors lost $7.7 and $9.7 billion, respectively, over the same three years! Example box 1.1 provides similar impressive financial results for Zara. Among the myriads of financial metrics, *net present value* (NPV) is of most interest. Financial theory has established that the value of an organization is well approximated by its NPV, which is the present value of its future cash flows minus the investment today

---

[2]Both qualifiers are important. After all, copying is the only strategy needed to retain the status quo. Similarly, if one-time superior performance suffices, one can just harvest the organization and be done with it.

that is necessary to generate those future flows.[3] (Its calculation will be discussed in detail in chapter 3.) NPV recognizes the longer term and temporal character of many decisions, allows us to incorporate risk and uncertainty, and is more robust than most other metrics because cash flows are harder to manipulate.

The goal of strategy can now be summarized by our first principle, which will be our yardstick for designing, evaluating, and improving strategy throughout the book:

Principle 1 (Value Maximization) The goal of strategy is to maximize the net present value of the organization.

In a market economy, the classic reasoning behind this principle is as follows: Separation of ownership and control is essential for most corporations, so authority has to be delegated. Owners typically prefer more wealth to less but have different preferences regarding risk and how they ultimately want to consume that wealth. If owners have access to competitive capital markets, however, they can choose the risk of their consumption plan by investing in a portfolio of more or less risky securities. Managers then do not need to know the risk characteristics of the owners and should not consult their own risk preferences. Their task is to increase the market value of each owner's stake in the firm. Brealey and Myers (2000) summarize that "it is good to know that managers can all be given one simple instruction: Maximize net present value." (The authors also discuss whether managers actually do this and the ethical ramifications of such actions.) The value maximization principle extends to non-profit organizations when we interpret maximizing net present value to mean maximizing the value stream it provides to its customers given its budget constraint.

Competitive strategy and the customer value proposition

With its goal defined, strategy's remaining task is to articulate specific plans to maximize the net present value of the organization. Large organizations do this in a hierarchical manner and specify several levels of strategy. At the highest level, *corporate strategy* defines the industries in which the organization will be active, configures business units for each industry, and acquires and allocates corporate resources to each business. Corporate strategy is like portfolio management: choosing a mix of industries to participate in and allocating resources to each to maximize the value of the entire organization is similar to investing in a mix of financial assets. For example, Toyota Industries Corporation was founded in 1926 by Sakichi Toyoda to manufacture and sell the automatic looms which he had invented and perfected. Since then, Toyota Industries has promoted diversification and expanded the scope of its business domains to include automobiles (vehicles contributed 49.6% to FY2006 corporate sales, engines (8.8%), car air-conditioning compressors (14.3%), and others (1.8%)), materials handling equipment (39.5%), logistics solutions (4.3%), electronics and others (3.3%) besides textile machinery (3.3%).

---

[3]Some managers prefer to use the simpler financial metric of *economic value added* (EVA), which is the net operating profit after taxes minus the opportunity cost of invested capital. While the explicit inclusion of opportunity cost is appealing from an operations perspective (think of the opportunity cost of holding inventory or excess capacity) bear in mind that EVA only considers current profits. Given that it excludes future cash flows, it can only be a proxy for the value of an organization.

A business unit formulates its *business* or *competitive strategy* to seek "a favorable competitive position in an industry, the fundamental arena in which competition occurs. Competitive strategy aims to establish a profitable and sustainable position against the forces that determine industry competition," according to Porter (1985). Competitive strategy uses two means to create sustainable value:

1. Choosing an attractive industry is the first fundamental determinant of a firm's capability to provide value. "The essence of formulating competitive strategy thus is to relate a company to its environment."[5] Porter's five-forces framework analyzes industry attractiveness by studying the bargaining power of suppliers and buyers, the threat of new entrants and substitute products or services, and the rivalry among existing firms.

2. Choosing an attractive competitive position within an industry is the second fundamental means of providing value. Positioning can be described in terms of the *customer value proposition*, or a clearly articulated set of benefits that the firm offers to customers. Customers ultimately make purchasing decisions based on the benefits or the value they derive from the product or service relative to its price. This value can be summarized by a *reservation price* which is the greatest amount a customer is willing to pay. When value exceeds price, the customer enjoys positive net value or *consumer surplus* by aquiring the product or service. When offered choices, customers will often buy the service or product that offers them highest consumer surplus.

For example, Zara's main business is the design, manufacture, distribution and retailing of clothing. It distinguishes itself from rivals by providing timely fashion for the masses. The customer value proposition thus emphasizes timely yet limited variety at modest cost and quality of materials.

To execute its competitive strategy, an organization further defines a financial strategy specifying how capital will be raised and invested; a marketing and sales strategy specifying how the market will be segmented and how the product will be positioned, priced, and promoted; and an operations strategy. To explain the latter, let us review what we mean by operations.

Three views of operations

The word operations stems from the Latin verb *operari* and noun *opus*, which mean "(to) work." Operations simply are activities, but it is typically understood that these activities are planned and coordinated and often involve a number of people. The Merriam-Webster (2007) dictionary says that an operation is "the performance of a practical work or of something involving the practical application of principles or processes. " From an academic perspective, *operations* is the study of work. Managers think of operations as the planning and execution of work, especially the creation and delivery of products and services.

When studying operations, it is helpful to adopt three different yet complementary views of operations. The resource view focuses on the assets used in the operation while the process view highlights the operation's activities. The financial analogy is that the resource view focuses on the balance sheet while the process view shows how assets are used in the generation of income. The third view characterizes the competencies of the operations, i.e. what it can and

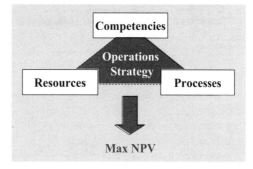

Figure 1.1 Operations strategy is a plan for developing resources and configuring processes such that the resulting competencies maximize net present value.

cannot do. We will explain these views in greater detail soon but this suffices to finally define our topic of interest.

The concept of operations strategy

We can now define the concept of operations strategy building on the meaning of its two elements, operations and strategy, as represented in Figure 1.1:

Operations strategy is a plan for developing resources and configuring processes such that the resulting competencies maximize net present value.

Operations strategy thus answers two questions:

1. What should operations be good at? Which competencies should it nurture?

2. Which operational system of resources and processes best provides these competencies?

Operations strategy is related to competitive strategy but has a distinct role. While competitive strategy is more about selecting industries and choosing the product attributes on which to compete, operations strategy focuses on enabling the execution of the business strategy–on how to best deliver the value proposition. For example, a competitive strategy for Toyota Motor Company was deciding whether to enter the full size pick-up truck market by launching the (upgraded) Tundra in 2007. Their operations strategy involved choosing assets and processes to best design, source, make, and distribute this new vehicle while developing competencies for future products.

Similarly, operations strategy relates to operations management but has a different focus, scope, and time scale. Operations management often means appropriately utilizing given assets and processes. Operations strategy focuses on

> **Example 1.2** Mercedes-Benz AG
>
> In 1993, Mercedes-Benz decided to build the first Mercedes-Benz passenger car factory outside Germany, in Tuscaloosa, Alabama. The plant was designed to produce the M-class, Mercedes-Benz's competitive response to the runaway success of the sport utility vehicles introduced by American car companies in the late 1980s. The U.S. location was chosen to circumvent the 25 percent import tariff on foreign-made pickup trucks.
>
> The supply of parts was coordinated by the Mercedes-Benz Consolidation Center-America, which was opened near the Tuscaloosa plant in Alabama to manage the parts and subassemblies from over 65 suppliers. Mercedes also developed a distribution network to transport the vehicles to 135 countries. The first M-class was sold in 1997 and actual demand quickly surpassed all forecasts and the annual production capacity of about 65,000 vehicles. The initial $300 million plant was expanded in 1998 and 1999 to about 80,000 vehicles at a cost of $80 million, but even that was insufficient. From 1999 to 2002, the M-Class was also produced by contract developer and manufacturer Magna Steyr in Graz, Austria (Magna Steyr is profiled in Example 7.6 on p. 265).
>
> Recently, DaimlerChrysler went through a similar process to decide on an operations strategy for the new R-class, featuring the Grand Sports Tourer. To prepare for the production of the R-class in Alabama, a $600 million expansion in 2004 doubled the factory size, doubled the workforce to approximately 4000, and doubled its production volume to 160,000 vehicles per year. *Source: Mercedes-Benz (1999)*

developing assets and configuring processes. Consequently, it is less about immediate, specific issues and more about future, general issues. For instance, operations management in a retail bank includes scheduling employees at each local branch (over the day, the week, and the month) to assist customers with their savings and checking accounts, mortgages, personal loans, debit cards, credit cards, and so forth. It also involves managing, for example, check clearing and the daily flow of information and cash at the back office. Operations strategy, however, would include deciding on the division and coordination of labor and processing between the many branch offices and the few back offices; choosing locations and capacities; deciding which activities to outsource or when to form alliances at the retail level while perhaps vertically integrating at the back office; and building internal capabilities for information technology.

Mercedes-Benz provides another example of decisions involving operations strategy. At the beginning of the 21st century, it announced its plans to design, produce, and sell a new line of consumer vehicles, the R-class (Example box 1.2). To further understand the typical questions that operations strategy must answer, we must dive deeper into the three views of operations.

1.2 | THE RESOURCE VIEW OF OPERATIONS

To coordinate and perform their activities, organizations need a wide variety of *real assets* or *resources*. We will make a distinction between real assets and *financial assets*. The terms real assets and resources refer to all the means needed to perform the activities excluding financial assets. To pay for the real assets, the

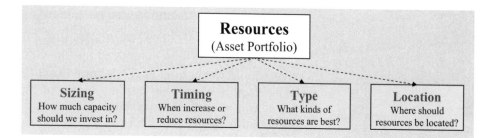

Figure 1.2 The resource view suggests four key questions to characterize resource strategy.

corporation typically sells "pieces of paper called financial assets, or securities. These pieces of paper have value because they are claims on the firm's real assets and the cash that they produce" (Brealey and Myers 2000, p.5).

Adopting a resource view

The *resource view* considers any organization (or any of its parts) as a bundle of real assets. Real assets are divided into two groups: tangible and intangible. Tangible real assets are human resources (people) and capital assets (property, plant and equipment as shown on the balance sheet). Intangible assets include relationships with suppliers or customers, intellectual property, reputation and brands, and knowledge and experience in processing, technologies, and markets. Often, tangible real assets "do" the work, while intangible assets embody the "know-how" to do the work.

In Example 1.2, Mercedes' bundle of real assets includes real estate in Alabama encompassing a plant with a variety of production and support equipment, such as presses, welding machines, and information systems, and staffed by 2000 employees. Its intangible assets include the supply base relationships it has formed, the process and product technologies that it employs, its knowledge of the local economic, legal, and social environment, its connections with logistics and transportation providers, and so on.

Viewing operations as a bundle of real assets is most useful when deciding on the amounts and types of resources the operation needs. This investment or capital budgeting decision, along with the allocation of resources to activities, is undoubtedly a major task of management. While this financing decision is the topic of the field of corporate finance and beyond the scope of what we will consider, resource investment and valuation of the operation in financial terms is also a key concern of operations strategy.

Four key questions to determine resource strategy

An organization's resource strategy must answer four key questions, shown in Figure 1.2. Together, these questions characterize the *asset* or *capacity portfolio* :

1. How many resources should we invest in? The answer involves capacity *sizing* which determines the capacity, in aggregate and per main resource

type. In Example 1.2, the aggregate amount of capacity was originally 65,000 vehicles per year. Chapter 3 will analyze how to answer this question.

2. When should we increase or reduce resources? Capacity *timing* represents the availability of capacity and the timing of capacity adjustments. The Mercedes capacity strategy includes the timing of capacity expansions: 85,000 vehicles per year in 1999 and 160,000 in 2004. We study this question in depth in Chapter 4.

3. What kinds of resources are best? The capacity *type* characterizes the nature of each resource. For example, is it a human (labor) or capital resource? To what extent can a capital resource operate unsupervised; i.e., what is the level of automation? What is the range of tasks that it can handle, from single-task (specialized) to multi-task (flexible)? For example, how is the 160,000 annual vehicle capacity split into capacity for the M-class and the R-class, and into assembly of the various engine configurations? Are the assets specialized to produce only the M-class or flexible to also produce the R-class? Chapter 5 is devoted to answering such questions about resource type and flexibility.

4. Where should resources be located? The capacity *location* decision deals with finding appropriate geographical sites and assigning roles to them. For example, how should the M-class plant location be chosen and what responsibilities should it have? For our Mercedes example, the location is Tuscaloosa, Alabama, but it would also include other locations if we were to consider the larger Mercedes supply chain. Chapter 6 will examine location decisions, including offshoring.

Indeed, location decisions are part of network strategy. Network strategy also includes topology or configuring connections between locations. For example, FedEx uses a hub-and-spoke or star topology for airplane routing, while most automobile companies use a tiered supply network or tree topology. Interconnections also specify the logistics (transportation) arrangements. Network strategy also specifies whether processes should be standardized or localized; e.g., should Tuscaloosa processes be similar to the German processes?

1.3 | THE PROCESS VIEW OF OPERATIONS

The purpose of resources is to work and generate value. The process view highlights how resources perform activities and add value.

Processes and activity networks

Processes are structured, recurrent activities that transform inputs into outputs. Some processes are well defined and documented, while others are less so and are called *routines* in everyday language. A process is also a network of activities

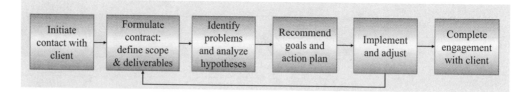

Figure 1.3 The operations of a consulting firm viewed as a process.

with specific precedence relationships among the activities—the relationships that specify which activities must be finished before another activity can begin. For example, most management consulting firms follow a structured sequence of activities for each engagement as illustrated by the activity network as in Figure 1.3.

We will use the terms activity network, process, and routine interchangeably. These terms embody an element of repetition but focus on the positive aspects: "Practice makes perfect" and recurrent execution makes analyzing and improving operations a worthwhile investment. One can argue that most great human accomplishments—in the arts[4], the sciences, sports, politics or economics—are the result of processes.

Adopting a process view and value stream mapping

The *process view* considers an organization (or any of its parts) to be an activity network or a collection of processes. A process can refer to detailed workflow, such as billing a customer or implementing an engineering change order, or to aggregate activities such as new product development or customer service. Adopting a process view means that we visualize instances of work, which we will call *flow units* (e.g., consulting engagements, patients, or orders), flowing through a network of activities. This *primary work flow* is typically accompanied by an *information flow* to coordinate the activities and a *cash flow* to support and reward them. *Flow charts* such as Figure 1.3 and *value streams* or *chains* are graphical representations of the process view of an organization. The value chain of Figure 1.4 shows the typical business processes found in most organizations.

Many organizations tend to focus on a subset of the typical business processes shown in Figure 1.4. For example, design companies such as Ideo help other companies innovate by designing products, services, environments, and interactions. Supply, demand and distribution management are the core activities of retailers, while on-going client service is a key activity in brokerage and corporate information services. Service and customer relationship management can also be an important process for product companies. For example, once a

---

[4]For example, Peter Paul Rubens, the Flemish painter from Antwerp (1577-1640), followed a well-defined process to conceive his art. Rubens started with a rough ink sketch, which he subsequently developed into a drawing or oil sketch. He refined the sketches into detailed drawings for which live models assumed the required poses. Then, guided by the sketches and detailed drawings, apprentices would paint in. Finally, "Rubens would come in at the end to touch things up (adjusting the price depending on how much he contributed)," according to Kimmelman (2005). He called Rubens "ridiculously gifted" and his process "Baroque art's luxury version of an assembly line, albeit an assembly line overseen by a genius, who employed assistants who were geniuses, too, like Anthony van Dyck."

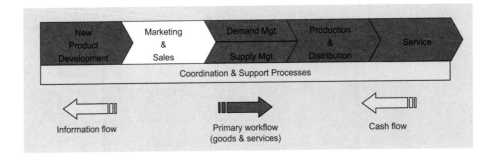

Figure 1.4 The value chain is the graphical representation of the process view an organization. The primary workflow is typically accompanied by an information and cash flow.

customer has bought a Mercedes, s/he will be constantly updated on new product introductions and promotions as part of "the Mercedes-Benz experience."

The benefits and importance of a process view

By necessarily starting with inputs (expressed customer demands) and ending with outputs (served customer demands), the process view is compatible with a customer-centric view of the world. Value stream mapping emphasizes this customer-centric view and defines value from the perspective of the customer: a value-added activity is an activity that benefits the customer.

The process view is a horizontal view of the organization that cuts through functional silos such as finance, accounting, production, marketing and sales. It emphasizes crucial inter-functional relationships among internal parties, as well as the interfaces and relationships with external customers and suppliers. By equating organizations with processes, the *business process reengineering* paradigm of the early 1990s has put operations on the agenda of top management at many organizations. By capturing both *structure* (or *architecture* or *design*) and *execution*[5], the process view is useful for analyzing the division and specialization of work following the dictum of Adam Smith, as well as for coordinating and evaluating execution. For example, how is the auto manufacturing process divided and coordinated between the original equipment manufacturer (OEM) and its suppliers? Given a process structure, what is the total marginal cost of the car manufacturing process from inputs to a finished vehicle? How long is an average consulting engagement from start to completion?

The process and resource views are complementary: the process view focuses on how work is done, while the resource view focuses on *who* or *what* performs the work. Both are necessary to understand operations well: Viewing the firm as a sequence of activities without considering its resources gives as incomplete a picture as viewing the firm as a collection of resources without considering how those resources are put to use. For example, the performance of

---

[5]Some authors differentiate between those two notions by using the word network to refer to the architecture or design of the operation, and management to mean execution. For example, the supply network would refer to the set of and the relationships with suppliers whereas supply management would refer to the way suppliers are handled.

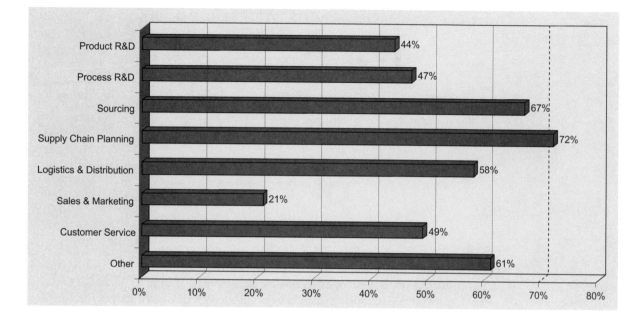

Figure 1.5 Operations strategy leaders do much more than production: they manage the value chain (Fig. 1.4). Note: Multiple responses possible. Source: von Hochberg, Rodrigues, and Grenon (2006).

a consulting company obviously depends on how it structures its activities, but also depends on the type and quantity of resources it allocates to those activities.

Operations leaders apply the process view and manage the value chain. Indeed, a survey by Booz Allen Hamilton shows that operations leaders manage much more than just production, according to von Hochberg, Rodrigues, and Grenon (2006). The bars in Figure 1.5 show the percentage of survey respondents who manage domains besides production, including more than 40 percent who oversee customer service and R&D.

Four key questions to determine process strategy

An organization's process strategy must answer four key questions, shown in Figure 1.6, that describe how we deal with the inputs, internal processes, outputs, and the future of each major customer-to-customer value stream:

1. Which activities do we perform internally, which are outsourced, and how do we manage suppliers? The *supply* or *strategic sourcing* process characterizes the interfaces and relationships with suppliers. Chapter 7 will analyze strategic sourcing decisions such as outsourcing (which activities are provided by third parties?), vertical integration (how far do we extend our activities upstream and downstream?), and supply network configuration (how many suppliers do we use and have relationships with?). For example, Mercedes owns engine plants, but outsources seat manufacturing and transportation within its production and distribution network. In con-

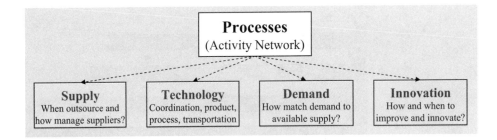

Figure 1.6 While processes have many facets, our process view will use four components, or drivers, to analyze an activity network.

trast, Guerlain, one of the oldest perfume houses in the world which was founded in 1828 in Paris, carefully controls both the design and manufacturing of its perfumes to ensure quality and brand protection. Only in 1998 did Guerlain first outsource the design of one of its new fragrances (Champs-Elysées).

2. Which technologies do our processes need? *Technology* characterizes how we process inputs to outputs. It includes the methods and systems employed, as well as the know-how and intellectual property. We will focus on four types of technology:

   (a) *Coordination and information technology* describes how we coordinate, communicate, and plan execution throughout the activity network. It lies at the core of modern banks for which timely information sharing and processing is paramount. Coordination is a typical managerial activity and includes the assignment of responsibility, incentives, measurement, and control. For example: do we have tightly centralized or distributed control? The supply of parts to Tuscaloosa is coordinated by the Mercedes-Benz Consolidation Center-America. Coordination is obviously important during planning. For example, managers often fail to coordinate financial forecasts, sales forecasts, marketing forecasts and operations forecasts. Collaborative planning and forecasting systems aim to correct this mistake. Coordination is equally important during execution: much of the challenge in managing operations is making events happen at the right times. Finally, coordination strongly depends on information technology such as communication technology (e.g., Internet, radio frequency identification RFID) and planning systems (e.g., enterprise resource planning ERP).

   (b) *Product technology* describes the design philosophy, product architecture, and product capabilities (often as perceived by the customer). For example, is an M-class sport utility vehicle designed in modules or as a single integral system? To what extent does the design take into account manufacturability, testability, or reusability?

   (c) *Process technology* describes the structure of the conversion process and methods used in its execution. *Network structure* describes the layout of the activity network in terms of locations and interconnections. For example, processes can be organized by activity or by product-line. Job shops such as consulting companies and tool-and-die shops often have a functional or process layout, whereas flow shops such as auto assembly plants and chemical processing plants usually have a product layout.

Process technology also includes conversion methods and abilities. For example, a semiconductor process is characterized by the wafer diameter and line width, among others. In June 2006, the majority of Intel's products were built on industry-leading 65nm technology, using 300mm wafers.

(d) *Transportation technology* describes how goods are exchanged among different activities in the network. It is a key driver in logistics and supply chain management, but also can describe how insurance policies are moved between the different processing steps.

3. How do we match demand to available supply? The *demand management* process characterizes the interfaces and relationships with customers. It includes demand planning and forecasting as well as tactical capacity allocation and order management. Demand management is an important driver in inflexible supply processes that cannot quickly adapt to changes in demand such as the core processes in airlines, hotels, and car rental companies. It also relates to *service* and *customer relationship management* (CRM), which are the processes involving any follow-up interaction with customers. We study demand and revenue management in Chapter 8.

4. How and when do we improve and innovate? *Improvement and innovation* characterize the processes and incentives to improve and innovate products and processes. It not only involves research and development activities, but also broader continuous improvement and learning throughout the organization. Chapter 6 will examine location decisions, including off-shoring. Chapter 10 will examine improvement and innovation.

1.4 | THE COMPETENCY VIEW OF OPERATIONS

The ensemble of resources and processes, which we will also refer to as the *operational system*, affects what an operation can and cannot do. This operational system together with the vaguer, but at least as important, concept of values characterize the competencies of the organization.

Values: operations' decision priorities

Besides resources and processes, values are a third factor that affect what an operation–and thus an organization–can and cannot do. Following Christensen and Overdorf (2000), we define *values* as the standards by which employees set priorities. Sure, some priorities are embodied or "programmed" into a process but many are not, even though prioritization decisions are made by employees at every level. Examples include judging whether an order or customer is attractive or not, whether a suggestion to improve a product or process is attractive or marginal, and whether an investment is worth making or not.

As organizations become more complex, consistent values are powerful mechanisms for employees to make independent but consistent decisions about priorities. As successful companies mature, "employees often start believing that the processes and priorities they have often used so successfully are the right way to do their work. Once that happens and employees begin to follow processes and decide upon priorities by assumption rather than by conscious choice, those processes and values come to constitute the organization's *culture*." (Christensen and Overdorf 2000)

Adopting a competency view

The competency view characterizes the abilities of the ensemble of the organization's resources, processes, and values. Competencies determine the set of outputs, products, and services that the operation will be particularly good at providing. For example, a premier management consulting company is good at providing high quality customized advice. An efficient operation such as McDonald's is good at delivering inexpensive food quickly, but from a standard and limited menu with a well-defined quality level. Zara, described in Example 1.1, is good at quickly delivering a large selection of new designs at a reasonable cost.

Where competencies reside changes over time: they start in resources, gradually migrate to processes, and eventually reside in values. Most of what gets done in start-up companies is attributable to resources, especially its people. Losing a person can be detrimental. As activities become more recurrent, processes are defined. As it becomes clear which business needs should be given highest priority, values emerge. Competencies then are rooted in well defined processes and values, and eventually reside in culture, rather than in resources. Processes and values then make organizational performance robust to changes in its resources. Even with hundreds of new recruits and departures per year, top management consulting companies remain successful because their processes and values are so strong that project staffing changes have little impact.

Four key questions to determine competencies

To determine an organization's competencies one can ask four questions, as visualized in Figure 1.7:

1. What is the total *cost* of operating, including variable and fixed costs? Cost is particularly important in competitive markets such as commodities and low margin businesses.

2. What is the total response or lead *time*, the time needed to transform inputs into outputs? Responsiveness is important in service and convenience-driven businesses, as well as in rapidly changing environments.

3. What is the ability to deliver *quality* outputs? Quality refers to the degree of excellence of the process, product, or service. It has design-related dimensions such as performance and features, as well as process-related di-

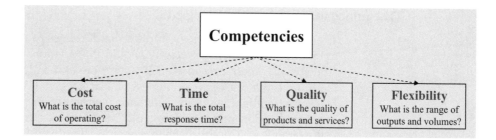

Figure 1.7 The competency view characterizes the abilities of an operation. Time, quality and flexibility are dimensions to differentiate from cost.

mensions such as durability and reliability. Quality is a key differentiator in luxury and high precision businesses.

4. What is the operations' *flexibility* to change inputs, activities, volumes, or outputs? Similar to quality, flexibility has several dimensions such as scope flexibility (the selection or range of products and services offered, including the level of customization), volume flexibility, and robustness, as we will see in Chapter 5.

The resource, process and competency views provide a 360-degree perspective on operations. The competency view is the most "outward-looking" and begs the important question: *which* competencies should an operation have or develop? This naturally connects to competitive strategy, which directly inspires our framework.

1.5 | A FRAMEWORK FOR OPERATIONS STRATEGY

In principle, operations strategy could emerge from a giant optimization program that automatically identifies the resources, processes, and competencies that maximize net present value. In practice, however, this quantitative approach cannot yet (and likely never will) formulate comprehensive strategies: the search space of all possible resource, process, and competency configurations cannot easily be represented mathematically, let alone be summarized into one financial measure that can be optimized.

Operations strategy therefore starts with qualitative arguments to characterize the appropriate types of resources, processes, and competencies. Subsequently, if more specificity is needed or desired, the value maximization principle can be used to optimize over that restricted search set. (We will use financial optimization to inspire optimal partial operations strategies such as optimal capacity and flexibility strategies later in this book.)

A key qualitative argument is provided by the principle of alignment or strategic fit, which is at the foundation of our operations strategy framework.

The principle of alignment: strategic fit

The term operations strategy implies that it relates to competitive strategy and to operations. But what precisely should this relationship be? The principle of strategic alignment provides an answer. One of the oldest ideas in the strategy literature is that the appropriateness of a strategy can be defined in terms of the fit, match, or alignment of organizational structure and resources with the environmental opportunities and threats (Chandler 1962; Andrews 1971). It gave rise to the famous SWOT approach to strategy: identify and align your strengths and weaknesses with the environmental opportunities and threats. In our setting, we can paraphrase this idea as:

Principle 2 (**Alignment**) Operations strategy should develop resources and configure processes such that the resulting competencies are aligned with the competitive position that a firm seeks over time.

The principle of alignment extends to the entire organization. McKinsey consultants Drew, McCallum, and Roggenhofer (2004) argue that the operating system must be aligned with what they call the *management infrastructure* (meaning organization, leadership, and performance systems) and the mindsets and behaviors (meaning values) of the organization. You may think of the operating system as the engine of a car: as high-powered as it may be, it won't go in the right direction without the appropriate dashboard information systems and a willing driver.

A framework for formulating operations strategy

The principle of strategic fit directly inspires a framework for formulating operations strategy that is represented visually in Figure 1.8. It can be thought of as answering three types of questions:

1. How does the organization seek to compete and provide value to its customers? For each targeted customer segment, how is the customer value proposition prioritized around cost, time, quality, and variety?

2. What must operations do particularly well? For each targeted customer segment, how are the operations' competencies prioritized around cost, flow time, quality, and flexibility?

3. Which resources and processes best provide that competency prioritization? For each targeted customer segment, how are the asset portfolio (sizing, timing, and location of each resource type) and the activity network (supply, technology, demand, and innovation management) configured?

The idea is that by answering these questions, a *tailored operational system* emerges: its resources and processes are configured such that its competencies best fit the customer value proposition specified by the competitive strategy. The sequence in which these questions are answered reveals a different perspective on operations strategy.

The *market perspective* first decides on competitive strategy and then specifies the competencies that operations strategy must develop by selecting and configuring the appropriate resources and processes. Behind this perspective is the

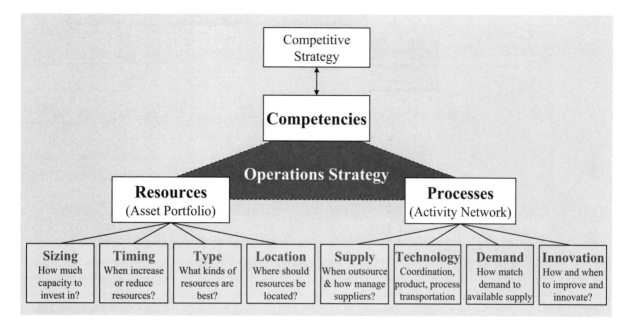

Figure 1.8 A framework for formulating an operations strategy.

premise that "structure follows strategy," as strategy-pioneer Chandler (1962) summarized in his book *Strategy and Structure*. This "top-down and outside-in" perspective ensures that operations and all parts of the organizations reflect the intended market position, and tends to create a customer-driven organization. For example, consumer goods companies such as Procter & Gamble and General Mills often let market research drive their strategies for new products and associated operations. Customer feedback strongly guides P&G's choice and improvement of its antiperspirant scents and product designs.

The *resource & process perspective* approaches the framework in the reverse sequence. This bottom-up and inside-out perspective starts from the premise that the building blocks of strategy are not products and markets, but processes and resources. "Competitive success then depends on transforming a company's key processes into strategic capabilities that consistently provide superior value to the customer." (Stalk, Evans, and Shulman 1992) This perspective ensures that the value proposition offered to customers can be well executed with the given operations. It tends to create a resource-driven organization, such as Honda. Honda's abilities and knowledge in engine technology is legendary and has been the driving force in deciding which markets to enter and which products to offer: it has entered markets that need a product with a high-performance engine.

As environments, strategy, and operations evolve, organizations must seek to maintain alignment by adopting both perspectives over time. In order to satisfy a new customer need, the firm may need to build new competencies, processes, and resources. Those processes and resources may later be used to invent new products and services that may drive, if not create, new markets. From this dual perspective emerges an operations strategy that "inextricably links a company's internal competencies (what it does well) and its external industry

	Zara's Inditex (2003)		H&M (2003)		
		% of sales		(@ 9.12 SEK/€)	% of sales
Net sales	4,598.9 €	100,0%	48,237.7 SEK	5,289.2 €	100,0%
Net income	446.5 €	9.7%	6,385.9 SEK	700.2 €	13.2%
Fixed assets	1,559.2 €	33.9%	6,124.0 SEK	671.5 €	12.7%
Inventories	486.4 €	10.6%	5,050.1 SEK	553.7 €	10.5%

Table 1.1 Financial summary of the Spanish Inditex group and the Swedish H&M.

environment (what the market demands and what competitors offer)" (Collis and Montgomery 1995).

1.6 | APPLYING THE FRAMEWORK: ZARA

Let us illustrate the framework in the setting of Zara.

Competitive strategy and the operational competency view

According to Example 1.1, Zara aims to distinguish itself in the eyes of the consumer by providing fast fashion and "cheap chic" styles. The value proposition thus seems to prioritize speed and selection, while keeping cost and quality comparable to that of competitors. In other words, selection and speed are the *order winners*, while cost and quality are necessary qualifiers to be in the game. Consequently, to execute this value proposition, its operations must be especially good at bringing many new styles quickly from design to retail shelves. Recall that 11,000 new styles per year are introduced and some of them within a three week design-to-rack time.

What makes Zara interesting from an operations standpoint is how it has configured its operational system to pull off such variety and speed, while keeping costs and quality reasonable. Let us now turn to Zara's resources and processes for new product design, manufacturing, and distribution.

Resource view

Zara's short design-to-rack times require short conversion times in, and immense coordination among, all major activities in the value chain. Consequently, Zara's operations strategy is characterized by high vertical integration because ownership allows tight coordination. Its capacity portfolio includes a design center, some manufacturing facilities (it also outsources manufacturing locally), two major distribution centers, as well as a controlling interest in 90% of the retail network (only 10% of its 724 stores are franchised). The design capacity of 11,000 new styles per year by its creative teams, made up of over 200 professionals, is in line with the timely fashion that Zara promises. Zara owns two central warehouses, both in Spain. The recent 123,000m^2 distribution center in Zaragoza has a distribution capacity of 80,000 garments per hour. It came on-line in fiscal year 2003 and has direct access to the highway and railroad network. Its proximity to

Zaragoza's airport favors fast handling of international cargo.

As shown in Table 1.1, the vertical integration of assets results in a high ratio of tangible fixed assets (property, plant, and equipment) of 33.9% of sales. It is perhaps less expected that the utilization of this deep investment in real assets is relatively low: the average capacity utilization is only about 50% and many facilities operate for only a single shift, according to Ferdows, Lewis, and Machuca (2004).

Process view

Supply. Zara's supply network is concentrated in Spain (only 25% of materials are sourced from the rest of Europe and 25% from the rest of the world, especially Asia). The physical proximity of suppliers ensures that Zara receives inputs quickly, enabling fast speed-to-market. Zara uses local facilities to produce the trendy products with most demand uncertainty while offshoring some manufacturing of basic products with more predictable demands. This targeted outsourcing strategy allows Zara to focus local capacity on the most time-sensitive production. (We shall see in Chapter 3 that low capacity utilization is to be expected when one seeks fast response times while being exposed to high demand volatility.)

Technology. Zara's process technology can postpone the dyeing of fabric: almost half the raw materials are purchased undyed (and sometimes so early that designs must be adapted to use them, as with silk from China). Local manufacturing processes have short setup times and run in small batches, while offshore manufacturing of more predictable demand can have longer lead times (Zara is said to have employed Toyota engineers to design its manufacturing and distribution system). Distribution is highly centralized to reduce the number of stocking points and the associated handling time and so that one store's upside demand fluctuations can offset another's downside. The hub and spoke delivery system uses the most appropriate transportation mode (truck, rail, or air) depending on the store location and the time-sensitivity of the product. It provides frequent deliveries (Thursday delivery is important in the fashion industry) with short lead times for reordering. This approach maximizes the flexibility of inputs and increases responsiveness while controlling working capital (inventory). Information technology enables the daily information flow between store managers, requesting products and providing customer preference feedback, and design and production sharing information on upcoming products.

Demand. Intentionally short style campaigns that are likely to run out of stock create a scarcity image. Customers visit stores frequently and are likely to buy what is available at that moment because that particular product may no longer be available next time. The combination of short campaigns and limited inventory reduces markdowns and leftovers.

Innovation. Fast new product design is a key enabler of Zara's strategy. Ideas inspired by urban hot spots, fashion shows, and store customers are transmitted to the creative teams. Design style platforms are created ahead of the season and are modified just before production based on feedback from retailers to incorporate the "concerns and demands of the public," i.e., the most recent fashion. This postponement of design styling requires fast and efficient information transfer, which is facilitated by organizing the creative teams by design styles (product-layout).

A firm believer that "people, cultures and generations, in spite of their differences, share a special sensitivity for fashion," Zara standardizes a majority of its designs but allows some adjustments to local taste. For instance, Zara originally insisted on a standard set of sizes for all countries but had to add smaller sizes for Japan and larger ones for the U.K. and Germany.

In conclusion, Zara has tailored the eight drivers of its operations strategy to its fast-fashion, cheap-chic value proposition.

Applicability of the Zara model: Should every retailer adopt it?

While Zara's operational system fits its competitive strategy well, it is not a panacea. A counter-example is the operational system of Sweden's Hennes & Mauritz AB, which operates the H&M clothing chain. H&M competes with Zara but has less of an emphasis on "new style velocity:" it produces much fewer new styles per year with a much slower design-to-rack time of 16 weeks, according to Tagliabue (2003). Without the stringent speed requirement, however, H&M has more leeway in configuring its operations which allows more outsourcing and higher capacity utilizations resulting in much lower fixed capital requirements. The lower safety capacity and responsiveness of the operating system is replaced by higher safety stock to buffer demand uncertainty.[6]

The Zara model is not used in other industries such as toy (e.g., Mattel, Inc.), cell phone (e.g., Nokia), or auto manufacturing. The reason may be that they lack a necessary condition for the Zara model to be profitable. Indeed, our analysis suggests that, at a minimum, a profitable application of the Zara model requires:

1. High customer willingness to pay for speed-to-market.

2. Short product life cycles with high demand uncertainty.

3. Low cost of excess capacity with low importance of scale economies.

4. Low cost of stockouts and distribution relative to inventory holding.

This reinforces this chapter's main message: great operations strategies are tailored to each company's strategy. While companies may share some elements, a complete tailored operations system is unique (to the extent that its strategy and industry are unique).

1.7 | THREE TOOLS TO TAILOR OPERATIONS

Tailoring is the technique of fitting the operational system to competitive strategy. It is diametrically opposed to the idea that there is a "one best way" to configure *any* operation, to borrow Frederick Winslow Taylor's words.[7] Rather,

---

[6]How would you mesh the claim that H&M has higher safety stock with the data of Table 1.1? Chapter 5 will explain it in terms of pooling.

[7]While Taylor's achievements are impressive, they did not include the idea of tailoring (despite the resemblance in names). Skinner (1969) is widely credited for drawing attention to fitted operational systems.

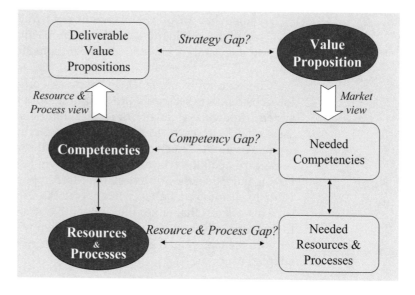

Figure 1.9 The strategic operational audit is a gap analysis to assess the degree of alignment and to develop improvement actions.

the best operations configuration depends on the mission of the organization. Given the daunting objective of tailoring, calling it a "technique" is not doing it justice: there is no simple recipe to tailor the entire operational system. Indeed, in a certain sense, this entire book is devoted to techniques for tailoring each driver of the framework. Nevertheless, the framework directly inspires a few guidelines to tailoring.

The strategic operational audit

A *strategic operational audit* "takes stock" of an organization's operation to assess its degree of fit with competitive strategy and to identify where improvements can be made. It consists of applying the top-down and bottom-up perspectives simultaneously and can be performed in three steps, as shown in Figure 1.9:

1. Start by understanding your customer and enunciating your competitive strategy in terms of the promised customer value proposition. Examine (audit) the current operational system: its resources, processes, and competencies. This step is represented by the three ovals in Figure 1.9.

2. Next, apply the resource & process views (bottom-up) to characterize the set of value propositions that current competencies can support well. Similarly, adopt the market (top-down) perspective to specify the competencies, as well as the best-aligned processes and resources, needed to execute the current competitive strategy. This second step is represented by the three rectangles in Figure 1.9.

3. Finally, assess the gaps between the current state and where we should be to ensure strategic alignment. Based on this assessment, we then de-

velop what Ansoff (1962) called "gap reducing actions" to improve strategic alignment. In our case, these actions involve changing the competitive strategy and/or changing the operations strategy.

Consider, for example, Dell Computer's original value proposition that allows customers to self-configure their desktop computer. Its aligned operational system features assemble-to-order flexibility and a quick response by a direct sales model. Recently, Dell also has been serving a growing laptop computer segment with the same operational system. It can be argued that this has led to some gaps at all three levels: customers seem to value touching a laptop before buying more than they do a desktop. More importantly, there seems less need or value to customize a laptop while it certainly is more difficult and costly to do so. This suggest that either the competitive strategy should be re-focused back to desktops, or that a new operational system with less flexibility would fit better with the laptop market segment. In other words, alignment may need to be adapted over time.

A balanced scorecard map

"The formulation of great strategies is an art, and it will always remain so. But the description of strategy should not be an art," according to Kaplan and Norton (2000). These pioneers of the balanced scorecard measure a company's performance from four major perspectives: market, internal operations, learning and growth, and financial view. They present a balanced scorecard map as a tool for organizations to communicate both their strategy and the processes and systems that will help them implement that strategy. They argue that such maps are needed, especially in the information age as organizations create an increasing proportion of value from intangible assets.

Adding the financial view (using the value maximization principle) to our framework yields the balanced scorecard map shown in Figure 1.10. This map can be used to communicate and integrate an operations strategy with the firm's financial and competitive strategy. The balanced scorecard tends to emphasize the learning and growth view and represents our earlier innovation lever as a separate view. The financial view specifies how the organization seeks to increase its net present value from a financial perspective. Given that NPV is the present value of the stream of future profits, the two financial levers are to increase revenues or decrease costs. The growth strategy must define its desired balancing point (represented by the "×" in Fig. 1.10) between emphasizing productivity or revenue growth.

Filling out this map, in addition to its use as a means of communication, may provide a useful exercise for an organization to distill its often implicit operations strategy. Kaplan and Norton (2000) provide the following evidence why constructing these maps is a useful team exercise. While the value proposition is key to competitive strategy, "approximately three-quarters of executive teams do not have consensus about this basic information." Similarly, they "readily acknowledge the importance of the learning and growth perspective, but generally have trouble defining the corresponding objectives." There is great power in team conversation and exercise. Describing operations using a balanced scorecard map has similar advantages to drawing process flow charts: it opens our eyes to obvious misalignments and brings out the best in us to improve align-

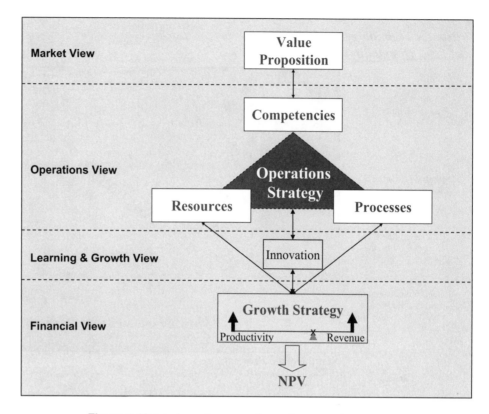

Figure 1.10 A balanced scorecard map for operations strategy.

ment and coherence in the organization.

The product-process matrix

Whereas the strategic operational audit and the balanced scorecard are high-level tools for improving fit, the *product-process matrix* focuses on the match between process technology and delivered product attributes.

As shown in Figure 1.11, the product-process matrix starts by evaluating the promised value proposition (or the product concept on the horizontal axis) and the process used to deliver value (on the vertical axis). It verifies alignment along one dimension, often by comparing the degree of variety in the value proposition with the degree of process flexibility. This product-process combination is then represented by a covered area in the matrix where the distance to the diagonal represents the degree of misalignment.

Tailored operations occupy the diagonal, which is the "sweet spot" of alignment. For example, the tailored operation for highly customized products and services ("customer solutions") requires a flexible process such as a job shop; this product-process combination is represented by position A in Figure 1.11. Top restaurants with three Michelin stars[8] fall in this category: they provide a con-

---

[8]The Michelin® guide awards up to three stars to the finest restaurants in Europe. Excellent restaurants receive one star. Two stars stand for a sophisticated and fine cuisine that deserves a detour. Exceptional cuisines that are worth a journey receive three stars. And exceptional they

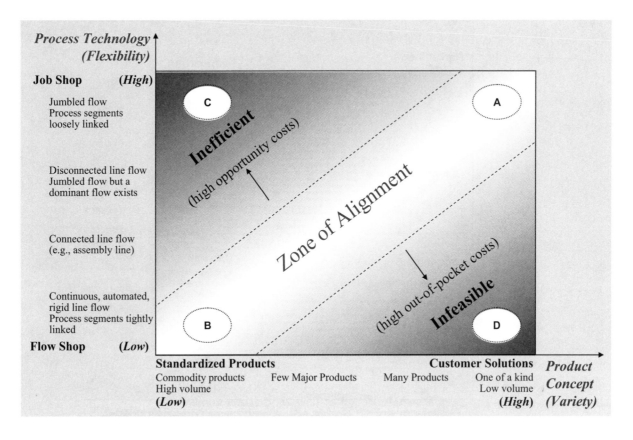

Figure 1.11 The product-process matrix is a tool to verify the degree of alignment between the product concept and the process technology.

tinually changing culinary experience for a select set of customers. In contrast, the tailored operation for standardized products such as high-volume commodity products is an efficient, highly-engineered process (position B). An example is the Chipotle chain of McDonald's owned restaurants: "Few restaurant chains can take it to the limit as well as Chipotle ... They make two things–burritos and tacos–very well", according to BestBite (2004).

Positions outside the diagonal signal misalignment. For example, three-star chefs who perpetually serve simple meals consisting of only burritos and tacos with their highly flexible job shop service process incur high opportunity costs (position C). Substantial savings would result from changing resources (including chefs) and streamlining the process into a flow shop. In contrast, asking Chipotle's process to change its menu daily would require high changeover costs. Asking it to deliver a three-star dining experience is virtually impossible (position D).

---

are: out of the 3,400 restaurants evaluated in the 2005 Michelin guide for the Benelux, only five restaurants (three in Belgium and two in the Netherlands) received the coveted three star status.

1.8 | GUIDELINES FOR OPERATIONS STRATEGY

Use a cross functional team with top-level involvement

The process view reminds us that operations touches upon all the functions in an organization. To formulate an effective operations strategy, it follows that a cross functional team that is familiar with all functions is necessary. It is equally important for senior leadership to be involved and committed to implement an integrative strategy.

Adapt alignment by balancing the market view with the operational view

Change is the only constant. Changes in customer needs, competition, and operational systems require periodic reviews of operations strategy. By balancing the external market view with the internal competency, resource, and process views, one can determine whether operations strategy should be re-aligned or adapted.

Tailoring operations involves all drivers in the framework

Aligning an operation with its competitive strategy requires that all drivers in the framework work together. Later in this book we will see that these drivers all interact, which prevents the delegation of each driver to a different functional manager. A horizontal approach is necessary and starts with the three qualitative tools from the previous section. Don't forget to also align the leadership infrastructure (metrics and incentives) as well as people's mindsets and behaviors.

Employ a qualitative approach first and refine this using a quantitative approach

Operations strategy is not an exact science; it requires judgment, experience, creativity, and luck. A qualitative approach is the typical way to start to formulating operations strategy. It also is the natural way to deal with people, a key improvement lever as shown in Figure 1.12. A quantitative approach then follows to refine and optimize, as we will do in the subsequent chapters to improve systems and methods; integration; planning; and reduce complexity. We thus aim to discuss most of the improvement levers in Figure 1.12.

1.9 | SUMMARY OF LEARNING OBJECTIVES

1. Explain the concept of operations strategy and discuss its impact on an organization.

Strategy is a plan to reach a particular goal. For corporations, the value maximization principle specifies that goal as maximizing their net present value. Competitive strategy seeks to accomplish this by deciding which markets to enter and which value proposition to offer to its customers. This value proposition

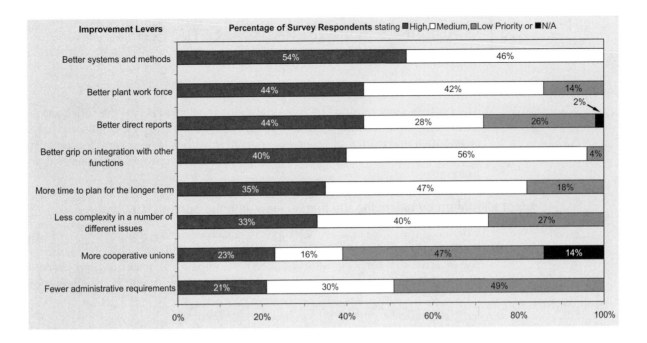

Figure 1.12 The typical improvement levers through which operations leaders create value, according to von Hochberg, Rodrigues, and Grenon (2006).

can be described by ranking the four dimensions of customer need: price, quality, responsiveness, and variety. Operations strategy is a plan for developing an operational system with competencies that maximize net present value. Integral to that plan is structuring interfaces with input and output, and capital and labor markets.

2. Adopt three complementary views to describe operations.

To describe operations, or the performance of work, it is helpful to adopt three complementary views. The resource view considers operations as a bundle of real assets. These tangible and intangible assets are the means of performing work. Deciding on the asset portfolio involves an investment decision. The firm finances this investment by selling financial assets, which are claims on the real assets and their cash flow. The process view highlights that operations are structured and coordinated networks of activities. The process view, which is graphically represented via a flow chart or value stream, takes on a horizontal, customer-centric perspective that is most useful for analyzing how the organization divides and coordinates work and produces value. The third perspective is the competency view, which characterizes the abilities of the ensemble of processes and resources. It describes what the operation excels at and is naturally linked to the customer value proposition.

3. Identify the key decisions and relationships in our framework for operations strategy.

> Our framework for operations strategy builds on the principle of alignment: the competencies of the operational system should be aligned with the competitive position that the firm seeks over time. Operations strategy formulation can thus start from the competitive position, ask what operations competencies are needed, and then choose the activity network and resource bundle compatible with those competencies. Instead of this market perspective, the sequence can be reversed using the resource perspective.

> The competency view involves decisions on the prioritization of cost, time, quality, and flexibility. The resource strategy involves sizing, timing, and deciding on the appropriate types and locations of resources. The process strategy decides on supply and demand management (the interfaces with inputs and outputs); internal technology (coordination and information, process, product, and transportation); and planning for the future through improvement and innovation management.

4. Use three tools to implement the principle of alignment and tailor operations strategy.

> Tailoring operations is the tool to achieve strategic fit with the competitive strategy. While the following chapters will investigate how to tailor each driver of an operations strategy, we discussed three qualitative guidelines for tailoring: the strategic operational audit, which is a gap analysis to assess the degree of strategic fit and to inspire improvement actions; the balanced scorecard map, which seeks to integrate the market, operations, and financial views of the organization; and the product-process matrix to verify alignment between process and product attributes.

> As a tailored operation, Zara provided an example of the framework and reinforced the key message of this chapter: all eight operations drivers reinforce each other and yield a uniquely tailored operational system whose competencies are aligned with its strategy.

DISCUSSION QUESTIONS

1. Which of the following are tangible or intangible real assets, and which are financial: a cappuccino maker, a coffee chain's (e.g., Starbucks) recipe and standard procedure to make cafe latte, a lease for a coffee shop, the coffee chain's culture and the provision of health-care benefits to half-time employees, the enterprise resource planning software, and the training program for new employees?

2. Consider several types of operations-related decisions that airlines make and characterize them as either strategic or operational.

3. Contrast the operational systems of a full-service airline (e.g., Lufthansa Airlines) with those of a low-cost airline (e.g., Ryanair). Are their operational systems (describe their processes and resources) tailored to their mission?

4. How would you measure the value that a firm provides to its customers? How do you determine what part of that value the firm captures?

5. What are the main disadvantages of the market view of operations strategy formulation? What are the main disadvantages of the resource view?

6. How would you characterize the view of operations strategy formulation that innovators take? Contrast, for example, the two major biotech companies Amgen and Genentech.

Visit www.vanmieghem.us for additional questions and updates.

FURTHER READING AND REFERENCES

▶ Ansoff (1962) and Chandler (1962) are among the first authors to write about strategic management and strategic alignment; Donaldson (2001) surveys fit studies. Porter (1985) discusses sources of competitive advantage. Drew, McCallum, and Roggenhofer (2004) discuss fit in the context of implementing lean operations.

▶ Skinner (1969) wrote the seminal article on operations strategy.

▶ Stalk, Evans, and Shulman (1992), Collis and Montgomery (1995) and Christensen and Overdorf (2000) provide further reading on the resource perspective on strategy.

Andrews, K. R. (1971). *The Concept of Corporate Strategy*. Homewood, IL: Irwin.

Ansoff, I. (1962). *Corporate Strategy*. New York: Irwin McGraw-Hill.

BBC (2005). History of the digital watch. www.bbc.co.uk/dna/h2g2/alabaster-/A1006534. May 29.

BestBite (2004). Restaurant review. *Atlanta Journal Constitution*. Dec. 24.

Brealey, R. A. and S. C. Myers (2000). *Principles of Corporate Finance* (Sixth ed.). New York: Irwin McGraw-Hill.

Chandler, A. D. (1962). *Strategy and structure: Chapters in the history of industrial enterprise*. New York: Doubleday.

Christensen, C. M. and M. Overdorf (2000). Meeting the challenge of disruptive change. *Harvard Business Review 78*(2), 67–76.

Collis, D. J. and C. A. Montgomery (1995). Competing on resources: Strategy in the 1990s. *Harvard Business Review 73*(4), 118–129.

Donaldson, L. (2001). *The Contingency Theory of Organizations (Foundations for Organizational Science)*. Thousand Oaks, CA: Sage Publications, Inc.

Drew, J., B. McCallum, and S. Roggenhofer (2004). *Journey to Lean: Making Organizational Change Stick*. New York: Palgrave, Macmillan Publishing.

Ferdows, K., M. A. Lewis, and J. Machuca (2004). Rapid fire fulfilment. *Harvard Business Review 82*(11), 94–102.

Kaplan, R. S. and D. P. Norton (2000). Having trouble with your strategy? Then map it. *Harvard Business Review 78*(5), 167–176.

Kimmelman, M. (2005). Peter Paul Rubens: From the assembly line of a genius. *The New York Times*. Jan. 14.

Mercedes-Benz (1999, May). Press release. www.mbusi.com/pr/pressreleases.html.

Merriam-Webster (2007). Online dictionary. www.m-w.com.

Porter, M. E. (1985). *Competitive Advantage: Creating and Sustaining Superior Performance*. New York: The Free Press, Macmillan Publishing.

Skinner, W. (1969). Manufacturing–missing link in corporate strategy. *Harvard Business Review 47*(3), 136–145.

Stalk, G., P. Evans, and L. E. Shulman (1992). Competing on capabilities: The new rules of corporate strategy. *Harvard Business Review 70*(2), 54–69.

Tagliabue, J. (2003). A rival to Gap that operates like Dell. Spanish clothing chain Zara grows by being fast and flexible. *The New York Times*. May 30.

Taylor, W. (1993). Message and muscle: An interview with titan Nicolas Hayek. *Harvard Business Review 71*(2), 99–110.

von Hochberg, P., M. Rodrigues, and G. Grenon (2006). Who manages manufacturing? *Strategy+Business* (44), 1–12.

Zara (2005, Feb). Company information. www.zara.com/v05/index.html.

Mini-Case 1 | THE SWISS WATCH INDUSTRY

[9]Swiss watches are legendary. Swiss watches once dominated the world: in the mid 1970s, 43% of the units sold worldwide were Swiss made. Then things changed. By 1983, Swiss market shares plunged to less than 15%, and 1000 of the 1600 Swiss watch companies closed. These massive closures were accompanied by a contraction of the labor market by two thirds.

At the brink of bankruptcy, the creditor banks of the two flagships of the Swiss watch industry, Swiss-French SSIH and Swiss-German ASU AG, asked the consulting firm Hayek Engineering for advice: *Should we shut down or can you design a new operations strategy?*

The worldwide watch industry

During the late 1970s, manufacturers from Japan and Hong Kong penetrated the watch market by using low-cost labor, quartz technology (developed, but not used in Switzerland) and mass production. Their inexpensive watches quickly gained an important market share. To compensate for the lost revenues from diminished market share, Swiss watchmakers raised prices.

By 1980, the world market for watches was about 500 million units per year and consisted of three segments. The low-end segment had prices up to about $75 and represented 450 million units out of 500 million. The middle segment with prices up to $450 represented 42 million units, leaving 8 million watches for the top segment.

Margin retreat left the Swiss with zero share of the low-end segment; only 3% of the middle segment; but 97% share of the luxury watches (which accounted for 0.4% of world unit watch sales).

Watch technology

Mechanical watches consist of two groups of parts: the visible exterior parts such as the case, the dial, and hands, as well as the interior "movement," which contains about 200 individual parts and is driven merely by a spring. After a long evolution, two main mechanical watch technologies emerged. The *lever* was used for expensive watches where jewels tipped the teeth in the movement. The *pin pallet* was used for cheaper watches.

The process to produce and assemble mechanical watches was labor intensive. Master artists would work in a library-style environment on well-lit work desks with microscopes where they would compile a piece of "living art" worth more than the sum of its parts. In the mid 20th century, most watches sold in jewelry shops for hundreds of dollars. Their full production cost consisted of approximately 60% labor, 20% materials and 20% depreciation.

In 1957, the Hamilton Watch Co of Lancaster, Pennsylvania, produced the world's first electric watch. Its traditional balance-wheel mechanism used a bat-

[9]Professor Van Mieghem prepared this case as the basis for class discussion rather than to illustrate either the effective or ineffective handling of a managerial situation. This case is based on an earlier version written by Professor Yehuda Bassok. Taylor (1993) and BBC (2005) are also acknowledged. No part of this case study may be reproduced without permission; direct all inquiries to permissions@vanmieghem.us

tery instead of a spring as power source. In 1960, the next advance in electric watches came from Bulova, a watch company founded in 1875 in New York City by Joseph Bulova, a 23-year-old immigrant from Bohemia. The Bulova corporation replaced the balance-wheel mechanism with the electronic vibrations of a tuning fork. It raised the beat of the watch from 2.5 beats per minute for a mechanical watch to nearly 2.5 million per second for an electronic watch. The tuning fork was kept vibrating by a battery-powered electronic circuit. The Bulova electronic watch was one of the first consumer products to use a transistor.

The Japanese watch industry

The electronic watch technology was embraced and enhanced by the Japanese watch industry. Since its inception in 1880, the Japanese watch industry was concentrated in the hands of three competitors: K. Hattori (which marketed the Seiko brand), Citizen and Orient. The three companies accounted for 50%, 30% and 20% of production in 1950, respectively. Japanese manufacturers used skilled labor commanding wages at a level of approximately 1/10 of those in Switzerland.

During the 1950s, Seiko pursued the goal of closing the technological gap between the Swiss products and its own products. They also developed a policy of standardizing the movements of the different watches and invested heavily in automatic equipment. This permitted Seiko to reduce labor to 35% of the full production cost of a watch in the late 1960s. Vertical integration of component manufacturing also permitted more rapid deployment of new technology and watch design. One industry observer estimated that the Japanese enjoyed a 15% to 45% variable cost advantage over the Swiss in the mid 1960s. During the late 1960s they initiated component fabrication and assembly operations abroad. Plants were located in Hong Kong, Singapore and Malaysia. Workers in all three locations earned about one third as much as did Japanese workers. In the early 1970s, Hattori-Seiko entered the American and European markets.

Meanwhile, the Swiss research lab CEH (Centre Electronique Horloger) developed a more accurate oscillator and produced the first wristwatch quartz movement in 1967. In contrast to the Swiss manufacturers who had refined their mechanical technology to catch up with Bulova, Seiko made a commitment to develop and produce both analog and digital Quartz watches. The popularity of quartz watches began to grow around 1976. By 1977, Seiko became the largest watch company in the world.

1. *How would you contrast the operations strategy of the traditional Swiss watch company with that of Seiko?*

2. *What information would you gather and what advice would you give? Would you close shop or recommend a new strategy for the Swiss watch industry? For the latter, use the framework describing your recommended value proposition and required changes in competencies and the operational system.*

Chapter

2

COMPETITION, COMPETENCIES, AND OPERATIONS

To govern is to choose.—John Fitzgerald Kennedy (1962).
Divide et impera!—Caius Iulius Caesar[1] (100 - 44 B.C.).

Learning Objectives

After reading this chapter, you will be able to:

1. Explain the concept of operational trade-off and discuss its impact on competition.
2. Implement competency focus to improve operational efficiency.
3. Analyze a competitive threat using trade-off curves.
4. Design strategies to improve competitive advantage through operations.

The first chapter introduced the competency view of operations as the natural link between competitive strategy and operations. This chapter will investigate this link in greater depth. A good operations strategy clearly stipulates which competencies are critical and which are of secondary importance. One can't have it all: operational competencies exhibit trade-offs and superior performance requires making choices. But where do these trade-offs come from and how can operations shape them to our competitive advantage? That is the subject of this chapter.

2.1 | THE CONCEPT OF OPERATIONAL TRADE-OFF

A *trade-off* is "a balancing of factors all of which are not attainable at the same time; a giving up of one thing in return for another" according to the Merriam-Webster (2007) dictionary. We acknowledge trade-offs when saying "you can't have it both ways." Trade-offs require customers and firms to make choices.

---

[1]These Latin words, meaning "divide and rule" but better known as "divide and conquer," are attributed to Caesar, who used the strategy they refer to with great success.

Trade-offs are at the heart of strategy because they determine market segmentation and prioritize operational competencies. Let us first review how we can capture customer trade-offs and then discuss how a similar concept applies to operations.

Customer utility, trade-offs, and market segmentation

As customers, all of us make trade-offs in our needs when making a purchase. When buying a car, we may trade-off aesthetics, performance, and safety while attempting to keep our budget constant. As described in Chapter 1, any product or service can be characterized by the four-dimensional attribute bundle of cost, timeliness, variety, and quality. Economics has demonstrated that the decision behavior of a rational consumer who is faced with a choice of bundles can be reasonably modeled by utility maximization. Each individual possesses a utility function that assigns to each four-dimensional attribute bundle the level of personal satisfaction. Customers simply choose the bundle within their budget that gives them highest satisfaction.

Customer trade-offs show how a customer can trade-off one or more attributes against the others, while holding her utility constant. Customer trade-offs are represented analytically by iso-utility or indifference curves that show the combinations of attribute levels that yield a constant utility. (The curves become surfaces when three or more attributes are involved.) Differences in preferences are manifested by different trade-off curves that allow firms to segment the market. To explain how this works, consider the Business Jet Group (BJG) of B/E Aerospace, discussed in Example 2.1.

An example of customer trade-offs and market segmentation

BJG is the world's leading manufacturer of cabin interior products for business jets. It creates completely customized cabins to meet any taste or purpose and offers the industry's largest selection of furniture, cabinets, appliances, and design elements. Recently, C&D Aerospace, which makes seats for commuter aircraft, has been trying to get into BJG's niche. Can a rival that is focused on standardization and cost-efficiency be a serious threat? How can operations help sustain and enhance BJG's differentiation strategy? We will address these questions throughout the chapter and start by illustrating how customer trade-offs allow BJG and C&D Aerospace to segment the market.

Consider the market for cabin interior products for small jet aircraft (up to 50 passengers): customers include corporations, wealthy individuals, and short-haul commuter airlines. Each of these customers has different preferences regarding size (individuals tend to prefer smaller jets), selection and customization (individuals tend to customize more), and total cost of ownership (airlines tend to be more sensitive to cost). Figure 2.1 shows the trade-off curves between levels of customization and the customer cost of ownership for similarly sized aircraft. Recall that each trade-off curve gives that customer a constant level of utility; overall, the figure shows two levels of utility $U_1 < U_2$. Given that customers prefer higher utility, they will prefer product offerings to the north-east of their trade-off curves. (Notice that the horizontal cost axis is inverted so that going east is more cost efficient.)

The fact that different individuals have different trade-off curves is exactly

---

Example 2.1 B/E Aerospace's Business Jet Group (BJG)

The Business Jet Group (BJG) of B/E Aerospace is the world's leading manufacturer of cabin interior products for business jets. The company offers the industry's broadest product line and gives its customers (manufacturers, modifiers, or owners of executive aircraft) the freedom to customize their cabin environment to meet any taste or purpose.

BJG offers the industry's most extensive selection of seats and sofas, executive cabinets, lighting products, passenger service units, coffee & cappuccino makers, wine chillers, microwave and steam ovens, oxygen systems, and air valves. By employing the industry's largest staff of engineers and designers, BJG can provide customized and integrated interior solutions for business jet aircraft. The company uses the newest technological advances in materials with state-of-the-art design hardware and software. Its products blend aesthetics and functionality.

BJG's operations strategy clearly guides how to make trade-offs. For example, it guides product design choices: "We must design the seats as light as they can be, but only as strong as they need to be. Of course keeping in mind quality, comfort, and performance," according to Arturo Callejas, Vice President of Operations. By offering the most complete business jet interiors product line, BJG has quickly become the industry leader. By emphasizing quality, service, and selection, it has established long-term preferred manufacturer relationships with essentially every manufacturer of new business jets and now supplies more than half of all executive aircraft seating, lighting, and air valves produced worldwide. *Source: Callejas (2004), B/E Aerospace.*

---

what allows firms to segment the market by choosing different strategic positions. Companies can then position themselves in the space of value-propositions and use the customer trade-off curves to segment the market. For example, in Figure 2.1, all else being equal, private jet owners prefer the value offering by BJG, while commuter airlines prefer that by firm C&D Aerospace.

Operational trade-offs

Just as individuals face trade-offs, so do organizations. Finite endowment of wealth and time limits the number and extent of objectives that an organization can attain simultaneously with its resources and processes. In theory, just like customer trade-offs are represented by iso-utility curves, so could operational trade-offs be represented by iso-NPV curves: these curves would show the competence combinations (e.g., of variety, response time, quality, and cost) that yield a given net present value.[2] The idea is that the organization would be indifferent between any of those combinations.

Because it is very difficult to characterize iso-NPV relationships, in practice, operational trade-off curves instead show the process cost to deliver a specific combination of quality, response time, and variety.[3] These costs are specific to

---

[2] For simplicity of representation, we will simply consider two-dimensional trade-offs and curves. When considering the trade-off among three or more competencies, the curves become surfaces.

[3] The appropriate type of cost depends on the situation. For example, marginal cost is important in a competitive setting with existing processes, while full unit cost is important in the planning phase of new processes.

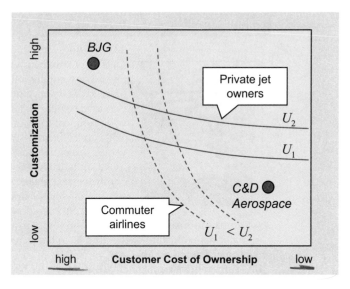

Figure 2.1 Customer trade-off curves show the combinations of product and service attributes that provide a constant level of utility. The figure shows two levels of utility, $U_1 < U_2$. Different types of customers have different preferences and trade-offs, which allows market segmentation. In this example, private jet owners prefer the value offering by BJG, while commuter airlines prefer C&D Aerospace.

the operational system and thus are shaped by operations strategy:

Principle 3 (**Trade-offs**) Operational competencies are governed by trade-offs that are defined by the operational system of resources and processes.

This principle says that an organization can't have it all because its competencies exhibit trade-offs due to the finite abilities of its resources and processes. But perhaps more importantly, the principle also says that operations strategy can shape and change the trade-offs by choosing the "right" resource bundle and activity network. What is "right" can be thought of qualitatively (competencies are aligned with the customer value proposition) or quantitatively (the NPV is increased).

2.2 | SHAPING OPERATIONAL TRADE-OFFS: EXAMPLES

Perhaps the most immediate impact of operations on competitive strategy is the ability to shape the trade-offs and choose an appropriate competency point. This is the counterpart of market segmentation and positioning and is crucial to sustain a strategic position. Let us start here with two concrete examples—one from

Example 2.2 Wilbur Chocolate

Wilbur Chocolate is an artisan producer of fine chocolate located in Lititz, Pennsylvania. The company, founded in 1865, was acquired in 1993 by Cargill, Inc., one of the largest private companies in the United States. Wilbur Chocolate's innovative product line serves the needs of the confectionery, bakery, food manufacturing, and dairy markets throughout North America.

Wilbur faces a growing demand for new products and partners with customers to create cutting edge products. Wilbur provides timely solutions for customers who are looking for a new flavor profile to add to their product line or for more flexibility in their ingredient functionality.

The same process is used to produce the majority of the company's variety: all chocolate consists of a fat (cocoa butter), flavors (cocoa powder, liquor, etc.) and a bulking agent (sugar). Several hundred different chocolate formulas and products can be produced in batches.

Source: Nisser (2007).

a manufacturing setting and one from a service operation—to illustrate how operations strategy can shape the trade-off curve by choosing the "right" process and resources.

Wilbur Chocolate: a trade-off between product selection and cost

To illustrate a trade-off involving variety similar to the one experienced by BJG, consider the simpler situation of Wilbur Chocolate, which produces hundreds of chocolate flavors and products using a single process (Example 2.2). Upon acquiring Wilbur, its parent company, Cargill, Inc., wanted to know how sensitive Wilbur's product cost is to changes in variety. Comparing this cost sensitivity to the customers' increased willingness-to-pay for innovative products was important in determining the amount of variety that the company should provide.

The selection-cost trade-off is a useful tool to help answer that question. If only a single chocolate-type is produced, the company could match its production to demand; the ensuing process is called a flow shop. If, however, several chocolate-types are produced, production must occur in batches and often use a cyclic schedule. For each chocolate, a cycle stock will be built up during its production to support its sales when other products are being produced.

To characterize the operational trade-off curve when N chocolates are made on a single batch process, we build up the minimal sustainable cost of producing the selection by capturing the major relevant cost drivers. Assume the full unit production cost includes $.70 for direct materials (cost of material inputs such as ingredients and packaging for one box of chocolate) and $.30 for overhead that is independent of selection (fixed costs such as depreciation and indirect labor, which we assume dominate variable labor costs). We then have that

$$\text{unit cost} = \$1 + \text{setup and holding cost.}$$

To find the minimal sustainable cost we must find the appropriate batch size that minimizes the sum of setup and inventory costs. The optimal batch size clearly depends on the annual holding cost (assume finished goods inventory incurs a unit annual holding cost H of $0.15, or 15% of $1); the changeover cost from one chocolate type to another (assume a setup cost S of $500 is incurred); and

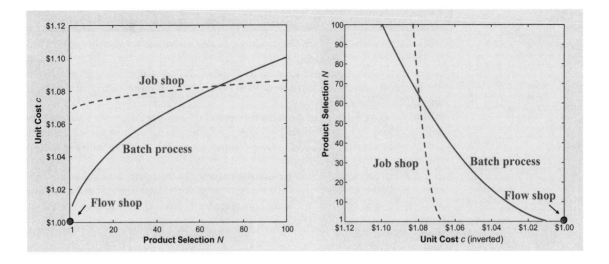

Figure 2.2 Selection-cost trade-off curves for three different processes: a flow shop which produces a single product, a batch process producing N products, and a highly flexible job shop (which has lower changeover costs but higher unit sourcing costs than a batch process). The figures show two equivalent representations of the same trade-off curves.

of the total volume (to keep things simple, assume that the total throughput rate of $R = 1,500,000$ boxes per year is split evenly over the N chocolate types). In this simple setting, the optimal batch size and associated unit cost is given by the economic lot sizing quantity for *make-to-stock* processes, reviewed in Appendix A on page 431:

$$\text{minimal unit setup and holding cost} = c_{HS}\sqrt{N} \tag{2.1}$$
$$\text{where } c_{HS} = \sqrt{2HS/R} = \$0.01.$$

The total unit cost thus is $1 + 0.01\sqrt{N}$. This square-root relationship between unit cost and selection is the trade-off curve of this process, and is shown in Figure 2.2 with a solid line in two equivalent representations. Notice that a single product company ($N = 1$) would neither need any changeovers nor cycle stock; a flow shop could continuously supply units at a cost of $1. In contrast, a company producing nine products would incur a unit cost of $1.03 where the three cents can be interpreted as a complexity cost.

Expression (2.1) shows how the company can *shape* its selection-cost trade-off curve: its only sensible levers are to increase total volume or flexibility. Once demand per product reaches a certain volume, one can dedicate a process to that product, obtaining a flow shop. In contrast, by decreasing changeover times, one can reduce cost while keeping selection constant–or increase selection while keeping cost constant. Such a highly-flexible process (e.g. a job shop) would be much less sensitive to changes in the breadth of selection. However, it would typically face higher material input costs due to the lower planned volume per product line. A typical resulting trade-off curve for a job shop is shown by the dashed line in Figure 2.2.

Example 2.3 Ameritrade's 5-Second Guarantee

Ameritrade develops and provides brokerage products and services for investment and portfolio management to individual investors and institutional distribution partners. Ameritrade started its operations in Omaha, Nebraska, after the deregulation of the U.S. brokerage industry in May 1975. It was one of the first firms to offer negotiated commissions to individual investors and was a founding member of the discount brokerage industry. In January 1996, Ameritrade was the first company to launch an online investing system for individual investors.

Ameritrade formulates its value proposition around flat pricing, fast executions, and real-time information. It recognizes that speed of execution is critical in today's capital markets where security prices move quickly. A greater execution delay increases the risk that the trade's execution price will differ from the market price at the time of submission. In 2004, it advertised its "5-Second Guarantee: Qualified S&P 500 Internet trades that take longer than 5 seconds to execute are commission-free." At that time, it charged a flat commission fee of $10.99 for any Internet trade. The average time to execute a trade was roughly 1 sec. in May 2004. On June 9, 2004, Ameritrade reported 144,000 average client trades per day in May. *Source: Ameritrade (2004).*

Ameritrade: a trade-off between quality of service and cost

Ameritrade, the trading company profiled in Example 2.3 that uses responsiveness as a competitive weapon, is an example of a service trade-off curve. Ameritrade's "5-Second Guarantee" states that any trade that takes longer than 5 seconds to execute is commission-free. Similar service guarantees are offered by Domino's Pizza (30 minute delivery guarantee otherwise the pizza is free), Lucky's supermarket ("three is a crowd" guarantees there will never be more than three people in line for a cash register), and Wells Fargo (which gives a $5 reward if you wait more than 5 minutes for service). Let us analyze the trade-off between a *quality-of-service guarantee* and its cost implications by focusing on Ameritrade.

We can derive this trade-off by calculating the cost of offering an advertised service guarantee of 5 seconds. The 5-second guarantee implies a lost revenue of $10.99 for each trade that takes longer than 5 seconds. This opportunity cost can be thought of as a warranty cost of poor quality of service. On average, it is:

$$\$10.99 \times \Pr(\text{execution time} > 5 \text{ seconds}).$$

Ameritrade can track the number of trades whose execution time exceeds the guarantee in order to have a proxy of the corresponding probability and warranty costs. If that data is not available, Ameritrade can resort to a queuing model of the service operation to estimate that probability. Queuing theory, the tool to analyze make-to-order processes and reviewed in Appendix C on p. 439, predicts that

$$\Pr(\text{execution time} > 5 \text{ seconds}) = \exp\left(-\frac{5 \text{ seconds}}{\text{average execution time}}\right) \quad (2.2)$$

$$= \exp\left(-\frac{5 \text{ seconds}}{1 \text{ second}}\right) = e^{-5} = 0.7\%,$$

given that the average time to execute a trade was roughly 1 second in May

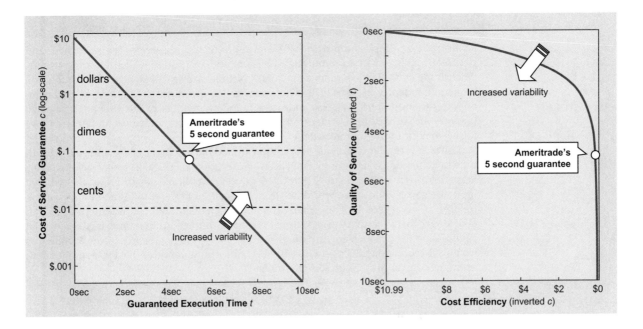

Figure 2.3 Equivalent representations of a quality-of-service vs. cost trade-off and Ameritrade's position. Increased variability in the timing or type of customer requests moves the trade-off curves in the direction of the arrows.

2004. At a daily trade volume of 144,000, this corresponds to a daily cost of $144,000 \times \$10.99 \times 0.7\% = \$10,663$, or \$3.9 million per year.

How would that modest number change if Ameritrade were to offer a tighter service guarantee, say of 2.5 seconds? Well, that would simply change the probability to $e^{-2.5}$. Sweeping over all possible service guarantees t yields the service-cost trade-off curve:

$$\text{cost of service guarantee per trade} = \$10.99 \times e^{-t}.$$

Figure 2.3 shows two equivalent representations of this trade-off. The left panel shows cost in a logarithmic scale as a function of the guaranteed service time. On the right, the panel shows the trade-off on a linear but inverted scale so that moving northeast improves both cost and service.

It is clear that the 5-seconds promise was a smart choice for Ameritrade. It was chosen to fall below the "knee" of its trade-off curve and thus resulted in a modest monthly cost. Had it offered a 2.5 second guarantee, its yearly lost revenue would have increased to \$47 million! Doubling the service quality would have multiplied unit cost by a factor of 12 as a consequence of the exponential relationship in the trade-off curve. (This factor would be even larger if demand were to increase when changing from 5 to 2.5 sec.)

Expression (2.2) of the trade-off curve shows how Ameritrade can *shape* its trade-off curve: its only sensible lever is to decrease the average trade execution time. (Reducing its commission below \$10.99 would reduce warranty costs but could also reduce revenue.) Given that average execution time equals average waiting time plus average service time, it must either decrease the average service time (by using faster computers or faster software) or the average waiting time. The waiting time formula, reviewed in Appendix C on p. 440, shows that Ameritrade must either increase its computer capacity (which will reduce utilization) or decrease the variability of customer requests (timing and/or type). This is important from a marketing perspective: if promotions were to increase the rate or variability in the timing or the type of trades, then waiting delays and warranty costs would have increased and moved the trade-off curves in Figure 2.3 in the direction of the arrows.

2.3 | PROPERTIES OF OPERATIONAL TRADE-OFFS

The two examples above highlight some general properties of trade-off curves.

The operational system and planned operating conditions shape trade-offs

The most important property of an organization's trade-offs is that they are defined by its operating system and are affected by all of its characteristics. Typically, trade-off curves assume a series of planned conditions consistent with the operations strategy. In our chocolate example, it was important to know the process architecture (a single production line, followed by finished good storage); the planned production volume; the operating policies (cyclic batch scheduling with identical batch size); and the cost structure of inputs, processing, and capacity. When those conditions materialize, the process competency vector of cost, quality, variety, and timeliness will fall on the trade-off curve.

Operational trade-offs provide competitive protection

One can argue that the existence of trade-offs is what makes operations relevant to strategy: in the same manner that competitive strategy deals with positioning in the customer needs space, operations strategy deals with positioning in the competency space that is hard to imitate. While heterogeneity in customer trade-offs drives market segmentation as we saw earlier, it is the trade-offs in operational competencies that provide competitive protection to a firm's strategic position. Like promises, value propositions are meaningful only when they can be delivered, which depends on the competencies of the operational system. One of the reasons organizations implement processes is to ensure consistent execution of its activities. Once a particular operational system is in place, others can only replicate its performance by copying it in its entirety, which is very costly.

To illustrate how trade-offs in operational competencies provide competitive protection, consider again the two jet manufacturers BJG and C&D Aerospace. The trade-off principle says that we can find operations that excel in flexibility but do not perform as well on other competencies. B/E has flexible design and manufacturing capabilities: it has custom product design processes and job shop production processes, all performed by highly capable employees, soft-

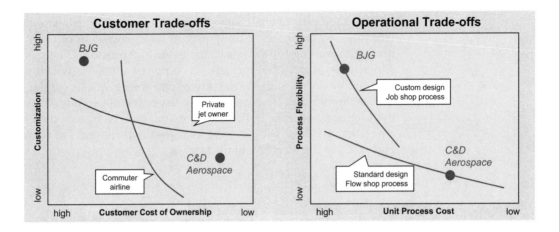

Figure 2.4 While heterogeneity in customer needs (left panel) allows firms to segment the market in the hope of establishing a quasi-monopoly position in a segment, the sustainability of that advantage is rooted in the existence of competency trade-offs. As shown on the right, C&D Aerospace will have difficulty competing in BJG's segment unless it completely overhauls its operational system.

ware, and hardware. In contrast, C&D Aerospace has configured its operational system to most efficiently make larger quantities of identical seats: its product design allows less selection and customization, and its assembly process has a more rigid activity sequence and is less flexible. Both processes and their associated resources have strengths and weaknesses that are manifested by square-root trade-off curves similar to those analyzed earlier, as shown on the right of figure 2.4. The fact that BJG's trade-off curve dominates C&D's at high levels of customization means that C&D Aerospace cannot move into BJG's niche without either running a big cost disadvantage or completely overhauling its operational system.

It is in this sense that operations strategy ensures not only ensures strategic fit, but its judicious use of competency trade-offs also makes the competitive strategy harder to imitate. Porter (1996, p. 70) put it nicely: "Rivals can copy one activity or product feature fairly easily, but will have much more difficulty duplicating a whole system of competing. ... The essence of strategy is choosing what *not* to do. Without trade-offs, there would be no need for choice and thus no need for strategy. Any good idea could and would be quickly imitated."

Time stamps and improvement

Trade-off curves are snapshots of particular instances in time. You should imagine them carrying a *time stamp*. As a firm improves its operations, its trade-off curve moves outward, which creates a region of new options for positioning: operational improvement can be used to cut costs, to deliver a higher level of non-cost competency, or to achieve a combination of the two.

For example, consider the selection-cost trade-off from the previous section and assume that the firm has become better in handling changeovers. This has

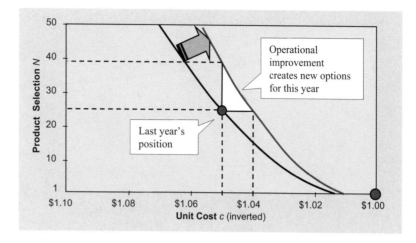

Figure 2.5 Operational improvement moves the trade-off curve outwards and opens up a region of new options represented by the shaded triangle.

decreased its setup cost from $500 last year to $320 this year. This 36% improvement has changed the selection-cost trade-off from $c = 1 + 0.01\sqrt{N}$ to $c = 1 + 0.008\sqrt{N}$, as shown in Figure 2.5. If the firm was offering a selection of 25 products last year at unit cost $c = \$1.05$, it now has the option to keep that selection unchanged and use the lower cost of $1.04 to either increase profits or lower prices; it can broaden its selection to up to 39 products without increasing costs; or it can use any combination inside the shaded triangle in Fig. 2.5.

Equivalent graphical representations of trade-offs

Trade-offs can be represented graphically in many equivalent ways depending on the choice and orientation of the axis. Operations researchers often represent the trade-off by drawing cost as a function of underlying parameters of interest, as in the left graph of Figure 2.2. From a strategy perspective, it is attractive to choose axes such that trade-off curves are downward sloping, as in the right graphs of Figures 2.2 and 2.3. That representation leads to a view where "going out north-east" is always desirable, yet trade-offs restrict us from getting it all. To have downward sloping curves that involve cost, however, one must typically invert the cost axis (which is equivalent to considering cost efficiency). Finally, notice that the visual shape of the curve (e.g., linear, convex or concave) also depends on the scaling of the axis, as illustrated by Figures 2.2 and 2.3.

Changing the value proposition: strategy effect

The trade-off principle predicts that costs will change when a firm changes its market strategy for instance by offering a higher level of variety while keeping its operational system unchanged. We will refer to this change in cost due to a change in market positioning only as the *strategy cost differential* Δc_{strat}. For example, consider the selection-cost trade-off from the previous section. Assume that our chocolate plant is currently producing 25 stock-keeping-units (SKUs),

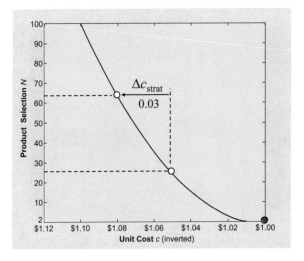

Figure 2.6 When a firm increases the level of variety offered to its customers while keeping its processes and resources unchanged, the change in strategy is reflected in the cost differential Δc_{strat}.

so that its unit cost would be $c = 1 + 0.01\sqrt{25} = \$1.05$ according to equation (2.1). If the company decides to increase its selection to 64 SKUs, while keeping its processes and resources unchanged, its unit cost would be $c = 1 + 0.01\sqrt{64} = \$1.08$. The change in strategy would thus imply a cost increase of $\Delta c_{strat} = \$1.08 - \$1.05 = \$0.03$, which can be read from the trade-off curve as shown in Figure 2.6.

Deviations from plan: sourcing and utilization effects

When actual operating conditions differ from the planned conditions, the actual cost to deliver the value proposition will differ from the cost suggested by the trade-off curve. We will refer to the change in cost due to a deviation from planned operating conditions (while keeping strategic positioning unchanged) as the *planned cost differential* Δc_{plan}. There are myriad possible causes for deviations from the underlying planned conditions, but two are worth highlighting: changes in the cost of inputs (direct materials or sourcing costs), and in the cost of resource usage.

When actual sourcing costs deviate from planned (or "standard") costs, the actual cost position of a company will differ from the planned cost leading to what we call a *sourcing differential* in costs. For example, if the actual sourcing costs of our chocolate plant are $0.66 instead of the planned $0.7, the sourcing cost differential $\Delta c_{plan\,(sourcing)} = 0.66 - 0.7 = -\$0.04.$ At a selection of 25 chocolate types, this would lower actual unit costs to $\$1.05 - \$0.04 = \$1.01$, as shown in the left panel of Figure 2.7.

When actual volumes deviate from planned volumes, the actual unit cost position will differ from the plan because fixed costs are now borne by a different number of goods or services. This results in what we call a *utilization*

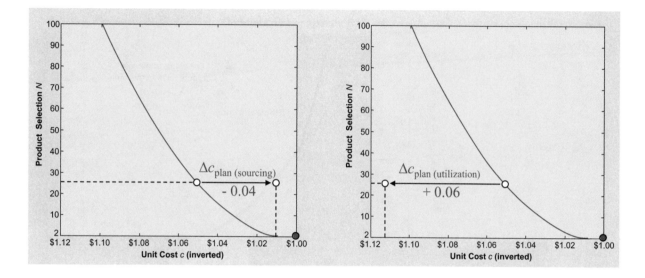

Figure 2.7 When actual conditions deviate from the plan, actual costs differ from the designed trade-off curve. Two reasons are differences in sourcing (left) or in utilization (right).

Analytics Box 2.1 Calculating utilization-driven cost differentials.

1. Compute the total fixed cost by multiplying the planned unit fixed cost allocation c_F by the "strategically-planned throughput rate" R_{strat}.

2. Find the unit fixed cost allocation at the actual throughput rate R by dividing the total fixed cost by R.

3. The resulting utilization cost differential is $\Delta c_{\text{plan (utilization)}} = c_F(R_{strat}/R - 1)$. Recall that capacity utilization is the ratio of throughput to capacity. Dividing numerator and denominator by capacity yields:

$$\Delta c_{\text{plan (utilization)}} = c_F\left(\frac{\text{throughput}_{\text{strat}}}{\text{throughput}} - 1\right) = c_F\left(\frac{\text{utilization}_{\text{strat}}}{\text{utilization}} - 1\right).$$

differential. For example, assume the actual sales volume of chocolate boxes is only 1,250,000, whereas the throughput rate planned under the operations strategy was $1,500,000$. The total fixed cost of $\$.3 \times 1,500,000 = \$450,000$ is now borne by only 1,250,000 chocolate boxes, leading to a higher fixed cost allocation of $\$450,000/1,250,000 = \$0.36$ per box. This utilization cost differential $\Delta c_{\text{plan (utilization)}} = \$0.36 - \$0.3 = \$0.06$ would raise actual unit costs to $\$1.05 + \$0.06 = \$1.11$, as shown in the right panel of Figure 2.7. American automotive companies experience similar phenomena when their pension obligations are spread over a smaller number of cars. Analytics Box 2.1 summarizes the calculations.

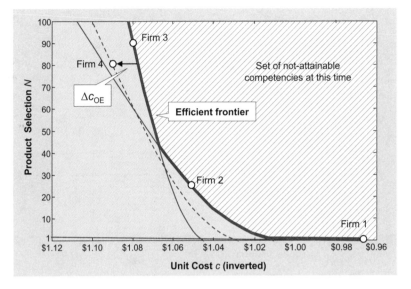

Figure 2.8 The efficient frontier is the outer envelope of all trade-off curves in an industry. As such, it defines the set of operationally efficient companies and the cost disadvantage Δc_{OE} of the remaining companies.

2.4 | OPERATIONAL EFFICIENCY AND THE FRONTIER

To analyze a firm's position in the competency space relative to competitors, it is useful to introduce the concept of *efficient frontier* .

The **efficient frontier** is a snapshot that traces the industry's lowest cost to produce specific competency bundles of variety, quality, and timeliness.

Imagine that we knew the operational trade-off curves of all the firms competing in a given industry. Then, we could find that industry's efficient frontier as the outer envelope of those individual firm trade-offs, all at a single point in time. The frontier thus defines the set of competencies that are currently achievable by best-in-class operational systems. For example, assume that our chocolate industry has four players with selection-cost trade-off curves as shown in Figure 2.8. (Recall that drawing only two dimensions implies that the level of other competencies, such as quality and responsiveness, is constant and similar for all four companies.) Assume for simplicity that all firms are operating under planned conditions so that their current positions, as indicated by the points labeled "Firm x," fall on their trade-off curves. Firm 1 is a single-product mass producer and defines the best-in-class operation for that competency. Firm 2 is a mid-volume batch producer, while Firm 3 is a small-volume, flexible job-shop. Firm 4 is below-best-in-class: the operations of Firm 3 could provide Firm 4's selection (80 SKUs) at lower cost (about a cent less).

Operational efficiency

We say a firm's competency bundle is *operationally efficient* if it falls on the frontier and its cost is the *efficient cost* for that competency bundle. While such firms have best-in-class systems, their challenge is to stay on the frontier by constantly improving and innovating, thereby pushing the frontier outward. (In daily language we say that the firm "pushes the envelope.") In contrast, a firm's competency bundle that is not on the frontier is inefficient.

A competency's **operational efficiency (OE)** is measured by its cost disadvantage Δc_{OE} relative to the efficient cost for that same competency bundle.

The cost disadvantage Δc_{OE} due to operational (in)efficiency[4] is the horizontal distance between its trade-off curve and the frontier, *ceteris paribus*. It measures how much better a world-class operational system would be at providing the same non-cost competency levels of variety, timeliness and quality. In Figure 2.8, Firm 4 has a cost efficiency differential of about $0.01, meaning that it could lower its cost by $0.01 by adopting more efficient resources and processes (those of Firm 3) without changing its value proposition.

It is important to remember that our notion of operational efficiency always refers to a specific level of competencies. Operational efficiency is measured relative to an objective and is not an absolute property. Some authors therefore call it *operational effectiveness*. For example, Firm 2 in Figure 2.8 can offer a selection of 25 SKUs efficiently because no operational system can do it at lower cost: $\Delta c_{OE} = 0$ for that competency bundle. In contrast, Firm 2 cannot efficiently offer a selection of 70 or 80 SKUs because Firm 3 can do that at a lower cost: thus, Firm 2 runs a positive cost disadvantage for that competency bundle.

How to estimate the frontier? Competitive intelligence!

Estimating the frontier requires competency information on all rivals in a particular industry. While such information is not readily available, substantial progress can made by combining various "competitive intelligence" approaches. One approach is to learn from trade associations and reports. Another is to estimate or re-engineer the trade-off curve of rivals by constructing hypothetical "best player" models that build on information from experts and suppliers. Some companies have even hired former employees of competitors (and have gone so far as to hire private investigators to observe competitors).

Who benefits from the frontier?

The efficient frontier is perhaps most useful for companies that fall below it. First, such operationally inefficient firms are at risk because competitors can duplicate their value proposition at lower cost. The larger their inefficiency (i.e., Δc_{OE}), the greater their risk (as we will later analyze in detail). Their challenge is to improve their operational system to eventually approach the frontier, which

---

[4]While the term operational *in*efficiency would be better, OE is standard. Similarly, one could use the term efficiency frontier; yet, efficient frontier is standard terminology in finance (as we will see in Chapter 9.)

brings us to our next point. Secondly, operationally inefficient firms can simultaneously improve on multiple dimensions by learning and adopting world-class operational systems. It is *as if* these firms don't face "real" trade-offs. While their current operations face trade-offs in line with the trade-off principle, these companies are so inefficient that they can improve on multiple dimensions without giving up on any. For example, if Firm 4 were to adopt the fast change-over tactics of Firm 3, it would gain cost efficiency without giving up on its selection offering.

Companies on the frontier, however, face real trade-offs: there are simply no better operational systems available at this point in time to allow them to simultaneously improve on multiple dimensions without giving up on any. Only through improvement and innovation can they push the frontier outward. In that sense, real trade-offs are those defined by the efficient frontier.

2.5 | OPERATIONAL EFFICIENCY AND PRODUCTIVITY

So far, our examination of trade-offs and operational efficiency has not involved any discussion of productivity. Remember that the goal of operations strategy is not to increase productivity, but to maximize value (recall Principle 1 on p. 5). Yet many business professionals continue to phrase the goal of operations as increasing productivity and mistakenly believe that a good operation is a low-cost operation. FedEx is among the most expensive delivery services, but few people would accuse it of running a poor operation. FedEx emphasizes guaranteed overnight delivery and is in complete agreement with our principles of value, alignment, and focus. A low-cost productivity emphasis could spell its demise. This is not to say that productivity has no role in operations strategy. To clarify, let us first review what is meant by productivity and then discuss how it relates to our story.

Defining productivity

Productivity measures the efficiency of transforming inputs into outputs over a given time period (monthly, quarterly, annually):

$$\text{Productivity} = \frac{\text{units of outputs}}{\text{units of inputs during a given time period}}.$$

Productivity is a physical measure of aggregate asset efficiency.

Different types of productivity come into play depending on which type of input, or "factor" in economic language, is under consideration. When we restrict our attention to the labor input, we derive the definition of *labor productivity*. For example, Harley-Davidson carefully tracks the number of powertrains per 1000 hours worked. Call centers track the number of phone calls handled by an agent during one hour. The car industry tracks labor productivity via the reciprocal measurement: the number of labor hours per assembled car. Similarly, one can define capital productivity, raw material productivity, energy productivity, etc.

Measuring productivity

A major problem with the traditional definition of productivity is measurement. Measuring physical units over a given time span is more tricky than one would expect. Two complications emerge because it involves comparisons both across time and within time. Consider, for example, comparing labor productivity in car assembly across time: labor productivity is measured today in the same manner as it was in 1913 when Henry Ford ran his first assembly line. However, comparing the present figures with those recorded back in 1913 would be fairly meaningless because the car produced today is only in the most superficial ways comparable to the Model T of 1913. Counting physical units does not account for the fact that cars typically become more and more advanced over time.

The second measurement issue is that most processes require several types of inputs. But how does one measure that in physical units? For example, the assembly of a car may require a certain amount of labor hours, but it also needs electricity, measured in kilowatt hours, and raw material of sheet steel, measured in kg, etc. One simply cannot add apples and oranges.

Total factor productivity (TFP) considers all inputs when looking at productivity and solves the additivity problem by converting all physical units into monetary units which can then be added. To address the inter-temporal comparison problem, one typically fixes a "standard base rate" to convert each input into money to eliminate any price or inflation effects.[5] Such fixed base rates, however, make it difficult to account for changes in the functionality and value of the product or service over time. Recognizing these problems, Lewis (2004) proposes that "productivity is simply the ratio of the value of goods and services provided to consumers to the amount of time worked and capital used to produce the goods and services."

The power of productivity growth and the global economy

The objective of productivity measurements is to track performance over time or to compare performance within a given time among various locations, organizations, industries, or countries. GDP per capita, which is widely regarded as the best single measure of standard-of-living and economic well-being, is driven by labor productivity:

$$\frac{GDP}{population} = \frac{GDP}{national\ labor\ hours} \times \frac{national\ labor\ hours}{population}$$

$$= labor\ productivity \times hours\ worked\ per\ capita.$$

Higher productivity increases the available surplus that can be distributed to consumers, employees, or shareholders. Differences in GDP per capita stem from productivity or utilization (i.e., hours worked per period per capita) differences. For example, while labor productivity in Western Europe and the U.S. has converged, the big difference is that Europeans have decreased annual labor hours per capita by 20 to 30% since the 1970s. In general, however, "productivity varies enormously around the world. The differences in productivity explain virtually all of the differences in GDP per capita," according to Lewis (2004). He posits that differences in wealth, poverty, and threats to global stability can

---

[5]Measuring TFP requires a variety of subtleties that are nicely reviewed in Appendix B in Hayes, Wheelwright, and Clark (1988).

be explained by differences in productivity. Armed with the most comprehensive international studies on productivity by industry section (conducted by the McKinsey Global Institute), Lewis distilled some contrarian conclusions.

Traditional actions that tend to increase productivity are capital investment, education, and incentive-based performance management. While these actions certainly help, Lewis found that "the importance of education of the workforce has been taken way too far. The truth of the matter is that regardless of institutional education level, workers around the world can be adequately trained on the job for high productivity." The best predictor of productivity, he argues, is product market competition because it disseminates better practices. This capitalist free market perspective was highlighted by Schumpeter (1942) as creative destruction. In Schumpeter's view, radical innovation by entrepreneurs is the force of sustained economic growth, even as it transforms industries by destroying established companies. This brings us back to operations.

The role of productivity in operations strategy

Ultimately, productivity stems from how we put our assets to work, which is exactly the concern of operations strategy. The latest empirical findings confirm what operations researchers have always been preaching: while attracting capital and high-caliber talented people is obviously important, the way we put that capital and talent to work is equally, if not more, important. A key component to productivity growth is improvement and innovation, which we will further explore in Chapter 10.

While productivity is a powerful predictor of economic well-being, there are several reasons why we must be careful when applying it in the context of operations strategy.

First, productivity comparisons at face value between operations within a company or across companies are meaningless unless one corrects for differences in operating conditions and strategic positioning. When doing so, "corrected" productivity is similar to our notion of operational efficiency in that it becomes a relative measure of how close a process is to the frontier *when keeping the level of strategic differentiation constant.*

Second, even after correcting for operating conditions and strategic positioning, one must be mindful that productivity nearly always boils down to cost minimization, which may not be the first priority of a differentiated (i.e., non-cost) strategic position. For example, Southwest airlines is lauded for its highly productive workforce. But should a full-service airline strive to serve its first-class customers with a similar productivity-focused workforce?[6] The principle of alignment implies that our operational system, including its performance measures, should be in line with our strategic priorities.

Third, productivity is a ratio or relative measure. As we will see in the next chapter, the value of an operation is typically a non-linear function of its inputs. It follows that maximizing a ratio such as productivity will not typically lead to the same outcome as maximizing value. Therefore, in our remaining journey, we will use the value maximization principle as our guiding objective and discuss productivity-related issues using our notion of operational efficiency.

---

[6]The threat analysis and strategic response sections provide a framework to address this!

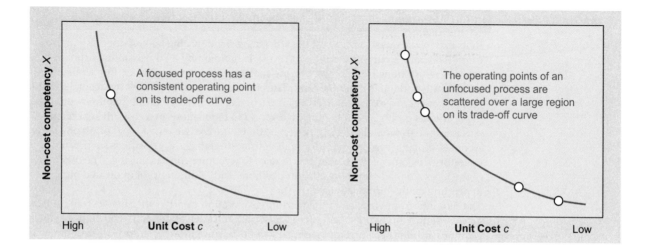

Figure 2.9 A focused operation (left) consistently operates at a single position on its trade-off curve. The opposite (right) is an operation with operating points scattered over a large region on its trade-off curve.

2.6 | How to Improve Operational Efficiency? Focus!

Bringing an organization to the frontier is a laudable goal, but how does one actually achieve that? There is obviously no simple recipe for being world-class, but one concept is often useful in pursuing this quest: operational focus. In the sciences, the Latin word focus means a point of convergence of rays. (The great astronomer Kepler first used it in that sense in his Pars Optica in 1604.) In everyday language, focus refers to a sharply directed or concentrated activity, attention, or energy. Let us discuss what focus means in operations.

The concept of focus in operations

A *focused operation* is an operation whose required competencies are restricted to a narrow set in the competency space of cost, variety, speed, and quality. The opposite is an operation that tries to deliver many divergent competencies.

How does the concept of focus relate to trade-offs? Focus can be phrased in terms of the point(s) on the trade-off curve where we choose to operate. A focused operation consistently operates on a single point on its trade-off curve, as shown in Figure 2.9. The opposite is an operation whose operating points are scattered over a large region on its trade-off curve. Scattering can occur at a given time or can be the cumulative result of oscillations of the operating point. Recall that every operation, whether it is focused or not, is governed by trade-offs. Thus, focus is a joint property of the operational system and of the way we choose to utilize that system. In other words, focus depends not only on the system, but also on the demands put on it.

For example, reconsider the four firms with trade-off curves as shown in

Example 2.4 Focusing recruiting at a Midwest bank

In its expansion quest, a Midwest bank is facing the daunting task of doubling its workforce. The bank's current recruiting process is handled by a 90 person department that receives requisitions from internal hiring managers. Upon receipt, the first available recruiter pulls and filters potential candidates from a database and sends ten resumes to the hiring manager based on the recruiter's particular knowledge of the requirements. The department's goal has been to quickly respond to requisitions in a cost-efficient manner. An operational study discovered, however, that there are two broad types of job positions. About 40% of the hires are made for high volume, high turnover positions such as ten-key operators, customer service, and inside sales that require constant hiring. The other 60% of the hires are made for more custom positions with a different set of desired attributes depending on the hiring manager.

The required competencies of the recruiting operation clearly differ between these two groups; setting up two focused processes would improve alignment. The high turnover positions are well specified and recruiters could be specialized on the ideal requirements. Focus and repetition of similar tasks in a flow process would yield the desired responsiveness and cost efficiency. The other custom positions, however, require more flexible and experienced recruiters that are knowledgeable about a wide variety of requirements involved by different positions such as executive, finance, mortgage lender, etc. Such search positions would be better handled in a project environment that can adapt to the specifics of the position. Clearly, some resources could be shared between the two processes. Chapter 5 will discuss the concept of chained flexibility to share resources while keeping most of the benefits from focus. *Source: Delaney (2007).*

Figure 2.8. Assume that Firm 4's president now accepts a long-term contract to produce large quantities of a single product, and decides to allocate that order to the same process that typically produces small, custom orders with short lead times. The positive outcome and typical rationale is that this increases asset utilization and reduces excess capacity. The downside, however, is the loss of operational focus: The firm may be producing both sets of orders simultaneously or it may be switching between them over time. Either way, the operating "points" of the process will be scattered over time and will thus define a diffused operating "zone." The acceptance of that long-term contract would thus lead to the loss of operational focus. Example 2.4 provides an example of a service operation that lacks focus and illustrates how to remedy that situation, which brings us to the next item.

How to focus an operation: tailored "divide and conquer"

The focus principle provides guidance on *how* alignment can be achieved. The first step is to partition products and services into groups with similar competency needs. The more homogeneous competency needs are, the more effective focus will be. The example in Figure 2.10 shows three groups of products and services with homogeneous needs. The configuration of these groups can be based on their products and services:

1. sharing similar priority rankings of required competencies in terms of cost, variety, timeliness, and quality. The Midwest bank in example 2.4 can group services on the basis of variety and customization in requisitions.

2. being at a similar point in their life cycle. As a product or service goes

through its *product life cycle*, its attributes change, and with it the required process competencies. For example, service, timeliness, and flexibility are more important in the introduction and decline phases of the life cycle, while cost and quality are crucial for mature products and services.

3. having similar locations, margins, volumes, and so on. It is natural to distinguish between high-margin and low-margin products, between products with predictable demand and products with uncertain demand, so on and so forth. Airlines do this by separating customers into different classes of service.

Finally, this is also a good time to consider *rationalizing* the product line and simplifying it by eliminating certain offerings or options that are seldom demanded.

The second step is to decide which resources and processes should be dedicated or focused to a certain group and which ones can be shared among all the groups. Extreme operational focus would design completely separate and specialized operational systems tailored (optimized) for each homogeneous group of products and services. In the example in Figure 2.10, extreme focus would mean three separate systems, each one focused on one product group. In our earlier example, complete operational focus would imply that Firm 4 produces the two sets of orders by employing two different processes. Each process would require restricted competencies ideally matched with the different needs of those orders: operation 3 for the customized orders and operation 1 for the standard, high volume order. Similar strategies would create separate flexible, manual processes for high-margin, low-volume, or unpredictable-demand products and services, while using efficient, automated processes for the others.

Balancing focus with sharing

Complete separation of operational systems is often not necessary nor advisable. A *tailored operational system* is the value-maximizing hybrid combination between two extremes: one single system shared by all groups and a separate focused system for each group. (In Figure 2.10 the tailored degree of focus is represented by "×" and specifies a hybrid combination.)

A tailored operational system separates those activities and resources that are key to providing the crucial competencies in the value proposition, while sharing all others. Notice that process separation does not necessarily require separate locations with associated investment and overhead expense. Sometimes, the existing facility can be divided both organizationally and physically into what Skinner (1969) calls a *"plant within a plant."* For example, key people and equipment needed for a given product or service can be collocated (for example, into software design groups or manufacturing cells), while administrative activities such as billing, accounting, human resources, and public relations are often shared. Similarly, sourcing or logistics can be shared if those processes have little impact on the key demand drivers.

Implementing focus thus comes down to deciding, for each group, the mix of separate and shared resources and processes that maximizes the value of the organization. While we will analyze that decision further in Chapter 5, it is important to remember for now that focus does not always mean completely separated

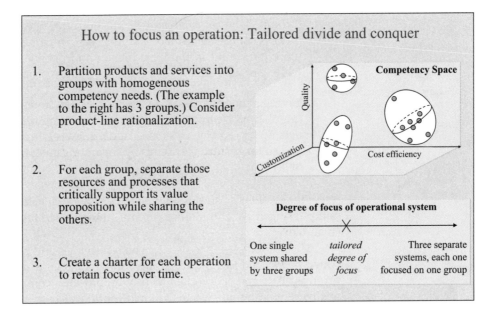

1. Partition products and services into groups with homogeneous competency needs. (The example to the right has 3 groups.) Consider product-line rationalization.

2. For each group, separate those resources and processes that critically support its value proposition while sharing the others.

3. Create a charter for each operation to retain focus over time.

Figure 2.10 Focusing the operation begins with partitioning products and services into homogeneous groups and then finding the best tailored combination of separate and shared resources and processes for each group. Creating charters for each operation serves as a reminder of its purpose.

operational systems; often a hybrid system where some activities and resources are dedicated to a particular product group while others are shared is better.

The benefits of operational focus

The main benefit of operational focus is:

Principle 4 (Focus) Operational focus increases operational efficiency.

In other words, a focused operation is more likely to have a competitive advantage because it would be closer to the frontier. This principle confirms the intuition that a clear, narrow objective is easier to achieve than a vague ensemble of incoherent objectives. Trying to be everything to all people necessitates compromises and thus, a mediocre performance. It results in an operation that does not excel anywhere, like operation 4 in Figure 2.8. In contrast, if the competencies that are required from a process are "focused" and consistent over time, then the operational system can be optimized accordingly. Consistently narrow demands allow faster learning, or, in the words of focus pioneer Skinner (1969) "simplicity and repetition breed competence." (Simplicity and repetition here refer to consistency in a narrow set of desired competencies. It may include a consistent focus on flexibility or customized service.) The result is a process with competencies that are more likely to be world-class and on the frontier.

Obstacles to achieving operational focus

If the principle of focus is so intuitive and attractive, why is it often forgotten, misunderstood, or ignored? Let us discuss some reasons.

First, growth and competitive changes may gradually turn focus into blur. Recall that an operation's focus depends on the demands we assign it. While an operation may start out focused, the pursuit of growth often means that new products and services with different customer needs are allocated to that same operation, which gradually loses focus. Similarly, changes in customer needs or competitor's positions may require a change in our competitive strategy and misalignment with the earlier focused processes. Maintaining focus is perhaps the most difficult strategy because it requires "saying no" to some new initiatives. Sometimes, organizations create mission statements or charters for each of its separate operations to maintain focus. Rather than promising everything (sadly, many operations strategies still pride themselves on offering service, quality, and flexibility while being most efficient), the charter should be clear on what the operation is good at and on what it should not do. A charter not only reminds everyone of the purpose of the operation, but also gives managers a good argument to say no to some requests.

Second, focus is often misinterpreted as a narrow product mix. While allocating a single product to an operation obviously makes it easier to focus that operation, a narrow product mix is not a necessary requirement. B/E Aerospace's Business Jet Group focuses on providing a large selection, just like McKinsey & Co. provides customized management advice. Life tells us that a focus on variety can sometimes be more valuable than a focus on monotony.

Third, achieving the benefits of the focus principle requires strategic alignment. The use of *flexible manufacturing systems* (FMS), as discussed by Jaikumar (1986) provides a classic example. He shows that in the 1980s both Japan and the U.S. were using FMS at roughly similar total volumes. A key difference, however, was that the average number of products made annually in the U.S. was 10 while the average in Japan was 93, almost ten times greater. While both can be argued to be focused operations according to our definition, only Japan realizes world-class performance because it also heeds the principle of alignment. Thus, while some U.S. companies were disappointed with flexible manufacturing systems, "the technology itself is not to blame–it is management that makes the difference."

Fourth, separate operational systems may not create maximal value due to either loss of economies of scale or increased risk. Depending on fixed costs and product volumes, strong scale economies may favor producing disparate products in a single process. With strong scale economies, Firm 4 in Figure 2.8 may be better off producing both custom and standard orders on a single process instead of investing in two focused processes.

Similarly, focus requires a strategic commitment, and in the face of uncertain and rapidly changing environments, it may be better to retain some flexibility as an operational hedge. In this sense, a focused strategy may be more risky than the hedging strategies we will discuss in Chapter 9. As successful companies mature, they may be forced to diversify to "regenerate growth and create value over the long term. ... Focus, in short, isn't always the best answer," according to Harper and Viguerie (2002).

new stuff production added to operation

2.7 | ANALYZING A COMPETITIVE THREAT

Once a firm has staked out a profitable position in a competitive industry, rivals may become interested in "sharing" some of those profits. Smart companies continuously scan the competitive landscape to assess whether any rivals are posing a threat to their established position. According to Intel's chairman Andy Grove, only the paranoid survive:

> "Business success contains the seeds of its own destruction. The more successful you are, the more people want a chunk of your business and then another chunk and then another until there is nothing left. I believe that the prime responsibility of a manager is to guard constantly against other people's attacks. The things I tend to be paranoid about vary. I worry about products getting screwed up, and I worry about products getting introduced prematurely. I worry about factories not performing well, and I worry about having too many factories. I worry about hiring the right people, and I worry about morale slacking off. And, of course, I worry about competitors. I worry about other people figuring out how to do what we do better or cheaper, and displacing us with our customers."Grove (1996)

Operational trade-off curves to analyze a competitive threat

We can use trade-off curves to analyze whether a competitor poses a threat to our current position. (In Chapter 10, we will return to threat analysis in the context of "disruptive technologies.") Let us assume that our value proposition entails a higher level of non-cost competency, denoted by X, than our rival's (the analysis for the reverse is similar). For example, if we were BJG and the rival is C&D Aerospace then X would represent customization. The question is whether this rival poses a threat to us, and if so, how serious that threat is.

It is to be expected that raising the competency level by ΔX incurs an extra unit cost Δc, as shown in Figure 2.11 on the left. But that cost differential reflects not only differences in operational efficiency, but also differences driven by our "more demanding" value proposition. Thus, to assess the threat we must make cost adjustments and estimate what our rival's cost would be if it were to compete with us head-on, promising the same value proposition as us, but using its own processes and resources.

The estimation of a rival's cost structure requires a substantial amount of *competitive intelligence* (known more euphemistically as *benchmarking*) and subjective judgment. The approach that we are about to present is arguably closer to a thought experiment or "what-if" analysis than to a precise, scientific technique.

Step 1: Adjust for operating conditions different from plan

To estimate the best or targeted performance of each operational system we must first control for operating conditions that are different from those planned. For example, assume that we are currently in an economic downturn so that our processes are running at lower utilizations than planned. This would increase

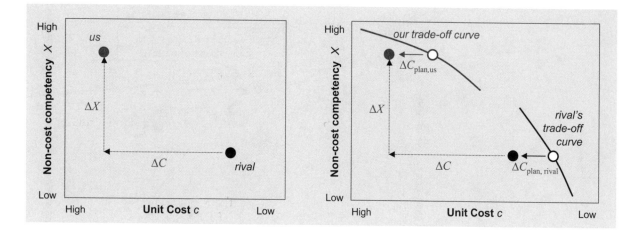

Figure 2.11 The first step in assessing the threat of a rival whose operational system is more cost-focused.

our current cost relative to what it would be under better conditions.

To estimate the best performance, we adjust the actual operating conditions to those for which processes and resources were strategically configured. The associated cost changes are captured by the plan cost differentials $\Delta c_{\text{plan, us}}$ and $\Delta c_{\text{plan, rival}}$. Adjusting for deviations from the plan yields positions that should be on each firm's trade-off curve, as shown in Figure 2.11 on the right.

Step 2: Adjust for differences in strategic positioning

The second step involves estimating how much our rival's cost would change if the rival were to increase its level of non-cost competency X to match ours while keeping its own processes and resources unchanged. This strategy cost differential Δc_{strat} is the outcome of a "what-if" analysis: what would change in the rival's cost structure if it were to match our level of non-cost competency X with its current operational system? The resulting adjusted position of the rival is represented by a diamond in Figure 2.12.

Clearly, the nature of operational adjustments depends on the type of competency. For example, if X is the breadth of product selection N, Δc_{strat} could include the increased cost of change-overs, inventory, and other complexity-related costs. If X represents responsiveness, Δc_{strat} may include the increased unit cost due to the lower utilization (or higher safety capacity) or faster transportation needed to guarantee faster responsiveness. If X represents a quality metric, Δc_{strat} may include the increased unit cost due to higher quality inputs and more testing and possible rework.

Step 3: Assess the threat by assessing our operational efficiency

The third step is to assess the seriousness of the threat. After adjusting for changes in operating conditions and strategic positioning, the seriousness of the threat is now directly related to the residual cost differential. The residual cost

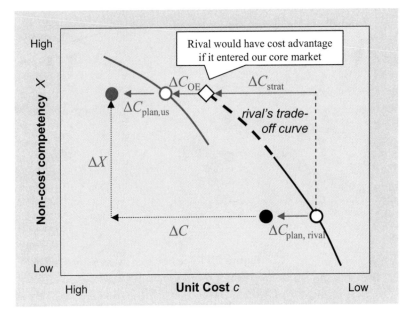

Figure 2.12 Steps 2 & 3: The seriousness of a rival's threat depends on its cost advantage due to operational efficiency Δc_{OE}, after adjusting Δc for changes in plan and strategy.

differential, denoted by Δc_{OE}, is due purely to operational efficiency and can be decomposed as shown on Figure 2.12:

$$\Delta c + \Delta c_{plan,\ rival} = \Delta c_{plan,us} + \Delta c_{OE} + \Delta c_{strat}.$$

By re-arranging terms, we can arrive at our rival's operational efficiency cost differential Δc_{OE}, which adjusts the gross cost advantage for differences in strategic positioning and operating conditions:

Efficiency cost differential Δc_{OE} = gross cost differential
$-$ strategy cost differential $-$ planned cost differential,

where the planned cost differential $\Delta c_{plan} = \Delta c_{plan,us} - \Delta c_{plan,\ rival}$.

The larger the adjusted cost advantage Δc_{OE}, the larger the competitive threat the rival poses to us. A large adjusted cost advantage Δc_{OE} (as shown on Figure 2.12) means that the rival would have a cost advantage if it entered our core market and replicated our customer value proposition using its own current operations. In contrast, if the adjusted cost advantage is negative, the threat is small because the rival would be at a cost disadvantage in such a case. For example, if the strategy correction Δc_{strat} is substantial, then a large gross cost advantage may not represent a threat because the rival's operational system cannot efficiently deliver our higher competency level. Strong operational trade-offs provide protection; the rival then simply isn't a real competitor.

2.8 | GUIDELINES FOR OPERATIONS-BASED COMPETITIVE ADVANTAGE

We can now turn our competitive cost analysis into operations-based strategies to improve competitive advantage. The idea is to seize the initiative and use the insights from the threat analysis to identify opportunities to reduce the threat while keeping an eye on customer evolution. In the 6th century B.C., Sun Tzu had already proposed a similar strategy: "The art of war teaches us to rely not on the likelihood of the enemy's not coming, but on our own readiness to receive him; not on the chance of him not attacking, but rather on the fact that we have made our position unassailable." (VIII. Variation in Tactics)

Study your own as well as your rivals' trade-off curves

Know not only your own cost structure but also that of your competitors. [After estimating trade-off curves, we can gain insight by performing competitive threat analysis to proactively improve our own operations by implementing all the factors that give our rival an advantage in operational efficiency.] By definition, these operational efficiency factors constitute cost improvements that can be made without hampering the strategic value proposition. This "pushing of the envelope" moves our trade-off curve outward and reduces the rival's relevant cost advantage (i.e., Δc_{OE}) and threat.

Operations leaders claim they focus on being cost competitive more than they focus on any other priority. Yet they actually know little about competitors' costs and, when making decisions, they typically don't leverage competitive information as much as they could, according to von Hochberg, Rodrigues, and Grenon (2006) and illustrated in Figure 2.13.

Strengthen your competitive position

[By increasing operational focus and strengthening relationships with suppliers, buyers, and labor and capital markets, we make it harder for our rival to copy us.] These actions increase our rival's strategy cost differential Δc_{strat}, thereby reducing Δc_{OE} and the threat.

The first strategy–learning from competitors–highlights a principle hailed by free-market proponents: [competition improves efficiency because smart firms adopt efficient practices from rivals after adjusting for differences in strategy. In contrast, strengthening our competitive position serves to establish a quasi-monopoly position and prevent head-on competition. Both strategies strengthen our current position and thwart our rival from moving into our core business; these are *defensive* strategies that should be implemented as soon as possible. However, even if our rival is not moving into our core business, our customers may move towards our rival's niche over time. The next longer-term strategy contemplates how to address such a risk.

Anticipate customer dynamics and strategic inflection points

A longer-term strategy should include market research to estimate customer utility dynamics. The viability of our competitive advantage crucially depends on

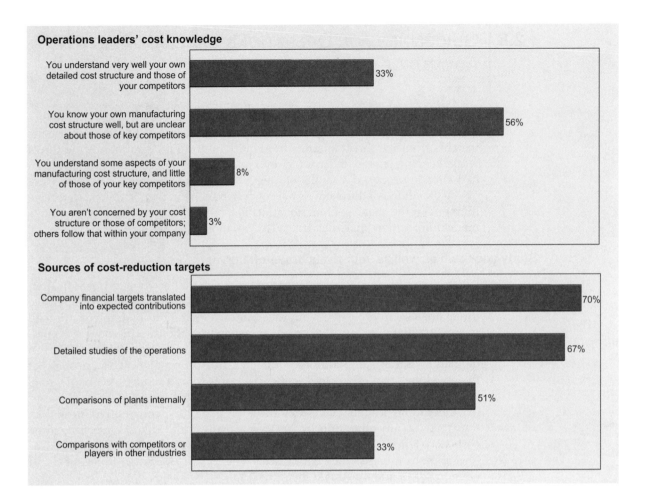

Figure 2.13 Operations leaders have limited knowledge about competitors' costs and don't leverage competitive information as much as they could, according to von Hochberg, Rodrigues, and Grenon (2006). The figures show the percentage of "yes" responses to each statement.

the net extra value, or utility, ΔU that customers derive from our products and services relative to our rival's. If this value advantage ΔU is decreasing or is already negative for some core customers, then the viability of our operational strategy is at risk and we must choose one of the three possible responses:

1. Fight: Can we improve our position by increasing the customer value ΔU or by improving our operational system? This would increase our differentiation ΔX and the strategy-related cost differential Δc_{strat}, thereby reducing Δc_{OE} and the threat.

2. Adapt or adopt. If our customer's needs are changing, we may need to adapt our operations strategy accordingly (recall the importance of adapting alignment from Chapter 1). Similarly, if our rival is on a superior track,

we may contemplate a restructuring and adopt our rival's value proposition or operational system.

3. Retreat. Or should we close our shop and exit the business altogether?

Our account of this longer-term strategy is a much condensed summary of corporate strategy. The moment when a corporation must decide to fight, adopt, or retreat is what Intel's chairman Grove (1996) calls a *strategic inflection point*, "a time in the life of a business when its fundamentals are about to change. That change can mean an opportunity to rise to new heights. But it may just as likely signal the beginning of the end." In the past, Intel has experienced both. In the mid-eighties, it exited the memory business because it couldn't stand the competition of Japanese rivals. That problem led Intel to instead focus on developing the value of the microprocessor, which turned out to be an extremely successful offensive strategy.

Be careful with cost and productivity numbers

Don't take cost numbers at face value. Rather, adjust for strategic positioning and volume (utilization) differences in order to arrive at the cost advantage due to operational efficiency, which is the meaningful cost number to compare rivals. Similarly, be mindful of productivity measurements because they may focus on cost without adjusting for strategy differences.

2.9 | SUMMARY OF LEARNING OBJECTIVES

1. Explain the concept of operational trade-off and discuss its impact on competition.

The bundle of operational competencies that a given operational system can provide is governed by trade-offs. An operational trade-off is a relationship among multiple competencies that specifies the cost needed to deliver a specific level of flexibility, responsiveness, and quality using a given operational system. Requiring a higher level of some competencies (e.g., flexibility and quality) may come at the expense of a lower level of other competencies (e.g., time responsiveness or cost efficiency). These trade-offs stem from the scarcity of operational resources, and their specific nature is determined by the way we configure the activity network and choose to deploy our resources. Trade-offs are snapshots taken at a given point in time which typically move as firms improve. Thus, operations strategy can shape these competency trade-offs.

The existence of trade-offs is at the essence of strategy. Customer choice is governed by trade-offs in utility. Heterogeneity in customer trade-offs allows the firm to segment the market and to position itself in a specific segment using a targeted value-proposition. The credibility, profitability, and sustainability of that market strategy depends on how operations strategy shapes the competency trade-offs and requires operating competencies. Credibility means that our processes must have the capability to deliver the value proposition. Profitability stems from choosing well-aligned processes and executing them better than our rivals do. Sustainability requires that these processes exhibit strong trade-offs so that rivals cannot straddle efficiently.

2. Implement competency focus to improve operational efficiency.

> The efficient frontier is the envelope of all competency trade-offs in a given industry at a given time; it specifies the lowest sustainable cost to provide a specific bundle of non-cost competencies. Efficient firms are those with competencies on the frontier. They are "world-class" because no other firm can provide such competencies at lower cost. A firm is more likely to be near the frontier if it employs focused operations. Operational focus means consistently requiring a narrow range of competencies; over time, this keeps the operating point on one point of the operation's trade-off curve.
>
> Focus facilitates process optimization and faster learning and thus increases operational efficiency. An operation can be focused by a three-step tailored divide-and-conquer approach. First, partition the portfolio of products and services into groups with similar needs. Second, decide which processes and resources should be dedicated to each group and which ones can be shared. Last, specify a charter for each focused process to help retain its focus. Remember, however, that there are various obstacles to achieving operational focus.
>
> Productivity measures the number of outputs produced by given units during a time period and is a measure of asset efficiency. Productivity measurement can be problematic but total factor productivity addresses some of these problems. While productivity is a powerful predictor of macroeconomic well-being, it must be carefully applied when comparing operations. Be mindful that productivity measurements often emphasize cost, which is beneficial as long as it does not come at the expense of other, sometimes more important, competencies. To compare apples with apples, we must correct for differences in strategy and operating conditions, which brings us back to our notion of operational efficiency.

3. Analyze a competitive threat using trade-off curves.

> Trade-off curves have several equivalent graphical representations which are useful to analyze differences in competency positioning between two firms. Such differences stem from variations in strategic positioning, inputs, and utilizations. Any remaining disparities stem from operational efficiency, which results from having better processes and resources. Operational efficiency is a measure of sustainability: we are at risk if a rival can offer our same strategic value-proposition with its current processes at a lower cost.

4. Design strategies to improve competitive advantage through operations.

> The analysis of a competitive threat using trade-off curves directly suggests strategies to improve competitive advantage. By learning from competitors and estimating their trade-off curves, we can proactively improve our own operations: we can implement all the factors that give our rival an advantage in operational efficiency. By definition, these operational efficiency factors constitute cost improvements that can be made without hampering the strategic value proposition. This "pushing of the envelope" moves our trade-off curve outward and improves our competitive advantage. The second defensive strategy is to increase operational focus and strengthen our relationships with suppliers, buyers,

and labor and capital markets. This would make it more difficult for our rival to copy our operational system and would improve the sustainability of our advantage. The third strategy is more long term and anticipates changes in the extra customer value that customers derive from our products and services relative to those of our rival. Depending on the dynamics in this extra customer value, the organization must make the strategic decision to fight, adopt, or retreat.

DISCUSSION QUESTIONS

1. Consider the retail financial services industry and three main players, such as Merrill Lynch, Schwab, and Ameritrade (or E-trade). What are the relevant dimensions that you would use to describe their relative value propositions? Which factors would you consider in order to derive and sketch their trade-off curves?

2. Where would you draw the frontier in Figure 2.11? How would you find it? Why don't we use the frontier in the analysis of competitive threats?

3. What role, if any, did the advent of the Internet have on the efficient frontier?

4. A company is introducing a new product line and must decide whether to build a separate operating system for that product line or whether to add that product line to the current operating system's workload. From an operations strategy perspective, what are the key factors/conditions that should be considered in making this decision? That is, when is a separate operating system preferred over an integrated one?

5. Discuss the pros and cons of United Airlines' low cost airline Ted using the concept of focus and "airline-within-an-airline."

6. The "plant-within-a-plant" is an attractive way for manufacturing organizations to achieve focus through process separation within a single location. To what extent does that attractiveness extend to a service organization? (Hint: Discuss the degree of a customer's physical interaction with the process.)

7. What is the relationship between capacity utilization, defined as average throughput (or sales) divided by processing capacity, and productivity?

CHALLENGE QUESTIONS

1. Does the fact that an operation is focused have an impact on the sustainability of a strategic position?

2. Is there a difference in the trade-off curve of a focused operation vs. an "un-focused" operation?

3. How would the selection-cost trade-off change when product demands are uncertain? (For example, each week's product demand is normally distributed with a known mean and standard deviation.)

4. For math fans: In the N-product lot sizing model of Appendix 2A, the impact of changeovers is covered only by a setup cost c_S. Characterize the selection-cost trade-off when changeovers not only incur a cost, but also a changeover or setup *time* t_S during which production is zero. (Hint: Here you must differentiate between available annual capacity and annual throughput or demand. Clearly, throughput is less than capacity because some productive capacity will be lost to changeovers.) Similarly, characterize the selection-cost trade-off when there is no financial cash cost c_S, but *only* a setup time t_S.

Visit www.vanmieghem.us for additional questions and updates.

FURTHER READING AND REFERENCES

▶ Skinner (1969) wrote the seminal article on the ideas of trade-offs and focus in operations. Harper and Viguerie (2002) provide some arguments against focus.

▶ Porter (1996) and Hayes and Upton (1998) discuss the role of operations and trade-offs in strategy.

Ameritrade (2004, Jul). Corporate website. www.ameritrade.com.

B/E Aerospace. Corporate website. www.beaerospace.com.

Callejas, A. (2004). Personal conversations. July 12.

Delaney, M. W. (2007). Chief sales officer, careerbuilder.com. Personal conversations. April 6.

FedEx Express (2000). Press release January 19. www.fedex.com/us/about/express-/pressreleases.

Grove, A. S. (1996). *Only the Paranoid Survive: How to Exploit the Crisis Points That Challenge every Company and Career* (First Edition ed.). Currency.

Harper, N. W. C. and S. P. Viguerie (2002). Are you too focused? *McKinsey Quarterly*, 28–122.

Hayes, R. and D. Upton (1998). Operations-based strategy. *California Management Review 40*(4), 8–25.

Hayes, R., S. C. Wheelwright, and K. B. Clark (1988). *Dynamic Manufacturing: Creating the Learning Organization*. New York: The Free Press, McMillan Publishers.

Jaikumar, R. (1986). Postindustrial manufacturing. *Harvard Business Review 64*(6), 69–75.

Kennedy, J. F. (1962, January 20). The inaugural anniversary address. National Guard Armory. "To govern is to choose. To appear to be unable to choose is to appear to be unable to govern". First attributed to Nigel Lawson, British Conservative politician.

Lewis, W. W. (2004). *The Power of Productivity: Wealth, Poverty and the Threat to Global Stability*. University of Chicago Press.

Merriam-Webster (2007). Online dictionary. www.m-w.com.

Nisser, R. D. (2007). Controller, Cargill Inc. Personal conversations. May 8.

Porter, M. E. (1996). What is strategy? *Harvard Business Review 74*(6), 61–78.

Schumpeter, J. A. (1942). *Capitalism, Socialism and Democracy*. New York: Harper.

Skinner, W. (1969). The focused factory. *Harvard Business Review 52*(3), 113–122.

UPS (2006, March). Annual report 2005. Quotation is on p. 2 of 10-K form.

von Hochberg, P., M. Rodrigues, and G. Grenon (2006). Who manages manufacturing? *Strategy+Business* (44), 1–12.

Mini-Case 2 | FEDEX V. UPS

[7]FedEx and UPS are two world-class service firms that provide overnight express as well as regular logistics services. Curiously, both competitors have chosen very different operations strategies as illustrated by the following quotations:

> "We strongly believe that the optimal way to serve very distinct market segments, such as express and ground, is to operate highly efficient, independent networks with different facilities, different cut-off times and different delivery commitments. " FedEx Express (2000)

> "Our express air services are integrated with our vast ground delivery system one system handling all products. This integrated air and ground network enhances efficiency, improves productivity and asset utilization, and provides us with the flexibility to transport packages using the most reliable and cost-effective transportation mode or combination of modes." UPS (2006)

FedEx was founded in 1972 by Fred Smith under the original name Federal Express. On an average day, FedEx processes more than 6.5 million shipments for express, ground, freight, and expedited delivery services. FedEx Express is the world largest express transportation company, processing about 3.3 million shipments daily through 10 hubs. Most of its overnight U.S. freight is processed at its superhub in Memphis, Tennessee. Historically, the company served mostly express requests but expanded in 1998 by acquiring the ground transportation company Roadway Package System. In 2000, the United States Postal Service signed a contract (currently valid until 2012) to process all its overnight and high-priority mail through the FedEx system.

Founded in 1907 as a messenger company, UPS grew organically into the world's largest package delivery company. In 1981, UPS purchased its first aircraft for use in airline delivery service. Today UPS Airlines is the 8th largest airline in the world (FedEx is larger by almost 100 airplanes). In 2006, the company delivered 15.6 million packages and documents on an average day, about 2.3 million of which were processed through its U.S. air network.

1. *Which company has greater operational focus?*

2. *How would you explain the different choice in operations strategy? Hint: Identify the key processes where the integrated UPS strategy may provide value compared to FedEx's, and vice versa, and compare the value of integration to the cost of integration. Based on this analysis, discuss the degree to which these companies have tailored their operations strategy.*

---

[7]Professor Van Mieghem prepared this case as the basis for class discussion rather than to illustrate either the effective or ineffective handling of a managerial situation. No part of this case study may be reproduced without permission; direct all inquiries to permissions@vanmieghem.us

Part II

The Resource View: Tailoring Real Assets

CAPACITY SIZING AND INVESTMENT

The most important questions of life are, for the most part, really only problems of probability. — Pierre-Simon Laplace (1812)

Learning Objectives

After reading this chapter, you will be able to:

1. Explain the concept of capacity strategy and discuss its challenges and importance.
2. Analyze two key capacity investment drivers: scale economies and uncertainty.
3. View and value capacity as a real option and optimize capacity investment.
4. Pick a position in the capacity-inventory-waiting strategy triangle.

Part I of this book introduced a framework for operations strategy and discussed the role of competencies and competition. Part II studies the resource view to understand how to structure an organization's bundle of real assets. We start with the capacity sizing and investment decision in this chapter. After discussing the key trade-offs and challenges in a capacity strategy, we study how scale economies and uncertainty impact capacity valuation. Maximizing this value suggests guidelines on how we can tailor an operations' capacity sizing decision. (Appendix 3A reviews discounting and present value calculations, as well as relevant operational issues.)

3.1 | CAPACITY STRATEGY AND KEY TRADE-OFFS

A capacity strategy is the long-term plan for developing resources and involves decisions on sizing, timing, type, and location of real assets or resources. Structuring the portfolio of real assets is a key part of operations strategy. Indeed, recall from Chapter 1 that operations strategy is a plan for developing resources and configuring processes such that the resulting competencies maximize net

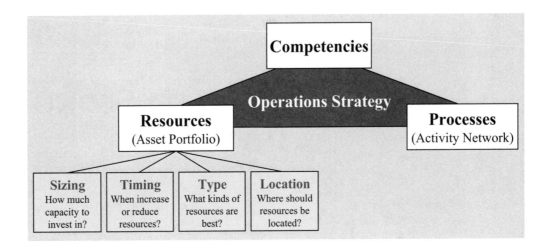

Figure 3.1 A capacity strategy involves decisions on the sizing, timing, type, and location of each resource in the processing network. This structuring of the real asset portfolio and configuring processes such that the resulting competencies maximize net present value is the task of operations strategy.

present value, as illustrated in Figure 3.1. Let us review the concept of capacity and the key trade-offs involved in capacity decisions.

The concepts of capacity and utilization

All organizations have a bundle of real assets or resources that perform their activities. Few real assets are available abundantly. A resource's limitations in processing are captured by its *capacity*, which typically represents the maximal sustainable output rate of that resource. The level at which we choose to operate that resource at any given time is the resource capacity *utilization*, typically a fraction of the resource capacity.

For example, recall that the Mercedes plant in Tuscaloosa (see Example 1.2 on page 8) had a capacity of 65,000 vehicles per year. If the economy slowed down so that annual demand decreased from 60,000 to 40,000, Mercedes could choose to reduce utilization from 92% to 62%. In reality, however, Mercedes had underestimated demand and, even though the plant ran at full utilization, some demand could not be met. In the short run, this meant that a customer had to either wait or buy another vehicle made by Mercedes or a rival. (Another option would have been to raise prices or manage demand as Chapter 8 will discuss.)

Capacity investment and characteristics

Not only are few real assets available abundantly, they are seldom free. Typically, the firm incurs a one-time *investment cost* to acquire a real asset, and an *operating cost* every time the asset is utilized. (Additional costs may include maintenance for capital assets, and training and retention for human resources.) While capacity refers to the amounts, or *stocks*, of various resources, *investment* refers to the change of that stock over time. Investment thus involves the cash flow stemming from capacity expansion and contraction in the expectation of future rewards.

According to Dixit and Pindyck (1994), investment decisions share three important characteristics in varying degrees; we will add multi-dimensionality as a fourth:

1. The investment is partially or completely irreversible meaning that one cannot recover its full cost should one have a change of mind.

2. There is uncertainty over the future rewards from the investment.

3. There is some leeway about the timing or dynamics of the investment.

4. Typically, a firm invests in multiple types of resources that have different financial and operational properties.

Decisions about the types and levels of investment are interdependent; the firm's productive capabilities depend on the complete vector of capacity levels, which we will call its *capacity portfolio*.

The importance of capacity investment

Capacity sizing and investment are important elements of operations strategy because they are risky undertakings with competitive repercussions. For example, seeking to beat rival British Airways, Richard Branson approved Virgin Atlantic Airways' $5.5 billion order—about double its annual revenues—of 13 Airbus planes on August 6, 2004, with an option to pick up another 13, nearly doubling its fleet. Given the uncertain future of European airlines, analysts said that Sir Richard's big order was a big gamble. Poor capacity gambles can lead to the demise of the company as illustrated by the case study of Webvan (see p. 423).

Capacity investment is not only a risky undertaking with competitive repercussions, it also impacts the entire supply chain. In February 2004, Apple Computer was forced to delay manufacturing of its new iPod mini, due to supply constraints on one of its parts—a one-inch hard drive made exclusively by Hitachi Global Storage Technologies (Example 3.1). Three months later, Hitachi announced a $200 million investment, adding 16,000 workers to its Thailand facility, and doubling the capacity of hard drive production from 30 million to 60 million units annually.

Key decisions and trade-offs in a capacity strategy

Capacity strategy decisions involve decisions on the sizing, timing, type, and location of each resource in the processing network, that involve several trade-offs.

Sizing means deciding on the capacity level. The key trade-off in that decision is between the cost of excess capacity and the opportunity cost of capacity shortage in terms of lost sales, customer waits, and competitive effects. The opportunity cost of capacity shortage can be mitigated by capacity expansion capacity or by various tactical countermeasures, such as raising prices, putting customers on a waiting list (i.e., backlogging), building inventory in advance, or subcontracting. Similarly, the cost of excess capacity can be alleviated by

> **Example 3.1** Apple Computer's iPod mini
>
> In February 2004, Apple Computer began shipping the smaller $249 version of its popular iPod to the U.S. market. The iPod mini was the world's smallest portable music player to hold up to 1,000 CD-quality songs. Apple said that it had received over 100,000 pre-orders for the iPod mini after introducing it the month earlier, and that the iPod mini would be available worldwide in April.
>
> A month later, however, Apple announced that it was moving the worldwide availability of iPod mini to July because U.S. demand was much stronger than expected and far exceeded the total planned supply through the end of June. Tight supplies of the cutting-edge one-inch hard drive made by Hitachi Ltd. forced Apple to delay the increase of production. "We're actually consuming just about all the 4 gigabyte, 1-inch drives they make," said Greg Joswiak, VP of hardware product marketing for Apple. Apple expected to ramp up its manufacturing of the iPod mini to meet worldwide demand in the July quarter.
>
> On May 17, 2004, Hitachi Global Storage Technologies announced an 8 billion Baht ($200 million) investment to double the capacity of hard drive production at its Thailand facility across a variety of product lines from 30 million to 60 million units annually. The funds were intended for productivity and technology improvements, as well as for adding new production lines and automation to allow for better usage of space. An additional 16,000 Thai workers were to be hired to support the planned manufacturing increase.
>
> *Source: Apple Computer Inc. (2004), Hitachi Global Storage Technologies (2004)*

contracting capacity as well as by countermeasures such as sales promotions, product line extensions, etc.

The second decision in a capacity strategy is the *timing* of capacity adjustments. In chapter 4 we will discuss various factors that make capacity timing challenging, but the key trade-off in timing comes down to comparing the cost of the capacity adjustment and the continuing or expected cost of excess (or shortage) capacity. For example, Mercedes continued to see strong demand for its M-class and spent an extra $80 million to expand its capacity to 80,000 vehicles in 1999. But even this was insufficient and a second expansion produced the M-class in a second location (Austria) from 1999 to 2002.

The third and fourth decisions in a capacity strategy involve the *types* of the resources we want and their *locations*. In practice, many types of real assets are deployed in the activity network for the production of several products and services. While economists distinguish between two major types of assets, labor and capital, there are many different types of human resources and capital resources. Each type of real asset has a certain resource capacity that may constrain the total output of the network. If that happens, the resource is called a *bottleneck*. Moreover, we can often choose from various types of resources and from various locations, depending on the network configuration. We shall study the type and locations decisions in chapters 5 and 6, respectively.

In this chapter we investigate capacity sizing in a single product, single resource setting and focus on the first two characteristics of investment: irreversibility and uncertainty. We will start with discussing why formulating a capacity strategy is challenging and then we will move into capacity valuation and optimal sizing.

3.2 | CHALLENGES FOR CAPACITY STRATEGY

In practice, formulating a capacity strategy is challenging for several reasons:

Capacity is a soft, malleable constraint

While capacity is conveniently modeled as a precise, rigid constraint on output quantities, in reality it is often a less precise, soft constraint. Managers sometimes say "we're running at 110% of capacity," meaning that they can get more output than theoretically rated, at least in the short term. This is especially true when the work flow is not automated, as in services. In such settings, capacity is a rather malleable constraint; it is merely the point beyond which marginal production costs increase sharply.

Capacity is like "black art"; it depends on so many factors

While our stylized notion of capacity as the maximal sustainable throughput allows us to focus on some important strategic issues, it is important to acknowledge that reality is more complex. Because its meaning allows a wide array of interpretations, capacity has been compared with "black art." For example, does maximal sustainable throughput mean that processing never stops? Or, do we exclude time for scheduled maintenance? Or, do we only include scheduled operating time? Also, capacity is a rate and thus specifies a number of units during a given time period. Capacity numbers thus depend on the number of working hours in the time period considered.

The truth is that, besides its increasing marginal cost interpretation, capacity is malleable because it is the result of all operational policies used in the activity network. Not only does system capacity depend on the resource bundle, it also depends on how execution in the network is handled. It depends on the product mix and on scheduling and routing decisions. It decreases with unforeseen downtimes in computer systems, machines, absenteeism, or inventory shortages. It increases with faster setup times, changeovers, learning, and higher reliability. In short, *actual capacity depends on everything*.

Even more importantly, while the long-term capacity numbers often are good approximations, sometimes they depend crucially on tactical activities taken on a smaller time-scale. Inventory and workforce scheduling, also known as *aggregate planning*, are two important tactical activities that can provide a relatively simple and quick lever to change monthly and even annual capacity, as we will see in Chapter 4.

Capacity frictions: leadtimes, lumpiness, and fixed costs

Capacity investment is hostage to many frictions , forces that prevent us from changing it quickly, precisely, and cheaply. Typically, it takes time to install new capacity. The *leadtime* is the lag time between the investment decision epoch and the availability of that new capacity. As in inventory management, capacity leadtimes increase the risk of capacity shortage caused by demand uncertainty. The basic approaches to protect against such risk are either to expand capacity earlier or to adopt larger capacity increments.

Capacity strategy analysis often simply assumes that capacity is endlessly divisible, so that it is a continuous variable whose investment can be *incremental* to match it with demand precisely. This is a valid assumption in settings where the number of possible capacity sizes is large, for example when deciding on the head count in a call center, the number of computers in a process, or the size of a plant. It also reflects ongoing or gradual capacity adjustments due to maintenance, training, and continuous improvement. Sometimes, however, capacity can only be installed in a small number of possible sizes. When capacity is not endlessly divisible, it is called *lumpy* and comes in discrete chunks which prevent us from precisely matching capacity with some demands. (Integer restrictions also make lumpy capacity harder to analyze.)

Even when physical capacity is finely divisible, installing capacity often incurs a fixed cost which introduces economies of scale that make incremental investment suboptimal. Training of new staff in a call center is an example of such fixed cost. As we will see shortly, fixed costs induce us to install capacity in chunks, even when it is physically divisible, just to spread out the fixed costs over a larger size in order to gain economies of scale.

Capacity requires large and irreversible investments

Frictions due to importance and irreversibility are of even greater impact than leadtimes, lumpiness, and fixed costs. Capacity decisions are at the core of strategy simply because they often involve the largest cash outlays that managers make. They have a first order impact on the value of the organization and on the success of operations strategy as indicated by the value maximization principle. Because of this far reaching impact on the value of the organization, capacity decisions require much thought, analysis, and planning so that they are made neither quickly nor frequently.

The key reason is that capacity decisions are not easily reversed. To the proverbial "businessman," easy means costless. In principle, when we can borrow from competitive capital markets, it is not the large amount of cash that makes capacity investment hugely important. Rather, it is the sad fact that we cannot fully recoup that cash if we later reverse our decision. We are not referring to the relatively small costs of borrowing. What is at stake here is simply the fact that old capacity is much like a used car: due to physical degradation you cannot trade it in and recover your initial investment. If you could, the investment would be *reversible* or *frictionless* and there would be no need for this chapter (and much of this book). If you can recover part of the initial investment, we call the investment partially reversible. Sometimes, however, your old capacity is worthless to others and no cash can be recovered. In that case the organization will never disinvest and the investment is *irreversible*.

Irreversible investment is not an academic invention. It is a good descriptor of investment in human resources and computers. The real situation may be even worse (from the perspective of the company, at least) if the organization has to *pay* to decrease investment. Such strong irreversibility makes companies hesitant to invest and has contributed to the onset of "Eurosclerosis,", the employment problem frequently attributed to rigid, slow-moving labor markets in Europe. Indonesia is experiencing similar dynamics since its 2003 labor "law requires that dismissed workers receive up to several years in severance pay; even employees who quit are entitled to payouts," according to Wright (2006).

Capacity decisions can be political

Capacity decisions are important organizationally and politically because they may impact large numbers of people within the firm and related to the firm (suppliers, municipalities, states, etc.). Given that they involve large amounts of money and people, capacity decisions may need negotiations with various stakeholders and interest groups. The prestige and power of a manager is often measured in terms of the size of her budget and her number of reports. Any capacity change may thus disrupt the status quo and start a political process. Sometimes, capacity investment is used as a carrot or a stick to achieve other goals. In June 2004, Siemens of Germany threatened to move capacity (and jobs) to Hungary if unions did not make concessions to reduce labor costs. The powerful IG Metall eventually agreed to increase the workweek to 40 hours, up from the celebrated 35-hour work week, for the same pay.

Measuring and valuing capacity shortages is not obvious

A key trade-off in capacity investment is balancing the cost of capacity with the opportunity cost of capacity shortage. While capacity costs are often known reasonably well, capacity shortages may not be. Given their importance, however, measuring or estimating capacity shortages (or excess demand) is crucial. Firms with corporate customers who place orders are more likely to observe all demand. While that may not be the case for retailers, they may implement some type of reservation system or can use their knowledge of when they ran out of capacity to estimate excess demand.

The economic cost of capacity shortage includes the opportunity cost of unsatisfied demand and potential loss of market share, both of which can only be estimated. Depending on the patience of customers, unsatisfied demand due to capacity shortage may result in one of the three short-term effects:

1. A *delay of sales* results when a customer signs on to a waiting list or backlog.

2. A *substitution* occurs when a customer chooses another product or service of the same firm. (In a multi-product or process context, the firm may design such "spill-overs" into its processes to reduce the capacity shortage cost, as we will see in Chapter 5.)

3. A *lost sale* results when a customer no longer wants the service or when she goes to a rival.

Sometimes, it is difficult to predict which of these three effects will materialize. For example, a customer may first sign up on a waiting list but that can still result in a lost sale if the wait is too long. Analyzing the two extreme cases of total backlogging (so that no sale is lost) and total lost sales provides estimates on the minimal and maximal short-term cost of capacity shortage.

The long-term impact of consistent capacity shortages may lead to a loss of customer goodwill and word-of-mouth, and will manifest itself in reduced customer adoption and smaller future demand. This may result in an untapped market potential, or more likely, in a market that never fully develops or that is "developed by a rival." For example, Boeing is profiting from the delay and shortage of the Airbus 380.

On the positive side, capacity shortage is equivalent to the absence of excess capacity, which may reduce risk when demand is uncertain (such as for new game consoles) or instill a sense of scarcity that may appeal to luxury buyers (or to Zara's fast fashion shoppers, as discussed in Chapter 1).

Capacity investment involves long-run planning under uncertainty

When formulating capacity strategies, we typically have in mind a long time-scale measured in months, quarters, or years. For example, the Harley-Davidson case study in Chapter 11 discusses "Plan 2003" which was presented in December 1993 to the board and contained a specific set of alternative strategies to double its production volume by 2003. In August 1995 (with still 8 years to go), a specific strategy was presented to achieve that goal. Such long planning horizons exacerbate the uncertainty faced when formulating a capacity strategy and therefore forecasting becomes critical.

3.3 | THE NECESSITY AND PRACTICE OF FORECASTING

Arguably the most vexing problem in capacity investment is the vast amount of uncertainty embodied in the future. Let us first review some important facts about forecasting.

Important elements in a forecast

Forecasts are predictions of the future. The value of capacity depends on how well it will be utilized. To estimate that value, we need a mental and analytic model that predicts all contingencies that can impact the future value of capacity utilization. This model should include a *forecast* of the evolution of the following factors:

1. Demand. Estimating demand evolution is a key input to capacity sizing.

2. Supply. As illustrated by Apple's iPod in Example 3.1, a firm's output also depends on the availability of inputs from existing and potential suppliers.

3. Technology. This includes not only how the cost of new capacity will evolve, but also expected improvements in competencies. Not only will new and better technologies become available over time, but learning and continuous improvements will increase existing capacity over time. For example, increasing *yields* has a dramatic impact on actual capacity and profitability in the semi-conductor industry. AMD's strategy to minimize "*ramp time*" has been credited for increasing AMD's lead in the processor race of 2000 by scaling up the speed and production of its Athlon chips before Intel could respond.

4. Competition and environment. Revenues, and thus the value of capacity decisions, depend on the actions of competitors. But also macro effects such as interest and exchange rates affect capacity value.

Uncertainty, variability, and volatility

It is a truism that the future is inherently uncertain. Useful forecasts therefore incorporate a measure of this uncertainty, which we will call *forecast error*. As forecast error decreases (it never disappears entirely), predictions become more precise, informative and useful.

Besides uncertainty, the future may also exhibit variability and volatility. Let us review what that means in the specific context of predicting a quantity X that evolves over time. Uncertainty means that we cannot accurately predict X's actual value in a given time bucket. Variability means that the actual demand varies over time. While that time variation is sometimes known accurately, for example with seasonality or long-term committed contracts, it usually entails some uncertainty. Volatility means that the variability over time may be fickle, rapid, and capricious. Given that volatility embodies uncertainty, we will use it as a synonym for uncertain variability.

The task of forecasting

Good forecasting recognizes that volatility precludes perfect predictions. Forecasting X means making a prediction of X_t and an estimate of volatility or forecast error at each point in time t:

$$\underbrace{X_t}_{\text{Forecast}} = \underbrace{\overline{X}_t}_{\text{Prediction}} + \underbrace{\varepsilon_{X_t}}_{\text{Volatility}}$$

The task of forecasting is to identify predictable values and to estimate the random component per time bucket.

There are many possible predictions and metrics of volatility, but the expected value and the standard deviation are often used. The predicted evolution captures trends and seasonality. A useful measure of relative volatility or forecast precision is the *coefficient of variation* (COV):

$$\text{coefficient of variation (COV)} = \frac{\text{standard deviation}}{\text{mean}}.$$

Three properties of forecasts

First, a forecast should contain all available information on the future evolution of X. It must reflect a good understanding of all possible outcomes with their likelihoods. Therefore, Cisco Systems, the leading supplier of network equipment and management for the Internet, brings both "the optimists" (marketing & sales) and "the pessimists" (finance & operations) to the forecasting table.

In theory, a forecast should contain all the statistical information that describes the future evolution of X, which is a time-sequence of random variables. For example, sales quantities in different time buckets could be independent and identically distributed (i.i.d.). The forecast should then state that sales is an i.i.d. process and it should specify one probability distribution. If sales have a growth trend, the forecast should specify not only the average growth rate, but also the statistics around the trend.

In practice, we often don't know the entire probability distributions, but a powerful result comes to the rescue. The central limit theorem says, informally, that the cumulative effect of many small and independent random effects is approximately normally distributed. This celebrated normal or Gaussian[1] distribution is fully characterized by two numbers only: a mean and a standard deviation.[2] Thus, the second key property of a forecast is that it should specify at least *two* numbers. In addition to the usual forecast of the expected value—also called a (single-) *point forecast*–it should also specify a measure of confidence of forecast error, like a range, standard deviation, or coefficient of variation. Mr. Trautman of Agilent Technologies, the measurement company spin-off of HP corroborates:

> "While some OEMs/IDMs may be willing to share their highly confidential point forecasts with their manufacturing partners, the problem is that these monthly forecasts are highly likely to change. If a contract manufacturer were to put capacity in place based solely on these forecasts, they would probably get it wrong.
>
> Instead, what contract manufacturers need are range forecasts that tell them the likelihood of demand falling within a certain range within a certain period of time."Gauntt (2004, p. 13)

A third property is that aggregate forecasting is more precise. For example, if the sales forecast for product line i has a coefficient of variation COV_i, then the coefficient of variation of the aggregate sales forecast is less than the weighted average of the COV_i. A stronger result holds when the product line sales are uncorrelated but have equal mean and COV; the aggregate sales forecast over n such product lines has coefficient of variation $COV/\sqrt{n}$.[3] In other words, it is easier to forecast a company's total revenues than its revenues per product line because individual variations (partially) cancel out. Related to the aggregation property is that longer term (absolute) forecasts are typically more uncertain: the standard deviation increases with the forecasting horizon. Specifically, if fluctuations from one period to the next are uncorrelated and identically distributed, then the standard deviation of the cumulative forecast grows with the square root of the unit of time.

Given the importance of forecasting to operations strategy, we summarize the three forecasting properties as:

Principle 5 (Forecasts) Forecasts should contain all available information on the future evolution of demand, supply, technology, competition and environment. At a minimum, each forecast must specify the expected value (mean) *and* volatility (standard deviation or coefficient of variation) by time bucket. Aggregate forecasts are more precise.

---

[1]The famous bell curve is named after the German mathematician Johann Carl Friedrich Gauss (1777-1855), who first characterized it while investigating the distribution of errors in measurements. Gauss' genius was apparent early on: His first-grade teachers were amazed when little Gauss, at the age of 7, summed the integers from 1 to 100 instantly by recognizing that the sum was 50 pairs of numbers that each add to 101.

[2]The continuous normal distribution is a good approximation for large positive discrete random variables with moderate volatility (COV< .5). For small discrete variables (e.g., items selling 3 or 4 units per month) or larger COVs other distributions (e.g., Poisson) are more appropriate.

[3]For math fans: Cauchy-Schwartz yields that the standard deviation of a sum is less than the sum of the standard deviations. (Strictly less unless the terms are perfectly positively correlated.) If the terms are uncorrelated, the variance of the sum equals the sum of variances which yields the stronger "square root rule."

This principle provides the guidance to what information should be gathered when constructing a forecast.

Forecasting in practice

Constructing a forecast for a single period requires the estimation of a probability distribution for a random variable. The "process of forecasting" strongly depends on the availability of data that you expect to be a useful predictor of the future. Appendix D (p. 443) reviews simple, yet powerful techniques that you can easily implement in a spreadsheet and that apply to the most likely settings that you will encounter. While more sophisticated techniques exist, good forecasting processes always keep data not only of actual realizations, but also of past forecasts. The latter is very helpful to estimate future forecast errors and volatilities.

Constructing a forecast for a quantity X_t that evolves over time typically requires more work. While sophisticated time-series forecasting is best left to experts, a simple yet powerful technique is to specify a set of specific *scenarios* of the evolution over time, also called a set of *sample paths*, with associated likelihoods. If a small number of sample paths are a good approximation of the evolution of the underlying quantity, then they allow effective *scenario analysis* that can be easily simulated in a spreadsheet. Scenario analysis is the typical tool to compute the expected net present value of a capacity strategy when demand is evolving over time, as reviewed and illustrated in Appendix 3A.

Organizational obstacles to good forecasting

Even though everybody accepts that a point forecast will almost never be "right," the exclusive use of point forecasts in planning persists in many companies. Obviously, people have an intuitive sense of the range of likely outcomes, but that information is "lost" in many companies' forecasts due to several reasons, including inappropriately designed information systems, long-held practices, and incentive systems. Forecasting is often a rather ad-hoc result of informal information gathering from many functions in an organization, including sales and marketing, operations, finance, and strategic planning. We said earlier that the important steps to establish forecasting competence are to include estimates of volatility or forecast errors and to keep data not only of actual realizations, but also of past forecasts. The latter is crucial to estimate forecast errors, but is also problematic because few people like to track "errors."

Besides its importance to operations strategy and planning of flow control, forecasting also serves other important goals. Managers often use a forecast as a "stretch goal." As such, they are averse to including margins of error in the forecast and to updating it, let alone revising it downward. Forecasts may also be related to financial reporting and expectation setting on Wall Street. Meeting quarterly forecasts sometimes becomes an overriding goal, as manifested by the hockey-stick effect where sales suddenly increase near the end-of-the-quarter. While there is no easy solution, it is important to separate goal-setting from forecasting actual outcomes.

Forecasting often results from agreements that entail a certain commitment so that forecasting is political and subject to gaming, especially when incentives enter the picture. For example, if operations managers are incentivized on cost, they will be averse to having excess capacity (and higher per-unit cost) and will tend to low ball capacity needs. In contrast, if sales managers are incentivized on revenue, they will be averse to having capacity shortages. In short, behind the analytical process of forecasting lurks an important political process. Understanding the latter is key to understanding why a company's forecasts are accurate or not.

The fact that actual performance can be modified via incentives also has a more conceptual implication. In operations management models, demand is often the generator of uncertainty and typically assumed to be exogenous. For example, it is often assumed that demand is unaffected by operational actions. While this may lead to a simple value-maximizing capacity level (as we will see shortly), in reality future demand may be dependent on that capacity level. (For example, the successful drug Enbrel was capacity constrained in its first years after introduction. People on the waiting list adopted other substitute drugs when they became available, reducing future Enbrel demand.) The other extreme would be to assume that demand is endogenous, reflecting practices where marketing and sales agree on a sales plan, each function doing whatever it takes to make it happen. Of course, reality is somewhere in between: demand, and forecasts in general, are neither completely exogenous nor completely endogenous.

3.4 | ECONOMIES OF SCALE IN CAPACITY INVESTMENT

Economies of scale or *increasing returns to scale* is a formal notion of "bigger is better" and often captures some realities in capacity investment. It means that the cost of doubling the size is less than double the cost of the original size. Let us denote the size of capacity by K and its associated capacity investment cost or capital expenditure (CapEx) by $C(K)$.[4] Capacity investment exhibits economies of scale if $C(2K) < 2C(K)$. This means that costs grow sublinearly, either due to the presence of a fixed cost component or due to decreasing marginal costs as shown in Figure 3.2. Scale economies implies that the per unit cost of capacity (i.e., average cost) $C(K)/K$ declines as the capacity size K increases and that the cost function is concave.

A linear CapEx function with economies of scale

The simplest capacity investment cost that exhibits economies of scale has a fixed cost component c_0 and a constant marginal cost c_K which is modeled by a linear[5] CapEx function:

$$\text{Linear CapEx function: } C(K) = c_0 + c_K K, \tag{3.1}$$

---

[4]Denoting capital and capacity by K seems to go back to Karl Marx's *Das Kapital*. Earlier, at the age of 29 and after being expelled from his native Germany and from France, Marx wrote *The Communist Manifesto* in Belgium in 6 weeks during 1847 based on a first draft by Engels.

[5]To be precise, this is an affine function...

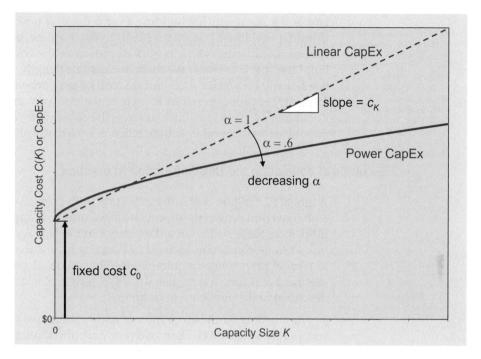

Figure 3.2 Capacity investment costs or capital expenditures typically exhibit economies of scale due to a fixed cost component c_0 or decreasing marginal costs modeled by parameters c_K and α.

as represented by the dashed line in Figure 3.2. The fixed cost may represent all the planning, real estate, and other costs that are (nearly) independent of the size of capacity. The marginal capacity investment cost is the additional cost to add one unit of capacity. The per unit cost of capacity is $c_K + c_0/K$ and decreasing simply because the fixed cost is spread over a larger capacity. This cost function captures the reality of economies of scale and is easy to manipulate analytically.

The power CapEx function

The linear CapEx function can be generalized to a "power" function that allows for decreasing marginal cost by adding a parameter $\alpha \in (0, 1]$ that measures the "degree" of scale economies:

$$\text{Power CapEx function: } C(K) = c_0 + \frac{c_K}{\alpha} K^\alpha,$$

as represented by the solid curve in Figure 3.2. (Notice that the affine function is recovered if $\alpha = 1$.) The cost per unit of capacity is $(c_0/K) + (c_K/\alpha K^{1-\alpha})$ and is again decreasing, but now due to two factors. As before, the fixed cost is spread over a larger capacity. In addition, if $\alpha < 1$, the marginal capacity investment cost or the derivative of C, $C'(K) = c_K K^{\alpha-1}$, is also decreasing. Smaller α yields a steeper decrease in marginal cost and stronger economies of scale.

The power relationship K^α in capacity investment cost has its roots in physics and is the argument for building ever bigger oil tankers and container ships. Consider building a box (say a plant, a vessel, a pipe, etc.). Its volume is a measure of its capacity, while its surface measures the cost of materials needed to build the box. If we scale the three dimensions (length, width, and height) of the box linearly by a factor k, its surface (cost) is proportional to k^2 while its volume (capacity) is proportional to k^3. Thus, the cost per unit of capacity is proportional to $k^{2/3}$. This result is known as the *cube-square rule* and suggests that the parameter α is around $2/3$. In practice, α is virtually always between .6 and 1.

Example of estimating the CapEx function in practice

A global \$2.5 billion dollar manufacturer with extensive field service operations embarked on a project to consolidate 256 worldwide applications into one Oracle E-Business Suite system in a data center in the U.S. As part of the planning, senior Deloitte consultant Richard L. Pérez had to estimate capacity requirements in term of raw storage requirements. This involved estimating the capacity investment cost function of disk drives as well as demand forecasting (as will be described in the mini-case in Chapter 4).

Rick estimated the economies of scale parameters from previous quotations and purchases of 150GB hard drives. Each installation of new hard drives incurred a freight cost of \$500 and required a visit by a system engineer which cost about \$150. These costs were insensitive to the number of drives installed so that the fixed cost component $c_0 = \$650$. The marginal cost parameters c_K and α were estimated through a linear regression in log-log scale. To see this, rewrite the power CapEx function to express the variable cost per unit of capacity and take logs:

$$\frac{C(K) - c_0}{K} = \frac{c_K}{\alpha} K^{\alpha - 1}$$

$$\Rightarrow \log \frac{C(K) - c_0}{K} = \log \frac{c_K}{\alpha} - (1 - \alpha) \log K.$$

The parameters α and c_K are thus found from the slope and intercept, as shown in Figure 3.3. Rick plotted some historical price quotes of the cost per hard drive as a function of the number of drives ordered in log-log scale. The best fitted linear curve had intercept $10^{4.1}$ and slope $-.157$, so that the degree of scale economies $\alpha = 1 - .157 = .843$ and $c_K = 10^{4.1}\alpha = 10^{4.1} \times .843 = \$10,613$ per 150GB drive.

3.5 | CAPACITY VALUATION AND VOLATILITY

Armed with an understanding of capacity, forecasting, and investment cost, we now turn attention to capacity valuation. Later we will size capacity by optimizing its value and distill managerial guidelines.

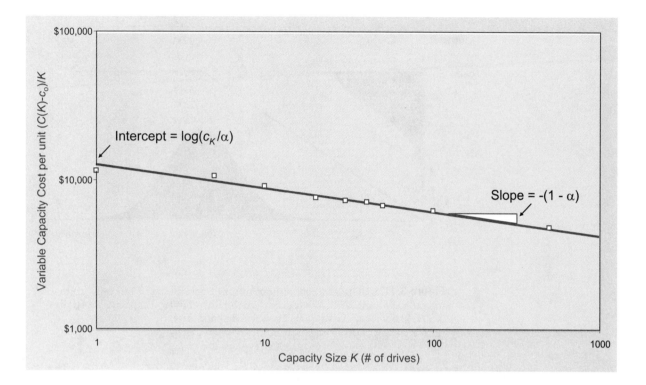

Figure 3.3 The economies of scale parameters c_K and α of the CapEx function can be estimated in a simple linear regression in log-log scale.

Capacity embodies real options or contingent decisions

You may find it useful to think of capacity as an option on a real asset, also known as a *real option*. An option is synonymous with contingent decisions. For example, after investment we can utilize the real asset at any level (depending on actual observed demand, for example) up to its capacity, but we don't have to. Capacity *caps output* and acts similar to a financial *put option*: the value of the capacity's output increases when demand increases but only up to a limit, as shown in Figure 3.4. Apple's iPod example (p. 74) demonstrates that resource output is the maximum of its demand, its supply and its capacity.

Besides the utilization option, capacity has also several other imbedded options. The capacity timing decision has an associated option value of delay: one may gain information by postponing the capacity decision, as Chapter 4 will illustrate. In a multi-product company, flexible resources have a switching or substitution option: they can switch to the more profitable product as needed, as we will see in Chapter 5. A global network has allocation options that move work to the optimal location, as Chapter 6 will discuss. Finally, investing in flexible and redundant capacity can reduce risk, as illustrated in Chapter 9.

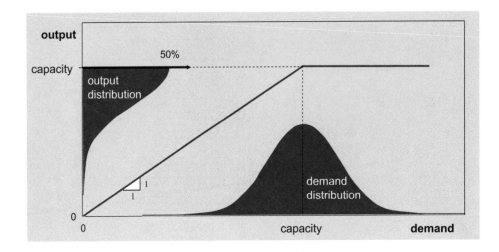

Figure 3.4 Capacity as a real option: output tracks demand but only up to the capacity limit. With symmetric demand uncertainty, a capacity shortfall is 50% likely if capacity equals expected demand.

Volatility degrades the value of capacity

The interpretation of capacity as a real option highlights its dependence on uncertainty. If either demand, supply, or processing itself is uncertain, the capacity constraint prevents us from enjoying all upside demand opportunity while we are fully exposed to the downside risk.

Assume, for example, that capacity equals the expected demand and that demand is normally distributed. Actual demand will then fall below or above the mean, each event occurring with probability 50%. If demand is below the mean, the output equals demand; otherwise a capacity shortage occurs and the output is capped at capacity. The output distribution thus equals the lower half of the normal distribution but has a point mass of 50% at the mean or capacity, as shown in Figure 3.4. In other words, the output is constrained on the upside with probability 0.5 while there is no protection on the downside. The average output will thus be *less* than the average demand. In addition, if the amount of demand uncertainty increases, the lower tail of the output distribution falls while the upside remains constrained by capacity so that the average output will fall.

The key insight is that the value of capacity typically decreases with more demand volatility:

Principle 6 (Volatility) Capacity is a real option whose value typically decreases when volatility increases.

This principle tells us that proper valuation of capacity must include volatility and the non-linearity imbedded in capacity that can restrict sales and thus profits. When financial valuation studies simply translate forecasted demand growth

> **Example 3.2** Wolfgang Puck's capacity value and shortfall
>
> Wolfgang Puck runs a restaurant (a service operation) next to the movie theaters in Evanston, a suburb of Chicago. Many of Wolfgang Puck's customers watch a movie after dining, but demand varies from day to day. To keep things simple, assume that the restaurant's demand before the 8:00pm movie is either "high" (120 customers) or "low" (80 customers) with equal probability. Notice that the expected daily demand is 100.
>
> Assume that the restaurant naively invested in seating and service capacity of 100. The number of customers that can be served thus would be either 100 or 80—notice that the upside variation is gone—with an average of 90. The expected capacity shortfall is $100 - 90 = 10$ customers or $50\% \times (120 - 100)$.
>
> Assuming a \$30 average profit margin per customer and 250 similar operating days per year, the expected annual value of the capacity investment would thus be $\$30 \times 250 \times 90 = \$675,000$ at best, not including any negative impacts for turning away some customers. Compared with the annual average demand value of $\$30 \times 250 \times 100 = \$750,000$, the non-linear capacity constraint caps the demand upside and reduces profits by 10%. Given that net profit margins of 10% are not unreasonable, capacity shortfalls can make or break the business.
>
> To further show how the value of capacity depends on volatility, let "high" be $100(1 + \sigma)$ and "low" $100(1 - \sigma)$, where σ is a constant between 0 and 1 that represents demand volatility. Notice that expected demand remains 100 but the expected daily capacity shortfall and the annual value of the capacity investment become:
>
> $$\text{shortfall} = 50\sigma \quad \text{and} \quad \text{annual value} = \$30 \times (100 - 50\sigma) \times 250.$$
>
> The shortfall thus increases when volatility σ increases and strongly degrades value. Simplistic capacity valuation that would ignore volatility would over-estimate value: in this example, a $\sigma = 30\%$ demand volatility would reduce the capacity value by 15%.

linearly into sales and profit growth they overvalue capacity. Example 3.2 provides a simple numeric example. The volatility principle also suggests that extra capacity would mitigate shortfalls. Let us investigate that further.

Measuring the capacity shortfall

The *capacity shortfall* in a given period measures the *excess demand*:

$$\text{capacity shortfall} = \begin{cases} \text{demand - capacity} & \text{if demand} > \text{capacity}, \\ 0 & \text{otherwise.} \end{cases}$$

Notice that the capacity shortfall is never negative and is measured in the same units that demand and capacity are measured. The capacity shortfall also measures lost sales (again in units of demand, not in financial units) if customers are too impatient to wait until capacity becomes available.

Typically, capacity is sized before we know demand for certain. To value capacity we then are interested in the expected capacity shortfall. This is easily calculated with a spreadsheet if our demand forecast is a discrete probability distribution (Appendix B on p. 435 reviews how to do it for general distributions, and the normal distribution in particular).

For example, consider the Wolfgang Puck restaurant of Example 3.2 whose capacity matched average daily demand of 100 customers during 6:00pm to 8:00pm. Heeding the forecasting principle, the manager kept track of actual

Probability	Demand	Shortfall
2.7%	50	0
5.0%	60	0
5.8%	70	0
8.8%	80	0
15.3%	90	0
20.0%	100	0
17.0%	110	10
13.8%	120	20
6.8%	130	30
4.0%	140	40
0.8%	150	50
Average:	100.12	8.50

Table 3.1 Daily demand forecast and capacity shortfall for Wolfgang Puck.

daily demand and observed the historical demand distribution with 11 scenarios shown in Table 3.1 (rather than the simple high-low distribution in Example 3.2). It is straightforward to compute the daily capacity shortfall for each demand scenario. The average capacity shortfall is about 8.5 customers. This means that, on an average evening, Wolfgang Puck was unable to seat 8.5 potential customers. If these customers are impatient (which they may be if they want to see their 8pm movie), this capacity shortfall would imply an 8.5% loss of revenue.

The impact of volatility and safety capacity on capacity shortfall

When capacity equals average demand, occasional shortfalls may arise if demand is volatile. In fact, shortfalls will happen with probability 50% if the demand distribution is symmetric around the mean, as illustrated in Fig. 3.4. Shortfalls can be reduced by raising capacity beyond average demand. The difference between capacity and average demand is referred to as *safety capacity*:

$$\text{safety capacity} = \text{capacity} - \textit{average} \text{ demand}.$$

Notice that safety capacity can be positive or negative. In the next section we will see that it is worthwhile to invest in positive (negative) safety capacity if the cost of a unit shortfall is high (low) relative to the cost of a unit extra capacity. Positive safety capacity is excess capacity; its purpose is to provide a safety net to capture higher-than-expected demand.

When demand is normally distributed, we can analyze how the expected capacity shortfall changes when we vary the amount of safety capacity and demand volatility. The analytics are reviewed in Appendix B on p. 435 but the results are shown in Figure 3.5. The figures show the expected capacity shortfall rate for various levels of demand volatility and safety capacity. We can make the following important observations:

1. The expected capacity shortfall increases strongly in volatility.

2. Safety capacity strongly reduces the shortfall and is most effective for highly volatile demand. Additional safety capacity, however, shows decreasing

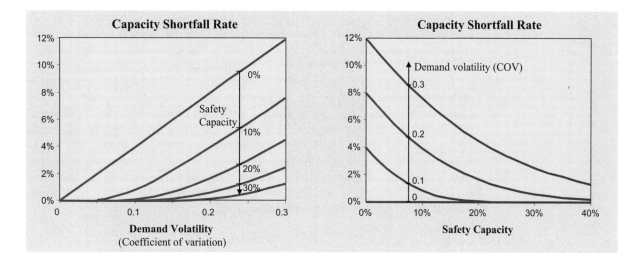

Figure 3.5 The expected capacity shortfall rate increases sharply in demand volatility but that effect is counteracted by excess or safety capacity (all values are relative to average demand).

marginal returns meaning that further shortfall rate reductions are increasingly more expensive.

With a magnitude of 5% or 10% you may wonder why expected capacity shortfall is such a big deal. Recall that those numbers are percentages of average demand or revenue. Given that operating margins of 10% of revenue are not uncommon in practice, reducing capacity shortfalls from 10% to 5% can double operating profits (and increase of net profits even more)!

3.6 | OPTIMAL CAPACITY SIZING

Now that we know how to evaluate capacity shortfalls, we can identify the optimal capacity size by maximizing net present value, according to Principle 1 (p. 5). The net present value of capacity equals the present value of utilizing the capacity minus the capacity investment costs. We have seen that the value of capacity degrades with volatility which increases the capacity shortfall. The key trade-off in capacity sizing thus is balancing the cost of capacity with the opportunity cost of capacity shortfall.

Optimal capacity sizing in a newsvendor model

To gain insight, let us first consider a simple model for which we can identify the optimal capacity size. This model is known as the newsvendor model and is reviewed in detail in Appendix B (p. 435). Let us quickly review its main logic.

Assume that capacity can only be used for a single period and that its size K must be decided on before observing the random demand D. A unit of demand yields an operating profit margin m if there is sufficient capacity, but incurs a shortfall penalty cost c_p otherwise. The marginal capacity investment cost is c_K.

To find the optimal capacity sizing condition, consider the following thought experiment. Should we invest in an extra unit of capacity beyond K? The marginal value would be an additional unit sold and a reduction of shortfall costs if demand $D > K$ but zero otherwise. The expected marginal value thus is $(m + c_p) \Pr(D > K)$ which decreases when capacity K increases. For this to be a profitable venture, it must be that $m + c_p > c_K$. In that case, increasing K increases NPV as long as this expected marginal value exceeds the marginal cost is c_K. At the optimal capacity size K^*, both are equal (assuming continuous demand and capacity) and the *optimal capacity sizing condition* is:

$$\text{Optimal shortfall probability } \Pr(D > K^*) = \frac{\text{marginal capacity cost } c_K}{\text{marginal capacity value } m + c_p}.$$

Thus, capacity should be chosen such that the probability of a capacity shortfall equals the financial ratio $c_K/(m + c_p)$. Equivalently, the probability that the capacity is sufficient to serve demand or the optimal *service probability* is:

$$\text{Optimal service probability } \Pr(D \leq K^*) = 1 - \frac{c_K}{m + c_p}.$$

When demand is normally distributed with mean R and standard deviation σ, then the optimal capacity level is $K^* = R + z^*\sigma$, where the optimal z-statistic is directly found with the normsinv spreadsheet function:

$$\text{Optimal } z\text{-statistic } z^* = \texttt{normsinv}(\text{optimal service probability}).$$

The problem set asks you to apply the newsvendor solution to the Wolfgang Puck example. The optimal capacity sizing condition also extends to a setting like Apple's iPod (Example 3.1) where we also face *supply uncertainty*. Instead of using the demand forecast only, we will then use the forecast of the minimum of demand and supply. The problem set offers you some hints on how to do this.

Insights from the newsvendor model

The optimal capacity sizing condition specifies the best trade-off between the cost of excess capacity and the cost of insufficient capacity. If both are equal, capacity should be sized to the median demand. Capacity investment should be more aggressive if shortage costs exceed capacity costs but more conservative otherwise.

The optimal sizing condition also tells us that the service probability or the probability that capacity is constraining output should be dictated by the financials. This means that the likelihood that an asset is a bottleneck should equal the ratio of its marginal capacity cost to its marginal value. In other words, optimal capacity investment will result in a network where the likely bottlenecks are expensive resources relative to their marginal value. Chapter 5 will further explore how to size resources in a network setting.

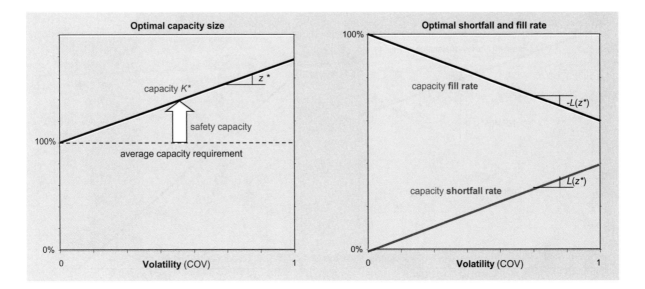

Figure 3.6 The optimal capacity size and safety capacity depend linearly on volatility for normal demand. Even though capacity may increase, it never increases sufficiently to prevent the capacity shortfall from growing.

Note that the optimal capacity size $K^* = R + z^*\sigma$ varies linearly with standard deviation when demand is normally distributed because the optimal z-statistic is independent of volatility. Equivalently, the optimal safety capacity, as a fraction of mean demand, is

$$\frac{\text{optimal safety capacity}}{\text{mean demand}} = z^* \times \text{coefficient of variation}.$$

In other words, an increase in relative volatility should lead to a proportional change in safety capacity, as illustrated in Figure 3.6. However, even though the optimal capacity may increase in volatility, its rise is insufficient to prevent the shortfall from increasing. (Typically, more volatility requires more safety capacity but safety capacity and z^* can be negative if capacity costs are large relative to margins and shortfall penalties.)

Also, the present value of optimal capacity sizing decreases linearly with volatility when demand is normally distributed (as shown in Appendix B on p. 435). Given that the optimal capacity increases linearly in volatility, so does the linear investment cost $C(K^*) = c_0 + c_K K^*$. As the difference between the present value and $C(K^*)$, the optimal NPV thus strongly decreases linearly in volatility as shown in Figure 3.7. (This agrees with the volatility principle and also generalizes Example 3.2 with a high-low demand distribution on page 87.) The impact of volatility on the attractiveness of the capacity investment option is dramatic: after a certain level of volatility, the value of capacity is insufficient to cover the investment cost and therefore we would do better to walk away from the investment option.

Lastly, now that we understand optimal capacity sizing under uncertainty,

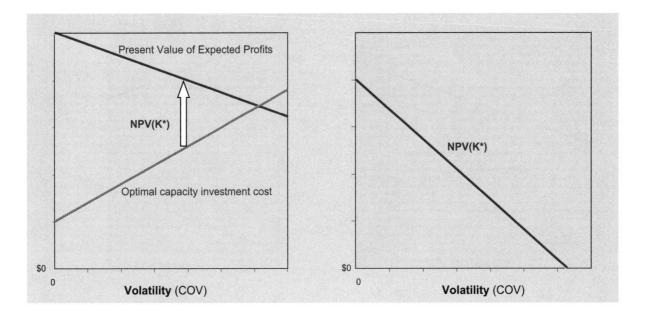

Figure 3.7 Under optimal capacity sizing, the present value, capacity investment cost, and NPV decrease linearly in volatility for normal demand. The investment thus becomes unprofitable beyond a certain volatility level.

the relevant question is: when should we care about safety capacity and volatility? Given operations strategy's task of value maximization, we should care when the volatility degradation on value is large. With normal demand, this volatility degradation relative to average demand equals:

$$\text{volatility degradation \%} \;=\; \left(1 + \frac{c_p}{m}\right) \times \underbrace{\text{COV} \times L(z^*)}_{},$$

$$=\; \text{financials} \times \text{optimal shortfall rate},$$

where $L(z)$ is a decreasing function of z, as shown in Appendix B (p. 435). Thus, the value loss from volatility is large when:

1. shortfall penalties are significant relative to contribution margins;

2. relative volatility as measured by coefficient of variation is high;

3. capacity costs are large relative to margins and shortfall penalties (so that z^* is small and standard losses $L(z^*)$ are high).

Capacity sizing in practice and capturing operations in NPV analysis

The general recommendation for capacity sizing from the newsvendor model—size to balance capacity cost with the expected opportunity cost of shortfalls by explicitly recognizing uncertainty—applies to practice. However, capacity sizing has additional complications in practice:

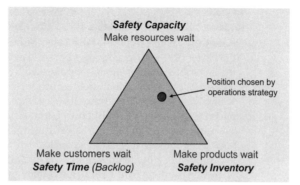

Figure 3.8 Operations strategy must position itself somewhere in the trade-off triangle of safety capacity, safety time (backlogging), and safety inventory to mitigate the degrading impact of volatility.

Capacity typically has a relatively long lifetime so one needs to balance the present value of its utilization with the capacity investment cost today. Such NPV analysis is typically done in a spreadsheet, as reviewed in Appendix 3A, where uncertainty is captured through scenario analysis or simulation. The appendix also discusses how to capture operational issues in the NPV analysis.

Capacity valuation should also take into account the option value of changing capacity in the future, a topic that we will discuss in the next chapter.

Finally, safety capacity is only one instrument to mitigate volatility and a good capacity strategy should also investigate other instruments, which we will do next.

3.7 | THE CAPACITY-INVENTORY-WAITING TRIANGLE

The previous section showed how safety capacity can mitigate the expected cost of mismatches between demand and supply. Safety capacity can be interpreted as making resources wait for above-average demand. Capacity shortfalls can also be alleviated by shifting supply or demand over time. In this section, we focus on shifting supply by either processing in advance of demand and making products wait in inventory, or processing after demand and making customers wait in a backlog. Chapter 8 will discuss how to shift demand over time.

The capacity-inventory-waiting strategy triangle

A good capacity strategy uses a tailored combination of safety capacity, safety inventory, and safety time to mitigate value degradation due to volatility (Figure 3.8). For example, a product company can produce in advance of demand and use inventory and capacity to buffer volatility. Consider, for instance, headphone manufacturer Koss Corporation featured in Example 3.3. Koss' President

---

Example 3.3 Koss Corp.'s inventory build-up strategy

Koss Corp. is the second-largest seller of headphones in the U.S. after Sony of Japan. In the early 1990's, Koss embarked on a lean inventory initiative following the virtues of the assemble-to-order model popularized by Dell Computer Corp. By the 1996 holidays, however, it was not able to deliver products. In fact, it was so far behind that it "needed to hire 450 people—three times its usual factory staff—to catch up. Training and new-hire mistakes heaped on $1 million in extra costs, a huge amount for a company that made $2.8 million on $36 million in sales" during fiscal 1996.

Soon after, President Michael Koss decided to switch from an assemble-to-order strategy to an inventory build-up strategy. While all employees initially resisted that change in operations strategy, Mr. Koss argued that, "unlike computers and some other electronics, headphones don't loose their value quickly. In addition, the interest expense for another month or two of inventory would be less than the cost of hiring more factory help for peak-demand periods." *Source: Ramstad (1999)*

Michael Koss argued that "unlike computers and some other electronics, headphones don't lose their value quickly" and believes that an inventory build-up strategy is better suited for his business than an assemble-to-order (ATO) strategy as employed by Dell Computer Corporation.

Using buffers to alleviate capacity shortfalls can also be effective in services. If customers are willing to wait (and sign up on a waiting or backlog list as for the iPod mini), then we can use waiting time as a second lever to buffer demand volatility. In Chapter 2 (page 41), we explored how Ameritrade's quality-of-service guarantee to limit customer waiting time depends on capacity; in this chapter we will investigate how to balance capacity investment with responsiveness.

The key take away is that a capacity decision should recognize that there are multiple counter measures to reduce the expected capacity shortfall. In this section, we analyze how operations strategy can pick a value-maximizing position in the capacity-inventory-waiting trade-off triangle shown in Figure 3.8. The newsboy model was one example of how to size safety capacity. In the remainder of this section we will consider two other model examples to help us identify "where we want to be in the triangle." The next example trades off capacity with inventory while the last analyzes the capacity-waiting trade-off. In Chapter 4 we will see how to solve capacity-inventory-waiting trade-offs in a spreadsheet.

Trading off capacity with inventory: the Koss model

Instead of serving customers in a make-to-order fashion, product companies may be able to make products in advance and hold them in inventory. That becomes especially effective in seasonal industries. Consider, for example, the headphone maker Koss which benefitted from an inventory build-up strategy to keep capacity level throughout the holiday season, as discussed in Example 3.3 (Mini-case 3 on p. 107 provides another example).

To understand the key trade-off between capacity and inventory, let us consider a stylized example of a company with seasonal demand like Koss. Assume for simplicity that the year has two seasons, each of equal length, and that most volatility stems from seasonality (and not from intra-season uncertainty). Specifically, let R denote the average demand rate and $R(1 \pm \sigma)$ the low and high sea-

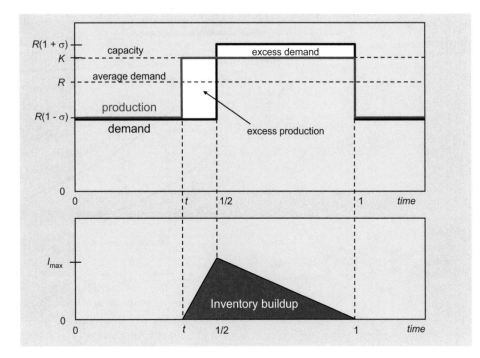

Figure 3.9 The optimal production and inventory build-up strategy for the Koss model produces in advance during low season to supply excess high-season demand.

son demand rates. The constant $\sigma \in [0, 1]$ is thus a measure of seasonal demand volatility: a value of $\sigma = 0$ corresponds to a perfectly stable or level demand rate R throughout the year while a value of $\sigma = 1$ models a purely seasonal demand rate that is zero half the year and $2R$ during the season.

The question that we want to address is: what is the optimal tailored capacity strategy to seasonal demand volatility? There are two extreme possibilities:

1. an *assemble-* or *build-to-order* (ATO or BTO) strategy that never builds in advance of demand. Its zero-inventory cost benefit however requires peak capacity investment.

2. a *level production* strategy that produces at equal levels throughout the year. Its benefit of minimal capacity requirements may however require substantial inventory to smooth any seasonal imbalance between production and demand.

Any capacity strategy in between those extremes tries to balance capacity costs with inventory holding costs. Let us analyze this trade-off and at the same time find out when ATO or level production is optimal.

Assume capacity K falls in between the two extremes of level production and build-to-order: $R \leq K \leq R(1 + \sigma)$. The optimal production strategy given that capacity is found as follows. It is convenient to use years as the time unit so

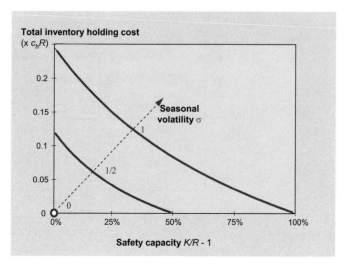

Figure 3.10 There is a strong trade-off between capacity and holding inventory that depends on the seasonal volatility of the Koss model.

that total production for the year must be $R \times 1$ year or R for short, which corresponds to an average capacity utilization of R/K. To minimize inventory we should produce at capacity during the high season. Given that capacity cannot meet peak-season demand, we must build the total excess peak-season demand in advance during the low season when we have excess capacity. To minimize inventory build-up, we will start the low season by producing at the demand rate and then by switching to full utilization near the end of the season to begin building inventory. This optimal production and inventory strategy is represented in Figure 3.9, where the switch-over time t is such that the excess production during the low season equals the excess demand during the high season.

   With the optimal production-inventory strategy known for an arbitrary capacity, the last piece of puzzle is to identify the capacity that maximizes value. For this Koss model, the solution can be found analytically as shown in Appendix 3B (p. 114). Here we focus on the insights:

1. There is a strong trade-off between capacity and inventory in the presence of seasonality, as shown in Figure 3.10 for medium and maximal seasonality. More volatility requires more inventory or safety capacity. Only with perfectly steady demand can we survive without safety capacity or inventory.

2. The optimal capacity size, shown in Figure 3.11, increases when the financial ratio c_h/rc_K increases, where c_h measures the annual unit *holding cost* and rc_K is the annual unit opportunity cost of capacity. This is the trade-off we expect: we substitute safety capacity for inventory as holding inventory becomes more expensive relative to capacity. This explains the excess capacity strategy of Zara (c.f., Chapter 1) whose fashion focus implies high inventory perishability and holding costs.

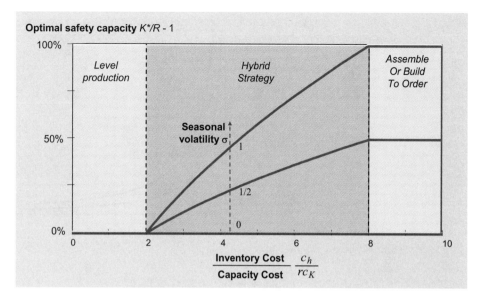

Figure 3.11 The optimal capacity size when pre-building inventory is possible depends on the financial ratio rc_K/c_h and on seasonal volatility. In the Koss model, the strategies of level production and ATO are optimal only for extreme values of the financial ratio.

3. The nature of the optimal capacity strategy itself depends on the financial ratio c_h/rc_K. A level production strategy is optimal if holding inventory is cheap relative to holding capacity, as in the case of Koss headphones, or if there is no demand volatility ($\sigma = 0$). In contrast, an assemble or build-to-order strategy (no seasonal inventory but maximal safety capacity to cover the peak) is optimal when capacity is cheap relative to holding inventory. That is arguably the case of assembly of personal computers at Dell (which is also less seasonal). For intermediate values of the financial ratio, a balance between inventory and capacity is optimal. For our model, this holds when $2 \leq c_h/rc_K \leq 8$ as shown in Figure 3.11.

4. Reducing seasonal volatility reduces capacity requirements and increases NPV, another manifestation of the volatility principle. Seasonal volatility can be reduced by processing multiple products with complementary business cycles such as lawn mowers and snow blowers using flexible resources. This strategy is also used effectively in services. Choice Hotels International Inc., a franchiser with brands including Comfort Inn, Quality and Clarion, and 1-800-Flowers.com, a provider of flowers and gifts, have an unusual agreement under which the companies essentially rent call-center employees to one another. "The deal works in part because the high season for hotel reservation calls is mid-May through early October, while Flower's call volume increases between October and May with surges at Christmas, Valentine's Day and Mother's Day," says White (2006). We will study seasonality and flexibility in the next two chapters.

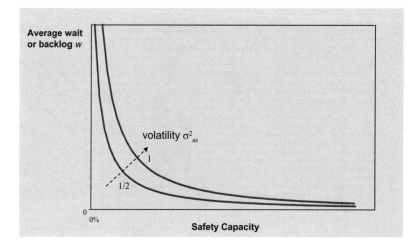

Figure 3.12 The trade-off between safety capacity and responsiveness, measured by average customer wait or backlog w, as a function of volatility.

Trading off capacity with waiting: the Wolfgang Puck model

Let us reconsider a service operation, such as the Wolfgang Puck restaurant, but assume now that our customers are patient and willing to wait if our operation is running at capacity. (It is indeed not unusual for Wolfgang Puck to have a wait.) Customers typically prefer immediate service and making them wait degrades their service experience and may result in lost goodwill. As before, let us simplistically model the entire impact of waiting on our service's financial performance by a penalty cost. Here it makes sense that the penalty increases the longer a customer must wait. Let c_w be the *waiting penalty* that is incurred per unit time that a customer is waiting.

Assume a stationary setting where demands in each period are independent. Let m denote the average unit margin of serving a customer. Capacity K is the average rate at which we can serve customers and R denotes the average demand rate. The average throughput (and sales) rate is the smaller of K and R. The expected operating profit for a capacity level K then becomes:

$$\text{expected operating profit rate} = \mathbb{E}(\text{sales rate}) \times [m - c_w \times \mathbb{E}(\text{waiting time})].$$

Queuing theory, reviewed in Appendix C on p. 439, estimates the average customer waiting time w as a function of demand, capacity, and volatility:

$$\mathbb{E}(\text{waiting time}) = \frac{1}{K}\frac{R}{K-R}\sigma_{as}^2 = \frac{1}{K}\frac{\rho}{1-\rho}\sigma_{as}^2,$$

where the volatility term includes the coefficient of variation in inter-arrival and service times: $\sigma_{as}^2 = 0.5(C_a^2 + C_s^2)$ and $\rho = R/K$ denotes capacity utilization. Clearly, to keep the average waiting time finite we must invest in safety capacity so that $K > R$. The expected sales rate or throughput then equals the average demand rate R. The *trade-off curve between capacity and waiting* embodied in the waiting time formula is shown in Figure 3.12 for two levels of volatility.

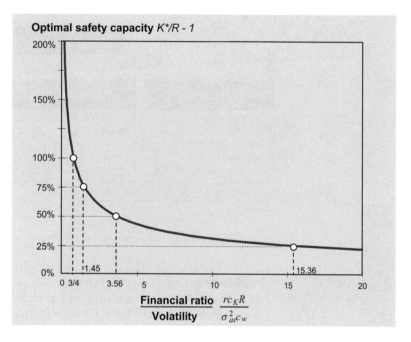

Figure 3.13 The optimal trade-off between capacity K^* and customer waiting or backlog cost as a function of the financial ratio rRc_K/c_w and volatility.

The optimal position on the trade-off curve maximizes net present value. This calculation is relegated to Appendix 3B assuming that the capacity cost function is linear in size with a fixed cost component: $C(K) = c_0 + c_K K$. The result is shown in Figure 3.13 and suggests the following recommendations for the capacity investment-waiting trade-off:

1. The optimal capacity size decreases with an increase in the financial ratio c_K/c_w, which measures the cost of capacity vs. the cost of waiting.[6] When waiting becomes relatively more expensive, the needed safety capacity increases very strongly and non-linearly.

   This is the trade-off we expect: when the organization incurs little cost from making customers wait (or back ordering), it will prefer building little expensive safety capacity. (Given that customers really wanted an iPod mini, they did defect and Apple's incurred waiting cost was low, suggesting that a capacity strategy with long waiting lists is not necessarily bad. The problem set asks you what this implies for capacity sizing and waiting times at a physician's office.)

2. Service firms enjoy economies of scale: the relative amount of needed safety capacity K^*/R decreases with an increase in average demand rate R.[7] This

---

[6]To be precise: r is the discount rate so that $rc_K R$ is the opportunity capacity cost per unit of time. Dividing by the opportunity cost of waiting per unit of time yields the dimensionless ratio $rc_K R/c_w$.

[7]The inherent economies of scale in queuing systems stem from the facts that waiting times are

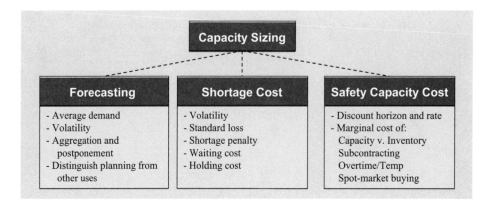

Figure 3.14 Three key drivers of capacity sizing with their levers.

explains the rise of consolidation in call centers and other service centers that enjoy these waiting economies of scale. McDonald's, for example, has a call center in Santa Maria, California, that takes drive-through fast-food orders from 40 outlets around the country and then sends them back to the restaurants by Internet, to be filled a few yards from where they were placed, according to Richtel (2006).

3. Firms with low opportunity cost of capital r should invest in high capacity.

4. The optimal capacity strongly increases with an increase in demand or service volatility, which is another manifestation of the volatility principle. This model also allows us to value the impact of variability reduction. For example, take $\sigma_{as}^2 = 1$ as a reasonable base case when arrivals are random (i.e., they follow a "Poisson process" for which $C_a = 1$) and service times are random (i.e., exponentially distributed with $C_s = 1$). Eliminating arrival uncertainty, e.g. by synchronizing or scheduling arrivals via a reservation system, would set $C_a = 0$ and reduce volatility to $\sigma_{as}^2 = 1/2$, allowing the optimal safety capacity to be cut in half! Exactly the same thing happens if we can standardize service times. Thus, reduction of volatility has a direct and strong impact on capacity investment but unless we can eliminate all volatility in demand and service, safety capacity is essential for services.

3.8 | GUIDELINES FOR CAPACITY SIZING

Capacity sizing is driven by three important factors: forecasting and balancing capacity surplus and shortfall costs. Our analysis of these three drivers, summarized in Figure 3.14, suggests actions that improve capacity sizing:

---

non-linear in capacity and that larger systems enjoy a decrease in relative variability due to arrival and service pooling; see Chapter 5 .

Improve forecasting

An informative forecast is the most important input for a good capacity strategy. The first-order objective of forecasting is to estimate average demand, which indicates rough capacity requirements. Estimating forecast errors is necessary to fine-tune safety capacity, inventory, or backlogging. Actions to improve forecasting include:

1. Track and analyze data. As quality-guru Deming once said: "In God we trust, all others must use data." The data should include not only actual realizations but also past forecasts so we can assess, correct for, and improve forecast errors. Appendix D (p. 443) summarizes simple forecasting techniques worth knowing.

2. Use forecasting errors. Forecasts should include all available information and opinions about the future, data which can be summarized in the form of a probability distribution. Assuming a normal distribution is often a good practice so that different scenarios and opinions can be summarized by a consensus (mean) and one volatility measure (standard deviation or coefficient of variation). Given that point-forecasts are virtually always wrong by definition, tracking forecast errors is a sign of smartness and strength, and by no means weakness. They give a historic estimate of volatility.

3. Reduce forecasting errors through aggregation and postponement. Forecast accuracy improves and seasonality reduces if we can make capacity decisions on aggregate estimates or if we can delay the sizing decision. Actions to improve forecast accuracy through capacity lead time reduction (postponement) and flexibility (aggregation or pooling) are discussed in the next two chapters.

4. Make a distinction between the planning and other functions of forecasting. Realize that forecasting also serves many other managerial roles including expectation and goal setting, incentive and performance measurement, political gaming, and financial expectations setting. Try to separate those effects from informative forecasting data for capacity planning.

Reduce capacity shortfall costs

The capacity shortfall cost is the product of the capacity shortfall magnitude (in units) and the financial cost of a shortfall. Our analysis suggests the following actions to reduce the shortfall cost:

1. Reduce the expected capacity shortfall with counter measures against volatility. We have analyzed safety capacity, inventory, and backlogging or waiting. These three counter measures are substitutes that mitigate capacity shortfalls. Operations strategy should use their value-maximizing combination which defines the optimal position in the capacity-inventory-waiting trade-off triangle of Figure 3.8.

2. Reduce the likelihood of a capacity shortfall by demand management. This may involve raising prices (to reduce demand) and proactive promotions

and revenue management techniques that reduce volatility by shifting and leveling demand over time, as we will analyze in Chapter 8.

3. Reduce the financial cost of a shortfall. The optimal point in the capacity-inventory-waiting triangle maximizes NPV and depends on volatility and financial ratios. The financial impact of a shortfall can be reduced by:

   (a) Reducing the penalty incurred per shortfall. The penalty covers the extra costs of shortfall mitigation from subcontracting, overtime, etc. Providing customers with substitutes may also reduce the penalty.

   (b) Reducing the waiting cost. Induce customers to be willing to wait. Often, behavioral strategies are effective in reducing customer waiting costs in terms of customer dissatisfaction and loss of future sales. Maister (1985) discusses various approaches such as making waiting customers comfortable, creating distractions and offering entertainment, and managing customer expectations of waiting.

   (c) Reducing the inventory holding cost by reducing the physical cost of storage or the opportunity cost (reducing the perishability and the cost of the stock).

Remember that the expected shortfall cost typically increases when volatility increases, even with optimal use of these counter measures. In other words, we can mitigate but not escape the degrading influence of volatility.

Reduce safety capacity costs

Optimal capacity sizing attempts to balance the marginal shortfall cost with the cost of excess capacity. The latter can be improved through the following actions:

1. Increase the life span of safety capacity. This reduces the effective discounted cost of capacity per period.

2. Use multiple forms of safety capacity. In addition to investing in excess capacity, a firm can create safety capacity through other methods such as franchising, subcontracting, overtime, temporary employees or by renting capacity or spot-market buying. These capacity timing actions are discussed in the next chapter.

3.9 | SUMMARY OF LEARNING OBJECTIVES

1. Explain the concept of capacity strategy and discuss its challenges and importance.

A capacity strategy is the long-term plan for developing resources and involves decisions on sizing, timing, types, and location of capacity under uncertainty. The key trade-off in capacity sizing is between the cost of excess capacity and the opportunity cost of capacity shortfalls due to lost sales, customer waits, or substitution to other products or competitors.

In theory, capacity simply is a precise, rigid upper constraint on throughput but the constraint is more nebulous in reality. Realized capacity depends on how we manage the process on a daily basis (tactical operations management and incentive management). Leadtimes, lumpiness, and fixed costs also introduce frictions that prevent us from changing capacity quickly, precisely, and cheaply. Most important, however, is the irreversibility and uncertainty in investment: we often cannot recoup our investment if we have a change of heart. Thus, companies must think twice before investing huge amounts of money.

2. Analyze two key capacity investment drivers: scale economies and uncertainty.

Capital expenditures often exhibit economies of scale: the investment cost per unit of capacity declines as the capacity increases. These economies of scale make it more efficient to install capacity periodically in chunks but reduce the reversibility of capacity investment. The linear and power function are two useful functions to model capital expenditures. Their parameters are easily estimated through a linear regression of cost per unit versus capacity size in log-log scale.

Arguably the most important driver in a capacity strategy is the forecast of demand, supply, technology, competition, and environment. Forecasts must start by estimating averages and trends, which indicate rough capacity requirements, and add volatility estimates to adjust safety capacity. Viewing capacity as a real option is a useful metaphor for understanding the crucial impact of volatility on capacity and the value of the firm. Capacity is like a put option in the sense that it "caps" output and prevents us from enjoying the upside of demand fluctuations. The result is that volatility typically degrades the value of capacity and any analysis that is based on expected values only will overvalue capacity. Safety capacity mitigates the strong degrading impact of volatility on value.

3. Value and optimize capacity investment.

Good capacity strategies should maximize the value of the firm, which depends on future operating profits. To value that future profit flow, we must discount it to arrive at its present value. Deducting the capacity investment cost then yields the net present value as a function of capacity. While discounting is a simple, mechanical process, easily executed in a spreadsheet, valuation is more tricky. Recall that "garbage-in is garbage-out," so it behooves us to carefully estimate the inputs of the discounting process. As explained in Appendix 3A, forecasting and analyzing the impact of capacity on volatility must be done in a pre-NPV analysis to estimate the expected operating profit flows. That is followed by a purely financial NPV analysis.

The optimal capacity size makes the best trade-off between the cost of excess capacity and the cost of capacity shortfalls. The simple newsvendor model shows that the value-maximizing capacity size is a function of volatility and the financial ratio of marginal capacity excess and shortfall costs. The optimal balance invests in safety capacity to mitigate the impact of volatility on NPV.

4. Pick a position in the capacity-inventory-waiting strategy triangle.

In addition to safety capacity, one can pre-build inventory or implement a waiting list or reservation system if customers are patient. Making product wait or making customers wait are substitutes for investing in safety capacity. As the cost of holding inventory or customers decreases, or as the volatility increases, these substitutes become more attractive. The volatility principle implies that we should use a combination of safety capacity, inventory, and waiting to mitigate the value degradation of volatility. Yet, even with an optimal use of these counter measures, we cannot escape the degrading influence of volatility. Therefore, reducing variability and uncertainty is often worthwhile.

DISCUSSION QUESTIONS

1. What does capacity mean in service operations such as the retail banking arm of Deutsche Bank or an Internet brokerage firm like Ameritrade or E-trade? What are the key challenges and frictions of their capacity strategy?

2. Discuss which of the three aspects of a capacity strategy (size, timing, and type) are mostly impacted by three different capacity challenges such as leadtimes, investment costs, and demand uncertainty impact. Why?

3. How does capacity investment affect the trade-off curves in Chapter2?

4. Why does the optimal trade-off between capacity and waiting shown in Figure 3.13 not depend on the margin of the product or service?

5. What does the optimal trade-off between capacity and waiting costs tell you about the staffing at highly-paid professional services? For example, how is wait that mere mortals will experience during medical specialist services related to the pay of the specialist?

6. In our analysis, we have implicitly assumed that capacity lives on indefinitely. How would our results change if capacity only has a finite useful life T?

7. What are the similarities and fundamental differences between capacity investment and inventory planning?

8. What would change to the capacity-inventory trade-off and optimal capacity strategy if inventory had a limited shelf life? For example, flu vaccine production for the Fall season falls in this category.

9. How can you apply the insights of inventory smoothing to service operations? (Hint: inventory is work done in-advance.)

CHALLENGE QUESTIONS

1. Capacity sizing should balance overage with underage costs. How is excess capacity (i.e., under utilization) captured when capacity is valued using discounted cash flow analysis in a spreadsheet?

2. Consider the Wolfgang Puck restaurant of Example 3.2 (p. 87) and approximate its daily demand forecast by a normal distribution with mean 100.12 and standard deviation 8.50. Assume that when demand exceeds capacity, we must turn away customers resulting in lost sales. To account for loss of *goodwill*, we will simply assume that turning away a customer costs Wolfgang Puck a *penalty* c_p of \$6.[8] Assume the restaurant operates 250 days per year and that capacity lives on for ever. What should the optimal restaurant capacity be if a marginal unit of restaurant capacity costs \$12,500?

3. In our analysis we have typically considered the simplest investment cost function that exhibits economies of scale: the fixed-cost function $c_0 + c_K K$. How would results change if you considered the power function?

4. Compute the expected capacity shortfall for an arbitrary capacity K when demands D_t are independent and all uniformly distributed over the interval $[R - \sigma, R + \sigma]$. (Thus the expected demand is R and $\sigma < R$ is a measure of volatility, proportional to the standard deviation.) What are its main drivers?

5. Continue challenge question 2 and compute the optimal capacity size K^*. How does it depend on volatility?

6. Assume that we also face supply uncertainty, in addition to demand uncertainty. To investigate this joint impact on capacity sizing, consider the simple setting where supply S_t and demand D_t are i.i.d. variables and take on three states each independently: the mean R with probability $1 - 2p$ or $R + \sigma$ w.p. p or $R - \sigma$ w.p. p. Investigate the impact of the volatility parameters p and σ. Hint: compute the probability distribution of $\min(S_t, D_t)$ and use that forecast as the input for the newsvendor solution.

Visit www.vanmieghem.us for additional questions and updates.

FURTHER READING AND REFERENCES

▶ The three following chapters will extend capacity investment to dynamic settings allowing for capacity timing, flexibility, and network location decisions. For more advanced treatments on capacity investment refer to Dixit and Pindyck (1994) and Van Mieghem (2003).

▶ Maister (1985) wrote the classic article on reducing waiting costs through behavioral strategies.

Apple Computer Inc. (2004). Press releases. Feb 17 and Mar 25.

Dixit, A. K. and R. S. Pindyck (1994). *Investment Under Uncertainty*. Princeton, NJ: Princeton University Press.

---

[8]The assumption of a constant marginal cost of turning away business is convenient analytically, but is a rather stark abstraction of reality in a business-to-business setting. When we can't supply part of an corporate order, the corporate customer may take its entire business to a more reliable supplier, or competitors may come in.

Gauntt, J. d. P. (2004, Oct). New rules for global component sourcing: the quality imperative in electronics. *Economist Intelligence Unit white paper*.

Hitachi Global Storage Technologies (2004). Press release. May 17.

Laplace, P.-S. (1812). *Théorie Analytique des Probabilités*.

Maister, D. (1985). The psychology of waiting line. In J. A. Czepiel, M. R. Solomon, and C. Suprenant (Eds.), *The Service Encounter*. Lexington, KY: D.C. Heath and Company, Lexington Books. available from davidmaister.com/articles/5/52/.

Ramstad, E. (1999). Koss CEO gambles on inventory buildup–Just-in-time production doesn't always work. *Wall Street Journal*. March 15.

Richtel, M. (2006). The long-distance journey of a fast-food order. *New York Times*. Apr. 11.

Van Mieghem, J. A. (2003). Capacity management, investment and hedging: Review and recent developments. *Manufacturing and Service Operations Management 5*(4), 269–302.

White, E. (2006). A cheaper alternative to outsourcing. *New York Times*. Apr. 10.

Wright, T. (2006). Indonesian labor rules take toll on investment. *Wall Street Journal*. Dec. 6.

Mini-Case 3 | Gujarat Apollo Industries Ltd

[9]Founded in 1972, the Apollo Group was named after Apollo 11 and is the parent of Gujarat Apollo Industries Ltd ("Apollo"). Located in Chennai, India, Apollo is India's No.1 manufacturer of road construction and maintenance equipment with a market share of over 60% in South Asia and recent sales in the Middle East and Africa. Its mechanical paver AP 400 M has been the choice of road construction companies in India for over 30 years.

Recently, Apollo has sold from 8 to 12 pavers per month at unit prices ranging from $75 to $85 thousand. Sales, however, are volatile with fluctuations based on government spending and seasonal factors due to the monsoon period from June to August, as shown in Figure 3.15. The company estimates that it was unable to meet between 10 to 20% of demand.

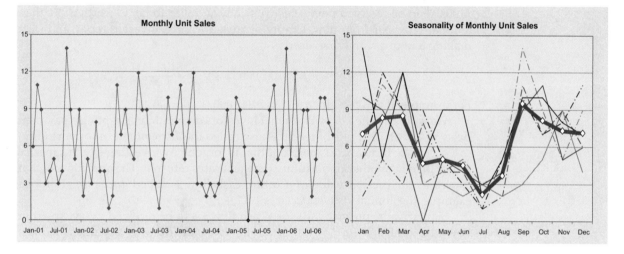

Figure 3.15 Monthly unit sales of Apollo pavers have been volatile from 2001 to 2006 (left panel). Averaging monthly unit sales yields the seasonal average monthly sales (thick line in right panel).

The capital cost to add an additional assembly line is about $540K, which would add about 4.3 units per month in capacity. Average gross margins are about 40% and the firm uses an annual discount rate of 10% to value investments.

1. *What capacity do you recommend for Apollo if it continues to build to demand?*

2. *What is the value of optimizing its capacity and inventory strategy? (Hint: adopt the Koss' model or read the next chapter and build a spreadsheet model.)*

---

[9]Devika Gupta, Chinmay Pandit, Dhruv Patel, Mani Sundaram, Ron Tamir and Professor Van Mieghem prepared this case as the basis for class discussion rather than to illustrate either the effective or ineffective handling of a managerial situation. No part of this case study may be reproduced without permission; direct all inquiries to permissions@vanmieghem.us

Appendix 3A | CALCULATING NPV FOR OPERATIONS STRATEGY

Capacity and operations strategies should maximize the net present value of the firm, according to the Value Maximization Principle (page 5). This Appendix reviews

1. how to discount future cash flows to compute net present value (NPV);

2. how to quickly estimate NPV; and

3. operational and financial issues to keep in mind when calculating NPV.

Discounting cash flows

Assume we invest $400,000 in capacity today and next year's operating profits from that capacity will be $100,000. What is the present value PV today of the $100,000 to be received next year? Typically, a dollar today is worth more than a dollar one year from now, simply because it can be invested today and start making a return r. In other words:

$$PV(1 + r) = \$100,000 \Rightarrow PV = \frac{\$100,000}{1 + r}.$$

For example, if $r = 10\%$, then $PV = \$100,000/1.10 = 90,909$.

We will call r the *rate of return* that investors demand for accepting a payment delay of 1 year. This rate of return is also called the *discount rate* or (opportunity) *cost of capital*. It measures the profit that is forgone by investing say in capacity rather than in another opportunity that generates return r. The analytic tool that expresses the present value of a future cash flow is called *discounting*. In our example, the annual *discount factor* is $1/(1 + r)$.

Similarly, the present value of a cash flow C_2 to be received two years from now satisfies $PV(1 + r)^2 = C_2$. Given that we can add present values (because they are all expressed in current dollars), we find the present value of a general cash flow $(C_1, C_2, ..., C_T)$ as:

$$PV = \sum_{t=1}^{T} \frac{C_t}{(1 + r)^t}.$$

This is called the discounted cash flow formula for horizon length T. Including the investment today (which is typically negative, e.g., $C_0 = -\$700,000$), we find the net present value:

$$NPV = C_0 + PV.$$

In the above, cash flows were received at the beginning of each year; i.e., the times t were integers. When cash flows can be received at any point in time t it is more convenient to express discounting in continuous time as follows:

$$PV = \sum_{t \geq 1} C_t e^{-rt},$$

where the continuous-time discount rate is slightly different from the discrete-time discount rate r. Equating discount factors yields:

$$r_{\text{continuous time}} = \ln\left(1 + r_{\text{discrete time}}\right).$$

NPV using spreadsheets or quick estimates

Computing NPV requires summing sequences and is typically done in a spreadsheet either "from scratch" or using a built-in formula. Let us illustrate the raw mechanics using the example of our investment of $400,000$ in capacity with a 9-year expected life. First, put the estimated annual operating profit flow sequence in a row. In our example, assume these are (in thousands of dollars):

Year t	0	1	2	3	4	5	6	7	8	9
Cash C_t	-400	100	120	110	90	80	100	105	120	85

Second, build a row of corresponding discount factors, starting with 1 in year 0 and finding the discount factor of year t by multiplying that of year $t-1$ by $1/(1+r)$. Third, derive the present value of each year's cash flow by simply multiplying it with its discount factor. In our example, assuming $r = 10\%$, we get:

Year t	0	1	2	3	4	5	6	7	8	9
Cash C_t	-400	100	120	110	90	80	100	105	120	85
Discount	1.00	0.91	0.83	0.75	0.68	0.62	0.56	0.51	0.47	0.42
PV	-400	90.91	99.17	82.64	61.47	49.67	56.45	53.88	55.98	36.05

Finally, sum all present values to yield the NPV (of $186.23 in our example).

A quicker method uses the built-in Excel formula NPV (which should have been called PV) as follows:

$$-400 + \text{NPV}(.1, \{100, 120, 110, 90, 80, 100, 105, 120, 85\}) = \$186.23$$

In practice, discounting and NPV calculations thus become spreadsheet exercises. There are, however, three simple cash flows whose present values are simple expressions that can be used for analytic models, to make quick estimates of more complex present values, and to gain intuitive understanding. These are annuities and perpetuities and their present values, summarized in Analytics Box 3.1, directly follow from a result from mathematics: the *geometric series* gives the sum[10] of the sequence of numbers

$$\sum_{t=0}^{T} \alpha^t = \frac{1 - \alpha^{T+1}}{1 - \alpha}. \tag{3.2}$$

Clearly, the present value of a positive cash flow increases as the rate of return decreases and as the length of the horizon T increases. Also, the present value of a variable positive cash flow can be approximated and bounded by the present value of an annuity of its average, its smallest, and its largest cash flow, respectively. In our example, a 9 year unit annuity at 10% has a present value given by equation (3.5) in Analytics Box 3.1 (p. 110):

$$PV_{\text{annuity}} = \sum_{t=1}^{9} \frac{\$1}{(1+.1)^t} = \$1 \left[\frac{1}{.1} - \frac{1}{.1(1+.1)^9} \right] = \$5.76$$

The average of the future cash flows is $101, its minimum is $80, its maximum is $120. Thus, the estimated NPV is $101 \times 5.76 - \$400 = \$182.40$, close to the actual of $186.23. The lower and upper bounds on the NPV are $60.80 and $291.20, respectively.

---

[10]This is directly verified by multiplying equation $x = 1 + \alpha + \dots + \alpha^T$ by α so that $\alpha x = \alpha + \alpha^2 + \dots + \alpha^{T+1}$. The difference between these two equations yields $(1 - \alpha)x = 1 - \alpha^{T+1}$.

Analytics Box 3.1 Simple Present Values: Perpetuity, Annuity, and Growth

A *perpetuity* is an infinite sequence of identical cash flows $(C, C, C, ...)$. When cash flows grow at a constant rate g, the sequence $(C, (1 + g)C, (1 + g)^2 C, ...)$ is called a *growing perpetuity*. A finite sequence of T identical cash flows $(C, C, C, ..., C)$ is called an *annuity* for T years. Their present values directly follow from the geometric series (equation (3.2), which also applies as T approaches infinity provided that $|\alpha| < 1$) and have simple expressions:

$$PV_{\text{perpetuity}} = \sum_{t=1}^{\infty} \frac{C}{(1+r)^t} = \frac{C}{r}. \tag{3.3}$$

$$PV_{\text{growth perpetuity}} = \sum_{t=1}^{\infty} \frac{(1+g)^{t-1}C}{(1+r)^t} = \frac{C}{r-g}. \quad \text{(provided } g < r) \tag{3.4}$$

$$PV_{\text{annuity}} = \sum_{t=1}^{T} \frac{C}{(1+r)^t} = C\left[\frac{1}{r} - \frac{1}{r(1+r)^T}\right] \tag{3.5}$$

$$= \texttt{PV(r,T,C)} \quad \text{(Excel formula)}$$

Operational issues to keep in mind when calculating NPV

Discounting cash flows is a simple, mechanical process: given a cash flow and a discount rate, its present value is easily calculated in a spreadsheet. In contrast, determining the net present value of an investment, or any valuation for that matter, requires judgment and knowledge of the specific investment project, the financial structure of the firm, and even capital markets in general. Valuation is more than discounting cash flows. The art and difficulty of valuation is in estimating the inputs (the relevant cash flow and the appropriate discount rate) for the discounting process and in interpreting its output. Operational decisions greatly impact the operating profit flows, so it is useful to model those decisions separately in a "pre-NPV spreadsheet" before embarking on discounting. The pre-NPV spreadsheet may contain the following items:

1. FORECAST OF DEMAND, SUPPLY AND MARGINS. Arguably, the most important elements of valuation are the demand, supply, and margin forecasts. The unit contribution margin m is the difference between unit revenue or price and unit variable cost. According to the Forecasting Principle, we must estimate not only their means over time, but also their volatility. In spreadsheets, forecasts can be modeled via a number of scenarios, where each scenario specifies a specific sample path for the demand D_t, supply S_t, and unit contribution margin m_t and the probability of that sample path. Recall that actual sales cannot exceed capacity, nor demand, nor supply. Thus, for each path, we would find the actual production quantity x_t as the minimum of D_t, S_t, and K_t. Multiplying by the unit margin m_t yields the operating profit for a given sample path. Finally, taking the expectation over all scenarios or sample paths then gives us the expected gross profit flow, which is the key input into the discounting process. Recall that capturing volatility explicitly is necessary to value capacity accurately.

2. CAPACITY ADJUSTMENTS. We first estimate the initial physical capacity level after the investment, denoted by K_0. Over time, companies continuously improve and these productivity improvements increase the effective capacity K_t. Capacity improvements due to learning and other efficiency improvements can easily increase capacity by 2 to 3% per year, if not more, depending on the industry. For example, in the high-tech industry of semiconductors and disk-drives, the increase in effective capacity due to yield improvements is dramatic and can be more than 50% per quarter. Such effects then dominate the entire valuation of capacity. Similarly, capital capacity may require periodic *maintenance* to slow-down physical *degradation* that may reduce effective capacity over time (or increase marginal production costs).

3. NEW PRODUCT AND PROCESS PLANS. Sometimes, it is useful to explicitly account for product model changes and product enhancements, as well as process changes and enhancement. Instead of incorporating their effect in capacity increases or margin changes, one can separate their cash flows to highlight their impacts.

4. MOVING BASELINE. The relevant cash flows in valuation are those that are "incremental," i.e., due strictly to the investment. If we did not invest, there would still be a cash flow, which we will refer to as the *baseline* or *status-quo*. To estimate the net value of a capacity investment, we should only include the difference between the cash flows from the operations with the investment and those under the status quo. Because it will enjoy operating improvements, the status-quo also changes over time (the *learning curve* is a useful tool to predict the cost effects of continuous improvement, as will be discussed in Chapter 10). This effect is called the *moving baseline*. If the process is complex, it is often easier to do two separate cash flow analyses—one for the base case and the other for the case when we invest— and simply find the NPV at the end as the difference between their present values.

Financial issues to keep in mind when calculating NPV

Once the gross profit flows from operations are known, a purely financial analysis follows to convert them into net present value. A general discussion of financial analysis is beyond our scope so we will only point out some important issues to bear in mind when valuing operations strategy:

1. CAPEX AND CONTINUATION VALUE. Estimate the capacity investment cost, including the purchasing and installation costs incurred up front. This is also called an initial *capital expenditure* or CapEx$_0$. In addition, there may be additional future capital expenditures (CapEx$_t$) for replacement parts or upgrades. Finally, there may be a salvage value when we dispose of the capacity at the end of its useful life, which would be a cash inflow at time T. If the capacity lives on beyond the horizon T that we analyze, we must include a *continuation value*, which is an estimate of the value of ongoing operations evaluated at time T. (Typically, the estimate is the value of a perpetuity of the operating profit. Notice that not including a continuation value is equivalent to saying the future has no value, which

could seriously underestimate the value of capacity.) Generally, however, estimating capital expenditures is easy compared to the rest.

2. DISCOUNT RATE AND RISK. Recall that the discount rate is the expected return that is forgone by investing say in capacity rather than in another opportunity that is subject to similar risks as the capacity investment. Identifying opportunities with similar risk is easier said than done. Determining the appropriate choice of the discount rate r is a central problem in finance. A common approach is to use a firm's *weighted-average cost of capital* (WACC), which is the weighted average between the return on its debt and on its equity. Estimating the latter isn't easy either, though.[11] More importantly, using the WACC is appropriate only if the risk of the investment is similar to the overall corporate risk.

In general, all risk should be captured in the cash flow forecasts, but only systematic (market) risk is factored into the discount rate. In practice, however, many corporations just specify a discount rate, often then called the *hurdle rate*, so investment proposals can be compared and gaming with the discount rate is prevented. For example, Boeing specifies a few discount rates depending on the nature of the project. The NPV analysis would then include the cash flow risk specific to that project. In this book, we will also be shamelessly simplistic and just assume a given discount rate to calculate the expected NPV so we can focus on operations rather than finance. (In Chapter 9, we will go beyond expected values to discuss risk-aversion.)

3. DEPRECIATION ACCOUNTING AND TAX SHIELDS. Benjamin Franklin wrote in 1789 that in this world nothing can be said to be certain, except death and taxes. The great economist John Maynard Keynes went even further, saying that the avoidance of taxes is the only intellectual pursuit that carries any reward. We must thus say something about taxes, albeit something rather basic. Taxes follow accounting rules set by governments. While they vary over time, most governments want to induce new investment (recall that investment is correlated with productivity growth, see p. 50). They do this by allowing corporations to spread the investment cost over several years, which is called *depreciation*, and to deduct that depreciation from taxable income.

While depreciation by itself is a pure accounting construct, its effect of reducing cash outflows due to its tax reduction on operating profit, or *tax shield*, is a real cash flow. Table 3.2 shows the mechanics to derive the tax shield, assuming our $400 thousand investment is depreciated straight-line over five years and the income tax rate is 40%. Even though the impact of the tax shield can be substantial, in the remainder we will ignore tax issues to focus on the operations.

---

[11]One approach uses the capital asset pricing model. But measuring the beta for an individual firm is not straightforward either. Interested readers are referred to Part Two on Risk in Brealy and Myers (2000).

	Year 0	Year 1	Year 2	Year 3	Year 4	Year 5	Year 6	Year 7	Year 8	Year 9
Gross Profit		100	120	110	90	80	100	105	120	85
- Depreciation		(80)	(80)	(80)	(80)	(80)				
Operating Profit before Tax		20	40	30	10	-	100	105	120	85
- Tax (at 40%)		(8)	(16)	(12)	(4)	-	(40)	(42)	(48)	(34)
Net Operating Profit after Tax		12	24	18	6	-	60	63	72	51
- Add back depreciation		80	80	80	80	80				
- CapEx + salvage or continuation value	(400)									
Free cash flow from operations	(400)	92	104	98	86	80	60	63	72	51
NPV (including tax shield)	$73.04									

	Year 0	Year 1	Year 2	Year 3	Year 4	Year 5	Year 6	Year 7	Year 8	Year 9
Gross Profit		100	120	110	90	80	100	105	120	85
- Tax		(40)	(48)	(44)	(36)	(32)	(40)	(42)	(48)	(34)
Net Operating Profit after Tax		60	72	66	54	48	60	63	72	51
- CapEx + salvage or continuation value	(400)									
Free cash flow from operations	(400)	60	72	66	54	48	60	63	72	51
NPV (excluding tax shield)	($48.26)									

Table 3.2 Accounting for depreciation (top table) of the capacity investment costs yields a reduction in taxes. Ignoring this tax shield underestimates the value of capacity, as shown by the bottom table.

Appendix 3B | CAPACITY-INVENTORY-WAITING TRADE-OFFS

This appendix shows the analytics behind the two examples in section 3.7.

Trading off capacity with inventory

Assume we have a capacity K in between the two extremes of level production and build-to-order: $R \leq K \leq R(1 + \sigma)$. Under the production and inventory strategy represented in Figure 3.9 on p. 95, the total excess peak-season demand is $(R(1+\sigma) - K)\frac{1}{2}$, which must be built in advance. The excess low-season capacity is $K - R(1 - \sigma)$, which can be used for building inventory. To ensure that we have sufficient inventory for the peak season, we must start building inventory at time t such that the total excess production covers the excess demand:

$$\underbrace{I_{\max} = (K - R(1 - \sigma))\left(\frac{1}{2} - t\right)}_{\text{maximal inventory buildup during } [t, 1/2]} = \underbrace{(R(1 + \sigma) - K)\frac{1}{2}}_{\text{excess demand during } [1/2, 1]}.$$

Solving for t yields the inventory building start time:

$$t = 1 - \frac{R\sigma}{K - R(1 - \sigma)}.$$

Given that inventory grows and declines linearly, the average inventory is $I_{\max}/2$ and is held over the time period $[t, 1]$. Let c_h denote the *holding cost* to keep a unit in inventory for a unit of time. The total inventory holding cost thus is

$$
\begin{aligned}
\frac{I_{\max}}{2}(1 - t)\, c_h &= \frac{1}{2}(R(1 + \sigma) - K)\frac{1}{2}\frac{R\sigma}{K - R(1 - \sigma)}c_h, \\
&= \frac{c_h}{4}R\sigma\left(\frac{2R\sigma}{K - R(1 - \sigma)} - 1\right).
\end{aligned}
$$

This equation shows the trade-off between capacity and inventory. (Clearly, inventory and capacity are substitutes and the trade-off curve increases with volatility, as shown in Figure 3.10 on p. 96 for the case of $c_h = 1$ and $\sigma = 1/2$ and 1.) Given that we meet all the demand at unit margin m, annual operating profits are:

$$\Pi(K) = mR - \frac{c_h}{4}R\sigma\left(\frac{2R\sigma}{K - R(1 - \sigma)} - 1\right).$$

To find the optimal trade-off between capacity and inventory, we maximize net present value NPV, the difference of present value $\text{PV}(K)$ minus the capacity investment cost $C(K)$. The operating profits are constant from year to year so that their present value is a simple perpetuity: $\text{PV}(K) = \Pi(K)/r$. The net present value of capacity thus is:

$$\text{NPV}(K) = \text{PV}(K) - C(K) = \frac{mR}{r} - \frac{c_h}{4r}R\sigma\left(\frac{2R\sigma}{K - R(1 - \sigma)} - 1\right) - C(K).$$

Assuming the fixed cost function $C(K) = c_0 + c_K K$ and setting the derivative of NPV equal to zero yields the optimal capacity level:

$$K^* = R(1 - \sigma) + R\sigma\sqrt{\frac{c_h}{2rc_K}} \Rightarrow \text{safety capacity} = R\sigma\left(\sqrt{\frac{c_h}{2rc_K}} - 1\right). \quad (3.6)$$

The corresponding maximal NPV of the capacity-inventory strategy is:

$$\text{NPV}(K^*) = \underbrace{\frac{mR}{r} - C(R)}_{} \underbrace{- R\sigma\left(\sqrt{\frac{2c_K c_h}{r}} + \frac{c_h}{4r} - c_K\right)}_{}$$

$$= \text{NPV(average demand) - PV(volatility degradation)}.$$

The boundary strategies of make-to-order and level production directly yield bounds on the financial ratio c_h/rc_K. A make-to-order strategy carries no inventory but requires maximal safety capacity to cover the peak demand. Setting $K^* = R(1 + \sigma)$ in the optimality equation (3.6) requires that $c_h/rc_K \geq 8$ for make-to-order to be optimal in this model. Similarly, a level production strategy has no safety capacity but maximal inventory buildup. Setting $K^* = R$ in equation (3.6) requires that $c_h/rc_K \leq 2$ for level production to be optimal in this model. If $\frac{c_h}{rc_K} \in (2, 8)$ a balance between inventory and capacity is optimal, as shown in Figure 3.11 on p. 97.

Trading off capacity with waiting

Appendix C on p. 439 estimates the average customer waiting time w as a function of the demand rate R, capacity K, and the volatility σ_{as}^2 in interarrival and service times as expressed by their coefficients of variations C_a and C_s:

$$w(K) = \frac{1}{K}\frac{R}{K - R}\sigma_{as}^2 \quad \text{where } \sigma_{as}^2 = \frac{C_a^2 + C_s^2}{2}.$$

Let m denote the unit contribution margin and c_w the cost incurred per unit of time that a customer is waiting. The expected operating profit rate then is:

$$\Pi(K) = R \times [m - c_w \times w(K)].$$

The optimal position on the trade-off curve $w(K)$ maximizes NPV, which is the difference of present value $PV(K)$ and the capacity investment cost $C(K)$. Given stationarity, the average operating profit remains constant over time. Thus, assuming our unit of time is a year, the present value of operating profits is a perpetuity:

$$PV(K) = \frac{\Pi(K)}{r} = \frac{mR}{r} - \frac{Rc_w w(K)}{r}$$

$$= \text{PV(average demand) - PV(expected waiting cost)}.$$

The optimal capacity K^* maximizes NPV so that the first-order optimality condition is $\text{NPV}'(K^*) = 0$ or $PV'(K^*) = C'(K^*)$. Assuming the fixed cost function $C(K) = c_0 + c_K K$, differentiation yields condition $\frac{\rho^3(2-\rho)}{(1-\rho)^2} = \frac{R}{\sigma_{as}^2}r\frac{c_K}{c_w}$, where utilization $\rho = R/K$. While we cannot solve for K^* in closed form, we can plot the inverse of $\frac{\rho^3(2-\rho)}{(1-\rho)^2}$ as a function of $\frac{rc_K R}{\sigma_{as}^2 c_w}$, as shown in Figure 3.13 on p. 99.

Chapter

4

CAPACITY TIMING AND EXPANSION

Times change and we change with them.—Latin proverb.

Learning Objectives

After reading this chapter, you will be able to:

1. Discuss the five different capacity timing strategies and their implementation.
2. Identify the key drivers of capacity timing and explain their role.
3. Value and optimize the option value of strategic timing and waiting.
4. Model tactical timing in the capacity-inventory-waiting triangle in a spreadsheet.

In this chapter, we will study the timing and adjustment of capacity, the second of a resource portfolio strategy's four major decisions, as shown in Figure 3.1 (p. 72). We will start with an overview of five different timing strategies and discuss their implementation options. To learn how to make better capacity timing decisions, we will then analyze key timing drivers and discuss two valuation tools: real options and aggregate planning. The appendix describes how you can optimize a linear capacity timing plan in Excel.

4.1 | FIVE CAPACITY TIMING STRATEGIES

In the previous chapter, the environment was stationary. Essentially nothing changed so that only capacity sizing was important (assuming that capacity lives on indefinitely). In this chapter, we will assume that we are blessed with a growing demand–(similar issues apply for declining demand) which requires a combination of capacity sizing and timing. First we will discuss the five major types of timing strategies you can choose from and ways to implement them. Then we will turn our attention to understanding timing decisions.

The importance of capacity timing and adjustment

If we face a changing or *non-stationary* environment, timing becomes an important component of a capacity strategy. For example, Harley-Davidson, the American icon of freedom and adventure, continues to enjoy increasing demand for its motorcycles. In 2006, it sold 349 thousand motorcycles, up from 81 thousand in 1993, which corresponds to a compound annual growth rate (CAGR) of 13%. To support such growth, Harley-Davidson must continually decide when and by how much to expand capacity; the case in Chapter 11 further investigates these decisions.

Timing capacity adjustments is a hot topic during growth as well as decline. For instance, when projected energy demands cooled, one electric energy producer saved an estimated $300 million by delaying the delivery of gas turbines previously ordered from General Electric during the infamous California power crisis of 2001 (Angelus and Porteus 2005).

1. Demand-chasing capacity strategy

In the absence of capacity adjustment frictions, timing would not be an issue: we would be able to instantaneously adjust capacity to mirror any demand change. Such *demand-chasing* capacity strategy can be used over small time windows. For example, call centers typically staff to match predictable demand fluctuations. Furthermore, Wal-Mart also matches work shifts in its stores with the ebb and flow of customer traffic. It aims to schedule its work shifts to track customer-demand curves in 10-minute segments and thus requires high flexibility from its employees. One store manager even went so far as to introduce an "open availability policy, which required workers to commit to work any day of the week between 7 a.m. and 11 p.m. or risk losing their jobs," according to Covert (2006).

Strategic capacity adjustment over larger time windows, however, is hostage to frictions, as discussed in Chapter 3. Long leadtimes, lumpiness, fixed costs, and irreversibility complicate quick, precise, cheap, and reversible capacity adjustments making a *demand-chasing* strategy difficult to implement. Most capacity strategies therefore fall somewhere between leading and lagging behind demand changes.

2. Leading capacity strategy

A *leading* capacity strategy builds capacity in anticipation of demand growth, as shown in Figure 4.1. This is the natural strategy used to introduce new products or services. For example, Mercedes-Benz used it successfully for its new M-class (see Example 1.2 on page 8). In contrast, when introducing its Internet grocery services, Webvan used an extreme form of capacity leading: it overbuilt capacity to an extent that ultimately led to the demise of the company, as illustrated by the case study on p. 423.

The advantages of a leading capacity strategy include:

1. *High service level* and low risk of losing customers to competitors. Given the abundant availability of capacity, utilization levels are not excessive so that responsiveness to customer orders is high and waiting times are small.

2. *Low capacity shortage risk*, which captures upward demand potential. Given

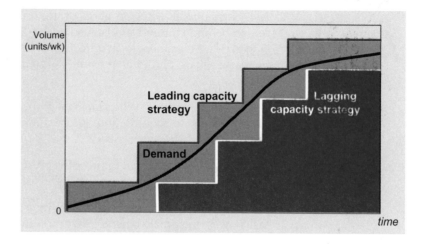

Figure 4.1 Most capacity timing strategies fall somewhere between the extremes of leading and lagging behind demand.

that demand is less than capacity, you observe true demand and have sufficient capacity to enjoy faster growth than expected.

3. *Market development.* The implicit belief that "if you build it, they will come" shows the company's faith in the attractiveness of the product and its ability to appeal to customers.

4. *Competitive barrier of entry.* The availability of excess capacity makes it less attractive for others to enter or expand.

5. *Insensitivity to capacity start-up problems.* Given that only a small part of the nominally-rated capacity increase is initially used, capacity yield losses can easily be accommodated and improved over time without impacting sales.

The disadvantages of a leading capacity strategy are the advantages of its counterpart, a lagging capacity strategy.

3. Lagging capacity strategy

A *lagging* capacity strategy expands capacity reactively after there is sufficient demand to use the majority of additional capacity. A good example is Harley-Davidson's capacity strategy: in spite of expanding capacity several times during the last decade, waiting times exceeding one year were not uncommon for popular models such as the Fat Boy Softail. This suggested that capacity expansion was lagging demand growth.

The advantages of a lagging capacity strategy include:

1. *High cost efficiency.* Given that capacity is only added after a strong indication of excess demand, capacity utilization is high. Small fixed cost allocations yield small unit product costs.

2. *Low excess capacity risk* and good protection against downturns. A major reason behind Harley-Davidson's lagging strategy is the company's aversion to risk, a testament to an unfortunate experience in the late 1970s when its market share plummeted from 77% to only 23%, leaving the company in dire straits.

3. *Option value of waiting.* When facing significant uncertainty, lagging strategies allow one to acquire more information and make better informed investments.

4. *Delayed capacity investment* reduces the present value of capacity expansion, a strong effect for companies with high cost of capital.

5. *Lesser dependence on forecasting.* Rather than forecasting future demand, the task now is to estimate whether there is sufficient excess demand to fill new capacity. When customers are patient and willing to sign up on a waiting list, as the ones of Harley-Davidson, the waiting list is a conservative estimate of excess demand. There must be more customers who don't sign up. In most cases, however, estimating excess demand and forecasting future demand pose similar difficulties.

6. *New or cheaper technology.* Lagging allows us to acquire the most recent technology, which is important in industries where the rate of innovation in capacity technology is high, such as in the semiconductor industry. Or, we may buy older technology that is now available at a lower price. When Toyota re-started its automobile operations after World War II, it bought used equipment from American companies.

7. *Increased control of channels and customer relationships.* When demand exceeds capacity, the firm can control the allocation of capacity to various channels, which gives an additional lever to reward "good" channels or customers. Such *turn-and-earn* allocation scheme in the automobile industry allocates an additional car to a dealer after each sale. This stimulates dealer sales efforts and induces dealerships to build larger and more attractive stores with better selection—a "win-win" situation.

4. Hybrid timing strategies and capacity requirements smoothing

Few capacity strategies are pure leading or lagging; most of them are a hybrid combination of the two. They employ several countermeasures to deal with demand changes and effectively position themselves in the capacity-inventory-waiting triangle discussed in Chapter 3 (recall Fig. 3.8 on p. 93).

With significant demand uncertainty and capacity leadtimes, a leading capacity policy is difficult to implement and one always runs the risk of being short of capacity. To alleviate that risk, a product company can build inventory during periods of excess capacity to fill later periods with excess demand, which is exactly what headphone manufacturer Koss did (Example 3.3 on p. 94). Relative to a leading strategy, such an *inventory-smoothing capacity strategy* increases average capacity utilization and allows the delay of capacity expansion. The result is a hybrid strategy between pure leading and lagging, as shown in Figure 4.2.

An alternative to pre-building inventory and making product wait is to pre–sell capacity and make customers wait. When customers are patient and willing

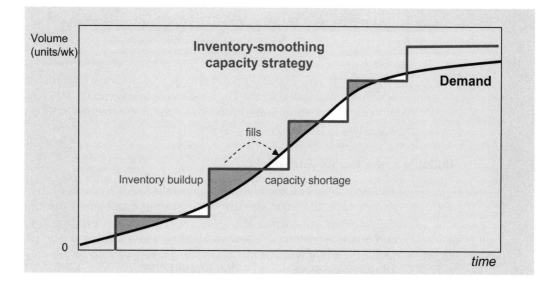

Figure 4.2 An inventory-smoothing capacity strategy is a hybrid between pure leading and lagging. Excess capacity builds inventory to supply the subsequent under-capacitated period. Its counterpart is backlogging-smoothing, which puts excess demand onto a waiting list.

to wait, one can put excess-demand customers onto a backlog list and serve them when the new capacity comes on-line. (Each chunk of capacity addition initially has excess capacity, which can be used to fill the backlog). This *backlogging-smoothing capacity strategy* is also a hybrid between leading and lagging. Chapter 8 will discuss other methods to manage and move demand when capacity is inflexible.

5. Follow-your-competitor timing strategy

The four capacity timing strategies discussed so far—demand-chasing, leading, lagging, and smoothing—base timing on experienced demand or on its forecast. Another option is to simply follow your competitor and build capacity when he does. Burger King, the international chain of fast-food restaurants, has followed this strategy within the U.S.: it typically enters markets that have no Burger King outlets within a three-mile radius of a McDonald's restaurant. We will further discuss the interplay of competition and capacity location in Chapter 6.

This follow-your-competitor timing strategy assumes that your competitor has superior information on future demand or that you have strategically chosen not to lead market development. Obviously, in practice you don't blindly follow your competitor (as such imitation has inherent dangers on industry capacity) but you can use his decisions as a signal to investigate whether you need more capacity as well.

4.2 | DIFFERENT WAYS TO EXPAND CAPACITY

Strategic capacity expansions can choose various ways to adjust capacity, most of which are illustrated in the Harley-Davidson case study in Chapter 11. Typical *capacity expansion* options, each with similar contraction options, can be listed according to their capacity adjustment size:

Building a new facility (Greenfield)

This adjustment method has the highest flexibility in terms of size and location of adding capacity, but is also the most expensive and incurs the longest leadtimes. A *"greenfield"* expansion allows a "fresh start" by using the latest technologies and a new workforce. A new location also gives the option of restructuring the network, as we will see in Chapter 6. Managers tend to like this option due to all the positive momentum that it builds. In contrast, closing down a facility is a painful activity, especially for the people who are let go, and is often executed only "upon expert consulting advice."

Expanding a current facility (Brownfield)

Adding floor space, employees, and equipment to a current facility is known as a *"brownfield"* expansion. Adding to a current location is a less drastic option than a greenfield, but also comes with more constraints.

External capacity provision: outsourcing, subcontracting, and alliances

Subcontracting refers to signing a contract with a third party to provide all or part of our capacity needs. Outsourcing, which will be discussed in detail in Chapter 7, typically refers to complete capacity reliance on a third party. Another form of adding capacity externally is to form an agreement or alliance between two or more parties. For example, Chapter 3 discussed the agreement between Choice Hotels International Inc. and 1-800-Flowers.com to rent call-center employees to one another. Franchising, the licensing of trademarks or process knowledge, is another form of external capacity provision that is often used by chain stores to allow fast expansion.

Process improvement and restructuring at current facilities

Good managers continually improve their operations, thus adding capacity without new "brick and mortar." Restructuring processes by reorganizing the flow, integrating activities, and replacing or adding equipment results in discrete capacity increases. Continuous improvement by speeding up changeovers and setups provides incremental additions.

Capacity increases of a few percentage points per year are normal, while in some industries drastic improvements happen through learning. Yield improvements in the semiconductor and biotech industry can result in major capacity increases. Unfortunately, adding capacity incrementally through process improvements or by "adding a sixth machine" does not enjoy economies of scale.

Example 4.1 From 24/5 to 24/7 at Poppies Inc USA

Poppies Inc. USA produces fresh and frozen pastries including eclairs, petit choux, and doughnuts in Site Rocky Mount, North Carolina. Each production run ends with a cleaning to remove all material in progress and sterilize all production equipment. Initially, Poppies operated 24 hours a day, five days a week, in other words, "24/5." Shutdown for the weekend required 8 to 10 hours of cleaning. Startup on Monday morning, which entailed heating up the ovens and a second sterilization, took an additional 4 to 5 hours. The entire shutdown and startup process represented a 10 to 12.5% capacity loss.

In August 2004, Poppies expanded capacity to fill strong growing demand by moving to 24/7 production. This not only added 40% capacity in production time but also eliminated startup downtime (equipment is now sterilized only once a week). Poppies' facility was smartly built with excess storage room that could now handle the extra raw materials inventory needed to sustain weekend production and the finished goods inventory built up over the weekend. Poppies decreased maintenance costs by choosing to schedule contractors during weekdays rather than during the earlier weekend down-time.

The largest drawback to a 24/7 operation is the human cost, according to Luc Kerkhof, Poppies' V.P.: "Absenteeism is higher on weekends and shift scheduling is complex and constantly changing. Existing workers experienced a decline in morale during the transition. Additionally, the operations manager is on call 24/7, and it was necessary to hire more indirect labor to share the workload." While Poppies' indirect labor jumped from 5.5% of fixed costs to 8.9% as a result of the move to 24/7 operation, these costs were easily outweighed by the vast productivity improvements. *Source: Kerkhof (2005).*

Adding a shift and 24/5 vs. 24/7 operations

Expanding the operating hours of a facility by adding shifts or working days significantly increases throughput and fixed asset utilization. Going to 24/7 operations represents the ultimate form of this strategy.

Expanding from 24/5 to 24/7 increased capacity by more than 40% at Poppies Inc., which is featured in Example 4.1. Continuous processing not only added two days of work per week but also eliminated shutdown and startup times. The downside of adding shifts and days, however, is the increased inventory storage requirements, increased supervisory needs, and additional human resource issues.

Tactical capacity adjustments: overtime, inventory buildup, temporary work

Occasional but not persistent demand surges can be accommodated by running overtime or adding temporary workers, which are means to implement a demand-chasing timing strategy. Amazon.com has been known to load buses with students and bring them to their facilities as temporary workers during the Christmas season. Manpower Inc., a $17.6 billion company headquartered in Milwaukee, WI, helps companies and individuals "win in the changing world of work." In 2006, Manpower placed 4.4 million associates into permanent, temporary and contract positions in 73 countries. Seasonal demand fluctuations can also be buffered by building inventory or keeping waiting lists, as analyzed in Chapter 3.

To understand and improve capacity timing decisions, we now turn our attention to modeling and valuing capacity timing strategies.

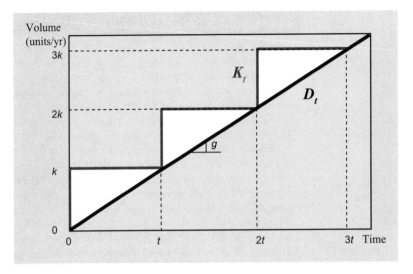

Figure 4.3 A simple timing model for a leading capacity strategy K_t with a linearly-growing demand rate D_t.

4.3 | A CAPACITY TIMING MODEL

To understand how different factors impact capacity timing and adjustment, we will first consider a theoretical model of a leading capacity strategy.

A simple timing model with economies of scale

The simplest model assumes that demand grows with a persistent, deterministic linear upward trend:

$$D_t = gt,$$

where g is the growth parameter. The capacity investment cost $C(k)$ for a capacity addition of size k exhibits economies of scale, as discussed in Section 3.4 on p. 82. We seek to characterize the leading capacity strategy that adds a constant capacity size k at times $0, t, 2t, 3t, ...,$ as shown in Figure 4.3.

The main benefit of the deterministic growth assumption is that the two decision variables, size k and time t, are dependent: knowing the capacity expansion size k is equivalent to knowing the expansion time t, so that only one independent variable remains. (With linear demand we simply have $k = gt$, but similar dependencies also exist with non-linear demand growth. Mini-Case 4 asks you to apply and extend this analysis to the case of exponential growth, where demand has a specific annual growth rate.)

The value maximization principle (p. 5) tells us that the optimal timing strategy maximizes net present value. A leading strategy with deterministic demand can always meet all demand so that the revenue stream is unaffected by changing the timing t (or size k). Therefore, maximizing NPV is equivalent to minimizing the present value of capacity costs. Because timing t is a continuous variable, we use *continuous-time discounting*: a dollar at time t is worth $exp(-rt)$ today. The present value of capacity expansion costs as a function of the timing variable t is

$$PV(t) = \sum_{n=0}^{\infty} C(k)e^{-rnt} = \frac{C(gt)}{1 - e^{-rt}},$$

where we used the geometric series (c.f., equation 3.2 on p. 109).

The importance of discounting with economies of scale

To appreciate the importance of discounting, consider the following thought experiment. Assume that you are running a firm whose time-value of money is negligible and which faces no borrowing constraints. It then matters little whether a dollar is put in capacity today or the next year, because a dollar in the future is worth as much as a dollar is worth today. Knowing that there are economies of scale in capacity costs, what would you do if you are faced with a growing demand? You would build all capacity today and none in the future in order to maximally exploit scale economies. Thus, without discounting, timing dynamics would disappear in this model.[1]

Optimal timing in the simple model

The optimal timing t^* minimizes the present value of capacity expansion costs. The necessary optimality condition for t^* is that the derivative of $PV(t)$ is zero. Denoting the derivative of $C(\cdot)$ by $C'(\cdot)$, differentiation of $PV(\cdot)$ yields the optimal timing condition for our simple timing model:

$$\frac{C(gt^*)}{C'(gt^*)} = \frac{g}{r}\left(e^{rt^*} - 1\right).$$

The optimal timing condition for two typical capital expenditure functions that exhibit economies of scale is shown in Figure 4.4. Optimal timing for the power function $C(K) = c_K K^{\alpha}/\alpha$ is shown on the left while timing for the linear function $C(K) = c_0 + c_K K$ is on the right.[2] Recall from page 82 that both the parameters $1/\alpha$ and the ratio of fixed cost to marginal cost c_0/c_K are measures of economies of scale. The key insight here is that timing increases with economies of scale.

Let us do a sanity check of the model and see what the predicted optimal timing between capacity expansions is for the power CapEx function. Recall that the parameter α typically falls between 0.6 and 1, with smaller values indicating stronger economies of scale (c.f. Chapter 3, p. 82). The associated optimal values of rt^* are between 0 and 1. Thus, for strong economies of scale, the model predicts the time between capacity expansions to be $t^* = 1/r$ or 5 to 10 years for typical annual discount rates of 10 to 20 percent. This is a sensible result that agrees with our observations of practice: for instance, Harley-Davidson had major, discrete expansions about every five years (in addition to continual process improvement).

---

[1] For finance fans: we are also ignoring the tax-shield from depreciation.

[2] For math fans: the timing condition for the power CapEx function is $\frac{e^{rt^*}-1}{rt^*} = \alpha^{-1}$, which is independent of g and c, and $e^{rt^*} - 1 - rt^* = \frac{r}{g}\frac{c_0}{c_K}$ for the linear CapEx.

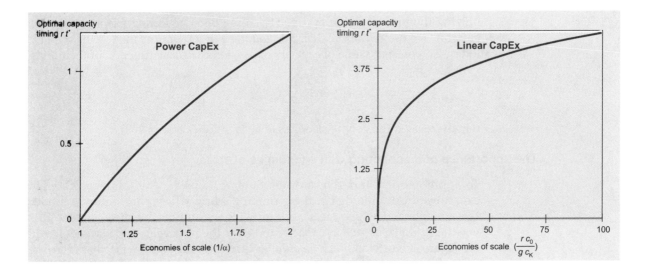

Figure 4.4 The optimal capacity timing as a function of economies of scale when the investment cost or capital expenditure CapEx for a capacity size K is given by the power function $c_K K^\alpha / \alpha$ (left) or the linear function $c_0 + c_K K$ (right).

Adding demand uncertainty to the simple timing model

The simple timing model assumes no uncertainty, zero lead-times, no backlogging, no competition, and no physical deterioration. Including any of those extensions complicates the analysis significantly. Surprisingly, however, adding demand uncertainty to the model does little to complicate insights.

In a classic operations research paper, Manne (1961) analyzed capacity timing when the demand has a linear growth trend with rate g, but also has a volatility σ around the trend.[3] Demand at time t is now normally distributed with mean gt (thus, the mean is the same as in the simple timing model) but with variance $\sigma^2 t$. Manne showed that such stochastic demand case has the same optimal timing as our simple deterministic timing model, provided that we replace the discount rate r by a *smaller* uncertainty-adjusted "equivalent discount rate" r' that decreases when volatility σ increases.

4.4 | KEY DRIVERS OF CAPACITY TIMING

The capacity timing model allows us to identify and understand the drivers of capacity timing.

---

[3]To be precise, Manne assumed that demand D_t is a *Brownian motion* with drift g and variance σ^2. This means that (1) D_t is continuous in t and its increments $D_{t+s} - D_s$ are (2) independent and (3) normally distributed with mean gt and variance $\sigma^2 t$.

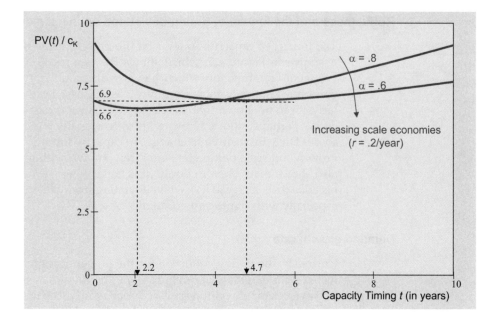

Figure 4.5 The present value of capacity investment costs is fairly robust to deviations from its optimal timing, especially with strong scale economies.

Scale economies

The optimal timing condition illustrated by Figure 4.4 shows that stronger scale economies increase the optimal time t^*—and thus the optimal size $k^* = gt^*$—between capacity expansions. We indeed expect stronger scale economies to induce larger, and thus less frequent, capacity additions.

Discount factor

The optimal timing condition for the power investment cost function illustrated by the left-hand graph in Figure 4.4 shows that the product of the discount rate r and the optimal timing t^* is constant for a given economy of scale α. Thus, the discount rate and optimal timing are inversely proportional. In other words, smaller discount rates increase the time between and the size of capacity expansions. Smaller discount rates lead to the same effect for the linear cost investment function.[4]

Smaller discount rates decrease the time value of money so that future investment is only slightly less costly in today's dollars. In the presence of economies of scale, we would then prefer to invest more today and less in the future. The fact that lower interest rates stimulate current investment is familiar to fiscalists and politicians.

---

[4]A larger discount rate r increases the financial ratio rc_0/gc_K and consequently the product rt^*. Because the product rt^* increases less than linearly, t^* decreases in r. To see this, assume that $r = 10\%$ and $rc_0/gc_K = 25$. Now let r double to 20% so that $rc_0/gc_K = 50$. This means that rt^* increases from about 3.5 to 4, so that t^* reduces from $3.5/.1 = 35$ years to $4/.2 = 20$ years.

Robustness and the impact of timing deviations on investment costs

The impact of capacity timing t on the present value of investment costs $PV(t)$ is shown in Figure 4.5, which shows PV as a fraction of c_K for the power investment cost function which has growth parameter $g = 1$. Increased scale economies not only increase timing, as discussed above, but also costs. Similarly, it can be shown that increasing the discount rate also increases timing and costs. Perhaps more interesting, however, is the fact that the present value of cost is fairly insensitive to changes in capacity timing. This is fortunate because growth and scale parameters are rarely known with great precision. Figure 4.5 also shows that, when in doubt, it is better to err towards delaying investment because costs increase less when deviating from the optimal timing to the right, especially with significant economies of scale.

Demand growth rate

Curiously, the timing condition for the power investment function seems unaffected by the demand growth rate g. The impact of the demand growth rate, however, depends on the specific capacity investment cost function and on the type of growth pattern. In the case of the linear cost function, for example, timing is impacted by the growth rate: a higher demand growth g reduces the financial factor rc_0/gc_K and thus also the timing, according to the right panel in Figure 4.4. In other words, with fixed costs, higher demand growth implies more frequent capacity additions.

Uncertainty or volatility in demand growth

Manne (1961) has shown that optimal capacity timing in a model with demand volatility is identical to the timing in the deterministic model provided that we use an equivalent discount rate. Given that the latter decreases when volatility increases, our simple timing model tells us that higher volatility increases capacity size, timing, and the present value of costs.

Therefore, more volatile growth leads to higher investment, which may at first seem to fly in the face of common financial sense. Given what we have learned from Chapter 3, however, we know to interpret a capacity increase due to uncertainty as safety capacity. The risk of running out early would lead to earlier capacity additions; thus, it is worth initially investing into some safety capacity in order to avert such contingency in the case of economies of scale. It can also be shown that the present value of capacity investment costs increases in volatility. The impact of volatility on capacity timing is thus another manifestation of Principle 6 (p. 86): volatility degrades the value of real assets and to counteract its impact, we must either invest in safety capacity or make either customers or products wait.

The effects of scale economies, discounting, demand growth, and volatility on the timing, sizing, and cost of capacity expansion are summarized in Table 4.1.

Capacity leadtimes

The combination of uncertainty and leadtimes is deadly for a capacity leading strategy because we cannot, at a reasonable cost, prevent the risk of capacity

Environmental Change	Optimal Response	Impact on cost
1. Greater scale economies	increase size and delay timing	increase cost
2. Smaller discount rates	increase size and delay timing	increase cost
3. Greater demand growth	*depends on investment cost*	*depends*
4. Greater demand volatility	increases size and delay timing	increases cost

Table 4.1 The effects of key drivers on optimal capacity timing and sizing.

shortage and its associated lost sales, backlogging, or substitution to other products. The solution here is to adopt a hybrid strategy using inventory build-up or backlogging. Similar to the impact of inventory-buildup on capacity sizing in Chapter 3 (see p. 94), the optimal amount of lagging depends on the trade-off between the cost of building capacities and the cost of holding inventory. In an industry where holding costs are low relative to capacity costs, lagging becomes more attractive than leading.

The impact of irreversibility on capacity adjustment timing

Few capacity adjustments are perfectly reversible, meaning that capacity investments often cannot be fully recovered when capacity is reduced. This makes managers more reluctant not only to invest, but also to adjust capacity.

To understand the impact of irreversibility, consider the following example. Assume we have installed capacity to support a daily demand of 100 units. Now, the economy is picking up and demand is growing. Due to frictions, we won't instantaneously adjust capacity to chase the demand. Only when demand has grown sufficiently, say to 150 units per day, do we decide to expand capacity. After a while, the economy cools down and demand slows down. Again, we won't instantaneously decrease capacity; only when demand has decreased sufficiently, perhaps even lower than 100 units per day, will we contract capacity. The reason for this effect is irreversibility: the salvage value from reducing capacity is less than the cost of adding capacity so that a reduction will not make up for a future expansion of equal size.

The resulting capacity dynamic exhibits *hysteresis*, which is named after a similar effect in physics where magnetic material can remain magnetized even after the magnetizing electric field is removed. Similarly, capacity dynamics exhibit *path dependence* meaning that they depend on past investment decisions; a reversal of an important capacity driver such as demand increase does not necessarily reverse the capacity dynamics.

Our example can be illustrated by Figure 4.6. Let K denote our capacity as usual and X_t the state of the economy at time t. Consider the point $s = K/X_t$, whose dynamics determine the optimal capacity adjustments. Irreversibility creates a hysteresis zone (the interval $[a, b]$) where capacity K is not adjusted. Only if the state of the economy X_t changes sufficiently to bring the point $s = K/X_t$ out of the region of inaction will capacity be adjusted. Accordingly, we expand capacity if X increases (the economy is heating up) sufficiently to bring s down to point a, but reduce it only if X decreases (the economy slows down) sufficiently to bring s up to point b. Capacity is not adjusted as long as the economy fluctuations are small, so that s remains inside the hysteresis zone (a, b).

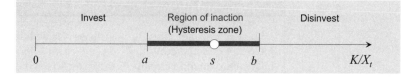

Figure 4.6 Irreversibility creates a hysteresis zone where capacity K is not adjusted unless the state of the economy X_t changes sufficiently to bring the point $s = K/X_t$ out of the region of inaction.

Dixit (1997) and Eberly and Van Mieghem (1997) analyze these optimal capacity dynamics under uncertainty and extend them to a capacity portfolio with multiple types of real assets. They establish two insights. Assume that increasing the capacity of resource type i by K_i costs $c_i K_i$, while a capacity decrease of K_i recovers $r_i K_i$. The degree of irreversibility of resource type i is then measured by the ratio of investment cost over resale value c_i/r_i, which drives capacity dynamics in two ways:

1. When investment becomes more irreversible, the hysteresis zone enlarges and the time between capacity adjustments increases. Managers become more reluctant to change capacity and investment and hiring will begin to exhibit periods of inactivity and episodes of accumulation and decumulation.

2. The sequence in which different capacity types are adjusted is fixed and depends on the degree of irreversibility. Capacity type i is adjusted more frequently than type j if the ratio of investment cost over resale values satisfies $c_i/r_i < c_j/r_j$. For example, assume labor markets are efficient, such that hiring and firing costs are of similar magnitude, while capital investment greatly exceeds capital disinvestment. Then the ratio c/r for human resources is close to 1 and much smaller than the ratio c/r for capital resources. Consequently, labor will be adjusted more frequently than capital. If not, both factors may be adjusted infrequently, as in the case of Eurosclerosis (c.f. p. 76).

Other factors that impact timing

In a competitive industry, timing and sizing decisions become more difficult because one must anticipate the impact of competitors' capacity additions. One must also weigh the costs and benefits of moving first against those of following one's rival. Also, if capacity degrades over time, it may need replacement at a more predictable time (than based on demand forecasts) as is the case in the electricity industry, where the life of nuclear reactors is finite. Finally, strong technological learning may drive future capacity costs downward, inducing us to delay capacity expansions.

The next two sections will review two tools to evaluate capacity adjustments: real options for strategic capacity adjustments that significantly change capacity, and aggregate planning for tactical adjustments.

Example 4.2 Acer: The Value of Capacity Expansion Postponement

Acer, a Taiwanese computer company, started operations by serving the lower-price segments in Asia. Later, in its quest for a global expansion strategy, it ruled out competing in the high-price segments served by established PC giants. Rather, it decided to expand into emerging markets by serving other low-price segments in Mexico, South-Africa, and Russia.

Postponing its global expansion had two benefits:

1. It allowed Acer to reduce its initial capital requirements.

2. The company could learn more about the product and service needs of its Asian customers. With this knowledge, it could size and tailor its later capacity expansion to better fit the needs of these emerging markets.

4.5 | STRATEGIC TIMING: THE OPTION VALUE OF WAITING

Strategic capacity timing often deals with the essential question: should we adjust capacity now or should we wait? The time frame considered is long (years) and the decision is complicated by vast uncertainty and significant financial impact. The timing decision should be based on both strategic and financial factors. The benefits of each action are very similar to those of a leading or lagging strategy. Real options, a fancy name for contingent decisions often analyzed using decision trees, provide a useful tool to quantify the financial benefits.

Definition of the option value of waiting

The value maximization principle favors the strategy with highest expected net present value. Thus, we should calculate the expected NPV of waiting and of immediate expansion, and then pick the strategy with highest NPV.

This strategy selection rule can be rephrased in terms of the *option value of waiting*, which is the difference between the expected NPV of waiting and the expected NPV of expanding now:

$$\text{option value of waiting} = \text{NPV(wait)} - \text{NPV(do not wait)}.$$

The strategy selection rule thus simply becomes: wait if and only if it has a positive option value. Let us illustrate the essentials of real option theory with an example.

A stylized example of waiting: Acer expansion

To illustrate real option valuation, consider a stylized model of Acer's expansion into the emerging markets of Mexico, South-Africa, and Russia, as described in Example 4.2. The question is whether Acer should expand now, or whether it should wait an additional year before expanding into the emerging markets.

The key reason for waiting is the belief that commercial success in emerging markets is highly correlated with success in the current Asian market. (Acer already has capacity in place to serve the Asian market. Aside from providing information regarding its future success, however, that capacity has no direct impact on our problem here.) Demand from these emerging markets is highly uncertain; marketing and sales reports predict that Acer's low-price PC will either be a blockbuster, a success, or a dud. Assume that the demand forecast for those three scenarios is, respectively: 200 thousand units per year with likelihood of 25%, 100 thousand units per year with 50% likelihood, or 30 thousand units per year with 25% likelihood.

The cost structure is assumed to be as follows. Capacity expansion incurs a fixed cost of $8 million plus a marginal cost of $50 per unit of capacity; i.e., adding production capacity of $100,000$ units per year costs $13 million. The process and product technology is commercially viable for four years (at that point a new technology would be needed, an issue we will ignore for now). Acer expects each PC to contribute about $80 in operating profits. A 25% discount rate is used for these types of investment projects.

NPV of "Expand Now"

If Acer decides to expand now, the optimal size of the capacity addition is 100 thousand units per year at a capital expenditure (CapEx) of $13 million (see discussion question). The scenario-contingent sales can be represented as in the top decision tree of Figure 4.7. Except for the medium demand scenario, the capacity decision is marked by a mismatch between supply and demand: in the blockbuster scenario sales are capped by capacity, while the low demand scenario has 70% excess capacity.

Ignoring shortage costs, the operating profits in these three scenarios are $8 million, $8 million, and $2.4 million, respectively, with an expected value of

$$25\% \times \$8 + 50\% \times \$8 + 25\% \times \$2.4 = \$6.6 \text{ million.}$$

The net present value thus is

$$\text{NPV}_{\text{now}} = -13 + \frac{6.6}{1.25} + \frac{6.6}{1.25^2} + \frac{6.6}{1.25^3} + \frac{6.6}{1.25^4} = \$2.6 \text{ million}$$

NPV of "Wait"

If Acer decides to wait, it can observe its commercial success in its current home market, which is highly correlated with its success in the emerging markets. Waiting thus gives Acer much better information on demand. Assuming for simplicity a perfect correlation, it can then make capacity decisions under certainty next year. When capacity investment is profitable, it allows a perfect match between supply and demand.

Thus, if demand is high, the capacity expansion will add 200 thousand units of capacity at a CapEx of $18 million. At medium demand, capacity addition is 100 thousand units per year at $13 million. In contrast, if demand is low, it is better not to invest, as illustrated by the lower decision tree in Figure 4.7. The expected capital expenditure is

$$25\% \times \$18 + 50\% \times \$13 + 25\% \times \$0 = \$11 \text{ million.}$$

the operating profits in the three scenarios are $16 million, $8 million, and $0, respectively, with an expected value of

$$25\% \times \$16 + 50\% \times \$8 + 25\% \times \$0 = \$8 \text{ million.}$$

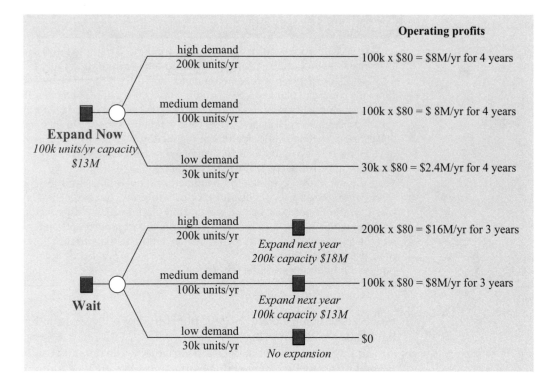

Figure 4.7 Acer's option value of waiting equals the NPV of the waiting strategy (lower decision tree) minus that of the expand-now strategy (upper decision tree).

The net present value becomes

$$\text{NPV}_{\text{wait}} = 0 - \frac{11}{1.25} + \frac{8}{1.25^2} + \frac{8}{1.25^3} + \frac{8}{1.25^4} = \$3.7 \text{ million.}$$

Acer's Option Value of Waiting

The incremental value of waiting relative to immediate investment is:

option value of waiting = $3.7 − $2.6 = $1.1 million.

With about 40% higher expected NPV, it is better for Acer to postpone its expansion and instead spend time learning from the commercial success in its home market.

Adding more options and complexity (abandonment and switching options)

In reality, information updating is not perfect because observed information signals are not perfectly correlated with the future, which remains uncertain. When managers update forecasts for projects with long leadtimes, they have further flexibility to downsize or even abandon the investment, and switch funds to other opportunities. Example 4.3 describes how Eli Lilly announced plans to

> **Example 4.3** Option to downsize and abandon at Eli Lilly
>
> In May 2002, pharmaceutical giant Eli Lilly announced plans to build a new insulin plant in Prince William County, VA. (Lilly introduced the first commercially available insulin in 1923, and its diabetes portfolio accounts for one-fifth of the company's revenue.) At the time, the company planned a $425 million, 600,000-square-foot facility with 700 employees, but the project's size was cut in half in 2005 because of reduced forecasted demand for its products. On January 11, 2007, the company announced that construction of the 300,000-square-foot insulin manufacturing facility, which was scheduled to be completed in 2009, would stop immediately. It estimated restructuring and asset impairment charges would be approximately $155 to $185 million.
>
> Scott Canute, Lilly's president of manufacturing operations, said the company expected worldwide demand for its insulin products to grow, but not at levels projected when plans for the Prince William site were put in place in 2003. Other factors impacting this decision were ongoing productivity gains, quality improvements and investments at existing sites currently manufacturing insulin products that would allow the company to meet expected demand.
>
> *Source: Eli Lilly press release, Jan. 11, 2007.*

build a new insulin plant in 2002, but shut down its construction in 2007, after having downsized it in 2005.

Timing is a managerial decision variable, while demand can be a continuous variable. In practice, one evaluates the expected NPV of a number of decision trees, each corresponding to a specific capacity timing with an associated set of discrete scenarios. These calculations would be similar to what we did here but would capture more detail. When the evolution of demand and uncertainty is complicated by numerous possibilities, one must build a simulation model to evaluate the NPV.

Factors that impact the option value of waiting

Deciding between moving now or waiting involves a trade-off between strategic and financial considerations. The main reason for moving now stems from the strategic decision to first develop a new market. In contrast, the benefit of waiting stems from better information (which reduces uncertainty and allows better capacity sizing) and from postponing investments which could have utilized newer or cheaper technology.

Typically, the option value of waiting is high if:

1. Initial uncertainty about customer requirements and demand is high *and* can be reduced significantly through forecast updating. Volatile industries where future demand (for a product at one location) is strongly correlated with current demand (for perhaps a different product at a different location) are good candidates for high option value of waiting.

2. Long remaining sales horizons are expected without significantly growing competition.

3. Future capacity costs less.

4. Committed capacity is flexible and the waiting decision essentially allocates capacity to a product or service. The next chapter will study the in-

terplay of flexibility and the option value of waiting.

The longer the postponement and the higher the discount rate, the higher the value of forecast updating and the lower the future capacity costs. The downsides of waiting longer, however, are:

1. Lost market development and first-mover advantage (potential loss to other competitors),

2. Additional months of lost sales, and

3. Lost opportunities for learning from operational experience and product and service improvement.

4.6 | TACTICAL TIMING: AGGREGATE PLANNING

When labor is reasonably "frictionless" and adjustable, changing the number of working hours per shift (or running *overtime*), the number of shifts per day, or the number of days per week is an effective and quick lever to change capacity. In addition, advance inventory buildup or a waiting list (back-orders) can accommodate temporary demand surges. Deciding on tactical capacity adjustments is known as aggregate planning.

Aggregate Planning

Graves (2002) defines *aggregate planning* as the "acquisition and allocation of limited resources to production activities so as to satisfy customer demand over a specified time horizon." Resource levels can be changed over time, where time is modeled as periods that typically represent days, weeks, or months. The total time horizon is typically a few quarters during which demand is assumed to be known with certainty.

The resources whose capacity can be adjusted are often restricted to the workforce size, inventory planning, subcontracting, and overtime scheduling. An aggregate plan would specify the various levels in each time period (day, week, or month), such as:

- the hiring and firing of temporary employees,

- overtime,

- subcontracting,

- inventory and backlog, and

- production and sales,

while satisfying all the organizational constraints posed by capacity, labor rules, storage, and demand.

Demand Forecast		Capacity Consumption		Financial Data	
Month	*Demand*	*Resource*	*Consumption*		
1	50,000	Labor	0.5 hrs/unit	Training cost/new employee	$3,000
2	55,000			Regular time hourly wage	$20
3	80,000			Overtime hourly wage	$30
4	95,000			Inventory cost/unit/month	$2
5	110,000			Back-order penalty/unit	$5
6	70,000			Direct Material cost/unit	$10
7	50,000			Sales price/unit	$80

Table 4.2 Input data for Koss' aggregate plan.

Deriving an optimal aggregate plan using linear programming

The great appeal of aggregate planning stems from its ease of specification and optimization. By calculating the operating profit associated with the aggregate plan, we can use optimization to find the plan that maximizes profits while satisfying the constraints that the organization faces.

A typical plan has many decision variables and many constraints, so that just finding a feasible plan is non-trivial. However, when the operating profit (objective) and all the constraints are linear functions of the decision variables, we can use the highly effective optimization tool of *linear programming*. Linear programming automatically finds a feasible and an optimal plan, and is available in most spreadsheet optimization tools. The appendix at the end of this chapter demonstrates the use of this tool in Excel.

An example of aggregate planning: Koss Corp.

Let us illustrate aggregate planning using a stylized example of Koss Corp., which faces strong seasonal demand for its headphones (see Example 3.3 on p. 94). Koss looks 7 months ahead during production planning and forecasts its demand as shown in Table 4.2. The assembly of headphones is predominately manual so that its main capacity constraint in the short term is labor. Its capacity consumption is half an hour per headphone, which is the inverse of labor productivity. Koss accommodates seasonal demand changes by adjusting its labor force, running overtime, building inventory ahead, or running backlogs. Adjusting the labor force is done primarily through temporary employees who receive training before joining the production workforce. The associated financials are summarized in Table 4.2 and also in a downloadable spreadsheet.

Download `AggregatePlan_Koss.xls` from www.vanmieghem.us

Decision variables for Koss Corp.'s aggregate plan

An aggregate plan for Koss Corp. specifies the following decisions for each month:

1. Workforce adjustments through hiring and firing.

2. Total overtime scheduled.

3. Planned inventory or backlog by the end of that month.

4. Monthly production and sales.

Other decisions such as subcontracting could easily be added.

Operating constraints for Koss Corp.'s aggregate plan

When making its planning decisions, Koss faces six types of operating constraints in our stylized example:

1. Workforce constraints. The number of employees in period t equals:

$$\text{employees}_t = \text{employees}_{t-1} + \text{hired}_t - \text{fired}_t.$$

2. Overtime constraints. The total number of overtime hours in a month cannot exceed 15 hours per employee (due to labor agreements).

3. Inventory constraints. These constraints are most easily expressed in terms of the *inventory position*, which equals the physical inventory minus the backlog. Thus, a positive inventory position equals the inventory on hand while a negative inventory position captures backlogs. Flow balance yields that:

$$\text{inventory position}_t = \text{inventory position}_{t-1} + \text{production}_t - \text{sales}_t.$$

4. Safety inventory constraints. Because a point demand forecast is rarely correct, the company holds 10% of the expected demand as safety inventory (better practices are reviewed in the next section).

5. Capacity constraints. Monthly production cannot exceed monthly capacity. Assuming that the assembly of headphones is predominately manual, production cannot exceed available monthly hours/(0.5 units per hour). The total available monthly hours equal overtime hours plus regular hours ((# of employees) × 20 days/month × 8 hours/day).

6. Demand constraints. Monthly sales cannot exceed monthly demand.

Other constraints such as limits on the number of monthly hires or on inventory and backlog could easily be added. In addition, all decision variables must be non-negative. In reality, some variables are integers, but allowing them to take fractional values provides a good approximation that significantly speeds up calculations and optimization.

Operating profit for Koss Corp.'s aggregate plan

In order to assess the attractiveness of a specific aggregate plan, we must compute its contribution to the company's operating profit. (Only profit components that are directly impacted by plan changes need to be captured.) The operating profit for a given month equals monthly revenues minus the following monthly costs:

1. Revenue = sales × $80.

Month	Hired	Fired	Employees	O/T	Inv.	Backlog	Production	Sales
0			150		5000	0		
1	6.3	0	156.3	0	5000	0	50000	50000
2	17.1	0	173.4	0	5500	0	55500	55000
3	106.3	0	279.7	0	15000	0	89500	80000
4	0	0	279.8	0	9500	0	89500	95000
5	0	0	279.9	0	11000	22000	89500	110000
6	0	4.7	275	0	7000	0	88000	70000
7	0	125	150	0	5000	0	48000	50000

Table 4.3 The operating profit-maximizing aggregate plan for Koss Corp.

2. Hiring and training cost = (# of employees hired per month) × $400.

3. Regular wages = (# of employees) × 20 days/month × 8 hours/day × $20/hr.

4. Overtime wages = (# of overtime hours per month) × $30/hr.

5. Inventory holding cost = inventory × $2.

6. Production cost (direct materials) = production × $10.

An aggregate plan for Koss Corp. and discussion

An aggregate plan can be easily obtained by maximizing the operating profit subject to the constraints. The result is shown in Table 4.3. The plan calls for hiring about 130 extra temporary employees (on top of the 150 regular employees) to accommodate the majority of the demand surge. Minor additional adjustments are made for advance inventory buildup in the third month ($15,000$ minus required safety stock of $10\% \times 80,000$ is $7,000$ units for buildup) and a backlog of $22,000$ units in the fifth month. The associated operating profit would be about $30 million.

Obviously, the plan is driven directly by the input parameters. If hiring or firing costs increase so that labor investment becomes more irreversible, workforce adjustments will decrease and overtime, inventory, or backlog will be used to accommodate demand changes. The beauty of linear programming is that it optimizes all these factors simultaneously and automatically. As such, aggregate planning prescribes a short-term optimal position in the trade-off triangle of capacity utilization (regular time, overtime, or subcontracted), inventory, and service and responsiveness (e.g., backlogging or lost sales), shown in Figure 3.8 on p. 93.

In practice, the plan would be used as a guideline and could be adjusted to reduce volatility and facilitate implementation. This can easily be done by adding or changing some constraints, re-optimizing, and verifying whether the decrease in profits is acceptable. For example, Table 4.4 shows an adjusted plan that has less backlog and smoother workforce reduction with virtually no reduction in profits (about $1 from optimal!). This way, near-optimal implementation-friendly plans are found easily through re-optimization.

Month	Hired	Fired	Employees	O/T	Inv.	Backlog	Production	Sales
			150		5000	0		
1	6.2	0	156.3	0	5000	0	50000	50000
2	17.2	0	173.4	0	5500	0	55500	55000
3	106.3	0	279.7	0	15000	0	89500	80000
4	0	0	279.7	0	9500	0	89500	95000
5	0	0	279.7	4195	11000	13609	97891	110000
6	0	30.9	248.8	0	7000	0	79609	70000
7	0	98.8	150.0	0	5000	0	48000	50000

Table 4.4 A near-optimal plan with less backlog and smoother workforce reduction.

Aggregate planning vs. strategic resource planning

Aggregate planning differs from strategic capacity adjustment in two significant ways. First, the resources under consideration are often restricted to the workforce size, inventory planning, subcontracting, and overtime scheduling. While nothing precludes the inclusion of capital equipment adjustments in the model, aggregate planning typically keeps capital equipment fixed during short planning horizons and seeks to find the best utilization and allocation of equipment to products over time.

Second, and more important, short to medium planning horizons completely disregard uncertainty. From a hierarchical perspective, aggregate planning operates at a lower level than strategic capacity planning (also known as *resource planning*), but at a higher level than *materials requirement planning* (MRP) and *capacity requirements planning* (CRP).[5] Appropriate planning models must strike a balance between complexity and realism. While resource planning (such as our simple timing model earlier) often neglects changes in inventory and overtime scheduling, the more detailed aggregate planning neglects uncertainty.

Stable industries or short-term plans may not suffer much from neglecting uncertainty, but few companies can forecast accurately half a year into the future. While one can always add safety buffers in the form of minimal safety stock requirements or extra workforce as safety capacity, linear programming does not tell you how to choose those safety levels, so one must resort to ad-hoc "fudge factors." Because of its assumption of certainty, the optimal aggregate plan also tends to be very sensitive to changes in parameters or demand forecast. Thus, the optimal aggregate plan's "nervousness" is a serious problem that hinders its practical implementation. Next, we will review some potential solutions.

---

[5]Despite its name, CRP typically verifies whether a production plan is feasible given the current capacity; that is, it checks the feasibility of resource *allocation* rather than planning resource investment or adjustments.

4.7 | SERVICE CONSIDERATIONS FOR CAPACITY ADJUSTMENTS

Most of the analysis in this chapter has assumed that the demand forecast is perfect. When service levels are important, capacity adjustments must take into account uncertainty and its impact on service. Unfortunately, identifying dynamic adjustments in such an environment while maximizing firm value is very difficult and is a topic of current academic research. Yet, our analysis in Chapter 3 suggests some reasonably simple approaches to incorporate most service level considerations.

Always start by incorporating forecast uncertainty

Service provisions in terms of availability (shortage probability) or responsiveness (leadtimes or waiting times) can only be planned well if we include forecast uncertainty. In practice, it often suffices to include the volatility (standard deviation) by time bucket, in addition to the mean. This volatility can then be used to build in a safety margin to guarantee availability or responsiveness, as we show next.

Add safety capacity or inventory to guarantee availability

If customers are so impatient that a shortage results in a lost sale, then adding safety capacity or inventory guarantees a minimal service or availability level. Chapter 3 showed that

$$\text{optimal safety capacity or inventory} = z^* \times \text{standard deviation},$$

where
$$z^* = \texttt{normsinv}(\text{service probability}).$$

Rough availability guarantees can easily be incorporated into a deterministic planning model as follows:

1. Add the service probability, which can be a strategic mandate or can be given by a newsvendor fraction (see p. 435), and the standard deviation (forecast error) of demand in each period as input parameters.

2. Inflate the expected demand forecast in each period by $z^* \times$ the standard deviation of that period to arrive at the peak demand curve.

3. Plan capacity or inventory levels to meet the peak demand curve.

This procedure is simple and useful in practice. It can be used in continuous-time optimization models (like the one in section 4.3) and discrete-time models (such as linear aggregate planning). It is a common approach to plan inventory in supply chains and capacity in call or data centers. For example, an aluminum producer requires "5-nines" availability at its data centers. Given that $\texttt{normsinv}(.99999) = 4.3$, the company plans its capacity to meet expected demand + 4.3 standard deviations, as shown in Figure 4.8. Mini-Case 4 asks you to investigate a similar approach.

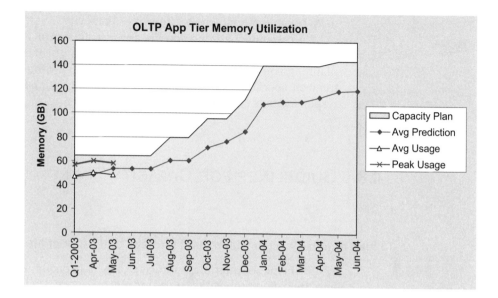

Figure 4.8 The capacity plan for memory in the data center of an aluminum producer requires a "5-nines" availability. Capacity in this case is thus sized and timed with 4.3 standard deviations above the average predicted demand. The plot also shows actual average and peak usage.

The downside of this procedure is that it is overly conservative as it assumes that demand would take on its maximal levels in *every* period. In reality, demand is not perfectly correlated over time and peaks in one period need not be sustained in the subsequent period. More realistic planning models heuristically reduce the required z value or, even better, optimize capacity by simulating demand. (Appendix 5 on p. 192 shows how to do this in a spreadsheet.)

Add safety capacity to guarantee responsiveness

Even when customers are patient, response times (leadtimes or waiting times) must be contained to guarantee an acceptable service. It seems that simply adding an upper constraint on the backlog in each period would suffice. After all, limiting the waiting list also limits waiting times. Following that argument, a first estimate for the maximal backlog is next period capacity $\times$ maximal response time[6]. This again is a linear constraint and can be directly incorporated into aggregate planning.

The problem with this reasoning is that it disregards any uncertainty in demand arrivals (or processing). When demand arrives at random times, queuing theory tells us that average waiting times increase almost exponentially when safety capacity decreases, as shown by Figure 3.12 (p. 98). Instead of adding a backlog constraint, response time guarantees require a non-linear constraint on safety capacity. Operating close to full utilization destroys service. It is surprising how many companies are bewildered when their operations turn into a total

---

[6]Remember Little's law: average inventory = average throughput times average flow time.

mess "even though there is some excess capacity."

Unfortunately, adding non-linear constraints to an aggregate planning model destroys its linearity and ease of optimization (which explains why commercial planning software disregards quality of service). One must either rely on customized special optimization logic or manually adjust capacities to satisfy the responsiveness constraints.

4.8 | GUIDELINES FOR CAPACITY TIMING AND ADJUSTMENT

To lead or to lag? Align with overall strategy and product life cycle!

The principle of alignment indicates that a capacity strategy must be aligned with the value proposition. Leading strategies are a better fit for companies that focus on innovation and service. To enable new product introduction and diffusion, one must first build capacity. Similarly, capacity shortages and back-orders with long waiting times are less likely if sufficient capacity is in place. In contrast, lagging strategies are more appropriate for companies that respond to market changes or that focus on efficiency.

The appropriate kind of timing strategy is correlated with the product life cycle, just like the appropriate process type discussed in Chapter 1. Typically, a leading strategy is used for product introduction while a lagging strategy becomes more appropriate in the later growth phases. For instance, Mercedes initially built M-class capacity for introduction, but expanded capacity only after demand became stronger than expected. In the decline phase, capacity can be contracted before demand declines in order to control end-of-lifecycle effects and prepare for follow-up products.

Include uncertainty and capacity frictions in capacity decisions

Capacity timing and adjustment are challenging due to uncertainty and capacity frictions (leadtimes, lumpiness, and irreversibility). To time and adjust capacity in a value-maximizing manner, one should incorporate uncertainty as well as frictions in the decision process. Both real options and aggregate planning (and its extensions) provide some tools to do so. As times change, companies must update forecasts and re-optimize capacity plans using a rolling horizon.

Timing and adjusting become easier, however, if we *reduce*, rather than just accommodate, the root problems of frictions and uncertainty. Some approaches are:

Streamline project management (reduce capacity leadtimes)

Shorter capacity leadtimes (see p. 75) allow us to postpone the adjustment decision while gathering more information and reducing risk. Good project management of capacity installation reduces the leadtime: working in parallel (concurrent design, engineering, and procurement) and streamlining the project activities (accelerating or eliminating hand-offs through better coordination between design, procurement, construction, and implementation; eliminating non-value added work; reducing rework by using standard designs or reusing previous designs) reduces the critical path leadtime.

Being well prepared can be equally effective in reducing leadtimes: it is important to first do the work that is independent of capacity sizing or timing. This includes project planning work, such as preparing relevant technology and supplier information, by collaborating well with capacity technology providers, and so on. This effectively takes these activities off the critical path and reduces the leadtime that factors into sizing and timing. Finally, reducing leadtime uncertainty has additional value (the construction business is notoriously unpredictable and this strategy requires adding safety time to the project).

Modularize capacity and construction (reduce lumpiness)

Breaking up a monolithic unit of capacity into modules allows us to adjust capacity in smaller chunks. This not only reduces initial costs, but also delays later additions and reduces risk. This explains why high-risk industries such as pharmaceuticals and semiconductors have worked so hard to modularize their process technology. *Modular capacity* also reduces the physical size, design, and installation complexity, thereby also reducing the leadtime. Eli Lilly now asks its Swedish vendor Pharmadule, the leading module manufacturer for the pharma industry, to ship completely finished modules which only need to be "assembled" on-site, vastly reducing on-site building time while increasing quality.

Modularizing capacity is difficult because it typically means sacrificing some economies of scale. Thus, companies should think about creating incremental capacity quickly, with little premium to larger chunks. One such approach is to commit with vendors to multiple modules with adjustable future deliveries.

Increase capacity adjustment flexibility (reduce irreversibility)

Investment becomes more irreversible when it cannot be recouped by reducing capacity. Adjustment flexibility thus increases when we reduce investment costs or increase resale value. By turning fixed investment costs into variable operating costs, leasing, subcontracting, outsourcing, and hiring temporary employees are the typical strategies used to mitigate the cost of capacity adjustment. Such actions are valuable in highly dynamic or uncertain settings even if their variable cost is higher than the cost of less reversible capacity.

Use adaptable, flexible, or reactive capacity and postponement (reduce uncertainty)

Adaptable capacity anticipates future contingencies by including options for fast and cheap adjustment later. Poppies' plant was built on an oversized piece of land with a large shell. The increased inventory resulting from moving to 24/7 could easily be accommodated. Over time, more equipment could be moved in to expand capacity when needed with little disruption to ongoing operations. In addition to this expansion option, adaptable capacity accrues more value in a multi-product or uncertain technology setting. Starting with generic or flexible capacity allows product or technology specialization to be postponed, thereby reducing risk, as the next chapter will show. *Reactive capacity* is an extreme form of postponement: instead of proactively deciding on capacity, building capacity when demand is known eliminates the need for forecasting.

4.9 | SUMMARY OF LEARNING OBJECTIVES

1. Discuss the five different capacity timing strategies and their implementations.

A demand-chasing capacity strategy simply adjusts capacity to match demand. Such strategy, however, is difficult to implement when capacity adjustment incurs frictions such as leadtimes, lumpiness, fixed costs, and irreversibility. Then, capacity timing strategies must choose whether to adjust capacity in anticipation of or in reaction to demand changes. Leading strategies are commercially attractive because they offer high service levels, can support demand surges, and send strong signals to customers and competitors. In contrast, lagging strategies boast high efficiencies, small risk, lower capacity costs, and are less dependent on forecasting. Leading strategies are a better fit for companies that focus on innovation, service, and growth, while lagging strategies are more appropriate for companies that respond to market changes or that focus on efficiency. The timing strategy also changes from leading to lagging as a product goes through its life cycle. A fourth strategy is a hybrid between leading and lagging and smoothes capacity requirements using inventory or backlogging. The fifth strategy involves a company following its competitor's timing strategy.

These timing strategies can adjust capacity in various ways. Depending on the adjustment size, strategic capacity adjustments may include new facilities, expanding existing facilities, or subcontracting or outsourcing. More tactical capacity adjustments derive from adding overtime, shifts, or workdays; building inventory in anticipation of seasonal demand surges; or from process improvement and restructuring.

2. Identify the key drivers of capacity timing and explain their roles.

Capacity timing and adjustment are challenging due to uncertainty and capacity frictions, such as capacity leadtimes, lumpiness, and irreversibility. Scale economies lead to chunky capacity adjustments, but discounting counteracts that effect. Higher discount factors (perhaps due to raising interest rates) make future investment less costly and decrease the size of today's investments while postponing future investments. Capacity adjustment also becomes less frequent as capacity reductions only recoup a small part of initial investment costs. Uncertainty, however, creates the greatest challenge: it requires additional capacity as a safety cushion, or to smooth adjustments using inventory or backlogging. Large capacity leadtimes increase the total uncertainty between the capacity decision and its availability, and require higher and earlier adjustments.

Both capacity timing and adjustment become easier if we *reduce*, rather than just accommodate, the root problems of frictions and uncertainty. Streamlined concurrent project management reduces capacity leadtimes. Modular capacity and construction reduces lumpiness. Leasing, subcontracting, outsourcing, and temporary labor all reduce irreversibility. Finally, adaptable and flexible capacity allows postponement and is less sensitive to uncertainty, as we shall examine in the next chapter.

3. Value and optimize the option value of strategic timing and waiting.

> Strategic capacity timing features long time frames and much uncertainty. The real options tool uses decision trees to quantify the financial benefits of strategic timing. The option value of waiting equals the difference between the NPV of postponed and immediate investment. It increases when future uncertainty can be significantly reduced through forecast updating and with long remaining sales horizons. Longer waiting, however, hurts commercial development and learning by doing.

4. Model tactical timing in the capacity-inventory-waiting triangle in a spreadsheet.

> Tactical capacity adjustments, also known as aggregate planning, change workforce, work time, inventory, and production levels over a short horizon assuming high forecast accuracy. It is easily formulated and optimized as a linear program in a spreadsheet. The major downside of aggregate planning is that it ignores uncertainty; this effect can be alleviated by periodically updating forecasts (using rolling horizons) and re-optimizing. It is better to incorporate forecast uncertainty and heuristically add safety capacity or inventory constraints in order to guarantee service levels, such as availability and responsiveness.

DISCUSSION QUESTIONS

1. What is the impact of a higher demand growth rate on the size of capacity additions?

2. How would you back up the statement: "If Acer decides to expand now, the optimal size of the capacity addition is 100 thousand units per year,"?

3. What is wrong with the practice of adding a safety constraint equal to a fraction of the demand in aggregate planning (as in the Koss Corp. example)? What do you suggest should be done?

4. What are the similarities and differences between modular and smart capacity?

CHALLENGE QUESTIONS

1. Revisit the Gujarat Apollo Industries Ltd. mini-case on p. 107. Apollo expects average demand to grow between 8 and 12 percent each year. Anticipating 5 years in the future, what capacity expansion strategy would you recommend? Investigate the sensitivity of your recommendation to changes in the annual growth rate and other model parameters.

2. How would you extend the simple analytic timing model to analyze a hybrid strategy of lagging and leading that uses inventory smoothing? (Hint: include inventory dynamics and holding costs, similar to the smoothing

analysis in Chapter 3. To capture the non-linear inventory build-up exactly, you need integration. Otherwise, use an approximation.)

Visit www.vanmieghem.us for additional questions and updates.

FURTHER READING AND REFERENCES

▶ Manne (1961) wrote the seminal article on the capacity timing. Dixit (1997) and Eberly and Van Mieghem (1997) analyze investment dynamics for a portfolio of assets. A survey of recent research on capacity investment is given in Van Mieghem (2003).

Angelus, A. and E. Porteus (2005). A capacity assembly problem. *Stanford University working paper.* June.

Covert, J. (2006). Wal-mart tightens work-shift rules. *Wall Street Journal.* May 3.

Dixit, A. K. (1997). Investment and employment dynamics in the short run and the long run. *Oxford Econ. Pap. 49*, 1–20.

Eberly, J. C. and J. A. Van Mieghem (1997). Multi-factor dynamic investment under uncertainty. *Journal of Economic Theory 75*, 345–387.

Graves, S. C. (2002). Manufacturing planning and control. *Handbook of Applied Optimization*, 728–746.

Kerkhof, L. (2005). Personal conversations. June.

Manne, A. S. (1961). Capacity expansion and probabilistic growth. *Econometrica 29*(4), 632–649.

Van Mieghem, J. A. (2003). Capacity management, investment and hedging: Review and recent developments. *Manufacturing and Service Operations Management 5*(4), 269–302.

Mini-Case 4 | TIMING OF IT EXPANSIONS

[7]A global $2.5 billion dollar manufacturer with extensive field service operations embarked on a project to consolidate 256 worldwide applications into one Oracle E-Business Suite system in a U.S. data center. This single center stored all the internal corporate data of the entire worldwide operations, including data from accounting ledgers, bill of material (BOM), factory routing, and purchase orders. Each day, additional data would be added to storage.

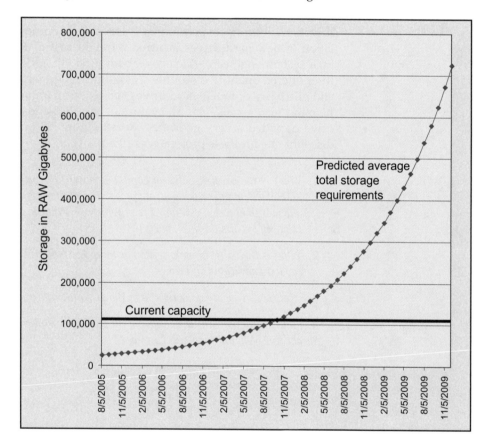

Figure 4.9 Predicted average demand for storage capacity relative to current available capacity.

As part of the planning, managers estimated capacity requirements in terms of the raw storage requirements. All systems ran on Oracle databases and computer programs were developed to extract historical data growth by business

---

[7]Richard L. Pérez and Professor Van Mieghem prepared this case as the basis for class discussion rather than to illustrate either the effective or ineffective handling of a managerial situation. No part of this case study may be reproduced without permission; direct all inquiries to permissions@vanmieghem.us

function. Then, with some research and testing of the systems, this data growth was translated into raw storage requirements. Finally, by predicting the growth in business function users (either through acquisitions or organic growth), demand for storage could be predicted remarkably accurately for a few years into the future. The result is shown in Figure 4.9 together with the current installed capacity of 110,800GB. This data is also available in a downloadable spreadsheet.

Download `MiniCase4_Data.xls` from www.vanmieghem.us

Given that the data store was forecasted to run out of capacity in November 2007, managers needed to devise a capacity expansion plan! Storage capacity is expanded by purchasing and installing an appropriate number of 150GB storage drives. Each capital expenditure exhibited scale economies because each installation of new hard drives incurred a freight cost of $500 and required a visit by a system engineer, which cost about $150. In addition, the drive manufacturer offered quantity discounts. A log-linear regression of previous quotations and purchases of 150GB hard drives yielded the parameters of the power CapEx function $\$650 + c_K K^\alpha / \alpha$. The values of $\alpha = .843$ and $c_K = \$10,613$ per 150GB drive provided a very good fit. (Recall Figure 3.3 on p. 85.) The company's discount rate for these projects was 20% per year.

1. *What is the present value of capital expenditures between Nov. 2007 and Nov. 2009 if a demand chasing strategy is followed that installs additional capacity just one month ahead of estimated requirements? What is the value of making a single capacity expansion in Nov. 2007?*

2. *What is the value of making two or more expansions? What are their appropriate capacity additions and times?*

3. *How sensitive are your results to the discount rate and other parameters?*

4. *How would your results change if the company required a "5-nines" service availability? What data would you need?*

Appendix 4 | LINEAR PLANNING OPTIMIZATION IN EXCEL

Linear planning models are surprisingly effective because they are easily implemented and optimized in standard spreadsheets, while they still capture many decisions and constraints. The generic linear planning model has a set of decision variables or activity levels x_i that have a linear contribution margin or value v_i to operating profit, but are subject to a set of linear organizational constraints.

The best plan specifies optimal activity levels x_i^* that maximize the operating profit. They are the solution to an optimization problem of the following form[8]:

$$\text{maximize operating profit} \sum_{\text{activities } i} v_i x_i$$

subject to

$$\sum_{\text{activities } i} a_{ji} x_i \leq K_j. \qquad \text{(capacity constraint for each resource } j)$$

$$\sum_{\text{activities } i} b_{li} x_i \leq D_l, \qquad \text{(demand constraint for each product } l)$$

$$\vdots \qquad \text{(other constraints)}$$

$$x_i \geq 0 \qquad \text{(non-negativity constraints).}$$

By smartly defining activities, a linear planning model can capture many decision problems that can be solved quickly using linear programming, which is embedded in Excel's Solver tool. You can do this in Excel in five steps that we illustrate with Koss Corp.'s aggregate planning model (p. 136).

Download `AggregatePlan_Koss.xls` from www.vanmieghem.us

Step 1: Define data (parameters)

It is good practice to keep all demand, operational, and financial data or parameters in one or multiple tables in Excel. This greatly facilitates the "what-if" analysis compared to the process of embedding the data directly into formulas. Figure 4.10 shows Koss Corp.'s data on rows 1 to 10.

Step 2: Define activities (decision variables)

There are eight activities at Koss Corp.: hiring, firing, scheduling overtime, and planning inventory, backlog, production, and sales. Each activity can change each month and we plan 7 months ahead. Thus, we define $8 \times 7 = 56$ variables that are tracked in the table on rows 13 to 21 in Figure 4.10. (That table also tracks the number of employees, which could be derived from hiring and firing and the starting number of employees.) It is also convenient to add an additional row (row 14) to track initial conditions on workforce, inventory, and backlog.

---

[8]The summation $\sum_i v_i x_i = v_1 x_1 + \cdots + v_m x_m$ is easily implemented in Excel as `sumproduct({`$v_1, v_2, \cdots, v_m$`}, {`$x_1, x_2, \cdots, x_m$`})`.

	A	B	C	D	E	F	G	H	I	J
1	Step 1: Data for Koss Corp.'s									
2	Demand Forecast			Operational Data			Financial Data			
3	Month	Demand					Training cost/new temp employee			$3,000
4	1	50000		Labor hrs/unit	0.5		Regular time hourly wage			$20
5	2	55000		Max overtime	15		Overtime hourly wage			$30
6	3	80000		hours/day	8		Inventory holding cost/unit/month			$2
7	4	95000		days/week	20		Backorder penalty/unit			$5
8	5	110000		SafetyStock	10%		Direct Material cost/unit			$10
9	6	70000					Sales price/unit			$80
10	7	50000								
11										
12	Step 2: Decision variables for Koss Corp.'s aggregate plan									
13	Month	# Hired	# Fired	# Employees	Overtime	Inventory	Backlog	Production	Sales	
14	0			150		5000	0			
15	1	6.2	0.0	156.3	0	5000	0	50000	50000	
16	2	17.2	0.0	173.4	0	5500	0	55500	55500	
17	3	106.3	0.0	279.7	0	15000	0	89500	80000	
18	4	0.0	0.0	279.7	0	9500	0	89500	95000	
19	5	0.0	0.0	279.7	4195	11000	13609	97891	110000	
20	6	0.0	30.9	248.8	0	7000	0	79609	70000	
21	7	0.0	98.8	150.0	0	5000	0	48000	50000	
22										
23	Step 3: Operating profit									
24	Month	Hiring cost		Wages	Overtime	Inventory	Backlog	Production	Revenue	
25	1	$18,750		$500,000	$0	$10,000	$0.0	$500,000	$4,000,000	
26	2	$51,563		$555,000	$0	$11,000	$0.0	$555,000	$4,400,000	
27	3	$318,750		$895,000	$0	$30,000	$0.0	$895,000	$6,400,000	
28	4	$0		$895,000	$0	$19,000	$0.0	$895,000	$7,600,000	
29	5	$0		$895,000	$125,859	$22,000	$68,046.9	$978,906	$8,800,000	
30	6	$0		$796,094	$0	$14,000	$0.0	$796,094	$5,600,000	
31	7	$0		$480,000	$0	$10,000	$0.0	$480,000	$4,000,000	
32	Total operating profit =	$29,984,938								
33										
34	Step 4: Constraints									
35	Month			Workforce	Overtime	Inventory	SafetyStock	Capacity	Sales	
36	1			3.7E-13	-2.3E+03	0.0E+00	0.0E+00	0.0E+00	0.0E+00	
37	2			-2.6E-13	-2.6E+03	-1.2E-10	0.0E+00	1.2E-10	0.0E+00	
38	3			0.0E+00	-4.2E+03	4.5E-11	7.0E+03	0.0E+00	0.0E+00	
39	4			0.0E+00	-4.2E+03	-1.2E-10	4.2E-11	0.0E+00	0.0E+00	
40	5			0.0E+00	0.0E+00	-2.4E-11	-8.7E-11	0.0E+00	0.0E+00	
41	6			2.6E-13	-3.7E+03	1.0E-10	0.0E+00	0.0E+00	0.0E+00	
42	7			0.0E+00	-2.3E+03	0.0E+00	0.0E+00	0.0E+00	0.0E+00	

Figure 4.10 Implementing linear planning in Excel. The screen shot shows an aggregate plan for Koss Corp. (see p. 136).

Step 3: Calculate operating profit

It is now easy to calculate all costs and revenues using the data and the activity levels (see the equations earlier on p. 137). It is often convenient to calculate the profit in steps. First, calculate the revenue or cost associated with each decision variable, as shown in the table on rows 24-31 of the financials in Figure 4.10. Then sum all the revenues and costs to arrive at total operating profit (cell C32).

Step 4: Define operating constraints

Step 4 adds another table containing all the constraints on the decision variables. The Koss example has six sets of constraints, discussed on p. 137 and captured in rows 36-42 in Figure 4.10. In spreadsheets, it is easiest to rewrite constraints so that the right hand side is zero. For example, the spreadsheet formulas for month 1 (row 30) are:

1. Workforce constraint (cell D36): `=D15-(D14+B15-C15)`

2. Overtime constraint (cell E36): `=E15-E$5*D15`

3. Inventory constraint (cell F36): `=F15-G15-(F14-G14+H15-I15)`

4. Safety stock constraint (cell G36): `=F15-E$8*B4`

5. Capacity constraint (cell H36): `=H15-(D15*E$7*E$6+E15)/E$4`

6. Sales constraint (cell I36): `=I15-B4`

Selecting cells D36:I36 and dragging them down automatically copies the right constraints into the other months.

Step 5: Optimize

In Excel, open the Solver dialog box under `Tools>Solver` and enter:
 `Set target cell`: enter profit cell `C32`
 `Equal to`: select `Max`
 `By Changing Cells`: enter decision cells `B15:I21`
 `Subject to the Constraints`: add the following constraints:

1. Workforce: `D36:D42=0`

2. Overtime: `E36:E42<=0`

3. Inventory: `F36:F42=0`

4. Safety Stock: `G36:G42>=0`

5. Capacity: `H36:H42<=0`

6. Sales: `I36:I42<=0`

7. Non-negativity: `B15:I21 >=0`

8. Require zero backlog at end of period: `G21=0`.

In the Solver dialog box, click on Options and select Assume Linear Model. This will vastly speed up calculations and a properly-coded Solver is guaranteed to find an optimal solution. (Unfortunately, in contrast to professional versions, the basic Solver add-in that comes free with Excel is not properly coded and sometimes produces erroneous answers. It is good practice to try several initial solutions.)

Chapter

5

Capacity Types, Flexibility and Consolidation

While the bringing out of yearly models results in many disadvantages and, for that reason, we are all against yearly models, I don't see just what can be done about it.— Alfred P. Sloan, Jr. (July 29, 1925)

Learning Objectives

After reading this chapter, you will be able to:

1. Describe the benefits and challenges of different types of capacity and flexibility.
2. Design products and processes for flexibility and mass customization.
3. Identify and value three key drivers of flexibility and explain their role in consolidation.
4. Tailor and optimize the capacity portfolio of a multi-product firm in a spreadsheet.

In the previous chapters, we implicitly assumed that a single measure of capacity was sufficient to describe all the resource needs of the entire organization. In this chapter, we will examine the choice of a resource portfolio in a multi-product organization. This involves determining capacity types and flexibility, the third component of a resource portfolio strategy, as shown in Figure 3.1 (p. 72). We start by describing the pros and cons of different types of capacity and flexibility and then discuss their implementation. Then we value and optimize network flexibility and quantify the benefits of consolidation. The appendix shows how to optimize flexibility using simulation in Excel.

5.1 | Different Types of Resources and Capacity

An integral part of operations strategy is the selection of the characteristics and types of resources and capacity. Given that we viewed capacity as resulting from physical resource constraints, this selection involves deciding on the types and capabilities of real assets that the organization needs. There are many types of real assets. Rather than attempting to give an exhaustive list, let us distinguish types along two dimensions that are important from an operations perspective.

Specialist or Generalist? Degree of flexibility

The Scottish political economist and moral philosopher Adam Smith proposed the "division and specialization of labor," which heralded the industrial age along with a dramatic rise in productivity and welfare. Instead of having generalists perform the entire process, Smith advocated the division of the process into activities performed by specialists. Deciding on the degree of specialization or the span of activities that an asset can perform is a key decision in operations strategy.

Specialists and *dedicated* assets perform a single or very limited range of tasks. Examples include highly-specialized professionals, a drill in a rigid fixture with a specific bit, or Henry Ford's original assembly line that was dedicated to one product. (Ford's famous saying about his Model T was that "you can have it in any color as long as it is black." Black paint dries fastest and maximizes capacity.) The benefits of specialization are efficiency and effectiveness. Recall from Chapter 2 how focus improves operational efficiency.

In contrast, *generalists* and *general-purpose* equipment can perform an endless variety of tasks. Examples include general management consultants and a typical household drill whose bit and orientation is adjustable to drill any hole in any type of material. Their great benefit is endless flexibility.

Flexible assets or resources can perform multiple tasks. Flexible or *cross-trained* operators are sometimes described as *agile*, indicating that they can swiftly move from one task at a workstation to a second task at another.

Flexible assets fall somewhere between specialized and general-purpose assets. *Scope flexibility* measures the degree of flexibility in terms of the breadth or scope of activities performed. Specialists exhibit minimal scope because their abilities are limited to performing one or a few tasks. (Obviously, the smaller the task, the more highly specialized and smaller the scope.) In contrast, generalists have maximal scope.

Labor or capital? Degree of automation

Another key distinction is made between human resources and capital assets. Economists sometimes aggregate human resources under the term *labor*, while non-economists may refer to certain capital assets as *equipment, machines,* or *technology*. Choosing the type of technology is also part of *technology management*, although this term also captures many other facets.

Most processes use a mix of labor and capital. *Automation* measures the degree to which a process can operate without human supervision. The degree of automation spans the spectrum from manual to fully automated. *Manual* processes typically utilize some capital equipment, but their operation also requires human presence. Typical examples include most service processes such as restaurants, airlines, and other transportation services. On the other extreme, fully automated processes operate without human supervision, sometimes continuously in the so called "24/7"-mode. For instance, glass manufacturing plants must operate continuously in order to prevent the molten glass from solidify-

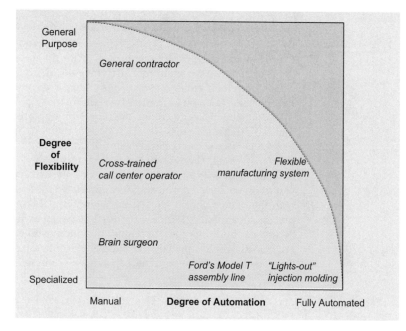

Figure 5.1 Resource abilities or capacity types can be described in terms of the scope of their activities and the mix of labor and capital employed.

ing. Other examples can be found in the processing industries of commodities, beverages, food, etc. Internet grocer Webvan started operations using highly automated distribution centers in stark contrast to Peapod's manual start-up processes (see case study on p. 415).

Most automated equipment may require human assistance for loading, unloading, or changeovers, but can otherwise run unattended. Such equipment works well when operated by a cross-trained or agile workforce. Many machining operations are automated, including the simple oven found in most homes.

Types and Alignment

In most environments, resource capabilities involve multiple dimensions. The degree of automation and flexibility can be combined to better describe capabilities. For example, agile manual processes, also known as agile worker-based production, are systems with cross-trained operators and equipment whose operation requires constant human presence.

The main question in this chapter is how to choose the right capacity types. The principle of alignment suggests that higher degrees of variety require higher degrees of flexibility, as illustrated by the product-process matrix (p. 26). Automation can provide higher consistency (quality), volumes, or lower costs. While both dimensions are independent in principle, increased automation typically comes with increased rigidity leading to a trade-off as shown in Figure 5.1. In the remainder of this chapter, we will focus on the flexibility dimension.

Example 5.1 Dynaco USA: Rationalization of Flexibility

Based in Northbrook, IL, Dynaco USA produces and sells high-speed industrial doors that open and close exceptionally fast. With lift speeds of eight feet per second, these doors of patented design minimize traffic flow disruptions, while shielding industrial facilities from their environment. These doors are constructed from a flexible reinforced PVC curtain sealed on both sides by an industrial zipper. Customers can fully customize their doors by choosing colors, the number and placement of windows, sizes, and customized mechanical parts.

In 2002, Dynaco started offering a line of standardized doors with a generic control panel. Customers could choose two types of motors (1Hp, 2Hp) and a door panel available in six colors and with up to 16 windows of only two sizes. The result was a classic win-win situation: industrial customers appreciated the lower price and were perfectly happy with the offered choice set. At the same time, the modular product design facilitated process streamlining. Window production, which used to be a bottleneck, was performed in advance and only the hot sealing of windows to doors was postponed to the actual order. With window production taken off the critical path, the total lead time was reduced from 50 hours to 35 hours while capacity was doubled. *Source: Wouters (2005)*

5.2 | BENEFITS OF FLEXIBILITY

"Flexibility means different things to different people. At the plant level, flexibility is about the ability to adapt or change," according to Upton (1995). There are numerous ways to adapt and change, but the crucial starting point is to define flexibility for your context: to what do you wish to respond, and in what time frame? Too often managers talk about what they've done to be flexible, but not why and why it matters.

The major objectives of flexibility are to increase scope, increase agility, or achieve robustness across a specified range. In this section, we will discuss the importance and the benefits of various types of flexibility. Yet, while flexibility offers several advantages, it is not always the preferred option. The next section explores the downsides of flexibility.

The strategic importance of flexibility

Both specialization and flexibility decisions are key elements of operations strategy and can provide a powerful source of competitive advantage. In August 2004, Toyota Motor Co. reported a quarterly profit of 2.6 billion dollars, which was higher than the combined profits of rivals General Motors and Ford Motor. Toyota credited simpler and more modular car designs, platform sharing, and flexible capacity for increasing its quarterly operating profit by $361 million.

Choosing the appropriate amount and type of flexibility is important. The experience of Dynaco, featured in Example 5.1, shows that a little flexibility goes a long way and is often preferred over full customization.

Resource flexibility questions are pertinent in every operation, including services. For example, to what extent should organizations cross-train their human capital? How can service teams be allocated to customer segments while simultaneously balancing the needs for customer knowledge and organizational flexibility?

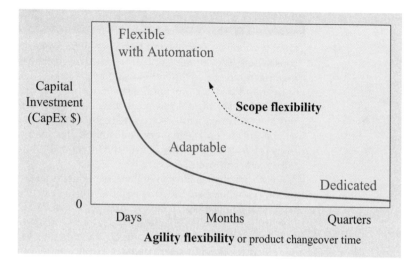

Figure 5.2 Scope and agility flexibility are closely related. In the pharmaceutical industry, full flexibility with automation can be very expensive.

Scope flexibility

Scope flexibility measures the breadth of activities that an asset can perform, as said earlier. It can refer to the ability to make a certain number of products. Scope flexibility allows an operation to adapt to a changing demand mix, to hedge mix uncertainty, and to increase scale economies by aggregating demands of several products and services (we will value these benefits in detail later in this chapter).

For example, Hitachi's new disk drive "mega manufacturing center" in Shenzhen, China will be capable of producing disk drives of varying form factors. The ability to produce new one-inch drives such as that of Apple's iPod mini (c.f., example 3.1 on p. 74) in addition to the traditional 3.5 inch drives gives the flexibility to meet future demand in the traditional IT and consumer segments.

Agility and scale flexibility

Agility-flexibility measures the speed at which an asset can change from one activity to another. Quick changeovers allow quick responses and the postponement of allocation decisions without much safety capacity or inventory. Google uses "agile programming," which uses continuous integration, short iterations, and test-driven development, to deploy new software. Chapter 10 will further investigate the role of flexibility and speed in innovation.

Agility and scope are closely related because scope flexibility assumes a minimal amount of agility, and vice versa. A plant that takes three months to change over can hardly be called flexible. In addition, agility and scope flexibility are also positively correlated with capital investment costs, as Figure 5.2 illustrates. For example, flexibility with automation has high agility but can be very expensive (and take a long time to build and validate) in the pharmaceutical industry, according to William A. Fox, Eli Lilly's senior engineering consultant.

Example 5.2 Robust Quality at Sony

Quality pioneers Taguchi and Clausing (1990) argue that quality robustness stems from consistency. They present a classic example involving the performance of Sony televisions manufactured at two different locations, San Diego and Tokyo.

Sony found that customers prefer pictures with a particular color density (let us call it a nominal level of 10) and become increasingly dissatisfied the more the color deviates from this level. Consequently, Sony set acceptable process specification limits of 10 ± 3. Sets shipped from San Diego were uniformly distributed within specs. However, shipments from Tokyo tended to cluster near the target of 10 though about 3 per thousand actually fell outside corporate specs.

Akio Morita, then chairman of Sony, explained that the Tokyo plant was striving for zero tolerances while San Diego was following instructions perfectly but only was staying within the limits of specification. A larger fraction of San Diego TV's (those farther away from 10) seemed unsatisfactory to customers compared to Tokyo's output. While Tokyo shipped all output without inspection and had to exchange a few TV's per thousand, Sony had to spend more to repair or replace those built in San Diego. Sony discovered that nothing is gained by shipping a product just barely meeting the corporate standard over a product that just fails.

Agility can also be interpreted as including *scale flexibility*, which measures the degree to which a resource can change its processing rate or production volume. AMD's use of flexible manufacturing processes to minimize its *"ramp time"* has been credited for increasing its lead in the processor race of 2000 by scaling up the speed and production of its Athlon chips before Intel could respond.

Robustness

Robustness means that performance (e.g., cost efficiency, quality, or responsiveness) does not vary much over the range of activities performed. Each resource has at least one activity that maximizes its performance. If deviating from that preferred activity steeply decreases performance, then the resource is inflexible. In contrast, if performance is fairly uniform across its range, then it is flexible. Robustness is especially important in guaranteeing quality (see Example 5.2) and in preventing a less-flexible, but lower-cost competitor from cherry-picking.

Tailoring the appropriate type of flexibility

The principle of alignment suggests that the implemented kind of flexibility should be tailored to the customer value proposition specified by competitive strategy. Scope flexibility is desirable for strategies that emphasize variety and customization. Then, the same set of resources can be used to process multiple products or services. Agility is important when competing on timeliness and responsiveness. Finally, robustness is most important for strategies that emphasize cost and quality.

5.3 | OBSTACLES TO ACHIEVING FLEXIBILITY

There is no such thing as a free lunch; likewise, the benefits of flexibility certainly do not come for free.

Flexibility is expensive and difficult to value

The greatest obstacle to achieving flexibility is the fact that flexible assets cost more than do their dedicated counterparts, while it is difficult to measure, value, and convey their benefits. Flexibility costs are typically less favorable both in investment and marginal production costs. A flexible resource's wider scope requires broader capabilities and thus higher investment costs than a dedicated resource would need, as Figure 5.2 showed. Similarly, loss of specialization benefits typically decreases productivity and increases marginal processing costs so that the unit contribution margins when using a flexible asset are lower than when using a dedicated resource.

In contrast to valuing its costs, valuing the benefits of flexibility involves estimating scale economies and uncertain forecasts (as we will see later), which are not easily explained to the unacquainted and are often open to interpretation.

Flexibility is not used appropriately

Many historic promises of flexible technology have gone unfulfilled, strengthening the beliefs of skeptics. The reason is not necessarily that the promise was not there. Rather, the potential was never exercised. Recall that scope flexibility is the ability to process a wide variety of products. If managers invest in flexible technology and subsequently use it to process a small set of products, one cannot infer that flexibility has little value. (Rather, one should infer that such managers have not heard of the principle of alignment.) Jaikumar's study on flexible manufacturing systems, discussed earlier in Chapter 2, summed it up well: "the technology itself is not to blame, it is management that makes the difference."

Flexibility is not well understood

A third obstacle is that it is often unclear which features of a process must be changed to enhance its flexibility. Conventional wisdom asserts that cross-training and computer integration increase flexibility, but Upton (1995) found three contradicting insights in his empirical study of paper factories:

1. The degree of computer integration was uncorrelated with increased flexibility in scope or agility. The reason is not that computer integration cannot be effective; it definitely is in supply chain coordination and replenishment. Rather, cost considerations may limit the scope of activities that the software can deal with, leading to the "there isn't a button for that" problem. Operators could once handle extreme demands, but computer integration eliminated that option.

2. While scope flexibility typically decreases with scale (large plants made a smaller range of products), agility-flexibility is not correlated with scale:

small operations are not necessarily more nimble at changeovers than large ones are.

3. Finally, most of the differences in plant flexibility could be explained by managerial action rather than by structural differences in processes. Unless managers make the goals of flexibility clear and reinforce them with aligned measurement systems, incentives, training, and mindset, the promise of flexibility remains unfulfilled. "People count more than machines," summarizes Upton (1995).

Complexity, competition, and customer perception

While economic theory hails the benefits of having more choices, increased flexibility requires more decision making and can lead to higher organizational complexity. In dedicated product-focused systems, less system-wide information and fewer decisions are needed, while authority, incentives, and goals are often clearer.

Competitive reasons sometimes preclude flexibility. For example, the majority of Hewlett-Packard's profits come from the sale of toner cartridges for its printers, a strategy similar to Gillette's strategy of selling cheap razors but expensive blades. Lower-priced copy-cat cartridges are the greatest danger to such a strategy. Given this competitive risk, it would be foolish for HP to design a common cartridge that would fit a majority of its printer models (even though that would reduce costs in the short run).

Finally, in addition to complexity and competition, one must carefully consider customer perception and reaction when deciding on flexibility. The experiences of Jaguar and Lexus are telling examples of the danger of platform sharing with lower-end vehicles. The Jaguar X-type shared the Ford Mondeo platform, while the Lexus ES300 shared the Toyota Camry platform. Both cars were questioned to be "real" Jaguars or Lexuses and customers questioned their incremental value above the "base car." (The wholesale part-sharing and selling of nearly identical finished products under different names or brands has become known as "badge engineering" in Germany.)

5.4 | PRODUCT DESIGN STRATEGIES FOR FLEXIBILITY

There are various approaches to increase the scope, agility, and robustness dimensions of flexibility. Some work on the process design, while others focus on the product design, although often both the product and the process are impacted. Here we review approaches that increase flexibility through *product* design; the next section considers process approaches.

Standard or universal design

A *standard* or *universal design* is a product design strategy that aims to satisfy different demands and needs with a single product or service. This strategy is illustrated by Henry Ford's statement that "you can have it in any color as long as it is black," or any standard (governmental) service. A universal design must decide which needs to cover. It can do this by aiming high, which results in high functionality at high cost, or by aiming low.

Typically, a successful universal design strategy is reserved for dominant companies or monopolies. Most companies use more flexible design strategies to offer more variety while retaining the operational benefits of some standardization. Commonality and modularity are two examples.

Component commonality and platform sharing

Component commonality is a design strategy whereby different products or services share a common component. Many restaurants have several dishes that share a common set of vegetables and side dishes. Swatch watches are designed to share a common interior (the "movement") while the exterior parts can differ. Ikea uses component commonality in its furniture.

Platform sharing is similar in concept to component commonality, but typically impacts a broader set of people and activities. Platform sharing originally referred to the practice of sharing a common wheelbase, powertrain, and other elements among different automobile models. Nowadays, the wheelbase can be long or short, narrow or wide—and a platform has become synonymous with "one group of engineers" who design several vehicles from a common vehicle architecture.

The benefits of platform sharing include:

- commonality in component design, manufacturing, sourcing, and inventory management,

- allowing mixed production on a single process (level loading of the assembly line),

- and level loading of new product development by staggering new product launches from the same platform.

For example, Volkswagen's "A5 platform," the fifth generation of its compact car platform, is shared by the 2003 VW Touran; 2004 VW Golf, VW Caddy, Audi A3, Seat Altea; 2005 Skoda Octavia and Seat Toledo; 2006 VW Jetta/Bora and Seat Leon; and perhaps a small crossover SUV in 2008.

Platform sharing brings significant cost savings. Nissan has reduced the number of platforms it uses from 34 in 1999 to 15 in 2004. The goal is to bring the number of platforms that the Renault-Nissan alliance uses down to 10 in 2010. "That's important because every shared platform can add $500 million-plus in annual savings for each carmaker. Renault will also share eight engine designs with Nissan." (Bremner, Edmonson, and Dawson 2004) Platform sharing also influences the location of product manufacturing. The Mercedes R-class discussed in Example 1.2 (p. 8) is produced in Alabama in part because it shares platforms with the M-class.

Modular design

Modularity is a design strategy where many different products or services are assembled from a set of modules or building blocks that are loosely coupled to the rest of the system. Modularity also promotes serviceability. It can also

---

Analytics Box 5.1 Modularity provides exponential scope flexibility

To appreciate the variety that can be achieved through modularity, consider this example. Assume a PC uses 10 modules, each of which have 5 different "grades," or choices; e.g., a 1Ghz, 1.5 Ghz, 1.8 Ghz, 2Ghz, and 3Ghz chip. The number of product combinations that can be designed from these $10 \times 5 = 50$ components is

$$5 \text{ (module 1 choices)} \times 5 \text{ (module 2 choices)} \times \cdots \times 5 \text{ (module 10 choices)},$$

which is 5^{10} or about 10 million! Scope flexibility thus grows exponentially in the number of modules:

$$\text{scope flexibility} = (\text{\# of choices per module})^{\text{\# of modules}}.$$

When the number of choices per module is high, an almost endless variety can be obtained from just a few modules or components.

Paint coloring is another example: adding a specific combination of the three or four basic color pigments—red, green, and blue (RGB) or cyan, magenta, yellow, and black (CMYK)—to white paint can produce any possible hue.

---

be applied to process design where a plant can be built in modules, allowing adjustment over time.

Modularity is the extension of commonality to multiple components that can be mixed and matched into a wide variety of end-products. The prototypical example of modularity is the personal computer composed of a modest number of interchangeable components such as a microprocessor, a hard drive, memory chips, video cards, keyboards, displays, etc. Similarly, executive education and consulting engagements are often based on a tailored subset of modules. Object-oriented programming applies object or modules that can be written and maintained independently of the source code of other objects. Containers apply modularity to transportation.

The crucial requirement is that all modules have standard interfaces so that they can easily be interchanged. Interface knowledge is sufficient for others to use the modules; the inner working and mechanisms of the modules can be kept private. Once interfaces are agreed upon, each module can be designed, maintained, and improved independently of others. The benefits of modularity affect all three types of flexibility:

- scope flexibility increases exponentially in the number of modules. This means that almost endless variety can be offered with a reasonably small number of modules, as illustrated by Analytics Box 5.1.

- agility in terms of fast product design and updating. Different modules can be designed or updated in parallel, thereby dramatically shortening the product design time compared to a sequential design. One can even introduce more frequent (but incremental) updates by updating one module at a time.

- robustness: low cost and high reliability due to re-using modules and scale economies. Modularity allows a divide-and-conquer strategy that reduces complexity and promotes operational focus, as discussed in Chapter 2.

These three benefits of modularity allow the disintegration of the value chain, a topic that we will return to when discussing outsourcing in Chapter 7.

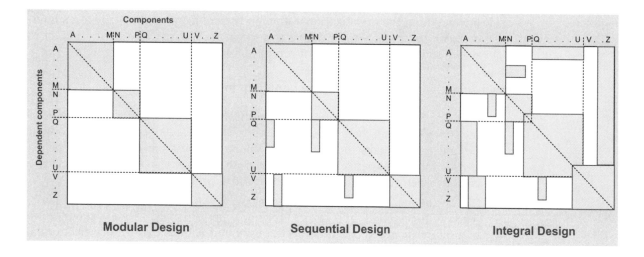

Figure 5.3 Design structure matrices show which components (left column) are dependent on other components (top row). For example, in the integral design, component A depends on components A-M, Q-U and W-Z (Loch, DeMeyer, and Pich 2006).

Diagnosing complexity

The design structure matrix (DSM) is a practical tool to map the complexity of a design or project. The DSM shows which components or tasks are dependent on or interact with other components or tasks. Interaction may take the form of, for example, information (one task requires input from the other), space or resources sharing, material (one task provides material used by the other), or constraints (one task may produce a system parameter that constrains the other task), according to Loch, DeMeyer, and Pich (2006).

For example, consider the three design structure matrices in Figure 5.3. In the matrix on the left, components A to M are coupled or "integrated," and form a subproject that must be managed by one team. Similar to N-P, Q-U and V-Z. The four subprojects, however, do not interact and thus can be executed and optimized in parallel.

In the middle matrix, components Q-R depend on A but not vice versa. Q-R thus are sequentially dependent on A and sequential execution is natural.

In the matrix on the right, however, even subprojects such as A-M and Q-U are interdependent. For example, A and Q-U are coupled even though they are in separate subprojects. The overall project is said to be very complex and integrated. Complexity typically is a function of the number of decision variables and the number of interactions among them. Consequently, Loch, DeMeyer, and Pich (2006) propose that the complexity of a design matrix can be roughly estimated as a product:

Complexity = (sum of all elements) x (sum of all interactions).

In practice, interactions occur in three domains simultaneously: the system domain (where components interact), the task domain (where project activities interact), and the organizational domain (where teams and stakeholders interact). For each of these three domains, a separate DSM may be drawn. Chapter 10 will describe the implications of complexity to innovation management.

The downside of modular design is the benefit of integral design

Modular designs have many advantages from a business or life cycle engineering standpoint, but there are still trade-offs. Whitney (2004) claims that modular designs tend to have more parts and favor "business performance" at the expense of technical performance. Modular design may also suffer from negative customer perception and a lack of competitive protection.

The opposite of a modular design is an *integral design* which has fewer parts, tends to be coupled, and favors "technical performance." Some examples are high-performance sport motorcycles, light and compact consumer electronics, precision machines and game software. In contrast to modular designs, integral designs tend to be more complex and do not lend themselves to a "divide-and-conquer" strategy. Yet they allow a better use of space (volume), mass, and energy during operations, according to Hölttä, Suh, and de Weck (2005).

Adaptable design

Adaptable designs can be adjusted to specific needs. The adjustment can be reversible or irreversible, and can be made from a finite or infinite selection of choices. For example, European pants are often sold by waist-size only, while the standard length is tailored after purchase. Length tailoring allows infinite choice and can be reversible (by cuffing) or irreversible (by cutting excess fabric). Software, as well as mechanical and electric designs, can have a finite number of "settings" that can be customized by the designer, the manufacturer, the dealer, or the customer. The result is a customized software that does not need debugging.

Adaptable and modular designs are often used in mass customization, as we will soon discuss. However, adaptable design is somewhat independent from standard, common, or modular design. Indeed, a standard microprocessor design can be made adaptable just by "turning off features" and purposely reducing functionality. (Chapter 8 will further examine this method of product differentiation and revenue maximization.) Modular designs like paint mixing can be infinitely adjustable.

Different impact on flexibility

Design methods cover a wide range in terms of their impact on scope flexibility. Universal, standard, and integral designs offer no scope flexibility, whereas the scope of modular designs is exponential in the number of modules, as illustrated in Figure 5.4. Single component sharing lies in between the two and allows a linear increase of the number of variants. Full custom design offers unlimited flexibility. Adaptable designs allow both scope flexibility and agility.

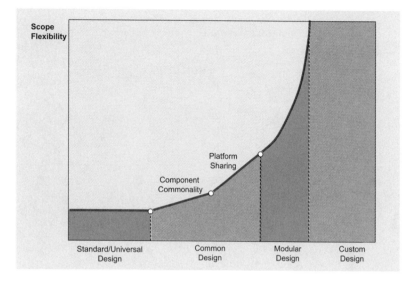

Figure 5.4 Product design strategies offer an increasing amount of variety, or scope flexibility.

5.5 | PROCESS DESIGN STRATEGIES FOR FLEXIBILITY

Just like products, *process* networks be designed to increase flexibility. Consider the operations of a credit card company, which includes setting up new accounts as well as answering service calls about credit card statements. The question is how to best allocate resources to those two tasks. Figure 5.5 illustrates five possible network designs to answer that question. Panel A shows the base-case design which uses two dedicated resources. New accounts and service calls are handled by two separate groups of employees. Let us investigate the four other potential network designs that increase flexibility.

Resource sharing

Asset or *resource sharing* means that different activities share the same, flexible resources, as represented by panel C in Figure 5.5. It is the process design counterpart of component sharing. In our example, a cross-trained call center operator can both service new account subscriptions as well as solve help requests. In manufacturing, the same flexible equipment can produce two products.

Resource sharing often requires centralization or collocation of the shared activities, which is not necessary in the case of dedicated processes (panel A in Fig. 5.5) nor in shared information-based services such as call centers.

Resource substitution

Resource substitution achieves an intermediate degree of flexibility between the ones obtained by dedicated and shared assets. Resource substitution, repre-

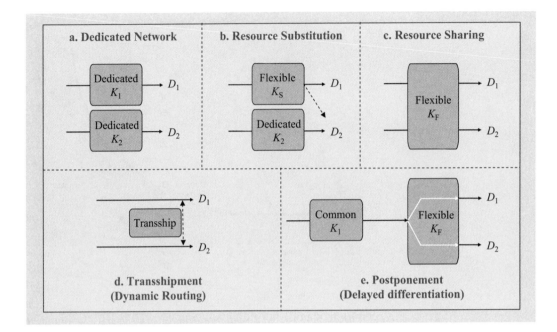

Figure 5.5 Several process design strategies to increase flexibility above a dedicated network (a). Resource sharing and substitution (top row) apply to a single stage in the value chain. Transshipment and postponement (bottom row) implicitly assume two or more stages.

sented by panel B in Figure 5.5, requires that at least one asset is flexible while the other asset can be dedicated. In our example, call center operators that service new account subscriptions can also solve help requests. The natural activities for each are to serve their allocated products, but the flexible asset has the option of substituting for the dedicated one in order to respond to unexpected deviations from the natural tasks. (We use a dashed line to stress the fact that substitution is typically used sparingly because it often incurs higher costs than performing the natural activities.)

Panel B shows downward substitution, which is often used in services such as car rentals, airlines and hotels where the higher service-class asset can also satisfy lower service-class demand. Such flexibility reduces the capacity shortage cost of the lower-service assets and can also be used for cross-selling.

Transshipment

Transshipment means re-locating assets, as represented by panel D in Figure 5.5. This practice is powerful in retail and distribution networks and helps match excess demand in one location with excess capacity in another. For example, if a customer requests an item that is out-of-stock, Nordstrom will transship it from the nearest location that has it in stock.

Transshipment is typically preceded by earlier processing activities in the value chain. For example, any of the "single-stage" network modules on the top row of Figure 5.5 could precede and be combined with transshipment. In a multi-product setting, transshipment can follow resource substitution when the two resources are in different locations. The result is *horizontal integration* without physical centralization.

Both transshipment and substitution flexibility introduce additional complexity into network control: dynamic decision making on routes, also known as *routing flexibility*, which requires real-time network information. (Therefore, the integration is also called *virtual centralization*.)

Postponed differentiation and late customization

Postponed differentiation and *late customization* delay customer-specific activities such as product assembly or service completion, so that earlier activities can be common to all customers. For example, HP manufactures printers in Vancouver in anticipation of worldwide demand but allocates and slightly adapts to specific markets only a few weeks before sales. The leading Norwegian ski manufacturer Madshus is about to start making skateboards based on a seven-layer ski sandwich technology, using a wood core and fiber. The core process is joint for both skis and skateboards. Garment producer Benetton can produce uncolored ("in greggio") garments in advance and postpone their dyeing until close to the sales season. The publication process of newspapers also uses postponement when common inserts are written and printed long before the front-page and the additional local news.

If assembly or completion is executed after the customer order is known, the process is called *assembly-to-order*(ATO). This network design can also be used in services. For example, a software company recently divided its engineering team into two groups: one group was focused on technology development and enhanced the software platform; the other team, called Professional Services, was more customer focused and used the platform to develop applications for the customer. By breaking up the process into two stages where the first one is common, represented by panel E in Figure 5.5, delayed differentiation finds an intermediate solution between dedicated and fully flexible processes. It is also at the core of mass customization.

5.6 | MASS CUSTOMIZATION

Mass customization is a compromise between mass production and full custom work. It balances the demand benefits of customization with the supply efficiencies of standardization by limiting customer choice to a pre-set range while increasing the flexibility of a flow process (Fig. 5.6). Thus, mass customization involves tailoring a product or service to each customer's wishes within certain limits, and delivering and administering it with a flexible flow process (a flow shop with negligible changeover times). It recognizes that many customers are looking to escape mass products, but do not mind mass production.

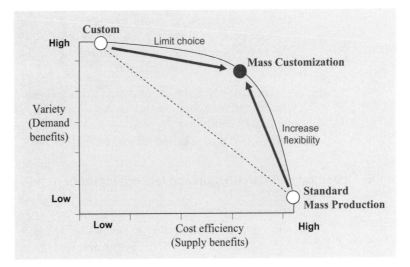

Figure 5.6 Mass customization is a compromise between mass production and fully customized work. It balances demand for variety and supply efficiency by limiting choice while increasing process flexibility.

Examples include both bricks and clicks

The mass customization matrix of Figure 5.7 shows how mass customization provides goods and services both through conventional channels and the Internet. Indeed, it can be argued that conventional retail channels have been providing mass customization for a long time. Restaurants, coffee shops like Starbucks, and insurance companies like American Family Insurance let customers choose from a menu and accordingly provide a tailored, flexible service, which can broadly be interpreted as mass customization. A similar process occurs with the provision of goods: Mercedes-Benz provides substantial mass customization of its vehicles so that few, if any, identical E-class vehicles roll of its assembly line in the Sindelfingen plant.[1] Furthermore, Build-a-Bear lets customers build their own stuffed animals in their store.

It was recent Internet companies, however, that have coined mass customization into a popular business term. The Internet is an effective channel to capture customer choice into the process, and has been used successfully in computer assembly (Dell), messenger bags (Timbuk2), tax preparation (H&R Block), and grocery delivery (Peapod, discussed in detail in the case study on p. 415).

Technology behind mass customization

Mass customization impacts three of the four technology types described in Chapter 1:

- Coordination and information technology are used to allow customers to self-design their product and transmit that information to the fulfillment

---

[1]The 2002 Mercedes E-Class had an astronomical 3×10^{24} different variations compared to the 157,584 units sold in Europe, according to Pil and Holweg (2004).

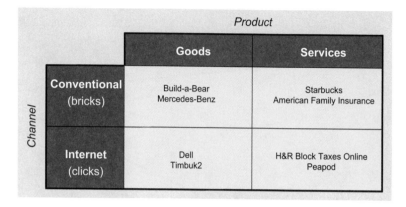

Figure 5.7 Mass customization provides goods and services both through conventional channels and the Internet.

process. The Internet removes customer and process collocation requirements and facilitates automating this information flow and including it in billing and order tracking.

- Product technology uses modularity and platforms along with adaptable designs. The product really is a menu of options and rationalized standardization (smart choice of options) is key.

- Process technology uses flexibility through postponement; at least the last process step must be able to quickly support a batch size of one. This inherent delay is mass customization's biggest downside: waiting.

How to create industrial intimacy?

When these technologies are carefully designed in concert, mass customized services can provide industrial intimacy. Kolesar, van Ryzin, and Cutler (1998) provide some suggestions on how to do achieve that, including:

1. Build customer knowledge into the service-delivery system. Customer relationship management (CRM) software is a typical tool.

2. Promote value-enhancing self-servicing. The use of travel web sites and self-service check-in transform service providers from work doers into self-servicing facility providers. Obviously, the essential trade-off remains between work done *by* the customer and work done *for* the customer.

3. Let customers design the product and integrate revenue management methods. For example, Amazon customers can choose direct overnight shipping or delayed bundled shipping. We will investigate revenue management further in Chapter 8.

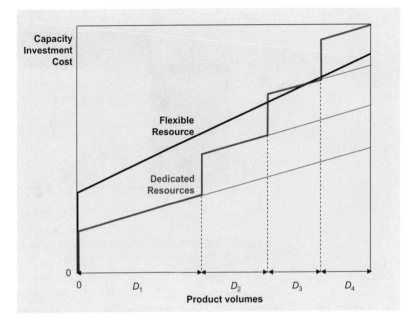

Figure 5.8 Flexible resources serve aggregate volumes and benefit more from economies of scale in capacity investment than do a set of dedicated resources.

5.7 | VALUING FLEXIBILITY AND CONSOLIDATION

All product and process designs for flexibility essentially embody some aggregation or contingent decision making. Therefore, the three main value sources or "drivers" of flexibility are:

1. scale economies (aggregating volumes),

2. risk pooling (aggregating volatilities),

3. allocation flexibility and information updating (real options).

Let us analyze each value source in detail.

1. Scale economies (aggregating volumes)

Aggregating volumes can yield scale economies at many stages in the value chain, including product design (of one product or re-use earlier designs); sourcing (centralized sourcing may benefit from quantity discounts); capacity investment (scale economies); transportation (coordinated or in bulk); storage (smooth and reduce cycle stock); and overhead. To illustrate this aspect, we examine scale economies in capacity and storage.

Capacity investment typically exhibits economies of scale. The flexible resource is scaled for aggregate volume and thus benefits more from economies of scale than does a dedicated resource, which is scaled for a single activity's volume. To analyze the essence of this value driver, consider the simplest setting where the annual demand D_i for product i is deterministic and constant over time. When dedicated resources are used, the capacity of product-i asset is D_i. Consider the fixed-cost investment function $C(K) = c_0 + c_K K$ and assume for simplicity that all dedicated assets have identical fixed and marginal costs. Adding a resource incurs a fixed cost which is represented by a vertical cost jump in Figure 5.8, which assumes four product volumes.

In contrast, if one flexible asset is used, only one fixed cost is incurred and capacity is sized to the aggregate demand $\sum_i D_i$. Higher scope requirements for the flexible resource imply more expensive capabilities that typically increase both fixed and marginal investment costs above those of a dedicated resource. In Figure 5.8 the fixed and marginal investment costs of the flexible resource are about double than those of a dedicated resource. Nevertheless, a flexible resource can have lower capacity investment costs by saving on fixed costs (or economies of scale in general). This value driver becomes more important when scale economies are larger and when numerous smaller volumes are aggregated.

To illustrate how a flexible resource also drives scale economies at other activities in the operational system, consider sourcing or transportation. Each incurs a fixed cost S per order or transport, which implies that they enjoy scale economies: N dedicated systems means incurring N fixed costs. With the optimal batch size (see Appendix 2A p. 431), the minimal annual inventory and setup cost is:

$$N \text{ dedicated systems} \quad : \quad \sqrt{2D_1 SH} + \sqrt{2D_2 SH} + \cdots + \sqrt{2D_N SH}$$
$$1 \text{ flexible system} \quad : \quad \sqrt{2(D_1 + D_2 + \cdots + D_N)SH}.$$

When all annual demands are similar, we see that the:

$$\text{relative consolidation savings from scale economies} = 1 - \frac{1}{\sqrt{N}}.$$

The value of flexibility thus increases as it replaces more dedicated systems. As shown in Figure 5.9, however, the marginal value decreases: consolidating 4 systems cuts costs by 50%, but consolidating an additional 4 only saves an additional 15%. However, this is good news! It shows that a little flexibility goes a long way. This insight can be extended to other settings and thus constitutes a new principle:

Principle 7 (Flexibility) The value of flexibility exhibits decreasing returns. "A little flexibility goes a long way" and is often preferred to full flexibility.

---

2. Risk pooling (aggregating volatilities)

Flexibility serves aggregate demand streams and enjoys not only economies of scale from aggregating average volumes, but also risk pooling from aggregating volatilities. Recall that the aggregation property of forecasting (p. 80) stems from the fact that, when aggregating two volatilities, individual fluctuations partly cancel out, thus reducing total relative volatility. This effect is also known as

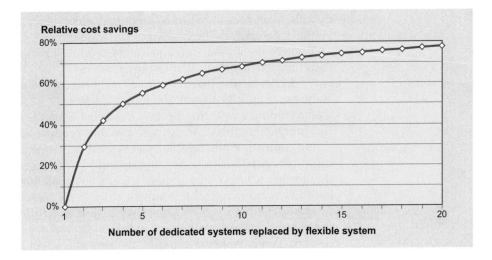

Figure 5.9 The relative cost savings from consolidating a number of dedicated systems into one flexible system shows decreasing returns.

risk pooling, diversification, statistical economies of scale, or the portfolio effect. Indeed, it is the fundamental reason for preferring financial portfolios.

To value risk pooling, we must quantify it. Recall from Chapter 3 that the standard deviation σ is one measure of the volatility of a random variable. Risk pooling means that the pooled risk is less than the sum of the risks: $\sigma_{\text{pool}} \leq \sigma_1 + \sigma_2$. The risk reduction depends not only on the standard deviations, but also on the correlation between two random variables (see Analytics Box 5.2). The more negative the correlation, the more likely that one variable's upside coincides with the other's downside (as represented in Figure 5.10) and the lower the pooled volatility. The relative reduction in volatility measures the:

$$\text{Risk pooling effectiveness} = 1 - \frac{\sigma_{\text{pool}}}{\sigma_1 + \sigma_2},$$

which decreases as the correlation or the difference in volatilities increases, as shown by Figure 5.10. Thus, risk pooling is most effective when we pool risks of similar magnitude that are negatively correlated. Yet pooling even weakly positively correlated risks can still reduce risk up to 30%.

The principle that "a little flexibility goes a long way" applies to risk pooling effectiveness. To see this, consider pooling N demands (either from N different products, locations, or postponed weeks of leadtimes). Assume, for analytical simplicity, that all demands have similar volatility σ and are uncorrelated. Then, the pooled volatility is $\sqrt{N}\sigma$ (apply equation 5.1 repeatedly) so that:

$$\text{Risk pooling effectiveness} = 1 - \frac{1}{\sqrt{N}},$$

exactly the same as the savings from economies of scale shown in Figure 5.9!
The financial value of risk pooling stems from:

Analytics Box 5.2 Quantifying Risk Pooling

Risk pooling means that aggregation reduces risk or volatility. Recall from Chapter 3 that the standard deviation σ is one measure of the volatility of a random variable, such as demand. Risk pooling also depends strongly on the correlation between two random variables D_1 and D_2. Let μ_i denote the mean and σ_i the standard deviation of D_i. The *correlation* coefficient ρ between D_1 and D_2 is a number between -1 and $+1$ defined as

$$\text{correlation coefficient } \rho = \frac{\text{covariance}}{\sigma_1 \sigma_2} = \frac{\mathbb{E}[(D_1 - \mu_1)(D_2 - \mu_2)]}{\sigma_1 \sigma_2},$$

where $\mathbb{E}$ denotes expectation. The standard deviation of the aggregate or sum of two random variables with correlation coefficient ρ is

$$\sigma_{\text{pool}} = \sqrt{\sigma_1^2 + 2\rho\sigma_1\sigma_2 + \sigma_2^2} \leq \sigma_1 + \sigma_2, \tag{5.1}$$

because σ_{pool} increases as correlation increases and $\rho \leq 1$. Setting $\sigma_1 = \sigma_2$ and $\rho = -1$ yields two additional bounds that together yield:

$$\max\left(\sqrt{\frac{1+\rho}{2}}, \frac{|\sigma_1 - \sigma_2|}{\sigma_1 + \sigma_2}\right) \leq \frac{\sigma_{\text{pool}}}{\sigma_1 + \sigma_2} \leq 1.$$

1. Reduced safety capacity or inventory. Recall that safety levels scale proportional to volatility (Fig. 3.6 on p. 91) so that their relative cost reduction equals the risk pooling effectiveness.

2. Increased revenues and service levels. Recall that expected shortfall also scales proportional to volatility (Fig. 3.6). With impatient customers, risk pooling reduces lost sales by the same proportion as does risk pooling effectiveness. Patient customers see shorter backlogs and waiting times.

3. Reduced profit variance risk, which is a form of operational hedging that we further discuss in Chapter 9.

Analytics Box 5.3 illustrates calculations for a product and for a service company. Notice the win-win effect: a company can choose to increase service levels while still reducing safety levels.

3. Allocation flexibility and information updating (real options)

The third value source stems from contingent decision making (real options) embedded in flexibility. Flexibility has a *switching option* that allows you to switch capacity allocation to the more profitable product. To see this, compare again two dedicated systems, each with capacity 100, to a flexible system with a capacity of 200. Assume the actual demand on Monday for each product is 120 and that product 1 fetches a contribution margin of $200 versus $100 for product 2. The dedicated strategy sells 100 units of each product. In contrast, the flexible system can switch capacity allocation and sell 120 units of product 1 and only 80 units of product 2. The value of the switching option on that Monday is a profit increase of 20 units $\times (\$200 - \$100) = \$2,000$.

Allocation flexibility allows dynamic profit maximization, whereas risk pooling is simply the passive aggregation of volatilities. This switching option retains

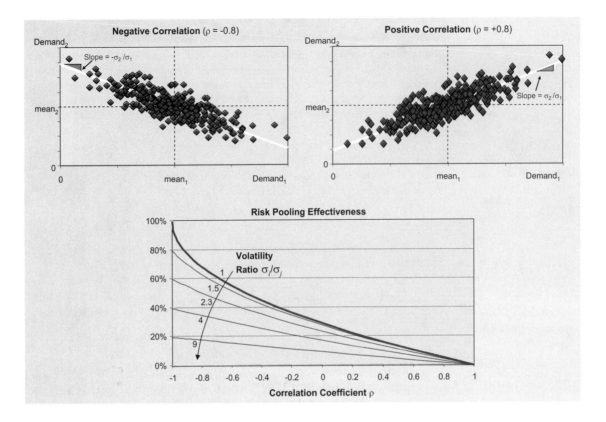

Figure 5.10 The effectiveness of risk pooling depends on the correlation coefficient. The top plots show sample points of two normal random variables; the symmetry axis has slope σ_2/σ_1. With a negative correlation (left), upside variations in one variable are more likely to go together with the other variable's downside variations, leading to lower pooled volatility. Risk pooling effectiveness is also reduced when the difference in volatilities grows (bottom).

value even with perfectly positively correlated demands, as long as products are heterogeneous in contribution margins.

The switching option is a special case of the option to postpone decision making. The benefits of scale economies, risk pooling, and allocation flexibility accrue even in a stationary setting where the demand forecasts do not change over time. When future demand is correlated with current demand, postponement allows you to observe more information, update forecasts, and make better decisions. For example, a flexible plant can be used for prototyping and for launching new (low-volume) products while observing market reactions or technology yields. After some time, forecasts can be updated (yet remain uncertain) and you may decide to "kill" a product, move it to a high-volume process, or replace it altogether by other products that use common components. This waiting option embedded in flexibility is valued using decision tree analysis, as we saw in section 4.5 on p. 131.

Analytics Box 5.3 The cost, revenue, and service value of risk pooling

Consider a product company such as Toyota. Assume the demand forecasts for two products have similar volatilities σ with correlation coefficient ρ. Platform sharing allows both products to be assembled to order on a flexible assembly line. The value of flexibility relative to two dedicated lines and deriving purely from risk pooling is:

1. Reduction in safety capacity: when service probabilities p in the dedicated and flexible system are equal and exceed 50%, the standardized safety level $z = \text{norminv}(p)$ is positive. The safety capacity of the flexible line equals $z\sigma_{\text{pool}} = z\sigma\sqrt{2(1+\rho)}$, which is less than $2z\sigma$, the sum of safety capacities in the dedicated systems.

2. Increase in revenues and service: keeping service probabilities and z equal, the flexible system enjoys a smaller shortfall of $\sigma_{\text{pool}}L(z)$ compared to $2\sigma L(z)$ in the dedicated systems. Fewer lost sales increase revenues from impatient customers. Patient customers experience smaller backlogs and waiting times.

To illustrate similar value drivers from risk pooling for service companies, consider Choice Hotels International and 1-800-Flowers who rent call-center employees to each other, as discussed in Chapter 3. Service operations are modeled by queuing systems, and serving two sets of customers by one group of flexible, cross-trained operators leads to risk pooling due to two effects: resource pooling and arrival pooling. Serving both service requests by a single resource pool prevents asynchronized idleness (in a dedicated system, server 1 can be idle while server 2 has a queue) and decreases statistical dependence among customers (in a dedicated system, server 1 can be tied up with a long type 1 service request which delays all type 1 customers, while in a flexible system server 2 can keep serving all customers). Arrival pooling means that the total relative volatility in arrivals to the flexible system is less than the sum of volatilities in dedicated systems. The joint result of arrival and resource pooling is that:

1. Safety capacity can be reduced to keep the same service levels (waiting times).

2. Revenues increase because less volatility leads to shorter lines so that fewer customers will abandon or balk. Patient customers again enjoy shorter waiting times.

Forecast updating captures more realism and nuance than does revenue maximization through contingent allocation. In our previous example, we implicitly assumed that the switching option of allocation flexibility was exercised after the complete resolution of Monday's demand uncertainty and that knowing Monday's product demands did not tell us anything about the demand for Tuesday. Either of these two strong assumptions can be relaxed. In this more realistic setting, the value of flexibility captures the (relative) amount of available information when the switching decision is made. Intuitively, the longer the firm can wait before locking in decisions, the better it can adapt to dynamically evolving market conditions.

In summary, the third value driver of flexibility stems from contingent decision making, which provides two real options: the option to wait for better information, and the option to switch capacity allocation.

Putting it all together: valuing consolidation, economies of scope, and tailored focus

Economies of scope refers to the incremental value obtained from sharing assets over several markets or products. Assets can be shared by "similar" products, such as by commonality and platform sharing in the auto industry, or by different markets. For example, the Coca-Cola Company derives economies of scope by sharing its distribution network not only over its traditional line of soft drinks, but also over its newer Dasani brand of plain water that was introduced in 1999. Similar scope economies apply to host-complement settings such as Gillette's razor-blade strategy, HP's printer-cartridge, and video players-DVDs.

Valuing economies of scope is similar to valuing consolidation. We should carefully analyze the value chain to identify activities that share assets. Following our framework above, we then value each asset sharing by assessing the value contribution of economies of scale, risk pooling, and real options. This valuation approach also allows us to determine the tailored degree of focus (recall Fig. 2.10 on p. 56), i.e., where we should share assets and where we should not.

5.8 | OPTIMIZING FLEXIBILITY FOR A MULTI-PRODUCT FIRM

Now that we know the costs and benefits of flexibility we must "tailor flexibility," by determining the appropriate amount of flexibility for the task at hand. According to the value maximization principle, "appropriate" means a usage that maximizes value.

But before we turn our attention to examples of tailored flexibility, let us first learn how to represent and optimize flexibility .

Representing capacity for a multi-product firm

Most organizations use many resource types to process several goods and services. In the previous chapter, we already learned how to model different types of resources in aggregate planning by representing their capacity constraints. That same approach can be used to represent and optimize flexibility.

The only complication is that the demand forecast needs more care: to properly capture the three value drivers of flexibility–scale economies, risk pooling, and allocation flexibility–we must not only forecast average demand volumes for each product, but also the total uncertainty embodied in *multi-product* demand . In order to illustrate this process, let us consider a simplified example of flexible technology.

A stylized example: Auto Co.

Auto Co. is introducing two car models and must decide on a capacity portfolio strategy: should it use two product-dedicated assembly lines, one flexible line, or a tailored combination of the two?

The two models, Afour and Bassat, share a platform but the Afour commands the higher price and unit contribution margin of $2000 versus the Bas-

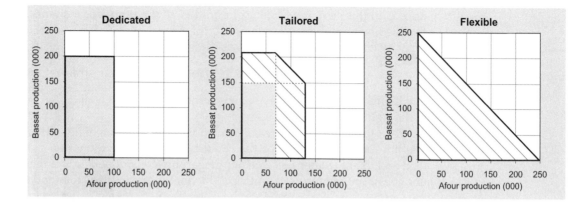

Figure 5.11 Auto Co. can invest in two dedicated capacities (left), one flexible capacity (right), or a tailored combination (middle). Flexible capacity is diagonally shaded.

sat's $1000. Investing in capacity involves a significant fixed cost and a variable cost that increases with the installed capacity size. For simplicity, we will assume that the fixed cost for the dedicated strategy equals that for the flexible strategy and hence does not impact our technology strategy choice. However, the capacity cost per unit for an Afour dedicated line is $800, slightly greater than the $700 for the Bassat line. A flexible line, however, costs $900 per unit of annual capacity.

Let us investigate Auto Co's optimal flexibility strategy using a capacity model that is easily analyzed in this downloadable spreadsheet.

Download `Flexibility_Auto.xls` from www.vanmieghem.us

Representing dedicated and flexible capacity

Assume Auto Co. invests in two dedicated assembly lines with annual capacities of $100,000$ Afours and $200,000$ Bassats. Any annual production volume of Afours below 100,000 and of Bassats below 200,000 is within capacity. If we use x_A and x_B to denote the annual production quantities of Afours and Bassats produced on its dedicated line, the capacity constraints of the dedicated strategy can be represented as:

$$x_A \leq 100,000 \quad \text{(dedicated Afour capacity constraint)}$$
$$x_B \leq 200,000 \quad \text{(dedicated Bassat capacity constraint)} \tag{5.2}$$

together with the nonnegativity constraints $x_A, x_B \geq 0$. In other words, the capacity of the two-product company Auto Co. is the set of production pairs (x_A, x_B) that satisfy the capacity constraints (5.2). A dedicated capacity strategy thus has a rectangular capacity region as represented by the left panel in Figure 5.11.

In contrast, if Auto Co. used a product-flexible line with capacity $250,000$, then any sum of production quantities up to $250,000$ units per year can be produced. In this case, it will be useful to denote the production quantities on the flexible line by different variables: x'_A for Afours and x'_B for Bassats. Thus, the capacity constraints for the flexible strategy are:

$$x'_A + x'_B \leq 250,000 \qquad \text{(flexible capacity constraint)} \qquad (5.3)$$

together with the nonnegativity constraint $x'_A, x'_B \geq 0$, which define the triangle in the right panel of Figure 5.11.

If Auto Co. decides to invest in a tailored combination of dedicated and flexible lines, the constraints for the capacity portfolio are the union of equations (5.2) and (5.3) together with the non-negativity constraints. Notice that we have one constraint per resource. Total production quantities for Afour and Bassat are $x_A + x'_A$ and $x_B + x'_B$, respectively. Their capacity region is represented by the "extended rectangle with cut-off corner" in the middle panel of Figure 5.11.

Capturing allocation flexibility: the switching option

Production levels are typically set in response to market conditions, but are constrained by earlier capacity investments. Recall that flexible capacity can switch its capacity allocation (and thus product mix) to maximize profit. The switching option is captured by making production levels (and thus the mix) contingent on observed market demands.[2] We introduce a series of activities, one for each possible demand realization, and find the contingent production levels as the solution that maximizes operating profit for a specific demand realization.

For example, assume Auto Co. has a capacity portfolio of two dedicated lines with annual capacity of $70,000$ Afours and $150,000$ Bassats, and a flexible line with capacity of $60,000$ units. If Auto Co. observes demand for $100,000$ Afour and $250,000$ Bassats, its optimal contingent production maximizes:

$$\text{operating profit} = \$2,000(x_A + x'_A) + \$1,000(x_B + x'_B) \qquad (5.4)$$

subject to

$$
\begin{array}{lll}
x_A \leq 70,000 & \text{(dedicated Afour capacity constraint)} & \\
x_B \leq 150,000 & \text{(dedicated Bassat capacity constraint)} & \\
x'_A + x'_B \leq 60,000 & \text{(flexible capacity constraint)} & (5.5) \\
x_A + x'_A \leq 100,000 & \text{(Afour demand constraint)} & \\
x_B + x'_B \leq 250,000 & \text{(Bassat demand constraint)} & \\
x_A, x_B, x'_A, x'_B \geq 0 & \text{(non-negativity constraints).} &
\end{array}
$$

This linear program is automatically solved in a spreadsheet using the Solver optimization tool, as described in Appendix 4 on p. 149. Our problem, however, is sufficiently simple and can be solved by hand: it is optimal to first allocate dedicated capacity and then allocate flexible capacity first to the highest margin product. In other words, the optimal contingent production levels are

$$x_A = 70,000; x_B = 150,000; x'_A = 30,000; x'_B = 30,000,$$

with an associated operating profit of $\$2,000 \times 70 + \$1,000 \times 180 = \$320$ million.

---

[2]The assumption that production levels can be set after annual market demands are known simplifies reality (where demand and production can vary over time). More realism is handled by adding more periods as in aggregate planning (Chapter 4).

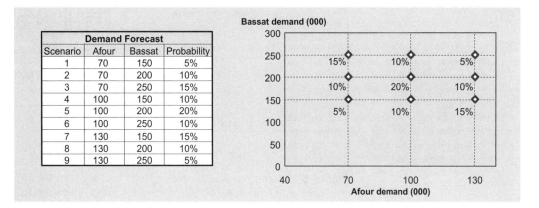

Demand Forecast			
Scenario	Afour	Bassat	Probability
1	70	150	5%
2	70	200	10%
3	70	250	15%
4	100	150	10%
5	100	200	20%
6	100	250	10%
7	130	150	15%
8	130	200	10%
9	130	250	5%

Figure 5.12 The demand forecast for Afours and Bassats. Uncertainty is captured via nine scenarios with associated probabilities. The forecast can be represented in a table (left) or a graph (right).

Capturing uncertainty in the demand forecast

The optimal flexibility strategy maximizes expected value, which depends on the demand forecast. To value flexibility, we must account for demand volatility. There are two ways to capture demand uncertainty in a capacity model: an elegant way and an easy way.

- The elegant way represents uncertainty through a multivariate probability distribution. For example, the forecast can be modeled by a normal distribution, which requires the estimation of the average demand per product and their covariance matrix. The resulting *newsvendor network* generalizes the single-dimensional newsvendor model of Chapter 3. Newsvendor networks can always be *optimized using simulation* (Appendix 5 shows you how to do this for Auto Co. in a spreadsheet) and sometimes analytically.

- The easy way assumes that uncertainty is represented through a number of scenarios that each have an associated probability. Figure 5.12 uses a table and a graph to show Auto Co.'s demand forecast with nine different scenarios. (In essence, scenarios are just a set of representative samples from the underlying probability distribution.)

Optimizing flexibility

Having chosen the "easy way," we now replicate our four activity variables nine times. We thus have one set for each scenario, in addition to three capacity portfolio variables. Figure 5.13 illustrates the decision variables for the Auto Co. example.

Notice that specifying the demand forecast and the decision variables is just an extension of steps 1 and 2 of linear planning optimization in Excel, described in Appendix 4 on p. 149. The remaining steps are unchanged; step 3 adds the capacity, demand, and nonnegativity constraints, as well as one set of constraints

Contingent Activities					Capacity Portfolio	
Scenario	x_A	x_B	x'_A	x'_B	Dedicated A	70
1	10	150	60	0	Dedicated B	150
2	70	150	0	50	Flexible	60
3	70	150	0	60		
4	70	150	30	0		
5	70	150	30	30		
6	70	150	30	30		
7	70	150	60	0		
8	70	150	60	0		
9	70	150	60	0		

Figure 5.13 After we add a set of activity variables for each scenario to the capacity variables, we can then use spreadsheet optimization to find the optimal capacity portfolio.

(5.5) for each scenario. Step 4 calculates the operating profit (5.4) for each scenario, takes expectations, and subtracts the capacity investment costs from expected operating profit to arrive at the value of the capacity portfolio. The only remaining step is to run the linear optimizer (Solver) to find the optimal capacity portfolio and contingent activities.

The outcome of this procedure, known as *stochastic linear programming*, is shown in Figure 5.13. A tailored capacity strategy is optimal. Let us discuss what that means.

5.9 | TAILORED FLEXIBILITY

Tailored flexibility refers to using the appropriate amount of flexibility for the task at hand. The flexibility principle states that the value of flexibility exhibits decreasing returns. In addition, more flexibility typically costs increasingly more. The result is that an intermediate amount of flexibility often provides the highest net present value. The appropriate amount of flexibility depends on the situation and follows from optimization. Let us review some examples of tailored flexibility.

A tailored capacity portfolio of dedicated and flexible resources

Flexibility is especially valuable in volatile environments with significant dynamic changes or uncertainty. Often the demands for products and services can be split into a guaranteed "*base volume*" and an uncertain "upper-*tail volume.*" In the Auto Co. example, the annual base volumes for Afours and Bassats were 70 and 150 thousand units, while the uncertain tail volumes were $130 - 70 = 60$ and $250 - 150 = 100$. The optimal capacity portfolio used dedicated capacity to fill the guaranteed base volume and flexible capacity for the volatile tail volume.

This method of using the resource type that best fits the task is derived from the principle of alignment. Using flexibility to serve guaranteed base volumes is not a good strategy: it is more expensive and leads to lower service levels.

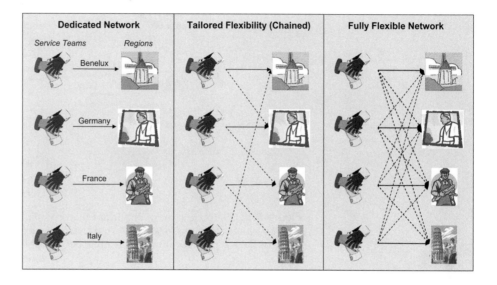

Figure 5.14 Service teams can be dedicated to regions (left) or can be fully flexible (right). Tailored flexibility assigns one "overflow" region to each service team such that the entire allocation is a "chain" (middle).

Similarly, trying to serve volatile tail volumes with dedicated capacity leads to lower firm value and service levels. The optimal amount of flexibility depends on the situation: it typically increases as demand volatility increases, demands are more negatively correlated, product margins are more heterogeneous, or the relative cost of flexibility compared to dedicated capacity decreases. (The analytical questions ask you to verify these properties.)

Tailored network flexibility: resource pooling and chained routing

The principle stating that a little flexibility is often optimal also applies to a network setting with many resource and product (or service) types. Consider, for example, a software company's multi-lingual customer support for Europe. The company has several options to organize its customer support, similar to those of Auto Co. It can organize support along linguistic regions, as illustrated by the left panel in Figure 5.14. This is similar to a dedicated network and benefits from focus and perhaps regional specialty. The downside, however, is lack of resource pooling; when the Italian team has excess capacity, it cannot help out an overloaded German team. In contrast, fully flexible teams that speak four languages can serve any region (right panel in Fig. 5.14). They act as one resource pool and enjoy strong risk pooling benefits. Requiring all teams to be fully flexible, however, is very expensive and often "overkill."

Tailored flexibility is a better solution. Jordan and Graves (1995) established that the principle of flexibility also holds in a network setting. They showed that the value of adding flexibility (allocating an additional market to a specific resource) exhibits decreasing returns. A loose measure of network flexibility is the number of network links (total number of languages spoken by service teams).

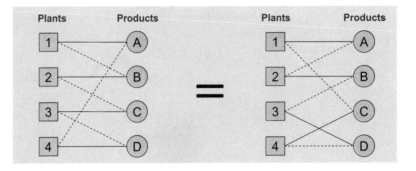

Figure 5.15 Chaining is more important than combining negatively correlated products. Assume products A and C are negatively correlated. Then
the two chained configurations have equivalent flexibility benefits.

In Fig. 5.14, the dedicated network has four links, while the fully flexible one has
16 links. While each additional dashed link increases value, the interesting finding is that adding four carefully-chosen links only has nearly the same value as
full flexibility. Compared to the dedicated network, it is most effective to allocate
each team to one additional region in such a way that all teams and regions are
connected via one *chain* of links (as in the middle panel of Figure 5.14).

Chaining allows resource pooling. To see this, imagine Germany is overloaded while Italy is almost idle. Then Italy can serve the Benelux, which allows the Benelux team to help out Germany. Chaining gives almost full network
flexibility while keeping resources mostly dedicated to their main activities (as
indicated by a solid link) and cross-trained in one other task that is performed
only sporadically (represented by a dashed link). This way, Italians who speak
Dutch but don't speak German can indirectly help the German team.

Tailored mix flexibility

Chaining can guide the strategic allocation of product mix to plants. It implies
that very different products (e.g., a minivan and a sports car) don't need to be
produced in the same plant to enjoy the benefits of flexibility. Success is possible
as long as different plants can at least produce two types of more similar vehicles and the product-plant allocation forms a chain. The mini-case asks you to
explore this further.

Total flexibility increases in value when the network produces substitutable
products that have low correlations. Platform and component sharing allow
cost-efficient mixed assembly of cars and small SUVs, while SUV demand drops
are compensated by car demand increases. But should such products be allocated to the same plant? Interestingly, chaining is more important than combining negatively correlated products in plants. Consider Figure 5.15 and assume
products A and C are negatively correlated. Equivalent flexibility benefits obtain
as long as the configurations form a chain, whether A and C are allocated to the
same plant (right panel) or not (left panel).

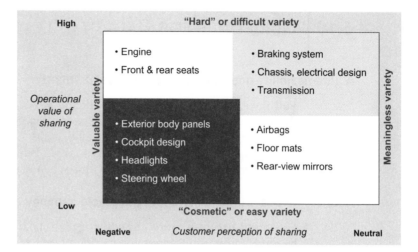

Figure 5.16 Tailored component commonality weighs the operational value of commonality against the commercial cost in terms of customer perception. The blue zone is preferred, while the dark zone must be avoided.

Tailored component commonality: maximize operational *and* customer value

Commonality must be carefully applied so as not to destroy customer value. The danger of platform sharing applies to commonality that only seeks to save cost. For example, a steering wheel is a highly emotional connection point between a driver and the car. Yet, Pontiac used the same steering wheel in its entire line from the minivan to the Grand Prix. Similarly, how would a Chevy Corvette driver feel knowing that the Chevy S-10 has the same radio receiver?

The appropriate amount of sharing recognizes the operational value of component commonality, as well as the cost in terms of customer perception (which ultimately drives customer valuations, pricing, and profitability). Customer perception of sharing internal components is often more neutral than sharing of external components that greatly impact the product design's look and feel. Similarly, variety of some components is easily achieved operationally, while for others it is very expensive.

Tailored commonality shares internal components that are expensive to customize ("hard" variety) while specializing external components that are easy to customize ("cosmetic" variety). The *commonality matrix* of Figure 5.16 may be a good starting point to tailor a commonality strategy. The blue zone is preferred, while the dark zone must be avoided. For instance, DaimlerChrysler differentiates its Smart cars by using interchangeable plastic body panels, while sharing the "hard" components where variety would be commercially meaningless.

5.10 | GUIDELINES FOR CAPACITY FLEXIBILITY

A little flexibility goes a long way when used smartly

Full flexibility is very expensive, but the flexibility principle says that a little flexibility used smartly often accrues most of its benefits at a fraction of the cost. Smart usage tailors to the setting: use flexibility for volatile tail-volumes, endow the network with minimal flexibility that pools resources through chaining, and align operational and commercial value when using commonality.

Reduce the cost of flexibility using adaptable capacity and setup time reduction

Flexibility becomes more attractive if it is cheaper. The cost of flexibility can be reduced by using adaptable capacity (see Chapter 4); by reducing the scope of flexibility to cover most, but not all, of the needs (the 80-20 rule often applies); and by smarter operations tactics that increase process flexibility (e.g., changeover time reduction allows mixed loading, transportation or processing).

How much flexibility do you really want? (Recall the obstacles.)

Flexibility is only valuable if it improves profits and should not be pursued just for its own sake. Do customers really value your increased flexibility? Will it help you competitively? Do any gains from postponement outweigh commercial costs? Do your costs decrease if you are more flexible? When you have excess dedicated capacity, there is little value to improving changeovers times and flexibility. Similarly, when demand significantly exceeds capacity, there is little value to flexibility since all resources are already fully utilized. After all, you first need more capacity before increasing flexibility. In other words, flexibility is most valuable when demand is comparable to capacity.

Integrate flexibility strategy with new product strategy

The value of flexibility depends on the delivered products and services. Include not only your current product portfolio, but also match your flexibility with the requirements of future product roll-outs. This is critical in biotechnology, where design, construction, start-up, and licensing of a biological production facility can take more than five years and requires commitment of funds prior to the release of final clinical data and the finalization of the manufacturing process. A process platform strategy whose main elements, through minor adaptations, can be used to manufacture multiple products becomes very valuable.

Be clear on the role of flexibility

To ensure flexibility is managed well, we must know what type of flexibility we need because that impacts the type of actions needed. For example, if flexibility is used for products with highly volatile demands, managing changeovers is important. For new products and prototyping, managing projects and critical paths is important. For low volume products that may be moved to dedicated capacity if commercially successful (flexibility as a launch strategy), good technology transfer skills are key.

5.11 | SUMMARY OF LEARNING OBJECTIVES

1. Describe the benefits and challenges of different types of capacity and flexibility.

> Organizations utilize different types of human and capital resources in their operations. This chapter studied how operations strategy can decide on an appropriate mix of these resource types. We paid special attention to how an organization can find the appropriate type, amount, and configuration of flexibility.
>
> Flexibility is about the ability to adapt and change. It is crucial to define flexibility for your context: to what do you wish to respond, and in what time frame? We identified three main objectives or types of flexibility. Scope flexibility is the ability to perform a variety of activities. Agility and scale flexibility allow quick changes in general, or specifically in volume. Robustness guarantees even performance over a wide range of activities. Scope is important for organizations competing on variety and customization, agility for speed and timeliness, and robustness for cost and quality.
>
> Flexibility, however, is no magic bullet. It is expensive, difficult to value, and is often not well understood nor used appropriately. Flexibility also leads to higher organizational complexity. Sometimes, specialization may provide higher value, competitive protection, and customer response.

2. Design products and processes for flexibility and mass customization.

> An organization's flexibility depends not only on the type of resources, but also on how its products and processes are designed and configured. Adaptable product designs increase flexibility over a standard or universal design while controlling costs. They adopt strategies such as component commonality and platform sharing, modularity, and full custom design. Processes also can be configured for flexibility through resource substitution, resource sharing, transshipment, or postponed differentiation.
>
> These product and process designs strategies, complemented with coordination and information technology, form the backbone of mass customization. As a compromise between mass production and full custom work, mass customization tailors a product or service to each customer's wishes within certain limits, and delivers and administers it with a flexible flow process.

3. Identify and value three key drivers of flexibility and explain their role in consolidation.

> Operations become flexible by aggregating or postponing activities such as design, processing, storage, distribution, and service. Accordingly, we identified and quantified three main value drivers for flexibility:
>
> 1. Scale economies from aggregating average volumes of different activities.
>
> 2. Risk pooling reduces total volatility by aggregating the volatilities of different activities. It is most effective when pooling volatilities of high but similar magnitudes that are negatively correlated. Risk pooling reduces safety capacity or inventory requirements while increasing service levels and revenues.

3. Real options use contingent decision making to improve profits. Dynamic profit maximization stems from postponed capacity allocation to the more profitable activity. The switching option gains value when product profitability is more heterogeneous and demands are more volatile. Postponing allocations allows forecast updating. The waiting option embodied in flexibility is most valuable in uncertain dynamic settings.

4. Tailor and optimize the capacity portfolio of a multi-product firm in a spreadsheet.

Flexibility exhibits decreasing returns but increasing costs so that an intermediate amount of flexibility maximizes value. To find the appropriate amount of flexibility, we must model and optimize the resource portfolio of a multi-product firm. In order to properly value risk pooling and allocation flexibility (two of the three value drivers of flexibility), we must capture uncertainty using scenarios or simulations.

The optimal configuration of flexibility is tailored to the organization's environment. Tailored flexibility uses a mix of dedicated and flexible capacities (where flexibility serves the volatile portion of demands), a "chained" allocation of activities to resources, and smart commonality for hard variety that has little commercial value.

These insights suggest answers to flexibility questions that are pertinent to many organizations. In stable environments, flexibility is seldom needed. Otherwise, partial flexibility or cross-training teams in a few different activities is sufficient, as long as the flexibility and activity assignments "form a chain" that creates a single resource pool.

DISCUSSION QUESTIONS

1. Alfred P. Sloan, Jr. "didn't see just what could be done about" the bringing out of yearly models. What do you see after reading this chapter?

2. *Agile automated production* (AAP) is an emerging manufacturing paradigm. Discuss its defining characteristics.

3. Which of the four main value drivers explain the value of mixing paint on demand by a retailer relative to the strategy where the manufacturer produces and delivers 100 different colors of paints to the retailer?

4. How does the delayed differentiation and allocation of HP printers to geographical markets benefit from the four value drivers?

5. One of the key pillars of the Toyota Production System is *heijunka*, a Japanese term for "make flat and level." How would you estimate the value of level loading in mixed production using a flexible assembly line?

6. Different products may require different production times and thus "consume" flexible capacity at different rates. How would that change the capacity constraints? Why didn't we capture that in the Auto Co. example?

(Hint: do some web research about how "takt time" of a car assembly line is determined.)

7. In what sense can we say that chaining and tail-volume flexibility are two sides of the same coin?

ANALYTICAL QUESTIONS

1. How would the optimal capacities in networks A and B of Fig. 5.5 compare? That is, what is the relationship between (K_1, K_2) in network A and (K_S, K_2) in network B?

2. Find the optimal dedicated strategy and the optimal fully-flexible strategy for the Auto Co. example and verify the statement that these strategies "lead to lower service levels" than the optimal tailored strategy. This can be accomplished through Excel, but there is a faster *and* more elegant way to do so (hint: these are essentially one-dimensional newsvendor networks).

3. Examine, using the downloadable spreadsheet `Flexibility_Auto.xls`, how the optimal tailored capacity portfolio for Auto Co. changes as the Afour becomes more (or less) profitable compared to the Bassat, and as the relative cost of flexibility compared to dedicated capacity decreases.

4. What is the correlation in Auto Co.'s demand forecast? Adapt Auto Co.'s demand forecast to investigate, using the downloadable spreadsheet, how optimal flexibility depends on demand volatilities and correlations.

Visit www.vanmieghem.us for additional questions and updates.

FURTHER READING AND REFERENCES

▶ Managerial references on flexibility include Anderson (2004) and Upton (1995).

▶ References on product design strategies for flexibility include Hölttä, Suh, and de Weck (2005), Ulrich and Eppinger (2003) and Whitney (2004).

▶ For further analysis of the configuration and value of flexibility, see Jordan and Graves (1995), Van Mieghem (1998), Iravani, Sims, and Van Oyen (2005) and Chod, Rudi, and Van Mieghem (2005).

Anderson, D. M. (2004). *Build-to-Order & Mass Customization; the Ultimate Supply Chain Management and Lean Manufacturing Strategy for Low-Cost On-Demand Production without Forecasts or Inventory*. CIM Press.

Bremner, B., G. Edmonson, and C. Dawson (2004). Nissan's boss. *Business Week*, 50–58. October 4.

Chod, J., N. Rudi, and J. A. Van Mieghem (2005). Valuing flexibility as a wait-and-switch option. Under review and available from the authors' websites.

Hölttä, K., E. S. Suh, and O. de Weck (2005). Tradeoff between modularity and performance for engineered systems and products. ICED 05, Melbourne, Aug. 15-18.

Iravani, S. M. R., K. Sims, and M. P. Van Oyen (2005). Structural flexibility: A new perspective on the design of manufacturing and service operations. *Management Science 51*, 151–166.

Jordan, W. and S. Graves (1995). Principles on the benefits of manufacturing process flexibility. *Management Science 41*, 557–594.

Kolesar, P. K., G. J. van Ryzin, and W. Cutler (1998). The new service factory: creating customer value through industrialized intimacy. *Strategy & Business 12*, 33–43. 3Q.

Loch, C. H., A. DeMeyer, and M. T. Pich (2006). *Managing the unknown*. New York: Wiley.

Pil, F. K. and M. Holweg (2004). Mitigating product varietys impact on the value chain. *Interfaces 34*(5), 394–403.

Taguchi, G. and D. Clausing (1990). Robust quality. *Harvard Business Review*, 65–75. Jan-Feb.

Ulrich, K. T. and S. D. Eppinger (2003). *Product Design and Development* (Third ed.). McGraw Hill.

Upton, D. M. (1995). What really makes factories flexible? *Harvard Business Review*, 74–84. July-August.

Van Mieghem, J. A. (1998). Investment strategies for flexible resources. *Management Science 44*(8), 1071–1078.

Whitney, D. E. (2004). *Mechanical Assemblies: Their Design, Manufacture, and Role in Product Development*. Oxford University Press.

Wouters, D. (2005). Personal discussions with vice president of Dynaco USA. June.

Mini-Case 5 | STRATEGIC NETWORK FLEXIBILITY USING FLEXCAP

[3]A large car company wanted to improve the flexibility of its network of 8 plants to produce its 16 product families. The motivation was twofold: automotive product demand is *very* uncertain (average forecast error exceeded 50% during the network configuration planning phase and remained so up to a few quarters before production) and the cost of unfilled demand or poorly utilized capacity is very high. Consequently, the company defined flexibility as the ability to build different product types in the same plant at the same time.

The company had good measures on the cost of flexibility, yet not much on the benefit. It wanted to know the best way of adding flexibility: Which plants should be capable of producing multiple products? How much flexibility does the company need to add? Is it better to add capacity or flexibility? In summary, what is the best configuration of network flexibility?

Answering these question involves maximizing the value (benefits minus costs) of network flexibility. Given available cost estimates, this boils down to estimating the benefits of flexibility and typically involves simulation (see Appendix 5). To assist the company's flexibility decisions, the FlexCap simulation tool was developed at MIT. That downloadable tool is explained here to help you explore similar questions for the two network flexibility problems below.

Download `FlexCap` from www.vanmieghem.us

The FlexCap tool: configuring a network

FlexCap is a simulation program that allows the exploration of alternative network configurations and their evaluations under uncertainty. When you open the FlexCap application you will see the four-plant, four-product system shown at the left in Figure 5.17. You can change the number of plants and the number of products under Model Parameters, a submenu of the Model menu. To "link" plants with products, pick up the blue arrow from the palette, click on a product, and then click on a plant to create a specific link. A link signifies that the product can be produced in the plant. Repeating this process can yield a network configuration as shown at the right of Figure 5.17. Links can be deleted by selecting the red circle from the palette and clicking on the link to be deleted. You can also directly specify the dedicated system or the chained system under the Model menu.

By double-clicking on a product you can change the parameters associated with each product: its selling price, stockout cost, and demand forecast. The demand forecast over some time period (say next year) is assumed to be normally distributed with given mean and standard deviation but is restricted to fall between the minimum and maximum demand. The forecast thus is a truncated normal distribution, and product demands are assumed to be uncorrelated.

By double-clicking on a plant you can change its capacity, thus limiting its

---

[3]Professor S. C. Graves from MIT graciously shared the FlexCap software and his assignments. Professor Van Mieghem adapted those to prepare this case as the basis for class discussion rather than to illustrate either the effective or ineffective handling of a managerial situation. This mini-case can be used without permission.

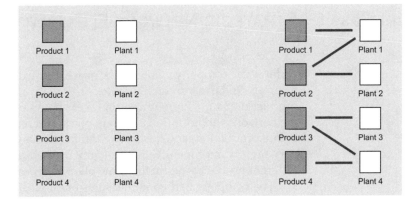

Figure 5.17 The FlexCap simulator opens with the 4 product-4 plant system shown at the left. You can modify products, plants, and their allocation by "linking" products and plants, as illustrated in the example to the right.

total production. You can specify the average capacity in terms of the number of units that can be produced, the standard deviation of capacity, or the minimum and maximum capacity. The capacity and demand numbers are expressed for the same time period, such as one year.

By double-clicking on a link you can change the capacity limits, production and transportation costs associated with each link. You also need to turn on the "enforce link capacities" command from the Options menu; the default is to ignore the link capacities. The link capacities determine the upper limit on production of a specific product in a specific plant (they can be ignored for this mini-case).

Note that if all products, plants, or links are identical, then their parameters can be changed together by selecting "Change all Products" from the Model menu. The software has one known bug–it requires positive standard deviations and crashes if you put in zero. Otherwise, it is pretty robust.

The FlexCap tool: simulating a network

The software allows you to simulate your configured network ("Simulate" in Model menu). On each run of the simulation, it samples a demand for each product and a capacity for each plant (random draws from a truncated normal distribution). Then, the software solves an optimization problem to determine the production quantities of each product in each plant for your specified network configuration.

You can choose from two optimization objectives. First, "Minimize Lost Demand" minimizes the capacity shortfall or amount of demand not satisfied; i.e., it maximizes the amount of demand that can be met. Second, "Minimize Costs" determines the production plan that minimizes the total cost of production, transportation, and stockouts.

The software reports the sales, average shortfall, average plant utilization, average total cost, and average gross revenue. The individual plant average utilizations are displayed in the plant icons. Individual product shortfalls are displayed in the product icons. The sales, cost and gross revenue numbers are only meaningful if you actually put the relevant costs into the model. The "Minimize Lost Demand" option does not consider cost, so you can use it without worrying about the various costs. The software also reports what the shortfall would be if you had "total flexibility"–that is, if each plant could produce all of the products.

A. The Auto Co. network problem

Consider an extended version of Auto Co., which would still be a simplified version of a real automotive company's setting. Suppose you have 6 plants, each with capacity of 100 and negligible standard deviation of 1, and 6 products, each with mean demand of 100 and standard deviation of 30. Auto Co. strives to minimize demand shortages and currently has a dedicated network; i.e., plant 1 can only produce product 1, plant 2 can only make product 2, etc. Auto Co. wants to know what the best way is to add flexibility.

1. *Consider adding flexibility to the dedicated network by making plants capable of producing more than 1 product. What is the best way to add flexibility? What are the benefits? How much do you need add?*

2. *Reconsider the dedicated system and suppose you could expand capacity at the plants. What are the benefits? How do they compare with adding flexibility?*

B. The Printer network problem

Suppose you have the opportunity to plan the manufacturing system at a greenfield site for a family of printers. You currently offer 8 printers whose annual demand is uncorrelated and forecasted as normally distributed with parameters as given in the following table (units are 000's):

Printer Type	A	B	C	D	E	F	G	H
Mean annual demand	80	80	60	60	40	40	20	20
Standard deviation of annual demand	10	30	10	30	20	5	10	5

The manufacturing system will entail a set of parallel lines. Each line will assemble and test printers; each can be dedicated to a printer type or can have some amount of flexibility. That is, a line can be designed to assemble and test any subset of the printer types.

Assume that each line will have a production capacity of 100,000 units per year, regardless of whether it is dedicated or flexible. The annualized cost for building and operating a dedicated line for any printer type is estimated to be $1,200,000. Suppose that the annualized cost to build and operate a flexible line is the cost for a dedicated line, $1,200,000, plus an estimate of $100,000 to $150,000 for each additional product that the line can make. (Thus, a line that can manufacture printers A, F and G will cost somewhere between $1,400,000 and $1,500,000 annually.) The unit contribution margin of each printer is $25; this is the difference between the revenue and the cost of material and distribution.

Use FlexCap to find a good capacity strategy for this facility.

Appendix 5 | OPTIMIZATION USING SIMULATION IN EXCEL

There are two ways to optimize under uncertainty in Excel:

1. the "easy way" models the demand forecast with a set of scenarios and uses a direct extension of linear planning optimization (Appendix 4 on p. 149), called stochastic linear programming. This method was described on page 176 where we optimized the flexibility of the Auto Co. example.

2. the "adaptable" way is to optimize using simulation.

This appendix describes optimization using simulation and finishes with a comparison of the easy way and the adaptable way. To illustrate, we use simultion to optimize the flexibility of the Auto Co. example (p. 176) in a downloadable spreadsheet.

> Download `Flexibility_Auto.xls` from www.vanmieghem.us

Step 1: Define data (parameters)

As mentioned in Appendix 4 on p. 149, it is good practice to keep all demand, operational, and financial data or parameters in one or multiple tables in Excel. This greatly facilitates the what-if analysis compared to subsuming the data into formulas. Figure 5.18 shows Auto Co.'s data on rows 1 to 7.

Notice that we approximate the demand forecast by a bivariate normal distribution. Hence, we only need five demand parameters: the average and standard deviation of each product, and the correlation coefficient. Here we chose 100 and 200 as averages, 30 and 50 as standard deviations, and a strong negative correlation ρ of -0.9. (The number 0.4359 in cell C7 is the value of the expression $\sqrt{1 - \rho^2}$; its purpose will become clear soon.)

Step 2: Define activities (decision variables)

The three decision variables are the dedicated Afour, dedicated Bassat, and flexible capacity (cells B11:B13 in Figure 5.18).

Step 3: Simulate demand and find contingent activities

This step requires some work. First we construct sampled demand scenarios from the bivariate normal distribution and then find the contingent activities for each demand scenario:

1. Draw two samples of the (univariate) standard normal distribution, Z_A and Z_B. Enter the formulae:

draw Z_A (cell A21): `=normsinv(rand())`

draw Z_B (cell B21): `=normsinv(rand())`

	A	B	C	D	E	F	G	H	I
1	Step 1: Data								
2	Normal Demand Forecast				Financial Data				
3		D1	D2		Contribution margin 1			$2,000	
4	mean	100	200		Contribution margin 2			$1,000	
5	std. deviation	30	50		Dedicated Afour capacity cost/unit			$800	
6	correlation		-0.9		Dedicated Bassat capacity cost/unit			$700	
7			0.4359		Flexible capacity cost/unit			$900	
8									
9	Step 2: Decision Variables								
10	Capacity								
11	Dedicated1	62							
12	Dedicated2	149							
13	Flexible	74							
14	CapEx	$220,228						NPV	$155,457
15									
16	Step 3: Simulate Demand & Contingent Activities								Step 4: Operating profit
17	Sample Mean		99.5	200.8	60.6	145.6	37.4	34.2	$375,686
18	Sample Std.Dev.		30.2	49.3					$28,545
19	Sample Correlation			-0.90					
20	Z_A	Z_B	D_A	D_B	x_A	x_B	x'_A	x'_B	Operating Profit
21	-0.17	0.84	95	226	62	149	33	41	$379,643
22	1.31	0.98	139	163	62	149	74	0	$420,389
23	-1.29	1.67	61	295	61	149	0	74	$345,064
24	-2.19	-0.85	34	280	34	149	0	74	$291,262
25	0.71	0.60	121	181	62	149	59	14	$405,959
26	0.47	2.32	114	229	62	149	52	22	$398,851
27	-1.58	-0.93	53	251	53	149	0	74	$327,716
28	-0.49	-0.21	85	218	62	149	23	50	$369,960
29	1.10	0.39	133	159	62	149	71	3	$417,634
30	0.89	0.51	127	171	62	149	65	9	$411,310

Figure 5.18 Spreadsheet to optimize flexibility through simulation in Excel.

2. Transform Z_A and Z_B into two correlated normal variables D_A and D_B that have means μ_A and μ_B, standard deviations σ_A and σ_B, and correlation coefficient ρ. This is achieved using the linear transformation[4]:

$$D_A = \mu_A + \sigma_A Z_A,$$
$$D_B = \mu_B + \sigma_B \rho Z_A + \sigma_B \sqrt{1 - \rho^2} Z_B.$$

In Excel, enter the formulas:

generate D_A (cell C21)   :   =B$4+B$5*A21
generate D_B (cell D21)   :   =BC$4+C$5*(C$6*A21+C$7*B21)

3. Now find the optimal contingent activities for this demand pair. For Auto Co., the optimal contingent production follows a greedy allocation rule: first allocate dedicated capacities, then allocate flexible capacity first to the

---

[4]For math fans: this procedure extends to higher dimensions. Recall that linear transformations of normal random variables remain normal. $D = \mu + AZ$ has desired mean vector μ and correlation matrix AA'. The matrix A is thus a square root of the desired correlation matrix.

highest margin product. In Excel, enter the formulas:

$$
\begin{aligned}
\text{dedicated Afour production } x_A \text{ (cell E21):} \quad &= \quad \texttt{MIN(C21;B\$11)} \\
\text{dedicated Bassat production } x_B \text{ (cell F21):} \quad &= \quad \texttt{MIN(D21;B\$12)} \\
\text{flexible Afour production } x'_A \text{ (cell G21):} \quad &= \quad \texttt{MIN(C21-E21;B\$13)} \\
\text{flexible Bassat production } x'_B \text{ (cell H21):} \quad &= \quad \texttt{MIN(D21-F21;B\$13-G21)}
\end{aligned}
$$

4. Calculate the associated operating profit. In Excel, enter the formulas:

$$
\text{operating profit (cell I21): } \texttt{=H\$3*(E21+G21)+H\$4*(F21+H21)}
$$

5. We're almost done! Selecting cells A21:I21 and dragging them down over 400 rows (until row 420) gives you 400 sample points of demand with contingent optimal profit. This is what makes Excel wonderful!

6. There is one small Excel idiosyncrasy to take care of. When optimizing capacity, the sample points must remain unchanged. Yet Excel redraws the random number with the rand-function with every calculation. To avoid that, copy the Z_A and Z_B samples (i.e., copy cells A21:B420) and paste only their values (using `paste special`) back into the same cells A21:B420.

Step 4: Calculate expected operating profit and NPV

Calculate the average expected operating profit:

$$
\text{expected operating profit (cell I17): } \texttt{=average(I21:I420)}
$$

(Row 17 also shows the sample averages to indicate how representative our sample is. If you prefer higher accuracy, increase the number of samples above our arbitrary choice of 400.) Subtracting the capacity investment cost yields the net value:

$$
\begin{aligned}
\text{capacity investment (cell B14):} \quad &= \quad \texttt{SUMPRODUCT(B11:B13,H5:H7)} \\
\text{NPV (cell I14):} \quad &= \quad \texttt{I17-B14}
\end{aligned}
$$

Step 5: Optimize

In Excel, open the Solver dialog box under `Tools>Solver` and enter:
    `Set target cell`: enter NPV cell `I14`
    `Equal to`: select `Max`
    `By Changing Cells`: enter decision cells `B11:B13`
In the Solver dialog box, click on `Options` and select `Assume Non-Negative` but de-select `Assume Linear Model`. Selecting `Use Automatic Scaling` and `Quadratic Estimates` often yields better results. It's always a good idea to re-optimize from a few different starting capacity numbers to verify that you find the globally best solution. (There is, unfortunately, no guarantee if you use the basic Excel Solver.)

Comparing the easy and adaptable way

The main advantage of stochastic linear programming is that it can automatically and accurately optimize both contingent activities and capacity. Its main downside for our purposes is that it requires you to specify uncertainty through a set of scenarios. Choosing representative scenarios is often not that obvious. (How would you do that if the forecast is jointly normally distributed with certain means, variances, and correlations?) Any what-if analysis requires you to change scenarios. Another downside is that associating a set of decision variables to each scenario quickly leads to a giant optimization program.

The main advantage of optimization through simulation is adaptability: it applies to any operating process that can be simulated (it doesn't need to be linear). The forecast can be specified through a distribution and scenarios are obtained automatically by simulating or sampling a set of outcomes. This allows easy "what-if" analysis of changes in forecasts by changing the means or volatilities and re-optimizing. The downside is that simulation only provides an estimation whose accuracy depends on the number of sampled points. In practice, accuracy for small problems is not an issue given that the data parameters themselves often are estimates.

Computer scientists will say that the more significant disadvantage is that optimization requires two "loops" and more time and computing power. For the small problems that we are interested in, however, "inner loop" optimization can be done using common sense so that only one optimization remains. For larger problems, the inner loop keeps the capacity portfolio constant and solves a linear program to find the optimal contingent activities and operating profit for each sample point. The outer loop then optimizes the capacity portfolio. Thus, a large number of optimizations is needed: with N sample points, each inner loop requires N linear optimizations, while the outer loop requires non-linear optimization. Nevertheless, implementing this two-round optimization is fairly easy: it requires less than a page of coding and realistic problems can still be computed almost in real time. Moreover, the inner-loop results can also generate gradients which can significantly speed up the non-linear optimization.

6

CAPACITY LOCATION, GLOBAL NETWORKS AND OFFSHORING

Location, location, location.—The proverbial sentence in real estate.

Learning Objectives

After reading this chapter, you will be able to:

1. Integrate location decisions with operations strategy and relate them to globalization.
2. Apply four types of location analysis: geographical and total landed cost, network, competitive, and focus.
3. Discuss several network choices: centralize or distribute? Localize or standardize? Integrate or separate? Offshore or onshore?
4. Value flexibility and currency exchange rate risk in global networks.

In the previous chapters, we studied the sizing, timing, and type of capacity changes. In this chapter, we will study the location decision, the fourth major decision of a resource portfolio strategy. We will start by discussing the forces behind globalization and propose a strategic framework for location decisions. Then we will review four types of location analyses that will help us understand network design choices and trade-offs. Finally, we will learn how to value global networks and guide global network strategy and offshoring.

6.1 | GLOBALIZATION AND OPERATIONS

Globalization refers to the various processes—cultural, social, political, economic, and technological—that lead to increased interaction among disparate locations across the globe. Globalization strongly impacts the design and management of the operational network, including the spatial spread, concentration, and integration of locations. We use the term *global operations*, or *global network*, to emphasize that process flows cross national boundaries. (In theory, in a truly global

Example 6.1 Tariffs lead Harley-Davidson to assemble in Brazil and Indonesia

In April 1995, Brazil raised its industry tariff on motorcycles from 20 to 70 percent. In addition to this industry tariff, other federal duties included import duties of 20%, social tax, social security contributions, and sales tax. This meant that Paul Izzo, Harley-Davidson's master dealer in Brazil, was paying more than 135% in federal duties on top of the price Harley-Davidson was charging. No wonder Harley-Davidson's exports to Brazil virtually stopped: in 1997, the company made 132,285 motorcycles but only 600 were exported to Brazil.

In response, Harley-Davidson Inc. petitioned for approval to assemble motorcycles in Brazil. In 1999, the company started importing U.S.-made components for assembly in Manaus, Brazil, an economic free-trade zone for motorcycle manufacturing and other industries. Local outsourcing of about 30 manufacturing operations and local assembly in its wholly-owned subsidiary in Manaus eliminated the industry tariff. The parts also qualified for lower import duty rates. By 2005, Harley-Davidson's sales in Brazil had more than tripled relative to 1997.

A similar response to more than 100% duties led to a dealer-operated "SKD (semi-knockdown)" construction in Indonesia. Harley-Davidson ships fully-assembled bikes to a third-party-owned Indonesian facility. There, the bikes are disassembled down to 20 to 30 parts or subassemblies, which are imported and then assembled back together!

network, no single location would have a "home" advantage. In practice, the term international operations still seems applicable.)

The importance of a global operations strategy

Today, operations strategy requires a global perspective because many companies continually investigate whether, and how, to serve an increasingly global market. An integrated global network provides valuable flexibility to respond to market, political and macroeconomic changes. For example, when the USD/EUR exchange rate fell in 2001-02, Poppies International, a Belgian industrial "patisserie," stopped exporting from Belgium to the U.S. and started supplying the U.S. solely from its North Carolina plant. A similar switch occurred in 2003 after Canada raised its import tax for non-NAFTA countries to 12%. Similarly, when Brazil changed its tariffs on motorcycles, Harley-Davidson decided to start a facility in Brazil ifself (Example 6.1).

In this section, we will follow Kouvelis and Niederhoff (2007) to explain why firms globalize operations. Then, we will assemble the forces behind globalization into a framework that integrates location decisions with the overall operations strategy. We will learn how to view location decisions as network choices and how to value an integrated global network.

Supply factors behind globalization

A common reason to establish operations in other parts of the world is to cut the costs of the input supply. We illustrate how location can affect three cost components: direct cost, capital cost, and taxes.

First, locating close to inputs can reduce direct costs. For example, paper plants locate in forested regions, aluminum smelters are near any hydroenergy power supply, and labor-intensive industries, such as the textile and toy industry, offshore to low-cost labor countries (even Zara sources staple T-shirts from

Asia). While offshoring can be a competitive necessity, chasing the lowest cost location seldom leads to sustaining competitive advantage.

The disk-drive industry provides a case in point. Following cost-reduction requirements from its biggest customer (IBM) in the early 1980s, Seagate Technology moved its disk-drive assembly to Singapore. While it did reap cost-savings in the short term, other disk-drive manufacturers quickly followed and competition for local talent rapidly increased labor costs. This led Seagate and its competitors to relocate subsequently to various other Asian countries, a practice that became known as "island hopping." A simplistic focus on direct labor cost is also dangerous when other costs (e.g., indirect costs, logistics and quality costs, overhead costs) comprise the bulk of total cost. This demonstrates why we must consider the impact of location on *total landed cost*, which is the total end-to-end cost from inputs to outputs at customers.

Capital investment costs can also drive location and globalization. New semiconductor plants can cost more than one billion dollars. To share costs and risks, several manufacturers enter into *joint venture* (JV) agreements. For example, in August 1994, Hitachi, Ltd. and Texas Instruments Incorporated (TI) announced plans to build a joint venture facility for the production of 16 and 64 megabit dynamic random access memory (DRAM) chips in Richardson, Texas. Unfortunately, operations started in 1996, just as DRAMs began an unprecedented and unforeseen price decline. The decline prevented the JV from building the adequate cash reserves necessary to sustain ongoing operations and invest in future growth. In February 1998, both partners agreed to end their JV arrangement and TI decided to take full ownership of the facility.

Taxes and local incentives are a third important cost factor driving location and globalization. Rainey and McNamara (1999) provide empirical evidence. State incentives such as tax breaks, subsidies, and other support helped Ireland attract pharmaceutical and electronics companies. Nowadays, the first step of the location strategy often consists of consultations and negotiations with regional and national governments.

Technological factors behind globalization

Access to the knowledge and skills of component suppliers, customers, competitors, employees, and research centers drives location. Some locations have developed certain specialized advantages. For example, watch manufacturers are clustered around Geneva, Switzerland. The "tie-city" of ShengZhou, China, is home to over 1,100 tie-manufacturing companies with an annual output of 300 million ties, or one third of the world supply. Japan and Germany are known for engineering high-precision machine tools. India has attracted offshored call center and software engineering operations. Competing in, sourcing from, or attracting talent from such location-dominated segments can drive globalization.

Improving infrastructure, including communication and transportation technology, has facilitated globally dispersed networks, which can further reduce operating costs. For example, Coca-Cola has hundreds of bottling plants around the globe that serve local markets in order to reduce transportation costs.

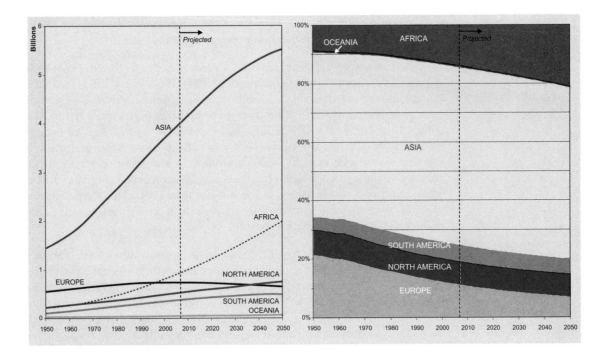

Figure 6.1 Each continent's population size (left) and share of the global population (right). (Adapted from www.census.gov)

Market demand factors behind globalization

A third reason to establish operations in other parts of the world is to improve market access and increase revenues. A picture tells more than a thousand words: consider the relative population sizes and growth of Asia and Europe (marked in contrast in the suggestive graphs of Figure 6.1). The graphs clearly highlight the increasing importance of the Asian market.

While certainly important, raw population size and growth are not the only factors. Density plays a major role and remains a major benefit for Europe and increasingly for Asia, according to Figure 6.2 (again, Asia's rise to prominence is all but certain). Purchasing power is obviously of great importance to revenue potential. As a stark example, only 10 million people live in Belgium's tiny 30,000 square kilometers. Yet their combined purchasing power (as measured by the 2005 GDPs of $372B v. $775B) is about half that of India, which is 100 times bigger in terms of both population (1,095 million inhabitants) and size (3,287,000 km^2). The Belgian per capita annual purchasing power is about $37 thousand, versus $707 in India.

Globalization can feed upon itself. Global companies with sophisticated global networks tend to intensify competition, thus forcing smaller companies to contemplate globalization just to keep up. Cultural globalization makes customers more aware of progress so that companies must introduce new products almost simultaneously at a global level (this contrasts with the old practice of ex-

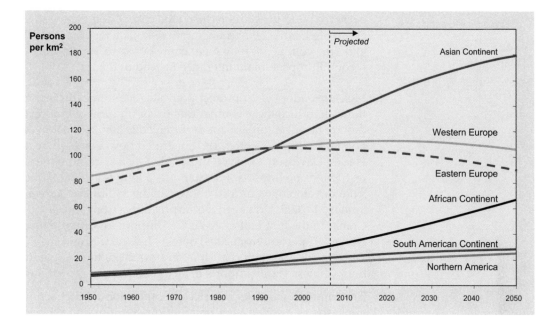

Figure 6.2 While Europe's population is stagnant and its share of the world is decreasing, its high density remains attractive (adapted from www.census.gov).

porting products that were advancing in their product life cycles domestically). Sometimes, global operations are used as a defensive tool against foreign competitors. For example, consumer package goods companies Kellogg and Nestlé both have large market share in their respective U.S. and European home markets, but limited presence in their competitor's home market: "The two companies maintain a gentleman's agreement of nonaggressive penetration of each other's home markets following unsuccessful past efforts and heavy revenue bleeding from subsequent retaliations," according to Kouvelis and Niederhoff (2007).

Local presence, content, and service considerations (such as lead-times, quality, and language) often dictate local operations. Local presence may help understand advanced local needs and sends a signal of commitment. All these aspects factored into Toyota's decision to build a plant in Valenciennes, France, and Mercedes-Benz's choice to build in the U.S., which has an advanced market of sport utility and other large vehicles (recall the M and R-classes of Example 1.2 on p. 8).

Macroeconomic and non-market factors behind globalization

Finally, various macroeconomic and non-market factors influence the selection of global locations. We will highlight three:

1. Currency risk and political stability are important considerations in global location decisions. For instance, the adoption of the Euro as the single

currency by 12 EU states reduced the cost of doing inter-state business and eliminated currency exchange rate risk. The fact that the UK chose not to join "the continent" may have contributed to Toyota's choice to build its second European plant in France instead of the UK.

2. Measures adopted to protect domestic economies from foreign competition can induce these competitors to set up local operations. *Tariffs* or duties are taxes on foreign goods, often collected by custom officers at entry points. Example 6.1 on p. 198 illustrated how a large increase in tariffs led Harley-Davidson to locate in Brazil. *Quotas* are time-measured quantity restrictions on imports. For example, a long tradition of quotas on textiles from developing countries known as the Multifiber Agreement ended on January 1, 2005. However, the surprisingly strong increase of imports from China (in the first half of 2005, U.S. imports of Chinese-made clothing increased 97 percent from 2004) quickly led the U.S. and the EU to place new "safeguards" on imports. Thus, in June 2005, the EU instituted quotas to limit Chinese textile imports to an 8–12.5 percent growth rate per year.

   Governments can take a variety of other non-market actions and regulations, some of which may unintentionally raise trade barriers. For example, in an attempt to curb congestion and acrid haze, China's 100 or so biggest cities have imposed motorcycle license restrictions, and in many cases, outright riding bans. Given that the majority of Harley-Davidson's customers live in or near cities, these measures have effects similar to those of trade barriers. Non-market actions by active customers can also influence preferences for location. For example, "after months of fevered lobbying and bitter debate, the Chicago City Council passed a ground breaking ordinance requiring "big box" stores, like Wal-Mart and Home Depot, to pay a minimum wage of $10 an hour by 2010, along with at least $3 an hour worth of benefits "(Eckholm 2006).

   Many economists view *protectionism* as a disguised tax on consumers (who pay higher prices) and a subsidy to local high-cost producers and even to foreign firms, who can command higher prices due to quantity restrictions. For example, the U.S. sugar lobby benefits sugar producers, as well as producers of substitutes such as fructose corn syrup.

3. Free trade zones and bilateral or multilateral treaties to reduce, if not eliminate, protectionism also impact globalization. The European Coal and Steel Community of West Germany, France, Italy, and the Benelux countries was formed in 1951 by the Treaty of Paris. The 1957 Treaty of Rome transformed it into the European Economic Community, which later became the European Union (EU) through the Maastricht Treaty in 1992. The EU inspired the formation of the North American Free Trade Agreement (NAFTA) among Canada, the United States of America, and Mexico in 1994. More global free trade policies are administered by the World Trade Organization (WTO), one of whose councils administers the General Agreement on Tariffs and Trade (GATT).

The factors behind globalization can be assembled into a framework that integrates location decisions with the overall operations strategy.

6.2 | STRATEGIC FRAMEWORK FOR LOCATION DECISIONS

A *location strategy* is a structured approach to deciding *where* to expand or contract capacity.

Location decisions as an integral part of operations strategy

Location decisions are multi-faceted and often idiosyncratic. Rather than letting location decisions be guided by a single-sided interest (e.g. a myopic focus on cost), however, it is important to view location decisions as an integral part of operations strategy. We can directly implement the general framework we developed in Chapter 1 and highlight the interaction of the location decision with the other levers of operations strategy (Figure 6.3).

This framework aligns and tailors location with competitive strategy by following three steps:

1. Start by reviewing the competitive strategy: what is the value proposition to customers and shareholders?

2. The location decision must be aligned with the competitive strategy by comparing the priority rankings of competencies that location should provide; i.e., what is the relative importance of cost, quality, flexibility, and responsiveness?

3. This ranking then guides how the various factors (discussed below) should be weighted in making the location decision. The factors can be categorized as mainly affecting assets (resource capacity) or activities (processes).

Let us first summarize the factors before illustrating their application. You will notice how they include the factors behind globalization.

Asset or Resource Capacity Factors

Location decisions are closely intertwined with capacity sizing, timing, and type decisions; together, they constitute a resource portfolio or network strategy. For example, a single location must be larger than two locations serving the same territory. Capacity additions with short leadtimes or highly advanced technology may favor familiar locations. In summary, the capacity sizing, timing, type, and location decisions are interdependent, as will be illustrated throughout this chapter.

Important elements to consider are:

1. Capacity sizing factors include:

   - working capital (inventory, cash, etc) and capital investment costs
   - taxes, financing, and local incentives (tax breaks, subsidies, etc.)
   - what part of total network capacity will the location provide?

2. Capacity timing factors include:

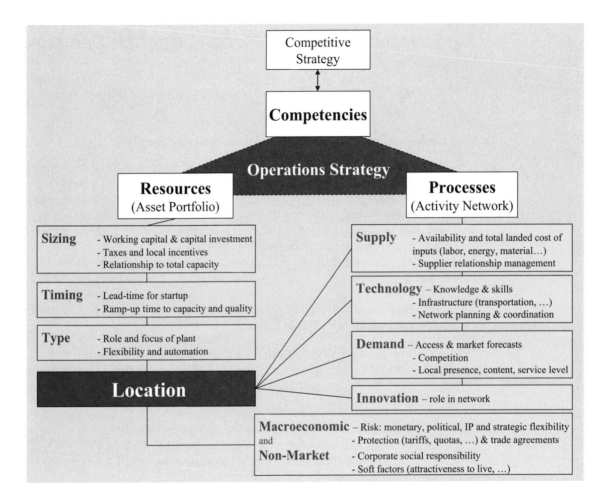

Figure 6.3 A framework for the location decision ensures its alignment with the overall operations strategy.

- lead-time for startup
- ramp-up time to full capacity, efficiency, and quality targets

3. Capacity type factors include:

- role and focus of the location (more on this later)
- degree and type of flexibility and automation

Activity or Process Factors

Location decisions closely impact how work gets done. Adopting a process view means considering:

1. Supply factors describe how location impacts input supply and include:

- availability and total landed cost of operating inputs, including labor *as well as* material, energy, and other inputs. The total cost should be adjusted for productivity, quality, and benefits (social security tax, health care, retirement, etc.)
- relationship management of the location's suppliers

2. Technology factors describe how location impacts internal processing and include:

- availability of knowledge, skills, and technology (both at the location as well as in the organization. Companies sometimes lack the appropriate people, planning, and management skills sets for a given network model or sourcing strategy.)
- state of infrastructure (services, transportation, utilities, etc.)
- coordination and interaction with the rest of the organization's processing network, including information and transportation flows.

3. Market demand factors describe the demand that the location will serve and include:

- access to markets and demand forecasts of sizes, densities, growths, and distances
- the degree, nature, and threat of competition,
- the importance of local presence, local content, and service levels

4. Innovation and improvement factors describe the role of the location in the organization's innovation and improvement processes. Sometimes, adding a location may force existing plants to take a step back in their improvement. For example, adding an offshore plant with long transportation leadtimes may require domestic plants to increase inventory levels.

5. Macroeconomic and non-market factors include other location-specific impacts on the operation, such as:

- risk considerations, including monetary risk (currency exchange rate risk, inflation, etc.), political risk, intellectual property (IP) risk, and strategic flexibility (which may increase geographical spread of facilities and limit employment to a maximal share of the local population in order to diversify risk and retain restructuring flexibility)
- tariffs, quotas, and other protectionist tools, as well as trade agreements
- corporate social responsibility (CSR)
- softer factors such as the attraction to live in a certain location (including social aspects and language)

Location decisions in practice

In practice, the relative importance of the factors depends on the situation, and the required degree of formal location analysis varies. Some examples of past location decisions illustrate typical idiosyncrasies:

When deciding on the location of its U.S. plant, Belgian "patisserie" Poppies International focused on market supply and demand factors. The competitive market decisions of pricing and service levels were taken as given. Consequently, the location decision was driven by the minimization of total supply chain costs. Because transportation was a major cost component, proximity to high demand density areas was important. Thus, a geographical analysis was performed, as described in Example 6.2. Three elements—proximity to a major airport, availability of large egg and cream supplies, and electricity costs— played a prominent role in Poppies' decision. The selection process was highly quantitative, forecasting total costs over ten years.

When Harley-Davidson needed to expand capacity in the mid 1990s (see the case study on p. 391), it hired a consulting company specialized in location studies. The supply factor included the ubiquitous labor considerations factors (availability, costs, qualifications, work ethic, and union friendliness), but broader non-market factors were also important. A site close to an airport with direct flights to Milwaukee, WI would have offered easy accessibility to and from headquarters. Attractiveness to live at a site was measured by the availability of local support services, such as hospitals, churches, recreational opportunities, housing, hotels, and education (measured using a five page comparative analysis of primary, secondary, and college education).

High-tech and high-talent companies often locate where their employees (engineers, scientists, bankers, etc.) live or would be willing to live. This strategy may generate a virtuous cycle, as in the case of Silicon Valley and Wall Street. Sometimes, locations are chosen solely on the basis of personal factors. For example, some international partnerships with the Kellogg School of Management originated from close personal relationships between the schools' deans. Another example of a company choosing its location based on personal factors is Warren Buffett's decision to locate his company (Berkshire Hathaway Inc.) in Omaha, NE, the town where he was born.[1]

Political decisions can also influence the location where activities are performed in a global network and may even prompt new locations. For example, a change in Brazilian tariffs led Harley-Davidson to start a facility in Brazil, as shown in Example 6.1. On Feb. 27, 2007, Toyota announced that it would invest $1.3 billion to build its eighth North American assembly plant in Mississippi. The state pledged $296 million in incentives to land the Toyota factory. Mississippi is the seventh state where Toyota operates a factory (it has 7 engine plants in addition to assembly plants in North America). G.M.'s vice chairman, Robert A. Lutz, said that Toyota had more influence in Washington than G.M. because of the number of states where it has plants (Maynard 2007).

---

[1]Buffett is renowned for his smarts, wealth, and frugality. He continues to live in the same house in Omaha that he bought in 1958 for $31,500. The current estimated value of his house is around $700,000, about one thousandth of a percent of his estimated net worth, according to Forbes (2005).

Example 6.2 Poppies International's Facility Location Decision

Poppies Int'l, headquartered in Zonnebeke, Belgium, produces fresh and frozen pastries including éclairs, petit choux, and doughnuts. In 2000, the company selected North Carolina as the site for its first U.S. plant after conducting a comprehensive location study. Transportation was an important cost component and trucking was the natural choice. Market density and infrastructure considerations narrowed potential locations down to seven, all close to interstate highways. The geographical analysis was complemented by three important factors:

1. Proximity to a "top 10" airport was deemed important for conducting national business and for corresponding with the Belgian home location.

2. The need for a large daily supply of eggs and fresh cream—the two key raw materials for cream puffs—required availability of at least two suppliers within a 300 mile radius.

3. Utility costs were carefully estimated because the high energy consumption by the baking and continuous "flash deep freezing" operations. Of special importance were electricity costs, which depend on average outside temperatures.

Seven potential locations were analyzed and a spreadsheet was used to estimate the total landed cost for each major market. Figure 6.4 illustrates the geographical analysis of expected total cost to serve its customer base for the St. Louis candidate location.

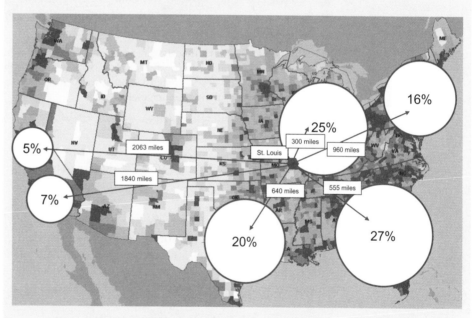

Figure 6.4: To locate its first plant the U.S., Poppies relied heavily on a geographical approach. Customer density suggested 6 major markets and total supply chain costs were estimated for 7 potential locations.

Poppies' spreadsheet analysis was noteworthy because it estimated total costs over a 10-year horizon, anticipating inflation and sales growth. Location had a significant impact: the difference (in the present value of total costs) between the lowest and highest cost location was about 16%. Interestingly, five years later, the actual costs were very close to the original forecast. *Source: Kerkhof (2005).*

Analytics Box 6.1 Total Landed Cost Calculations

The total landed cost is the total end-to-end cost to transform inputs to outputs at customers. It is estimated by tracking flow units along their routes through the activity network and recording incurred costs along the way. Following Pyke (2007), consider, for example, the typical total landed cost components for a network with an offshore plant and a domestic distribution center (DC):

1. Inbound raw materials and services: purchasing cost at the offshore plant.

2. Inbound logistics: the cost of moving inputs to the offshore plant.

3. Manufacturing and inventory cost at the offshore plant.

4. Overhead at the offshore plant and domestically: consider the incremental costs of management, staff, and support (IT, legal, etc.)—but be careful not to double count costs that appear in other categories. When assessing product-to-plant allocations, distinguish variable overhead (which depends on volume; e.g., setups, maintenance) from fixed overhead (which is independent of volume, such as some utilities, management staff, and depreciation).

5. Outbound logistics: consider cost and leadtimes for (i) customs, duties and taxes, (ii) offshore plant to offshore port, (iii) offshore port to domestic port, (iv) domestic port to domestic DC, (v) fulfillment at DC, (vi) DC to customers. Pipeline inventory will increase if lead-times increase or are more variable. (Use standard formulas for cycle and safety stock, see, for example, Chapters 6 & 7 in Anupindi et al. 2006.)

6. Inventory at domestic DC, which will also increase if lead-times increase or are more variable.

7. Make sure to include other incremental costs, such as supplier relationship management costs (including travel cost for managers to visit suppliers), translation costs, and other soft costs (hassle of managers getting up at 3:00 a.m. to place phone calls to their supplier, etc).

6.3 | FOUR TYPES OF LOCATION ANALYSES

There are four broad types of analyses that can be used to further evaluate and quantify the impact of the supply, technology, demand, and macroeconomic factors in the location decision. Each type of analysis tends to highlight a subset of the factors. Each situation thus calls for a specific analysis, depending on which location factors are dominant.

Geographical or spatial analysis and total landed cost

A *geographical* or *spatial analysis* quantifies the market supply and demand factors of the location decisions. It is part of the typical location analysis when transportation costs constitute a significant fraction of total cost. Poppies International's location decision for its U.S. plant used customer density and supply chain cost analysis, as described in Example 6.2 (p. 207). Some other industries with significant transportation costs are the cement industry and the fiberglass insulation industry (where transportation constitutes up to 20 percent of total cost).

Figure 6.5 A major appliance manufacturer used this map of 2003 U.S. customer density, along with other information to make decisions about where to offer premium service operations.

Spatial analysis starts with estimates of market demand per region (or customer density) and of the number of facilities that are needed (see next sections). Potential locations are often identified by infrastructure considerations such as proximity to highways, railroads, or airports, or analytic approaches such as gravity location or optimization models, as described in detail by Chopra and Meindl (2007). The spatial analysis ends by comparing all the potential sites' total landed costs (Analytics Box 6.1).

Spatial analysis is also useful for fine-tuning service offerings. For example, a global appliance manufacturer used a density map of its U.S. customer base (Figure 6.5), along with other information, to make decisions about where to offer premium service operations.

Network analysis

Network analysis considers the entirety of the company's locations and interconnections. Such analysis highlights a part of the technology factor and can be used in conjunction with spatial analysis or risk assessment (later in this chapter we will use a network analysis to value flexibility in global networks).

Network analysis also captures the interdependency of the location decision with capacity sizing and timing. Let us consider the interaction between location and timing to incorporate possible future expansions (location and sizing is analyzed in the next section). To frame ideas, consider Acciona Energy, a world leader in renewable energy, which has two wind turbine factories in Spain, and one in China. In 2006, the company decided to start manufacturing operations

Figure 6.6 Location strategies should anticipate future additions. The central location A may be best during market development. However, if market growth is expected, it may be better to start at location B or C to have a better network (B & C) in the long run.

in North America with an initial focus on the production of 1.5MW wind turbines in the U.S. A geographical analysis may identify Indiana (location A in Figure 6.6) as a good location for Acciona Energy's U.S. plant during early market development.

If demand is expected to grow significantly, however, that central location may not provide the best starting point for future additional locations. Rather, a position like B or C in Fig. 6.6 may incur some higher costs initially but would allow a lower cost network (B & C) in the long run. If customer proximity is an important competitive driver, one may even establish both "beachhead" locations from the start and later expand them.

Competitive analysis

When demand or customer proximity is an important source of competitive advantage, the location strategy may be more driven by *competitive considerations* which can result in the grouping together of competitors. For example, car dealerships tend to cluster. Another example involves politics: as election cycles draw near, both Democrats and Republicans tend to move to the center to attract as many voters as possible.

The collocation of competitors is in line with predictions from game theory, as Harold Hotelling showed in 1929 with his classic model and analysis of competitive location. The idea goes as follows. Suppose that two competing car dealerships are deciding on a location along Main Street and that customers tend to favor the dealer closest to them. The central location is optimal for a single dealership. Hotelling (1929) predicts that this same central location will

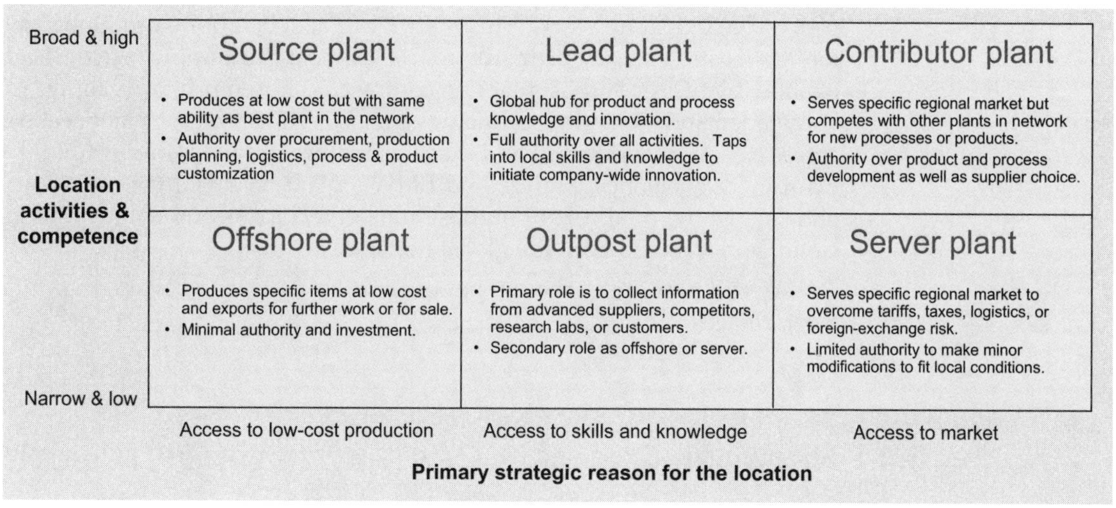

Broad & high	**Source plant**	**Lead plant**	**Contributor plant**
	• Produces at low cost but with same ability as best plant in the network • Authority over procurement, production planning, logistics, process & product customization	• Global hub for product and process knowledge and innovation. • Full authority over all activities. Taps into local skills and knowledge to initiate company-wide innovation.	• Serves specific regional market but competes with other plants in network for new processes or products. • Authority over product and process development as well as supplier choice.
Location activities & competence	**Offshore plant**	**Outpost plant**	**Server plant**
	• Produces specific items at low cost and exports for further work or for sale. • Minimal authority and investment.	• Primary role is to collect information from advanced suppliers, competitors, research labs, or customers. • Secondary role as offshore or server.	• Serves specific regional market to overcome tariffs, taxes, logistics, or foreign-exchange risk. • Limited authority to make minor modifications to fit local conditions.
Narrow & low	Access to low-cost production	Access to skills and knowledge	Access to market

Primary strategic reason for the location

Figure 6.7 A strategic role matrix for facilities (Ferdows 1997).

be chosen in equilibrium by two competing dealers, who then each will serve half of Main Street. Notice that it would be socially optimal for one dealer to move to the left quarter of main street and the other to the right quarter. Even though both dealers would keep their same market share (and customers would be better off), no dealer will choose that location independently because it would allow the competitor to relocate and garner a higher market share.

Facility role or focus analysis

The location strategy also specifies the role and competencies of a specific site, which is closely related to deciding on operational focus, discussed in section 2.6 on p. 53. Some authors use the term *facility strategy* to denote how the size, location, and type (or role) of individual facilities are chosen.

In order to decide on the role, we must assign activities and responsibilities to individual facilities. For example, the electronics industry often separates the workflow by activities into R&D, component manufacturing, and assembly and test. These activities are then quite naturally allocated to parent plants, component plants, and assembly and test locations.

The strategic role of a site not only assigns activities (i.e., a part of the value chain) but also clearly specifies responsibilities and competencies as part of the global network. To help articulate this strategic role, Ferdows (1997) suggests that managers start their facility focus analysis by answering two basic questions about each facility:

1. What is the primary strategic reason for the facility's location?

2. What is the scope of its current activities and competencies?

The answer to these questions leads to the strategic role matrix (Figure 6.7), where foreign plants are categorized by the primary strategic reason of their location (horizontal axis) and the scope of their activities and competencies as part of the global network. This matrix can also be applied to globalization: a foreign location chosen primarily for its low cost (the supply factor) is called an offshore plant. An outpost plant, in contrast, is chosen primarily for its access to knowledge and skills (the technology factor), while a server plant seeks market access (the market demand and macroeconomic factors). For example, Toyota's plant in Valenciennes, France, and BMW's plant near Spartanburg, South Carolina, serve the dual role of outpost and server plants. Over time, these plants could gain larger roles in the global network.

We will now apply these types of analyses to discuss several important network choices.

6.4 | NETWORK CHOICES: CENTRALIZE OR DISTRIBUTE?

Location decisions shape the ultimate operating network. Here we use spatial analysis to study the interaction between capacity size and location, which explains the desired spatial network concentration.

Factors favoring a centralized network

Centralization, or consolidating operations in a single location, is typically observed when "bigger is better." In the previous chapter (section 5.7 on p. 170), we saw that consolidation allows resource sharing. We then derived its value from three main sources: economies of scale, risk pooling, and real options.

Recall that economies of scale, or increasing returns to scale, stem from aggregating volumes and result in unit costs that decline in size. Aggregating volumes can yield scale economies at many stages in the value chain, including product design (of one product or re-use earlier designs), sourcing (centralized sourcing may benefit from quantity discounts), capacity investment (section 3.4), inbound transportation (coordinated or in bulk), inventory (volume aggregation smooths and reduces cycle stock per unit), and overhead. Any batch process that spreads a fixed cost over more units enjoys scale economies (as manifested by the square root law of the EOQ model in Appendix A).

Risk pooling stems from aggregating volatilities and results in reduced safety capacity and safety inventory, increased revenues and service levels, and reduced profit variance risk (recall Analytics Box 5.3 on p. 175). Risk pooling increases the efficiency of large service processes such as call centers (recall Fig. 3.13), as well as centralized distribution systems such as Amazon's.

Sometimes, centralized networks can better guarantee consistent and uniform quality than distributed networks can. For example, FedEx and UPS use central hub-and-spoke networks for their air transportation. Inbound planes arrive and unload before midnight. Automatic re-sorting loads outbound planes that leave early in the morning. As such, the centralized hub-and-spoke network guarantees overnight delivery. Moreover, air transportation is a highly fixed-costs business that is only slightly impacted by distance, in sharp contrast with ground transportation, which favors distributed networks.

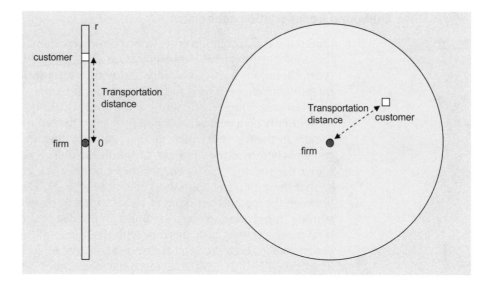

Figure 6.8 Representation of transportation costs from a centrally located firm to a customer base dispersed linearly (left) or spatially (right).

Factors favoring a distributed network

Distributed networks that operate in many locations are implemented when "closer is better." One prototypical example is the distribution sector, which includes supermarkets and shopping facilities whose revenues depend on attracting dispersed customers through proximity. Another example is businesses that actually deliver to dispersed customers. Both settings face cumulative transportation costs from one point to a set of customer points dispersed over an area. Such outbound transportation costs increase super-linearly with the size of the served area. The resulting total landed cost then exhibits decreasing returns to scale. This favors serving a large area from multiple dispersed locations, each serving a subarea. For example, UPS and FedEx have a distributed network of storage and forwarding locations for ground transportation.

Transportation costs can measure customer convenience and explain why retail banking features distributed networks. Fast response time requirements, as in fire-fighting operations and emergency care, also impact transportation costs and thus favor the close proximity of facilities to customers.

Distributed networks also have many intangible benefits. For instance, in January 2001, Toyota's new plant in Valenciennes, France produced its first Yaris. Even though Toyota already had a plant in the UK, it chose France to "produce where the market is" and to prove its engagement to Europe. The expectation was that Toyota's local presence would improve the understanding of its market needs (especially in small cars) and would expedite the adoption of the brand.

Outbound transportation economics

Outbound transportation costs from a central location to a distributed set of customers (or, equivalently, transportation costs incurred by customers to visit a central location) increase rapidly and non-linearly in the sales area and consequently encourage a firm to have many local plants. To see this, consider the simplest case where customers are uniformly distributed over a line and served individually by a centrally located firm, as in the left display in Figure 6.8. Customers in the top half of the market are at an average distance of $\frac{1}{2}r$ from the center, where r is the "radius" of the linear delivery zone. Normalizing customer density to 1 customer per meter, there are r customers in the top half so that their total transportation distance is $r \times \frac{1}{2}r$. Recognizing the symmetry between the top and bottom half yields a total transportation distance of r^2. Assuming transportation costs are linear in the distance traveled, this means that total transportation costs increase with the square of the radius of the linear delivery zone. Thus, the total transportation cost to serve an area of double the length is $(2r)^2 = 4r^2$, which exceeds the total cost of $2r^2$ when the two locations would each serve an area of length r.

A similar argument applies to customers that are uniformly distributed spatially, say over a circle where total transportation costs[2] are proportional to r^3. Again, the average unit transportation cost (total cost/number of customers) is proportional to $r^3/r^2 = r$.

In summary, average per unit transportation or landed costs between a central location and a distributed set of customers increase in scale.

Trade-offs and optimal area to serve per facility

The key point is that the total network cost per unit includes a set of costs that decrease and another that increase with the size of the served area. The total cost per unit thus reaches a minimum at a specific size (as shown in Figure 6.9), which is a facility's optimal geographic coverage. This optimal size is the value-maximizing trade-off between increasing and decreasing returns, and determines the extent to which the network should be centralized or distributed.

6.5 | NETWORK CHOICES: LOCALIZE OR STANDARDIZE?

When operating in several locations, operations strategy must decide to what extent resources and processes at different locations should be similar.

Factors favoring standardization ("copy-exactly")

Resources and processes used in research and development often vary greatly from those used in high-volume production facilities. Typically, a team of R&D engineers would optimize the process in a development facility and a new set of engineers would transfer and adapt the process for high-volume production. This was not the case at Intel, which adopted its *Copy Exactly* facility strategy,

---

[2]Then one needs some calculus to find the total transportation distance of $\frac{2\pi}{3}r^3$.

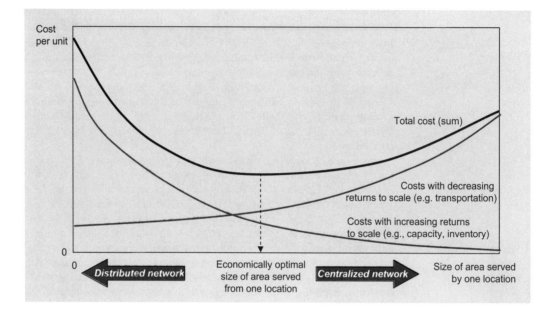

Figure 6.9 The degree to which a network should be centralized or distributed depends on the optimal area size to serve from one location. This optimal size trades off costs having increasing returns to scale with costs having decreasing returns.

described in Example 6.3. Standardizing resources and processes between R&D and production facilities decreases ramp time and improves yields, which are important achievements for innovators. The *Copy Exactly* strategy also improves productivity by sharing learning and not reinventing the wheel.

Standardized facilities create one giant capacity pool with great flexibility to allocate and shift demand seamlessly among facilities. This not only mitigates demand-supply mismatch risk, but also creates redundancy and robustness. Furthermore, standardization creates economies of scale in purchasing equipment and allows centralized global sourcing, which will further be explored in Chapter 7.

Factors favoring localization and tailoring

While corporate and operations managers may favor standardization, there are benefits to tailoring resources and processes to the needs of each location. This is especially important if customers prefer, or local regulations require, some customization. Accenture and many other consulting companies try to roll out "global methodologies," but client teams often say that their project is unique or requires customization. By their very nature, the formal processes needed to enforce and preserve standardization may slow down and even stifle local improvements. Yet, there is always a tension between standardization and progress: standards must be changed from time to time, yet "it's not a standard if it changes too frequently."

> **Example 6.3** Intel's "Copy Exactly" Facility Strategy
>
> Intel introduced its "Copy Exactly" factory strategy in the mid-1980s and completed its implementation in 1996. Intel credits "Copy Exactly" with enabling the company to quickly bring factories online with high-volume practices already in place, hence decreasing time to market and increasing yields. Rapid productivity and financial gains followed. In 1997, VLSI Research estimated that revenues per manufacturing employee increased from $114,000 in 1985 to $461,000 in 1995. Meanwhile, the company's revenue increased by three times during those 10 years, while the number of factory workers decreased by 30 percent.
>
> "Copy Exactly" solves the problem of getting production facilities up to speed quickly by duplicating everything from the development plant to the volume-manufacturing plant. In particular, it means that it ensures that the process devised at the development facility is fine tuned not just for performance and reliability, but also for high-volume production. To do that, managers from high-volume facilities participate in the development plant as new process technologies are created. When "Copy Exactly" was first implemented, only equipment and process output parameters were copied exactly to the high-volume plant. During the last decade, Intel has widely expanded the functions that were duplicated in high-volume factories. Now, everything at the development plant—the process flow, equipment set, suppliers, plumbing, manufacturing clean room, and training methodologies—is selected to meet high volume needs, recorded, and then copied exactly to the high-volume plant. *Source: Intel (2007).*

Allowing facilities to evolve separately may also be more cost and time-effective than requiring each facility to increase its level of flexibility. Uneven process or supplier capabilities across locations may also prevent effective standardization.

6.6 | NETWORK CHOICES: INTEGRATE OR SEPARATE?

Location decisions not only interact with the spatial concentration of the network but also with the flexibility within the network.

Global network alternatives

Consider, for example, a firm serving two markets, a domestic market and an offshore market, each with a market specific product. Global network strategy here involves two major decisions: spatial network concentration and network integration, or flexibility. With two markets, deciding on spatial concentration involves choosing between one centralized location (either domestic or offshore) or two distributed locations. Deciding on network integration means choosing the number and type of possible allocations from resources to markets, which affect network flexibility. These allocations are represented by routes in the six global network alternatives represented in Figure 6.10. In the previous chapter, we learned how chained allocations lead to tailored network flexibility (p. 181). Thus, global network design must decide on location (spatial concentration) as well as integration (flexibility).

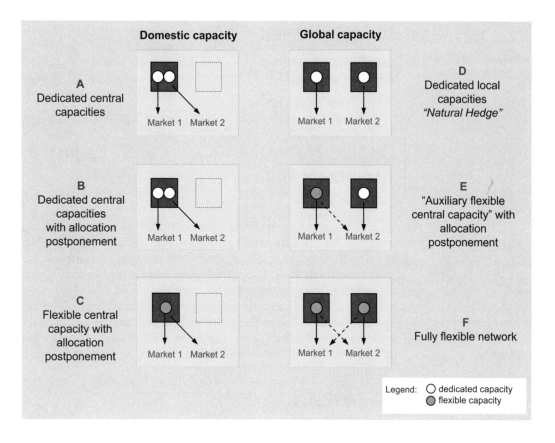

Figure 6.10 Global network choices for a two market setting. Both markets can be served by domestic capacity (left) or by global capacity (right). Both cases can differ in the amount of operational flexibility in the network.

Separate networks

In a separable network such as network D in Figure 6.10, resource-market allocations can be disentangled and each allocation can be managed separately and independently. The main benefits of separate, or dedicated, networks are market focus (with resulting efficiencies) and operating simplicity (needs minimal coordination).

Integrated networks and network flexibility

In integrated networks, one location can serve multiple markets (e.g., networks A, B, C, E, and F in Figure 6.10) or multiple locations can serve one market (e.g., networks E and F in Figure 6.10).

The amount of network flexibility depends on the degree of integration and on each location's capacity flexibility. The least flexible network has two dedicated capacities with long lead-times such that all production and market allocation must be done before demand is observed. It is useful to separate the total lead-time into production and transportation lead-times. With short transportation lead-times, market allocation can be postponed to save on transportation costs. With flexible capacity and short production and transportation lead-times, production allocation can be postponed to better match demand with supply. In addition, capacity investment can be reduced through risk pooling benefits.

6.7 | GLOBAL NETWORK VALUATION: FLEXIBILITY AND CURRENCY RISK

To value the operational flexibility embedded in integrated global networks, we must model relevant costs, revenues, and risks. In the previous chapter, we learned how to value and optimize the amount of flexibility in a network exposed to demand risk. Global networks add currency exchange rate risks, as well as increased transportation costs, tariffs, and other duties. Valuation involves estimating costs, demands, and currency exchange rates for a set of representative scenarios. It also requires optimizing production and allocation decisions in each scenario. Production and capacity allocation decisions depend on the level of network flexibility inherent in the operating system. Let us start with a simple example.

Global network example[3]

Consider a global firm operating in Europe and the U.S. that is exposed to demand and currency risk. Suppose that the unit sales price is €20,000 in Europe and $20,000 in the U.S.; similarly, the unit cost is 10,000 in local currency. Suppose that currencies are correlated with demand and that there are two, equally likely future scenarios (states of nature):

1. U.S. demand is 100k units, Euro demand is 50k, and the exchange rate is $1/€.

2. U.S. demand is 50k units, Euro demand is 100k, and the exchange rate is $2/€.

Assume that the unit cost of transportation, tariffs, and duties is $6,000 and that the firm aspires to high service levels. The firm wonders what the value is of having an integrated global network with production facilities in both continents.

Domestic capacities (networks A, B, and C in Fig. 6.10)

Assume that the firm would produce only in the U.S. If the firm must allocate and transport before seeing actual demand (network A), it would produce 100 thousand units for the U.S. and 100 thousand units to be exported to Europe. Total production costs are 200k units × $10k = $2 billion plus 100k units × $6k = $.6 billion in transportation, tariffs and duties. Revenues in dollars depend on the particular scenario:

---

[3]This example builds on the global manufacturer's dilemma example by Professor John R. Birge.

1. 100k × \$20k (U.S.) + 50k × €20k × \$1/€ (Europe) = \$3 billion.

2. 50k × \$20k (U.S.) + 100k × €20k × \$2/€ (Europe) = \$5 billion.

The average operating profit is \$4 billion - \$2.6 billion = \$1.4 billion.

If the firm can postpone production and allocation until it sees which scenario will occur (network B), it can save considerably. Expected revenues equal the \$4 billion of network A, but costs are contingent:

1. 150k × \$10k (U.S.) + 50k × \$6k (export) = \$1.8 billion.

2. 150k × \$10k (U.S.) + 100k × \$6k (export) = \$2.1 billion.

The average cost is \$1.95 billion and operating profit is \$4 - \$1.95 = \$2.05 billion.

Notice that if the firm uses dedicated (i.e., separate) capacities for each market, it would need to invest in 100 thousand units of capacity for each market, or 200 thousand in total. In contrast, if it were to use flexible capacity (network C), only 150 thousand units of capacity are needed.

Dedicated global capacities (network D)

If the firm produces and sells locally and can postpone production, operating profits per scenario are:

1. 100k × \$(20k-10k) + 50k × €(20-10)k × \$1/€ = \$1.5 billion.

2. 50k × \$(20k-10k) + 100k × €(20-10)k × \$2/€ = \$2.5 billion.

The expected profit is \$2 b. While this is slightly lower than in networks B and C, it provides a natural hedge; because both revenues and costs are in the same currency, the total cash flow risk is ±500M, compared to ±850M with domestic capacities.

Integrated global network with allocation flexibility (networks E and F)

If the firm integrates its global network with 100 thousand units of capacity in each continent (network D) by including contingent transshipment, it can do better by optimizing scenario-dependent production and allocation. This is typically done with a stochastic linear program or by using optimization via simulation, as described in Chapter 5 on p. 176 and p. 192.

In our simple example, this can be done by hand: in scenario 1, production costs are equal in both markets so local production saves transportation and import fees. In scenario 2, however, production costs in Europe are double those of the U.S., and the difference exceeds exporting costs so that U.S. production should be maximized. The resulting expected operating profit is \$2.1 billion according to Table 6.1.

An optimized integrated global network

If we also optimize the amount and the location of capacity in the network, we find the optimal network configuration shown in Table 6.2. Compared to the dedicated global network D, the value of global network integration and optimization in this example equals \$200 million or 10%. Compared to network

Allocation Decisions				
Scenario	U.S. →U.S.	Euro→Euro	U.S. →Euro	Euro→U.S.
1	100,000	50,000	0	0
2	50,000	50,000	50,000	0

Operating profit and expected value					Capacity	
Scenario	Revenues	Cost	Profit		U.S.	100k
1	$3,000M	$1,500M	$1,500M		Europe	100k
2	$5,000M	$2,300M	$2,700M			
Expected	$4,000M	$1,900M	$2,100M			

Table 6.1 An integrated global network with allocation flexibility.

Allocation Decisions				
Scenario	U.S. →U.S.	Euro→Euro	U.S. →Euro	Euro→U.S.
1	100,000	50,000	0	0
2	50,000	0	100,000	0

Operating profit and expected value					Capacity	
Scenario	Revenues	Cost	Profit		U.S.	150k
1	$3,000M	$1,500M	$1,500M		Europe	50k
2	$5,000M	$2,100M	$2,900M			
Expected	$4,000M	$1,800M	$2,200M			

Table 6.2 An optimal global network.

C, where the flexible domestic capacity is only 150,000 units and has a value of $2.05 ± .85 billion, the value of integration and optimization is $150 million with a reduced cash flow risk of ±700M. Notice, however, that the optimal network must have 50,000 units of extra flexible (U.S.) capacity in order to be able to exploit upside risk.

This is an example of operational hedging via allocation flexibility, which can improve value *and* decrease risk. In Chapter 9, we will further investigate whether the exchange rate risk of offshoring is better hedged operationally or financially (e.g., using futures).[4]

Key insights for optimal integrated global networks

While our example was quite simple, its logic and insights can be generalized to networks with more locations, products, demand, and currency exchange risks. For the optimization, we just add more scenarios which can also account for dynamic evolution. The important insights are:

1. It is valuable to integrate global networks through flexible capacity, contingent allocations, and transshipments, especially as costs and revenues differ across locations and as demand and exchange rates become more volatile. This is because operational flexibility allows us to capture more of the upside and decrease our exposure to the downside.

---

[4]Offshoring allows companies to hedge exchange rate risk via both flexible production and the ability to institute foreign denominated debt that is collateralized on foreign assets (thus providing a natural hedge).

2. To be able to exploit the upside, the network needs extra capacity. There is no such thing as a free lunch: to exercise allocation switching options, the network needs sufficient excess capacity. Excess capacity becomes more valuable when product margins are high compared to capacity costs.

3. The best global network configuration can be determined by optimizing the amounts and locations of capacity. The optimization must incorporate demand and exchange rate risks in addition to costs.

The last insight suggests a network perspective to offshoring.

6.8 | OFFSHORING

Offshoring means locating operations abroad.

The evolving reasons behind offshoring

The traditional reason behind offshoring is to lower operational costs; yet, the other factors in our framework are rapidly gaining importance. For example,[5] Emerson Electric started operating in China in the mid 1980s and enjoyed strong labor cost reductions, from $1.50/hr in Mexico to $0.20/hr in China. Still, they quickly saw that China had market opportunities and more important capabilities, such as flexibility, infrastructure, and a supply base capable of providing their direct material (which comprise 50% of cost). Over the last ten years, the company realized that they can even execute a small volume, high mix strategy in China because they can have more engineers there than in the U.S. Similarly, Eaton Corporation's objective for "going to China" was to gain market access, understand the market, and provide the right value to penetrate the market. After offshoring to Malaysia and Singapore, Motorola has pursued China since the 1980s, hoping to follow their market (growth in China exceeds growth in the U.S.) and increase responsiveness (reduce cycle time to respond and tailor to local requirements).

Paradoxically, offshoring can lead to *shorter* leadtimes than onshoring in labor-intensive environments with high seasonal demand volatility. While this effect is evident in manufacturing (Example 6.4), it can also apply to offshored R&D, like pharmaceutical drug development, which allows for cheaper and faster failure of projects and thus quicker ultimate success. While it does not reduce project risk, offshoring can allow more "shots on goal" rather than "make the goal easier to score on."

An ongoing study (Fig. 6.11) confirms that 73% of offshoring arrangements are pursuing growth, with 32% of those initiatives involving product innovation and design, R&D, or engineering.

Risks of offshoring: macroeconomic and non-market factors

Offshoring shares the risks of remote foreign operations, including:

---

[5]Source: personal conversations with managers at Emerson, Eaton, and Motorola. May 12, 2007.

> **Example 6.4** Norman's offshoring strategy leads to shorter leadtimes
>
> Norman International Inc., founded in 2001, produces custom-made window shutters at its Chinese manufacturing facility, and exports the products to its L.A. facility for distribution in U.S. markets. Because Norman is the only company in the industry to produce custom-made shutters in China, it enjoys a huge cost advantage. Thus, it can offer more selections at a higher quality than most of its U.S. counterparts in terms of frame types, colors, materials, and specialty window shapes. This has resulted in a 2006 sales revenue of $100 million that is expected to grow at 30–40% annually for the next 3 years.
>
> Norman's value proposition is to provide consistently high quality shutters within a consistently short lead-time and with wider selection at lower costs than its counterparts. Higher quality can be achieved at lower cost because high quality shutter production is very labor intensive. For example, a smooth and lustrous surface requires multiple hand-sanding and finishing operations, which is cost prohibitive in the U.S. Interestingly, shorter lead-times are possible because of a higher safety capacity in China. Due to high labor costs in the U.S., most U.S. counterparts do not buffer seasonal demand fluctuation through excess capacity, and thus require longer lead-times (ranging from 4—14 weeks). *Source: Chou et al. (2007).*

1. Competitive risk: an offshoring strategy that chases low cost is easily imitated (e.g., island hopping–discussed earlier).

2. Currency risks, which were magnified by the Asian financial crisis of the late 1990s.

3. Political risks never disappear. The fear of terrorism makes it difficult to operate in certain countries. A key risk for China is how it will handle its growing divergence in wealth (what will China do after the Beijing Olympics?).

4. Intellectual property (IP) risk is significant in some emerging countries. According to Eaton Corp., a typical strategy to contain that risk is IP compartmentalization, which breaks up a project or product into smaller parts that are executed or manufactured at different locations.

5. Health and environmental risk, and corporate social responsibility. In 2007, various countries from Latin America to Asia rejected Chinese-made toothpaste. Chinese wheat gluten tainted with the chemical melamine was blamed for dog and cat deaths in North America. Other products turned away by U.S. inspectors included toxic monkfish, frozen eel, and juice made with unsafe color additives. In June 2007, the U.S. Consumer Product Safety Commission announced a voluntary recall of dozens of Thomas & Friends Wooden Railway Toys. Some of the wildly popular toy train sets were manufactured in southern China and contained potentially poisonous lead paint. Fairly or not, people "have a limited attention span when it comes to human rights problems on the other side of the world. But the prospect of lead paint in your child's nervous system tends to focus the mind"(Leonhardt 2007).

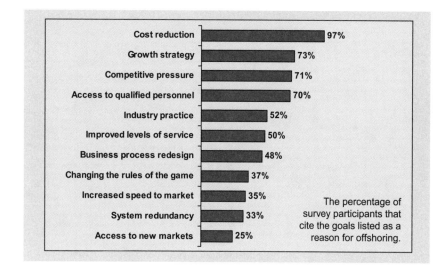

Figure 6.11 Reasons for offshoring according to a survey by Lewin et al. (2006) that tracks hundreds of offshoring projects in 104 U.S. companies.

Risks of offshoring: operational factors

Logistics costs and lead-times are key operational risks of offshoring. Moving products or services across national boundaries incurs tariffs, brokerage costs and other import taxes. The longer supply chains not only incur higher costs, but also longer and more variable lead-times which reduce market responsiveness and increase inventories. Potential quality concerns only exacerbate these risks. Maintaining a domestic backup source is an effective instrument to mitigate these risks.

While offshoring is easier when the product or service is digitizable, the service risk still remains. Dell and many others have offshored U.S. call center operations to India, hiring workers who are well versed in the English language. Given that customers prefer listening to a familiar accent, however, Capital One in the UK closed all its call centers in India.

Factors favoring a global network and even onshoring

Offshoring can be viewed as a specific network strategy. For example, if we consider the U.S. and Asia, there are four possible network strategies as illustrated in Figure 6.12. From our preceding discussion about network flexibility, it follows that in a risky environment, the integrated global network is more valuable than the local network.[6]

Global networks are also increasingly pursued by companies in developing

---

[6] As a matter of fact, the global network is typically the optimal one; offshoring and onshoring (networks 3 and 4) can only arise as boundary solutions to the optimal network design. Lu and Van Mieghem (2007) show that onshoring can be optimal under high demand uncertainty when the price differential between the domestic and foreign market is high while the manufacturing cost differential is less than the transportation-tariff cost.

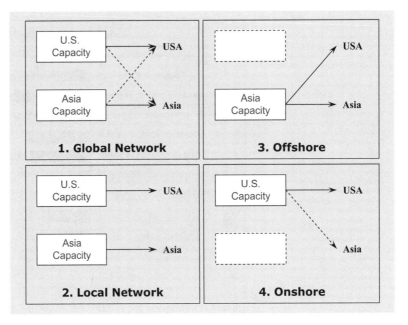

Figure 6.12 Offshoring is viewed as one of four possible network strategies.

countries, and may lead to 'reverse offshoring.' For example, Chinese electronics manufacturer Sichuan Changhong is building a $30 million factory in the Czech town of Nymburk with a capacity of 1 million flat-screen televisions a year (Rocks 2007). Similarly, Taiwan's Foxconn Technology Co. makes millions of computers and electronic gear for HP, Cisco Systems, and Apple at its sprawling 200,000 worker facility in south China. Yet, it also has a fast response, $80 million factory employing 5,000 people in Pardubice, Czech Replublic.

The reasoning behind these Central European plants illustrates the factors that favor a global network and even onshoring:

1. High scale economies with substantial domestic markets favors onshoring. For example, Sichuan Changhong's high volume plant in Nymburk enjoys economies of scale and provides access to the Euro zone.

2. A competitive strategy based on speed favors domestic capacity. Operating in Central Europe allows quick response to changes in demand. "When customers want things basically yesterday, you can't afford to have them sitting on a ship for 35 days," according to Chang, Foxconn's operations chief.

3. There may be high tariff-transportation costs relative to the production cost savings from offshoring. This applies to heavy or bulky items and to items with relatively low direct labor content. Protectionism can also make importing expensive. For example, locating in the Czech Republic, Sichuan Changhong reduces transportation costs to the Euro zone and evades the 14% Euro tariff on televisions made in China.

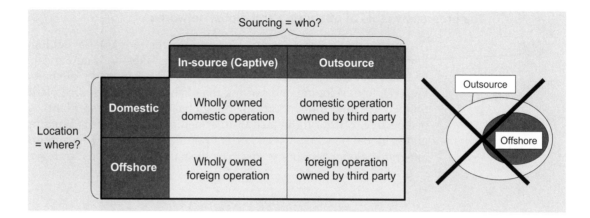

Figure 6.13 Offshoring and outsourcing are answers to different questions: where is an operation performed versus who owns it?

4. High currency exchange rate risk typically favors the natural hedge embedded in the global network. It may even lead to onshoring if there is a substantially profitable domestic market. Locating in the Euro zone provides natural hedging.

5. High demand volatility along with high price differences favors a global network, and even onshoring, if capacity is expensive. Assume, for example, that a product sells for $100 in Europe but only $50 in Asia. If capacity is expensive, it is likely that demand exceeds supply, in which case the more profitable European market will get allocation priority. The resulting profit increase and savings in tariff-transportation costs may outweigh the higher production cost of Central Europe over China.

Distinguish between offshoring and outsourcing

While the casual observer may associate offshoring with outsourcing, both are independent concepts; not all offshoring involves outsourcing. Offshore outsourcing is only one of four possible strategies in the offshoring-outsourcing matrix of Figure 6.13. The rows specify where an operation is performed, and the columns describe who owns the operation. Outsourcing will be studied in the next chapter.

Captive offshoring is illustrated by GE, American Express, and British Airways, who all own call centers in India (Gauntt 2004). The Indian workers handle calls from the U.S. and are employees of the American firm.

In contrast, offshore outsourcing is the relocation of industry activities to another country; it is similar to trading and applies equally to goods and services. For example, Mass General Hospital outsources some X-ray diagnosis to radiologists in India.

The progressive role of offshoring and global networks

An offshoring strategy designed to capture cost advantages seldom yields a long-term competitive advantage. Offshoring takes on a new meaning when its role broadens over time from seeking a cost advantage ("offshore plant" in Fig. 6.7), to developing and serving the offshore market (source plant), and ultimately creating innovations for the global company (lead plant). From this perspective, offshoring is just an intermediate step towards building an integrated global network. Given current population and growth projections, such integrated global network seems to be the natural operations strategy.

6.9 | GUIDELINES

Think globally: consider costs *and* revenues

Globalization is almost certain to increase given current population and development trends. This necessitates a global operations strategy. Global networks allow an organization to relocate activities to their optimal location, which provides a tremendous opportunity for cost reduction. The McKinsey Global Institute estimates that adding offshore locations to the network followed by a re-optimization of the value chain can reduce cost by up to 70%.

Importantly, this reduced cost base gives companies the opportunity to substantially reduce prices in both old and new markets, and to expand demand and profits. For example, if a carmaker dropped the unit price of a vehicle by 30%—from $10,000 to $7,000—demand would nearly double over time, from 22 million to 41 million units sold (factoring in typical price elasticities), according to Farrell (2004).

Global network flexibility is valuable

While globalization improves cost and revenue potentials, it also increases the stakes and exposes the organization to more risk. Integrated networks with allocation flexibility not only provide an operational hedge against supply, demand, political, and macroeconomic risks, but they can also exploit the upside and add value. Chapter 9 further explores risk mitigation and operational hedging.

Tailor the locations in your network

Successful global organizations tailor their networks to their strategies and local conditions. For example, while offshore textile production of basic apparel is to be expected, domestic facilities are more appropriate for Zara's fast fashion strategy. The framework, network trade-offs, and valuation study in this chapter can be used to optimally fit your global network to your strategy, industry, and market needs.

6.10 | SUMMARY OF LEARNING OBJECTIVES

1. Integrate location decisions with operations strategy and relate them to globalization.

> Rather than letting location decisions be guided by a single motive such as cost reduction, successful location decisions must be approached strategically. The desired competencies must be aligned with the corporate strategy and the location decision must be integrated with the other elements of operations strategy.
>
> The strategic framework considers the interaction between location and the required size, timing, type and flexibility of the organization's capacity portfolio. The framework also integrates the location decision with the organization's activity network. The important elements to consider are the impact of location on the supply management of inputs, the site's technology, the market demand, and the organization's innovation processes. Last, but not least, is the consideration of macroeconomic and non-market factors.
>
> In practice, the importance of each factor depends on the organization. This framework explains why firms globalize their operations: increasing markets and decreasing costs are primary reasons. Improved access to inputs, suppliers, or technology also drives globalization, as do macroeconomic and non-market factors. Protectionist measures such as tariffs and quotas favor localized operations, as do free-trade zones or monetary unions.

2. Apply four types of location analyses: geographical and total landed cost, network, competitive, and focus.

> Four main types of analyses can guide location decisions. A geographical or spatial analysis is needed when proximity or transportation costs are important. Such an approach uses customer density or demand per region and calculates the total landed cost of serving customers from a set of candidate locations. Closely related is network analysis, which focuses on the interaction between sizing, timing, and flexibility of each location in the network.
>
> When location is an important factor to draw customers, competitive considerations may drive location decisions. Game theory predicts collocation as an equilibrium outcome. When demand is expected to increase significantly, locations should anticipate future expansions. The fourth analysis considers the strategic role and focus of each location as part of the necessary organizational competencies.

3. Discuss several network choices: centralize or distribute? Localize or standardize? Integrate or separate? Offshore or onshore?

> Location decisions interact with network strategy. Strong scale economies (e.g., from capacity investment, batching, or pooling) favor centralized networks, while decreasing returns to scale (e.g., from transportation) lead to distributed networks. The optimal trade-off determines a facility's size and location. Network strategy also decides to which extent locations should have standardized resources and processes, and how integrated or connected the network should be.
>
> Offshoring can be viewed as one of several potential network strategies. The qualitative and quantitative insights from this chapter can be used to determine

when offshoring, an integrated global network, or onshoring is most appropriate. Considering global population and development trends, global networks will only increase in value. Re-locating activities to their optimal location results in cost reduction; lower prices then expand markets and revenues. Yet, the main message of this book remains: the optimal network should be tailored to your strategy and the conditions you face.

4. Value flexibility and currency exchange rate risk in global networks.

Valuing flexible global networks requires modeling costs, revenues, and risks. Currency exchange rate risks and tariffs, taxes, and transportation costs are important elements in global valuation. Operational flexibility uses contingent allocations and transshipment to exploit upside variations. This flexibility is especially valuable if costs and revenues differ across locations and if demand and exchange rates are highly volatile. Optimizing a global network entails adding capacity at specific locations in order to optimize revenues as well as costs.

DISCUSSION QUESTIONS

1. INSEAD and the University of Chicago each have a campus in Singapore. INSEAD's is located at 1 Ayer Rajah Avenue while Chicago's address is 101 Penang Road. How would you explain the fact that both institutions are located on the other side of the world but less than 5km apart?

2. ITW owns two companies, Berkel and Hobard, that produce and sell food slicer machines. Berkel is located in South Bend, IN; Hobard is in Richmond Hill, GA. In 2007, ITW was contemplating merging the two food slicer operations. What analysis would you recommend to decide on the location of the merged operations?

3. "Domestic locations provide quicker responses to customer demands than offshore locations can." Discuss why, and whether, this is true.

4. "Offshoring is preferred when the manufacturing cost savings from offshoring outweigh the incremental transportation, taxes, and tariffs." Discuss why and when this is true.

Visit www.vanmieghem.us for additional questions and updates.

FURTHER READING AND REFERENCES

▶ Hayes and Wheelwright (1984) give an early account of location strategy in operations. Chopra and Meindl (2007) provide further analytic models of, and trade-offs between, location and transportation decisions. Lu and Van Mieghem (2007) analyze multi-market facility networks and discuss offshoring.

▶ References for global operations include Dornier, Ernst, Fender, and Kouvelis (1998), Farrell (2004), Ferdows (1997), and Lee and Lee (2007).

Anupindi, R., S. Chopra, S. D. Deshmukh, J. A. Van Mieghem, and E. Zemel (2006). *Managing Business Process Flows: Principles of Operations Management.* New Jersey: Prentice Hall.

Chopra, S. and P. Meindl (2007). *Supply Chain Management: Strategy, Planning & Operations.* Prentice Hall.

Chou, H.-C., D. Kobayashi, V. Malhotra, K.-L. Nien, and C. Recktenwald (2007). Norman shutters case. Final course project for OPNS454 at the Kellogg School of Management.

Dornier, P.-P., R. Ernst, M. Fender, and P. Kouvelis (1998). *Global Operations and Logistics: Text and Cases.* Wiley.

Eckholm, E. (2006). Chicago orders 'big box' stores to raise wage. *The New York Times.* July 27.

Farrell, D. (2004). Beyond offshoring: Assess your company's global potential. *Harvard Business Review*, 82–90. December.

Ferdows, K. (1997). Making the most of foreign factories. *Harvard Business Review*, 73–88. March-April.

Forbes (2005). Homes of the billionaires. *Forbes.com.* Mar 10.

Gauntt, J. d. P. (2004, Oct). New rules for global component sourcing: the quality imperative in electronics. *Economist Intelligence Unit white paper.*

Hayes, R. H. and S. C. Wheelwright (1984). *Restoring our Competitive Edge: Competing through Manufacturing.* New York: John Wiley & Sons.

Hotelling, H. (1929). Stability in competition. *Economic Journal 49*, 41–57.

Intel (2007). Virtual press kit: Copy exactly factory strategy. www.intel.com/pressroom/kits/manufacturing/copy_exactly_bkgrnd.htm as of June 20.

Kerkhof, L. (2005). Personal conversations. June.

Kouvelis, P. and J. Niederhoff (2007). On the globalization of operations and supply chain strategies: A conceptual framework and its application. In H. Lee and C.-Y. Lee (Eds.), *Building Supply Excellence in Emerging Economies*, pp. 3–37. N.Y.: Springer.

Lee, H. and C.-Y. Lee (Eds.) (2007). *Building Supply Excellence in Emerging Economies.* Springer.

Leonhardt, D. (2007). A lesson that Thomas could teach. *New York Times.* Jun. 20.

Lewin, A. Y., M. Peacock, C. Peeters, J. Russell, and G. Sutton (2006). 2nd bi-annual offshore survey results. *Duke University CIBER/Archstone Consulting.*

Lu, L. X. and J. A. Van Mieghem (2007). Multi-market facility network design with offshoring applications. *Mfg & Service Operations Management.* Under review.

Maynard, M. (2007). Toyota to build $1.3 billion plant in the land of Elvis and honey. *New York Times.* Feb. 28.

Pyke, D. F. (2007). Shanghai or Charlotte? The decision to outsource to China and other low cost countries. In H. Lee and C.-Y. Lee (Eds.), *Building Supply Excellence in Emerging Economies*, pp. 67–92. N.Y.: Springer.

Rainey, D. V. and K. T. McNamara (1999). Taxes and the location decision of manufacturing establishments. *Review of Agricultural Economics 21*(1), 86–98.

Rocks, D. (2007). Offshoring: Made in China–Er, Veliko Turnovo. Mainland manufacturers are spending millions on Central European plants. *Business Week.* Jan. 8.

Mini-Case 6 | MEXICO OR CHINA? MANAGING A GLOBAL NETWORK

[7]A $10 billion high-tech U.S. manufacturer of wireless transmission components was at a crossroads regarding its global network. The company faced intense global competition which placed significant pressure on margins and working capital productivity. The company had two assembly plants, one in China and another in Mexico. The question that operations strategy had to address was how these plants would best be allocated to global market requirements.

Background: demand, costs and assembly

Global demand for wireless transmission components is fragmented, with less than 15% of revenue coming from products that are sold in multiple geographic areas. North America is the single largest market embracing nearly 50% of demand but its growth is slow. Asia Pacific is the high growth market with 25% of demand share. Europe is the third major market. While aggregate demand within a market is fairly predictable, SKU-level demand is highly uncertain due to product commoditization, price sensitivity, and short product life cycles of only 1-2 years (Table 6.3).

Assembly and test of wireless transmission components are labor and capital intensive: assembly operations are mostly manual while testing also requires equipment. The company's two assembly plants have similar technical capabilities. The Chinese facility enjoys lower costs, but has a relative labor productivity of 75% (Table 6.4). It also faces capacity constraints on test equipment that can be alleviated through a one-time capital purchase of new equipment. The higher cost Mexico facility has significant excess capacity and operates at less than 50% utilization with 80% productivity.

Raw materials comprise a significant cost component and are purchased from cost competitive Asian sources for all global needs. Global sourcing requires additional working capital in order to maintain sufficient safety inventory of finished goods (to protect against demand variability) and large pipeline inventory of products (to be staged and transported globally).

Finally, transportation costs constitute a high fraction of total cost because end products are air freighted to quickly respond to high demand variability. Air freighting can be up to 10 times more costly than sea freighting on a per unit basis; however, lead times are 5 days versus 30 days. The company's cost of capital is 15%. All data is also available in a downloadable spreadsheet:

> Download `Case-MexicoChina.xls` from www.vanmieghem.us

Tailored global operations strategy proposal

The company has designed a tailored global operations strategy that satisfies demand through a mix of local and offshore sourcing models. The Chinese plant would serve the entire Asian and European markets, as well as the base demand

---

[7]Cort Jacoby and Ruchir Nanda from Deloitte Consulting and Professor Van Mieghem prepared this case as the basis for class discussion rather than to illustrate either the effective or ineffective handling of a managerial situation.

| Product SKU | Monthly unit sales | Std Dev. unit sales | BOM cost | Weight (Lbs) | Labor Times (hrs) | | | | Sales Mix | |
					Manual	Test A	Test B	Other	China	US
LEX 100021	67,200	20,160	$518	13.50	1.68	1.20	0.23	0.20	0%	100%
LEX 100022	54,400	24,480	$165	13.50	0.73	0.60	0.23	0.13	0%	100%
LEX 100023	52,000	31,200	$1,329	10.50	8.62	4.20	1.68	0.20	15%	85%
LEX 100024	38,240	7,648	$2,091	16.50	13.90	6.06	2.45	0.33	10%	90%
LEX 100025	27,520	2,752	$1,439	12.15	7.33	5.31	1.84	0.29	25%	75%
LEX 100026	27,200	1,360	$956	12.38	5.13	3.24	1.42	0.27	25%	75%
LEX 100027	26,400	7,920	$702	13.65	4.95	2.22	0.82	0.20	0%	100%
LEX 100028	25,120	11,304	$1,952	18.00	2.42	3.60	2.24	0.27	100%	0%
LEX 100029	24,960	14,976	$751	8.48	5.10	2.58	0.89	0.20	77%	23%
LEX 100030	22,880	4,576	$1,350	14.55	7.33	5.40	1.70	0.29	30%	70%
LEX 100031	22,560	2,256	$840	11.33	4.91	3.06	1.31	0.20	30%	70%
LEX 100032	20,960	1,048	$1,072	8.55	5.32	4.20	0.35	0.53	35%	65%
LEX 100033	19,200	5,760	$1,400	13.50	4.84	4.46	0.77	0.22	0%	100%
LEX 100034	18,080	8,136	$2,040	15.90	13.90	6.03	2.45	0.33	11%	89%
LEX 100035	17,280	10,368	$789	11.85	5.87	3.60	1.17	0.20	0%	100%
LEX 100036	17,200	3,440	$1,229	17.03	9.90	6.30	1.40	0.20	27%	73%
LEX 100037	16,640	1,664	$727	12.30	4.66	3.81	0.82	0.27	0%	100%
LEX 100038	16,240	812	$2,088	24.75	6.97	5.10	2.08	0.20	0%	100%
LEX 100039	16,160	4,848	$633	13.50	4.77	2.55	0.47	0.13	100%	0%
LEX 100040	15,200	6,840	$528	14.40	4.22	2.04	0.54	0.20	0%	100%
LEX 100041	14,880	8,928	$1,255	15.30	11.26	8.10	1.40	0.20	13%	87%

Table 6.3 Product data on sales, bill of material cost, weight, labor times, and sales mix.

of high volume North American products. The Mexican plant would serve only the local North American market: it would assemble all its low volume products, as well as provide surge capacity for the high volume North American products.

The company wants to understand how to manage the key trade-offs among transportation cost, demand variability, and lead-time in its global network.

Questions

1. *Quantify the Total Landed Cost for both locations for three scenarios: % of China shipments by sea = 100%, 50%, and 0%. Based on this analysis, how should the trade-off between the transportation mode and lead-time be assessed? How can air shipments be minimized while maintaining a high on-time fill rate to customers?*

2. *What are the key criteria to consider in assigning products-to-plants? How should "base" demand be differentiated from "surge" demand? What steps can be taken to determine the optimal allocation mix?*

3. *Given the dynamic nature of the industry, what key performance indicators should be used to evaluate and assess the strategy on an ongoing basis?*

Outsourcing Markups		
SKU Costs Additional Data	*Markup*	*Comments*
Raw material inbound freight	2.00%	of BOM costs
Average SGA	5.00%	of BOM + Labor + Inbound Freight costs
Profit	8.75%	of BOM + Labor + Inbound Freight + SGA costs

Labor Variables		
Labor Rates	*China*	*Mexico*
Manual & Others	$6.50/hr	$10.50/hr
Test A	$7.50/hr	$11.50/hr
Test B	$18.50/hr	$16.50/hr
Productivity	75%	80%

VAT			
VAT Recovery Loss		*Markup*	*Comment*
China	America	4.00%	VAT charges are computed on total
Mexico	America	0.00%	costs (inbound freight, labor, SGA & profit)

Outbound Lane Rates				
Origination	*Destination*	*Lane Type*	*Standard Cost*	*Fuel Surcharge Cost*
China	USA	Air	$6.50/kg	$0.55/kg
China	USA	Sea	$0.65/kg	N/A
Mexico	USA	Truck	$0.85/kg	N/A

Lead Times		
	China to US	*Mexico to US*
Production	7 days	7 days
Deployment	7 days	3 days
Transit Ocean	25-30 days	N/A
Transit Air	4-5 days	N/A
Transit Truck	N/A	5-8 days
Customs	2 days	2 days

Table 6.4 Corporate data on outsourcing markups, labor rates, tax, transportation, and lead times.

Part III

The Process View: Tailoring Activity Networks

7 | STRATEGIC SOURCING, SUPPLY MANAGEMENT, AND OUTSOURCING

We used to bend all the sheet metal, mold every plastic part that went into our products. We don't do those things anymore, but somebody else is doing it for us.— John Young (1993), former CEO of Hewlett-Packard.

Learning Objectives

After reading this chapter, you will be able to:

1. Explain the concept of strategic sourcing and integrate it with operations strategy.
2. Use a framework to choose a supply relationship and guide the outsourcing decision.
3. Apply three tools to improve outsourcing: total cost of ownership, structured contracts, and multi-sourcing.
4. Illustrate how technological change affects sourcing and value chain disintegration.

In Part 1 of this book, we introduced a framework for operations strategy and studied competencies and competition. In Part 2, we learned how to configure the operational system's resources. Now we start Part 3, which will teach us how to structure operational processes. In this chapter, we will analyze two essential components of operations strategy: the questions of who should perform an activity or process in the value chain, and how we should manage the supply relationship.

7.1 | STRATEGIC SOURCING: CONCEPT AND FRAMEWORK

Strategic sourcing refers to the process of deciding on appropriate supply relationships for each activity in the value chain. It typically involves:

- Identifying the activity, its requirements, and potential qualified suppliers.
- Deciding who will perform the activity (in or outsource; make-or-buy).

Example 7.1 Cortina NV's offshore outsourcing strategy

Since starting as a small shoe factory in 1950 in Belgium, Cortina has consistently specialized in "first price shoes," or product quality and service at the lowest cost. During the 1960s, Cortina started sourcing shoes from Italy and by 1980 shoe production was completely outsourced to China. Initially, finished shoes were purchased from Chinese manufacturers, but since 1987 Cortina has gradually moved away from this "pick-up" (pure purchasing) strategy, instead focusing on in-house design while outsourcing production. Today, Cortina is one of the largest shoe importers in Europe, sourcing yearly more than 20 million pairs of shoes from about 50 to 60 suppliers. Annual sales exceed 100 million euros and grow more than 10% annually.

Every three months, the Cortina development team, consisting of a dozen Belgian designers, develops a fashion collection of more than 3,000 new shoe styles. Complete designs, indicating styles and dimensions, as well as materials and colors, are sent electronically to China. At Cortina's Wholly-Owned Foreign Enterprise (WOFE), about 80 Chinese employees make samples of ladies' shoes, while other potential manufacturers produce samples of other shoes. A staff of about 70 Chinese Cortina employees spread over four offices inspects the samples and stays in permanent Internet contact with the Belgian designers. Approved samples are sent to Belgium and shown to retailers who place orders for delivery in 4 months.

In addition to local inspection, the staff of 70 employees also source materials, approve and audit suppliers following Cortina quality standards, outsource and follow-up with production, and control quality, outbound logistics, and administration. Cortina's Belgian-based logistics division manages the importing of 2,200 incoming containers per year, warehousing, and the more than 3,000 outgoing trucks to retailers throughout Europe. *Source: Dumarey (2005)*

- Supplier relationship management (SRM): defining, establishing, and managing the bilateral relationship (often, but not always, involving contracting) to align incentives.

In this section, we will use some examples to discuss the importance of strategic sourcing. We will then provide a framework that integrates sourcing with operations strategy.

Sourcing in practice

Shoe designer and distributor Cortina NV, profiled in Example 7.1, outsourced production to China in 1980. After 25 years of experience, Cortina has become one of the largest shoe importers in Europe, sourcing more than 20 million pairs yearly of shoes from about 50 to 60 suppliers. Cortina has never considered bringing production back in-house, but rather has been constantly increasing its design and logistics competencies. In contrast to Cortina's offshore outsourcing, Zara's sourcing strategy is characterized by extensive vertical integration and mainly domestic production, as discussed in Chapter 1.

Increasing globalization coupled with decreasing communication and transportation costs also enable new service operations strategies, where entire business processes are outsourced and sometimes offshored. Based in Bangalore, India, Chillibreeze turns client data and figures into PowerPoint presentations. Several U.S. hospitals are examining X-rays over the Internet, working with radiologists in Australia, Israel, and increasingly, India.

Identification of Needs	Supplier Identification	Supplier Communication	Negotiation of Terms	Supplier Liaison	Logistics Management
"What we need"	*"Who can provide it ?"*	*"Here's what we want"*	*"How much, when, at what price"*	*"Here's how it's going"*	*"Control the flow"*
▪ Establish product requirements ▪ Understand technical direction ▪ Formulate 3-5 year strategy	▪ Determine make-vs.-buy ▪ Pick sole-vs.-multiple suppliers ▪ Understand supplier capabilities; technical & mfg	▪ Document product requirements ▪ Formulate a Request for Quote (RFQ)	▪ Develop contract agreements	▪ Manage the scorecard ▪ Communicate with suppliers	▪ Convey forecasts ▪ Control inventory costs ▪ Manage end-of-life cycle

Figure 7.1 Sun Microsystems' approach to sourcing and supply management (Farlow, Schmidt, and Tsay 1996).

Sourcing strategies change over time; after all, we live in an age of outsourcing. For example, General Motors used to make seats itself, like most car companies. Nowadays, GM Europe buys seats from its three major tier 1 suppliers: Lear, Faurecia, and Johnson Controls. Some firms have gone so far as to become "virtual" manufacturers, owning many designs and brands but making almost nothing themselves. An example of this vertical disintegration is the production of a Barbie doll. According to Grossman and Helpman (2005), Mattel procures raw materials (plastic and hair) from Taiwan and Japan, and conducts assembly in Indonesia and Malaysia. It buys the molds in the U.S., the doll clothing in China, and the paints used in decorating the dolls in the U.S.—all of which is a testament to globalization.

The make-or-buy decision is not a black or white choice. Strategic sourcing also defines the nature of the supply relationship, which can fall on a continuum between a transactional market exchange ("arm's-length" relationship) and a close and intimate relationship to vertical integration. The close collaboration of Japanese manufacturers, such as Toyota and Honda, with their suppliers is well known and is so effective that rivals strive to imitate it. For example, General Motors does not only receive seats from Lear, but is also increasingly collaborating with Lear on the design, development, and testing of seats and many other systems of the car's interior (including wiring harnesses, head liners and door panels). Lear is also responsible for integrating all the parts that go into the system. Ensuring that this supply relationship works well requires close and constant cooperation, and strong project and supplier management skills.

Strategic sourcing is followed by tactical supply management, or the execution of the supply flow, including purchasing and logistics. The combination of the strategic decisions and the tactical execution is referred to simply as *sourcing*, as illustrated by Sun Microsystems' approach to sourcing shown in Figure 7.1.

> **Example 7.2** Toyotas CCC21 sourcing program
>
> In the late 1990s, Toyota heard from a rival executive that it was paying too much for parts compared to its peers. Insulted by the commentary, Toyota launched an internal study that pitted the company, component-by-component and car-by-car, against other models. The result took months to compile and shattered the myth about the companys cost advantage, according to Toyota's CEO, Katsuaki Watanabe. Out of hundreds of components and vehicle systems, Toyota was the winner in just over half. It was considered outright humiliating.
>
> Then-purchasing chief, Mr. Watanabe pushed Toyota and its parts suppliers to tweak the way they designed. They made 173 components and systems simpler and less expensive without affecting quality. In one effort, Toyota worked with suppliers to consolidate countless specifications for wire harnesses. That strategy produced tens of millions of dollars in savings.
>
> In total, the Construction of Cost Competitiveness for the 21st Century, or CCC21, program saved one-trillion yen ($8.68b), equivalent to a 30% cut in the companys procurement costs during 2000-2004! *Source: Shirouzu (2006)*

The importance of strategic sourcing

Strategic sourcing determines what we do and how we interact with others. It shapes the operational system and is similar to any business strategy: it makes a case for creating a competitive advantage and increasing NPV. (In high-tech industries, a sourcing strategy is also known as a *commodity business plan*.) In many industries, globalization and advances in technology facilitate the disintegration of the value chain, thereby increasing the importance of structuring and managing supply networks. The term *global sourcing* emphasizes that the network encompasses the globe.

Strategic sourcing recognizes the long term (that's the beauty of NPV!) and becomes a driver for continuous improvement not only in cost, but also in quality, timeliness, and flexibility. When done well, good sourcing yields annual cost reductions, increases "spend productivity," *and* increases the speed of innovation and new product development.

Sourcing also has great financial impact and leverage (Example 7.2). Purchasing is the biggest single cost for most businesses, accounting for about 60% of the average company's total cost. This means that even small improvements in sourcing can have a great impact. Consider for example the retail industry, where purchasing represents about 85% of the cost of goods sold (COGS). Reducing purchasing costs by 10% increases gross margins from 15% to 23.5%. This 56% increase typically flows through to the bottom line and leads to an even higher relative increase in net income. After price changes, reducing purchasing costs is the most powerful profit lever. Given this high leverage, it should not be surprising that improving sourcing efficiency has received much attention lately.

Sourcing decisions as an integral part of operations strategy

Strategic sourcing is not a simplistic focus on extracting cost reductions from suppliers. In fact, suppliers are antagonized by short-sighted strategies with dismal long-term results, such as lack of quality, trust, and innovation. Such strategy is illustrated by the results of the actions of GM's infamous global pur-

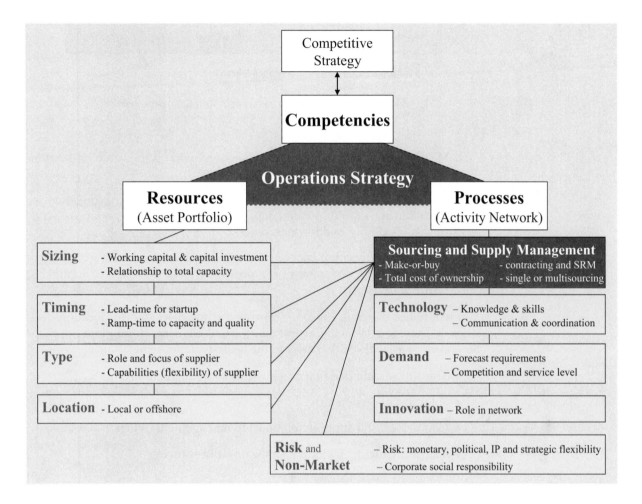

Figure 7.2 Strategic sourcing and supply management are an integral part of operations strategy.

chasing czar, Lopez, in the 1990s.[1]

In contrast, strategic sourcing supports and drives the competitive advantage and NPV of the firm. It is broad in scope and is part of the process of configuring the firm's operational system and integrating it with external parties. Therefore, effective strategic sourcing follows a structured, analytical process in order to integrate sourcing strategy with the overall operations strategy.

To help in that process, we can directly implement our general framework from Chapter 1 to highlight the interaction of sourcing and supply management with the other levers of operations strategy (Figure 7.2). The approach to align and tailor sourcing with competitive strategy follows the three familiar steps:

---

[1]José Ignacio Lopez de Arriortua headed GM's purchasing in North America during 1992-93. "During this period he is credited with saving GM approximately $4 billion in expenses, and potentially causing irreparable harm to the long-term supplier relationships key to GM's future competitiveness." Moffett and Youngdahl (1998)

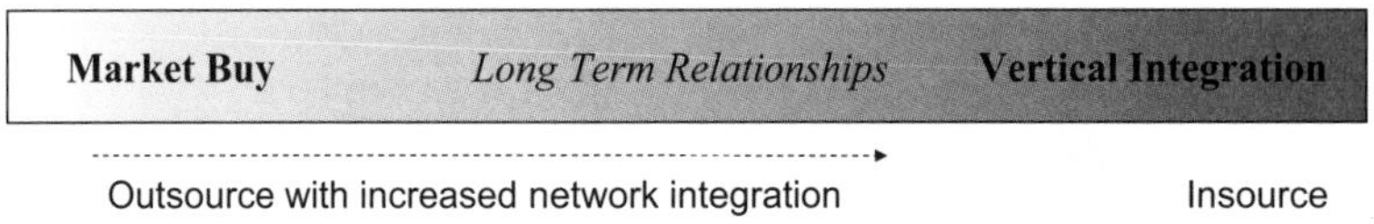

Market Buy	*Long Term Relationships*	**Vertical Integration**

Outsource with increased network integration   Insource

Figure 7.3 The spectrum of possible sourcing relationships.

1. Start by reviewing the competitive strategy: what is the value proposition to customers and shareholders?

2. The value proposition then indicates the priority ranking of competencies that sourcing should consider; i.e., what is the relative importance of cost, quality, flexibility, and responsiveness?

3. This ranking then guides how the various elements affecting assets (resource capacity) and activities (processes) should be weighted in making sourcing decisions.

You will notice that this approach mirrors the one discussed for location decisions in Chapter 6. We will illustrate the various elements throughout the chapter and emphasize those that are specific to strategic sourcing:

- The outsourcing decision and possible sourcing relationships

- Total cost of ownership

- Contracting and supplier relationship management (SRM)

- Tailored sourcing, including single or multi-sourcing

7.2 | THE SPECTRUM OF SOURCING RELATIONSHIPS

Sourcing relationships fall on a continuum between a transactional market exchange ("arm's-length" relationship) on the one extreme, and vertical integration on the other, as illustrated by Figure 7.3. *Insourcing* means that the supply relationship is internal. *Outsourcing* refers to having an external party supply the activity. Let us discuss the relative advantages of each.

Benefits of Outsourcing using Market Exchange

The simplest form of sourcing from external sources uses a transactional market exchange and is more commonly known as *purchasing* or *procurement*. While it technically represents the simplest and most extreme form of outsourcing, purchasing often refers to the tactical sourcing of off-the-shelf goods or services using an arm's-length relationship.

The benefits of outsourcing through "arm's length" relationships, or by "using the market," include (we list the relevant factors in the strategic framework of Figure 7.2 in parentheses):

1. Operational and strategic focus (Competencies). Outsourcing some activities allows the firm to solely focus on those activities at which it excels. Later we'll see how to link core competencies to sourcing.

2. Cost and risk pooling efficiencies (Sizing and Location). External specialists may have greater economies of scale and scope. They may also enjoy risk pooling by serving many other customers and market segments. When outsourcing is combined with offshoring (recall Chapter 6), additional cost efficiencies may accumulate.

3. Operational and financial flexibility (Timing, Type, and Risk). Outsourcing reduces capital commitments (e.g., fixed assets), thereby "liberating the balance sheet." If structured correctly, outsourcing allows capacity to scale up and down quickly and flexibly among products, thus mitigating demand risks.

4. Access to the latest technologies and innovation (Technology and Innovation). Few companies have the scale and the resources to stay updated with all the latest technologies. Outsourcing can give access to proprietary technology or other intellectual property. Sun Microsystems depends on its suppliers to remain "leading edge" and believes that vertical integration would result in less innovation.

5. Market competition enhances efficiency and incentives for improvement (Demand). If there are several potential suppliers, the firm has choices and gains more insights in true costs. In contrast, insourcing creates an internal monopoly that may be reluctant to change. Thus, it may provide lower quality service and higher costs than those of external parties that must compete for business. Free market enthusiasts will remind us that the collapse of the USSR is proof that a planned economy just does not work as well as the invisible hand of the market.

Benefits of Insourcing and Vertical integration

Economists refer to the value chain (it starts with raw materials and ends with the distribution and sales of goods and services) as the *vertical chain*. The degree of any company's *vertical integration* is a measure of the extent of activities in the vertical chain that it performs or owns. We also can describe the direction of integration: forward (meaning towards end-customers) vs. backward (meaning towards suppliers).[2] Both Ford Motor Company and General Motors used to be highly vertically integrated (see Example 7.3).

Arguments in favor of vertical integration include:

1. Control (Size, Timing, Type). By supplying an activity internally, the firm controls the delivered volumes, quality, and speed to market. In contrast, outsourcers may become hostage to suppliers who may gradually raise prices or reduce quality of service, especially when they have capacity shortages. For example, disk drive manufacturer Seagate Technology is strongly vertically integrated, which enables it to fully control cost and speed to market. It makes its own silicon heads, which read magnetic information from discs.

---

[2]The terms "upward" and "downward" would be more consistent with "vertical" integration.

Example 7.3 Vertical integration in the early automobile industry

In 1913, Henry Ford's assembly line for the Model T heralded the age of mass production. Ford did not rely on the market's invisible hand to organize the fast supply flow of parts. Instead, he vertically integrated the entire supply chain to solve coordination, information, and incentive problems. Ford owned a rubber plantation in Brazil, iron mines in Minnesota, and transportation systems such as ships and rail to connect raw materials to the Highland Park manufacturing and assembly facilities. A far move into backward integration guaranteed that a flow of supply fed the flow of production.

Ford's ultimate centralization of decision-making in one person had its own weaknesses. These weaknesses, along with rising prosperity and the changing character of business and consumption, gave rise to General Motors (GM) and Chairman Alfred Sloan's strategy of "a car for every purse and purpose." Alfred Sloan's GM was also highly vertically integrated, but it stimulated flexibility and innovation by decentralizing the empire into independent profit centers that were "managed by the numbers" from a small headquarter. In the 1980s, GM was the most integrated car manufacturer, with 70% of the parts of each car supplied by internal divisions.

2. Aligned incentives promote optimal investments (Size and Technology integration). If the supply technology is specific to one user (economists call this *asset specificity*), external suppliers will have little incentive to invest because such investments are susceptible to ex-post expropriation. Suppliers also typically invest less than what is optimal for the entire value chain (even without asset specificity) simply because they only gain a part of the total margin. Vertical integration aligns incentives and removes two problems, known as the *holdup problem* and *double marginalization*. Later we will see how structured contracts can align incentives.

3. Operational and transaction cost efficiency (Location and Technology). Vertical integration may be more efficient than incurring the transaction and coordination costs of dealing with suppliers. Interaction costs include managing the relationship, and monitoring and coordinating the exchange of information, goods, and services. By joining sequential processes and eliminating handoffs or transportation, internal processing may be cheaper than buying from external parties.

4. Learning by doing (Type, Improvement, and Innovation). Even Sun Microsystems, a firm believer in a leveraged business model that outsources most of its manufacturing, owns a motherboard assembly facility in Milpitas, California. Not only does this facility provide extra capacity in addition to the supplier's, but it also ensures that Sun understands the technology and can effectively perform design for manufacturability and testability, factors that are paramount to achieving reasonable yields. It also allows Sun to develop new products in total secrecy. Similarly, McDonald's, a strong advocate of outsourcing through *franchising*, owns and operates several restaurants itself. This ensures that the company understands restaurant operations, and allows for new product testing. It can also alleviate incentive problems (for example, for highway restaurants with few return customers).

5. Protection of proprietary assets, technology, and other intellectual prop-

Pro	Con
• Operational and strategic focus (core)	• Strategic risks:
• Cost and risk pooling efficiencies:	• Dependence/Loss of control
•Scale economies	• Leakage of proprietary skills/ information;
•Risk pooling	• Incentive problems (hold up, dual marginalization)
• Operational and financial flexibility (scaling)	• Transaction costs
• Access to technology/innovation	• No "learning by doing/owning"
• Market competition/discipline	

Figure 7.4 Summary of the advantages and disadvantages of arm's length purchasing, an extreme form of outsourcing.

erty (Risk). For example, Eli Lilly considers its manufacturing capabilities to be an important competitive strength. When its blockbuster drug Ceclor went off patent in 1992, no generic manufacturer was capable of making it at a competitive price; thus, Lilly's in-house manufacturing expertise gave it an extra year of market exclusivity. It is difficult to know in advance what is "outsourceable." When IBM outsourced the processor and operating system of its personal computer in the early 1980s, it did not foresee the future valuations of Intel and Microsoft. Suppliers may become even more powerful and forward integrated, leading to a "hollowed out company."

Making is the opposite of buying. The benefits of insourcing are the weaknesses of arm's-length market outsourcing, as summarized in Figure 7.4.

Long-Term Relationships: Partnerships and Alliances

Restricting supply relationships to vertical integration and market exchange is similar to viewing the world in only black and white only. Reality, however, is more complex; more specifically, supply relationships are usually hybrids between the two extremes. This means that a firm can *both* make and buy (a particular form of dual sourcing that we will discuss later), or that the relationship can be somewhere between owning and operating all—or none—of its supply assets. The latter are called partnerships and alliances, and can vary from long-term relationships to joint ventures. Long-term *partnerships* are "successful ongoing relationships that are based on trust that has been built up over many years rather than in the words of a legal contract," according to Sun Microsystems. Strategic *alliances* are joint ventures, where "two or more firms agree to collaborate on a project, or to share information or productive resources" (Besanko et al. 2000).

Renault-Nissan BV, an Amsterdam based company set up to drive integration between the two companies, is an example of a strategic alliance. Renault is the controlling shareholder of Nissan, with a 44% stake in the company. The neutral site is the venue for monthly meetings between 8 board members, four from each company, who make decisions on joint activities such as product design and engineering, computer systems, and purchasing. "Already, about

	Commitment to competitive pricing	
high	**Trust-based partnerships**	**Balanced Sourcing**
	• May not provide clear incentive to drive improvement • Assumes supplier goal congruence • Supplier may capture all value creation	• Fully leverages supplier capabilities • Drives improvement at both customer and supplier • Requires significant customer capability
	Unleveraged Purchasing	**Darwinian Rivalry**
low	• Typifies the clerical mentality of traditional purchasing • Focuses on price rather than total cost • Leaves lots of money on the table	• Requires significant purchasing clout • Eliminates supplier lethargy but may instill resentment • Does not drive synergistic improvement

Commitment to cooperative relationship (vertical axis, low to high)

low   **Commitment to competitive pricing**   high

Figure 7.5 Booz Allen's "balanced sourcing" matrix (Laseter 1998).

70% of the parts used by the two auto makers are jointly purchased by the alliance."(Bremner, Edmonson, and Dawson 2004) The alliance is showing remarkable strength. As a couple, Renault-Nissan is the fourth largest car company in the world, after GM, Toyota and Ford. Renault builds its Clio compact and Scenic minivan at Nissan plants in Mexico, while Nissan makes its Frontier pickup at a Renault plant in Brazil. They have also embarked on a plan to share platforms, reducing them to 10 in 2010.

Several parameters define a supplier relationship and its position on the relationship spectrum (Fig. 7.3), including:

1. Degree of integration: What is the extent of integration as measured by the customer capital involvement in the supplier's operation? The resulting arrangement may be a stand-alone or independent contractor, joint venture/alliance, or wholly owned subsidiary.

2. Responsibility: To what degree does the buyer retain control of outsourced service activities?

3. Comprehensiveness: To what degree are activities outsourced? Are we outsourcing execution only (e.g., maintenance), processing of information (e.g., invoicing), core activities tied to operational results (e.g., order processing), or the entire business (e.g., contract manufacturing)?

Balancing cooperation and competition

The major difficulty in strategic sourcing is balancing cooperation and competition. Depending on the relative importance in a company's sourcing strategy of either establishing a cooperative relationship or receiving the lowest price, Laseter (1998) identifies four types of supplier relationships, as shown in Fig 7.5.

GM's infamous global purchasing czar Lopez set the benchmark for the "Darwinian rivalry" approach to sourcing (lower right quadrant in Fig 7.5). This one-dimensional approach uses competitive bidding and other techniques to extract the absolute lowest price from suppliers. Essentially, this price-based sourcing approach pits the interest of the supplier against those of the buyer. Each side reveals as little as possible, for fear of giving the opposing side an edge (Jackson and Pfitzmann 2007).

On the other extreme is a one-dimensional focus on cooperation, which results in a "trust-based partnership" as epitomized by some Japanese businesses (upper left quadrant in Fig. 7.5). Many organizations today are increasingly preaching the importance of maintaining trusting relationships with suppliers, and are sometimes afraid of upsetting the supplier. "They ask senior managers to have faith, because the benefits are qualitative and the results will come only in the long run. Avoiding being put on the hook for near-term results has real appeal, and cooperating with suppliers, in fact, comes naturally for many buyers. ... The reality is that most buyers worry more about the prospect of shutting down an internal plant as a result of supplier delivery or quality problems than about the reality of absorbing a higher price from a supplier" (Laseter 1998).

Few large companies today treat sourcing as if it simply involves processing purchase orders by clerks or expediters, which leads to "unleveraged purchasing" (bottom left quadrant in Fig 7.5).

"Balanced sourcing" aims for long-term sourcing relationships that are neither overly trusting nor too adversarial. The balance is much more difficult to achieve than any of the other three approaches; companies such as Toyota, Cisco Systems, and Sun Microsystems provide good examples of this. (Example 7.2 shows how Toyota was perhaps too trust-based and moved towards competitive pricing while collaborating in long-term relationships; in other words, it was moving towards balanced sourcing.) This approach always includes a reasonable profit margin for the suppliers, as well as incentives for lowering cost, improving quality, expanding innovation, and making design changes in subsequent years.

How to reach balanced or knowledge-based sourcing

In fact, balanced sourcing is another name for strategic sourcing. It is in line with the value proposition or competitive strategy. It is broad in scope and requires multifunctional teams to leverage supplier capabilities and drive improvement at both the customer and the supplier. Finally, it follows a structured process that displays a depth of analytic rigor and reflects a level of understanding (including on total cost considerations) that often exceeds that of the suppliers.

Jackson and Pfitzmann (2007) refer to balanced sourcing as knowledge-based sourcing, thus emphasizing information sharing and insight. With this approach, buyers and suppliers have a long-term commitment to improving each other's capabilities. They begin by working together to eliminate wasted effort and inefficiencies. Jackson and Pfitzmann describe that during meetings with suppliers at Honda Motor Company, executives write their proposed actions and agreements on a whiteboard. When all these items have been discussed, the meeting is over. The contents of the whiteboard are then typed up and two copies are printed; the supplier and the automaker sign them, and the contract is complete. Thereafter, both sides work together to execute the plan.

Jackson and Pfitzmann (2007) suggest four changes necessary to implement knowledge-based sourcing:

1. Establish suppliers as strategic long-term partners.

2. Set up an ongoing system to eliminate waste through collaboration across the supply chain.

3. Get it right the first time. Because the price-based approach favors cost reduction over quality, suppliers know that redesigns are likely and may even overdesign the product to hit cost reduction targets after launch. In contrast, with knowledge-based sourcing, the engineers are pulled from the project a short time after product launch. That way, manufacturing can focus its attention on in-plant productivity improvements, rather than on retooling for product redesigns.

4. Respect and develop human capabilities. Balanced sourcing requires a profound sense of cooperation together with deep product and process knowledge.

Obviously, balanced sourcing is not always appropriate. If a company is buying a part or a component just once and is unlikely to require the supplier in the future, there is little need to spend resources on improving operational and systemic output, according to Jackson and Pfitzmann.

7.3 | A FRAMEWORK FOR THE OUTSOURCING DECISION

The starting point: identify the activity and its requirements

Any sourcing strategy including an outsourcing decision must first identify the activity or process under consideration, its requirements, and potential qualified suppliers. This necessitates a clear specification of the scope of activities in the value chain (design, production, distribution, service) that is being considered.

Clearly defining what we require from the activities is equally important. Requirements take various forms depending on the activity under consideration. For example, when an airline analyzes the option of outsourcing its call center, it must consider the quality of service in terms of time responsiveness and the range and depth of questions that can be answered. Notice that these requirements have little to do with the core business of flying airplanes. Requirements can also be broader and less specific: are we considering mere execution of a well established process or do we also need higher value-added knowledge and expertise? For example, outsourcing commodity processes such as simple shoe manufacturing mainly involves "purchasing hours" ("hands" or machines), while outsourcing software development also needs knowledge and expertise.

After identifying the activity and its requirements, the decision framework from Figure 7.6 can guide the outsourcing decision by addressing the following five questions, which we illustrate in the context of Cortina's situation (Example 7.1 on p. 236).

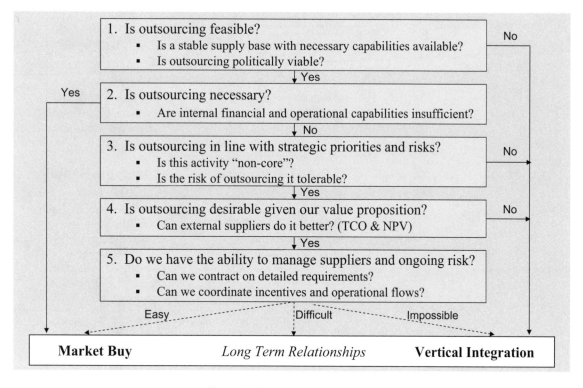

Figure 7.6 A framework for the outsourcing decision.

1. Is outsourcing feasible?

Verifying whether outsourcing is even an option is done by considering the supply market and the political and larger consequences of outsourcing. Outsourcing is only feasible if a financially stable supply base is available, consisting of at least one supplier with the necessary capabilities. This is the case for shoe and textile manufacturing. In contrast, when Harley-Davidson considered expanding capacity in 1995, they did not have the option of outsourcing the chrome plating of motorcycle metal parts; there was a lack of suppliers that could chrome at the necessary jewelry quality and volume (see the case study on p. 391).

Feasibility should also consider governmental regulations and potential non-market customer responses to outsourcing. For example, defense department contractors are under stringent requirements that may not allow outsourcing to foreign companies. Those companies that outsourcing initiatives to Asia should be mindful of acceptable human conditions (otherwise, customer indignation and consumer boycotts may remind companies not to use sweatshops). Under that caveat, outsourcing manufacturing is feasible for both shoe designer Cortina and retailer Zara.

2. Is outsourcing necessary?

Limited financial and operational means and capabilities may preclude performing the activity inhouse and instead necessitate outsourcing. Limited resources

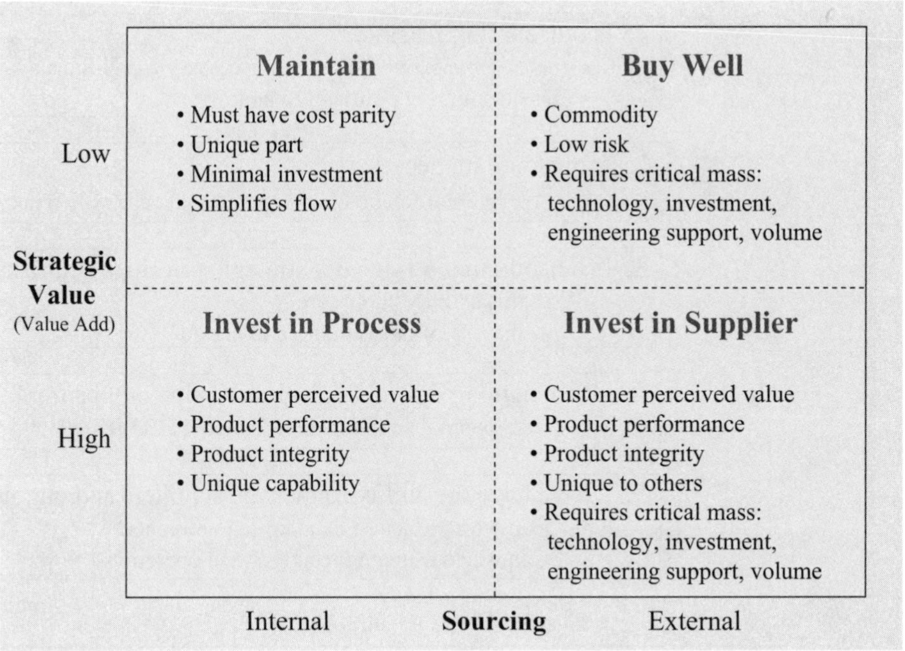

	Internal ⟵ Sourcing ⟶ External

<table>
<tr><td rowspan="2">

Low</td><td>Maintain
• Must have cost parity
• Unique part
• Minimal investment
• Simplifies flow</td><td>Buy Well
• Commodity
• Low risk
• Requires critical mass:
   technology, investment,
   engineering support, volume</td></tr>
</table>

Strategic Value (Value Add)

Low	**Maintain** • Must have cost parity • Unique part • Minimal investment • Simplifies flow	**Buy Well** • Commodity • Low risk • Requires critical mass: technology, investment, engineering support, volume
High	**Invest in Process** • Customer perceived value • Product performance • Product integrity • Unique capability	**Invest in Supplier** • Customer perceived value • Product performance • Product integrity • Unique to others • Requires critical mass: technology, investment, engineering support, volume

Internal   **Sourcing**   External

Figure 7.7 The core competency matrix can guide sourcing strategy.

are often a binding constraint for small companies. For example, Cortina estimates that it would need to employ about 8,000 people to manufacture more than 20 million pairs of shoes annually. This is a tall order for a family company with fewer than 200 employees. Large companies such as Zara have more latitude. However, the required resources are sometimes daunting, even for large companies. For example, Sun Microsystems concentrates on semiconductor design of its SPARC microprocessors and on workstation system design. However, it outsources all semiconductor manufacturing. For this *"fabless"* company to become an *"integrated device manufacturer"* such as Intel or AMD would require multi-billion dollar investments (a chip manufacturing plant easily costs a billion dollars).

3. Is outsourcing in line with strategic priorities and risks?

Competitive strategy clearly defines the so-called *"core"* activities. They are activities that are critical to the business, that differentiate the company from competitors, and that provide a competitive advantage. A company tries to perform its core activities better than rivals do; core activities are typically performed internally. Non-core activities are all other activities where a firm only wants to be competitive with rivals. Consequently, they are candidates for outsourcing. Chapter 11 discusses how Harley-Davidson uses the *core competency matrix* shown in Figure 7.7 to guide its sourcing decisions. Core activities occupy the lower left quadrant and are typically insourced. Cortina NV regards shoe design, supply chain logistics, and sales as core competencies.

The risks of dependence and loss of control of proprietary assets and intellectual property are sometimes too large to consider outsourcing, as discussed earlier.

4. Is outsourcing desirable given our value proposition?

If outsourcing is an option, the next step is to question whether it would be more desirable than insourcing. The answer should consider both qualitative fit with the value proposition (how we prioritize cost, quality, time, and variety) and economic attractiveness. For example, given that design-to-rack timeliness and almost continuous style changes are necessary to execute Zara's value proposition of fashion items, the company can only outsource textile manufacturing to local, well-coordinated suppliers. For reasonably stable items such as T-shirts, however, offshore outsourcing to Asia is in line with the value proposition (of both Zara, and say, The Gap).

If outsourcing is qualitatively aligned with the competency priorities, the question is whether its *total cost* is less than insourcing in the long term. This requires estimating the net present value of total costs. Sometimes, insourcing yields a simpler, faster, or more efficient operational flow, such that even a non-core activity is still better insourced (upper left quadrant in Fig. 7.7).

5. Can we contract and manage suppliers and ongoing risk?

If outsourcing has "survived" the first four tests, the final test is whether we can align incentives in the bilateral relationship (often, but not always, involving contracting) and have the capability to manage the relationship over time at a tolerable risk.

The ability to specify detailed contracts to outsource an activity greatly depends on the underlying product and process architecture. As the activity becomes more complex and develops more interactions with other activities in the network, it becomes harder to detail all the contingencies and the cost of coordination and changes rises (economists call this incomplete contracting.). Products and services that are composed of modules with enumerable and quantifiable interfaces are easier to outsource than those with countless and almost inseparable interactions (recall the modular versus integral product design discussion in Chapter 5). Electronic designs typically have clearly defined interfaces (in terms of voltage, current, and frequency) and are thus easier to modularize and outsource. In contrast, mechanical designs with high architectural complexity are harder to separate and outsource. The ability to contract and the extent of outsourcing therefore is strongly dependent on product and process technology, a topic we will return to at the end of this chapter.

In the following three sections, we will turn our attention to three tools that address questions 4 and 5: total cost of ownership and risk balancing through contracts and multi-sourcing.

7.4 | TOTAL COST OF OWNERSHIP

The fourth step in the outsourcing framework is to evaluate the attractiveness of outsourcing by considering both the qualitative test of alignment with competitive priorities, as well as the quantitative economic test using the concept of total cost of ownership. Originally, the *total cost of ownership* (TCO) accounted for all the costs associated with buying and owning an asset. Nowadays, the application of the TCO concept has been broadened to include the evaluation of the total cost of sourcing and of using any activity provided by a given supplier following a three-step process:

1. Determine all network activities that are materially impacted by sourcing.

2. Identify and quantify the cost drivers of each activity.

3. Sum the costs of the activities generated by each supplier to derive the TCO of each supplier.

Step 1: Determine the activities to be captured in TCO

The total cost of ownership should account for all costs incurred during the entire sourcing process. This includes the strategic activities of supplier identification, selection, contracting, and relationship management. It also includes the tactical activities of purchasing, receiving, storage, usage, and disposal.

For example, Sun Microsystems estimates that establishing a new supplier relationship, including supplier certification, takes from six months to a year and costs more than half a million dollars just in management time and travel. Such a cost would be included in the TCO, causing it to always exceed the purchasing price.

Step 2: Identify and quantify cost drivers using activity-based costing

TCO is typically calculated via activity-based costing (ABC), which identifies and estimates the cost drivers of each activity captured in the TCO. Cost drivers are factors that raise the cost of a given activity.

Cost driver identification is facilitated by adopting a process view of the entire sourcing process. Figure 7.8 provides a generic list of cost drivers (corresponding to the matrix entries) for each activity (corresponding to columns). Cost drivers are categorized by the "level" (corresponding to rows) that affects the cost; i.e., does cost increase per unit sourced, per order sourced, or per selected supplier? TCO allows for a comprehensive valuation model by further categorizing the cost drivers into those that directly impact cash and those that impact non-cash factors, such as:

- quality costs due to yield losses, inspection, increased safety stock, etc.

- lead time costs reflected in increased safety capacity or inventory, expediting, lost demand, etc.

- variety costs stemming from setup, changeover, and administrative and managerial complexity costs.

	Acquisition	Reception	Possession	Utilization	Elimination
Supplier Level	•Total purchase discounts				
	• Supplier vetting costs • RFP costs • Contract administration costs • Supplier change costs	• Litigation costs for breach of contract		• Engineering costs • Personal training costs • System adaptation costs	
Order Level	• Payment delay savings or costs	• External transportation costs			
	• Ordering costs	• Receiving costs • Invoice and payment processing costs • Quantity testing costs • Quality testing costs • Litigation costs for problems with quality	• Internal transportation costs	• Quality control costs • Production delay costs	• Waste collection costs
Unit Level	• Price • Product discounts			• Intrinsic efficiency • Replacement costs	• Recycling costs or revenues • Disposal fees or revenues
	• Service costs for installation and assembly • Testing costs		• Inventory holding costs • Order picking costs	• Production failure costs • Product failure costs • Maintenance costs • Installation costs	• Costs of removing obsolete materials • Disposal management costs

Figure 7.8 Calculating TCO requires the identification of the cost drivers (table entries) for each sourcing related activity (columns). Cost is incurred per supplier, per order, or per unit in the order. It and can be categorized as cash (top rows) or non-cash (shaded bottom rows). (Degraeve and Roodhooft (2001))

Once the cost drivers have been identified, they must also be quantified. This is the most data-intensive step of computing the TCO. Assume, for example, that sourcing affects transportation and that part weight and distance are key cost drivers. One then builds a linear cost model that predicts transportation costs as $a \times$ (part weight) $+ b \times$ (distance). Cost quantification requires the estimation of the coefficients a and b, using historical and forward-looking cost data and statistical regression analysis. Depending on the cost driver, the data may stem from supplier's invoices, maintenance records, depreciation records, etc. Roodhooft et al. (2005) provides a detailed case study that describes how to calculate the TCO of a utility supplier to a large industrial site that consumes large volumes of different types of energy on a daily basis.

Step 3: Calculate the TCO of each supplier

The final step is to derive the TCO of each supplier by aggregating the costs of the activities that are generated by one of them. When usage occurs over a long time span, the TCO should be the present value of all costs.

Total cost of ownership vs. total landed cost (TLC)

In Chapter 6, we introduced total landed cost (TLC) to evaluate location decisions. TLC is related to TCO, but also has some differences:

TLC is used mostly in product-location sourcing decisions (the location factor in the framework of Fig. 7.2). It focuses on the total cost incurred from sourcing at a certain location to the point of consumption. The timeframe for TLC economic analysis ends at the purchasing epoch or time of consumption.

TCO is used mostly in capital expenditures (such as IT systems implementation, plant equipment, etc.) and direct material purchasing decisions, including supplier selection. The timeframe for TCO economic analysis includes the entire equipment or product lifecycle. TCO thus incorporates all the elements of TLC, but also includes post-purchase costs, such as startup cost, ramp-up cost, and the cost of quality, maintenance, repairs, returns, staff training, etc. TCO thus also relates to the sizing, timing, type, and technology factors in the framework of Fig. 7.2.

Multiple uses of TCO in strategic sourcing

The most important reason to compute the TCO of each supplier is to help determine whether the economics of outsourcing are better than those of insourcing. If this is so, the TCO can help support supplier selection. Sun Microsystems interprets TCO quite literally, stating that it is "better to buy from people" with a lower TCO.

The insights from the TCO analysis can be used to improve coordination and performance across the supply chain. Instead of limiting the TCO analysis to within the firm, it can also be extended to the firm's supplier and customer processes. Cooperation facilitates the sharing of data, but even adversarial suppliers may provide some cost information.

TCO is a typical tool used in balanced or knowledge-based sourcing. Companies that know their supplier's TCO—and thus their cost structure—can use that knowledge to drive win-win continuous improvement. Toyota is a beautiful example. While a typical North American car company has hundreds of suppliers for fasteners, Toyota has exactly five global suppliers. One of those suppliers summed up the difference as follows: "Toyota does not jerk us around. Instead, they visit and help us and actually know our cost structure better than we do. They don't come and demand a price below our cost. Rather they give us a fair price, which allows us a fair margin, and they will work with us to reduce our costs."Toyota supplier of fasteners (2004)

Finally, performing a TCO analysis for customers can be a persuasive sales tool. In the Roodhooft et al. (2005) case study, a utility provider performed a TCO analysis for one of his larger customers. The analysis documented the cost savings for the customer when using the supplier's offering instead of internal or other external sources. Performing a total cost analysis for customers also became an added service offering of the supplier. Most importantly, perhaps, it yields a better understanding of customer needs and powerfully communicates what a firm's products and services are worth to the customer.

Scorecard for:		Commodity Rated:		Done on:	
Category	**Subcategory**	**Data or Comments**	**Max Points**	**Actual Points**	**Score**
Quality	Receiving Inspection		-8		
	Total Failure Rate (RPM/DPM)		20		
	Failure Verification/ Retest		2		
	FA/Corrective Action		8		
	Purge or Stop Ship		-10		
	PPA, DOA, or Field Problems		-10		
	Quality Subtotal:		30		pts
Leadtime/ Delivery/ Flexibility	Leadtime		10		
	On-time Delivery		15		
	Flexibility		5		
	L/D/F Subtotal:		30		pts
Technology	Product		9		
	Manufacturing		16		
	Technology Subtotal:		25		pts
Support	Materials/ Purchasing		10		
	Sustaining Technical		5		
	Support Subtotal:		15		100 pts
Performance Matrix Total			100		
Price Index			1		
Score = performance matrix * price index			100		
Total Cost of Ownership = [(100 - Score) / 100] + 1				Goal: 1.0	

Table 7.1 Sun Microsystems' supplier scorecard for electrical components (Farlow, Schmidt, and Tsay 1996).

Communicating TCO using supplier scorecards

The cost drivers from the TCO analysis can be represented in the form of a *supplier scorecard* that can be shared with the supplier. Instead of contracts and litigation, Sun Microsystems uses the scorecard shown in Table 7.1 to track and influence supplier performance and behavior.

As with any measurement system, firms should be careful in the design of supplier scorecards so that they give the desired incentives. In theory, categories should be scaled and weighted to assure they line up with total cost. In practice, weights should at least reflect the strategic value proposition of the firm. Also, good scorecards are designed in cooperation with the suppliers because suppliers tend to change their operations to maximize their score. For that same reason, scorecards should include all the relevant cost drivers in the TCO to prevent potential gaming behavior by suppliers who have an incentive to improve on the measured dimensions, but shirk on other hard-to-measure or overlooked dimensions. In practice, however, most companies track no more than a handful of categories: quality, delivery responsiveness, and cost improvement being the typical ones. If there are too many categories, they tend to lose their stimulus, require complex and costly data collection, and may lead to conflicting supplier goals.

We now investigate structured contracts and multi-sourcing as two tools to improve coordination and balance risk with suppliers.

7.5 | STRUCTURED SOURCING CONTRACTS

After identifying the activity and its requirements and selecting a supplier, the third and final step in strategic sourcing involves negotiating the terms of the bilateral relationship and managing the relationship over time. This may be achieved through informal supplier scorecards (see above) or through more formal contracting. In this section, we will analyze how well-structured contract agreements set clear expectations and can also align the incentives of the buyer and the supplier.

Increased outsourcing also increases the value of the supply relationship; nurturing this intangible real asset becomes increasingly important. An important component of supplier relationship management (SRM) is the process of measuring execution against the sourcing agreement or contract. Cooperative actions such as sharing production schedules, risk, and knowledge become increasingly important in nurturing and improving this relationship. (Taylor and Plambeck 2007) describe how informal agreements, or "relational contracts", can be simple, yet effective relationship management tools. In the remainder, we discuss how structured agreements or contracts can be used to accomplish similar objectives.

Outsourcing complicates flow coordination

Sourcing from external parties complicates the coordination of both information and material flows due to decentralization and dependence.

First, suppliers make decisions based on their incentives and information, both of which typically differ from those of the buyer. This may lead to decisions that are sub-optimal for the value chain as illustrated by the *double-marginalization* problem: by capturing only a part of the total returns, the supplier has lower incentives for investment and improvement than would be optimal for the value chain as a whole.

Second, there are externalities in processing network decisions in the sense that a decision made in one part of the network may have an impact somewhere else. For example, an upstream cost-sensitive supplier may be more interested in running at high utilizations, thereby restricting its flexibility to respond to changing downstream demands. Therefore, the downstream player may have to buffer itself by increasing safety capacity or inventory.

Figure 7.9 Whereas collaboration technology shares information, structured contracts align business objectives and balance risk.

How to improve coordination and align incentives

How can we improve supply chain performance and mitigate performance losses stemming from the lack of centralized network control? To do so, we must attack the root of the problem by "internalizing externalities & homogenizing asymmetries." In other words, the solution must design mechanisms such that agents incorporate the full extent of their actions and take into account network-wide information. The most drastic implementation of this solution is vertical integration, which in theory leads to one team with identical incentives and information.

In order to improve outsourcing relationships, the solution must focus on *collaboration technology*, which allows the sharing of information about designs, forecasts, capacities, and transactions. By dramatically increasing the speed of information flows, collaboration technology decreases cycle times and inventories. It does not, however, internalize externalities, which is exactly what structured contracts aim to do.

Structured contracts aim to align business objectives and balance risk as an attempt to produce integrated work flows with greater throughput and profitability. While collaboration technology focuses on execution, structured contracts aim for collaboration at the management and planning levels, as illustrated in Figure 7.9.[3]

Simple versus structured contracts: Service Level Agreements (SLAs)

A *contract* is a set of rules that control the three flows in a processing network: the flow of material, information, and cash, as shown in Figure 7.10. To be effective, the contract should be specified in terms that are verifiable by an independent third party (the "judge") and its stipulations should be enforceable.

Commonly-used simple contracts focus on specifying the financial terms to modify or align incentives. Some examples are:

1. *Fixed-price* or *price-only contracts* specify a fixed price per transaction unit, or for the entire sourced project or service. (*Transfer price* arrangements between internal groups in a company also fall into this class.) A lower

---

[3]I am grateful to Colin Kessinger for sharing Figures 7.9 and 7.11.

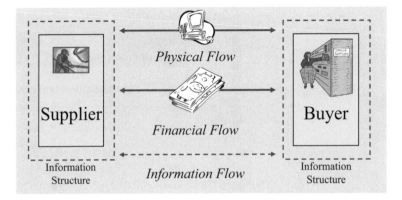

Figure 7.10 A contract is a set of rules that control the three network flows.

price typically induces a buyer to buy more but reduces supplier profits and incentives to serve the relationship well.

2. Under a *cost-plus contract* (also known as a time-and-materials contract), a customer agrees to reimburse the supplier for its total costs and to also pay whatever sum will give the supplier its desired profit margin. While many contract manufacturers use this form of contract because of its simplicity, its deficiency is that the supplier lacks incentive to reduce costs.

3. In contrast, under a *gain or profit sharing contract*, parties agree on the baseline cost of providing a service. If the actual cost exceeds the baseline cost, the provider receives the difference. Otherwise, the difference is split between the two parties in an agreed ratio. While this contract induces improvements, it also is the most expensive contract to negotiate and monitor because parties have to define precise cost projections for every situation. Subsequent negotiations are almost inevitable when actual costs are higher.

Cost-plus and gain sharing contracts also extract a price from the contractor by revealing its costs and profits, thus betraying its future negotiating position. Fixed-price contracts are not affected by these shortcomings: they let providers keep rewards from innovation, are less costly to negotiate, and require no monitoring. Combinations of these simple contracts are possible: e.g., a fixed price contract with a partial cost reimbursement.

Notice that these simple contracts emphasize cost. *Structured contracts* are richer contracts that clearly specify commitments (liabilities) and contingency options (rights) in terms of quality, timeliness, flexibility, as well as prices and quantities. One example is shown in Figure 7.11. A structured contract can be thought of as defining a supply *service level agreement* (SLA). Structured contracts that capture these four main competencies can be designed to tailor the outsourcing agreement to competitive priorities.

We will now consider a few examples that illustrate how structured contracts can align business objectives and balance risk.

AVAILABILITY AND RESPONSIVENESS		PRICE
Quantities guaranteed available within 3 month lead time		$400 per unit
Quarter 1	1000 units per month	
Q2	1000 units per month	
Q3	2000 units per month	
Q4	3000 units per month	
Additional quantities guaranteed available within 1 month		$425 per unit
Quarter 1	400 units per month	
Q2	400 units per month	
Q3	800 units per month	
Q4	1000 units per month	

NON-PERFORMANCE
1% of unit price for every day late, applied at end of 6 months by buyer

BUYER LIABILITY (COMMITMENT)		PRICE
Quantities buyers commits to buy		$400 per unit
Quarter 1	100 unit per month	
Q2	100 unit per month	
Q3	400 units per month	
Q4	400 units per month	

Figure 7.11 A structured contract specifies a service level agreement in terms of contingent quantities, quality, information and liabilities, and prices.

Base Case: price-only contract and double marginalization

Consider a simple price-only supply contract as a base case. Imagine a bookstore that buys a new novel from a publisher at a wholesale price of $10 and sells it for $20. Formally, the three flows in this price-only contract for a perfectly reliable supplier with ample capacity (i.e., the publisher fills each order perfectly) are: (1) information flow = the bookstore's order quantity q; (2) financial flow = the wholesale price; and (3) physical flow = product quantity q.

Demand for the novel is uncertain and is forecasted to be on average 5000 units with a normally-distributed forecast error (standard deviation) of 3000 units. No matter what quantity the bookstore buys, it will still be exposed to overage and underage risks. An unsold novel may be discarded, thereby resulting in a loss of $10. In contrast, a stockout results in lost sales and a corresponding margin of $20 − $10 = $10. Under the terms of this contract, the bookstore can maximize its expected profit by appropriately balancing both risks. The optimal balance follows from a newsvendor solution (see Appendix B on p. 435) and results in a guaranteed service level with:

$$\text{Service probability under price-only contract} = \frac{C_u}{C_o + C_u} = \frac{\$10}{\$10 + \$10} = 50\%.$$

In other words, the bookstore should order the mean demand of 5000 units; it will have an equal $50\% - 50\%$ probability of having leftovers or lost sales. Notice that the supplier is not exposed to any risk and is guaranteed a contribution profit of $(\$10 - \$2) \times 5000 = \$40,000$, assuming a marginal production and delivery cost of $2.

In contrast, the supply chain as a whole has an overage risk of only $2 but a larger underage risk of $18. Thus, its optimal service level is:

$$\text{Supply chain-optimal service probability} = \frac{\$18}{\$2 + \$18} = 90\%.$$

If a contract achieves supply chain-optimal profits, then it is said to be *coordinating* or *efficient*. The price-only contract is clearly inefficient because it suffers from double marginalization: the bookstore orders a quantity smaller than the supply chain-optimal quantity, because it captures only its own margin and disregards the publisher's margin. In other words, it has higher overage risk but lower underage risk and thus is more conservative in inventory management. Compared to the centralized supply chain, this strategy results in lower availability and sales. By simply transferring responsibilities (e.g., asking the vendor to make the ordering decisions and manage inventory), one doesn't eliminate double marginalization inefficiencies. Instead, we need to balance risks.

Buy–Back Contracts

Consider a buy-back contract under which the supplier agrees to buy back any unsold product at a buy-back price of $6. A buy-back contract thus stipulates a wholesale price as well as a buy-back price (obviously, to avoid arbitrage, the buy-back price is less than the wholesale price). The impact of this contract is that the bookstore's overage cost decreases to $\$10 - \$6 = \$4$, while its underage cost remains $10. The bookstore is willing to order more, so its optimal service level with this buy-back contract increases to:

$$\text{Service probability under buy-back contract} = \frac{\$10}{\$4 + \$10} = 71\%.$$

The buyback contract will increase availability and reduce overage risk, thus becoming attractive to the buyer. The total overage risk is now shared by the supplier. This doesn't necessarily mean that the buyer is extracting surplus at the expense of the supplier. As long as the additional profit from the order increase outweighs the expected costs of the returned items, the supplier, as well as the buyer, will have higher expected profits with the buyback contract.

Contracts that provide either credits for unsold items (without physically taking them back) or price-support (where wholesale prices decrease when sales prices decrease) are essentially buy-back contracts. Obviously, they cannot be implemented for free because they require trustworthy information sharing of overage quantities or retail prices.

Revenue and Profit Sharing Contracts

Revenue and profit sharing contracts can yield a similar balance of risks. For example, consider a revenue sharing contract under which the buyer agrees to share 45% of the revenue with the supplier, while the supplier decides to sell books at the strongly reduced wholesale price of $3. The impact of this contract is that the bookstore's overage cost decreases to $3, and its underage cost decreases to $20 \times 55\% - \$3 = \$8$. Again, the bookstore is more willing to order more in this scenario than under a price-only contract. Thus, its optimal service level increases to:

$$\text{Service probability under revenue sharing contract} = \frac{\$8}{\$3 + \$8} = 73\%.$$

Revenue sharing contracts have become very popular in the video rental industry after Blockbuster adopted them in 1998. Earlier, Blockbuster paid about $60 per copy and rented it for $3, according to Cachon and Lariviere (2001). So it had to rent each copy about 20 times just to break even, only to replace it a few weeks later with a copy of the next hot movie. However, with a revenue sharing agreement with the studio of say 50%, Blockbuster can buy a copy for less than $10. Even though Blockbuster keeps only about half the revenue, say $1.5 per rental, it breaks even after a mere six rentals, thus justifying the purchase of many more tapes.

Profit sharing contracts also balance risk but have the advantage of not distorting the relative marginal cost (MC) to marginal revenue (MR) ratio. This means that if the retailer sets profit-optimizing prices such that $MC = MR$, the price coincides with the supply chain-optimal price. Profit or gain sharing contracts, however, have the downsides discussed earlier.

Options and Quantity Flexibility Contracts

Risk can also be balanced by stipulating contingent contracts where, for example, buyers commit to minimal quantities but also have the option to change orders as "demand visibility" grows closer to the point of sales. By limiting the magnitude of allowed order changes, risk sharing between buyer and seller can be controlled and balanced. Benetton is a classic example: the company not only uses quantity flexibility contracts, but also tailors its production to different capacity types.

When to consider structured contracts?

Structured contracts specify commitments and contingent options. When structured correctly, they align incentives (mitigating the double marginalization problem) and improve overall performance in the supply chain by allocating capacity to buyers and balancing risks between supplier and buyer. Given their structure, they have value if:

1. There is significant demand uncertainty.

2. The marginal cost to produce additional items is less than the incremental revenue they generate; larger quantities then increase supply chain profits.

3. The contingency terms can be monitored easily.

These conditions are satisfied in the publishing, apparel, entertainment, and computer industries. Obviously, while the contract may improve total supply chain profits, the specific choice of contract terms depends on the expected profits, risk tolerances, and bargaining power of the supplier and the buyer. Minicase 7 asks you to further analyze these issues.

> **Example 7.4** GM's multi-sourcing inefficiencies in mixed-model JIT production
>
> GM Europe uses multi-sourcing for the seats of its Opel Corsa and Meriva models, which are produced in its Figueruelas (Zaragoza, Spain) plant using the just-in-time philosophy. Originally, Lear was the single supplier for the seats of the Opel Corsa. But when the Opel Meriva was introduced in 2003, its seats were put up for bidding; Johnson Controls won that business even though the Meriva shares its platform with the Corsa and has similar carry-over front seats, but different rear seats. The Johnson Controls plant is located in Figueruelas, next door to Opel, while Lear's plant is about 30km away, in Epila.
>
> GM-Opel has two assembly lines in its Figueruelas (Zaragoza, Spain) plant: one single purpose Corsa line and one mixed Meriva and Corsa line. Given that Lear and Johnson deliver their seats separately to separate gates, Opel had to re-sequence the Corsa and Meriva seats at its mixed line.

7.6 | MULTI-SOURCING AND TAILORED SOURCING

In addition to TCO scorecards and structured contracts, multisourcing can also be used to balance cooperation and competition in the supplier relationship. Multi-sourcing can also be tailored to the specific competitive priorities as suggested by the principle of alignment. Competitive strategy may require conflicting competencies such as low cost and high responsiveness or flexibility. Strategic fit then can be improved by using a sourcing portfolio. The combined use of multiple supply sources, each of which is different and possesses unique advantages, is better than any single-sourcing strategy.

Multi-Sourcing

Companies generally use multiple suppliers for a single input to either ensure a reasonable price by encouraging competition, or to mitigate the risk of total dependence on a single supplier. The key challenge of *multi-sourcing* is balancing those benefits with the increased complexity cost of handling additional suppliers and with potentially reduced supplier cooperation.

GM Europe divides its seat sourcing, including design and manufacturing, among three major suppliers: Lear, Faurecia, and Johnson Controls. For example, Faurecia designed the seat for the 2003 Opel Vectra and was also awarded a small portion of seat assembly in the UK plant, while Lear did the volume assembly in the Rüsselheim homeplant where the Vectra was introduced. Similarly, Sun Microsystems uses three tier 1 suppliers for memory chips and gives each supplier "a slice of the pie" (10-40% of the program). However, a persistent use of multi-sourcing can sometimes lead to inefficient outcomes. Example 7.4 illustrates that additional sequencing provisions may be required to bring multi-sourced parts at the right time to the point of use in the right order.

The benefits of multi-sourcing can also be obtained by using a single sourcing strategy for each product, component, or location, while using multi-sourcing across their ensemble. For example, Toyota tends to favor single suppliers for each plant, but uses multiple suppliers across its entire network. Similarly, Sun Microsystems uses single sourcing for projects such as application-specific integrated circuits (ASICs), but rotates multiple suppliers across projects.

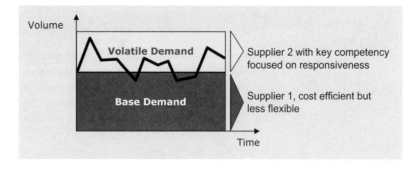

Figure 7.12 Tailored dual sourcing allocates the guaranteed base demand far in advance to a cost-efficient supplier, and the uncertain volatile demand to a responsive supplier.

Make-and-Buy Dual Sourcing

Make-and-buy is a particular form of dual sourcing where one sources both internally and externally. It is a hybrid solution between vertical integration and outsourcing. Benetton is a classic example: while it outsources about 70% of production to a network of contractors, it also has internal production facilities. Similarly, Sun Microsystems outsources a majority of its workstation motherboard assembly operations, but also operates similar assembly in its fully owned motherboard assembly plant in Milpitas, CA.

Possible dimensions along which sourcing can be tailored

Multi-sourcing aims to balance cooperation with the benefits of competition and risk control. The principles of alignment and focus tell us that benefits increase if we seek different requirements from each source. Thus, the typical dimensions cover the trade-offs between responsiveness, variety, quality, innovation and cost:

1. *Volume and responsiveness-based sourcing* splits a given product's volume into a "guaranteed" part and an uncertain, volatile part. Each volume part is allocated to the source that is best configured to deal with either certain or volatile demand, as Figure 7.12 illustrates. This is often accompanied with a lead-time requirement: by its very nature, base demand is certain and, in a manufacturing setting, can be produced in advance in an efficient process. However, volatile demand may require fast response capabilities.

   For example, Benetton outsources base demand in order to enjoy the low cost of contractors with 7 month leadtimes, but covers short-term variations with internal, fast capacity. Sun Microsystems, on the other hand, may outsource the volatile portion to guarantee high utilization of its internal processes. Services, such as call centers or transportation, often rely on contractors for peak demand swings. Volume-based multi-sourcing is also commonplace in utility sourcing; it operates on the commitment to purchase a specified amount over a specified period of time for a fixed price to cover its base demand, and by supplementing it through internal production (or spot market sourcing) to cover peak demand.

2. *Product or customization-based sourcing* uses different suppliers for different products, depending on each product's reward, risk, and customization requirements. Timbuk2, for example, manufactures its customized messenger bags internally in San Francisco, but outsources its standard bags to its Asian supplier. Smartly configured service operations also assign standard service requests to lower-cost resources, while complex requests go to highly-capable, experienced (but more expensive) people.

3. In *quality-based sourcing*, different supply sources are used depending on the quality requirements. When a high level of accuracy or excellence is required, companies may rely on external expertise.

4. In *innovation-based sourcing*, new products may be produced in-house, while stable, older, or service products may be outsourced.

Once the multi-sourcing strategy is decided upon, the next question is how to allocate quantities to suppliers; we will address that question in Chapters 8 and 9.

7.7 | TECHNOLOGY, SOURCING, AND VALUE CHAIN DISINTEGRATION

The costs and benefits of outsourcing are strongly dependent on technology. As product, process, and coordination technologies change over time, so does the extent of outsourcing and industry integration. To demonstrate the interaction between the sourcing and technology factors in our strategic sourcing framework (Fig. 7.13), let us consider some examples.

Technological changes and disintegration in the electronics industry

The extent of outsourcing in the electronics industry has increased dramatically and continues to change in response to technology changes. IBM used to be highly vertically integrated, owning disk drive manufacturing plants, semiconductor "fabs" (fabrication plants), printed circuit board, and computer assembly plants in addition to renowned research and development centers and sales and service organizations. But manufacturing and even design is increasingly being outsourced as the company becomes more focused on service and brand management.

Technological changes are highly correlated with disintegration in the electronics industry: e.g., electronic *product design technology* has easily defined interfaces and thus is amenable to modularization. *Process technology* has become increasingly sophisticated (mainly due to continuous miniaturization), increasing the required expertise and the cost of process technology. In order to address these rising requirements companies have followed Adam Smith's adage of "division and specialization of labor." Electronic designs are divided into modules

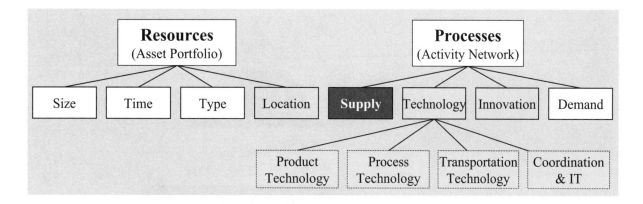

Figure 7.13 Technological changes affect sourcing, value chain (dis)integration, globalization, and innovation.

than can be standardized across the industry, thus allowing manufacturing to be outsourced to specialists who enjoy industry-wide economies of scale. The resulting sophisticated yet cheap "chips" (integrated-circuits) then can be recombined into even more complex electronic systems that allow better and faster *information technology*. Add this to the miniature electronic parts that are cheap to *transport* (relative to their value), and a virtuous cycle results: more outsourcing and disintegration yields more powerful and cheaper information technology that allows more effective and efficient coordination with suppliers, and thus more outsourcing. This explains why the electronics industry is by far the most global and disintegrated industry: purchasing and outsourcing accounts for more than 80% of the cost of goods sold.

During disintegration towards global sourcing, industry structures evolve. The original equipment manufacturer (OEM), such as IBM and HP, started outsourcing manufacturing to a *contract manufacturer* or an *electronic manufacturing service* (EMS) such as Flextronics or Solectron. Some OEMs like Dell increasingly focus on logistics and sales, outsourcing design to *original design manufacturers* (ODM) such as Arima or Compal (the majority of notebook computers are designed and manufactured by ODMs, mostly based in Taiwan and South Korea). Interestingly, some ODMs increasingly want to build and sell their own brands. And so the pendulum may swing back to integration if marketing forces outweigh technological forces.

Technological changes and disintegration in the automobile industry

The automobile industry is undergoing a similar but slower restructuring, moving away from Henry Ford's vertical integration model (Example 7.3). During the 1950—1970s, Toyota started rocking the auto industry by implementing different process and coordination technologies. "Like Ford's, the Toyota production system is based on the work flow system. The difference is that, while [Ford] worried about warehousing parts, Toyota eliminated the warehouse," according to Ohno (1988), the architect of the Toyota Production System. Non-core parts

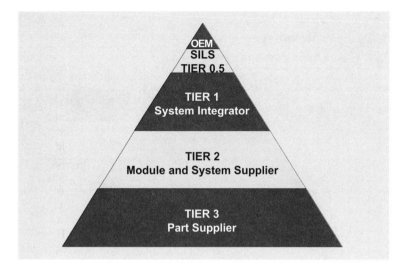

Figure 7.14 The tiered supply system is a manifestation of the disintegration of the automobile industry. (Shipping in line sequence (SILS) is explained in Example 7.5.)

were outsourced and shipped just-in-time of need. The advantages of the Toyota Production System were so great that they started changing the industry's structure. In the 1980s and 1990s, GM followed suit and started shifting "from vertical integration to horizontal integration. They sold their part producing divisions like Delphi and acquired competitors like Saab and started joint ventures with Fiat." (Fisher 2003)

Value chain disintegration is manifested by a *tiered supply system*, a hierarchical sourcing strategy. There, the OEM outsources systems to Tier 1 suppliers, who in turn outsource modules to Tier 2 suppliers, who then outsource parts to Tier 3 suppliers, as shown in Figure 7.14. Example 7.5 illustrates the responsibilities the tiered supply system presents for GM's Opel division.

Disintegration in the auto industry is progressing more slowly than in the electronics industry because of differences in product and transportation technology (process and information technology is similar). Mechanical product design is inherently more integral (recall Chapter 5) and difficult to modularize, because mechanical interactions are harder to isolate and separate than electronic designs. Rather than being specified by a few numerical interfaces, vehicle strength, rigidity, vibration and acoustics properties all depend on the totality of the vehicle design and are a complex function of the interaction among different vehicle subsystems. Product or part standardization incentives are weaker. While many parts, such as engines, could easily be standardized, car manufacturers tend to view those as "core" to their product differentiation strategy and derive disproportional profit from them; larger engines easily command several thousand dollars premium despite their marginal cost of a few hundred dollars. Standardization and outsourcing would diminish that source of differentiation and revenue maximization. Finally, mechanical parts tend to be heavy and

Example 7.5 Outsourcing using a tiered supply system for the Opel Vectra

Leanfield, the brand new GM-Opel production facility in Rüsselheim, Germany, assembles the Opel Vectra sedan and three other car lines that share the Opel Epsilon platform. Opel, the *original equipment manufacturer* (OEM), has outsourced the sequencing of most parts to MAN-Ferrostaal, which operates a sequencing center, called a business mall, next to the Leanfield as a "tier 0.5" supplier. About 100 tier 1 suppliers ship their parts to the business mall (usually in Kanban), ready to use or pre-configured to minimize final variance work. MAN-Ferrostaal picks the parts following an EDI pull signal from Leanfield and *ships in line sequence* (SILS) to the Leanfield using a sophisticated shuttle system.

Lear corporation is a tier 1 supplier and a system integrator of the Epsilon platform interior components, such as wiring harnesses, headliners, door panels, and seats. As a system expert, the tier 1 integrator is responsible for developing, testing, and supplying the parts and has unique project management skills to source and manage the tier 2 suppliers. GM's Tier 1 suppliers supervise the advanced product quality process and the process failure modes and effects analysis. They also ensure that fixtures and tools are procured in a timely manner, and that the production part approval process and production test are performed for all incoming components.

Given the high complexity of the systems, tier 1 suppliers partner with tier 2 suppliers for modules and subsystems. For example, the Canadian company Collins & Aikman develops and produces the cup holder subsystem of the Opel Vectra rear seat. Then, the tier 2 supplier is responsible for sourcing his group of tier 3 suppliers. For example, Collins & Aikman buys components like springs and plastic parts from tier 3 suppliers. Tier 3 suppliers are experts in single part manufacturing. They supply similar parts to other OEM's tier 1 or tier 2 suppliers, and enjoy economies of scale and utilize highly efficient technology over several life cycles of their parts. (*Fisher 2003*)

Example 7.6 Magna Steyr AG: contractor for total vehicle assembly

Magna Steyr AG is located in Austria and majority-held by Magna International, a first tier automotive supplier with its headquarters in Canada. It is the leading non-OEM car designer and manufacturer in the world. Originally a bicycle and motorcycle producer called Steyr-Daimler-Puch, Magna-Steyr increasingly focused on the automotive industry in the 1980s, especially on four-wheel drive off-road vehicles.

Its first success story was the designing and manufacturing of the Mercedes-Benz G-class. This was followed by the manufacturing of the VW Golf Country in 1990, the Jeep Grand Cherokee (1994), the development and manufacturing of the all-wheel drive version of the Mercedes-Benz E-Class 4MATIC (1996), the production of the M-Class (1999, see also Example 1.2), and the development and production of the Saab 9-3 convertible and the BMW X3 (2003).

bulky, making their transportation (and thus outsourcing) relatively expensive.

Despite these obstacles, outsourcing is increasing; some companies outsource even total vehicle assembly. Increased competition and cost pressure in the automotive industry and focus away from capital intensive manufacturing may increase assembly outsourcing by OEMs. Magna Steyr (Example 7.6) is proof of the concept that Tier 1 suppliers can benefit by assuming more value-added activities, similar to the ODMs in the electronics industry.

Technology changes and disintegration in services and business processes

In contrast to manufacturing, many service operations involve co-production with customers. When the physical presence of the customer is required, it is difficult to separate the service product from the service process. Outsourcing the entire process is then almost equivalent to selling the business and is only an option for "non-core" service activities. Many corporations outsource food service, maintenance, and other support activities.

If the product and process can be separated, however, breaking up the process and outsourcing some of its parts is feasible. The condition is that it does not significantly degrade the service product experience. Such a separation is possible if the service is predominantly an information product, as in the case of accounting, diagnosis, service calls, and financial services. Information technology then allows the product to be digitally transmitted to suppliers, and business process outsourcing would follow similar dynamics as do manufacturing.

Let us now turn these insights into some guidelines for practice.

7.8 | GUIDELINES FOR SUCCESSFUL SOURCING

Tailor sourcing to competitive strategy

Strategic sourcing supports and drives the competitive advantage and NPV of the firm. Tailored sourcing applies the principle of alignment to the design of a sourcing strategy that matches the value-proposition of the good or service. It fits the specific prioritization of quality, responsiveness, variety, innovation, and cost. It goes well beyond the method many organizations use to approach sourcing strategies (as one-size-fits-all plans to "rationalize the supply base" and "form long-term supplier relationships").

Rather, tailored sourcing specifies for each item or service what should be bought, from which suppliers, and under what terms. Tailored sourcing recognizes the long term impact and drives continuous improvement in the company-specific value dimensions (quality, responsiveness, variety, innovation, and cost). In short, tailored sourcing becomes a source of competitive advantage.

Use multifunctional teams and relationship managers

Strategic sourcing is broad in scope. When critical and extensive activities are outsourced, such as complete interior designs (including seats) in the automobile industry or call centers in a service industry, a company's fate depends on the success of the supply relationship. Outsourcing experts such as Cisco and Sun Microsystems recognize the need for strong management skills that vastly surpass clerical purchasing skills. They employ commodity managers who are "non-traditional, as they typically come from non-procurement backgrounds and often have general business or technical backgrounds" (Farlow et al. 1996). In addition to managing the supplier relationship, they are expected to fully understand the supplier's technological and manufacturing capabilities as well as future technology trends. Commodity managers also act as the liaison between internal design teams and suppliers, holding weekly meetings with members of engineering, material planning, and marketing groups. In short, they are relationship managers who may control multi-billion dollar budgets (they operate at the management and planning level and are not involved in tactical purchasing).

Decide on facts and evaluate the total cost of ownership

Successful sourcing follows a structured process that displays a depth of analytical rigor and reflects a level of understanding that often exceeds that of the suppliers. The analytical tool here is the total cost of ownership (TCO), which prevents a narrow focus on price only in both supplier selection and the management of the ongoing relationship.

Use a supplier portfolio

Multi-sourcing combines the individual strengths of each supplier into a portfolio that outperforms any single supplier while minimizing risk. The portfolio should consist of suppliers with different capabilities. Typically, they should also differ in importance so that one can differentiate the few strategically important suppliers ("core suppliers", "partners") from more key suppliers, and others. Close relationships are built and maintained with the strategically important suppliers. The longevity of the relationship is what matters most, not the cost of one supply.

Coordinate sourcing across locations and functions

Coordination (if not centralization) of sourcing prevents duplication of effort in supplier identification, selection, certification, and contracting. Coordinated sourcing deepens relationships and awards scale economies to both the buyer and the supplier at the same time. Remember, however, that location decisions differ from sourcing decisions. (See Figure 6.13—p. 225 in Chapter 6—for the conceptual difference between offshoring and outsourcing.)

Adapt sourcing to anticipated changes in technology

The examples in the previous section of the electronics, automobile, and other industries demonstrate that technology can have a crucial impact on the attractiveness of outsourcing and the ability to manage suppliers (steps 4 and 5 in the outsourcing framework of Fig. 7.6 on p. 247). The examples also suggest that sourcing strategies should adapt to changes in product, process, and coordination technology. Specifically, outsourcing becomes more attractive when:

1. Product technology is modular with simple interfaces, and modules can be standardized across the industry.

2. Process technology can be separated from product technology and is highly specialized, or benefits from strong economies of scale or scope, or risk pooling.

3. Transportation and information technology: transportation of goods and transmission of information is relatively inexpensive compared to the product or service value.

7.9 | SUMMARY OF LEARNING OBJECTIVES

1. Explain the concept of strategic sourcing and integrate it with operations strategy.

   Strategic sourcing decides on the appropriate supply relationship for each activity in the value chain. It starts by identifying the activity, its requirements, and any potential qualified suppliers. It specifies who will performs the activity (in or outsource) and under which conditions. Finally, it establishes and manages the supplier relationship to align incentives.

   Strategic sourcing amounts to configuring the operations system and its interfaces with suppliers. To ensure that the resulting operation works well and is aligned with the competitive strategy, sourcing must be integrated with all the parts that comprise operations strategy. Our general framework can help in that process by highlighting the interaction of sourcing and supply management with the other levers of operations strategy (Figure 7.2).

2. Use a framework to choose a supply relationship and guide the outsourcing decision.

   Sourcing relationships fall on a spectrum between the extremes of a transactional market exchange (simply called purchasing or procurement) and vertical integration. The advantages and disadvantages of "arm's-length" purchasing are summarized in Figure 7.4 on p. 243. Outsourcing that is based on long-term relationships aims to combine the benefits of both market exchange and vertical integration.

   A five-step framework may assist in the outsourcing decision. Sometimes, the answer can be derived directly from two "go, no-go" conditions: outsourcing may be infeasible (e.g., lack of supply base) or necessary (e.g, insufficient capabilities for insourcing). Otherwise, one should check whether outsourcing is aligned with the strategic priorities and risks, whether external suppliers can supply it better (i.e., at lower total cost), and whether we have the ability to contract and manage the relationship and the ongoing risk.

3. Apply three tools to improve outsourcing: total cost of ownership (TCO), structured contracts, and multi-sourcing.

   The major challenge in strategic sourcing that uses long-term relationships is to balance cooperation (seeking the benefits of vertical integration) and competition (a major benefit from market exchange). A win-win situation for the buyer and supplier can be achieved when multifunctional teams consider all relevant dimensions to the relationship, and drive improvement at both customer and supplier. We considered three tools to drive improvement while instilling some price discipline: total cost of ownership supplier scorecards, structured contracts, and multi-sourcing with a supplier portfolio.

   The total cost of ownership (TCO) captures all costs that are impacted by a supply source change. TCO is data-intensive, and is built up using a process view of the operation and activity-based costing. In addition to supplier selection, TCO information can be communicated in supplier scorecards to enhance communication and improvement. By extending TCO analysis to both suppliers and customers, it becomes a powerful tool to improve the entire value chain and to communicate your product or service value to your customers.

Structured contracts specify commitments and contingency options and can be designed to shape and balance risks and incentives between buyer and supplier. Even relatively simple structured contracts such as buy-back and revenue or profit-sharing contracts can be effective. Options and quantity-flexibility contracts allow for more sophisticated risk control. The adoption and the choice of contract depends on their individual implementation costs (information sharing and verification), bargaining power, and the preferences of the supplier and the buyer.

Multi-sourcing uses a portfolio of different suppliers; as each supplier has different strengths, a careful combination of suppliers yields better results than single-sourcing. Multi-sourcing aims to ensure reasonable prices and mitigate the risk of supplier dependence. By strategically selecting suppliers, one can also tailor the properties of the sourcing portfolio to the competitive priorities. Multi-sourcing can be tailored along volume and responsiveness, product or customization, quality, and innovation requirements.

4. Illustrate how technological change affects sourcing and value chain disintegration.

Examples of the electronics, automobile, and business services industries demonstrate the impact of technology on sourcing strategies and on the (dis)integration of the value chain. Outsourcing and disintegration increases when (i) product technology is modular and standardized, (ii) process technology can be separated from product technology and exhibits economies of scale or benefits from risk pooling, and (iii) transportation of the goods or information transmission is relatively inexpensive compared to the value of the product or service.

Discussion Questions

1. A power tool company has been manufacturing its cordless power tools (sold in the U.S.) in Mexico. Now, it contemplates outsourcing manufacturing to Malaysia. Which factors should it consider when comparing the total cost of ownership of both strategies? What data would it need to compile?

2. Consider the power tool company of question 1: how could it design a multi-sourcing strategy that uses both Mexico and Malaysia as manufacturing locations?

3. Newell Rubbermaid's supplier scorecard, a representative example of many scorecards used in practice, measures quality, service level, productivity, and responsiveness and compiles a supplier score by weighing each component at 25%. How do you think those weights were chosen? Discuss their importance and how they should be chosen.

4. Which of the structured contracts in the bookstore example of section 7.5 would the publisher accept, and which ones would the bookstore accept? Hint: evaluate the expected profits of both parties for each contract and compare them with the base case of the price-only contract.

Visit www.vanmieghem.us for additional questions and updates.

FURTHER READING AND REFERENCES

▶ Further references to managing supplier relationships include Cachon and Lariviere (2001), Chapman, Dempsey, Ramsdell, and Reopel (1997), Gauntt (2004), Jackson, Iloranta, and McKenzie (2001), Farlow, Schmidt, and Tsay (1996), Fisher (2003), and Laseter (1998).

▶ For more discussions on vertical integration and market exchanges, see Besanko, Dranove, and Shanley (2000) for an economic perspective or Slack and Lewis (2001) for an operations view.

▶ Examples of Total Cost of Ownership calculations and applications in supply chains include Chopra and Meindl (2007), Degraeve and Roodhooft (2001), and Roodhooft, den Abbeele A., and Peeters (2005).

▶ Insightful historic overviews of the automobile industry include Hounshell (1984), Ohno (1988) and Womack, Jones, and Roos (1990).

Besanko, D., D. Dranove, and M. Shanley (2000). *Economics of Strategy*. New York: John Wiley & Sons.

Bremner, B., G. Edmonson, and C. Dawson (2004). Nissan's boss. *Business Week*, 50–58. October 4.

Cachon, G. P. and M. L. Lariviere (2001). Turning the supply chain into a revenue chain. *Harvard Business Review*, 2–3. March.

Chapman, T. L., J. J. Dempsey, G. Ramsdell, and M. R. Reopel (1997). Purchasing: No time for lone rangers. *McKinsey Quarterly*, 31–40.

Chopra, S. and P. Meindl (2007). *Supply Chain Management: Strategy, Planning & Operations*. Prentice Hall.

Degraeve, Z. and F. Roodhooft (2001). A smarter way to buy. *Harvard Business Review*, 22–23. June.

Dumarey, E. (2005). Personal conversations with Mr. Dumarey, CEO of Cortina NV, and company profile at www.cortina.be. Spring.

Farlow, D., G. Schmidt, and A. Tsay (1996). Supplier management at sun microsystems: Managing the supplier relationship. *Stanford University GSB case*. study S-OIT-16, supervised by Charles A. Holloway.

Fisher, H. (2003). First tier in automotive environment. Unpublished Master's Thesis with J. A. Van Mieghem, advisor. Kellogg School of Management & WHU.

Gauntt, J. d. P. (2004, Oct). New rules for global component sourcing: the quality imperative in electronics. *Economist Intelligence Unit white paper*.

Grossman, G. and E. Helpman (2005). Outsourcing in a global economy. *Review of Economic Studies 72*, 135–159.

Hounshell, D. A. (1984). *From the American System to Mass Production 1800-1932*. Baltimore and London: Johns Hopkins University Press.

Jackson, B. and M. Pfitzmann (2007). Win-win sourcing. *Strategy+Business* (47), 1–8.

Jackson, T., K. Iloranta, and S. McKenzie (2001). Profits or perils? the bottom line on outsourcing. *Strategy+Business*, 1–13.

Laseter, T. M. (1998). *Balanced Sourcing: Cooperation and Competition in supplier relationships*. Jossey-Bass Publishers. A Strategy & Business Book.

Moffett, M. H. and W. Youngdahl (1998). José Ignacio Lopez de Arriortua. *Thunderbird Case*. Number A02-98-0003.

Ohno, T. (1988). *Toyota Production System: Beyond Large-Scale Production*. Portland, Oregon: Productivity Press.

Roodhooft, F., V. den Abbeele A., and F. Peeters (2005). Total cost of ownership as a tool for inter-firm cost management: a case in the Belgian utilities industry. *KU Leuven Research Paper*, 18. Number 0534 available from www.econ.kuleuven.be/eng/tew-/cteo/Reports.aspx.

Shirouzu, N. (2006). As rivals catch up, Toyota CEO spurs big efficiency drive. *Wall Street Journal*. Dec 9.

Slack, N. and M. Lewis (2001). *Operations Strategy*. New Jersey: Prentice Hall.

Taylor, T. and E. Plambeck (2007). Simple relational contracts for capacity investment: Price-only vs. quantity-commitment. *Manufacturing and Service Operations Management 9*, 94–113.

Toyota supplier of fasteners (2004). Personal conversations.

Womack, J. P., D. T. Jones, and D. Roos (1990). *The Machine that changed the world: The story of lean production*. HarperCollins Publishers.

Young, J. (1993). *The Chicago Tribune*, 15. Feb 21, section 1.

Mini-Case 7 | BOSE 301SE: SOURCING AND CONTRACTING

[4]Bose Corporation is planning to release a special Christmas edition of its popular 301 speakers. Lance Dixon, director of Purchasing and Logistics for Bose, is negotiating a special order with his preferred supplier, G&F Industries. After implementing a successful JIT II program, G&F has increased its manufacturing capabilities, thus becoming a full service supplier of full speaker systems for small, special orders. Given that customer disappointments are not conducive to building the Bose brand, Bose decided that all 301SE's must be produced before December to ensure their sufficient availability at the beginning of the short Christmas season.

Ursula von Trapp, Bose's marketing executive for special programs, has performed market research and analyzed sales of similar past offerings. She recommends a target price of $200 per speaker pair, for which she predicts the demand forecast as illustrated in Figure 7.15.

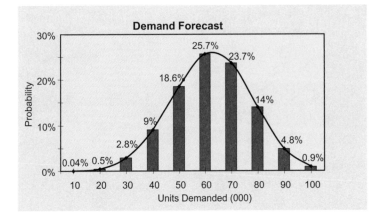

Figure 7.15 The demand forecast for 301SE is specified using 10 scenarios.

John Argitis, president of G&F, has agreed to a $120 wholesale price per 301SE pair. G&F incurs a cost of $60 to manufacture and deliver a pair to Bose. Bose can sell any left over stock at the end of the Christmas season to discounters in Belgium at an expected salvage price of $40 per pair.

Lance, a clever negotiator, proposes G&F to buy back from Bose any 301SE's that are left over at the end of the Christmas season for $70 per pair (G&F can also salvage such pair to the Belgian discounter for $40). On the other hand, Tom Beesen, VP of Manufacturing at Bose, is an ardent proponent of vertical integration and suggests bringing the 301SE in-house.

1. *What production level should G&F plan for? Should it accept Lance's proposal?*

2. *Would vertical integration improve profitability?*

---

[4]Professor Van Mieghem prepared this case as the basis for class discussion rather than to illustrate either the effective or ineffective handling of a managerial situation. No part of this case study may be reproduced without permission; direct all inquiries to permissions@vanmieghem.us

Chapter

8

DEMAND AND REVENUE MANAGEMENT

There is no utility other than that for which people are willing to pay.—Dupuit (1844).

Learning Objectives

After reading this chapter, you will be able to:

1. Explain the concept of revenue management and integrate it with operations strategy.
2. Identify the conditions for and obstacles to effective revenue management.
3. Design products to achieve customer segmentation and price discrimination.
4. Analyze time segmentation with dynamic pricing and capacity constraints.
5. Apply two tools for capacity segmentation and reservation: overbooking and dynamic capacity allocation.

In Part 2 of this book, we learned how to configure the operational system's resources. Now, in Part 3, we are analyzing how to structure the operational processes to utilize the resources in a value-maximizing manner. In the previous chapter, we studied input management (sourcing and supply management). In this chapter, we will turn our attention to output management. We will investigate how demand and revenue management can be integrated with operations strategy in order to simultaneously improve firm profitability and customer service.

8.1 | DEMAND AND REVENUE MANAGEMENT: CONCEPTS

Broadly interpreted, the concept of demand management includes all the activities that influence the demand for products and services. This includes many, if not all, marketing activities, as well as sales and service activities. Given that this book is about operations strategy, we are interested in how operations can contribute to demand management. Much of operations deals with matching

---

Example 8.1 American Airlines' response to PeoplExpress

Robert Crandall, Chairman and CEO of American Airlines, recalls his company's response to PeoplExpress' deep discounting in 1978:

> "We could match deeply discounted fares and risk diluting our entire [reservations] inventory, or we could not match and certainly lose market share. Yield management gave us a third alternative–match deeply discounted fares on a portion of our inventory and close deeply discounted inventory when it is profitable to save space for later booking higher value customers. By adjusting the number of reservations which are available to these discounts, we can adjust our minimum available fare to account for differences in demand. This creates a pricing structure which responds to demand on a flight-by-flight basis. As a result, we can more effectively match our demand to supply" (Smith et al. 1992).

Other airlines soon followed American's pioneering example, and the rest is history: revenue management gave "full-service" airlines the tools to attract many of PeoplExpress's customers (while preserving their high-end customer base). This drove PeoplExpress' load factors down to unsustainable levels. By November 1986 PeoplExpress was no more.

---

supply and demand, often by tailoring the production processes to the demand characteristics. But when the existing operational system is inflexible, operations strategy must match demand to available supply in a value-maximizing manner. *Revenue management* refers to the collection of demand management practices that aim to maximize the revenue of available supply.

The growing importance of revenue management

Going to a ball game used to be so simple. All you had to do was walk up to the ticket window at the ballpark and buy a seat. But if you ask for a seat today, and you are faced with numerous options to choose from. In 1987, tickets to the Dodgers games sold for $7, $6, and $4. In 2007, the Dodgers sold 24 categories of seats at 104 different price points, depending not only on where you sit, but on when you buy your seat and whether you buy it for one game, some games, every game, individually, or as a group (Shaikin 2007).

Revenue management takes the age-old business practice of price discrimination (tailoring the price to an individual's willingness-to-pay so as to extract more revenue) to new heights. With CRM and ERP systems, advances in information and optimization technology have made it commercially feasible to apply price discrimination in real time and at a level of customer specificity that was previously impossible. Movie theaters, buses, trains, amusement parks, and restaurants have long practiced revenue management techniques by offering discounts to children, students, or and senior citizens. But those are crude, sledgehammer approaches compared to the fine, scalpel techniques that are possible today.

The deregulation of the U.S. airline industry in 1978 is often cited as the start of "modern" revenue management. The new deep discount carrier PeoplExpress started advertising its Newark-Buffalo weekday flight at a price of $70 for "every seat and every flight"(Sloan 1981). With the emergence of deeply discounted fares established airlines were faced with two unattractive responses.

Example 8.2 Peapod: online grocery shopping and delivery

Peapod is an Internet grocer pioneer that delivers goods to its customers using its own fleet of vehicles. When brothers Andrew and Thomas Parkinson founded Peapod in 1989, they pioneered the online grocery delivery concept with just 400 households in Evanston, a suburb of Chicago. By 2007, Peapod had become America's leading Internet grocer, delivering to 1,500 zip codes and over 12,700,000 households across 18 U.S. markets. Peapod is a wholly owned subsidiary of international food provider Royal Ahold, and works in partnership with Ahold USA supermarket companies including Stop & Shop and Giant Food.

By 2007, Peapod had completed more than 10 million deliveries to 270,000 customers. Using its own fleet of vans and trucks, deliveries are made either from two central warehouses or any of 16 smaller warerooms (adjacent to supermarket partners Stop & Shop and Giant Food). Holding excess delivery capacity or adding trucks and drivers at the spur of the moment is expensive. Instead, Peapod uses its proprietary SmartMile revenue management system to profitably match demand to delivery supply. A substantial fraction of demand is moved to available capacity supply by dynamically turning on or off available delivery time slots and offering discounts for lowly-utilized delivery slots. Automated routing with GPS tracking allows tailored planning (longer delivery slots for less accessible drop off locations) and real-time updating. For a fee as low as $6.95, most customers can place orders for delivery as soon as the next day (within a two-hour window) or even days or weeks in advance. These capacity and price controls improve capacity utilization and revenues, while also increasing customer satisfaction.

Source: Peapod (2007) and Chapter 13

American Airlines, however, found a third, successful response: it introduced revenue management techniques (Example 8.1). In 1992, American Airlines estimated the quantifiable benefits of revenue management at $1.4 billion over the previous three years. They expected an annual revenue contribution of over $500 million to continue into the future.

In the early 1990s, revenue management spread to the car rental and hotel industry. At the threat of being liquidated by its parent General Motors, National Car Rental implemented revenue management and optimized pricing and car reservation and allocation methods. But two years later in 1994, National was among the fastest growing car rental companies. Similarly, Marriott Hotels had increased revenue from its rooms by more than 4% by the mid 1990s. In 2003, Marriott estimated that its new centralized "One Yield" revenue management system, which handled 62 million reservations at 2,800 properties, delivered incremental profits of $6.7 million (Thibodeau 2005).

By 2000, revenue management practices had spread to many other industries, including banking, entertainment, Internet groceries (Example 8.2), logistics, manufacturing, retail, media broadcasting (Araman and Popescu 2007) and real estate. For instance, Camden Property Trust uses the M/PF Yieldstar Price Optimizer to automatically update the prices of its rental apartments. The Yieldstar technology uses data, such as the number of vacancies and forecasted market conditions, and mathematical optimization (instead of human intuition) to optimize rental rates for individual apartments. About 25% of Camden's rent growth was directly related to its Yieldstar implementation (Dunham 2006).

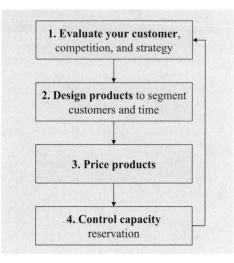

Figure 8.1 Revenue management follows a four step process and is continuously updated.

Revenue management as an integral part of operations strategy

To match demand with supply in a value-maximizing manner, revenue management must be integrated with the overall operations strategy. To help align revenue management with the operations' competencies, resources, and other processes, four steps can be followed, as illustrated in Figure 8.1:

1. Evaluate your strategy, competition, and customer. Of course, the opportunities arising from revenue management techniques depend on your strategy as well as the actions of your competitors. Fiercely competitive markets allow little price flexibility, while niche strategies may not want to dilute their focus by serving additional segments. Yet, understanding customer purchasing behavior and valuations is key: What do customers need and value? Besides price, how important is flexibility in the purchasing decision? Do valuations change significantly over customers or over time?

2. If so, there is an opportunity to serve them better and improve profits by designing products tailored to each group and time period. This involves bundling asset use with qualifying service restrictions (such as an advance purchase, weekend stay-over, or unrestricted airline ticket). By selling each product at different prices, customers can choose or self-select, thereby segmenting the market and partially revealing their valuation.

3. Price the products based on customer purchasing behavior, valuations, and forecasted demand curves. Subsequent price optimization will suggest prices that maximize profits.

4. Control the capacity that is allocated to the various products.

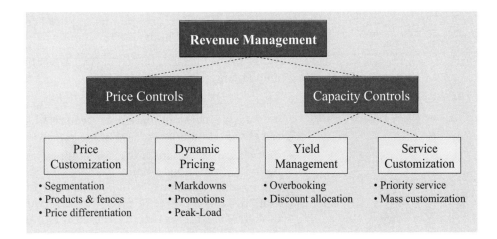

Figure 8.2 Typical revenue management techniques predominantly control either the price or quantity side of revenue.

The four-step revenue management process should periodically, if not continually, be revisited to adapt to changing conditions.

In the remainder of this chapter, we will discuss these four steps in detail; we will finish the chapter by reviewing how revenue management is an integral part of operations strategy. First, we will categorize the typical revenue management processes (remainder of this section) and discuss potential obstacles (next section).

Price controls

Revenue equals price times quantity. Revenue management practices can accordingly be categorized as processes that aim to improve revenue by predominantly controlling price or quantity (capacity), as illustrated in Figure 8.2.

Price controls are techniques that vary prices in order to influence demand. Pricing is arguably the most intuitive and widely used form of revenue management. It is useful to make the distinction between strategic and tactical pricing. Strategic pricing refers to the setting of long-term, average prices that take into account competitive behavior as well as customer valuation and cost (basic economic theory tells us that profit-maximizing prices equate marginal revenues with marginal costs).

In contrast, revenue management through price controls typically refers to tactical price changes among customers or over time:

1. *Price discrimination and customization* is the tactic of adjusting price to groups or even individual customers. It aims to extract a substantial part (if not all) of each customer's willingness-to-pay. It is common to discrimination among groups of customers by offering different products, and such practice is well-studied in economics. Customizing price to individual customers, the ultimate form of price discrimination, is widely practiced in sales, in contract negotiations, and in make-to-order quotations, but more

as an art than a science: "despite its importance, there is little available research in this area." (Philips 2003).

2. *Dynamic pricing* is the tactic of varying price over time in response to changes in demand or supply conditions:

- *Markdown pricing* decreases price over time in order to clear leftover inventory. A commonplace practice in retail, it reflects decreasing customer valuation near the end of the season.
- *Promotional pricing* includes discounting, normally within a limited period. "Promotions are ubiquitous in the retail world: a recent retail survey estimated that 60% of all retail sales involved some sort of promotion. ... The power of promotions derives from the fact that they can often be targeted to particular customer segments in ways that are not possible through list prices" (Philips 2003).
- *Peak-load pricing* increases prices during periods of high demand while supply remains constant. It is widely practiced in industries with fixed supply but changing demand over the day, week, or season. For instance, telecommunication companies offer inexpensive or even free nights or weekends; the entertainment industry sells matinee and late night shows at a discount; the transportation, rental, and vacation industries increase prices during peak season; and many utility companies change prices during the day (many Belgian households have a dual electricity meter and may shift electricity-intensive tasks to off-peak).

In addition to these tactics of controlling *posted prices* that customers can see, there are also *price discovery* mechanisms, in which customers determine prices through their own actions during the transactions. These include different forms of auctions, group buying, and negotiations (Sahay 2007).

Capacity controls

Capacity controls are techniques designed to influence demand by restricting the availability of supply (while keeping prices fixed). As before, revenue management through capacity controls typically refers to tactical changes in availability (in contrast to strategically bringing a limited quantity to the market).

1. *Yield management* uses reservation systems and booking controls to accept and allocate demand to available capacity. This strategy originated in the airline industry (where demand is highly volatile) and aims to maximize the revenue (or "yield") of each unit of capacity by smartly reserving it ahead of capacity consumption.

2. *Service customization* is the tactic of adjusting a service (or even a good) to an individual customer. While service customization shares some characteristics with yield management (such as the control of available capacity), it does not require the use of reservation systems. Service customization also applies to make-to-order or service-to-order environments. Service customization may involve the use of priority systems (e.g., FedEx's overnight versus regular delivery) and mass customization (recall Chapter 5 where we also discussed revenue and profit maximization through flexibility).

8.2 | OBSTACLES TO REVENUE MANAGEMENT

Before we analyze the four steps in revenue management, it is important to recognize potential implementation obstacles.

Data mining, forecasting, and optimization

Revenue management techniques stand or fall with the availability of representative and detailed forecasts. Substantial valid data sets are required to forecast demand curves by market segment, product, and time of purchase. While the Internet has vastly increased the availability of data, good customer behavior modeling and statistical techniques are still necessary to set up data capturing and to extract relevant forecasts. Finally, serious computational power is needed for price and capacity optimization, especially if revenue management is to be applied in real time (such as on the Internet). For smaller businesses, the cost of full state-of-the-art automated real-time revenue management may outweigh its benefits; instead, a few basic revenue management tools may be sufficient.

Competition and automated revenue management

Few businesses are monopolies; thus, their prices depend not only on demand characteristics, inventories, and capacities, but also on competitors' actions. Competitive revenue management can quickly become complex and is not yet full understood in a network setting. For example, consider the airline industry, where two airlines may compete for customers on a single flight-leg (horizontal competition), but may also serve each other's customers on connecting flights (vertical competition). Airlines may form alliances that allow each airline to sell tickets for flights operated by any alliance partner (an arrangement called *code sharing*).

Competitive revenue management is an active research area that is generating new insights. For example, Netessine and Shumsky (2005) show that optimal allocation levels depend on the type of competition: under horizontal competition, the total assets protected for high-price customers are larger than what a monopolist would protect (so high-price customers are better off). Under vertical competition, the protection level may be higher or lower than the monopoly level, depending on the quantity of connecting demand.

The technical equilibrium underlying competitive revenue management is not always smooth or well-behaved. Therefore, computerized systems that use automated optimization may generate capacity controls that exhibit non-intuitive behavior. For example, they may suggest a significant increase in a booking limit without any significant change in demand (Netessine and Shumsky 2005). Managers need to be aware of the potential problems.

Treat your best customers well

It is crucial that the best (most valuable) customers do not resent your revenue management techniques. As we will see, good revenue management increases firm profits while improving service along some dimension that is important to customers that pay the high price. When that important message is not heeded

> **Example 8.3** Amazon and Coca-Cola's experience with non-market factors
>
> In October 2000, it was reported that Amazon had engaged in dynamic pricing of DVDs after customers discovered price differences of more than 40% depending on the log-in profile used. Customer response was so furious that Amazon CEO Jeff Bezos publicly apologized and refunded 6,896 customers an average of $3. "We've never tested and we never will test prices based on customer demographics," Bezos told the Associated Press. In a similar snafu, chairman Doug Ivester told the Brazilian magazine Veja in 1999 that Coca-Cola was considering vending machines that boost prices during hot weather. "In final summer, ..., the utility of a chilled Coca-Cola is very high. So it is fair it should be more expensive. The machine will simply make this process automatic"(BBC 1999). Negative customer reaction caused Coke to deny it would ever use such a vending machine. The public relation fiasco was recalled when Ivester was ousted in December 1999.

and revenue management is perceived as unfair, strong customer reactions follow. Be mindful of Amazon's experience (Example 8.3) of extracting higher prices from the customers it knows best, its loyal customers.

Social concerns and fairness (non-market factors)

The economic benefits of price discrimination, and thus the incentives to implement revenue management techniques, are obvious. In addition, the ability to implement revenue management techniques is increasing, with better information systems and optimization software. However, strong social obstacles still exist.

Few customers enjoy discrimination or other revenue techniques such as overbooking and dynamic pricing. Example 8.3 reports a telling Coca-Cola experience. Krugman (2000) summarizes the main criticism: "dynamic pricing is undeniably unfair: some people pay more just because of who they are," referring to the sophisticated practices of Internet retailers. In addition to unfairness, the practice of purposely degrading a product just to separate the market is not easily defensible from a social perspective.

Thus, while revenue management often increases both firm profits and customer surplus (i.e., total welfare), negative popular reaction may diminish any benefits it may have. Privacy and anti-discrimination concerns may lead to government regulations. In February 2005, the European Union mandated specific, minimal compensations from airlines to customers who are denied boarding due to overbooking or flight cancelation. Similar regulations are to follow for international train and boat traffic.

8.3 | CUSTOMER SEGMENTATION AND PRODUCT DESIGN

The first and second step in implementing revenue management involve understanding and segmenting customers by designing products. Segmentation, or separating demand into various segments, is extremely important when applying many revenue management techniques. Let us start with a simple example.

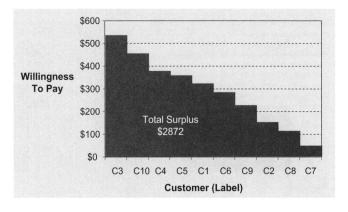

Figure 8.3 The willingness to pay of a sample of 10 customers.

Club Bora Bora example

Assume you would like to employ revenue management techniques for the operations of Club Bora Bora, an exclusive vacation resort in French Polynesia. You have started by collecting information on how much customers value a day at your club (for example, you sampled 5% of the people who expressed interest in staying at Club Bora Bora on a given day). Your estimates of each customer's valuation, expressed in terms of their *willingness to pay* (WTP) or *reservation price*, are:

Customer	$C1$	$C2$	$C3$	$C4$	$C5$	$C6$	$C7$	$C8$	$C9$	$C10$	Sum
WTP	$323	$151	$534	$378	$358	$284	$50	$113	$225	$456	$2,872

Armed with this information, your optimal pricing strategy is to charge each of these individuals their reservation price if they would present them as your customers. The maximal revenue you could possibly collect is the sum of all reservation prices, which is the total customer valuation or surplus of $2,872. Imagine sorting all customers by their willingness to pay as in Figure 8.3, and then charging them the according, fully-customized prices. Identifying and charging each customer's reservation price, a method called *perfect* or *first-degree price discrimination*, represents the ideal form of revenue maximization. Perfection, however, is not of this world; neither is perfect price discrimination because we seldom have perfect information on customers. While we can't be perfect, we can do fairly well by employing the following strategies:

All good revenue management starts with a forecast. If we cannot have perfect customer information, we can at least model and predict their reservation prices using an inverse demand function.[1] We can also use statistical analysis to identify the best fitting function to our data. For our limited data set, a simple linear regression using a spreadsheet shows that the best linear inverse demand function is:

$$p = 565 - 50q.$$

Assuming our 5% customer sample is representative of the entire customer population, our total demand function is $D(p) = 20 \times (565 - p)/50 = 226 - 0.4p$.

---

[1]Traditionally, the demand function specifies the demand as a function of price. The inverse demand function predicts the price for a given quantity.

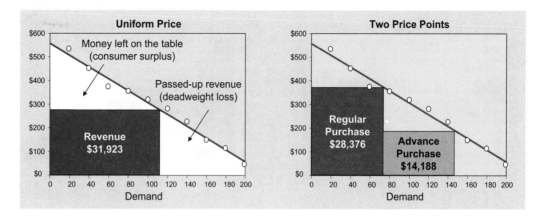

Figure 8.4 Relative to uniform pricing, revenue can be increased by 33% by segmenting customers into two groups and using optimal price discrimination.

Club Bora Bora: charging a single price

If we treat all customers equally, we must charge each the same price. The optimal price maximizes total revenue and is thus derived from a simple optimization problem. Remember that customers derive net value, and thus will pay the price only if their willingness to pay exceeds the charged price. For a given price p, the total sales quantity is thus $D(p)$ with associated revenue $pD(p) = 226p - 0.4p^2$. Simple price optimization (see Appendix 8) yields the:

$$
\begin{aligned}
\text{optimal single price} &= \frac{1}{2}\$565 = \$282.5, \\
\text{associated sales quantity} &= 226 - 0.4 \times 282.5 = 113, \\
\text{associated revenue} &= 113 \times \$282.5 = \$31,923
\end{aligned}
$$

Perfect price discrimination would recover the total customer surplus. Using the actual customer sample, the total customer surplus is $20 \times \$2,872 = \$57,440$. Using the linear demand approximation, the total customer surplus is the area under the demand curve:

$$
\text{total surplus} = \$565 \times 226/2 = \$63,845.
$$

In other words, a single price captures only half of the total surplus (assuming linear demand functions); our customers were willing to pay more (representing money left on the table in the left panel of Figure 8.4) and we could have potentially sold to more customers (passed-up revenue). We can do better by segmenting our customers and charging tailored prices to each segment.

Club Bora Bora: segmenting customers into two groups

Imagine that we have a variable or an instrument that is correlated with a customer's willingness to pay. For example, low valuation customers are more price-sensitive and may be willing to purchase in advance at a lower price, while high value customers may buy at the last moment at full price. In this case, it is optimal to sort and group customers, and charge them different prices by creating two "products:" advance and regular purchase. Let us optimistically assume that customers self-select perfectly between these two products: all customers with valuations exceeding the full price p_1 buy at the last moment at that price, while customers with lower valuations between p_1 and the advance price p_2 buy in advance.

Thus, the quantity demanded by the regular segment is $D(p_1)$, while the quantity demanded by the advance segment is given by $D(p_2) - D(p_1)$. The associated total revenue is:

$$\begin{aligned} \text{Revenue} \;&=\; \text{regular purchase revenue} \;+\; \text{advance purchase revenue} \\ &=\; p_1 D(p_1) \;+\; p_2\left(D(p_2) - D(p_1)\right) \\ &=\; p_1\left(226 - 0.4p_1\right) \;+\; p_2\left(p_1 - p_2\right)0.4 \end{aligned}$$

$$(8.1)$$

Price optimization (see Appendix 8) yields:

$$\text{optimal prices:} \quad p_1 = \frac{2}{3}\$565 = \$376.67 \text{ and } p_2 = \frac{1}{3}\$565 = \$188.33$$

$$\text{sales quantities:} \quad 226 - 0.4p_1 = 75.33 \text{ and } (p_1 - p_2)0.4 = 75.33$$

$$\text{associated revenue:} \quad 75.33 \times \$376.67 + 75.33 \times \$188.33 = \$42,563$$

Segmenting customers by designing two products sold at different prices increases revenue by $\$10,640$ or 33% relative to uniform pricing. It has two effects: raising the price for customers with a high willingness to pay reduces money left on the table (right panel of Figure 8.4) and allows the company to give a discount to the other customers, reducing the passed-up revenue. While this inter-segment subsidy often results in negligible net effects on customer surplus compared to a single price, company revenue and thus total welfare (the sum of customer surplus and company revenue) increases, given that more customers are willing to make the purchase (150.67 versus 113, an increase by 1/3 or 33%).

Club Bora Bora: customer segmentation with capacity constraints

Such an increase in sales, however, cannot be accommodated by the limited room capacity of 120 at Club Bora Bora. To mitigate capacity shortages, revenue management typically raises the price. Again, optimal prices maximize revenue but now a capacity constraint is added to the price optimization problem:

$$\begin{aligned} \textit{Maximize} \quad &\text{Revenue} \;=\; \text{regular revenue} + \text{advance revenue} \\ \textit{subject to} \quad &\text{Sales} \;=\; \text{regular sales} + \text{advance sales} \quad \le \text{capacity} \end{aligned}$$

Total revenue remains as in equation (8.1), while the capacity constraint becomes

$$226 - 0.4p_2 \le 120.$$

Constrained price optimization (Appendix 8) yields:

$$\text{optimal prices:} \quad p_1 = \$415 \text{ and } p_2 = \$265$$

$$\text{sales quantities} \;:\quad 226 - 0.4p_1 = 60 \text{ and } (p_1 - p_2)0.4 = 60$$

$$\text{associated revenue} \;:\quad 60 \times \$415 + 60 \times \$265 = \$40,800$$

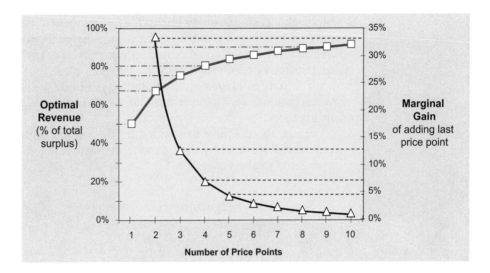

Figure 8.5 The improvement in revenue from customer segmentation and optimal differentiated pricing (for a linear demand curve).

As before, sales quantities are split evenly among the two segments. The capacity constraint has the effect of increasing both prices, although the brunt of the price increase is carried by the low value segment. Even though capacity is about 20% short compared to the ideal capacity of 150, tailored revenue management using constrained price optimization mitigates the revenue fall to less than 5%.

Club Bora Bora: the value of adding more price points

The example showed that segmenting the customer base into two groups and offering two price points increased revenues by one-third. The incremental value of additional price points quickly decreases, however, because there is less and less consumer surplus to be captured. As derived in Appendix 8 and illustrated in Figure 8.5, revenue gains quickly taper off as more price points are added. Going beyond a handful of price-points is rarely valuable, especially because the implementation and leakage cost increases (for instance, successful firms such as Southwest Airlines use just a handful of price-points).

Let us summarize the insights gained from the example.

Product design: fences and leakage

Perfect price discrimination is seldom possible, but imperfect differentiated pricing often is. This so-called *second-degree price discrimination* is implemented by designing differentiated "products." By selling each product at a different price, customers can choose or self select, thereby partially revealing their valuation.

The key idea behind designing these differentiated products is that they attract different customer groups that are correlated by willingness-to-pay, while their marginal production cost is roughly the same. From an operational perspective, different products are thus essentially identical real assets. Sometimes,

Example 8.4 Product design fences in revenue management (Maglaras 2002)

- Time of purchase or usage restrictions. In the travel industry, advance purchases can often be made at a discount price compared to spot purchases. Matinee tickets can only be used for morning or afternoon shows (which is a form of dynamic pricing, as discussed below).

- Location of purchase. Car rental companies (naively) change their prices depending on the country that is selected when making a reservation.

- Purchase restrictions. Cancelation or change fees increase product separation and aim to discourage people from switching among products (for example when a price declines). Requiring a Saturday-night-stay is a popular restriction to separate leisure from business customers.

- Purchase volume restrictions. Discount products are often only available in individual quantities to prevent resale ("scalping"). Sometimes, however, special discounts apply only to groups as a form of quantity discounts.

- Duration of usage restrictions. In the car rental and recreation industries, single-day rentals are usually more expensive than the price per day associated with a weekly-rate.

- Customer affiliation and loyalty programs, which can be used to separate and retain customers, as well as to gather more or better data.

products can be physically differentiated, as in the publishing industry where pricier hardcover books attract readers who value novelty while soft-cover books are sold at a discount (their marginal production cost differs by a few dollars at best, much less than their price difference).

Often, however, product design for revenue management purposes leaves the physical asset unchanged, instead adding qualifying restrictions or "fences" to its purchase or usage (Example 8.4). While customers may value a product highly in practice, customers may buy it only at the low price in theory. Fences prevent this "buying-down" by purposely degrading the low-price product by adding restrictions or disabling features. The bundling of the physical asset with restrictions represents the *product*, also called a *fare-class* in the transportation industry. The airline industry provides the typical example: identical seats in the same economy class are sold at different prices with different purchasing restrictions. Electronics manufacturers and software vendors may also sell the same high-end product, with some features purposely disabled, at a lower price. It is not a new practice to purposely degrade a product in order to separate the market. Almost two centuries ago, French economist Dupuit (1849) wrote about the railroads:

> It is not because of the few thousand francs which would have to be spent to put a roof over the third-class carriages or to upholster the third-class seats that some company or other has open carriages with wooden benches... *What the company is trying to do is prevent the passengers who can pay the second-class fare from traveling third-class; it hits the poor, not because it wants to hurt them, but to frighten the rich.*

Effective product designs use features and fences that strongly correlate with customer preferences and reservation prices. Effective product design is not only more art than science, but its induced segmentation often exhibits "leakage" or "spill" when certain customers choose products other than those intended for them. For example, leakage occurs when a Chicago-based consultant on assignment in San Francisco buys a one-way ticket to San Francisco on Monday and a series of Friday-Monday return tickets from San Francisco to Chicago, thereby circumventing the Saturday-night stay fence. Inexhaustible customer creativity may force companies to continually redesign or increase fences.

Demand modeling and forecasting

Nearly all revenue management techniques rely on forecasts of demand curves to help design products and optimize price and capacity controls. Demand curves are more general descriptions than demand functions. In addition to describing a relationship between demand and price, demand curves also include the dependence of that relationship on various exogenous parameters such as income, advertising spending, gender, age, weather, time, and competitors' prices. When any of these parameters change, the demand function may "move."

Demand curve forecasting typically involves modeling customer preferences and statistical techniques (such as regression) to estimate demand models, whose configuration requires experience and art. Aggregate models (such as the linear demand model of Bora Bora Club) are only one way of modeling customer preferences; refer to Talluri and van Ryzin (2004, Chapter 7) for other approaches, such as utility models, or stylized choice models like the multinomial logit. It is more valuable to capture more variables in the demand curve only if the variables can be well estimated; however, this requires substantial amounts of valid data points. It follows that demand modeling is "an area where the established revenue management firm has an advantage over the newcomer" (Bell 2004).

Recall from Chapter 3 and Appendix D that forecasts should include an expected value (point forecast), as well as a measure of accuracy (forecast error or standard deviation). The fact that forecasts are never perfect directly implies that static, deterministic revenue management will also suffer from demand-supply mismatches. To mitigate the effects of capacity shortages or left-over capacity, one can update prices over time or include safety capacity controls, as the upcoming sections will investigate.

When should we consider customer segmentation and differential pricing?

Implementing customer segmentation and price discrimination can be valuable when the following conditions are met:

1. The valuation of an identical asset unit varies considerably over the customer base. If not, there is no value to be gained from separating customers into groups and charging them tailored prices.

2. Customers can effectively and efficiently be segmented into groups with similar willingness-to-pay. This requires sorting variables or fences (such as purchase history, willingness-to-pay in advance, location, etc.) that can be bundled with the asset into a product. Effective segmentation means that customers self-select the product designed for them without much leakage (or buy down). Efficient segmentation requires that the design and administration of the separate products is not too costly.

3. Customer valuation of each segment (product) can be forecasted with reasonable accuracy. Forecast errors should not be too high relative to the mean.

These three conditions imply that just a handful of price points are typically sufficient. Finer segmentation reduces the number of potential customers per segment, thereby (i) reducing the variation of valuation within each segment, (ii) making it harder to efficiently design effective products, and (iii) increasing the relative forecast error due to loss of aggregation or pooling.

Differential pricing is particularly attractive for high fixed cost, low marginal cost operations. If there is a low marginal cost, it becomes attractive to serve additional customers at a low price. In the extreme case of information goods, the price would tend to zero. To recover high fixed costs (which is important if one is to consider a similar investment in the future), it is paramount that a high price segment is maintained. As business becomes more informatized, fixed costs increase while marginal costs decrease. In the publishing industry, there is a long practice of separating customers by first providing hardcover books at higher price and only later selling the soft-cover versions. While the marginal production cost of soft-covers is perhaps a couple dollars cheaper than hardcover books, the separation is done mostly to cover the high fixed costs of publishing. This effect will become more and more important as more goods and services are digitalized.

8.4 | TIME SEGMENTATION AND DYNAMIC PRICING

Dynamic pricing is the tactic of varying price over time in response to changing supply or demand conditions. Seasonal or peak-load pricing adjust prices for temporal changes in demand while supply remains constant. Markdown and promotional pricing apply price changes when the supply is changing (clearing leftover inventory) or when it differs from the forecast, while demand may also be changing. Other reasons for implementing dynamic pricing are stochastic demand variability and lack of perfect information about underlying market conditions (which, for example, can be "learned" in the first few weeks and then used for pricing in remaining weeks).

Seasonal discounts and peak-load pricing

Club Bora Bora experiences lower demand during the fall season. Assume that the lower valuations and demand quantities for a single night stay are reflected in the lower demand curve:

$$D_{\text{low season}}(p) = 180 - 0.4p.$$

If the same prices ($p_1 = \$415$ and $p_2 = \$265$) as before would be used for the off-season, sales and revenue would be:

sales quantities : $180 - 0.4 \times 415 = 14$ and $180 - 0.4 \times 265 - 14 = 60$
associated revenue : $14 \times \$415 + \$60 \times 265 = \$21,710.$

Room utilization would fall to $74/120 = 61.67\%$; revenue would fall to $\$21,710/\$40,800 = 53\%$. Both can be improved by adjusting the price to off-season demand. Repeating the earlier price optimization, but now using the low season demand curve yields:

$$\text{optimal low season prices:} \quad p_1 = \$300 \text{ and } p_2 = \$150$$
$$\text{sales quantities} \quad : \quad q_1 = 60 \text{ and } q_2 = 60$$
$$\text{associated revenue} \quad : \quad 60 \times 300 + 60 \times 150 = \$27,000.$$

By offering a low-season *discount* of $\$115$, room utilization increases to 100%, and the revenue improves significantly (yet lower "pricing power" caps maximum revenue at $\$27,000$ compared to $\$40,800$ in peak season).

Seasonal or peak-load pricing is attractive when demand exhibits strong seasonality. The presence of capacity constraints along with seasonality only increases the yield of dynamic pricing. This explains the popularity of seasonal pricing in the entertainment, transportation, rental, restaurant, recreation, and utility industries under the forms of matinees, early bird specials, weekend rates, etc.

The only "real" implementation work of seasonal pricing is to segment demand over time and forecast demand curves for each time-bucket (at a minimum of two—seasonal and off-season demand). Computation of seasonal pricing is straightforward with the use of a simple optimization program, while listing is often done by offering "discounts" during off-season. When price changes are difficult to sell or implement, an approximate solution is to use and change capacity controls, as the next section will illustrate.

Selling off a fixed supply: markdowns and promotions

Assume a retailer stocked 144 units of a summer safari-look women's shirt to sell over an 8 week season. Market research forecasted a maximum willingness-to-pay of $\$50$ and a steady weekly demand of maximally about 60 units (in reality, valuations may decrease over time as we'll discuss below). Assuming that WTP is uniformly distributed over customers, each week then shares the same weekly demand function of

$$D(p) = 60 - 1.2p.$$

With ample stock, the optimal retail price and sales quantity would be $\$25$ (often listed as $\$24.95$) and 30 units, respectively. Because this would exceed the expected weekly availability of 18 units ($144/8$ weeks), the optimal stock-constrained price can be found through the equation $18 = 60 - 1.2p$ or:

$$p = \frac{60 - 18}{1.2} = \$35.$$

Halfway into the season, the retailer reviews inventory and finds that sales have been slower than expected. While the expected inventory after 4 weeks was $144 - 4 \times 18 = 72$, the actual stock is 88. Assuming the demand curve remains valid for the remaining weeks, it is then optimal to markdown the shirts and sell 22 units per week to clear the remaining inventory by the end of the season. The associated optimal markdown price is then

$$p_{\text{mark-down}} = \frac{60 - \text{actual remaining weekly inventory}}{1.2} = \frac{60 - 22}{1.2} = \$31.67$$

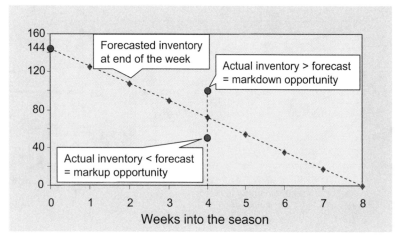

Figure 8.6 Dynamic pricing opportunities arise when the inventory moving forward differs from forecast.

Figure 8.6 illustrates the two types of revenue opportunities through dynamic pricing that can arise when selling a fixed capacity or inventory (144 units) over a season. A markdown opportunity occurs if demand has been slower than expected. With actual inventory moving forward and exceeding the forecast, the firm can improve expected future revenue by reducing all future prices. Similarly, when demand has been unexpectedly high, the firm can extract additional revenue from a more constrained inventory by raising all future prices.

The example shows that the optimal dynamic price decreases with the actual amount of remaining inventory, where the unconstrained price of $25 provides a price floor (if the supply exceeds the optimal monopoly quantity, it is better not to sell the excess). As illustrated in Figure 8.7, the optimal dynamic price also decreases as the remaining selling time decreases (i.e., as we approach the end of the season). For example, assume that the remaining inventory is 88 units with n weeks left in the season. The market-clearing price for this weekly supply of $88/n$ is $(60 - 88/n)/1.2$. Again, if there is at least one week left, the unconstrained price of $25 acts as price floor.

Instead of determining the optimal price adjustment at a particular point during the season, a similar procedure can be followed to determine the optimal time to implement a predetermined markdown.

In reality, customers with high valuations may arrive early in the season, causing the demand curve to shift downward after every selling week. Dynamic pricing then allows the retailer to sell to the customers with high valuations early in the season, while marking down (or up) to adjust for lower valuations and actual selling conditions as reflected by actual remaining inventory positions. The optimal price path is again found by optimization. Dynamic optimization (as described in Analytics Box 8.1) can easily handle updating of remaining inventory and demand forecasts.

Dynamic pricing to sell a fixed inventory over a given season improves revenues when sales are volatile so that the inventory trajectory does not follow the

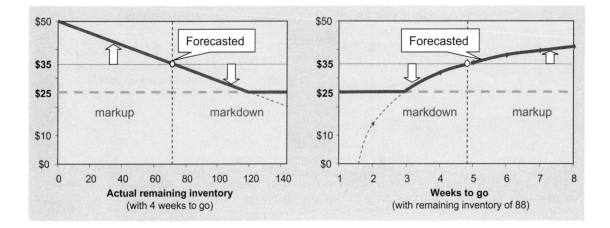

Figure 8.7 Optimal dynamic price as a function of remaining inventory (left) and sales-weeks to go (right). The unconstrained price of $25 acts as a price floor.

expected (typically straight) trajectory. The impact of dynamic pricing increases as the end of the season approaches, or as actual inventory begins to differ significantly from forecasted needs.

Dynamic pricing on the Internet: CRM, cross-selling, and sourcing

Dynamic pricing can be interpreted as the process of tailoring prices to consumer characteristics when consumers randomly arrive over time. This is essentially a euphemism for price discrimination. Internet retailers practice dynamic pricing when they update prices depending on the "potential buyer's electronic fingerprint—his record of previous purchases, his address, maybe other sites he has visited—to size up how likely he is to balk if the price is high. If the customer looks price-sensitive, he gets a bargain; if he doesn't he pays a premium"(Krugman 2000).

Thus, dynamic pricing on the Internet exploits the immense amounts of easily accessible data, but the same vast amount of customer traffic also requires that pricing and other revenue management techniques are automated. Experienced dynamic pricers have developed sophisticated statistical models that predict a specific customer's price sensitivity; think of it as updating a particular slope of the demand curve for each customer. The models are coupled with an automatic generation of discounts. The irony of this is that loyal and returning customers are more accurately analyzed, and thus can be "more accurately priced."

Dynamic pricing can also be extended to dynamically cross-sell or bundle products or services, which is widely acknowledged as an important part of *Customer Relationship Management* (CRM). Amazon is particularly strong in recommending books or music that may well complement the product that a particular customer considers buying. This multi-product dynamic revenue management problem is much more complex: given estimated consumer preferences and product inventories, two key questions are how (1) to select packaging com-

> **Analytics Box 8.1** Dynamic price and markdown optimization.
>
> The optimal price path to sell a fixed inventory over time adjusts for changes in demand forecasts as well as for actual remaining inventory positions. This price path can be calculated by solving the following price optimization problem each week. For each week (or period) t from 1 to the end of the season T, the optimal prices p_t are the outcomes of the optimization (easily solved in a spreadsheet):
>
> $$\textit{Max } \text{Revenue\_to\_go} = p_t D_t(p_t) + p_{t+1} D_{t+1}(p_{t+1}) + ... + p_T D_T(p_T),$$
> $$\textit{subject to} \qquad D_t(p_t) + D_{t+1}(p_{t+1}) + ... + D_T(p_T) \leq I_t.$$
>
> Here, $D_{t+i}(\cdot)$ is the updated forecast or demand function for week $t+i$ (that is, for sales in i weeks hence) and the capacity constraint ensures that the total future sales do not exceed the actual remaining inventory I_t available at the beginning of week t.
>
> When solving the optimization problem at the beginning of week t, only the price for the current week p_t is actually used. Re-optimizing for the following week then gives its optimal price, adjusting for updated demand forecasts and actual selling conditions. This procedure is repeated until the beginning of the last week.
>
> Additional constraints can be added to restrict price volatility if so desired.

plements and (2) how to price the product package to maximize profits. Most techniques are proprietary heuristics. Netessine, Savin, and Xiao (2006) are the first to investigate optimal dynamic cross-selling. Their research paper shows that optimal dynamic cross-selling (which anticipates the impact of current actions on future revenues) is valuable when inventory levels are of similar magnitude to expected demand.

Dynamic pricing is also used to estimate demand curves by measuring demands at different price points. Recently, dynamic pricing has also been used in sourcing. For example, Sun Microsystems' eProcurement lets suppliers adjust their prices dynamically (this form of dynamic bidding is a form of price discovery that is called a *reverse auction*).

When should we consider time segmentation and dynamic pricing?

It can be valuable to implement dynamic pricing when one or more of the following conditions are met:

1. Demand quantities are seasonal, while capacity is fixed. Off-season promotions can move peak demand to fill demand valleys, thus improving average utilization and reducing capacity shortages. In addition to seasonal inventory (Chapter 3) and capacity adjustment (Chapter 4), dynamic pricing is a third strategy to deal with seasonality.

2. Customer valuations for the asset are seasonal. Value-based pricing should thus update prices accordingly (regardless of whether supply is fixed or perishable).

3. Demand quantities, valuations, or underlying market conditions are uncertain. Dynamic pricing can then have periods of price experimentation to learn demand or market parameters, followed by periods of optimized price based on the estimated parameters.

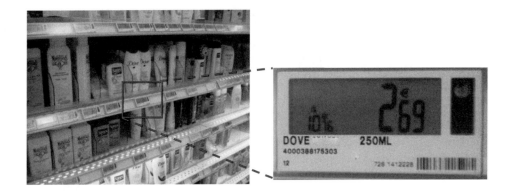

Figure 8.8 Electronic displays allow wireless updating of prices at Carrefour supermarkets (Ninove, Belgium, 2005).

4. Prices can easily be changed. Information technology increasingly reduces the cost of changing prices. It only takes a few keystrokes to change a price on the Internet. Even in traditional retailing, electronic displays, as shown in Figure 8.8, allow wireless updating of prices.

5. Asset supply is perishable and demand is volatile. Markdowns improve the likelihood that assets are sold before perishing.

6. Assets are sold both in advance (in bulk) and on the spot market, which we will further analyze in Examples 8.6 and 8.7 below.

8.5 | CAPACITY RESERVATION AND OVERBOOKING

In theory, if demand is known with certainty (as we implicitly assumed until now), price controls suffice and exactly direct optimal capacity usage. In the economic analysis of the Club Bora Bora example, the answer was simple: accept 120 orders (equal to capacity), allocating 60 rooms to the high price and the remainder to the low fare.

Capacity pre-sales, yield management, and operations strategy

In practice, demand is rarely known with certainty; posted price controls can still result in demand-supply mismatches. In Chapter 3, we saw that operations strategy must position itself somewhere in the capacity-inventory-waiting triangle (Fig. 3.8 on p. 93) to buffer against uncertainty. To reduce mismatches, a firm can use a combination of excess capacity (let assets wait for customers), excess inventory (let products wait for customers), or excess time (let customers wait on a reservation or backlog list). *Yield management* is the practice of pre-selling capacity and making customers wait on a reservation list.

In Chapter 3, we studied the trade-off between the cost of making customers wait and the cost of adding capacity in order to optimally size capacity. After capacity is sized, but before all demand is known, we can use yield management to reduce capacity surplus and shortage costs. When pre-selling a fixed amount of capacity while demand is uncertain, yield management addresses the fundamental question of when to accept or reject an order (acceptance results in reserved capacity). Yield management uses capacity controls, which are techniques that influence demand and maximize revenue by restricting the availability of supply (while keeping total capacity and prices fixed). We will approach the solution in two steps:

1. Decide how many reservations to accept in total. If we anticipate order cancelations, then selling more reservations than actual available capacity can improve actual capacity utilization and revenue. This practice is also called *overbooking* and is analyzed in this section.

2. Decide how to segment capacity and how many reservations to accept for each capacity segment. Capacity segmentation, the operational counterpart of customer segmentation, will be analyzed in the next section.

Let us first illustrate overbooking with an example before we generalize insights.

Example: overbooking at Club Bora Bora

For the main season, Club Bora Bora has listed an advance purchase price of $265 and a regular price of $415. It expects to sell about 60 rooms to each segment, as predicted by the deterministic price optimization. While the total room capacity is 120, past experience has shown that, on average, 10 room reservations are either canceled late or their customers do not show up.

As a solution, the resort can overbook and accept 130 reservations, 10 beyond capacity, in order to compensate for late cancelations and no-shows. The risk, however, is that there will be fewer cancelations than predicted. Then, a customer with a confirmed reservation would be denied a room and would have to be lodged elsewhere. Club Bora Bora estimates that associated oversale cost, after refunding any reservation fees and accounting for the compensation for inconvenience, the cost of other accommodation, and loss of goodwill, is $640. What is the value of this overbooking policy and how can the resort do better?

Without overbooking, $120 - 10 = 110$ rooms would be occupied on average. At an average price of $(\$265 + \$415)/2 = \$340$ per room, this results in an average revenue of $110 \times \$340 = \$37,400$.

With overbooking, 10 additional reservations are sold, increasing revenue by $\$340 \times 10 = \$3,400$, or 9%, to $\$40,800$. If the number of cancelations was 10 for certain, it is optimal to overbook by exactly the number of cancelations (Figure 8.9). The result would be a perfect match between demand and supply: capacity is 100% utilized and sold. The value of overbooking thus cannot exceed:

$$\text{Maximal value of overbooking} = \$40,800 - \$37,400 = \$3,400 \text{ or } 9\%.$$

In reality, however, the number of cancelations is uncertain and the firm faces two risks: capacity surplus and shortage risks. When more cancelations occur than compensated for, capacity is underutilized (wasted or spoiled) and

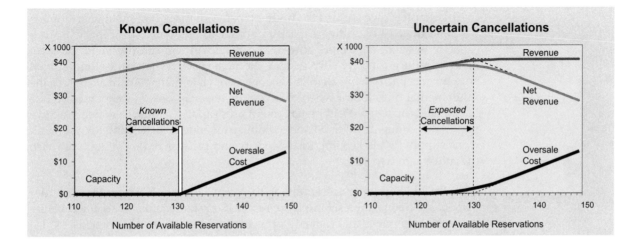

Figure 8.9 When the number of cancelations is known (left), it is optimal to overbook by an equal amount. In reality, cancelation rates are uncertain (right), and the optimal overbooking quantity may differ from expected cancelations, depending on volatility and financial data.

revenue is lost. In contrast, when fewer cancelations occur, the firm incurs a net cost for excess demand. Thus, the risks depend on the volatility of cancelations in the forecast. Assume the forecast is normally distributed with mean 10 and standard deviation 5. If the firm accepts 10 excess reservations, the average capacity surplus and shortage can be calculated (using the techniques in Appendix B):

$$\text{Expected capacity surplus } = \text{Expected capacity shortage} = 2 \text{ rooms.}$$

The expected mismatch cost of $2 \times \$340$ (revenue of 2 unused rooms) plus $2 \times \$640$ (shortage penalty of 2 over-sold rooms) or $\$1,960$ decreases the maximal revenue of $\$40,800$ to $\$38,840$. Compared to the non-overbooking option, the

$$\text{Expected value of overbooking} = \$38,840 - \$37,400 = \$1,440 \text{ or } 3.8\%.$$

Optimal overbooking

The optimal overbooking level balances the risks of capacity surplus and capacity shortage. This is easily derived using a "newsvendor" model (Chapter 3 and Appendix B) but from a different perspective: the physical capacity is known and fixed but we must decide on an overbooking level that can minimize total capacity surplus and shortage risk. The relevant "demand" is the number of cancelations, which reverses the typical situation of shortage and surplus, as illustrated in Figure 8.10.

If we make one additional reservation, we increase the risk of being overbooked but decrease the risk of having surplus capacity or spoilage. Let p be the probability that we will be overbooked. In the Club Bora Bora example, the

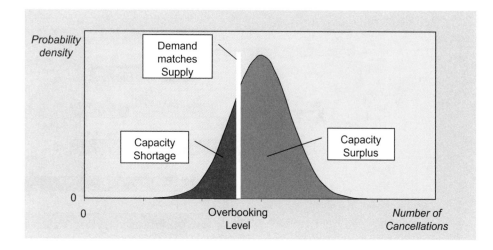

Figure 8.10 The optimal overbooking level balances the risks of capacity shortage and capacity surplus.

marginal impact on the expected mismatch cost is the expected shortage cost of $640p$ plus the expected surplus cost of $340(1 - p)$. The optimality condition sets the marginal profit to zero and yields:

$$\text{Optimal shortage probability} = \frac{\text{regular margin}}{\text{regular margin} + \text{shortage penalty}} \quad (8.2)$$

$$= \frac{\$340}{\$340 + \$640} = 35\%.$$

Be careful when interpreting this: it does not mean that 35% of all customers would be denied a room. Rather, it means that the hotel would be overbooked 35% of the days, thus only impacting customers who were forecasted to be no-shows (typically a small fraction of all customers). Similarly, it is likely that a flight is overbooked,[2] yet only a very small fraction of all passengers are denied (either voluntarily or not) a seat (Figure 8.11).

The optimal overbooking level can be directly computed using the Excel function `norminv`:

$$\text{Optimal overbooking level} = \texttt{norminv}(.35, 10, 5) = 8 \text{ rooms.}$$

Thus, it is optimal to err on the conservative side and accept 8 reservations beyond capacity, thus 128 in total. Again, the expected capacity surplus and shortage can be calculated to be:

$$\text{Expected capacity surplus} = 3.15 \text{ rooms.}$$
$$\text{Expected capacity shortage} = 1.15 \text{ rooms.}$$

---

[2]Bailey (2007) reports "bumping" cost data for three US Airways flights in 2007 that suggest that the cost of not overbooking enough is around $315, and the cost of overbooking too much is between $200 and $255. This would correspond to optimal shortage probabilities of 55% to 61%. Obviously, this is only a point estimate and overage and underage costs vary significantly from flight to flight.

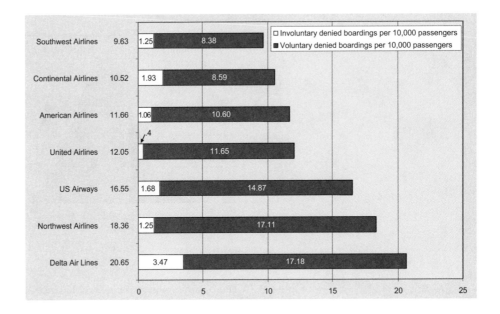

Figure 8.11 Number of denied boardings per 10,000 passengers on U.S. flights during January-March 2007. Source: DOT (2007)

The expected mismatch cost reduces to $3.15 \times \$340$ (surplus cost) plus $1.15 \times \$640$ (shortage penalty) or $\$1,807$. The expected revenue equals the maximal revenue of $\$40,800$ minus the expected mismatch cost or $\$38,993$. Compared to no overbooking, the

$$\text{Expected value of optimal overbooking} = \$38,993 - \$37,400$$
$$= \$1,593 \text{ or } 4.3\%.$$

Compared to simply overbooking the expected number of cancelations, the value of optimization is:

$$\text{Incremental value of optimal overbooking} = \$38,993 - \$38,840$$
$$= \$153 \text{ or } 0.4\%.$$

Magnitudes of fractions to a few percentage points are fairly representative values of revenue management techniques. Given that these improvements directly fall to the bottom line, they can have a considerable impact on large volume, low margin businesses.

Capacity reservation and overbooking in practice

In addition to the obvious industries of travel, recreation, logistics, and rental markets, capacity reservation and overbooking techniques can be used by any business that supplies capacity by reservation. Example 8.5 illustrates the pre-selling and overbooking of manufacturing capacity when cancelation numbers and rates are forecasted.

Example 8.5 Capacity reservation and overbooking in manufacturing

An apparel manufacturer of women's summer safari-look shirts is taking orders from retailers. Advance orders are priced at $10 per unit and can be produced at a marginal cost of $6. In the past, retailers have canceled orders after updating their demand forecasts to correct for "better demand visibility" as the selling season approaches. Given an available capacity of 100,000 units, the manufacturer is considering taking orders in excess of capacity to compensate for expected cancelations.

Overbooking may lead to capacity shortages that are accommodated by a fast, but expensive backup supplier at a cost of $11 per dress. The net shortage penalty cost thus is $11 − $10 = $1 so that equation (8.2) yields:

$$\text{optimal shortage probability} = \frac{\$4}{\$4 + \$1} = 80\%.$$

If the number of canceled units is forecasted to be $20,000$ on average with a forecast error (standard deviation) of $10,000$, the normal approximation suggests

$$\text{optimal overbooking level} = \text{norminv}(.8, 20000, 10000) = 28,416.$$

The manufacturer maximizes expected profits by taking reservations for $128,416$ units. If the cancelation rate (i.e., the fraction, instead of the number, of reservations that are canceled) is forecasted to be 20% on average with a forecast error of 10%, then the optimal overbooking level satisfies the equation

$$\text{optimal overbooking level } Q = \text{norminv}(.8, 20000 + 0.2Q, 10000 + 0.1Q).$$

Including the additional cancelations on the overbooked reservations increases optimal overbooking. Indeed, solving the equation using Excel Solver yields $Q = 39,696$.

Overbooking can be very important. For example, Bailey (2007) quotes W. Douglas Parker, the chief executive of US Airways, as saying: "Why do we do so much of it? We will overbook as long as we allow people to no-show for flights; 7 to 8 percent of our customers are no-shows." The potential impact is huge. US Airways had a revenue of $11.56 billion in 2006 and would have lost out on $1 billion or more of that had it not overbooked, according to the company. And with profit of just $304 million in 2006, the airline could have gone bankrupt without overbooking.

Be careful with oversale costs and shortage penalties

While the optimal overbooking quantity easily follows from a newsvendor model, determining the correct net shortage penalty can be tricky. As Example 8.5 illustrates, sometimes it may be more clear to express the optimal shortage probability as

$$\text{optimal shortage probability} = \frac{\text{regular margin}}{\text{regular margin} - \text{margin on a shortage}}. \tag{8.3}$$

First, notice that the margin on a shortage must be negative to yield a valid shortage probability (≤ 1). In other words, the firm incurs a net loss or a penalty for each shortage. If not, then it is optimal to accept every order or reservation, *provided the shortage margin remains constant*. This brings us to the second point:

In reality, total shortage costs increase nonlinearly with the level of over-booking, causing the marginal penalty cost to increase. In the airline industry, more overbooking of a flight increases the compensations needed for passengers to volunteer to take a later flight and the likelihood "that unaccommodated passengers will have to be transported on another airline. ... If too few passengers volunteer to take a later flight in exchange for the airline's final compensation offer, then involuntary oversales occur. Involuntary oversales cause an additional cost through loss of customer goodwill" (Smith et al. 1992).

In reality, shortage penalties increase as the time of capacity usage nears because it is harder to find back-up accommodations in the last minute. Airlines therefore track and update cancelation forecasts, using sophisticated models with non-constant penalty shortage costs.[3] Our static model simply assumes a constant average shortage penalty.

When and how much to overbook?

Overbooking should be considered when:

1. We have a reliable forecast of cancelations, no-shows, and shortage penalty costs. It is important to track past cancelation and no-show data.

2. The net shortage penalty is not too large compared to the regular margin (when there is no capacity constraint).

Notice that overbooking increases asset access and availability, one measure of customer service level, at the expense of increasing the shortage cost. Small levels of overbooking (with small shortage probabilities) make both the customers and the firm better off, an important message that should be communicated to customers.

The optimal level of overbooking depends on the ratio of additional revenue to oversale cost, and the uncertainty in the cancelations forecast. When both are of similar magnitude, overbooking to compensate the expected cancelation is a good practice. As the shortage cost rises relative to the regular margin, however, one should be more conservative and reduce the overbooking level.

The optimal booking level also depends on the volatility of the cancelation forecast. It decreases as volatility rises if the shortage penalty exceeds the regular margin, and increases otherwise. Similar to the capacity shortage cost, the expected cost of being overbooked (the mismatch cost) increases in variability.

Reducing the negative impact of overbooking

The sum of capacity shortage and surplus risks can be reduced by decreasing cancelation rates or by decreasing the shortage penalty.

Cancelation rates can be decreased by limiting a customer's cancelation flexibility. This is the main idea behind a non-refundable deposit when making a reservation or adding restrictions (JetBlue Airways only sells non-refundable tickets; thus, no-shows lose the value of their tickets). Some industries require a partial payment when making a reservation; it is partially refundable until a

---

[3]"On average, about half of all reservations made for a flight are canceled or become no-shows. American Airlines estimates that about 15 percent of seats on sold-out flights would be unused (spoiled) if reservation sales were limited to aircraft capacity" (Smith et al. 1992, p. 11).

certain time before capacity usage, when the full payment is due and it becomes non-refundable. Keep in mind that lowering the attractiveness of the "product" typically lowers the demand or the price it can sell for.

Surplus costs can be decreased by last-minute discounts and stand-by tickets to fill surplus capacity at the last minute.

Shortage penalties can be decreased by:

- Having a process to deal with overbooked customers. Be prepared!

- Having back-ups such as external capacity providers or other internal capacities. Few overbooked customers mind *"trading-up,"* the practice of giving an overbooked customer a substitutable, but higher-quality asset. For instance, the company can give a customer a premier rental car when no more economy cars are available (there is also a more annoying practice of *"selling-up,"* when firms try to stimulate customers to trade-up for money).

- Using more "flexible products," a topic worth having its own section:

New flexible products, callable products, and dynamic reallocation

Recently, new products are being used to decrease both surplus and shortage costs. They improve matching demand and supply by allowing dynamic reallocation from oversold capacity units to other undersold units.

Dynamic reallocation in its simple form, also known as "replaning" in the airline industry, means that "a customer holding a reservation for a product would be contacted a few days before delivery and 'incentivized' to change their reservation to another product. This creates inventory for high-paying customers when in a stockout or fully overbooked situation. A revenue gain occurs when a new customer will pay more for the product than it costs to incentivize a booked customer to switch product, including the cost of the alternative product" (Bell 2004).

Callable and flexible products further enable and structure dynamic reallocation. A callable product is sold at a discount (low-fare p_L), but grants the capacity supplier the option to recall the capacity at some price p (with $p_L < p < p_H$ to avoid arbitrage) after some (or all) high-fare demand is observed. Flexible products consist of a set of two or more assets (e.g. airline flights) serving the same market. A customer choosing the flexible product is guaranteed to be served by one of the alternatives. He is not informed which of the alternatives until a later date. (This is similar to opaque fares on Hotwire and Priceline that do not tell you a precise time, only a window.) A flexible product is a callable with initial discount and guaranteed re-accommodation.

The main benefits of dynamic reallocation are:

- Resource pooling: by being able to move customers over various assets, we are "pooling" all our asset capacity. Moving customers to lower utilized assets fills up valleys and reduces peaks, thereby smoothing capacity utilization (a similar effect as that of Peapod's system as described in Example 8.2).

- Demand induction: since flexible products are inferior, they can be priced lower than a low-fare product without cannibalizing low-fare demand.

Dynamic reallocation thus creates more capacity and better service for the best customers, increases surplus for low end customers, and improves expected revenue for the capacity provider. Therefore, it is a "win-win-win" situation (Gallego, Kou, and Philips 2004).

Flexible products and dynamic reallocation bring us to the topic of how to manage allocation between products.

8.6 | CAPACITY SEGMENTATION AND ALLOCATION

The operational counterpart of customer segmentation is capacity segmentation. When different "products" require identical units of capacity, the company must decide how to divide and allocate capacity to each one. For example, when airlines sell identical seats in the economy cabin at different prices with different purchasing restrictions, they must decide to segment and allocate the economy cabin to the different products.

Let us first illustrate these ideas and calculations with an example before generalizing the insights.

Example: segmenting capacity at Club Bora Bora

Recall that deterministic forecasting and price optimization suggested that Club Bora Bora should list an advance purchase price of $265 and a regular price of $415 for its main season, with the expectation of selling about 60 rooms to each segment. In reality, the actual number of reservations and cancelations is uncertain. We already saw that the Club Bora Bora should overbook and take 128 reservations for its 120 room capacity. Assume now that the regular demand is uncertain with a mean of 60 and a standard deviation 30. How should the hotel allocate its 128 reservations slots to the advance and regular purchase segments?

Given that the advance segment reservations are made before the regular reservations, we must decide how many advance reservations to accept. This number is called the *advance booking limit* for advance reservations. Enforcing such a booking limit is equivalent to protecting a number of reservation slots for the regular price because:

advance booking limit + regular protection level = total bookings.

As a reference case, assume that the hotel simply protects the average regular demand of 60 rooms. This means that its advance booking limit is $128 - 60 = 68$ rooms. The expected regular requests that will not be able to make a reservation equals the expected capacity shortage, which can be calculated (using the techniques[4] in Appendix B):

Expected regular shortage = 12 rooms.

---

[4]Expected shortage is $\sigma L(z) = 30L(0) = 12$.

Optimal capacity segmentation

Protecting the average demand is not necessarily optimal. The optimal advance booking limit can be derived as follows. Imagine that we receive an advance reservation request. If we accept it, we will gain an advance purchase revenue of $265. If we don't accept it, instead stopping or "closing" advance booking, then we *may* sell the room later at the regular price. We thus must trade-off accepting a lower revenue now with foregoing a likely higher revenue later. Let p be the probability that the room will be sold at the regular price. Revenue then is maximized by accepting the advance purchase as long as

$$\$265 \geq \$415p.$$

If we were to take no advance reservations, the probability of selling 128 rooms at the regular price is very small. As we increase the advance booking limit and fewer rooms are available for regular purchase, the probability p of selling a room at regular price increases and eventually nears 100% if we were to allow 128 advance reservations. In other words, there typically exists an optimal advance booking level which is such that

$$\text{optimal regular shortage probability } p = \frac{\text{advance margin}}{\text{regular margin}} = \frac{265}{415} = 64\%. \quad (8.4)$$

In other words, it is optimal to keep accepting advance reservations as long as their profit exceeds the expected profit of a regular reservation, which is known as *Littlewood's rule* (Littlewood 1972). Beyond that point, the availability control of discount reservations should be turned off.

To infer the optimal allocation that yields this shortage probability, we must know how p depends on the two demand forecasts. In the simplest case, it is assumed that there is ample advance purchase demand to buy up to the advance booking limit. In that case, the optimal probability that a regular request can be accommodated equals the complement of the shortage probability, or $1 - p$. Again, assuming a normal approximation, we find the corresponding *protection level* as

$$\text{optimal protection level} = \texttt{norminv}(36\%, 60, 30) = 49 \text{ rooms.}$$

This means that the optimal advance booking limit is: $128 - 49 = 79$ rooms. The corresponding expected regular shortage can again be calculated (using the techniques[5] in Appendix B):

$$\text{Expected regular shortage} = 18 \text{ rooms.}$$

Thus, compared to the base case of allocating the expected regular demand, the net value of optimized capacity allocation thus stems from taking $79 - 68 = 11$ more advance reservations and having, on average, $18 - 12 = 6$ fewer regular reservations. Disregarding cancelations, the

$$\begin{aligned}
\text{value of allocation optimization} \quad &= \quad \text{expected extra revenue} \\
&= \quad 11 \times \$265 - 6 \times \$415 = \$425.
\end{aligned}$$

---

[5]The z-statistic of the optimal protection level is $(49 - 60)/30 = -0.37$, and the expected shortage is $\sigma L(z) = 30L(-0.37) = 18$.

Example 8.6 Capacity segmentation and allocation in manufacturing

Reconsider the apparel manufacturer of women's safari-look summer shirts from Example 8.5. The manufacturer offers retailers a discount when orders are placed well in advance of the summer season. Advanced orders are priced at $10 per unit and can be produced at a marginal cost of $6. In contrast, regular orders are priced at $16.72. The 67% surcharge (obviously advanced orders would be marketed as a 40% discount opportunity) reflects the higher cost of expediting, perhaps including a backup supplier at a cost of $11 per dress. While the regular orders are preferred (they yield a higher margin of $5.72 versus $4), their demand is forecasted to be only 50,000 on average, while available capacity is 100,000 units. The advance orders fill up left-over capacity. How should the manufacturer allocate his available capacity of 100,000 units to the discounted advance orders?

He faces the same risk as the Club Bora Bora hotel does. Accepting one additional advance order brings in an advance margin of $4, but decreases capacity available for regular orders by one. The risk is that there might be insufficient internal capacity for regular orders, in which case expedited external capacity would be required at a margin of $16.72 − $11 = $5.72. Thus, the expected displacement cost is $5.72p, where p is the probability of higher cost production. The optimal regular protection level is such that (8.4) yields:

$$\text{regular shortage probability} = \frac{\$4}{\$5.72} = 70\%.$$

If regular demand is forecasted to be 50,000 on average with a forecast error (standard deviation) of 30,000, the normal approximation suggests:

$$\text{regular protection level} = \text{norminv}(.3, 50000, 30000) = 34,268.$$

The manufacturer should accept up to $100,000 − 34,268 = 65,732$ advance orders (or $128,416 − 34,268 = 94,148$, compensating for the cancelations of Example 8.5.) The expected operating profit with optimal capacity allocation is $426,273, compared to $417,541 when allocating to the mean. The value of allocation optimization thus is $8,731, or 2.1%.

Relative to simply allocating the expected number of regular reservation, the value of optimization thus is again on the order of 1% (recall that the best possible revenue was $40,800.)

Capacity segmentation for capacity buyers and sellers

Smart capacity allocation can be used by any business that supplies or purchases capacity to or from at least two segments. Suppliers can implement capacity segmentation when they have both long-term, contractual customers as well as spot customers. For example, a specialty steel mill may have long term contracts that guarantee a maximal response time to customer orders, but may also accept orders on the spot market. Long-term contracts are desirable because they guarantee a minimum capacity utilization, but such long-term or bulk orders typically receive a discount. Moreover, their specific arrival times and order quantities may not be known far in advance. The question then is: how is capacity allocated to long-term and spot orders? In other words, what is the optimal portfolio of contracts? Example 8.6 illustrates how to answer these questions.

Buyers deciding on an optimal sourcing strategy face a similar problem. When actual demand (and thus sourcing quantity) is uncertain, how much sourc-

Example 8.7 A sourcing portfolio of long-term contracts and spot purchasing

A manufacturer assembles printers in Vancouver, Canada, for sale in North America and Europe. European monthly demand is stable and is expected to be similar to past demand, with an average of 32,108 units and a standard deviation of 6,244 units. The company is reevaluating its sourcing portfolio of transportation capacity to Europe. It can sign a long-term contract and reserve shipping capacity at $35 per unit per month, or procure capacity in the spot market at an expected price of $56 per unit. What is its optimal transportation sourcing strategy?

The manufacturer faces a capacity reservation and allocation problem similar to that of the Club Bora Bora hotel. Committing to one additional shipping unit in long-term capacity costs only $35 but reduces the risk of more expensive spot market purchasing. The latter saves an average of 56p$, where p is the shortage probability (i.e., the probability that demand exceeds long-term capacity). Consequently, the expected marginal transportation cost is $35 - $56p$. The optimal shortage probability thus is:

$$\text{shortage probability} = \frac{\text{advance reservation ``margin''}}{\text{spot market ``margin''}}$$

$$= \frac{-\$35}{-\$56} = 62.5\%.$$

The long-term contract should cover all transportation needs 37.5% of the time, or:

$$\text{advance capacity reservation level} = \text{norminv}(0.375, 32108, 6244) = 30,118.$$

The expected capacity shortage of the long-term capacity is $6,244L((30118 - 32108)/6244) = 3,611$ units. Expected transportation costs are $30,118 \times \$35 + 3,611 \times \$56 = \$1.256$ million. Committing long-term capacity to the expected needs of $32,108$ units would decrease shortages to $6244L(0) = 2,491$ units, but would increase expected transportation costs to $32,108 \times \$35 + 2,491 \times \$56 = \$1.263$ million. Optimization of the sourcing portfolio thus reduces expected monthly transportation cost by $6,905 or 0.5%.

ing should be committed to in advance, and how much sourcing should be decided on at the last minute at a higher price (be it from the same supplier, another supplier, or the spot market)? Example 8.7 illustrates how to answer these purchasing questions.

Capacity segmentation in practice: displacement costs and selling-up

In practice, various complications arise that may not be covered in the basic model. Often, the model's parameters (demand forecasts, prices, and costs) change over time, requiring forecasts to be updated and controls to be dynamically adjusted. We can extend the basic model to a dynamic setting using the concept of displacement cost.

The *displacement cost* is the opportunity cost of reserving assets for current demand. The general capacity reservation rule becomes: accept a current request if its revenue (margin) exceeds the displacement cost. In our simple setting, the displacement cost of accepting a discount request is the expected revenue from selling later at regular price; there, the displacement rule is identical to Littlewood's rule. In general, the displacement cost can be calculated using three steps:

1. Update the future demand forecast for each product and asset.

2. Compute the best allocation of future demand (as predicted by the forecast) and of remaining capacity to products.

3. Determine the displacement cost as the reduction in expected profit if the remaining capacity is reduced by the amount required by a new request.[6]

The advantage of the displacement cost method is that it can be extended to much more sophisticated settings such as multi-night stays (at hotels), group reservations, multi-product settings (including bundling and cross-selling), and network settings (logistics or airline networks). The three-step method clearly shows how the displacement cost depends on the current forecast and the remaining capacity.

The displacement cost can also be used to capture more complex consumer behavior such as buying-up. Consumers may be less definite in their preference between the regular and discounted product, and could switch between the two. Sometimes, consumers looking to place an advance reservation can be "talked into" making a reservation at the regular price, a practice known as "buying or selling-up." The displacement cost of accepting a discount reservation now depends on the likelihood that the asset can be sold later at the regular price, augmented by the likelihood that the discount price customer chooses to pay at the regular price when told that the discount is not available (also known as the sell-up probability $p_{sell-up}$). Thus, the greater the likelihood of selling-up, the greater the displacement cost. (The problem set asks you to evaluate the impact of selling-up on advance booking limits.)

When and how much should we allocate capacity at a discount?

Allocating a chunk of capacity to discount sales and protecting the rest to regular sales is valuable when:

1. We have an updated forecast of regular future demand (and of the sell-up probability).

2. Regular demand is insufficient to consume all available capacity.

3. Discount sales increase the overall capacity utilization and the expected profits.

4. The value of allocation optimization increases when regular demand is highly volatile and the discount differs from 50%.

The efficiency of capacity allocation depends on the prices and the effectiveness of the fences used to separate the discount segment from the regular segment. As an extreme example, if the discount segment is not priced properly, it could lead to a large fraction of regular demand switching to the discount segment ("buy-down").

---

[6]For analytics fans: the optimal allocation is easily found using a linear program that maximizes profits subject to remaining capacity and future demand constraints. The displacement cost can then be computed in terms of the shadow prices (also called *bid prices*) of the capacity constraints.

The amount of capacity allocated to the discount segment depends on the discount (as a fraction of regular price) and the regular demand forecast volatility. When the discount is about 50%, it is a good practice to protect the mean regular demand. As discounts become smaller, one should become more conservative and reduce the protection level. Similar to optimal capacity sizing (Figure 3.6 on p. 91), the optimal regular protection level also depends on the volatility of the regular demand forecast: it decreases as volatility rises if the discount is less than 50%, and increases otherwise. Like the capacity shortage cost, the expected cost of having insufficient capacity for regular sales increases with variability.

Notice that smart discount allocation increases average utilization and thus asset access and availability, one measure of customer service level. This requires a discount greater than 50% (a frequent case in the airline industry[7]) but comes at the expense of increasing the shortage cost.

8.7 | SUMMARY OF LEARNING OBJECTIVES

1. Explain the concept of revenue management and integrate it with operations strategy.

Demand management includes all the activities that influence the demand for products and services. It is sometimes viewed as the counterpart of supply management as both are intimately related. When the operational supply system is inflexible, we must attempt to best match demand to available supply. Revenue management is the combination of various demand management practices that aim to maximize the revenue or profits of available supply. The implementation of revenue management follows a four step process that should be periodically updated:

1. Evaluate your strategy, competition, and customer.

2. Design products to segment customers or time.

3. Price the products to maximize value.

4. Control the capacity that is allocated to the various products.

Revenue management is an integral part of competitive and operations strategy. It interacts directly with the elements in our framework that are shaded in Figure 8.12. Customer segmentation and product pricing must be aligned with the customer value proposition, a key component of competitive strategy. This affects the required competencies of the operational system: the priority ranking of cost, quality, responsiveness, and flexibility. Revenue management typically occurs after capacity investment (size) and is most useful if capacity is constrained and lacks flexibility (type) to easily change over time. In a sense, demand management can act as a partial substitute for capacity adjustments and

---

[7]The median ratio of high to low airline economy fare is 2.6, which corresponds to an average discount of $1 - 1/2.6 = 61\%$ (Netessine and Shumsky 2005).

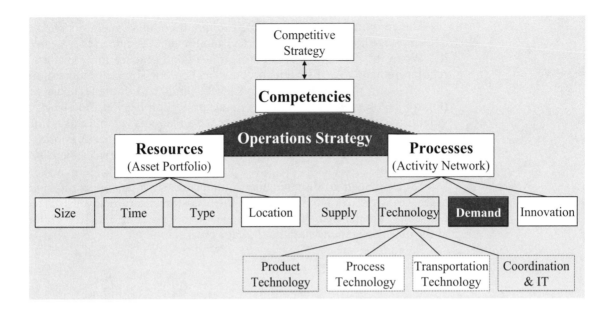

Figure 8.12 Demand and revenue management is an integral part of operations strategy and interacts with the shaded elements in our framework.

flexibility. Revenue management requires smart product design, and a substantial amount of information and optimization technology. As we will illustrate below, its techniques can also be used to configure sourcing portfolios. In summary, effective revenue management must be aligned with the entire operations strategy.

2. Identify conditions for and obstacles to effective revenue management.

Before implementing revenue management techniques, one should verify whether the expected benefits (specific conditions are given below per item) outweigh the potential obstacles. These hurdles include the cost of data mining, forecasting, and optimization, and concerns about social fairness. Good revenue management educates all stakeholders: it informs customers and ensures that the best customers are treated well. It involves both sales and operations, ensuring that both parties understand the products, prices, available capacities, and backup processes. Finally, it communicates anticipated changes with suppliers. As such, demand and revenue management is an integrated component of the operations strategy.

3. Design products for customer segmentation and price discrimination.

When purchasing behavior, needs, desired flexibility, and valuation differ significantly among customers, there is an opportunity to serve them better and improve profits by designing products tailored to each customer segment. In this case, product design involves bundling asset use with qualifying service restrictions, or fences. Popular fences may restrict the time, quantity, or location of purchase, the changing or canceling of the purchase, or the time and duration of usage. By selling each product at a different price, customers can choose or self-select, thereby segmenting the market and partially revealing their valuation. Price discrimination increases the revenue from high-end customers, while the discounted prices increase the total customer base, asset utilization, and sales.

Pricing involves demand curve forecasting for each product followed by price optimization. In practice, fences are imperfect and leakage occurs when customers buy-down and select a lower priced product than the product designed for them. While a greater number of products allows for finer segmentation, the value of adding more price points decreases because there is less incremental customer surplus to be gained while the administration and leakage costs increase and forecasting becomes more difficult. Therefore, a handful of price points often suffice.

4. Analyze time segmentation with dynamic pricing and capacity constraints.

When demand or supply changes over time, forecasts must be continually updated and prices must be dynamically adjusted. Popular dynamic pricing strategies involve markdowns (to sell a fixed supply) and peak pricing or promotions (to move demand to off-season). Sophisticated dynamic pricing updates prices for each particular customer and may suggest complementary products. A dynamic pricing opportunity exists when demand or supply changes over time or when assets are sold both in advance (in bulk) and on the spot market. The value of the opportunity depends on the cost of making a price change.

5. Apply two tools for capacity segmentation and reservation: overbooking and dynamic allocation.

The fourth step in revenue management involves controlling the capacity that is allocated to the various products. Capacity controls are the counterpart of price controls and add value when demand forecasts are imperfect, or when competition restricts pricing flexibility. Deciding how many products to sell in aggregate (capacity reservation including overbooking) and what quantities of each product type to sell (capacity segmentation and dynamic allocation) are two important capacity controls, known together as yield management.

Overbooking should be considered whenever customers are expected to cancel orders and the net shortage penalty is not too large. Being prepared by having backups and using flexible products (e.g., dynamic reallocation) reduces the net shortage penalty and increases the value of overbooking. Reserving capacity for each segment ensures that appropriate capacity amounts are sold to the targeted demand segments. If forecasts have significant uncertainty, the company would be prevented from selling too much or too little capacity at a discount. Capacity overbooking and dynamic allocation techniques should be considered by any firm that is buying or selling capacity.

DISCUSSION QUESTIONS

1. Explain which revenue management techniques can be used in to media broadcasting.

2. How can flexible products be used to improve revenue and customer surplus in the hotel and recreation industry, logistics, and manufacturing?

3. How does the optimal regular protection level (equivalently, the advance booking limit) change if advance customers are likely to buy at the regular price when told that the discount is not available? (Hint: compute the displacement cost as a function of $p_{\text{sell-up}}$, the likelihood of selling up an advance customer to the regular price.)

CHALLENGE QUESTIONS

1. How would you determine the optimal protection level for regular capacity reservations if the advance purchase demand is not guaranteed to consume all the slots that we allocate for it? Specifically, assume that demand for advance reservations can falls anywhere between 500 and 1000 with equal likelihood, and that the demand for regular reservations can fall anywhere between 250 and 600 with equal likelihood (thus, both demands are independent and uniformly distributed). Assume that total available capacity is 900 and that the ratio of advance purchase price to regular price is 50%.

2. How would the effectiveness and the value of optimal capacity allocation change if demands are correlated?

Visit www.vanmieghem.us for additional questions and updates.

FURTHER READING AND REFERENCES

▶ Classic articles on revenue management for airlines include Littlewood (1972), Belobaba (1989), and Smith, Leimkuhler, and Darrow (1992).

▶ Revenue management is a relatively recent, but rapidly growing field in operations. Talluri and van Ryzin (2004) provides a state-of-the-art overview of the field. Other relevant articles include Araman and Popescu (2007), Bell (2004), Gallego, Kou, and Philips (2004), Netessine and Shumsky (2005), Netessine, Savin, and Xiao (2006), and Philips (2003).

Araman, V. and I. Popescu (2007). Stochastic revenue management models for media broadcasting. *Management Science*. Under review. Available at http://faculty.insead.edu/popescu/.

Bailey, J. (2007). Bumped fliers and no plan B. *The New York Times*. Mar. 30.

BBC, N. (1999). World: America's Coke plan to charge by degrees. www.bbc.co.uk/1-/hi/world/americas/492475.stm. October 28.

Bell, P. C. (2004, August). Revenue management for MBAs. *INFORMS OR/MS Today*, 22–26.

Belobaba, P. B. (1989). Application of a probabilistic decision model to airline seat inventory control. *Operations Research 37*(2), 183–197.

DOT (2007). Air travel consumer reports for 2007. U.S. Department of Transportation's Office of Aviation Enforcement and Proceedings (OAEP), airconsumer.ost.dot.gov/reports/atcr07.htm.

Dunham, K. J. (2006). Technology proves a boon for some landlords. *Wall Street Journal*. June 28.

Dupuit, J. (1844). On the measurement of the utility of public works. *International Economic Papers (1952) 2*, 83–110. trans. R. H. Barback.

Dupuit, J. (1849). On tolls and transport changes. *International Economic Papers (1962) 11*, 7–31. trans. E. Henderson.

Gallego, G., Kou, and R. Philips (2004). Revenue management of flexible and callable products. Discussed by Philips at the 2004 Kellogg Operations Workshop.

Krugman, P. (2000). What price fairness? *The New York Times*, A35. October 4.

Littlewood, K. (1972). Forecasting and control of passenger bookings. *AGIFORS Symposium Proceedings 12*, 95–117.

Maglaras, C. (2002). Overview of revenue management. B6833 class slides, Columbia Business School.

Netessine, S., S. Savin, and W. Xiao (2006). Revenue management through dynamic cross-selling in e-commerce retailing. *Management Science*.

Netessine, S. and R. A. Shumsky (2005). Revenue management games: Horizontal and vertical competition. *Management Science*.

Peapod (2007). Personal conversations with Peapod managers and corporate information. www.peapod.com.

Philips, R. (2003). Teaching pricing and revenue optimization. *INFORMS Transactions on Education 4*(1). ite.pubs.informs.org/Vol4No1/Philips/.

Sahay, A. (2007). How to reap higher profits with dynamic pricing. *Sloan Management Review 48*(4), 53–60.

Shaikin, B. (2007). Baseball thinks outside the box to sell seats; complex pricing helps the Dodgers, Angels and others increase revenue. *Los Angeles Times*. Mar. 27.

Sloan, P. A. (1981). Peoplexpress airline table advertisement of april 30, 1981. www.airtimes.com/cgat/usc/peopleexpress.htm as of Aug. 7, 2006.

Smith, B. C., J. F. Leimkuhler, and R. M. Darrow (1992). Yield management at American Airlines. *INFORMS Interfaces 22*(1), 8–31.

Talluri, K. T. and G. J. van Ryzin (2004). *The theory and practice of Revenue Management*, Volume 68 of *International Series in Operations Research & Management Science*. Kluwer Academic Publishers.

Thibodeau, P. (2005). Marriott links two data streams with revenue management system. *Computerworld*. March 14.

Appendix 8 | PRICE OPTIMIZATION OF LINEAR DEMAND

Analytical price optimization is tractable when the demand function is linear because revenue is then a quadratic function of price, causing marginal revenue (the key quantity in optimization) to again be linear. Let p_{max} be the maximal price anyone is willing to pay and q_{max} the maximal quantity that could be sold. The corresponding linear demand function then is:

$$D(p) = q_{max}\left(1 - \frac{p}{p_{max}}\right)$$

$$= a - bp \qquad \text{with } a = q_{max} \text{ and } b = \frac{q_{max}}{p_{max}}.$$

A good benchmark to compare revenues with is the maximal consumer surplus, which is the triangular area under the demand curve:

$$CS_{max} = \frac{1}{2}p_{max}q_{max} = \frac{a^2}{2b}.$$

Single price

Revenue is $pD(p) = ap - bp^2$ so that marginal revenue is $a - 2bp$. The revenue maximizing price sets marginal revenue equal to marginal cost, which is assumed to be zero when products are already in stock, or:

$$p^* = \frac{a}{2b} = \frac{1}{2}p_{max}.$$

The associated optimal quantity and revenue can be found through:

$$\text{sales} = \frac{a}{2} = \frac{1}{2}q_{max}$$

$$\text{revenue} = \frac{a^2}{4b} = \frac{1}{2}CS_{max}$$

Two price points

Price discrimination with two prices requires solving the following price optimization:

$$\begin{aligned}
\text{Revenue} &= \text{regular purchase revenue} &+& \text{advance purchase revenue} \\
&= p_1 D(p_1) &+& p_2\left(D(p_2) - D(p_1)\right) \\
&= p_1\left(a - bp_1\right) &+& b\left(p_1 - p_2\right)p_2
\end{aligned}$$

(8.5)

Optimal pricing equalizes the marginal revenues from both segments and sets them equal to zero:

$$a - 2bp_1 + bp_2 = bp_1 - 2bp_2 = 0,$$

Thus, $p_1 = 2p_2$ so that $a - 4bp_2 + bp_2 = 0$ or:

$$p_1 = \frac{2}{3}p_{max} \qquad \text{and} \qquad p_2 = \frac{1}{3}p_{max}$$

$$q_1 = q_2 = \frac{1}{3}q_{max}$$

The associated optimal quantities and revenue can be found through:

$$\text{sales} \quad = \quad q_1 = q_2 = \frac{1}{3}q_{\max}$$

$$\text{revenue} \quad = \quad \frac{2}{3}CS_{\max}$$

Two price points with a capacity constraint

The capacity constraint only impacts pricing if it is binding, meaning that capacity is less than total unconstrained sales, or $K < \frac{2}{3}q_{\max}$. In that case, revenue can be maximized by selling all capacity, meaning that total sales equal:

$$D(p_2) = a - bp_2 = K$$

In other words, $p_2 = (a - K)/b$. Substituting the value of p_2 into equations (8.5) and optimizing over p_1 yields $p_1 = p_{\max} - K/2b$.

Equivalently, the higher regular price is set to extract the maximal revenue of the remaining surplus, which again is the linear demand with slope b and intercept K/b so that $p_1 - p_2 = K/2b$. Thus, the optimal prices are:

$$p_1 = p_{\max} - K/2b \qquad \text{and} \qquad p_2 = (a - K)/b,$$

with associate quantities and revenue:

$$\text{sales} \quad = \quad q_1 = q_2 = \frac{1}{2}K$$

$$\text{revenue} \quad = \quad (a - \frac{3}{4}K)K/b$$

N price points

The symmetric solution of the two-price-points extends to the general case of n price points:

$$p_1 \quad = \quad \frac{n}{n+1}p_{\max} \qquad \text{and} \qquad p_i - p_{i-1} = \frac{1}{n+1}p_{\max}.$$

$$\text{sales} \quad = \quad q_i = \frac{1}{n+1}q_{\max}$$

$$\text{revenue} \quad = \quad \frac{n}{n+1}CS_{\max}.$$

Chapter

9

RISK MANAGEMENT AND OPERATIONAL HEDGING

Chance favors the prepared mind.—Louis Pasteur (1822–1895)

Learning Objectives

After reading this chapter, you will be able to:

1. Explain the concepts of risk management and operational hedging, and integrate them with operations strategy.

2. Identify, assess, and value operational risks.

3. Distinguish tactical from strategic risk management, and operational from financial hedging.

4. Explain and tailor four operational hedging strategies.

In this chapter, we will study risk management, an integral part of operations strategy. We will start by viewing risk management as an ongoing process. We will discuss the various sources of risk that companies are exposed to and proceed with a methodology to assess those risks. The goal of risk assessment is to improve how we react to risk and to proactively reduce our exposure to it. The remaining sections will illustrate how operations can help in mitigating specific risks.

9.1 | RISK MANAGEMENT: CONCEPT AND PROCESS

Defining hazards and risk

Before describing the concept of risk management, we must first define some terms. *Hazards* are potential sources of danger. In a business setting, danger can mean anything that may have a negative impact on the firm's net present value. Hazards have a harmful impact, but they may or may not occur.

Example 9.1 What is risk? Different viewpoints

From the pages of the presidential commission on risk management:

> "Risk is defined as the probability that a substance or situation will produce harm under specified conditions" (Presidential-Congressional Commission 1997).

From the pages of economics:

> "Risk refers to situations in which we can list all possible outcomes and we know the likelihood that each outcome occurs" (Pindyck and Rubinfeld 1989).

From the pages of finance:

> "Risk can be defined as the possibility that the actual return will deviate from that which was expected" (Van Horne 1993).

In everyday language, *risk* refers to an exposure to a chance of loss or damage. ("We risked losing a lot of money in this venture"; "Why risk your life?") Risk thus arises from hazards *and* exposure: it does not exist if exposure to a hazard does not or will not occur (e.g., if you live on top of a mountain, you are not at risk of flooding). The interpretation of risk as *an undesirable possible consequence of uncertainty* suggests that risk is a combination of two factors:

1. The probability that an adverse event or hazard will occur.

2. The consequences of the adverse event.

Financial versus operational risk

While it is intuitive to associate risk with a probability and an undesired outcome, be aware that there are other interpretations of risk, as illustrated in Example 9.1. In finance, risk is "the possibility that the actual outcome is likely to diverge [or deviate] from the expected value." (Sharpe 1985). In finance, risk is equated with uncertainty in payoffs, which we will refer to as *profit variability risk*. Risk then implies the existence of some random variable whose standard deviation or variance can be used as a measure of risk. Notice that this view calls any uncertainty in outcomes, whether favorable or not, risk. The key distinction from the common interpretation of risk is the absence of "danger" or an "adverse event."For instance, people don't typically say that they are at risk of running the lottery.

Operational risks are risks that stem from operations, i.e. from activities and assets. Any potential source that generates a negative impact on the flow of information, goods, and cash in our operations is an operational risk. The inclusion of cash flowing through the operation implies that financial and operational risks are not mutually exclusive. But the goal of operations is to maximize expected firm value by matching supply with demand. Any possible mismatch between supply and demand, excess or shortage, is undesirable and is called *mismatch risk*. Chapter 3 showed that mismatch risk increases with volatility; this chapter will investigate methods to mitigate this risk.

Example 9.2 Risk Management by Procter & Gamble

Only hours after a tornado hit P&G's Pringles plant in Jackson, Tennessee on Sunday May 4, 2003, the brand contingency team started the recovery processes. Employees from the only other Pringles plant in Mechelen, just outside of Brussels, were flown in to help reconstruction. By Wednesday, P&G determined that its major equipment would be fine, and put its major U.S. customers on allocation. By Saturday, a temporary roof had been installed; on Monday, May 12, a limited production of its most popular flavors was resumed.

Meanwhile, production in Belgium was maximized and re-routed to supply some of the Jackson plant's Latin American and Asian customers. According to the Mechelen plant:

> "Already in the second week of May, first Raw & Pack Material orders were placed at our suppliers with stretched leadtimes which enabled Mechelen to switch its production schedule by the end of the third week (the 2 lines with the capability to run Asian product–14 case count versus 18 case count– started to run the Asian brand codes).

> "First, shipments to the Asian market left Mechelen by the end of May! In total Mechelen delivered 11,100,000 200g cans and 7,500,000 50g cans! On top of this achievement, Mechelen produced specific flavors for Japan that were never ran before (a special Operations-QA-PD team was formed to qualify our lines for these specific flavors).

> "As a consequence of this massive support, the inventories in Mechelen for the Western European market were heavily eroded. Due to this low inventory the Mechelen organization was further stretched to provide good service levels for Western Europe. We discovered some opportunities in our supply chain (which would be more difficult to find when they were hidden under stock).

> "Net: Mechelen protected the Asian business with huge flexibility and strengthened its own supply chain by doing that" (Van Campenhout 2004).

Risk management: concept and examples

In general, *risk management* is the broad activity of planning and decision-making designed to deal with the occurrence of hazards or risks. Risks include both unlikely but high-impact disruption risks, as well as more common volatility in demand, internal processing, and supply. Procter & Gamble provides an example of managing disruption risk. On Sunday May 4, 2003, 1,200 workers at the company's Pringles plant in Jackson, Tennessee, heard warning sirens and rushed to evacuation areas. About 18 minutes later, tornados hit and badly damaged the plant's roof, while subsequent rain damaged truck loads of potato chips. The south end of the building was demolished and required reconstruction. With the sole Pringles plant in the Americas shut down, P&G had no choice but to suspend all U.S. distribution, armed with only a six-week supply of Pringles already in stores or en-route. It was estimated that it would take at least one month before shipments could resume, causing a huge blow to one of P&G's biggest brands. (According to the company, people eat 275 million chips per day, generating annual sales above $1 billion.) But the company was prepared: by 3a.m., the brand contingency team and an entire recovery process (described in Example 9.2) was set in motion. We shall return to the importance of tactical risk management through fast risk discovery and recovery.

Figure 9.1 Risk management as an ongoing process with four steps.

Strategic risk mitigation involves the structuring of global networks with sufficient flexibility to mitigate the impact of hazards. For example, BMW enjoys demand risk mitigation through its global operations network by building cars in Germany, Britain, the U.S., and South-Africa. Out of the annual 160,000 Z4 roadsters and X5 sport "activity" vehicles built in 2003 in its Spartanburg, South Carolina plant, about 100,000 were exported, mostly to Europe. At the same time, BMW imported about 217,000 cars from Europe to reach annual U.S. sales of about 277,000 cars.

Partial balancing of flows through global manufacturing networks (such as those of BMW or DaimlerChrysler's) or service networks (such as large consulting and accounting companies) can also mitigate currency exchange risk. For example, Michelin, the world's biggest tire maker, drew 35% of its 2003 annual sales from North America. While this would normally expose the French company to dollar-euro currency exchange risk, Michelin was not worried about exchange rates. They compensated for the loss caused by translating American revenues into euros by purchasing raw materials that are priced in dollars.

In contrast, companies like Porsche, which builds cars mostly in Germany, must raise local prices to make up for currency changes (a dangerous approach that almost wiped Porsche out in the U.S. in the early 1990s). Otherwise, it must absorb the changes in the form of lower profits, or may resort to financial hedging instruments that we will describe below.

Risk management as a process and integral part of operations strategy

Now that we know what is meant by risk, we can proceed with the topic of this chapter: managing risk through operations. It is useful to think of risk management as a four-step process, as illustrated in Figure 9.1:

1. Identification of hazards: the first step in any risk management program is to identify the key potential sources of risk in the operation.

2. Risk assessment: the second step is to assess the degree of risk associated with each hazard. Then we must prioritize hazards and summarize their total impact into an overall risk level of the operation.

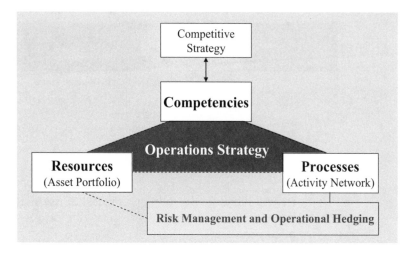

Figure 9.2 Operational hedging is a process of strategic risk mitigation. It involves structuring resources and processes to reduce future risk exposure. Therefore, operational hedging is an integral part of operations strategy.

3. Tactical risk decisions: this step describes the appropriate decisions to be taken when a hazard is likely to occur soon, or when it has already occurred.

4. Implement strategic risk mitigation or hedging, which involves structuring the operational system to reduce future risk exposure.

To adapt to change and to incorporate learning and improvement, risk management must be approached as a process; these four steps must be executed and updated recurrently. We will investigate the role of learning further in the next chapter.

It is useful to make a distinction between tactical and strategic risk management. Tactical risk management uses mechanisms to detect whether a specific hazard is likely to occur soon. Then, it executes contingency plans. For instance, P&G used warning sirens and followed a contingency plan to deal with the tornado strike on May 4, 2003, in Jackson, Tennessee (Example 9.2).

In contrast to dealing with the occurrence of a specific hazard, strategic risk management is concerned with mitigating future risk exposure. Operational hedging, a subset of strategic risk management, refers to the adjustment of strategies and the structuring of resources and processes to proactively reduce, if not eliminate, future risk exposure. For instance, P&G's Pringles operations comprise two manufacturing plants with sufficiently flexible processes enabling them to partially take over each other's work. This operational system provides a form of insurance that resulted in the tornado strike having limited financial impact.

In summary, operational hedging is an integral part of operations strategy (Fig. 9.2) for two reasons: it is a necessary process in each operation, and it involves structuring the entire operational system. The remainder of this chap-

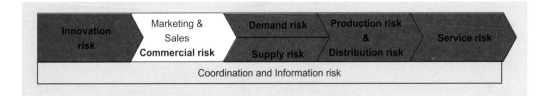

Figure 9.3 Identifying operational risks using the value chain.

ter will illustrate the four-step process of risk management, meanwhile describing how risk management interacts with the operational system's resources and other processes.

9.2 | IDENTIFICATION OF OPERATIONAL HAZARDS

The first step in any risk management program is to identify any potential sources of danger. According to one manager who participated in many risk assessment processes: "One lesson I learned is that hazard identification is one of the most difficult steps in the process. Without a clear and robust framework, it is nearly impossible to identify all critical hazards." Now, we will describe one approach to help this identification process.

An organization is most affected when a danger affects its ability to serve the customer's needs. Although a danger might impact an operation, the effects on the organization and its future are limited if the customer does not suffer from that impact. To identify important risks, it is useful to adopt the customer's perspective by asking: what is my customer's worst nightmare?

The answer then can be linked to operational risks that stem from our activities and assets. Recall from Chapter 1 and Fig. 9.2 that any operation can be viewed from three perspectives: as a bundle of competencies, processes, or resources. Adopting these three views directly suggests three approaches that should be combined to identify operational hazards.

Identifying operational risks using the competency view

Linking competency failures to customer nightmares is probably the most direct way to focus the mind on important operational risks. What is the impact of a failure in quality, flexibility, timeliness, cost, or quantity? If operations strategy is well aligned, this importance should correspond to the priority ranking of the competencies in the value proposition.

While this link is direct, competency risks must be linked to processes or resources if we want to mitigate them.

Identifying operational risks using the process view

Potential hazards can be identified and categorized by considering each activity in the value chain, as shown in Figure 9.3. Depending on the stage in the value chain where the negative impact may happen, we have:

1. *Innovation risk* represents any exposure to hazards that originate during research and development. The pharmaceutical industry provides a good example: a new drug or compound may turn out to not have sufficient efficacy, potency, or safety to be approved by the relevant governmental agency. Another example is Intel, which recently pulled the plug on the development of a 3Ghz Pentium chip, its fastest microprocessor for personal computers, because it proved to be too difficult to manufacture.

2. *Commercial risk* represents any exposure to hazards that originate in marketing and sales and negatively impacts revenues. It includes the risk that new products or services are not adopted, cash risks (e.g., lower sales prices than expected), or receivables risks (when customers don't pay).

3. Closely related are *demand and supply risks*, which refer to any uncertainty in quantities demanded or supplied for a given product or service at a given time. Typical examples include retail risks, in which case we may have leftover stock that must be discounted, or insufficient supply (stock-outs, underages). Supply risks may also refer to *sourcing risk*, which stems from interaction with suppliers. It may include risks in information (the wrong order was communicated or the order was not received), risks in goods (the wrong quantity or quality of goods was received), or risks in cash (the supply ends up being more expensive than expected). For example, a supplier may claim not to have received an order, or may have sent the wrong amount or type of supply. The shipment may have been lost or stolen. A supplier may have a capacity or yield problem, or may even undergo a catastrophic event such as terrorism, sabotage, or financial bankruptcy.

4. *Processing and distribution risks* include any exposure to hazards that originate in our internal processing and distribution networks. There may be labor issues, worker safety hazards and non-ergonomically designed work environments, or maintenance failures that affect capacity availability. Inventory may be at risk of spoilage, damage, or loss. Unexpected operator errors, yield problems, accidental damage, and delays may increase cost above expectations. Distribution channels may be at risk of logistics provider failure, route or transportation mode disruptions, and other hazards (similar to sourcing risks).

5. *Service risk* refers to exposure to hazards during after-sale service interactions. This may include lack of procedures to deal with product returns, problems, and service inquiries.

6. *Coordination and information risks* refer to uncertainty in coordination and information. They may stem from internal miscommunication and often result in internal demand-supply mismatches. Examples include information technology system failures in hardware, software, local, and wide

area networks. Other information risks include forecasting risks, computer virus risks, and errors during order-taking and receiving.

Some industries, such as the pharmaceutical industry, also use the term *technical risk* to refer to the innovation risk of launching a new technology or drug. It is distinct from ongoing operational risk and commercial risk: while a drug may be approved and be no longer at technical risk, it still remains to be seen whether it will have sufficient demand at reasonable prices for it.

Identifying operational risks using the resource view

One can also consider each asset in the operational system and identify associated potential hazards. In practice, one would investigate the key assets in the operation. We can classify assets, and corresponding risks, into three types:

1. *Capital asset risks* are exposures to hazards originating from property, plants, and equipment. These include exposures to property and environmental liability, equipment unreliability, as well as financial risks related to maintenance and perhaps future resale. They can also include working capital such as inventory and receivables risk.

2. *People risks* include safety, health, operational dependence, operator and management errors, resignations, turnover, absenteeism, sabotage, stealing, and more.

3. *Intangible asset risks* include policy risks, intellectual property risks, reputation, culture, and more.

Surrounding background risks

No value chain operates in a vacuum. Aside from operational risk, the operating system is subject to various hazards that originate from its surroundings. Depending on the source, we can categorize types of background risks as:

1. *Natural risk*: In addition to operation-specific hazards, nature is capricious and can expose organizations to natural hazards such as earthquakes, heavy rains, lightning, hail storms, fires, and tornados. The exposure typically depends on the location of the organization. For example, coastal properties are exposed to coastal storm hazards such as hurricane storm surges, flooding, erosion, and wind.

2. *Political risk*: This risk includes any negative, unexpected change in laws and regulations (political stability is typically preferred). Examples include a breach in business contracts without recourse to legal action, unexpected strengthening in environmental or labor laws, unexpected currency devaluations, or an outbreak of war.

3. *Competitive and strategic risk* refers to the potential negative impact of competitors' actions, or environmental and technological changes that reduce the effectiveness of the company's strategy.

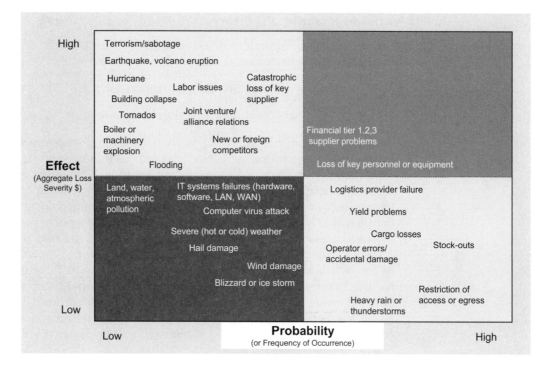

Figure 9.4 A subjective risk map is a graphical representation of the risk assessment for a specific organization done with the help of expert opinions. It shows the impact versus the likelihood of occurrence for each hazard.

Who should identify potential hazards?

Everyone involved in the operation should be able to identify potential hazards. Naturally, people closest to the activities or assets often have the best knowledge. For example, account managers, service representatives and technicians are most knowledgeable in identifying service risk. In contrast, supplier relationship and purchasing managers are the natural parties to identify sourcing risk. This means that risk identification requires a multi-functional team that can interact with functional specialists.

9.3 | RISK ASSESSMENT AND VALUATION

The second step in any risk management program is to analyze the degree of risk associated with each hazard. The goal of risk assessment is to indicate which areas and activities in the value chain are most susceptible to hazards.

Qualitative risk assessment: the theory

Recall that risk is an undesirable consequence of uncertainty. Risk assessment thus involves, for each hazard identified in step 1, the estimation of:

1. the impact (vulnerability) on the organization if the hazard were to occur

2. and its probability of occurring during the operation.

The result can be displayed in a *subjective risk map*, an example of which is shown in Figure 9.4. The word "subjective" reminds us that this risk map is based on expert opinion only and not on statistical analysis. Obviously, the risk map is company-specific: the risks carry different weights depending on the competitive strategy and the industry. For example, for a commercial bank, IT systems failure would have a much greater impact than would a hurricane.

Risk assessment is completed by ranking hazards to locate the highest-risk activities. This can be done qualitatively by combining the impact and probability for each hazard into an overall risk level. The risk map in Figure 9.4 classifies hazards into three risk levels. High risk hazards occupy the upper right quadrant and create high damage with high probability. Medium risks are unlikely hazards with high impact (also called *disruptions*) or frequent, low impact hazards (recurrent risks). Low risks stem from unlikely hazards with low impact, and occupy the lower left quadrant.

Qualitative risk assessment: examples from practice

Every good operations periodically assesses risks. For example, Figure 9.5 shows how the National Interagency Fire Center (National Interagency Fire Center 2002) assigns risk levels (extremely high, high, medium, or low) for helicopter operations depending on the hazard's probability or frequency (unlikely, seldom, occasional, likely, or frequent) and impact (negligible, moderate, critical, or catastrophic).

Debit card companies and other financial companies conduct risk assessment programs periodically. According to one debit card product manager:

> "We had to go through *every* possible operational risk to our business annually, provide an estimate of impact of a hazardous event (on a scale of 1 to 5, covering a range of dollar values) as well as the likelihood of the event happening (also on a scale of 1-5). If you provided a top-two score high impact and high probability event, you were asked to present to the bank's risk management committee, which consisted of senior and executive managers and was headed by the bank's newly formed enterprise risk manager. They would expect to see your action plans if the event occurred, as well as the steps you've taken to mitigate the risk.
>
> "As part of the BASEL II requirements, all banks must conduct this type of thorough assessment for all areas of their business. Failure to meet the BASEL standards can results in sanctions by banking oversight committees (Fed, OCC, etc.) that could affect banks abilities to lend, to lend at good rates, to get approval for M&A, etc. It is a quite exhaustive accounting of operational risks. Admittedly, many estimates were just educated guesses by line managers and,

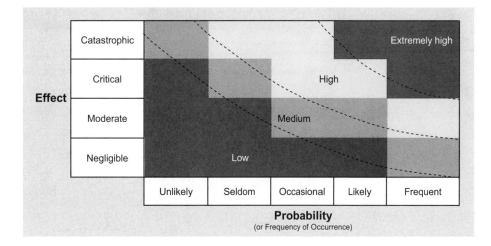

Figure 9.5 Qualitative risk assessment assigns an overall risk level to each hazard, depending on its probability and its impact.

of course, it also took a lot of time out of managers' days to focus on events that most likely weren't going to happen... In the end, though, the risk assessment process helped everyone realize where we were vulnerable. It also helps bank management have a much broader understanding of the entire risk exposure and brought operational risk management to the executive board level."

Some risks, such as political risks, are difficult to assess, compared to calculating the technical risk of product approval or the statistical risk of poor forecasting. Yet, where there is a will, there is a way. According to one risk assessment team, "one way to help dimension political risk is to compare the political risks of one country relatively to the risks faced in other countries the firm operates in. One team member found research that provided political risk indexes for various countries throughout the world. Other resources to help quantify what seemed to be a rather nebulous topic include the World Bank's Multilateral Investment Guarantee Agency and numerous consulting firms and insurance providers."

Quantitative risk assessment: risk metrics

The qualitative approach can be quantified by estimating the financial impact and probability of each hazard from past data and experience. A hazard's "risk level" can then be quantified by its expected impact, which is equal to the financial impact multiplied by the probability of occurrence. Constant risk levels are then represented by hyperbolic curves in risk maps, as illustrated by the dotted lines in Figure 9.5.

Besides the methods that assess the expected value of a hazard, there are many other ways of quantifying risk. These are most easily described by letting X denote the (financial) effect of a hazard or random event (i.e., X is a random

Example 9.3 How to calculate Value-at-Risk (VaR)

Value-at-Risk at $x\%$ is the answer to the question: how much can be lost with $x\%$ probability over a pre-set horizon? Suppose you currently have a portfolio worth $1 million, and its annual return is normally distributed with mean 10% and standard deviation 30%. What is your value-at-risk at 5%?

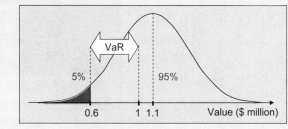

Calculating value-at-risk at 5%.

Your value-at-risk at 5% can be calculated in two steps, as illustrated in the figure above:

1. Find the 5% quantile of next year's value. In our example, Excel gives us that number as `norminv(.05,1.1,.3)` = $0.6 million.

2. Find the VaR as the difference between the 5% quantile of future value and the current value. In our example, the VaR is $1 - 0.6 = \$.4$ million.

This means that there is only a 5% chance that you will lose more than $400,000.

---

variable) and $\overline{X}$ its mean or expected value $\mathbb{E}X$. Recall that financially, risk is considered to be the possibility that actual outcomes deviate from expected ones. A basic risk metric is *variance* (or its square root, the standard deviation), the expected squared deviation around the mean:

$$\text{variance} = \mathbb{E}(\overline{X} - X)^2 = \sigma^2.$$

Variance and standard deviation treat positive deviations from the mean ("the upside") symmetrically with negative deviations ("the downside"). Statistical measures that exclude upside deviations are arguably more natural metrics of risk, because they only capture the undesirable consequences of uncertainty. A popular downside risk measure is *Value-at-Risk* (VaR). It measures the worst expected loss at a given confidence level by answering the question: how much can I lose with $x\%$ probability over a pre-set horizon? Example 9.3 illustrates how to calculate VaR. Other examples of downside risk metrics are:

$$
\begin{aligned}
\text{below-mean semivariance} \quad &= \mathbb{E}((\overline{X} - X)^+)^2, \\
\text{below-target } t \text{ semivariance} \quad &= \mathbb{E}((t - X)^+)^2, \\
\text{expected below-target } t \text{ risk} \quad &= \mathbb{E}(t - X)^+,
\end{aligned}
$$

where the notation X^+ means the positive part of X, i.e., $X^+ = \max(0, X)$.

Valuing risk with preferences and utility functions

Measuring risk directly in terms of the downside volatility of outcomes is certainly informative, but such raw risk metrics do not allow us to easily compare risks. For example, do you prefer a risky project with a value variance of $1 to another with a variance of $100? Surely, you would want to know the expected value before answering! As a matter of fact, if your preferences depend on expected values *only*, you are said to be *risk-neutral*.

Most people, however, are *risk-sensitive*, which means that their preferences do not depend only on expected value. Deciding between two risky projects then requires trading off risk with expected return. Making this trade-off is difficult in general, but under standard rationality assumptions we can use a utility function to summarize risk preferences. A utility function u simply maps outcomes into a decision-maker's utility. A risky outcome X_1 then is preferred over outcome X_2 if and only if the expected utility of the first exceeds that of the second.

It directly follows that a risk-neutral manager would have a linear utility function, so that only expected outcomes matter. For example, consider choosing between two projects: the first project has a payoff of $100 for sure, while the second's payoff has an expected value of $100, but is normally distributed around that mean with standard deviation σ. A risk-neutral manager derives equal expected utility from both projects and is indifferent between them.

In contrast, risk-averse managers have concave utility functions, which reflect their higher sensitivity to downside than upside. To see this, consider a concave function such as the negative exponential

$$u(x) = 1 - e^{-\gamma x},$$

shown in Figure 9.6. The parameter $\gamma > 0$ represents the manager's sensitivity to risk and is called the *coefficient of absolute risk aversion*. As the coefficient of risk aversion γ increases, the utility function becomes more concave and more sensitive to downside variations. Notice that the upside has a maximal utility of 1, while the downside is unlimited. The marginal utility of $1 above the mean is less than that of $1 below the mean. In other words, a risk-averse manager gets *more* utility from reducing the downside by one unit than from increasing the upside by one unit. It follows that downside variation is not offset by equal upside variation, and that the expected utility from a random outcome with mean 100 is strictly less than a certain outcome of 100. A risk-averse manager dislikes volatility.

Mean-variance frontiers

Risk-averse valuation with expected utilities typically requires calculus, but there is one useful exception. When payoffs are normally distributed, their expected exponential utility can be expressed by the simpler *mean-variance preference*:

$$\text{Mean-Variance preference } MV = \mu - \frac{\gamma}{2}\sigma^2,$$

where μ is the expected payoff and σ^2 is its variance. Expected utility increases with the mean payoff, but decreases if the actual outcome is more likely to deviate from its expected value (as indicated by a greater variance) or if the manager is more risk-averse (as indicated by a greater coefficient of risk-aversion).

Mean-variance preferences are at the core of modern financial *portfolio management* and provide a good inspiration for operations strategies for risk mitigation. The original idea was first formulated in 1952 by Nobel laureate Harry Markowitz, who employed mean-variance preferences. He started by observing

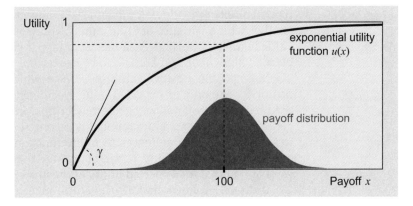

Figure 9.6 Risk-averse managers have concave utility functions, thus preferring a unit reduction of the downside to a unit increase of the upside.

that individual investors are not interested in the expected value of their portfolio only. If that were the case, portfolios would consist of one asset only: that with the highest expected return.

Most investors hold diversified portfolios because they are concerned with risk as well as expected value. Markowitz used the variance of portfolio value as a measure of risk. Not only are mean-variance preferences reasonable models to describe the decisions of a risk-averse investor, but variances of a portfolio are also easily computed as a function of the covariances between any pair of assets in the portfolio. Markowitz thus presented a mathematical approach to optimal portfolio selection depending on the investor's risk-aversion, represented by the coefficient of risk aversion γ.

Optimal portfolio selection can be illustrated graphically as follows. Imagine that you calculated the expected value (return) and variance (risk) of all possible portfolios that can be bought with a given budget. Now represent each portfolio by one point on a risk-return graph, as shown in Figure 9.7. Then, the optimal portfolio can be derived in two steps:

1. Only portfolios that lie on the northwestern frontier, called the *mean-variance frontier*, should be selected; these are called *efficient* portfolios (any other portfolio is dominated by an efficient one with the same expected return but less risk, or the reverse).

2. Once the frontier is known, the final step is to estimate the investor's coefficient of risk-aversion γ, in order to identify the optimal portfolio with the point on the frontier with tangent $\gamma/2$. Indeed, the investor maximizes his expected utility by maximizing his mean-value preferences, which are straight lines in the risk-return graph.

Before we use this approach for strategic risk mitigation and operational hedging, we must consider step 3 of the risk management process.

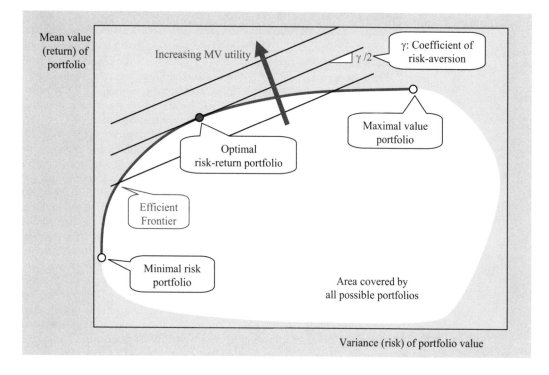

Figure 9.7 Graphical representation of Markowitz's optimal portfolio selection. The optimal risk-return trade-off for a manager with coefficient of risk aversion γ is the point on the efficient frontier with a tangent of $\gamma/2$.

9.4 | Tactical Risk Decisions

The third step of the risk management process is to let our risk assessment guide us in developing a plan of appropriate tactical decisions to be taken when a specific hazard is likely to occur, or when it has already occurred. Good tactical risk management involves three activities: risk preparation, risk discovery, and risk recovery.

Risk preparation

To be successful in later risk recovery, organizational risk preparedness is key. This means that companies have formulated proactive and reactive plans: what to do if risk levels are elevated, and contingent actions to take after the hazard occurs. In addition to making plans, they also practice the plans with fire drills, backup routines for power losses, and so on.

Example 9.4 Risk discovery and recovery: Nokia v. Ericsson

At 8pm on Friday, March 17th, 2000, a lightning bolt hit an electric line in New Mexico and, somehow, resulted in a fire at the Philips NV's semiconductor plant in Albuquerque. While the sprinkler system extinguished the fire in less than 10 minutes, it also destroyed the clean room during that process, and with it, millions of cell phone chips that were destined for its two largest customers, Nokia and Ericsson. But how the two companies responded to the crisis couldn't have been more different.

At Nokia, computer screens indicated delays of shipments from some Philips chips even before Philips called Nokia's chief component-purchasing manager Tapio Markki on Monday, March 20th. Philips said the fire impacted some 4 million handsets and that there would be a one week delay. Given that it was about to introduce a new generation of cell phones based on the Philips chips, Nokia decided to further look into the issue and offered to fly two Nokia engineers to Albuquerque to help with the recovery. Philips declined the offer and said on March 31, two weeks after the fire, that they would need more weeks to repair the plant, and that several months worth of chip supplies could be disrupted.

Nokia went into textbook crisis management mode. Of the five parts, two were indispensable: one was made by various suppliers around the globe, while the other one was an application specific integrated circuit (ASIC) made only by Philips. A Nokia team, headed by current chairman Ollila, flew to Philips' headquarters in Amsterdam and spoke directly with Philips' CEO, Cor Boonstra, in an attempt to find alternate supply. Nokia demanded capacity information about all Philips plants and insisted on rerouting the capacity. "The goal was simple: For a little period of time, Philips and Nokia would operate as one company regarding these components," said Nokia's Korhonen. As a solution, Philips used its plants in Eindhoven to produce more than 10 million units of the ASIC chip, and also freed up a Shanghai plant for Nokia. Meanwhile, Nokia engineers redesigned some of their chips so they could be produced elsewhere, and they worked further with Albuquerque to boost production.

Ericsson, in contrast, treated the initial call from Philips as "one technician talking to another." When Ericsson's top management finally learned about the problem several weeks later, it was too late. Philips had no more spare capacity left and no other suppliers were capable of providing the parts Ericsson needed. Thus, Ericsson came up millions of chips short in a rapidly moving cell phone market. The company said they lost at least $400 million in potential revenue. At the end of 2000, its mobile phone division announced a staggering $1.7 billion loss and vowed that it would never be exposed like this again. In January 2001, Ericsson exited the handset production business completely. *Source: Latour (2001)*

Risk discovery

In order to execute proactive plans, one must monitor risks and have a fast system of hazard detection or discovery. Reconsider the P&G Pringles plant example (Example 9.2 on p. 315). When it became likely that the plant was in the path of an oncoming tornado, management decided that the risk level was sufficiently high to evacuate the plant. The anticipatory risk decision was to turn on the sirens as a signal to everyone that the earlier-designed evacuation procedure was in effect.

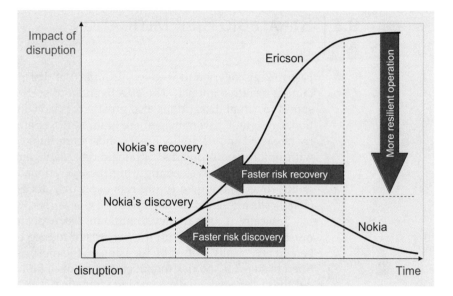

Figure 9.8 Faster risk discovery and recovery, along with a more resilient operation, is paramount in mitigating the impact of disruptions (adapted from Sheffi 2005).

Risk recovery

Once disaster has struck, risk recovery executes contingency actions such as finding other supplies, temporarily changing prices to ease demand, providing substitutes when actual demand significantly differs from plan, or using backup suppliers or processes. For example, when Grainger, which supplies maintenance and operating parts, had its East Cost facilities hit by electricity blackouts or hurricanes in Florida, they switched to internal power generators; by using this quick backup strategy, Grainger did not miss a single order fulfillment. Similarly, once a tornado struck at P&G, managers immediately started a recovery operation by calling the corporate brand contingency team.

Fast risk discovery and recovery is paramount to containing the negative impact of a disruption. The differential reaction to the unforeseen problems at a Philips semiconductor plant by two of its customers, Nokia and Ericsson, provides a case in point (Example 9.4). Nokia quickly switched sourcing to other back-up facilities and suppliers with little impact to ongoing operations, while Ericsson's slow response along with its unhedged single sourcing strategy is reported to have cost it $400 million in lost sales.

In summary, in good tactical risk management, companies are prepared, use risk discovery mechanisms, and have quick risk recovery plans. By the very nature of a crisis, however, there still is a fair amount of unforeseen decision making to be done. The first step is to examine options for addressing the risks. Then, make decisions about which options to implement. Finally, take actions to implement the decisions. Naturally, the appropriate decision maker for these contingent decisions is more senior the higher the risk level.

9.5 | STRATEGIC RISK MITIGATION

Fast risk discovery and recovery from actual disruptions is paramount in containing negative impact. The effectiveness of such tactical risk decisions to respond to actual disruptions also greatly depends on the flexibility of the operational system. Crisis management is similar to operating a hospital's emergency room: speed and flexibility are the most important competencies to quickly deal with unforeseen problems. Strategic risk management, the fourth step in risk management, involves configuring the operational system for speed and flexibility so as to mitigate future risk exposure. Its goal is to design what Sheffi (2005) calls a resilient organization.

Typically, it costs money to mitigate risk exposure. Strategic risk mitigation must balance that cost with the benefits of reduced risk exposure. The greatest benefit is typically gained by focusing on the most risky hazards (that were identified in step 2 of the risk management process) first. Let us discuss how to carry out the cost-benefit analysis behind strategic risk mitigation.

The value-maximizing level of risk mitigation (risk-neutral)

Risk mitigation strategies fall on a continuum between risk acceptance and risk elimination. Many hazards have such a small risk that one simply accepts their exposure. For example, passengers and freight forwarders accept the inherent risks of flying. Sometimes, risks can be eliminated. For instance, P&G could eliminate tornado risk by relocating its plants to areas where tornados are highly improbable.

Typically, the marginal benefit of risk mitigation decreases while its cost increases, so that the appropriate risk mitigation level falls in between the extreme strategies of risk elimination and risk acceptance. For example, consider mitigating shortage risk by adding safety stock. Figure 9.9 depicts the costs and benefits of reducing shortage risk by adding safety stock for product with a sales price of $5, a unit cost of $1, and a normally-distributed demand forecast with mean and standard deviation of 1 million. When stocking the average demand, the shortage probability is 50%. Shortage risk mitigation requires adding safety stock. Complete shortage risk elimination would yield expected revenues of $5 million, but would require exorbitant safety stock. A risk-neutral manager is better off mitigating 80% shortage risk because that maximizes expected profits, according to the newsvendor model (see p. 435).

Strategic risk-return trade-offs for risk-averse managers

Risk-averse managers care about profit risk as well as expected profits. They are willing to give up some expected profits for a reduction in profit risk.[1]

When managing a single asset such as capacity or stock, profit risk can be decreased by reducing the asset level. Reconsider our earlier example of mitigating shortage risk by adding safety stock. With an abundance of stock, short-

---

[1]This is simply a statement of fact, not a prescription. In fact, Chapter 1 explained that managers of publicly held companies should maximize expected value, because shareholders can diversify risk on their own by engaging in portfolio management consistent with their own risk-reward preferences.

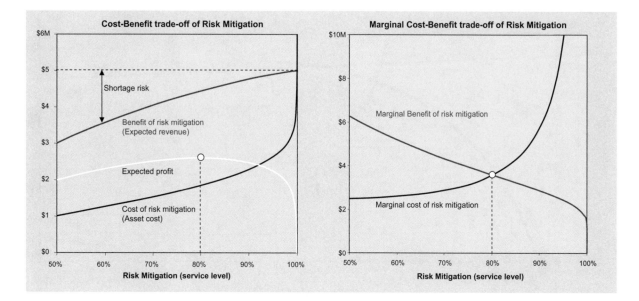

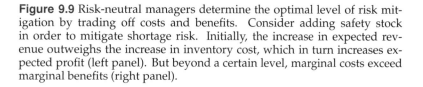

Figure 9.9 Risk-neutral managers determine the optimal level of risk mitigation by trading off costs and benefits. Consider adding safety stock in order to mitigate shortage risk. Initially, the increase in expected revenue outweighs the increase in inventory cost, which in turn increases expected profit (left panel). But beyond a certain level, marginal costs exceed marginal benefits (right panel).

ages are eliminated and sales equal demand. The manager then is exposed to total demand risk, and profit standard deviation is maximized (equal to $5 \times$ 1 million demand standard deviation). By reducing the stocking (and thus service) level, sales are capped by inventory and profit risk decreases (to $5 \times$ the standard deviation of the minimum of demand and stocking level). Figure 9.10 depicts the mean and variance of profits as a function of the service level. Using Markowitz's approach, the appropriate level of risk mitigation for a manager with a coefficient of risk aversion γ is specified by the point on the frontier with a tangent of $\gamma/2$. By moving southwest along the frontier, we give up some expected profit and thus decrease profit variance risk.

Periodic updating and continuous risk management

Strategic risk mitigation includes a procedure to keep risk assessment up to date. Business risks continually change over time and risk management must evolve accordingly. Just like periodic financial portfolio rebalancing and health checkups, periodic updating of risk management is a smart preventative move. Grainger, for instance, reviews each risk plan every six months and updates if there is a business change. It also performs real tests, as well as "desktop exercises" of its risk plans on an annual basis.

In the remainder of this chapter, we will turn our attention to various strategies that can be used to mitigate operational risk.

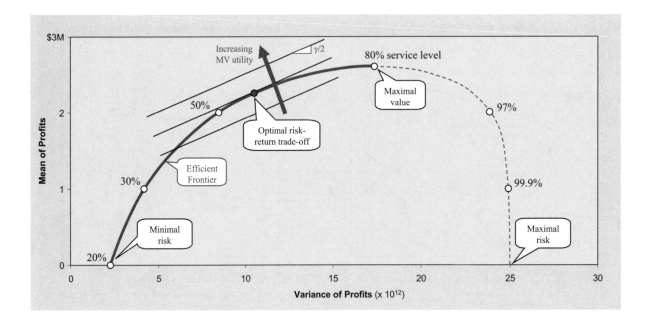

Figure 9.10 Increasing inventory or capacity increases service level and reduces shortage risk, but increases profit variance risk. The optimal risk-return trade-off for a manager with a coefficient of risk aversion γ is the point on the efficient frontier with a tangent of $\gamma/2$.

9.6 | FOUR OPERATIONAL HEDGING STRATEGIES

Hedging refers to any action taken to mitigate a particular risk exposure. It often involves counterbalancing acts that take on one risk to offset another. Most businesses hedge or insure to reduce risk, not to make money. In theory, a perfect hedge eliminates risk without impacting mean value. In practice, however, hedging impacts both risk and value. Using Markowitz's visualization, hedging becomes more effective as the frontier becomes flatter, so that risk reduction only comes with a small value loss.

The insurance industry uses three means to mitigate its risk: it builds reserves to meet claims, pools risks over many clients (this diversification reduces its total risk), and transfers remaining risks to reinsurers using contracts. Operations can also use these three generic risk mitigation strategies; in addition, there are also an arsenal of operations management techniques to reduce risk.

These four generic strategies to mitigate risk using operational instruments, i.e. *operational hedging*, are summarized in Example 9.5. Let us review these four strategies qualitatively; the remainder of this chapter will quantify and tailor them to a particular situation.

> **Example 9.5** Four generic operational hedging strategies
>
> 1. RESERVES & REDUNDANCY
>
>   - safety capacity, safety inventory, safety time, warranties (reserves)
>   - multi-sourcing, multiple locations and transportation modes, back-up assets and processes (redundancy)
>
> 2. DIVERSIFICATION & POOLING
>
>   - operating in diverse markets (diversification)
>   - serving diverse markets with one resource (demand pooling)
>   - using diverse suppliers for one resource (supply pooling)
>   - allocation flexibility of suppliers, designs, resources, activities, and outputs
>
> 3. RISK-SHARING & TRANSFER
>
>   - alliances and partnerships
>   - outsourcing with structured supply contracts
>   - entering financial hedging contracts with third parties
>
> 4. REDUCING OR ELIMINATING ROOT CAUSES OF RISK
>
>   - postponement with quick response (decrease risk exposure)
>   - supplier collaboration and improvement
>   - root cause analysis and variance reduction (Six Sigma, total quality management)
>   - robust product and process design, including process relocation

1. Reserves and redundancy

A core risk mitigation strategy is to invest in reserves, assets held in excess of expected requirements "just-in-case." In Chapters 3 and 4, we analyzed how to size safety capacity, inventory, and time as a buffer against uncertainty.

In general, redundancy refers to an excess over normal requirements or duplication. In engineering, redundancy is the duplication of critical system component to increase system reliability, often through backup assets or processes, such as Grainger's backup power generators. In the normal course of operations, these redundant assets or processes are not needed.

2. Diversification and pooling

Diversification refers to serving multiple risks (e.g., product demands) from one portfolio or network. This popular risk mitigation strategy is also known as "not holding all the eggs in one basket." There are several ways of pooling risks with operations, each with a different impact:

A. *Pure diversification and natural hedging* refers to serving two markets with separate, dedicated resources. This reduces total profit variance risk because variability in one market partially offsets variability in the other (unless both risks are perfectly positively correlated). Supplying countries from local operations is an example of pure diversification that is also known as *natural hedging*. It mitigates profit variance risk arising from local demand risk as well as currency exchange risk. Notice that pure diversification does not impact expected value and differs from reserves and redundancy.

B. *Demand pooling* refers to serving multiple demands from one resource, such as a centralized warehouse that stocks one product to serve multiple areas, or a single facility that supplies multiple markets. Similarly, *supply pooling* means serving one demand from multiple suppliers; a typical example is multi-sourcing of a single component. In Chapters 6 and 7, we described the benefits of processing at multiple locations or sourcing from multiple suppliers.

Demand and supply pooling are special forms of diversification and risk-pooling. By "betting on two horses," they provide the profit variance risk mitigation benefits of pure diversification that are valued by risk-averse investors. In addition, as demonstrated in Chapter 5, they reduce mismatch costs, safety capacity, and safety inventory, while improving service. (See Analytics Box 5.3 on p. 175; recall that resource sizing is driven by the aggregate standard deviation.) Thus, in contrast to pure diversification, demand and supply pooling also brings benefits to risk-neutral managers (but less so as correlation increases or if risks have dissimilar magnitudes).

C. *Allocation flexibility and information updating* refers to pooling *heterogeneous* risks with a *flexible* network. The embedded real options achieve more powerful operational hedging than do static demand or supply pooling. For example, consider serving continental Europe and the United Kingdom from a single process in Belgium. If the process has sufficient flexibility to postpone country allocations, it can first observe actual demands and exchange rates and then maximize revenues by steering the allocation to the more profitable country. It is exactly this type of dynamic pooling that was effective in the Pringles and Nokia examples.

In addition to the embedded risk mitigation of pooling, allocation flexibility and other real options can increase expected profits. Chapter 5 called this the revenue maximization option of flexibility, which becomes more valuable as the pooled risks become more heterogeneous. This "active" operational hedging highlights an interesting advantage over financial hedging or pure insurance: operational hedging not only mitigates risk but can also add value by exploiting upside variations. We will illustrate this quantitatively in the next few sections.

Redundancy and diversity through flexible networks are related. For example, consider P&G's network for Pringles production has two plants. Each plant's main mission is to serve its own geography, so that neither plant is redundant, strictly speaking. The flexibility embodied in the network, however, does allow the Belgian plant to serve as a backup for the Jackson plant, illustrating its relationship to redundancy.

3. Risk sharing and transfer

Instead of bearing all the risk ourselves, we can share it with partners, alliances, or suppliers. In Chapter 7, we described how structured contracts can balance risk between a supplier and buyer. Later in this chapter, we will discuss how a company can share and even transfer risk by entering into financial hedging contracts with third parties. The obvious example of sharing risk is taking on insurance contracts.

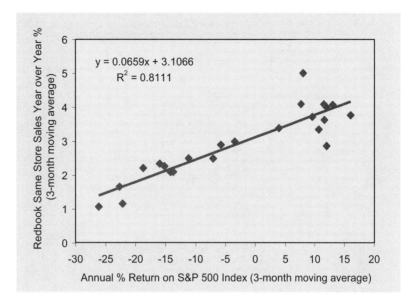

Figure 9.11 Redbook's same-store sales growth rate is highly correlated with the annual return on the S&P 500 Index (Gaur and Seshadri 2005).

4. Reducing or Eliminating Root Causes of Risk

In addition to these three insurance-like techniques, operations research has also emphasized risk reduction by quick response, supply chain collaboration and continuous improvement. As we will review in the next chapter, continuous improvement uses root cause analysis and an entire arsenal of techniques for variance reduction. It cannot be overemphasized that, in the long run, eliminating problems is better than mitigating their impact. Toyota is living proof.

9.7 | FINANCIAL HEDGING OF OPERATIONAL RISK

Financial hedging uses financial instruments to mitigate risk. Let us discuss some examples of how financial hedging can mitigate operational risk and how it relates to operational hedging.

Hedging demand risk with options

Demand for discretionary items such as apparel, consumer electronics, and home furnishings is often correlated with economic indicators. Gaur and Seshadri (2005) present evidence that the correlation can be quite significant. For example, The Redbook Average (a seasonally adjusted average of same-store sales growth in a sample of 60 large U.S. general merchandise retailers representing

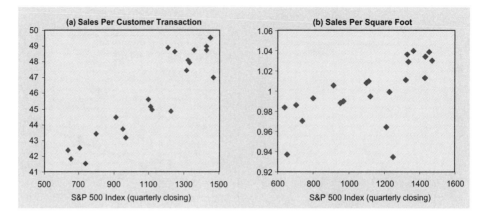

Figure 9.12 Quarterly sales per customer transaction (a) and per square foot (b) at Home Depot are correlated with S&P 500 Index (Gaur and Seshadri 2005)

about 9,000 stores) monthly time-series data from Nov. 1999 to Nov. 2001 had a correlation coefficient of 0.90 with same-period returns on the S&P 500 index ($R^2 = 81\%$, see Figure 9.11). In addition, that value of R^2 is correlated with the fraction of discretionary items sold as a percentage of total sales.

Similar results hold on the firm-level. Figure 9.12 shows that sales per customer transaction and sales per square foot at The Home Depot (a retail chain selling home construction and furnishing products) are both significantly correlated with the S&P 500 index.

Theoretically, the correlation between sales and a financial instrument can be exploited to mitigate demand risk by buying a (tailored) call option on the financial asset.[2] Consider a retailer who must order inventory today but faces a leadtime of 4 weeks. Assume for simplicity that demand is perfectly correlated with the S&P 500 index. Buying call options on the index with exercise price corresponding to the inventory and exercise date one month from now would provide a perfect hedge, as shown by Figure 9.13.

In reality, the correlation is imperfect and the hedging transactions are more complex (involving a tailored family of different calls) but we can take away the main insights: financial hedging can significantly mitigate profit variability risk. (For this specific example, however, a healthy dose of caution is appropriate, given that Home Depot is part of the S&P 500; thus, the correlation is to be expected and may not be a reliable predictor of future performance.)

In well-functioning financial markets, arbitrage arguments show that the options are priced at a level equal to their expected return. Financial hedging then reduces variance risk without impacting the expected return. Risk-averse retailers will then increase their order sizes closer to the risk-neutral (newsvendor) level. In addition, financial market information can be used to update demand forecasts.

---

[2] A call option gives its owner the right to buy the asset at a specified exercise price on or before the specified exercise date.

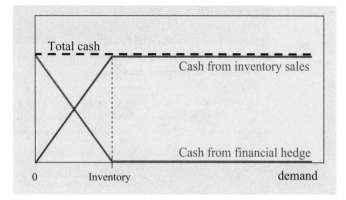

Figure 9.13 When demand is correlated with a financial asset, inventory risk can be mitigated by buying a call option on the financial asset. If the correlation is perfect, a financial option with an exercise price corresponding to the inventory would provide a perfect hedge.

Hedging demand risk with (weather) derivatives

When demand is correlated with weather conditions, demand risk can be mitigated using financial weather derivatives. For example, Japanese insurer Mitsui Sumitomo sells derivatives based on the snowfall in a particular location. Retail ski shops could use that derivative to hedge against low snowfall that could impact sales. At the same time, Mitsui Sumitomo could sell the opposite derivative to a snow removal company. This example shows how intermediaries such as Mitsui can sometimes improve markets by balancing risks.

In addition to snowfall, weather derivatives can include specifications on rainfall, temperature, and wind. In 2002, Mitsui Sumitomo issued a weather-derivative contract to a soft drink wholesaler based on the number of hours of sunshine. If the number of sunshine hours recorded in the July–September quarter fell below a certain predetermined threshold, Mitsui would pay the company a pre-determined amount.

Hedging currency risk with forward contracts and swaps

Global firms like Michelin, BMW, and Porsche are exposed to currency exchange rate risk. Two popular risk mitigation strategies are natural hedging (produce and sell locally) and financial hedging involving forwards and swaps.

In a *foreign exchange forward market*, you can buy and sell currency for future delivery. If you are going to receive €500,000 next month, you can insure yourself by entering into a one-month *forward contract*. The forward rate on this contract is the price you agree to receive in one month when you deliver the €500,000. Forward contracts are customized transactions between you and a bank. More generally, you can manage risk by entering into a *swap*, which is a contract between two parties specifying the exchange of a series of payments at specified intervals over a specified period of time.

For main currencies and specific amounts and delivery dates rates, there are

Example 9.6 Should we use financial hedging with futures, or operational hedging?

Consider a global manufacturer with production facilities in Europe and the U.S. that is exposed to demand and currency risk. The firm wonders whether it should hedge financially or operationally.

Suppose that the unit sales price is €20,000 in Europe and $20,000 in the U.S.; similarly, the unit cost is 10k in local currency. Suppose that currencies are correlated with demand and that there are two states of nature, each equally likely:

1. U.S. demand is 100k units, Euro demand is 50k, and the exchange rate is $1/€.

2. U.S. demand is 50k units, Euro demand is 100k, and the exchange rate is $2/€.

Hedge Option 1: a natural hedge produces and sells locally with operating profits per state:

1. $1,000M in U.S. + €500M in Europe at $1/€ = $1,500M

2. $500M in U.S. + €1,000M in Europe at $2/€ = $2,500M

The expected profit is $2,000M, with a variability risk of ± $500M.

Hedge Option 2: a natural hedge combined with a financial hedge that sells 500M future euros for $1.50 per euro (the expected financial return is zero and we neglect small transaction costs). The operating profits per state are:

1. $1,000M (US) + €500M (Europe) + $750M - €500M (future) = $1,750M

2. $500M (US) + €1,000M (Europe) + $750M - €500M (future) = $1,750M + €500M at $2/€ = $2,250M

The expected profit is again $2,000M but with a reduced risk of ± $250M.

Hedge Option 3: an active operational hedge where we only produce in the low cost location—in Europe in state 1 and in the U.S. otherwise. The operating profits in each state are:

1. Sales: $2,000M in U.S. + €1,000M in Europe. Cost: € 1,500M in Europe. Net = $2,000M - €500 at $1/ € = $1,500M

2. Sales: $1,000M in U.S. + €2,000M in Europe. Cost: $1,500M in U.S. Net = $500M + €2,000M at $2/ € = $3,500M

The expected profit is $2,500M, an increase in value of 25% over the passive hedges!

Hedge Option 4: the active operational hedge of Option 3 combined with a financial hedge would yield an expected profit of $2,500M with reduced variance.

standardized contracts, called *futures*, that are traded on currency future markets. In well-functioning financial markets, arbitrage arguments imply that future rates equal the expected rate so that forwards and futures do not impact expected value (neglecting small transaction costs). Example 9.6 revisits the global manufacturer example of Chapter 6 (p. 218) to illustrate natural, operational, and financial hedging. As predicted, natural and financial hedging reduce profit variance without affecting expected profits. In contrast, active operational hedging can use allocation flexibility in the global network to produce and sell at the most advantageous location, thereby increases expected profits (combining that with financial hedging further reduces variance without impacting expected value).

Differences between financial and operational hedging

A firm can simultaneously use both financial and operational hedging. For example, consider a domestic manufacturer that must invest in domestic capacity to produce goods that will be sold in a foreign market. The firm can use financial currency forward contracts to hedge currency risk. To further mitigate that risk, it can use ex-post operational flexibility.

Sometimes, complementing operational hedging with financial hedging may not be possible. For example, the planning horizon for a production facility may exceed 10 years. While operational hedging can be used, it is unlikely that financial hedging is available over that time-horizon. Financial hedging of capacity is also problematic if there is no capacity futures market that can replicate the capacity's cash flows (a swap can always be constructed if a counter party is available).

Whether a company should use both financial and operational hedging is the topic of current academic research. The answer depends on the type of financial contract, the operational system, and the correlation between the underlying financial asset and the operational risk under consideration. With perfect correlation, operational flexibility and financial hedging can complement each other, as Example 9.6 illustrates. Yet the optimal amount of operational flexibility that a firm should invest in depends on whether it engages in financial hedging or not. Chod et al. (2006) show that financial hedging with linear contracts increases the desired level of operational flexibility, while option contracts decrease it.

9.8 | TAILORED OPERATIONAL HEDGING

Earlier we said that risk management is an integral part of operations strategy. In this section, we will illustrate how risk management interacts with resource decisions (capacity size and type) and sourcing decisions. Furthermore, we will demonstrate how some generic operational hedging strategies can be tailored to specific situations.

Tailored natural hedging at Auto Co.

To illustrate the concept of tailored hedging, let us analyze how to tailor pure diversification to a particular setting. Consider, for example, a company that faces correlated demand risk, and manufactures two products, each on its own dedicated line. The question is how to size the capacity portfolio to mitigate risk. Mean variance analysis of profits provides an answer.

To illustrate mean variance analysis of a capacity portfolio, let us use the specific Auto Co. example introduced in Chapter 5 (p. 176). Recall that Auto Co. manufactures two models, the Afour and the Bassat. Assume first that Auto Co. has an investment budget of $100 million.

The profit mean and variance for an investment budget of $100 million can be calculated for the demand data using simulation-based optimization (described on p. 192). Figure 9.14 plots the results for $100 million investments

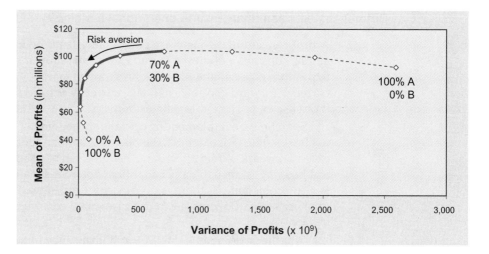

Figure 9.14 Pure diversification results from serving two markets with dedicated resources A and B. The percentages show the relative resource investment for a given budget. A risk-averse manager can operationally hedge by rebalancing towards resource B, which serves the lower profit variance market.

that vary their allocation to Afour and Bassat capacity. A risk-neutral manager would maximize expected profits by investing $70 million in product line A and the remaining $30 million in B. In contrast, a risk-averse manager should move down the frontier (in bold in Fig. 9.14) and rebalance capacity towards B.

But why B? Given that market A's demand has a standard deviation of $30,000$ with a unit contribution margin of $\$2,000$, the standard deviation of its (budget-unconstrained) contribution is $60 million. Compare this with the $50 million for market B, whose demand has a standard deviation of $50,000$ with a unit contribution margin of $\$1,000$.

The general insight gained here is that firms can tailor their operational hedge by rebalancing dedicated capacities towards the resource that serves the market with lower profit variance. The Auto Co. example shows that this doesn't need to be the market with the lowest demand risk or the highest contribution margin. Rather, it is the product of these two factors that counts. Recall from our risk pooling discussion in Chapter 5 (p. 174) that the effectiveness of this operational hedge increases as the pooled risks become more similar in magnitude and more negatively correlated. Indeed, a perfect zero-variance hedge would be obtained if both markets had equal profit variances and were perfectly negatively correlated.

Tailored redundancy and dynamic pooling with allocation flexibility at Auto Co.

To illustrate active operational hedging, continue considering the Auto Co. example, enriched with two additional options. First, the firm can borrow investment funds, meaning that it has no budget constraint. Second, the firm can not only invest in the two dedicated resources, but also in a product-flexible line.

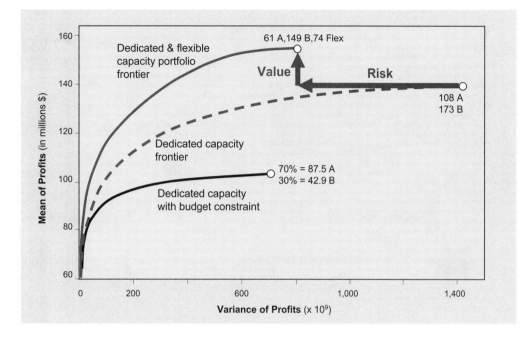

Figure 9.15 Adding flexibility not only mitigates profit variance risk through pooling (frontier is to the left of the dedicated capacity frontier) but also increases value by exploiting upside variations through contingent revenue maximization (frontier is above dedicated frontier).

The capacity portfolio now consists of three assets. The flexible line has higher capacity investment costs but pools *and* exploits demand uncertainty. Given that flexible capacity serves as a substitute to the dedicated resources, it can also be interpreted as a form of adding reserves in the form of adding *redundancy*.

Figure 9.15 shows the magnitude of risk mitigation and the value enhancement of hedging with operational flexibility compared to pure diversification with dedicated assets. The system with the $100 million investment budget is dominated by relaxed budget constraints: mean profits and profit variance risk increase, thus reflecting higher investments (108,000 A and 173,000 B annual car capacity versus 87,500 A and 42,900 B). In contrast, adding the option of investing in an additional flexible line here cuts profit variance risk roughly by 50% while increasing value by more than 10%. This shows that flexibility is attractive even to risk-neutral investors.

Risk-averse investors can further tailor the optimal operational hedge by rebalancing the capacity portfolio in two directions, as suggested by Figure 9.16: to do so, they must increase the shares of the flexible capacity and of the resources serving the lower profit variance market (B). The latter reflects the pure diversification effect inherent in pooling, while the former demonstrates the profit variance risk mitigation power of flexibility (notice that the operational hedge can be so powerful that a risk-averse manager may even increase capacity relative to the risk-neutral levels). The tailored capacity balance depends on the

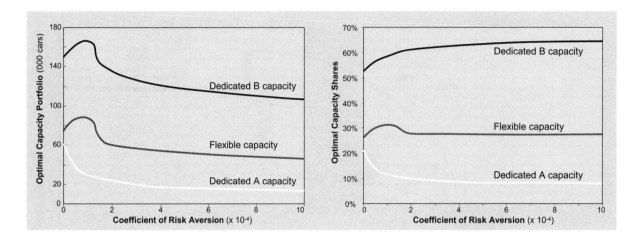

Figure 9.16 Risk-averse managers tailor the operational hedge by rebalancing the capacity portfolio toward (1) more flexibility and (2) resource B, which serves the lower profit variance market.

manager's coefficient of risk aversion, as well as on the demand and processing network data.

Tailored operational hedging: base demand, tail-pooling, and chaining

The appropriate capacity mix between flexible and dedicated capacity illustrates another tailoring dimension. Tailored flexibility, analyzed earlier in Chapter 5, serves mostly the uncertain part of the demand distribution (also known as tail risk), while most of the predictable "base demand" is allocated to dedicated resources. Benetton provides another example: garment production of its base demand is allocated to a set of efficient subcontractors up to two quarters ahead of the season. Flexible in-house capacity produces garments quickly, thereby minimizing demand risk.

Tailored flexibility also works in service operations. Service representatives may be mostly dedicated to a certain product or region (base demand). As long as the resource-product allocations form a chain, service representatives can help out colleagues who are overloaded. Pooling benefits accrue while specialization benefits are enjoyed the majority of time. Tail-pooling thus balances specialization (favoring dedicated resources) and pooling (favoring flexible resources) benefits.

Temporal tailoring of scale flexibility allocates quick response capacity to peak demand. Electricity capacity illustrates temporal tailoring in a single product setting: nuclear power serves base demand continuously while various levels of fossil fueled generators (including even jet generators) pick up peak demand.

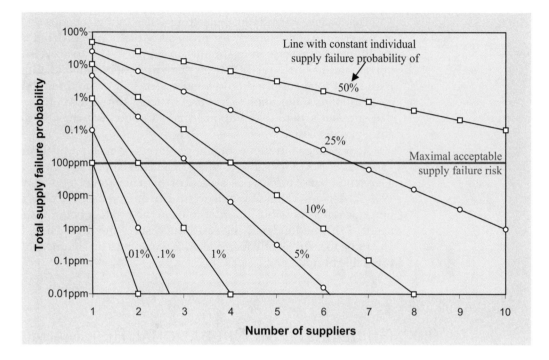

Figure 9.17 Tailored redundancy uses the appropriate number of suppliers depending on the maximal acceptable supply failure risk (100 parts per million here) and the failure probability of an individual supplier.

Tailored redundancy and multi-sourcing for supply and project risk

Multi-sourcing is a powerful strategy to mitigate supply failure risk. Consider the U.S. flu vaccine supply problem in 2004, when a major supplier (Chiron) was forced to close down due to violations of regulatory quality standards. The U.S. had roughly split the majority of its expected need of 100 million flu vaccines over Chiron and one other supplier. Because of the long lead times (about 8 months), it had little recourse; thus, flu vaccines were put on allocation, causing a serious political outcry. This was in marked contrast with the U.K.'s hedged strategy, which uses 6 suppliers for a target demand of only 14 million.

Tailored redundancy selects the appropriate number of suppliers based on the maximal acceptable supply failure risk and the failure risk profiles of individual suppliers. For example, consider the simplest situation where supply risk is all or nothing (similar perhaps to Chiron's flu vaccine problem) and the failure probability p is the same for all suppliers and independent of one another. Supply totally fails only when all suppliers fail. The probability of total supply failure when using N suppliers thus is p^N. Figure 9.17 shows this relationship in a log-linear plot. This determines the minimum number of suppliers needed to diversify supply risk below a maximal tolerable level. Clearly, more suppliers are needed if they are more unreliable or if maximal acceptable risk levels are tighter.

This insight extends to the setting where supply failure is manifested by an uncertain or *random yield* (or probability that a unit ordered is of acceptable quality) and can differ from supplier to supplier. The analysis is much more involved and has only recently been done by Federgruen and Yang (2007). They found that total supply should be allocated to a tailored number of suppliers, each supplier's allocation being proportional to the mean-to-variance ratio of that supplier's yield distribution. That allocation scheme also minimizes variable sourcing costs.

Redundancy through common platforms or even parallelism can also mitigate project risk. For example, when Toyota develops a new car, it often produces a large number of prototypes, several of them in parallel (Sobek, Ward, and Liker 1999). It decides which type will eventually be commercialized as close to market introduction as possible, in order to have the product better respond to market needs. While redundancy increases the costs of the R&D stage, it gives Toyota an option to significantly increase project revenues by commercializing the most profitable prototype.

9.9 | GUIDELINES FOR OPERATIONAL RISK MANAGEMENT

Implement an operational risk management process

In most companies, risk management is the responsibility of the CFO. In addition to financial risks, companies should also acknowledge, identify, and assess operational risks. Setting up a formal operational risk management process under a senior operations manager is a necessary first step. For example, Grainger has a "business continuity department" of about 15 people that anticipates, evaluates, and mitigates operational risks.

Use a multi-faceted approach tailored to the type of risk and product life cycle

No single size fits all. Risk mitigation should use the right mix of multiple financial and operational hedging strategies, depending on the type of risk. For example, supply risk of short life cycle products is best mitigated with supplier diversification and demand management techniques such as contingent substitution and pricing. For long life cycle products, inventory, contingent supply, and continuous risk monitoring of suppliers may be more appropriate. Make the distinction between intermittent and recurrent supply risks.

Not only the length, but also the stage in the product life cycle determines appropriate tactics. Technical innovation risk in the pharmaceutical industry is mitigated by redundancy (developing several designs in parallel), faster and earlier drug trials (testing), and retaining flexibility so important decisions can be postponed (e.g., by using modular facility construction).

Use a portfolio approach

While each risk needs a tailored response, remember that the organization's total risk exposure enjoys portfolio diversification benefits. Such a portfolio approach often justifies investment in redundant assets or more expensive flexible assets.

Realize that operational hedging may incur additional costs

There is no such thing as a free lunch. The benefits of operational hedging may involve additional hidden costs. For example, multi-location processing incurs a loss of scale, requires procurement from a wider supply base, slows down the learning curve process, and may produce less-consistent quality. Good risk management tries to reduce these costs over time.

Reducing risk is more powerful than mitigating exposure

In the long run, reducing and eliminating sources of risk is often more profitable than mitigating their impact with fences, counterbalancing actions, or band-aids. For example, exposure to demand uncertainty can be mitigated through pooling and reserves like safety inventory or capacity. Yet, initiatives like lead time reduction, postponement, quick response, better forecasting, and information sharing reduce the demand uncertainty (and with it, the need for mitigation).

Operations management has a rich heritage in eliminating the root cause of "problems" as illustrated by the success of the Toyota Production System and continuous improvement programs such as lean operations, Six Sigma, and total quality management. Such operations improvement programs, which we will study in the next chapter, should be an important component of any risk management program.

9.10 | SUMMARY OF LEARNING OBJECTIVES

1. Explain the concepts of risk management and operational hedging, and integrate them with operations strategy.

Risk is an undesirable consequence of uncertainty. Risk management is the planning and decision making process designed to deal with the occurrence of hazards. It can be viewed as an ongoing process with four steps:

1. Identification of hazards or key potential sources of risk in the operation.

2. Risk assessment of each hazard to categorize and prioritize risks.

3. Tactical risk management deals with the occurrence of a particular hazard.

4. Strategic risk mitigation or hedging to reduce future risk exposure.

Operational hedging is a form of strategic risk mitigation that involves designing a resilient operational system. Effective operational hedging is an integral part of operations strategy because it affects the configuration of all the resources and processes. It also must be aligned with the competitive strategies and required competencies. For example, firms that compete on high quality or responsiveness will typically find it optimal to invest in more risk mitigation than would firms competing on low cost.

2. Identify, assess, and value operational risks.

Operational risks can be identified by adopting the competency, process, and resource views of operations. Consider each key competency, activity, and resource in the operational system and identify potential sources of risk. In addition, identify any surrounding background risks such as natural, political, competitive, and strategic risks.

Risk assessment involves assessing the risk level of the identified hazards by estimating their likelihood and potential effect. This can be done using a subjective qualitative risk map and refined by quantifying risk metrics, such as variance of outcomes or downside measures such as semivariances and value-at-risk. To connect risk assessment with decision-making, however, one must estimate the decision maker's risk attitude and the way one trades off various risk levels with expected value. A useful and fairly implementable approach is Markowitz's mean-variance analysis. In that, one must represent all possible network configurations by their expected profits and variance of profits. Optimal risk-return trade-offs fall on the northwestern frontier and have a tangent specified by the risk-aversion coefficient.

3. Distinguish tactical from strategic risk management, and operational from financial hedging.

Tactical risk management uses mechanisms to detect when a specific hazard is soon likely to occur, and executes contingency plans. Good tactical risk management is similar to crisis management: it has practiced plans for fast risk discovery and recovery. In contrast to dealing with the occurrence of a specific hazard, strategic risk management is concerned with mitigating future risk exposure. It involves building a resilient operation that configures resources and processes such that disruptions have only a minor impact. In addition to operational hedging (configuring a resilient operational system), risk mitigation can also be achieved through financial means such as options, (weather) derivatives, and forward contracts. While financial and operational hedging can be done simultaneously, hedging with operational flexibility not only reduces risk, but can also increase value by exploiting upside variations.

4. Explain and tailor four operational hedging strategies.

The appropriate level of mitigation typically falls somewhere between the extreme cases of risk elimination and acceptance and should be based on a risk-return analysis incorporating your risk-aversion level. We have emphasized operational hedging, which typically uses four generic strategies: add reserves and redundancy, diversify and pool risks, share and transfer risk, and reduce or eliminate the root causes of risk.

Smart operational hedging tailors the strategy to a particular situation. Tailoring can be done qualitatively and can be refined through optimization. It is important to remember to use a multi-faceted approach and to consider the organization's total risk exposure as a portfolio. Finally, while risk mitigation is important, it should go hand-in-hand with the time-honored operations tradition of reducing sources of risks through root cause analysis and continuous improvement, a strategy that is often more profitable in the long run and that we will discuss in the next chapter.

DISCUSSION QUESTIONS

1. In the presence of substantial technical risk, some firms develop multiple designs in parallel. How does this fit with the four generic operational hedging strategies?

2. In daily conversations, risk means the possibility of an adverse outcome. Explain why a volatility metric that treats upside and downside variations in the same manner (e.g., standard deviation or variance) can be a sensible measure of risk.

3. How would you quantify the mismatch risk exposure of a risk-neutral retailer (chapter 3 may be useful)?

4. Which operational risks (as described in the section on identifying operational hazards) are addressed by the actions in Example 9.5?

ANALYTICAL QUESTIONS

1. Determine the ideal forward contract in hedges 3 and 4 in Example 9.6.

Visit www.vanmieghem.us for additional questions and updates.

FURTHER READING AND REFERENCES

▶ References to joint financial and operational hedging include Gaur and Seshadri (2005), Chod, Rudi, and Van Mieghem (2006), and Ding, Dong, and Kouvelis (2007).

▶ References to operational hedging of demand and supply risks include Chopra and Sodhi (2004), Federgruen and Yang (2007), Tomlin (2006), Sheffi (2005) and Van Mieghem (2007)

Chod, J., N. Rudi, and J. A. Van Mieghem (2006). Operational flexibility and financial hedging: Complements or substitutes? Working paper.

Chopra, S. and M. S. Sodhi (2004). Managing risk to avoid supply chain breakdown. *Sloan Management Review*. Fall 2004.

Ding, Q., L. Dong, and P. Kouvelis (2007). On the integration of production and financial hedging decisions in global markets. *Operations Research* 55(3), 470–489.

Federgruen, A. and N. Yang (2007). Selecting a portfolio of suppliers under demand and supply risks. *Operations Research*. forthcoming.

Gaur, V. and S. Seshadri (2005). Hedging inventory risk through market instruments. *Manufacturing and Service Operations Management* 7(2), 103–120.

Latour, A. (2001). Trial by fire: a blaze in Albuquerque sets off major crisis for cell-phone giants—Nokia handles supply shock with aplomb as Ericsson of Sweden gets burned—Was Sisu the difference? *Wall Street Journal*. Jan. 29.

National Interagency Fire Center (2002). Interagency helicopter operations guide. www.nifc.gov/ihog/pdf/chapters/ch03.pdf.

Pindyck, R. S. and D. L. Rubinfeld (1989). *Microeconomics*. Macmillan Publishing Company.

Presidential-Congressional Commission (1997). Final report on risk assessment and risk management, volume 1. www.riskworld.com/Nreports/1997/risk-rpt/html-/chp1box1.htm.

Sharpe, W. (1985). *Investments* (3rd Edition ed.). Prentice Halls.

Sheffi, Y. (2005). *The Resilient Enterprise*. The MIT Press.

Sobek, D., A. C. Ward, and J. K. Liker (1999). Toyota's principles of set-based concurrent engineering. *Sloan Management Review 40*, 67–83.

Tomlin, B. (2006). On the value of mitigation and contingency strategies for managing supply-chain disruptions risks. *Management Science 52*(5), 639–657.

Van Campenhout, M. (2004). Private correspondence on "Mechelen's position on handling the consequences of the Jackson tornado". October, 22.

Van Horne, J. C. (1993). *Financial Management and Policy* (8th Edition ed.). Prentice Hall.

Van Mieghem, J. A. (2007). Risk mitigation in newsvendor networks: Resource diversification, flexibility, sharing and hedging. *Management Science*. forthcoming.

Mini-Case 9 | DELL COMPUTER

[3]PC assembler Dell Computer is introducing two special Christmas products: a desktop and a laptop computer. Demand for computers is notoriously volatile and difficult to forecast with any degree of confidence. Marketing therefore uses three scenarios for projected quantities of laptops and desktops that will be demanded during the season. The first scenario has a likelihood of 30% and shows a demand of 4500 laptops and 1500 desktops, abbreviated as $D = (4500, 1500)$. The likely scenario has demands $(3500, 3500)$ with 50% likelihood, while the third scenario (20% likelihood) projects demands $(2000, 3500)$.

Dell must sign sourcing contracts with its suppliers in advance of the season. The two products have product-specific boxes, but have a common CPU. Laptops will be priced at $1300, and desktops will sell for $1000. The sourcing cost is $200 for a laptop box, $150 for a desktop box, and $500 for a CPU. Dell will put the CPU in the appropriate box in assemble-to-order fashion. For simplicity, ignore this marginal assembly cost.

1. Dell has set its sales plan to be $(3500, 3500)$ and therefore is planning to sign a sourcing contract with its suppliers, thus committing itself to buying 3500 laptop boxes, 3500 desktop boxes and 7000 CPUs. What is the expected total profitability of this sourcing contract? (Assume for simplicity that all leftover components are disposed of at zero cost.)

2. What is the optimal sourcing contract that Dell should commit to with its suppliers? That is, what quantities $(Q_{\text{laptop}}, Q_{\text{desktop}}, Q_{\text{CPU}})$ should Dell order to maximize its expected firm value? (Assume for simplicity that all leftover components are disposed off at zero cost.)

3. Compare your optimal sourcing contract with the sales-plan-driven contract of $(3500, 3500, 7000)$ and interpret it in terms of operational hedging: what exactly are you hedging and how do you obtain the hedge?

4. Give two other operational hedging techniques that Dell should consider.

5. Assume now that Dell is risk-averse, in the sense that it is willing to give up some mean value for a reduction in variance. How would your recommended sourcing contract of part 2 change?

---

[3]Professor Van Mieghem prepared this case as the basis for class discussion rather than to illustrate either the effective or ineffective handling of a managerial situation. No part of this case study may be reproduced without permission; direct all inquiries to permissions@vanmieghem.us

Chapter

10

IMPROVEMENT AND
INNOVATION

If a man empties his purse into his head no one can take it away from him. An investment in knowledge always pays the best interest.—Benjamin Franklin (1706-90)

Learning Objectives

After reading this chapter, you will be able to:

1. Explain the *process* of improvement and its role in operations strategy.
2. Identify different types of learning and their impact on improvement and innovation.
3. Apply the learning curve as a tool to predict aggregate cost dynamics.
4. Diagnose complexity and potential unforeseeable uncertainty in innovation projects and manage them by using sequential learning or parallel selectionism.
5. Connect operational improvements with customer valuations of competing products in order to predict whether an innovation is sustaining or disruptive.

In this chapter, we will view improvement and innovation as processes that build operational competencies. We will describe different types of learning and each one's role in improvement and innovation. Drastic improvements and innovation are often characterized by unforeseeable uncertainty; we will discuss two approaches to manage innovations. Last, we will analyze the role of operational improvements in innovation projects to characterize sustaining versus disruptive innovations.

10.1 | IMPROVEMENT AS A PROCESS

Change is the only constant. Customer expectations and preferences change, as do competitors' competencies and value propositions. Let us explain what that means for operations strategy.

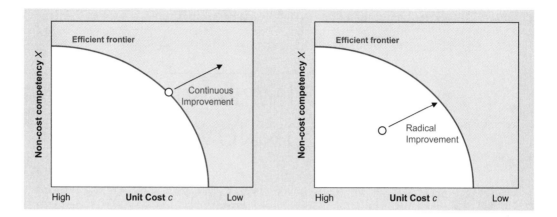

Figure 10.1 Depending on a firm's position relative to its rivals and the frontier, operations strategy can configure a continuous (left) or a radical (right) improvement process in line with the priorities defined by competitive strategy (the arrow).

The importance of improvement in operations strategy

A fundamental concern in operations strategy is how to stay ahead of rivals and how to adapt and align operational competencies to changing customer preferences. Recall from Chapter 1 that the task of competitive strategy is to define our customer value proposition by taking into account changing customer preferences. This value proposition defines the priority ranking of desired competencies such as cost, quality, responsiveness, and flexibility. The task of operations strategy is to develop resources and processes such that the resulting competencies are aligned with competitive strategy.

To understand how change relates to improvement, it is useful to adopt the competency view and the concept of the efficient frontier introduced in Chapter 2. In theory, we can then identify two improvement strategies, depending on our position relative to that of our rivals:

1. Our operation is world-class and our firm is at the efficient frontier (left panel in Fig. 10.1, which is more likely to happen if operations strategy has been deployed successfully). The challenge then is to stay ahead, which requires continuous improvement. During that process, we push the efficient frontier outward in the direction of the required competency priorities as defined by the value proposition.

2. We are not best-in-class and our firm's position is below the efficient frontier (right panel in Fig. 10.1). The task of operations strategy then is to quickly get to the frontier, again in the direction of required competency priorities, which may require radical change.

In practice, both modes of improvement are used. Continuous improvement is occasionally interspersed with radical change, which is often prompted by the arrival of new technologies or changes in the external environment. Let us discuss how these improvements are implemented in practice.

Radical improvement: reengineering

In operations, radical improvement typically involves a drastic restructuring of the operational system and of how work gets done. It often includes the adoption of different resources and processes. In the 1990s, information technology allowed radical change in operations. This led to the *reengineering* movement, which advocated the "fundamental rethinking and radical redesign of business processes in order to achieve dramatic improvements in critical contemporary measures of performance such as cost, quality, service and speed," according to its advocates Hammer and Champy (1993). The classic example of reengineering is the accounts payable process at Ford Motor Co. Ford eliminated invoices, instead basing payments on receipts of shipments. The result was a radically different, streamlined process.

In Chapter 1, we said that the *business process reengineering* paradigm of the early 1990s, which equates organizations with processes, has put operations on the agenda of top management at many organizations. Nowadays, many reengineering ideas and objectives have been merged with the process view and practices such as process streamlining and the elimination of non-value-added activities (both activities are part of lean operations, as we will soon see). Reengineering is now similar to quantum change restructuring, which is required to resolve the misalignment between strategy, operations, and customers. Dell's strategic operational audit (Chapter 1) provides a current example.

Continuous improvement as a process

Continuous improvement is the aggregate result of numerous small improvements in the way work gets done that people are constantly making throughout the organization. In his study of 1,435 companies, Collins (2001) describes traits of "good-to-great" companies (such as Walgreens, Kroger, and Gillette) that consistently follow a disciplined process of continuous improvement in core competencies. For example, Collins found that good-to-great companies don't use technology to ignite a transformation, but that they find new uses for widely-available technology. However, *the* unquestionably best example of a company that uses a process of continuous improvement to keep pushing the frontier is Toyota. What may be less understood is that the Toyota Production System (TPS) really has two simultaneous processes that are distinct but also interconnected: a production process to make a product, and an improvement process that makes the production process better. Our focus here is on the latter.

Continuous improvement through the elimination of waste is at the foundation of the Toyota Production System, where it is called *kaizen*, or "change for the better." (example 10.1 describes this in the words of the master himself, Taiichi Ohno.) It can be viewed (perhaps somewhat philosophically) as a process that constantly revisits the following steps (Fig. 10.2):

1. Compare the performance of the <u>actual</u> operation with that of the <u>ideal</u> operation (which is perfectly synchronized with demand at lowest cost). Any deviation Δ along any competency dimension (quality, responsiveness, flexibility, cost, etc.) is waste, variability, or inflexibility. A more positive interpretation of Δ is that it represents an opportunity for improvement.

> **Example 10.1** Continuous Improvement at Toyota
>
> According to Taiichi Ohno, the creator of the Toyota Production System, "the most important objective of the Toyota system has been to increase production efficiency by consistently and thoroughly eliminating waste. This concept and the equally important respect for humanity are the foundation of the Toyota production system."
> When asked "What is Toyota doing now?", Ohno (1988) gave a very simple answer:
>
> > "All we are doing is looking at the time line from the moment the customer gives us an order to the point when we collect the cash. And we are reducing that time line by removing the non-value-added wastes".
>
> Simple but brilliant. It shows the essence of continuous improvement.

2. Identifying waste in practice is not trivial yet essential for improvement to continue. Therefore, great emphasis is placed on making waste visible through orderly workplace organization and visual management that shares information at a glance and allows for quick responsive management. Visual information tools include information boards, signs, clearly indicated walkways and work spaces, and more. Visual controls such as lights ("andon" in TPS) and standard work sheets draw attention to any problems or deviations from the norm. Process measurement is continuous; from time to time, the system is stressed with new demands or challenges to identify waste (this raising of performance targets is similar to management by objectives). For example, if reducing the allowed inventory storage space has no impact on performance, it clearly removes waste. If performance suffers, then the next step is required:

3. Investigate the root cause of identified problems. This step is the hardest of the entire continuous improvement process as it relies on a positively-inclined human infrastructure that is willing and capable to eliminate those problems. It involves using the entire arsenal of good operations management techniques, including waste and variability reduction tools.

Continuous improvement: "lean" and waste reduction

Womack, Jones, and Roos (1990) introduced the term "lean" to describe the Toyota Production System. Nowadays, lean tools refer to the various techniques that aim to reduce waste from non-value-added activities. They aim to synchronize the operations with demand by establishing continuous flow processing (organizing in flow layout with work stations in close proximity, thus allowing transfer batch size reduction), pull control, quality at the source, and flexibility. Standardized operations allow waste identification and facilitate flexibility. (A more detailed discussion of lean implementations is beyond our scope in this book.)

An important element here is to eliminate non-value-added activities (where value is always defined from the customer perspective) through process streamlining. For example, when Target received too many customer complaints about defects in electric cables it sold, it worked with its supplier. There was an excess of cable inventory, which prevented operators from seeing where defects arose. The first step was to use lean tools to structure, clean, establish flow, and sort out

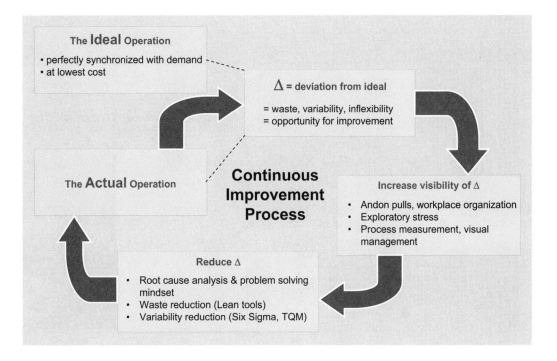

Figure 10.2 Here, continuous improvement is viewed as a process that constantly compares actual and ideal performance. It increases the visibility of this deviation so that the entire organization can reduce it.

waste. Once that was accomplished, the second step involved collecting data and reducing variability.

Continuous improvement: "Six Sigma" and variability reduction

Variability reduction improves performance because it reduces the fraction of output that is unacceptable to customers (Fig. 10.3). Variability can be reduced using various techniques such as statistical process control and robust product and process design (recall Example 5.2 at p. 158). Variability reduction has been popularized through the use of various programs, including total quality management (TQM) and Six Sigma.

Six Sigma was introduced by Motorola in 1986 as a new method of standardizing the way defects are counted (in response to increasing complaints from the field sales force about warranty claims). The word "Sigma" emphasizes variability by referring to the symbol σ, which represents the standard deviation of the process output. The number 6 emphasizes extremely small process variability that leads to less than 3.4 errors per million when the process output is normally distributed and critical customer requirements are 6σ away from the process mean.

Such low variability at the individual part or step is necessary in complex systems that have many parts or steps. Yet, the beauty of Six Sigma is that it allows a quick response, resulting in a robust operation that is resistant to un-

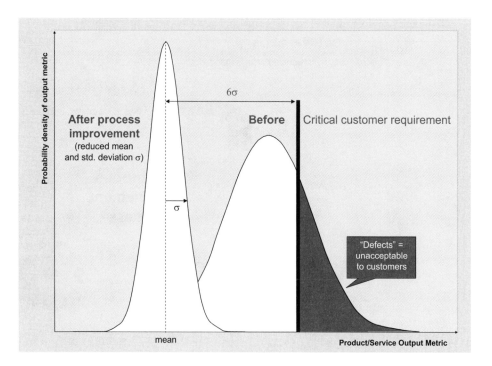

Figure 10.3 Process improvement through variability reduction reduces the fraction of output that is unacceptable to customers. Here the improved process capability is Six Sigma (critical customer requirements are 6σ away from the process mean).

avoidable unforeseen problems. To see this, assume that the process parameters would change (say the narrow distribution in Fig. 10.3 shifts to the right by one standard deviation; i.e. the process goes "out of control"). Statistical process control would then detect that change very quickly and root cause analysis would start to bring the process back in control. Meanwhile, the number of defects actually reaching customers remained extremely small (going from 6σ to 5σ would still keep errors below $2/10,000$).

The Six Sigma problem-solving framework and work-breakdown structure can be easily remembered using the acronym DMAIC:

- Define the problem to determine what needs to be improved.

- Measure the current state against the desired state.

- Analyze the root causes of the business gap.

- Improve by team brainstorming, selecting, and implementing the best solutions.

- Control the long-term sustainability of the improvement by establishing monitoring mechanisms, accountabilities, and work tools.

> **Example 10.2** Six Sigma Plus at Honeywell
>
> Honeywell has taken its continuous process improvement methods to a new level. As its overall strategy, Six Sigma Plus combines all the improvement tools it has developed over the years. Six Sigma is Honeywell's principal engine for driving growth and productivity across all its businesses and functions, from design and engineering to manufacturing, and from sales and marketing to supply management.
>
> Honeywell has realized billions in cumulative savings from Six Sigma-related activities by relentlessly focusing on eliminating waste and reducing defects and variation. Six Sigma methodology (Define, Measure, Analyze, Improve, and Control) is applied to a wide variety of projects, not only to the elimination of variation in processes.
>
> Honeywell's Six Sigma Plus skill sets include Lean Enterprise, Activity Based Management, Honeywell Quality Value Assessment, Total Productive Maintenance and Growth projects, among others. (Honeywell 2007)

General Electric and Honeywell successfully applied and popularized Motorola's Six Sigma methodology as part of leadership development, going far beyond counting defects. GE turned Six Sigma into an overall high-performance system that executes business strategy using four steps:

1. Align executives to the right objectives and targets using a balanced scorecard (recall Chapter 1).

2. Mobilize improvement teams using DMAIC.

3. Accelerate results by using action learning and by integrating all teams so that the cumulative impact on the organization is "accelerated."

4. Govern the process through visible executive sponsorship, review, and sharing best practices with other parts of the organization.

Nowadays, the lean and Six Sigma improvement paradigms are combined into "Lean Six Sigma" or "Six Sigma Plus" paradigms (Exhibit 10.2).

10.2 | LEARNING AND IMPROVEMENT

Learning and problem solving are often at the core of improvement processes, as demonstrated by their role in lean operations and Six Sigma. Let us discuss various types of learning and their relationship to improvement.

Operational Learning vs. Conceptual Learning

The organizational learning literature breaks down the learning process into two activities, conceptual learning and operational learning. *Conceptual learning* tries to understand why an event occurs by assessing cause-and-effect relationships and designing a theory to explain the event, similar to the scientific method. In contrast, *operational learning* is experience based; it is done by actually working through problems, implementing solutions, and observing the results.

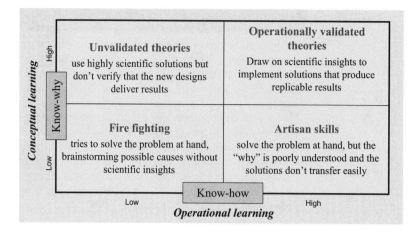

Figure 10.4 Only improvement projects based on operationally validated theories deliver a positive bottom-line impact (Lapré and Van Wassenhove 2002).

To achieve true organizational learning with measurable bottom-line results, improvement projects must combine both modes of learning. They must promote a better understanding of why a solution works and they must know how to implement the solution. The importance of combining both learning modes was demonstrated by a study of more than 100 improvement projects at the Belgian manufacturer Bekaert, the world's largest independent producer of steel wire. Lapré and Van Wassenhove (2002) found that only 25% of Bekaert's improvement projects actually delivered factory-wide improvements, meaning that the total productivity of the plant or the organization improved. In contrast, 50% of the projects had no impact while, surprisingly, 25% actually had a negative impact. The researchers found that successful projects shared two characteristics: "they produced process knowledge that was well understood and broadly relevant, and the knowledge was transferred to other parts of the factory—an outcome that's by no means automatic."

Lapré and Van Wassenhove (2002) measured the relative amount of operational and conceptual learning of each project, and mapped all the projects onto a matrix like the one shown in Figure 10.4. The purpose behind such a categorization is to determine whether a recently developed improvement can be generalized and applied to different settings at other places. If you can't explain why you are doing something, that action must necessarily be restricted to localized efforts and cannot have company-wide impact. If you don't know how to replicate the results, a similar outcome occurs.

In summary, to drive company-wide improvements, one needs operationally-validated theories. There is good science explaining why a certain approach solves a problem; the implementation of that approach has been validated in a real-life operational setting. This is exactly how Toyota manages its improvement process:

"We found that, for outsiders, the key is to understand that the

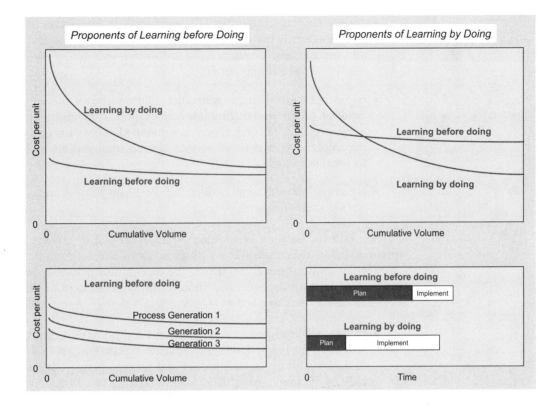

Figure 10.5 The different beliefs about cost per unit and total project time by proponents of learning before doing (left displays) and proponents of learning by doing (right).

Toyota Production System creates a community of scientists. Whenever Toyota defines a specification, it is establishing sets of hypotheses that can then be tested. In other words, it is following the scientific method. To make any changes, Toyota uses a rigorous problem-solving process that requires a detailed assessment of the current state of affairs and a plan for improvement that is, in effect, an experimental test of the proposed changes. With anything less than such scientific rigor, change at Toyota would amount to little more than random trial and error—a blindfolded walk through life" (Spear and Bowen 1999, p. 98).

Learning by doing vs. Learning before doing

The adage that "practice makes perfect" advocates learning by doing, which refers to the capability of people to improve by repeating the same activity. Along with restricting the scope or complexity of the task, learning by doing explains the productivity improvements when following Adam Smith's dictum to divide and specialize labor.

Proponents may argue that learning by doing, among others:

- "unleashes" the creativity of the workforce and its power to improve. This idea hinges on the belief that those who execute the task know it best and are the best problem solvers (leading eventually to a lower cost in Fig. 10.5's upper right panel).

- encourages a dynamic organization that minimizes planning time and focuses on adaptation during implementation. This hinges on the belief that not everything can be foreseen and planned, so one may as well learn during implementation (leading to a shorter total project time in Fig. 10.5's lower right panel).

- is compatible with a continuous improvement process and essential to Toyota's system of *kaizen*.

In contrast, learning before doing advocates that improvements should be planned before execution starts. It uses analysis, virtual prototyping, role play, simulation and optimization during the design and planning of products and processes. Afterwards, execution should simply implement the plan.

Proponents may argue that learning before doing, among others,

- "unleashes" the power of science and technology to improve. This idea hinges on the belief that highly educated specialists are in the best position to design and optimize product and process plans, which determine the bulk of the total cost (always leading always to a lower cost in Fig. 10.5's upper left panel).

- encourages a safe and efficient organization that promotes knowledge sharing and ensures that complex processes will work. This idea hinges on the beliefs that (i) people can learn from their peers' experiences, insights, and knowledge and prevent themselves from repeating mistakes (a key reason behind BP's "peer assist" process); (ii) complex processes such as developing a new airplane or global supplier network must be planned and controlled (learning by doing would be cost-prohibitive and dangerous).

- is compatible with step change and even drastic improvement (in between successive projects or generations in Fig. 10.5's lower left panel).

In practice, different situations require different types of learning, and both can be combined as we will see later. Let us first describe a tool that is useful in settings of learning by doing and continuous improvement.

10.3 | THE LEARNING CURVE

People engaged in repetitive tasks learn by doing. If data of this phenomenon is gathered, a learning curve is found, which is useful in predicting capacity requirements, costs, and profitability. Let us discuss this concept and its application.

Year	Bits/die	Line width (micron)	Cost (milli-cents/bit)	Cumulative bits sold
1974	4.1E+03	6	8.02	2.00E+12
1977	1.6E+04	3.5	2.89	3.00E+13
1980	6.6E+04	2.3	1.37	3.00E+14
1983	2.6E+05	1.3	0.395	2.00E+15
1986	1.1E+06	1	0.196	1.00E+16
1989	4.2E+06	0.8	0.105	5.00E+16
1992	1.7E+07	0.5	0.038	2.70E+17
1995	6.7E+07	0.35	0.019	1.25E+18
1998	2.7E+08	0.25	0.01	6.25E+18

Table 10.1 Industry data on transistor density, cost, and cumulative production (Schmidt and Wood 1999).

The learning curve concept

The *learning curve* shows how learning by doing translates into "improvement." In its strictest interpretation, it depicts the relationship between direct labor hours per unit and the cumulative number of units produced. A broader cost formulation known as the *experience curve* (which was used in the top panels of Fig. 10.5) relates the average value-added cost per unit to cumulative units. Thus, experience is measured by the cumulative number of units produced, while improvement is measured by the direct labor hours or the marginal cost.

An example: the learning curve and Moore's law

To illustrate the learning curve, let us start with an example from the semiconductor industry (which will also allow us to say something about Moore's law). Table 10.1 shows industry data since 1974 on the transistor density of chips, which is expressed as "bits/die" (a bit corresponds to one transistor switch and a die to the piece of silicon that holds the transistor). The table also shows the cost per bit as well as the cumulative production of bits.

The cost formulation of the learning curve plots the cost per bit as a function of cumulative production. It typically starts out high and decreases at a decreasing rate as shown in the top panels of Fig. 10.5. The magnitudes of the data in Table 10.1, however, define such a large range that the plot is best shown in log-log scale (Figure 10.6).

A striking observation to be made is that the data pretty much defines a linear relationship, with a slope that is visually (if you want to be more precise you can run a least squares regression) estimated as:

$$\lambda = \text{slope} = \frac{1 - (-2)}{19 - 12} = \frac{3}{7} = 0.43.$$

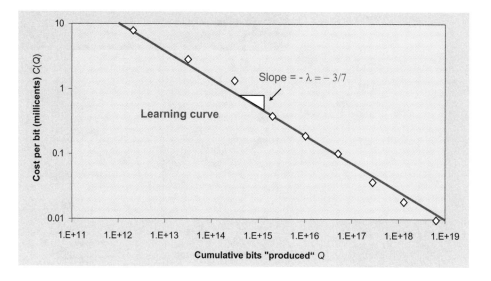

Figure 10.6 The learning curve for the semiconductor industry is the best linear fit to historical data in log-log scale.

Mathematical representation of the learning curve and learning rate

It has been observed in many industries that the learning curve is approximately linear on a log-log scale. Let us investigate what that means. At the same time, we will turn the learning curve into a useful tool by representing it mathematically.

Let Q denote the cumulative units produced, and let C_Q denote the marginal value-added cost of the Q-th unit. The learning curve then is the (least squares minimizing) linear fit to historical (Q, C)-data:

Learning curve (log-log) $\quad : \quad \log C_Q = \log C_1 - \lambda \log Q$

$$\Rightarrow \quad C_Q = C_1 \times Q^{-\lambda}, \tag{10.1}$$

where C_1 is the marginal cost of the first unit and λ is the slope measured on a log-log scale.

To understand the practical meaning of the slope λ, consider what happens to cost when volume doubles. Compare the marginal cost of the $2Q$-th unit with that of the Q-th unit using equation (10.1):

$$C_{2Q} = C_1 \left(2Q\right)^{-\lambda} = 2^{-\lambda} C_1 Q^{-\lambda} = 2^{-\lambda} C_Q.$$

In other words, the percentage cost reduction from doubling the cumulative volume is constant and is called[1]:

Learning rate $L = 1 - 2^{-\lambda}$.

---

[1]It is standard in the literature to define $2^{-\lambda}$ as the learning rate, which leads to statements like "a flat learning curve has a 100% learning rate," even though there is no improvement. Our definition is more intuitive.

Thus, the fact that the learning curve is approximately linear in log-log scale means that labor hours or cost per unit are reduced by a certain percentage whenever cumulative volume doubles. Thus, the learning rate of a process is a fraction; i.e., $0 \leq L \leq 1$. And if, say $L = .3$, we say that we have a "30% learning curve." A higher learning rate means that we are "better" in translating experience into improvement.

In 1977, Intel cofounder Robert Noyce said:

> "Between 1960 and 1977 annual usage of transistors has increased by 2000 times, or has doubled 11 times, in the past 17 years. This stunning increase promotes continual cost reductions of 28% for each doubling of volume" (Noyce 1977).

Returning to our semiconductor example, the associated learning rate there is

$$L = 1 - 2^{-3/7} = 26\%,$$

which means that Noyce's observation pretty much applied until at least 1998!

The applications and limitations of the learning curve

While the mathematical representation of the learning curve is very precisely defined, its rigor is rather illusionary. In fact, the learning curve is not a scientific theory in the sense that it is not grounded in physical or economic laws. Rather, it is a purely empirical observation of the continuous improvement results from learning by doing. While there are various ways of learning and improvement, the learning curve assumes that one must produce to learn and that repetition breeds competence.

Even so, the learning curve can be a useful tool in practice. In a certain sense, the key insight gained from the learning curve is that learning by doing is "predictable." This means that we can predict future costs with reasonable accuracy. Industry-specific, historic estimates of learning rates are well documented. This predictive power makes learning models especially useful during capacity planning, timing, and budgeting, when designing realistic cost reduction programs, and for checking whether the implementation of new processes is "on track" or not.

For example, Procter & Gamble is an avid user of the learning curve. The company keeps vast records of historic yield data when it starts up new filling dispensing lines (a typical P&G plant has about 10 such lines, each costing about $2 million). When starting up a new line, managers keep close track of yields to see whether the implementation is "on track." Assume, for example, that the target yield of a line is 98%, but that the yield is only 60% three weeks after start-up. Should we worry? The learning curve then allows managers to estimate how long it will take to reach 98% yield by usual learning by doing. Exceptional action is needed only if that time is judged too long.

To fully understand the learning curve, we will relate it to economies of scale and productivity growth in the remainder of this section.

The learning curve vs. economies of scale

The learning curve implies that the marginal cost per unit decreases with the *cumulative volume produced*. In contrast, economies of scale means that the average

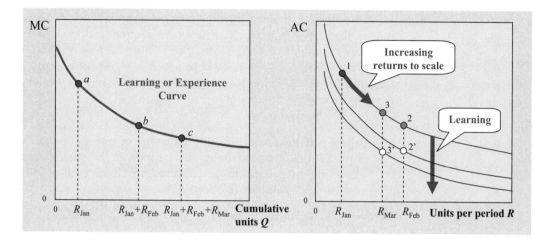

Figure 10.7 The learning curve implies that marginal cost decreases with cumulative production (left). Economies of scale implies that average cost decreases with volume per period, or throughput (right).

cost per unit (AC) decreases with increasing *volume per period*, or *throughput rate* (p. 82 in Chapter 3).

To understand the difference, consider the following example of a process that exhibits economies of scale. Assume that January production is less than February production, and that March production falls in between. Denoting monthly production volumes or throughput by R_i for month i, we have: $R_{Jan} < R_{Mar} < R_{Feb}$. Economies of scale then imply that the average unit cost in February is less than that in March, which is less than that in January, as illustrated by points 1, 2 and 3 in the right-hand panel of Figure 10.7. Think of spreading the *fixed costs accrued over a period* over more units as a driver of economies of scale. Consequently, if we produce the same volume each period with a process that enjoys economies of scale, the average cost will be constant each period, as will the marginal cost of the last unit produced each period.

In contrast, if the process enjoys learning, the learning curve predicts that the marginal cost of the last unit produced each period will decline over time. The driver behind learning economies is continuous improvement resulting from learning by doing. This implies that the required inputs and resources per unit decrease with cumulative volume $Q_t = \sum_{i \leq t} R_i$, leading to a decrease in marginal cost. In our example, the marginal cost will decrease from January to February to March, as shown by points a, b and c in the left-hand panel of Figure 10.7, where each point represents the marginal cost of the last unit produced that month. Given that production in February is larger than production in March, the cost decrease from a to b will be larger than that from b to c.

In summary, to decrease average cost during a period with economies of scale, one must increase production during that period. With learning economies, one can reduce marginal cost by continuing producing over time, leading to a downward shifting of the average cost curve over time. If we combine economies of scale with learning in our example, we can think of learning as driving down the average-cost curve from month to month (although the effect is really continuous over time), leading to average cost $2'$ in February and $3'$ in March, as shown in Figure 10.7.

The learning curve vs. productivity growth

Recall from Chapter 2 that labor productivity measures the average direct labor hours per unit during a given length of time (e.g., one year). Productivity growth then compares productivity of last year with that of this year. Thus, traditional models of productivity improvement assume that labor hours, or more broadly unit costs, can be reduced by a predictable percentage over a given length of time (e.g., one year). In contrast, the learning curve assumes that costs are reduced by a predictable percentage when cumulative production is doubled.

The relationship between the rate of productivity improvement and the learning rate depends on the time it takes to double cumulative production. To see this, consider a company that doubles cumulative production in only one year and has a learning rate of $L = 20\%$. Then, the unit cost of the last item produced this year is only 80% of the unit cost of the last item produced last year. In other words, productivity growth would also be 20%. In contrast, if cumulative production only increases by 50% during the year, the marginal cost has decreased, or productivity has grown, by about 12.2%, which is only a little higher than half the learning rate.[2]

Thus, the greater the production (or sales) growth rate, the faster cumulative production grows during a given time period. Higher cumulative production brings us down the learning curve faster, yielding lower costs faster if the learning rate is higher. Put another way, productivity growth is driven by the compounded effect of the production growth rate and the learning rate.

Constant production growth yields "exponentially fast" learning

Science often predicts that many physical and societal processes follow "exponential" dynamics, meaning that these processes have a constant growth rate in *each time period*. Accordingly, we say that learning is *exponentially fast* if the cost per unit decreases at a constant rate per unit of time. Given that the learning curve assumes a constant cost savings rate each time production doubles, exponentially fast learning requires a constant production (and thus sales) growth rate over time. The effect then is that we move down the learning curve by a fixed amount *each year*.

Exponential learning is highly desirable, but a constant sales growth is rarely sustainable in business. For example, to gain a constant cost decrease of $L\%$ each year, we must double production each year. For U.S. auto sales, which are about 15 to 17 million per year, this would require annual sales to grow as 32, 64, 128, 248, ... This would mean that four years from now, every U.S. citizen would buy a new car that year, two the year after, and so on. Doubling sales each year also means that each year's production must equal the total cumulative production of that product during all preceding years!

There are, however, some special industries that, quite miraculously, are en-

---

[2]The learning curve yields that $C_{1.5Q} = C_1 \cdot (1.5Q)^{-\lambda}$ and that the slope $\lambda = -\log(1 - L)/\log 2 = .322$. Thus, the cost when increasing cumulative production by 50% is $C_{1.5Q} = C_Q \cdot (1.5)^{-.322} = 0.877 C_Q$.

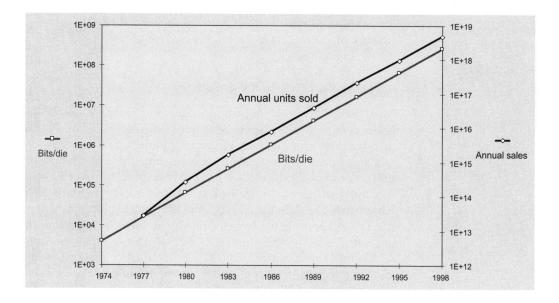

Figure 10.8 Constant sales growth yields exponentially fast learning in the semiconductor industry and is manifested by Moore's law.

joying exponential learning: the semiconductor industry and the disk drive industry are two examples. Exponential learning may perhaps be observed in the case of products that enjoy "network economies," such as cell phones, although network effects typically taper off quickly as the product adoption reaches saturation.

A famous example of exponentially fast learning is given by Moore's law, which addresses the growth rate of the transistor density or "bits" on a chip: "Gordon Moore was the first in 1964 to predict the future progress of the IC. He suggested that its complexity would continue to double every year" (Noyce 1977). By the 1980s, Moore's law had been revised to a doubling every 18 months (Schmidt and Wood 1999). Figure 10.8 plots the data from Table 10.1 and suggests that this exponentially fast learning has continued until at least 1997. Analytics Box 10.1 confirms that the doubling time has remained 18 months.

10.4 | INNOVATION AND UNFORESEEABLE UNCERTAINTY

Until now we have analyzed improvement. From here on, let us turn our attention to innovation.

Analytics Box 10.1 Moore's law and exponentially fast learning.

Figure 10.8 plots both the transistor density (bits/die) and yearly production data from Table 10.1. Instead of plotting cost versus cumulative production in a log-log scale as is required for the "traditional" learning curve, exponential learning plots the metric (here the transistor density or annual production) in year t, denoted by $n(t)$, versus time in a log-linear scale. In that scale, both metrics lie on a line so that the annual growth rates of both transistor density and annual production are constant. Together with the learning (recall that we estimated a 26% learning rate for the cost per transistor), this implies that transistor production has enjoyed exponentially fast learning.

We can compute how long it takes for transistor density to double as follows. Exponential learning estimates a linear fit, given as:

$$\log n(t) = a + bt.$$

The "doubling time" Δt follows from

$$\log 2n - \log n = (a + b(t + \Delta t)) - (a + bt) = b\Delta t.$$

Recalling that $\log 2n - \log n = \log 2$, we conclude that the

$$\text{doubling time } \Delta t = \frac{\log 2}{b}.$$

The slope b can be visually estimated for both metrics

$$b_{\text{density}} = \frac{9 - 4}{1998 - 1974} = 0.21 \text{ and } b_{\text{production}} = \frac{19 - 13}{1998 - 1974} = .25$$

which gives a doubling time for transistor density of 1.43 years (17.2 months) and of 1.20 years (14.4 months) for production.

Improvement vs. innovation

Improvement means making something better, while innovation is about creating something new. In theory, this distinction sounds simple enough. Yet in practice, improvement and innovation are closely related because both are processes that result in change; their difference is in the implied extent of the change. Innovation is traditionally understood as a significant or radical change. However, some companies innovate through incremental changes that may or may not accumulate to a radical change.

From an operations perspective, the distinction between improvement and innovation is relative to the time scale on which change occurs. This directly implies that learning is related to both improvement and innovation (and we will soon see how the interaction between the two can determine the impact of innovation on industry structure).

Let us leave the philosophical discourse behind now. An extensive discussion of innovation management is also outside the scope of this text. Rather, we will focus on how operations and improvement can impact innovation, and what new techniques are needed to deal with innovation.

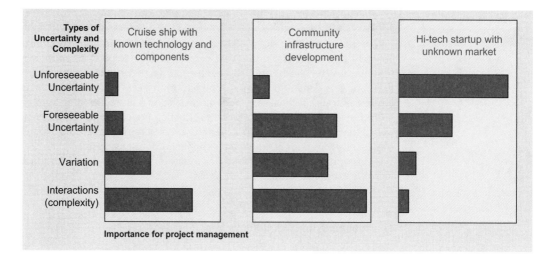

Figure 10.9 The presence and importance of different types of uncertainty and complexity in managing improvement and innovation projects depends on the nature of the project (Loch, DeMeyer, and Pich 2006).

Innovations embody unforeseeable uncertainty and unknown unknowns ("unk unks")

Throughout the book, we have analyzed how operations can deal with complexity, variability, and uncertainty. But thus far, we have assumed that variability and uncertainty was foreseeable, meaning that we knew the relevant random variables, their probability distributions, and their interaction and evolution over time. Mathematically, we could represent the future in a decision tree with known probabilities in order to plan and configure the operational system using real options and dynamic contingent optimization. Using this so-called "planning approach," we learned, for example, how to value flexibility and risk management, and how to size safety capacity, inventory, and time. The importance and extent of complexity, variation, and foreseeable uncertainty depends on the nature of the project (Fig. 10.9).

When managing radical change, however, one must acknowledge that there may be unknown unkowns ("unk unks"), variables that the manager is not aware of. Unforeseeable uncertainty is intrinsic to new product development, to problem solving in engineering projects, to implementing new manufacturing or information technology, and to venture startups. Indeed, new ventures can seldom foresee all market and technology uncertainty, as illustrated by a classic quotation:

"When a new venture does succeed, more often than not it is in a market other than the one it was originally intended to serve, with products and services not quite those with which it had set out, bought in large part by customers it did not even think of when it started, and used for a host of purposes besides the ones for which the products were first designed" (Drucker 1985, p. 189).

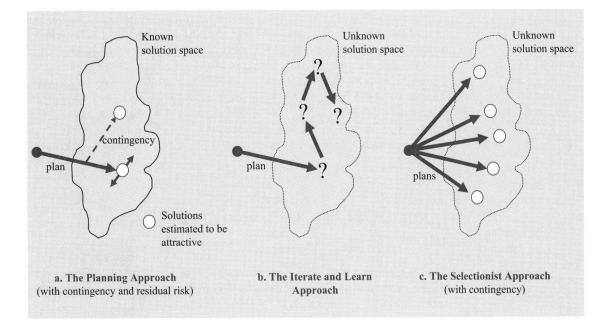

Figure 10.10 The three fundamental approaches to manage under uncertainty. The planning approach manages foreseeable uncertainty and complexity. Unforeseeable uncertainty inherent in innovation requires a learning or a selectionist approach (Loch, DeMeyer, and Pich 2006) .

Approaches to manage unk unks

In their book *Managing the Unknown*, Loch, DeMeyer, and Pich (2006) identify three fundamental approaches to managing uncertainty (10.10). The planning approach (which was used throughout this book) manages foreseeable uncertainty (defined over a "known solution space") and complexity through contingency planning (we can interpret this approach as one form of learning before doing). However, the unforeseeable uncertainty that is inherent in innovation makes it impossible to plan all contingencies. Managing unforeseeable uncertainty therefore requires a trial-and-error form of learning or a selectionist approach. (Pich, Loch, and DeMeyer 2002) show that these are the only two approaches that are conceptually available to manage unk unks.

While trial-and-error learning is related to learning by doing, it emphasizes "actively searching for new information and flexibly adjusting activities and targets to this new information, applying new and original problem solving (not only triggering pre-set contingency plans) as new information becomes available. It has characterized the development of many breakthrough technologies such as Motorola's pager, Corning's fiber optics, Apple and HP's personal digital assistants, and Sun's Java" (Sommer, Loch, and Dong 2007).

The selectionist approach tests several plans in parallel and selects the one that works best ex-post. In Chapter 9, we interpreted pursuing multiple paths in parallel as managing risk through flexibility and redundancy. We described how Toyota develops new products by producing numerous prototypes, several of them in parallel, then picking a winner as close to market introduction as possible. This is an effective method if market preferences have unforeseeable uncertainty. Similarly, pharmaceutical companies start the search for new drugs by initially conducting many molecule discovery projects in parallel (but narrow down closer towards drug trials and commercialization). Selectionism is constantly conducted by free market economies (the market chooses which approach or firm is most successful) and venture capitalists (who fund many startup projects, a few of which may hit it big, while most will get killed).

10.5 | MANAGING UNK UNKS AND COMPLEXITY IN INNOVATION

It is helpful to know that innovation projects have unforeseeable uncertainty (unknown unknowns or unk unks) and complexity, but how can operations help in managing these unk unks? Which approach (planning, learning, or parallel selectionism) will offer better outcomes? In this section we will summarize the state-of-the art research and advice by Loch, DeMeyer, and Pich (2006).

A diagnosis process for uncertainty and complexity

When starting an innovation project, it is helpful to diagnose uncertainty and complexity at the outset. Such a diagnosis process can follow five steps:

1. Start by identifying the goal of the project. Who are the stakeholders that may influence the outcome of the project? Do we have some understanding of the causality of actions and effects in the project?

2. Then, break the overall project into pieces (divide and conquer!). What are the key subprojects or modules? Who are their major players and stakeholders?

3. Perform risk management for each piece. Adopt the risk management process described in Chapter 9: identify potential hazards and assess the risk associated with each one. Develop tactical contingency plans for each major risk (i.e., use the planning approach shown in Fig. 10.10).

   Also, identify any knowledge gaps by probing assumptions and asking what you know and what you don't know. While unk unks cannot be foreseen by definition, this step can identify areas of potential unk unks through a highly iterative and gradual process.

4. Estimate the complexity of each piece, and of the overall project. As we saw in Chapter 5 (p. 163), complexity can be estimated by using design structure matrices for the system domain (where components interact), the task domain (where project activities interact), and the organizational domain (where teams and stakeholders interact). This analysis highlights the interaction between different project pieces and suggests which pieces can be pursued independently or sequentially, and which ones require an integrated approach.

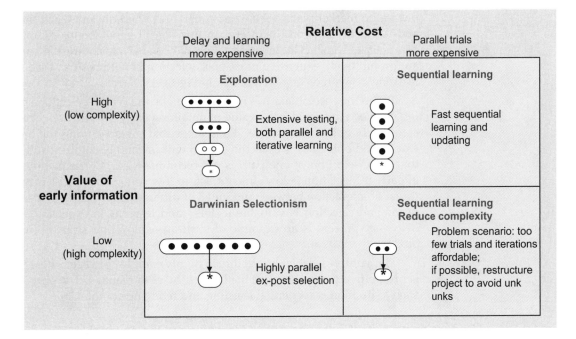

Figure 10.11 Innovation projects with significant unforeseeable uncertainty can use a tailored management approach that depends on their relative cost and the value of obtaining information early (adapted from Loch, DeMeyer, and Pich 2006).

5. Finally, manage each piece by using a tailored approach of contingency planning, learning by doing, and parallel selectionism, a topic worthy of its own section.

Using a tailored combination of planning, learning, and selectionism

Depending on the uncertainty and complexity of each piece of the innovation project (piece), a different management approach may be most appropriate. In other words, the different approaches can and should be combined, and used not for whole projects, but mixed and matched for *pieces* of the project.

In general, projects with foreseeable uncertainty can be well managed by traditional risk management (the contingency planning approach). Pre-specifying the best path to reach good outcomes is exceedingly difficult for highly complex subprojects so that pursuing different paths in parallel can be beneficial.

Subprojects that are threatened by complexity and unk unks require a combination of selectionism and flexible iteration and learning. The appropriate combination depends on the project-specific cost and the benefits of each approach (Figure 10.11).

Clearly, highly parallel ex-post selection is appropriate when it is expensive to delay the project and the cost of running parallel trials is low. For example, the successful credit card company Capital One uses such 'Darwinian selectionism' (lower left box in Fig. 10.11). "It rapidly develops many new ideas, tries them out in the market place, sees what works and what doesn't, back the winners, and ruthlessly kills off the losers. In this way, it generates more 'hits' than its competitors" (Loch, DeMeyer, and Pich 2006, p. 147). In contrast, if parallel trials are prohibitively expensive or ex-post selection is not possible, then sequential learning is favored (upper right box in Fig. 10.11).

When the cost situation is not so obviously in favor of selectionism or learning, we need to consider the value of obtaining early information. This is where complexity enters the picture. Remember that pre-specifying the best path to reach good outcomes is exceedingly difficult for highly complex subprojects so that early selection of one path is not recommended. Consequently, the value of early information is low. In contrast, in low complexity projects there is less threat of interaction between unk unks in different modules so that early exploration and selection is valuable if delay and learning is expensive. The drug discovery process is an example of such an exploration strategy (upper right box).

High unforeseeable uncertainty in highly complex projects where parallelism is prohibitively expensive are the hardest cases to manage. The only solution in such a situation is sequential learning and reducing complexity.

Reduce complexity if selectionism and learning are too expensive

Developing a new airplane can be a daunting project. Parallel trials typically are not affordable and time delays due to learning are very expensive. The development of the supersonic Concorde plan in the 1960s entered novel technological terrain with many technical unk unks. Parallel trials were not an option. The result was a schedule slippage by four years due to testing needs, and a budget overrun of an initial estimate of £135 million to £1.1 billion.

The development of the Boeing 777 provides an example of the value of reducing complexity in such environment. Boeing developed the 777 in response to the Airbus 340; development time and costs were kept low by using previously proven technology components (Loch, DeMeyer, and Pich 2006).

Another effective way of reducing complexity is to reduce the level of interactions between subprojects. As discussed in Chapter 5, the reduced complexity of modular designs allows for fast parallel design and updating, and disintegration of the value chain; re-using modules reduces cost while increasing reliability.

Remember, however, that adding more people to a project (even if it is late) may actually worsen the outcome because the added burden of communication increases complexity.[3] This idea is known as Brook's law in software development. Brooks (1995, p. 17) provides a memorable analogy in *The Mythical Man-Month*: "When a task cannot be partitioned because of sequential constraints, the application of more effort has no effect. The bearing of a child takes nine months, no matter how many women are assigned."

---

[3]When n people must communicate, the number of communications is of the order $n(n-1)$. When n grows, the associated complexity cost may quickly outweigh the benefits.

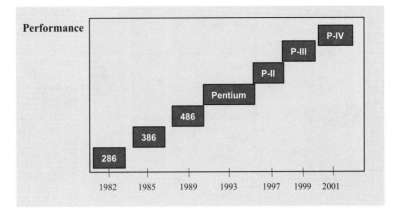

Figure 10.12 Intel followed a high-end encroachment strategy by innovating on the high-end.

10.6 | INNOVATION, IMPROVEMENT, AND ENCROACHMENT

Let us now connect improvement and innovation in order to investigate how an innovator can benefit from operational improvements such as improved functionality and decreased cost. In this section, we will consider the setting of a firm that innovates its own product offering, whereas the next section discusses how an innovator can compete against an incumbent.

High-end versus low-end encroachment: examples from Intel

Intel has continually upgraded its product offering of microprocessors, from the 286 model in 1982 to the Pentium IV in 2001 (Figure 10.12). Historically, Intel's newest products have been high-end innovations that supersede the previous models in terms of performance (processing power). The new models were priced at a high level, and initially sold to the "best" customers, where the best customers are defined as those who are willing to pay the most for this type of product. Schmidt and Wood (1999) call this a *high-end encroachment* strategy because the new product encroaches on the existing market from the high end. That is, the new product is bought by high-end customers at a high price.

High-end encroachment entails some risks, however. It moves the company's brand into higher performance regions, thereby exposing itself to low-end competition. Meanwhile, some of its customers may postpone purchasing as they have become accustomed to later price drops.

Perhaps in light of these risks, Intel modified its strategy when introducing the Celeron microprocessor in the late 1990s. The Celeron did not supersede the current model in terms of performance, but rather sold to lower-end customers who wanted sub-$1000 computers. In other words, it encroached on the low-end of the market, a strategy referred to as *low-end encroachment*.

To understand the impact of continuous improvement on high-end and low-

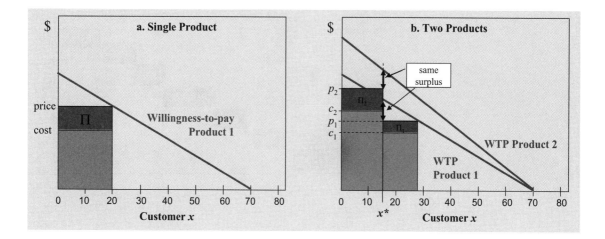

Figure 10.13 With a single product (left panel), the willingness-to-pay curve equals the demand curve. With two products (right panel), customers choose the product that gives them the highest surplus. Customers to the left of the indifferent customer x^* buy product 2, and the others buy product 1 as long as their surplus is positive.

end encroachment, let us build a model that links innovation and learning to product positioning and customer valuation.

A Monopoly Model of Encroachment

A customer's valuation of a product is traditionally described by her willingness-to-pay or *reservation price*, which is the maximal price she is willing to pay for the product. Ranking customers in decreasing willingness-to-pay and depicting their reservation prices then yields a reservation price curve, as shown in Figure 10.13 on the left.

When customers are offered one product only (as in the left panel of Figure 10.13), the reservation price curve equals the demand curve for that product: all customers with valuations above the price will buy the product. The intersection of the price and the demand curve directly yields the sales volume (on the x-axis). The highlighted rectangles represent the profit Π, and the cost.

In contrast, when customers have a choice between two products (right panel of Figure 10.13), the two reservation price curves do not equal the demand curves for each product. Rather, customers will choose the product that gives them highest surplus (the difference between their willingness-to-pay and the price of the product). Clearly, the sales of product 1 depend not only on its price, but also on the price of the other product. The market split between the two products and their profitability is determined by the customer x^* who derives the same surplus from either product and thus is indifferent between them.[4] The firm can

---

[4]Depending on the relative slope of the reservation price curves, the customers to the left of the indifferent customers buy one product while the customers to the right buy the other. In the right panel of Figure 10.13, the reservation price curve of product 2 is steeper than that of product 1, so that the customers to the left of x^* buy product 2.

now set optimal prices by optimizing its total profit.

Over time, the firm will reduce its cost through continuous improvement (as predicted by the learning curve) while perhaps at the same time increase the functionality of the product. This may translate into higher reservation curves if customers value the increased functionality. By using the learning curve to predict costs and by forecasting reservation price curves, the firm can use the model at each point in time and thus anticipate changes in its optimal prices, and resulting sales and profitability.

The impact of continuous improvement on encroachment (monopoly)

In the example of Figure 10.13 (right panel), product 2 is valued higher by every customer because its reservation price curve is above that of product 1. If product 2 is the new product, it is called a *superior innovation*; otherwise, product 1 is called an *inferior innovation*. In addition, if its reservation price curve is steeper than that of the "old" product, then the customers with highest willingness-to-pay will buy it and the superior innovation will encroach on the high-end.

Over time, continuous improvement will reduce costs. An interesting insight to be gained from the learning curve, however, is that the relative cost decrease is highest at product introduction, later tapering off. It is much easier for a new product to double cumulative production. Thus, the cost of the new product will decrease faster than that of the old product. As a result, the new product will gradually take over the market and supersede the old product (similar to the effects of Intel's high-encroachment strategy).

10.7 | INNOVATION, IMPROVEMENT, AND COMPETITION

While nothing prevents a monopolist from positioning its new product below the old one and encroaching from below, they rarely do so in practice *unless* competition looms. Indeed, low-end encroachment is a fairly common strategy by an entrant who introduces a new product to compete with the incumbent's entrenched product. In this section, we will broaden our discussion to include the role of competition in improvement and innovation.

Competing through low-encroachment innovation: the disk drive industry

The hard disk drive industry provides a classic example of low-end encroachment. Unlike the microprocessor market, where Intel has sustained a market leadership position from generation to generation, the disk drive market created a new market leader with each generation. Between 1975 and 1990, the computer hard disk drive industry underwent a transition from a standard product size of 14 inches, to 8 inches, to 5.25 inches, and subsequently to even smaller "form factors" as shown in Figure 10.14. (Recall from Example 3.1 that Apple's iPod-Mini uses a cutting-edge 1-inch drive.) Unlike Intel's constant leadership in the microprocessor market, each generation in the disk drive industry had a new market leader. Watching the market shifts was like observing a game of mu-

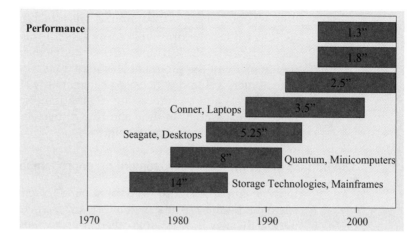

Figure 10.14 The disk drive market had a new leader for every generation.

sical chairs (indeed, players have been driven out of the industry over time): the leader switched from Storage Technologies, to Quantum, to Seagate, to Conner Peripherals, respectively.

The vertical axis in Figure 10.14 implies that disk drive performance grew over time as smaller and smaller drives were developed. Yet, that oversimplifies the fact that performance is not so readily expressed along one dimension. Previous buyers measured performance primarily based on storage capacity (a new smaller drive initially had less capacity than its predecessor, but grew over time), while initial buyers of a new smaller drive measured performance based more on physical size.

Competitive Model of Innovation

To understand encroachment innovation strategies in a competitive setting, we must extend our model in two directions:

1. A customer's valuation of a product can depend on multiple attributes. To explain the dynamics of the disk drive industry, we must have at least two attributes: one valued by the original main market (storage capacity) and another not valued by the main market (such as physical size or form factor), but which may attract new customers.

   Modeling customer valuation of multiple attributes can be done using *conjoint analysis*, where customers value each attribute in isolation. A product then is a particular combination of attributes. In the simplest setting, we then derive a customer's reservation price for a particular product as the sum of the worth of that product's attributes. With the reservation price curves of each product in hand, we can now determine each product's demand using the indifferent customer approach explained above. The result is that we can predict each product's market demand as a function of the reservation curves and the product prices. (Mini-case 10 asks you to explore this further.)

2. The model must capture competition in the sense that each firm controls

its own price, but its demand also depends on its competitor's price. The Nash equilibrium concept can predict optimal prices under strategic firm behavior. This equilibrium can be computed either in Excel or analytically (the results are provided by Schmidt and Porteus 2000).

As in the earlier monopoly case, both firms will continuously improve their operations and reduce their cost or increase the functionality of their product, which may translate into higher reservation curves if customers value the increased functionality. By using the learning curve to predict costs and by forecasting reservation price curves, firms can use the competitive model at each point in time to anticipate market outcomes.

The dynamics of competitive encroachment: disruptive technologies

In the disk drive example, the new product was initially inferior on the dimension valued most by the mainstream buyers (storage capacity), but was superior on another dimension (size). Because the new product is not attractive to its main customers, the incumbent is not particularly worried about it and keeps improving its product along the dimension valued by its own customers (storage capacity). Often, however, that improvement rate exceeds the rate needed by customers and thus may not result in increased willingness-to-pay.

Meanwhile, the entrant is also improving its product by improving its storage capacity and cost. As we saw before, the learning curve favors the innovator who can more quickly and more often double cumulative production (by starting from 0) than can the incumbent. The result is that the innovator can decrease cost faster than the incumbent can, which may offset the increased costs of higher storage. Even though the innovator's rate of improvement may also exceed the rate that customers need, its product becomes gradually more attractive to a larger segment of the market, including the original mainstream customers. Even if customer reservation prices do not change, the end result remains the same: the originally inferior product improves sufficiently to overtake almost the entire market, while the incumbent appeals only to the highest end of the market which is increasingly shrinking in size. Ultimately, the at-first inferior innovation pushes the old product out of the market.

According to Christensen (1997), the incumbent's loss of market position resulted from its failure to recognize the manner in which the newcomer's smaller sized entry into the marketplace encroached on the mainstream product. The entrant's product did not (initially) appeal to the incumbent's mainstream customers, instead appealing to fringe customers who were not buying the incumbent's product anyway (Figure 10.15). Over time, however, the trajectory of improvements in the smaller drives (namely, increases in storage capacity) led to their acceptance by these same mainstream customers; this is exactly the phenomenon that we have called low-end encroachment. Christensen refers to an initially inferior innovation that ultimately dominates original leaders as a *disruptive innovation* or *disruptive technology*.

Insights on new product introductions and preventing failures

The key take-away from the model is that the decision of whether to introduce a new product or not is really determined by how reservation price curves and costs are expected to change over time. The model simplified reality by assum-

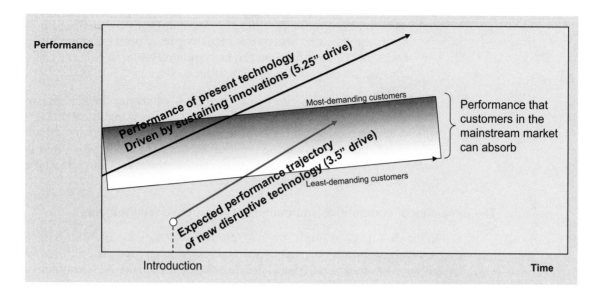

Figure 10.15 A disruptive innovation encroaches from below. In the disk drive industry, the innovator was initially inferior in terms of the traditional attribute valued by its main customers (storage capacity), but it was superior in an attributed that appealed to fringe customers (size). Over time, the learning curve benefits the innovator who eventually takes over the market.

ing those curves and prices are known. Of course, both of them are subject to a substantial amount of uncertainty in reality. We intentionally disregarded uncertainty so that we could highlight the different ways in which a new product can encroach on an existing market.

The model also gives us insight into how an incumbent may recognize a disruptive technology before it is too late, when it can cause failure. Disruptive technology follows a low-end encroachment strategy. In other words, it seems that the adage that you should "listen to your customers" may not always be a good one. However, this adage may indeed be sound if one takes a broader view of who your customer is and what your "customer" is "telling" you: a true market-oriented perspective goes further than simply asking existing customers what they want. It seeks a fuller understanding of latent or unexpressed needs. It looks beyond existing customers, striving to understand the future needs of future customers. Recall from Chapter 2 (p. 59) that smart companies continuously scan the competitive landscape and assess whether any rivals are posing a threat to their established position. According to Intel's chairman Grove (1996), only the paranoid survive:

> "Business success contains the seeds of its own destruction. The more successful you are, the more people want a chunk of your business and then another chunk and then another until there is nothing left. ... And, of course, I worry about competitors. I worry about other people figuring out how to do what we do better or cheaper, and displacing us with our customers."

10.8 | GUIDELINES FOR IMPROVEMENT AND INNOVATION

Establish a process for improvement and innovation

Operations views improvement and innovation as a process, a structured set of activities that can be managed like any other process. World-class companies continuously improve by relentlessly eliminating waste (lean) and reducing variability (Six Sigma).

While creativity, insight, and invention are intrinsic elements in innovation, successful innovators such as Ideo have a well structured approach that guide that process. But be mindful about the goals of your process. One key message of this book is that the operational system should be tailored to strategic objectives. In contrast to enforcing consistency, innovation processes should excel at flexible trial-and-error and selectionism while allowing accompanying variability and failures. Hindo (2007) reports how 3M is struggling to find a balance between consistency (and Six Sigma) and creativity.

Build a human infrastructure conducive to improvement

Continuous improvement is the cumulative result of all the people in the organization. Equally important to waste elimination is Toyota's respect for humanity (Example 10.1). Toyota does not just preach that people are its most important asset—it truly believes that investing in their knowledge and skills is necessary to build competitiveness. Its managers are expected to be able to do the jobs of everyone they supervise and also teach their workers how to solve problems according to the scientific method. The leadership model applies as much to the first-level "team leader" supervisors as it does to those at the top of the organization (Spear and Bowen 1999, p. 103).

Continuous improvement favors the innovator

When starting from scratch, cumulative output is easily and frequently doubled and cost drops quicker than for an incumbent. In this sense, continuous improvement from learning by doing favors the innovator, and the models we discussed can be used to manage and predict market outcomes. At the same time, this is a reminder that incumbents should not disregard even inferior innovations. Two millennia ago, the Roman poet Ovidius had already said: "add little to little and there will be a big pile."

Prepare for unknown unknowns

Significant improvement projects (like innovations) may suffer from unforeseeable uncertainty. While unk unks by definition cannot be known at the outset, we should "know that we don't know" and prepare for unk unks by using a sequential learning or a parallel selectionism approach, or a combination of the two.

The impact of unk unks can be mitigated by gathering information from the start (communication among designers, producers, and customers such as in concurrent design and engineering) and controlling complexity (by modularizing and standardizing selectively).

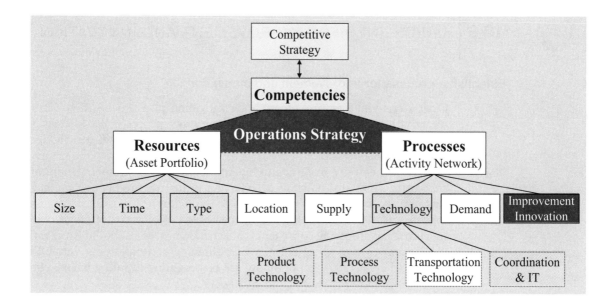

Figure 10.16 Improvement and innovation management is an integral part of operations strategy. We emphasized the interaction with the shaded elements in our framework.

10.9 | SUMMARY OF LEARNING OBJECTIVES

1. Explain the *process* of improvement and its role in operations strategy.

From an operations perspective, continuous improvement is the process of striving towards the ideal. Popular improvement processes include lean operations, which seeks to visualize and eliminate waste (any deviation between the actual and the ideal operational system), and Six Sigma, which aims to reduce variability.

Building capabilities for improvement and innovation must be an integral part of the theory and practice of operations strategy. As we near the end of our journey, let us review how improvement interacts with the other elements of our framework (Fig. 10.16).

First, competitive strategy defines the priority ranking of competencies that operations strategy should nurture. This provides a guide to whether improvement processes should emphasize cost, time, quality, or flexibility. Second, improvement processes impact resource requirements: they reduce the size and allow the postponement (time bucket in Fig. 10.16) of capacity expansions. Third, improvement and innovation may have unforeseeable uncertainty, which can be best handled through flexibility (type) or parallel trials (time). Reducing complexity in products, process, and communication is an effective way to reduce unforeseeable uncertainty and accelerate improvement and innovation.

2. Identify different types of learning and their impacts on improvement and innovation.

> Learning can be categorized into conceptual and operational learning. Conceptual learning applies the scientific method to "knowing why" an improvement works: it poses theories of cause-and-effect relationships and tests these theories. Operational learning knows how to implement an improvement. To drive company-wide improvement, one needs to combine both types of learning.
>
> Learning before doing is closely related to conceptual learning: it emphasizes analysis, virtual prototyping, simulation and optimization during the design and planning phase of improvement projects. In contrast, learning by doing is done through experience and is similar to operational learning.
>
> Learning before doing impacts product and process design and is emphasized during innovation to, for example, introduce new functionality. Learning by doing emphasizes continuous improvement to incrementally improve cost, time, quality and flexibility.

3. Apply the learning curve as a tool to predict aggregate cost dynamics.

> The learning curve is an empirical observation of changing input requirements (labor hours or cost) as a function of experience. The relationship is typically linear in log-log scale, which means that cost decreases by a constant fraction whenever cumulative output is doubled. As such, the learning curve is useful in budgeting to predict cost and capacity requirements as a function of forecasted volumes.

4. Diagnose complexity and potential unforeseeable uncertainty in innovation projects and manage them by using sequential learning or parallel selectionism.

> Drastic improvement projects, such as innovations, often cannot foresee all the variables that may impact eventual project success. There is always the possibility of unknown unknowns (unk unks) propping up for which no contingency planning exists (given that they were unknown during planning). Yet, managers can diagnose the threat of unk unks by identifying knowledge gaps and estimating project complexity. Depending on the extent of unforeseeable uncertainty and complexity, the two fundamental approaches to deal with unk unks are sequential learning and parallel selectionism. Sequential learning involves learning by doing in fast iterations. Selectionism runs parallel trials and selects the best at the end. Obviously, in practice both approaches are combined.

5. Connect operational improvements with customer valuations of competing products in order to predict whether an innovation is sustaining or disruptive.

> The interplay between operational improvements and innovations can (to some extent) predict the market dynamics and outcomes. An innovation may add new functionality through design (learning before doing), thus increasing the willingness-to-pay of some customer segment. Operational improvement may decrease cost through experience (learning by doing); the learning curve favors the innovator because cumulative production doubling is easier and more frequent when starting from 0 production than it is for an existing product. A sustaining innovation is superior in functionality to the existing product. Like any innovation, the high-end encroachment decreases cost faster than the existing product and eventually dominates the market. A disruptive innovation is

typically inferior along the dimension that is valued by existing customers, yet superior along another dimension that is valued by fringe or new customers. Over time, however, the learning curve favors it over the existing product while it may also improve along the traditional dimension, eventually taking over the market.

DISCUSSION QUESTIONS

1. Consider a firm that enjoys economies of scale in production and learning. Assume that January production of 3000 units is less than December (Christmas!) production of 5000 units, and that February production of 4000 units falls in between. Draw a chart showing the average cost (vertical axis) as a function of monthly production volume (horizontal axis) and clearly indicate the average cost in December, January, and February.

2. In this chapter, we learned how operations can impact competition through innovation. Summarize that discussion by discribing the key operational drivers and dynamics (i.e., without appealing to differences in customer personalities or communication) behind a "disruptive technology."

Visit www.vanmieghem.us for additional questions and updates.

FURTHER READING AND REFERENCES

▶ For the learning curve: Hayes and Wheelwright (1984) and Schmidt and Wood (1999).

▶ Our discussion on high-end and low-end encroachment reflects the work of Glen M. Schmidt and co-authors, who analyzed Christensen's innovator's dilemma: Schmidt and Porteus (2000), Christensen (1997), and Christensen and Raynor (2003).

Brooks, F. P. (1995). *The Mythical Man-Month: Essays on Software Engineering* (20th Anniversary ed.). Addison-Wesley.

Christensen, C. M. (1997). *Innovator's Dilemma*. Boston: Harvard Business School Press.

Christensen, C. M. and M. E. Raynor (2003). *The Innovator's Solution*. Boston: Harvard Business School Press.

Collins, J. (2001). *Good to Great: Why Some Companies Make the Leap... and Others Don't*. Collins.

Drucker, P. (1985). *Innovation and Entrepreneurship: Practice and Principles*. New York: Harper & Row.

Grove, A. S. (1996). *Only the Paranoid Survive: How to Exploit the Crisis Points That Challenge every Company and Career* (First Edition ed.). Currency.

Hammer, M. and J. Champy (1993). *Reengineering the Corporation: A Manifesto for Business Revolution*. New York: Harper Press.

Hayes, R. H. and S. C. Wheelwright (1984). *Restoring our Competitive Edge: Competing through Manufacturing*. New York: John Wiley & Sons.

Hindo, B. (2007). At 3M, a struggle between efficiency and creativity. *Business Week*. Jun. 11.

Honeywell (2007). About us: our culture: continually improving. www.honeywell.com/sites/honeywell/ourculture.htm.

Lapré, M. A. and L. N. Van Wassenhove (2002). Learning across lines: The secret to more efficient factories. *Harvard Business Review*. October.

Loch, C. H., A. DeMeyer, and M. T. Pich (2006). *Managing the unknown*. New York: Wiley.

Noyce, R. (1977). Microelectronics. *Scientific American 237*(3).

Ohno, T. (1988). *Toyota Production System: Beyond Large-Scale Production*. Portland, Oregon: Productivity Press.

Pich, M. T., C. H. Loch, and A. DeMeyer (2002). On uncertainty, ambiguity and complexity in project management. *Management Science 48*(8), 1008–1023.

Schmidt, G. M. and E. L. Porteus (2000). The impact of an integrated marketing and manufacturing innovation. *Management and Service Operations Management 2*(4), 317–336.

Schmidt, G. M. and S. C. Wood (1999, Jun). The growth of Intel and the learning curve. *Stanford University Graduate School of Business publication* (S-OIT-27).

Sommer, S., C. H. Loch, and J. Dong (2007). Mastering unforeseeable uncertainty in startup companies: an empirical study. *Organizational Science* ((under review)).

Spear, S. and K. H. Bowen (1999). Decoding the DNA of the Toyota Production System. *Harvard Business Review*, 97–106. Sep-Oct.

Womack, J. P., D. T. Jones, and D. Roos (1990). *The Machine that changed the world: The story of lean production*. HarperCollins Publishers.

Mini-Case 10 | QUANTUM-SEAGATE: COMPETING ON INNOVATION

[5]Andrea Forward[6], engineering manager at Seagate Technology, was adamant in her support of a new development program for a 5.25 inch disk drive. "Look, I know this thing is going to be an expensive product to develop, and I know there just doesn't seem to be much of a market for 5.25 inch drives at the present time. But I've been talking to one of my engineer friends who now works for this young and upcoming computer startup, Apple. They think they can grow a market for personal desktop computers using such a drive, and a relatively lower-capacity, 5.25-inch drive would be perfect for such a computer."

"Hold on just a minute," countered Kwon Suzuki, VP of Marketing. "I just got back from the big Computer Expo, where I talked with all the leading computer companies such as DEC. They were raving about the 8-inch drive from Quantum and how well it was performing as a replacement for the old 14-inch drive. These customers said nothing about wanting a smaller drive. What they wanted was even more capacity in that 8 inch drive. If we want to compete against Quantum and encroach on their market, we should develop a higher-capacity 8-inch model. As I said, all that these big users could talk about was capacity, capacity, and more capacity. You engineering types are always looking to do something technically driven, but if it won't sell, what good is it?

Tell you what, Andrea. There's this new methodology I've been hearing about: conjoint analysis. We survey potential customers, find out what key attributes that these customers are looking for in a product, and then find out just how much value each customer places on each attribute. Why don't we try out this new technique, and let the customers tell us what to do?"

Several weeks later, Andrea and Kwon got together to review the conjoint results.

"Well, I'm not quite sure just exactly where all this is going to take us but I've got a ton of good information," started Kwon. "We talked to all the primary users of disk drives in today's market. First, we contacted mainframe users and had them go through the necessary exercise as prescribed by the conjoint method. Second, we surveyed companies such as DEC who make the high-volume units that I am going to call mid-range computers, to distinguish them from the personal desktop computers you mentioned earlier. Quantum's customers are predominantly mainframe and mid-range users. And it's just like I told you earlier. They want more capacity in that 8-inch drive and show relatively little desire for a 5.25-inch form factor. No wonder Quantum is focusing much of its efforts on providing more capacity.

"More about that later. But more importantly, you got me thinking beyond these existing customers. It's risky, but yes, maybe we should also consider that

[5]Professors Glen M. Schmidt (University of Utah) and Jan A. Van Mieghem (Northwestern University) prepared this case as a basis for class discussion rather than to illustrate either the factual, effective, or ineffective handling of a managerial situation. No part of this publication may be reproduced without permission; direct all inquiries to permissions@vanmieghem.us

[6]This case study is historical fiction in that the characters and exact numbers are fictional, but the case is intended to offer a sense of what transpired in the disk drive industry in the late 1970s and early 1980s.

third possible group of customers you mentioned: those who might buy that new Apple desktop personal computer. And then, just to satisfy our curiosity, we peered even further into the future on this. We came up with a possible fourth group of users that might want disk drives for a portable type of computer. Some people are envisioning a computer that an engineer might want to take to a work site so that she can collect and analyze her data and write her report on-site, for example; something like a very powerful portable calculator. And after some heavy brainstorming we decided there might even be some specialty uses for other little devices that you could carry around and store data in. Maybe something like a little pocket-sized "personal assistant" that holds your daily calendar. Or maybe something that a forklift driver could carry around, to keep track of inventory levels in a warehouse.

"Anyway, as you can see, this analysis left us with the following five possible customer groups: mainframe users, mid-range users, desktop users, portable computer users, and specialty users. Here's where it gets interesting: among all these potential users, we found two key things that these customers were all concerned with to some degree. First, they wanted to know, just how much data will the disk drive store? And secondly, they wanted to know, physically, just how big is the disk drive?

"Regarding the two parameters of storage capacity and physical size, we were able to glean the following information. We found that, other things being equal, all of these potential customers prefer more capacity. Not a surprise, is it? However, not everybody is willing to pay the same amount for a given level of capacity. If you think about mainframe users, they clearly value capacity the most. Mid-range users value capacity only slightly less. The potential desktop users are more accepting of a drive with limited capacity, and futuristic users of those portable computers are even more willing to give up storage capacity. Finally, for those specialty devices that we could envision, we had to sort of guess, but we felt big capacity levels would be of very little value, at least relative to the way a mainframe user values capacity.

"In fact, we found that if we plot the value (or part-worth) that each customer places on a disk drive of a given capacity, starting with the mainframe user who values this capacity most highly, we get something like the graph shown in Figure 10.17. This graph shows that there are 1.275 million potential customers in this total market, broken down into the five groups I mentioned earlier. But even within any one of these groups, some customers value capacity more than others. In fact, the mainframe customer who values capacity the least is similar to the mid-range user who values capacity the most. So we can conveniently approximate this relationship using the straight line shown in Figure 10.17. In other words, the first customer, who is the customer valuing capacity the most, would effectively pay $2,415 for 60 megabytes (MB) of capacity in a disk drive. We call this her part-worth for capacity, as this is only part of what the disk drive is worth to her. She will also pay some additional amount depending how compact the drive is, as we will see later. Other customers aren't willing to fork over that much money for the 60MB drive: willingness-to-pay for capacity decreases linearly with each customer until we get to the last customer (namely, the 1.275 millionth customer), who would pay nothing. Effectively, this last customer needs only a miniscule level of capacity, with no use for higher levels of capacity.

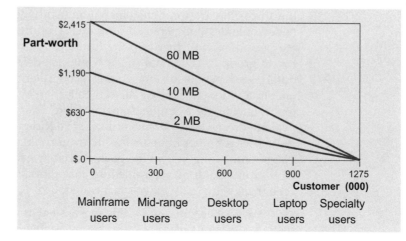

Figure 10.17 The value (part-worth) that each potential customer places on storage capacity.

"Now, not so surprisingly, we found the reverse relationship for physical size. In other words, mainframe users don't really care much about physical size. At least they don't care as much as the mid-range users, who in turn don't value compactness as much as desktop users, who don't value compactness as much as portable computers users, who don't value compactness as much as specialty users. In fact, if we plot the value (or part-worth) that these same 1.275 million customers place on compactness, we end up with a graph something like that shown in Figure 10.18. At one extreme, a mainframe user has a part-worth of $1,085 regardless of size, while at the other extreme a specialty user has a wide disparity.

"Perhaps we can use this type of analysis to figure out what each customer will pay for any given disk drive. We can call this amount the customer's reservation price, and calculate it as simply the sum of the two part-worths for capacity and physical size. This framework gives us a way of thinking about what it takes to actually make a sale to a customer. We have to price our disk drive at a level below that customer's reservation price, and if there is a competitor, our disk drive has to provide that customer with more value than the competitor's disk drive can. Or else our customer will buy the competitor's product."

"I think I'm beginning to get it," replied Andrea. "That's why Quantum's 8 inch drive is doing so well right now. Look, Quantum recently upped the capacity of its 8 inch drives, but the mainframe users still want more, more, more. The mid-range customers also love it, as they still primarily favor more capacity over smaller physical size! So to keep its customers happy, that's what Quantum is focusing on: more and more capacity. I understand Quantum is extremely profitable with their 8-inch drive and can produce it at a cost of $2,800. What if we assume, for simplicity, that they basically have a monopoly on the market? I've heard they sell about 150,000 units. Would your data support that number?

"At the same time, I have a hunch that your data suggests we can encroach

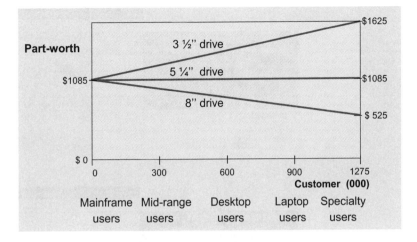

Figure 10.18 The value (part-worth) that each potential customer places on physical size.

on Quantum's market in a seemingly non-threatening way. What if we do indeed pursue the 5.25-inch form factor? I mean, let's get specific. From an engineering perspective, I think we can develop a 5.25-inch drive with 10 MB of capacity. At the time of introduction, production cost would be $2,100, but it will go down as we grow our volume. Also, I think we can increase the drive's capacity at a rate of about 50% per year. And I think customers will then increase their willingness-to-pay for our drive, because as capacity increases, it will come closer to meeting their appetite for capacity.

"I suspect Quantum will continue to increase the 8-inch drive's capacity as well. While Quantum's customers will expect continually increasing capacity in an 8-inch drive over time, I'm not sure they will actually be willing to pay more as capacity goes up, given how much capacity those drives already have. For simplicity, let's assume that willingness-to-pay for the 8-inch drive remains constant as its capacity goes up from here. With regard to Quantum's production cost, they will be able to reduce cost per MB but I don't think they can reduce per-unit cost like we can, because they are already further down the learning curve.

"To be specific, what if we assume that the disk drive characteristics and customer willingness-to-pay change over time as shown in Tables 10.2 and 10.3? Which customer segments do you think would buy our drive, how much market share would we get over time, and how much profit would we make? Would our drive encroach on Quantum's 8-inch product? How might it impact their profitability? I think we need to answer at least some of these questions before making a decision."

Discussion Questions

1. If you were Seagate, would you introduce a 5.25 inch drive? Estimate pricing, market share, and profitability at introduction, and also at one year,

	Years since introduction					
	0	1	2	4	6	7
Capacity of 8" drive, MB*	60	90	135	300	680	1025
Maximum willingness-to-pay for 8" drive*	$3,500	$3,500	$3,500	$3,500	$3,500	$3,500
Minimum willingness-to-pay for 8" drive*	$525	$525	$525	$525	$525	$525
Production cost of 8" drive	$2,800	$2,800	$2,800	$2,800	$2,800	$2,800

*These values apply to a drive of the MB level as given in the first row of the table.

Table 10.2 Expected changes in characteristics related to the 8-inch drive.

	Years since introduction					
	0	1	2	4	6	7
Capacity of 5.25" drive, MB	10	15	22	50	115	170
Maximum willingness-to-pay for 8" drive*	$2,275	$2,300	$2,375	$2,500	$2,700	$3,000
Minimum willingness-to-pay for 8" drive*	$1,085	$1,110	$1,185	$1,310	$1,510	$1,810
Production cost of 5.25" drive*	$2,100	$2,050	$2,011	$1,950	$1,900	$1,880

*These values apply to a drive of the MB level as given in the first row of the table.

Table 10.3 Expected changes in characteristics related to the 5.25-inch drive.

two years, four years, six years, and seven years after introduction.

2. If you were Quantum, how would you react to Seagate's new product introduction strategy?

3. One "view of the world" is that new products diffuse through the market because of communication. Some personality types buy these products because of communication external to the social system (these customers are sometimes called "innovators"), while others require communication internal to the social system (these are "imitators"). At first, only "innovator-types" buy the product. Then "early adopters" become convinced, followed by the "early majority." The "late majority" types are risk-averse and are exceeded in their reluctance to convert only by the "laggards." How does the reservation price perspective compare with this marketing view?

4. What are the possible scenarios under which the electric car might make inroads into the automotive market? Describe both a low-end and high-end encroachment strategy. In your discussion, identify who the first customers are, what segments the market grows from, and so on. In what time frame do you envision that the electric car, or some other alternate fueled vehicle, will gain popularity? Which of these strategies would you choose if you were a manufacturer?

Part IV

Integrating Case Studies

HARLEY-DAVIDSON MOTOR COMPANY

[1] Dave Storm, Vice President of Strategy for Harley-Davidson Motor Company, reflected on the struggles and successes that Harley-Davidson has faced over its turbulent history. Harley-Davidson had come a long way and overcome many obstacles since its inception, but times had changed and so had the challenges. The determination and will to succeed within the organization was, however, stronger than ever. Harley-Davidson had felt a sense of pride at the success of their latest expansion to 100,000 motorcycles per year. Their plans had been successfully executed well ahead of schedule. Ten years ago, no one within the organization would have imagined that so many people would want to buy Harley-Davidson motorcycles. Never in their wildest dreams would they have thought that they would be capable of producing so many. However, the company had underestimated the demand for their product and in the heavyweight motorcycle market as a whole. With demand growing rapidly, Harley-Davidson's constrained production capacity was insufficient to meet demand. Excess demand, estimated to be more than 10% above capacity, resulted in waiting lists of up to 2 years depending on the model. Harley-Davidson was practically inviting potential customers to buy from their competitors!

Dave asked Jim McCaslin, Vice President of Harley-Davidson's York Assembly facility, to join him and the rest of the management team at the Head Office in Milwaukee to finalize the company's response to the latest surge in demand. The management team had devised several alternative strategies to counter their gradually sliding market share and to continue the phenomenal growth that the company had been enjoying recently. The problem they faced was choosing the best strategy, and time was rapidly running out. On June 3, 1996, they would present their recommendations to the Board of Directors on the best way to deal with their constrained production capacity in a rapidly growing market.

HISTORY (1903-1992) AND COMPANY INFORMATION

Harley-Davidson Motor Company, the only remaining major American manufacturer of motorcycles, has had a long and exciting history. William Harley and the Davidson brothers (Walter, Arthur, and William) built the first Harley-Davidson motorcycle in 1903 in a shed in Milwaukee, Wisconsin. By 1909, Harley-Davidson had introduced a more powerful motorcycle, incorporating a new engine that has become the company's standard to this day: the V-Twin (named after the

---

[1]This case was prepared by Troy Anderson, Mark Bruno, Shaun Usmar, and Professor Van Mieghem as the basis for class discussion rather than to illustrate either the effective or ineffective handling of a managerial situation. The cooperation of Harley-Davidson management is gratefully acknowledged. No part of this case study may be reproduced without permission; direct all inquiries to permissions@vanmieghem.us

55° angle at which the two cylinders are juxtaposed). Doubling the power of its predecessors, it carried riders at a then unbelievable 60 miles per hour. The motorcycle craze caught on, and by 1911 there were over 150 other brands of motorcycles competing for space on America's roads. Soon thereafter, a new use for motorcycles appeared. Already popular for police use, Harley-Davidson motorcycles began to be used to support the infantry in World War I. Over 20,000 Harley-Davidson motorcycles had been called into action by the end of the war.

Although there was initially a strong demand for these bikes, the introduction of the Model T automobile and the subsequent effects of the Great Depression devastated the motorcycle market. By 1931, only three U.S. manufacturers had survived: Harley-Davidson, Excelsior-Henderson and Indian. Even though annual company sales dropped sharply to 3,700 motorcycles, Harley-Davidson survived thanks mostly to a strong dealer network, police and military use, conservative business management, and strong exports.

In 1941, the U.S. and Allied forces once again turned to Harley-Davidson for help. Harley-Davidson supplied all of its production—more than 90,000 units during World War II. This was the beginning of a new trend. Immediately after WWII, people were eager to get back to motorcycling. An increase in discretionary income coupled with an improved road system throughout the U.S. fueled an explosive demand for motorcycles. To help meet this booming demand, Harley-Davidson converted an airplane propeller plant on Capitol Drive in the Milwaukee suburb of Wauwatosa into additional manufacturing facilities in 1947. Harley-Davidson's success grew even more when Indian, its oldest and closest competitor, went out of business. Much of the reason for their demise was their inability to deal with the volatility of the market demand. Harley-Davidson was able to cope better, thus becoming the sole survivor in the U.S. motorcycle industry since 1954.

But the company did not rest on its laurels. It leapt forward in 1957 by introducing the Sportster motorcycle ushering in a new era of heavyweight motorcycles. The 1950s and 60s also saw the explosion of the American "motorcycle culture," with black leather jackets becoming not only a statement of fashion, but also of a lifestyle. The tough "Wild Ones" image, made popular by the Marlon Brando movie of the same name, labeled motorcycle enthusiasts as "outlaws." (In fact only a small minority of all motorcyclists fit this image.)

In 1965, Harley-Davidson ended family ownership with a public stock offering and was later purchased by the American Machine and Foundry Company (AMF) in 1969. AMF had great plans for Harley-Davidson; indeed, AMF's financial strength and resources helped the motorcycle company meet the demands of the rapidly expanding marketplace. In 1974, the company moved its chassis manufacturing and final assembly operations to an old AMF plant in York, PA. (The engine and transmission operations remained in Milwaukee, along with the corporate headquarters.) When AMF purchased Harley-Davidson, they were producing 14,000 motorcycles a year, but by 1975 they increased production to 75,403, including lightweight motorcycles.

This rapid growth in production quantities was, however, a poor indicator of success. Beginning in 1969 and continuing into the 1970s, huge numbers of low priced motorcycles were imported from Japan, dramatically reducing Harley-Davidson's market share. The ferocious competition coupled with motorcycle quality problems, which surfaced as a result of the company's rapidly expanding production, caused major problems for Harley-Davidson.

In 1981, AMF wanted to sell Harley-Davidson after 11 years of ownership—but there were no willing buyers. Working against the odds and driven by a love for the product and a belief in the company's potential, 13 members of the Harley-Davidson management team purchased the company from AMF for $81.5 million in a highly leveraged buy-out. They could not have done so at a more challenging time. In the face of a worldwide decline in the heavyweight motorcycle market, the Japanese manufacturers decided to ship their excess inventories to the US, thus massively overloading the market and depressing prices. This, coupled with extraordinary interest rates and inflation, could have meant the demise of Harley-Davidson. After complaining about inappropriate competitive practices to the International Trade Commission (ITC), President Ronald Reagan imposed a 5-year tariff on imported Japanese heavyweight bikes. This gave Harley-Davidson just enough room to move. Through a combination of streamlined operations, improved quality and manufacturing techniques, and by designing new models, Harley-Davidson was able to win back market share from its competitors. By 1986, it was in a position to return to public ownership, and by 1987 it petitioned the ITC to remove the tariffs one year early. Harley-Davidson was on its way to becoming an American success story.

Company Structure

The parent Harley-Davidson Inc. operates in two segments: motorcycles and related products, and financial services. Its motorcycle segment consists primarily of its wholly-owned subsidiary Harley-Davidson Motor Company, which designs, manufactures, and sells heavyweight motorcycles. It also sells a broad range of related products including motorcycle parts, accessories, and apparel. The Financial Services segment comprises Eaglemark Financial Services. Eaglemark provides financial support services such as financing and insurance to Harley-Davidson's participating North American dealers and domestic retail customers.

The Heavyweight Motorcycle Industry

The heavyweight motorcycle market in which Harley-Davidson operates includes all motorcycles with an engine displacement of 651cc or above. By the early 60s, Japanese manufacturers started to move from producing smaller lightweight motorcycles to producing Harley-Davidson look-alikes. These bikes were faster, less expensive, and more technically advanced in terms of electric systems and engine designs. By the late 70s, the big four Japanese producers—Honda, Yamaha, Kawasaki and Suzuki—were producing so many heavyweight bikes that they sent their excess production to the U.S. This, combined with a massive downturn in the demand for heavyweight bikes, spelled trouble for Harley-Davidson. Between the early 70s and 1984, its market share dropped almost continuously. Its domestic market share dropped from 77.5% in 1973 to 30.8% in 1980. It was not until 1988 that Harley-Davidson managed to increase its share to 46.5%, a level it has maintained and even increased until today (Fig. 11.1 and Table 11.1).

Consumers

In order to understand Harley-Davidson customers, one must understand the Harley-Davidson "mystique." People ride "Harleys" not so much as a means of transport, but rather as a lifestyle. Many owners are affiliated in some way to the Harley Owners Group (HOG). Harley-Davidson motorcycles exude freedom and adventure. To their owners, Harleys are as American as the Stars and Stripes or the Bald Eagle. It is, however, more than just national pride that drives these owners. To them, their motorcycle has a personality. It has heart and spirit; it is not just a mechanical marvel, but is another member of the family. This "family loyalty" is demonstrated by Harley-Davidson's 95% customer retention ratio. There must be very few companies who play such a large part in their customer's lives that their customers willingly tattoo its brand name logo on their bodies (Figure 11.2). Harley-Davidson is one such company.

Despite the renegade image with which Harley-Davidson owners are often associated, not all customers fit this image. In fact, the trend over the last ten years has been towards more mature and better-educated owners. The typical U.S. Harley-Davidson motorcycle owner is a male in his early forties, with a household income of approximately $66,000, who purchases a motorcycle for recreational purposes and who is an experienced motorcycle rider.

Product Segments

The heavyweight class of motorcycles is comprised of four segments: standard, which emphasizes basic transportation and cost; performance, which emphasizes handling and speed; touring; and custom. The touring segment includes motorcycles equipped for long-distance touring with fairing, windshield, and saddlebags. By comparison, the custom segment emphasizes styling and individual owner customization. These motorcycles are highly customized through the use of chrome trim and accessories. While Harley-Davidson pioneered the touring segment, it is best known for creating the custom motorcycle featuring the distinctive styling associated with certain classic Harley-Davidson motorcycles, as shown in Figure 11.3.

Harley-Davidson has concentrated on the touring and custom segments, currently manufac-

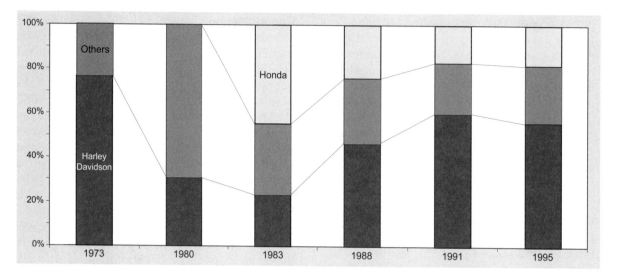

Figure 11.1 North-American heavyweight motorcycle market shares.

	(Units in Thousands)		
	1995	1994	1993
North America:			
Total registrations	140.3	124.9	109.5
Harley-Davidson registrations	77	69.5	63.4
Harley-Davidson market share percentage	54.90%	55.70%	57.90%
Europe:			
Total registrations	139.9	128.7	129.8
Harley-Davidson registrations	15.3	14.2	13.1
Harley-Davidson market share percentage	10.90%	11.00%	10.10%
Japan/Australia:			
Total registrations	35.5	34	31.8
Harley-Davidson registrations	7.9	7.6	6.6
Harley-Davidson market share percentage	22%	22%	21%

Table 11.1 Worldwide heavyweight (750cc+) motorcycle registration data.

turing and selling 23 different models of heavyweight motorcycles, with suggested retail prices ranging from approximately $5,100 to $18,200. These motorcycles are based on variations of four basic chassis designs: the Sportster, Dyna, Softail and Touring bike chassis. They are powered by one of three air cooled, twin cylinder engines of "V" configuration, which have displacements of 883cc, 1200cc, and 1340cc, respectively.

With its smaller engine displacement, the Sportster model represents Harley-Davidson's only "entry level" option for potential first-time motorcyclists. It provides the ideal way for consumers who lack the ability or the confidence to handle heavier bikes to enjoy the thrill of riding a

Harley-Davidson. It is also the greatest selling bike in the history of the company.

Market & Competitors Up until the 1960s, Harley-Davidson had a virtual monopoly on the domestic heavyweight motorcycle market. Since then, however, the U.S. and international heavyweight motorcycle markets have become highly competitive. Major competitors like Honda, Yamaha, Kawasaki, and Suzuki have financial and marketing resources that are substantially greater than Harley-Davidson's, and also have much larger corporate revenues.

Out of these competitors, Honda has historically posed the biggest threat. It entered

Figure 11.2 When was the last time you felt this strongly about anything?

the worldwide motorcycle production industry in 1963 when its first production facility outside Japan—Honda Benelux N.V. in Belgium—started producing lightweight scooters. Honda has since expanded into all facets of the motorcycle industry. By looking for high-end extensions to their sport lines, Honda now produces a range that closely follows that of Harley-Davidson (see Table 11.2). It sells the popular Gold Wing line of touring bikes and three successful custom lines: the Valkyrie, Shadow and Magna. Honda now sells around 5 million motorcycles a year, thus giving it a 50% share of worldwide unit sales! Honda's 1995 motorcycle revenues, however, were only $3.7 billion (out of a $40 billion total revenue for Honda), compared to Harley-Davidson's $1.35 billion (see Table 11.3).

Yamaha poses the next biggest threat with its classic American motorcycles: the Royal Star, V-Star and the Virago. Generally, the custom and touring motorcycles are the most expensive and most profitable vehicles in the market.

Currently, Harley-Davidson dominates the 651+cc market in the U.S. with a 50% market share. The next highest competitor is Honda with around 20%. The situation overseas is slightly different. Although Harley-Davidson has managed to capture a 16% share in the Pacific Rim—mainly Japan and Australia—its situation in Europe is more precarious. In Europe, which has a larger heavyweight market than the U.S. does, Harley-Davidson only holds a 6% share. As a result, the company has been looking towards both Europe and Asia as growth markets for the future.

Although Harley-Davidson has led the industry in domestic sales of heavyweight motorcycles for the last ten years, its market share is shrinking. This is primarily due to Harley-Davidson's continued inability to ramp up production at a rate fast enough to meet the growing market demand.

Operations Harley-Davidson operates two main facilities. Its Capitol Drive plant in Wisconsin produces engines and transmissions for both the Sportster and super heavyweight models. Its facility in York, PA, performs all final assembly. Due to its strong nationalistic roots, Harley-Davidson has chosen to outsource very few of its components and as a result produces many of its parts in-house. Even at times when the company's livelihood was threatened, Harley-Davidson refused offers from both Honda and Yamaha to provide their advanced V-twin engines.

But how could Harley-Davidson compete with the Japanese? They used robots and cheap labor to create a lower cost structure. After a few trips to Japan in the early 80s it became apparent to Vaughn Beals, then Chairman of the Board, that hidden magic was not the reason for the Japanese success. "We were being wiped out by the Japanese because they were better managers. It wasn't robotics, or culture, or morning calisthenics and company songs—it was professional managers who understood their business and paid attention to detail, " Beals said. The Japanese methods seemed to work. In the early 80s, only 5% of Japanese machines coming off the assembly line

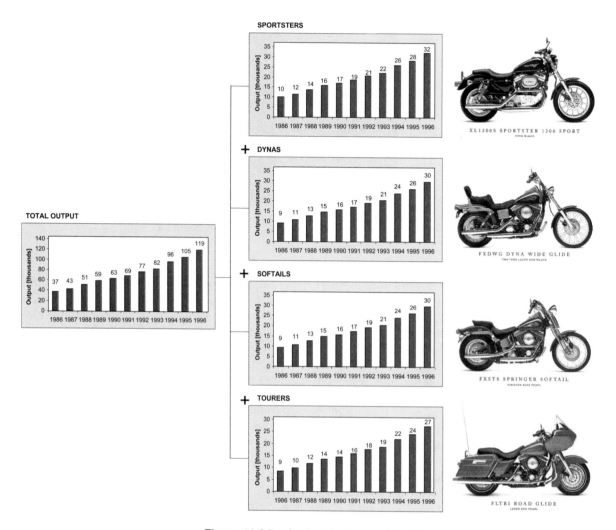

Figure 11.3 Production Output per Model

failed to pass inspection, compared with 50—60% of Harleys. Furthermore, the Japanese were able to reduce costs and increase quality by achieving 20—30 inventory turns per year compared to Harley-Davidson's 4.

Don Gogan, a recent graduate of Kellogg's Masters in Manufacturing Management program, is now a Product Plant Manager at the Capitol Drive facility. He recollected that in order to beat, or at least join the Japanese, Harley-Davidson had to play their game. That game included learning and embracing three practices, known as the "Productivity Triad" Employee Involvement (EI), Just-In-Time inventory (JIT), and Statistical Operator Control (SOC). EI involved enlisting the full participation of all employees to solve problems and control quality. In this way, everyone would be responsible for the success of the company. JIT, or MAN (Materials As Needed) as Harley-Davidson named it, involved reducing costly inventory levels and supplying the assembly line with small quantities of materials only when needed. Finally, SOC gave all employees sufficient training to help them measure the quality of their own output, and consequently assure quality throughout the process.

Harley-Davidson was one of the first companies in the U.S. to adopt these lean manufactur-

Harley-Davidson		Honda	
Model	**MSRP**	**Model**	**MSRP**
Sportster		*ST*	
XLH Sportster 1200	$7,610	ST 1100 ABSII	$14,299
XL 1200S Sportster 1200 Sport	$8,395	ST 1100	$11,799
XL 1200C Sportster 1200 Custom	$8,670		
XLH Sportster 883	$5,245	Pacific Coast (800cc)	$6,699
XLH Sportster 883 Hugger	$5,945		
Dyna		*Shadow*	
FXDL Dyna Low Rider	$13,750	Shadow Ace	$8,699
FXD Dyna Super Glide	$10,865	Shadow Ace 750	$6,299
FXDS-CONV Dyna Convertible	$14,100	Shadow VLX Deluxe	$4,999
FXDWG Dyna Wide Glide	$14,775		
Softail		*Valkyrie & Magna*	
FLSTC Heritage Softail Classic	$15,275	Valkyrie (1520cc)	$12,799
FXSTC Softail Custom	$14,125	Magna	$7,499
FLSTS Heritage Springer	$17,145		
FLSTF Fat Boy	$14,595		
FXSTS Springer Softail	$14,765		
Tourers		*Gold Wing & Tourers*	
FLTR/FLTRI Road Glide	$14,850	Gold Wing Aspencade	$15,199
FLHT Electra Glide Standard	$12,725	Valkyrie Tourer	$14,199
FLHTC/FLHTCI Electra Glide Classic	$14,975		
FLHTCUI Ultra Classic Electra Glide	$18,065	**Yamaha**	
FLHR Road King	$14,725	Royal Star (1300cc)	$13,999
FLHRCI Road King Classic	$15,960	Royal Star Tour Classic (1300cc)	$14,599
		V-Max (1200cc)	$10,499
		Virago (1100cc)	$7,699

Table 11.2 Comparison of Heavyweight Motorcycle Prices

ing practices—and the results were impressive. Inventory turns increased from 5 to 20, the percentage of completed motorcycles coming off the line rose from 76% to 99%, and productivity rose by 50%. None of these changes could have been made without the involvement of the employees and their unions. Employee and union involvement is deeply rooted into Harley-Davidson's corporate culture.

Dealers The dealer network was also crucial to Harley-Davidson's success. Nationally, it comprised 600 independent, but primarily exclusive, dealers. The symbiotic relationship between the company and its dealers proved critical to Harley-Davidson's survival during troubled times. Whether it was by buying excess inventory to improve Harley-Davidson's cash flow, or by repairing poor quality bikes that they had received in order to make them fit for sale, the dealers stayed loyal during the difficult years.

THE 1992 CAPACITY DECISION

With the market improving due to a resurgent economy, Harley-Davidson looked to continue improving its operations to keep up with increasing demand. Jeff Pharris, a Strategic Planning Manager, recollected the large demand for bikes in 1992. With longer waits for bikes, noticeable also for employees (the staff received no preferential treatment), Harley-Davidson had its finger on the pulse of the market through product ownership and first-hand observance of the entire channel.

Harley-Davidson knew that wait times and the general backlog of orders it had from its dealers, not to mention some of the opportunistic pricing practices of the dealers, meant ever-growing demand. Despite Harley-Davidson's perception of itself as a niche player, this "niche" was becoming larger—more and more people wanted to ride a Harley-Davidson.

Not wanting to throttle back on customers' demands, Harley-Davidson knew it needed to add supply. At the time, Harley-Davidson was quite averse to adding capacity due to its experience with the volatile and cyclical motorcycle business.

INCOME STATEMENT (IN 000):

	1995	1994	1993	1992	1991
Net Sales	$1,350,466	$1,158,887	$ 933,262	$ 822,929	$ 701,969
Cost of goods sold	(939,067)	(800,548)	(641,248)	(572,927)	(500,715)
Gross profit	411,399	358,339	292,014	250,002	201,254
Income from financial services	3,620	-	-	-	-
Selling, admin. and engineering	(234,223)	(204,777)	(162,675)	(154,942)	(119,182)
Income from operations	180,796	153,562	129,339	95,060	82,072
Interest income (expense), net	96	1,682	994	(2,259)	(3,381)
Other income (expense), net	(4,903)	1,196	(3,249)	(1,611)	(1,355)
Provision for income taxes	64,939	60,219	50,765	34,530	29,045
Income from operations	111,050	96,221	76,319	56,660	48,291
Extraordinary items, net of tax	1,430	8,051	(88,204)	(2,875)	(11,319)
Net income (loss)	**$ 112,480**	**$ 104,272**	**$ (11,885)**	**$ 53,785**	**$ 36,972**

BALANCE SHEET (IN 000):

	1995	1994	1993	1992	1991
Working capital	$ 104,028	$ 189,358	$ 142,996	$ 96,232	$ 64,212
Finance receivables, net	213,444	-	-	-	-
Total assets	**1,000,670**	**676,663**	**527,958**	**475,026**	**424,045**
Short-term debt, including current	2,691	1,431	4,190	912	29,062
Maturities of long-term debt					
Long-term debt, less current maturities	18,207	9,021	2,919	1,453	38,130
Finance debt	164,330	-	-	-	-
Total debt	**185,228**	**10,452**	**7,109**	**2,365**	**67,192**
Shareholders' equity	**494,569**	**433,232**	**324,912**	**335,380**	**238,000**

CASH FLOW (IN 000):

	1995
Net cash provided by operating activities:	$ 171,877
Net Income	112,480
Adjustments to reconcile NI to cash:	
Depreciation and Amortization	42,329
Net changes in Working Capital	14,937
Other	2,131
Net cash used in investing activities:	(187,821)
Net Capital Expenditures	(112,985)
Other-Net	(74,836)
Net cash provided by (used in) financing activities:	(10,478)
Net increase (decrease) in cash and equivalents:	**(26,422)**

Source: Harley-Davidson Company 1996-10K

Table 11.3 Selected Financial Statement Data of Harley-Davidson

Therefore, Harley-Davidson was going to try to expand capacity at existing plants first through process improvement and restructuring, and externally only as needed. In this way, Harley-Davidson could always stay ready for any expected dip in demand and still be profitable.

Concerns   Approaching 1992, Harley-Davidson had seen it all: fantastic pre-war demands, post-war booms and recessions, the recessions of the 1970s and 80s, a leveraged buyout, the loss of significant market share, and finally a resurgence in demand. Indeed, Harley-Davidson's familial firm memory has been tainted with boom and bust cycles throughout its history. This made management and key decision-makers reluctant to just add supply due to an upturn in the waits and dealer ac-

tions, a feature that many newer recruits could not understand at first.

Throughout this boom and bust cycle, debtors and investors alike upset any feeling of comfort within the organization. Indeed, it was just this relationship, coupled with the weight of past debt obligations, that influenced Harley-Davidson's decision to avoid taking on further debt in its 1992 capacity decision. As a result, the option of adding another plant was considered to be out of the question. Consequently, Harley-Davidson was prompted to fund the 1992 expansion internally. Below are some of the steps Harley-Davidson took and their pertinence to the more recent 1996 capacity question.

Outsourcing Since Harley-Davidson was not going to expand by adding a new facility, the question of outsourcing work became a much-discussed option. Jeff Pharris knew the significant returns on investment achieved in the auto industry by outsourcing. Only 55% of Harley-Davidson's cost-of-goods-sold (COGS) was related to purchased goods. Many companies produced parts similar to Harley-Davidson's and could be approached to supply the company. It was a well-known fact that after-market suppliers make it possible to build a Harley-Davidson from scratch (at significantly higher expense).

Jeff Pharris found himself wishing on a number of occasions that they would begin outsourcing; he felt that much of the value that Detroit appreciated could be easily replicated here. But he also knew and understood the concerns of the longer-time employees in the firm that a too extensive use of outsider's parts could perhaps detract from the value of the Harley-Davidson brand.

Rationalization of Operations Once the company decided not to build new facilities, the optimal use of available space at existing facilities became a priority. This required rethinking machining and assembly of parts within these facilities. First, Harley-Davidson decided to integrate some machining and assembly, using a daring new process architecture where machining cells would be positioned in close proximity to the assembly line, feeding it directly without storage and handling.

Second, all machining and parts activities were scrutinized to see which activities could be outsourced. Harley-Davidson categorized part manufacturing activities according to their strategic value and whether they were proprietary or also could be purchased externally. Investment and outsourcing decisions were prioritized according to the position of each activity in the core competency matrix shown in Figure 11.4.

The matrix looks at strategic value (high or low) and internally versus externally sourcing components. Strategic value is attributable to characteristics that distinguish a component from its mimickers, either quality-wise or cosmetically. When looking at the outsourcing decision, it was important to consider who was supplying the part and perhaps to whom else that company supplied.

Third, and last, the strategic planners proposed a project status monitoring system that projected cost-of-goods-sold (COGS) figures for given future volumes. Management committed to deliver the COGS figures on the pro-forma profit and loss statement for the future. This approach was well understood and appreciated by the board, which approved the $80 million capital investment required for the plant's restructuring.

Harley-Davidson accomplished the expansion from an 75,000 unit to 100,000 unit capacity ahead of schedule and did it without any external funding. In a year and a half, Harley-Davidson had accomplished what was originally estimated to take three years, and the operations group delivered the COGS figures!

MORE GROWTH IN DEMAND

Harley-Davidson had increased its output by nearly 10,000 units in 1995 alone (Fig. 11.3 on p. 396), yet its market share continued to steadily decline (Fig. 11.1 on p. 394). Compared to 1993, industry registrations of domestic heavyweight motorcycles were up 14.5%. The company ended 1994 with a domestic market share of 56.1% compared to 58.4% in 1993. Market share slid further to 55.8% in 1995, despite a significant increase in output over the same period. This decrease was a reflection of Harley-Davidson's constrained production capacity in a growing heavyweight motorcycle market. The strong growth in the heavyweight motorcycle segment in recent years was underpinned by strong economic indicators, growing demand for leisure goods and greater disposable income amongst Harley-Davidson's target consumers. They needed to act quickly once again to take advantage of this trend or risk further loss of market share to competitors.

A basic look at the supply and demand situation for Harley-Davidson suggested the need to either increase prices to increase profits and better match supply and demand—or to increase capacity to meet demand and regain lost market share (Figure 11.5). On the other hand, the pragmatists within the organization pointed out the dangers of uncontrolled growth as experienced in the early

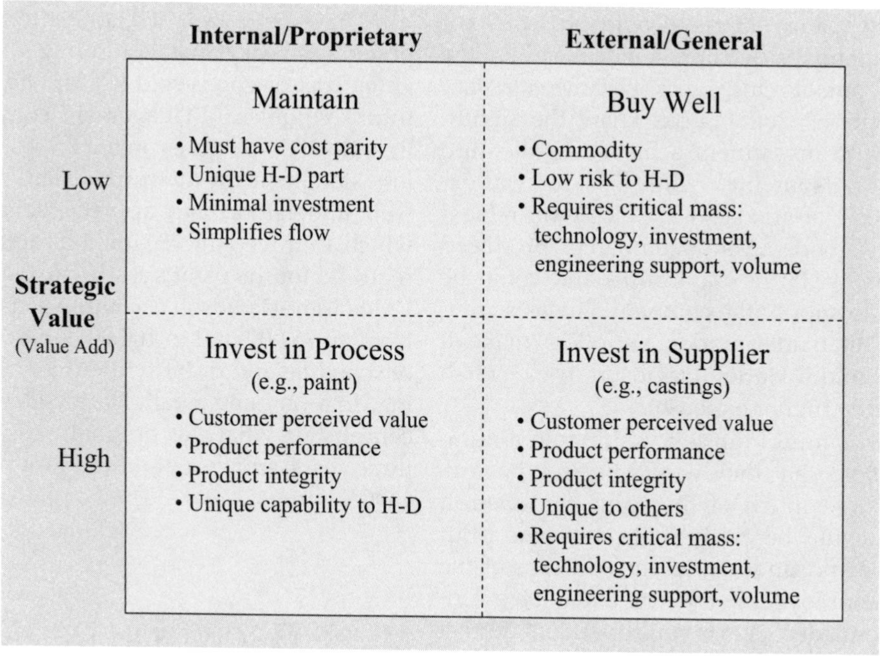

	Internal/Proprietary	**External/General**

Low	**Maintain**
	• Must have cost parity
	• Unique H-D part
	• Minimal investment
	• Simplifies flow
		Buy Well
		• Commodity
		• Low risk to H-D
		• Requires critical mass:
		  technology, investment,
		  engineering support, volume

Strategic Value (Value Add)		

High	**Invest in Process**
	(e.g., paint)
	• Customer perceived value
	• Product performance
	• Product integrity
	• Unique capability to H-D
		Invest in Supplier
		(e.g., castings)
		• Customer perceived value
		• Product performance
		• Product integrity
		• Unique to others
		• Requires critical mass:
		  technology, investment,
		  engineering support, volume

Figure 11.4 Investment and outsourcing decisions were prioritized according to the position of each activity in the core competency matrix.

70s under AMF ownership, or the risk of alienating the market with excessively high prices.

Dave Storm knew that Harley-Davidson also had to consider the risks of expanding and having the market for heavyweight motorcycles disappear as it did in the early 80s, when yearly demand for light and heavyweight bikes plummeted from 400,000 units down to 100,000 units in only 18 months. This sharp drop in demand had caused Harley-Davidson to reduce its yearly output from 50,000 units down to 28,000 units. They did not want to risk returning to the dark days of survival in a soft market with excess capacity and employee layoffs.

In 1995, the management team took all these factors into account, and then decided on four primary success criteria against which any decision would be evaluated and later measured:

1. The speed of increasing the volume of 1340cc bikes (higher margin and higher demand motorcycles).

2. Maintaining good labor relations.

3. Maintaining focus on the company's core-competencies and customer needs, as well as fostering optimal engineering-manufacturing relationships as a means to achieve this.

4. Controlling costs (capital, operating expenditure, overheads, etc.) and risk: Harley-Davidson should be able to withstand a "disaster scenario" such as a 30% drop in demand without loosing excessive amounts of cash.

The Harley-Davidson team realized that they were no longer the niche player that they had once been. They were now a well-respected growth company (Fig. 11.3 on p. 398), adored by loyal customers and Wall Street investors alike. If they continued to grow, they needed to take advantage of the booming demand for their product.

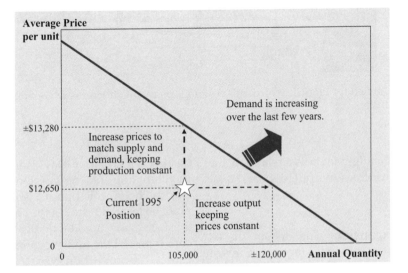

Figure 11.5 Conceptual representation of strategic choices.

STRATEGIC CHOICES

Increase prices The simplest action involved maintaining existing output levels, but raising prices to increase profits and to capture a greater portion of consumer spending surplus for the company. This would provide an easy way to match supply and demand without requiring additional capital investment, or significant changes to the production process. Just how much more would consumers be willing to pay? And what would the long-term implications be? What if the economy slows down in the future?

Change the product mix The next option was to eliminate the legendary Sportster from the product line-up and using the freed-up capacity for the high-margin Softail and Tourer lines. Proponents of this option pointed out that the Sportster was the company's lowest margin product (Table 11.4) by far, and that the demand for the bigger bikes was so great that they would easily be able to sell the increased output, thereby capturing the greater margins associated with these products. Furthermore, Harley-Davidson was probably best known for its big bikes. The capital expenditure required to change over the current facilities to exclusive

big-bike production was also minimal, estimated[2] at $20 million. It required only limited equipment investment and plant and equipment setup changes that could be depreciated over 5 years.

Continuous improvement and outsourcing The last option that did not require any significant investment in new facility construction ("brick and mortar") was to continuously improve and optimize existing facilities to maximize output, while outsourcing most non-core activities. By spending around $10 million per year, this approach would allow the company to increase capacity by 10% annually to a maximum of 150,000 bikes per annum. Each modest incremental capital investment could be depreciated over 5 years. They had already embarked upon a more conservative version of this outsourcing strategy in the previous 1992 capacity expansion. Jeff Pharris in particular, was a firm believer in outsourcing as many non-core activities as possible, and felt that it was the most cost effective and time effective way to increase output in the short term. A responsible approach to further outsourcing non-core activities and component manufacturing along with some

---

[2]Dollar figures have been modified to ensure confidentiality.

	Average Price	Average Direct Cost	Contribution Margin
Sportser	$7,000	$5,000	$2,000
Dyna	$12,000	$8,500	$3,500
Softail	$15,200	$10,700	$4,500
Tourer	$17,000	$12,500	$4,500

Table 11.4 Product Information (figures are modified to ensure confidentiality).

re-arrangement of equipment, was a relatively low risk opportunity to increase output to 150,000 bikes per year.

"Brownfields" expansion The first of the expansion alternatives that would require an investment in brick and mortar was a "brownfields" expansion. This would involve the extension of the existing manufacturing facilities at Milwaukee and York, thereby allowing Harley-Davidson to increase its capacity over the course of 2 years to a maximum of 200,000 units per annum. It was felt that this level of production would allow Harley-Davidson to meet demand in the medium to long term, and thereby ensure continued growth and increased profitability. The capital investment required with this option was, however, fairly significant: it would require a $100 million investment spread over the next three years, each depreciated over 10 years.

"Greenfields" expansion The final option that was considered involved building a new plant that would allow Harley-Davidson to achieve a total capacity of 210,000 units per annum after incremental ramp-up. This option, the most capital intensive of all the alternatives, would require a total layout of $180 million during the next three years, each depreciated over 10 years. It involved many issues that the company was not accustomed to

dealing with. Harley-Davidson had no experience with building and commissioning new plants. If it was to choose this option, where would the new plant be located? Should the company build a flexible facility, or should it dedicate the plant to a specific type of bike and reconfigure the existing facilities? If production was dedicated to a specific product, would it be better to build the higher-margin big bikes in this new facility, or the Sportsters? Should the new plant be integrated and perform all machining and assembly activities for a product line, or should it focus on a particular function such as machining, engine manufacturing, or final assembly?

Choosing an option Neither Dave nor Jim was sure which of these many choices would be the best for Harley-Davidson in the long run. There were so many uncertainties. All that they could be certain about was that if they did not make a decision shortly, they would run the risk of losing further ground to their Japanese competitors and to new American custom bike producers. (Rumors said that Polaris, a recreational vehicles company, and a new company, registered as Excelsior-Henderson[3], were planning to enter the heavyweight custom motorcycle market.) The management team had only a day left before they would have to make a recommendation which would be aligned with Harley-Davidson's strategy and financially attractive to the Board.

---

[3]The original Excelsior-Henderson Motorcycle Company folded in 1931, and the trademark fell into disuse after its parent went bankrupt in 1992.

DISCUSSION QUESTIONS

1. Describe and evaluate Harley's operations strategy (using the framework of Chapter 1).

2. Demand uncertainty is a major factor in strategic capacity decisions. How does Harley-Davidson take uncertainty into account in its planning processes? How does HD's history affect its decision-making process?

3. What factors should HD consider when analyzing the alternatives?

4. What is your recommendation to Harley-Davidson? Assess your plan's fit with HD's strategy and assess its financial attractiveness: complement your qualitative analysis with an NPV analysis. (Use a discount factor of 12%; marginal tax rate is 37%.)

SEAGATE TECHNOLOGY

[1]On July 10, 1997, Ron Verdoorn, Executive Vice President of Seagate Technology and Chief Operating Officer of its Storage Products Group, was reading the capital appropriation request for the *Barracuda 9LP* and the *Cheetah 9LP*. The *Barracuda 9LP* and the *Cheetah 9LP* were two of Seagate's new high-end disk-drive product families that were scheduled to go into volume production in the first calendar quarter of 1998. The capital appropriation request called for a $103 million capital investment in two final assembly facilities, one for the *Barracuda*, one for the *Cheetah*, and one joint test facility. The capacities of the new facilities would enable the execution of the master production plan, which was derived by the Material Division based on a sales forecast by the Marketing Division.

While the capital investment plan was definitely reasonable, Ron was wondering whether the plan would provide Seagate with a sufficient hedge against demand uncertainty, which was intrinsic to the sales forecast in a highly volatile disk drive industry.

Company Background   Seagate Technology, Inc. is a data technology company that provides products for storing, managing, and accessing digital information on the world's computer and data communications systems. At more than $8.9 billion in revenue for its fiscal year ending in June 27, 1997, Seagate is the largest independent disk drive company in the world (Table 12.1).

Seagate was founded in 1979 in Scotts Valley, California, and went on to ship more than 100 million disk drives by 1997.

Seagate designs, manufactures, and markets disk drives for use in computer systems ranging from notebook computers and desktop personal computers to workstations and supercomputers, as well as in multimedia applications such as digital video and video-on-demand. Seagate leads the disk drive storage industry by offering the broadest product line, including disk drives with 2.5, 3.5, and 5.25inch form factors and capacity points up to 23Gigabytes. The company sells its products to original equipment manufacturers ("OEMs") for inclusion in their computer systems or subsystems, and to distributors, resellers, dealers and retailers.

Seagate has pursued a strategy of *vertical integration* and accordingly designs and manufactures rigid disk drive components such as recording heads, disks, disc substrates, motors, and custom integrated circuits. It also assembles certain key subassemblies for use in its products including printed circuit board and head stack assemblies. Products are manufactured primarily in the Far East, with limited production in the United States and the Republic of Ireland.

As of June 27, 1997, Seagate employed 111,000 persons worldwide, approximately 93,000 of who were located in the company's Far East operations.

---

[1]This case was prepared by Professor Van Mieghem as the basis for class discussion rather than to illustrate either the factual, effective or ineffective handling of a managerial situation. Portions of it are based on Seagate's 1997 10-K form. Selected data in the case are based on estimates. No part of this case study may be reproduced without permission; direct all inquiries to permissions@vanmieghem.us

(Data in thousands)

Fiscal Year Ended	6-27-1997	6-28-1996	6-30-1995	7-1-1994	7-2-1993
Net sales	$8,940,022	$8,588,350	$7,256,209	$5,865,255	$5,195,276
Gross profit	2,022,255	1,581,001	1,373,385	1,170,821	909,872
Income from operations	857,585	286,969	459,301	473,097	-195,442
Income before extraordinary gain	658,038	213,261	312,548	329,685	-267,605
Net income	658,038	213,261	312,548	329,685	-267,605
Total assets	6,722,879	5,239,635	4,899,832	4,307,937	3,470,970
Long-term debt, less current portion	701,945	798,305	1,066,321	1,176,551	941,882
Stockholders' equity	$3,475,666	$2,466,088	$1,936,132	$1,634,700	$1,228,829

Source: Seagate Technology 1997-10K

Table 12.1 Selected financial statement data.

Disk Drive Technology Magnetic disk drives are used in computer systems to record, store, and retrieve digital information. Most computer applications require access to a greater volume of data than can economically be stored in the random access memory of the computer's central processing unit (commonly known as "semiconductor" memory). This information can be stored on a variety of storage devices, including rigid disk drives, both fixed and removable, flexible disk drives, magnetic tape drives, optical disk drives and semiconductor memory. Rigid disk drives provide access to large volumes of information faster than can optical disk drives, flexible disk drives or magnetic tape drives—and at substantially lower cost than high-speed semiconductor memory.

Although products vary, all rigid disk drives incorporate the same basic technology shown in Figure 12.1. One or more rigid disks are attached to a spindle assembly that rotates the disks at a high constant speed around a hub. The disks (also known as media or disk media) are the components on which data is stored and from which it is retrieved. Each disk typically consists of a substrate of finely machined aluminum or glass with a magnetic layer of a "thin-film" metallic material.

Rigid disk drive performance is measured by four key characteristics:

1. Average access time, which is the time needed to position the heads over a selected track on the disk surface;

2. Media data transfer rate (expressed in megabits per second), which is the rate at which data is transferred to and from the disk;

3. Storage capacity (expressed in megabytes or gigabytes–"MB" or "GB"), which is the amount of data that can be stored on the disk; and

4. Spindle rotation speed (commonly expressed in revolutions per minute–"rpm"), which has an effect on the speed of access to data.

Read/write heads, mounted on an arm assembly similar in concept to that of a record player, fly extremely close to each disk surface, and recording data on and retrieving it from concentric tracks in the magnetic layers of the rotating disks.

Upon instructions from the drive's electronic circuitry, a head positioning mechanism (an "actuator") guides the heads to the selected track of a disk where the data will be recorded or retrieved. The disk drive communicates with the host computer through an internal controller. Disc drive manufacturers may use one or more of several industry standard interfaces, such as SCSI (Small Computer System Interface).

Disk Drive Market Rigid disk drives are used in a broad range of computer systems, as well as for multimedia applications such as digital video

Figure 12.1 Disk drive technology.

and video-on-demand. Users of computer systems are increasingly demanding additional data storage capacity with higher performance. They use more sophisticated applications software, including database management, CAD/CAM/CAE, desktop publishing, video editing and enhanced graphics applications. Furthermore, they increasingly operate in multi-user, multitasking, and multimedia environments. Additionally, there is a sizable market for rigid disk drives in the existing installed base of computer systems, some of which require additional storage capacity.

The computer system market includes four major segments: desktop personal computers, mobile computers, workstation systems, and server/multi-user systems.

The personal computers (desktop and mobile) market in 1997 was characterized by a minimum storage requirements for entry-level personal computers of 810MB to 1.7GB. Seek times ranged from 12.5msec down to 10.5msec. The entry-level capacities continue to increase. In addition, users of personal computers have become increasingly price sensitive. Seagate's objective for the desktop and mobile personal computer market is to design drives for high-volume, low-cost manufacture.

Smaller footprint systems, such as mobile, laptop, notebook, and ultra-portable computers require rigid disk drives in form factors of less than 3.5inches. These small form factors emphasize durability and low power consumption in addition to capacity and performance characteristics found in their desktop functional equivalents. Personal digital assistants and hand-held pen-based computers may use 1.8inch or 2.5inch hard disk drives or flash memory such as PCMCIA cards for additional memory. These mobile applications also emphasize low power consumption as well as very high degrees of durability.

Workstation systems include high performance microcomputers, workstations, servers, and minicomputers. Applications are computing or data intensive, so that workstation systems typically require rigid disk drive storage capacities of 2GB and greater per drive, average seek times of 8msec and rotation speeds of 7,200rpm to 10,000rpm. Due to the leading edge characteristics required by end-users of workstation systems, manufacturers of such systems emphasize performance as well as price as the key selling points.

Server/multi-user systems are large systems that include mainframes and supercomputers. Typical applications such as business management systems, transaction processing, parallel processing and other applications require intensive data manipulation. Also included in high-end applications are systems designed for video-on-demand and near-line storage. Users of these systems generally require capacities of at least 4GB per drive with average seek times of 8msec and rotation speeds of 5,400rpm to 10,000rpm. End-users of large systems are less concerned than users of smaller systems with the size, weight, power consumption, and absolute cost of the drive.

As with workstation systems, the OEM typically designs drive products into these systems with emphasis on performance, reliability and capacity. In this market segment, data storage subsystems that contain large numbers of disk drives are commonly used. Because data integrity is paramount, high device reliability and maintainability are key features. Mainframe, supercomputer and digital video systems also benefit from very high data transfer rates (up to ten times those of small computer systems).

With the proliferation of multimedia applications, the demand for increased drive capacities continues to increase at an accelerating rate. After all, sound and moving pictures require many times the storage capacity of simple text.

Disk Drive Products Seagate's products include over 50 rigid disk drive models with form factors from 2.5 to 5.25inches and capacities from 1GB to 23GB. Seagate believes it offers the broadest range of disk storage products available. It provides more than one product at some capacity points and differentiates products on a price, performance, and form factor basis. Seagate typically devotes its resources to developing products with industry leading performance characteristics and to being among the first to introduce such products to the market. The company continuously seeks to enhance its market presence in emerging segments of the rigid disk drive market by emphasizing its established capabilities in high-volume, low-cost production.

The *Marathon* and *Medalist* disk drive product lines are targeted for the personal mobile and desktop computing market, respectively. However, the high-end workstation and server/multi-user systems market is served with the *Barracuda, Cheetah* and *Elite* product families.

The *Barracuda* family of 3.5inch drives, introduced in 1992, had the highest rotation speed (7,200rpm) of any drives produced at that time. In fiscal year 1997, Seagate introduced two new products in the *Barracuda* family, the *Barracuda* 4LP and the *Barracuda* 4XL, with 4GB and 4.5GB respectively. The *Barracuda* 4XL, which began volume production during the fourth quarter of fiscal 1997,

was designed to provide a balance of price and performance for the maturing workstation market.

In August 1996, the Company announced the 3.5inch *Cheetah* family—the world's first disk drives to offer rotation speeds of 10,000rpm for increased data throughput and lower latency times. The *Cheetah* drive is targeted towards the very high performance segment of the market. Volume production of the *Cheetah* 4LP and the *Cheetah* 9 began in the third and fourth quarters of fiscal 1997, respectively. Seagate revealed its fifth generation *Barracuda* 9LP and its second generation *Cheetah* 9LP in early fall 1997, with volume production scheduled to begin in the first calendar quarter of 1998.

Finally, the *Elite* product line covers the high-end 5.25inch market. In the third quarter of fiscal year 1997, production commenced on the Elite 23, a high performance, 5.25inch disk drive with 23GB of formatted capacity, a rotation speed of 5,400rpm, and mean-time-between-failures (MTBF) of 500,000 hours.

Disk Drive Industry and Competition The rigid disk drive industry is intensely competitive, with manufacturers competing for a limited number of major customers. In addition to the product performance dimension described earlier, the principal competitive factors in the rigid disk drive market include product quality and reliability, form factor, price per unit, price per megabyte, production volume capability, and responsiveness to customers. The relative importance of these factors varies with different customers and products.

Seagate experiences intense competition from a number of domestic and foreign companies, some of which have far greater resources. Seagate competes with independent rigid disk drive manufacturers, such as Quantum and Western Digital Corporation, who have 1997 revenues of $5.3B and $4.1B, respectively. Seagate also faces competition from customers, including IBM, Toshiba, NEC and Fujitsu Limited. These customers continually evaluate whether to manufacture their own drives or purchase them from outside sources. They also sell drives to third parties, thus resulting in direct competition with Seagate. IBM's Storage Division, for example, has successfully invested in mobile disk drive technology and has now captured a 40%

share of the global mobile disk drive market.

The rigid disk drive industry is characterized by ongoing, rapid technological change, relatively short product life cycles and rapidly changing user needs. This, together with intense competition, has resulted in an industry with a history of declining prices. The price per megabyte of disk storage has dropped at a steady pace of about 40 percent per year from 1980 through 1995–even faster than the price drop for computer memory chips (Figure 12.2).

In addition, the famous volatility of demand for computer products and peripherals translates into highly fluctuating demand for disk drives. Seagate often must accommodate changes in orders of up to 20% within only two weeks of production.

Competitors offer new and existing products at prices necessary to gain or retain market share and customers. To remain competitive, Seagate believes it is necessary to continue reducing its prices and aggressively enhancing its product offerings. In addition, Seagate's ability to compete successfully will also depend on its ability to provide timely product introductions and to continue to reduce production costs. The company's establishment and ongoing expansion of production facilities in Singapore, Thailand, Malaysia, China, and Ireland are directed toward such cost reductions.

Product and Process Development Seagate's strategy for new products emphasizes timely and cost effective development and introduction of products that offer functionality and performance equal to or better than competitive product offerings. Seagate believes that its future success will depend upon its ability to develop, manufacture and market products which meet changing user needs; the products must also successfully anticipate or respond to changes in technology and standards on a cost-effective and timely basis. Accordingly, the company is committed to the development of new component technologies, new products, and the continuing evaluation of alternative technologies.

The upcoming introduction of the two new products under discussion, the *Barracuda 9LP* and the *Cheetah 9LP*, was thus in line with Seagate's ongoing strategy. The *Cheetah* boasted faster seek

time (5.2 vs. 7.1msec) and a higher throughput rate (21 vs. 15.3Mbytes/sec). The *Barracuda*, on the other hand, was 15% more energy-efficient and enjoyed the *Barracuda* family's reputation for a high level of reliability. While the primary market for the *Cheetah* is in enterprise servers, both drives appeal to high-end workstation users for graphic imaging applications. At about $1090 for a 9.1Gbyte drive, the pricing for the new *Cheetah* family would be approximately 15% above the industry-leading *Barracuda* series.

Seagate develops new disk drive products and the processes to produce them at six locations: Longmont, Colorado; Moorpark and San Jose, California; Oklahoma City, Oklahoma; Bloomington, Minnesota; and Singapore. Generally speaking, 3.5inch form factor drives intended for desktop personal computer systems are produced in Longmont, Moorpark, and Singapore. Moreover, 2.5inch form factor drives intended for mobile personal computers are developed in San Jose. Oklahoma City is responsible for the development of 3.5inch disk drives with capacities and interfaces intended for use in minicomputers, supermicrocomputers, workstations and file servers. Finally, Bloomington is responsible for 3.5inch and 5.25inch products principally intended for use in systems ranging from workstations and superminicomputers to mainframe and supercomputers, as well as newer digital video and video-on-demand markets.

In addition to developing new products and components, the company devotes significant resources to product engineering aimed at improving manufacturing processes, lowering manufacturing costs, and increasing volume production. Process engineering groups are located with the disk drive development groups and the reliability engineering groups in the locations listed above. Most of Seagate's volume production, however, is done in locations remote from these groups and the development of the volume processes is completed at the volume manufacturing sites.

Manufacturing Strategy Seagate's manufacturing managers face difficult challenges. Because of surging global demand, their facilities frequently run at full capacity. Changes in technology along with short product life cycles force frequent equip-

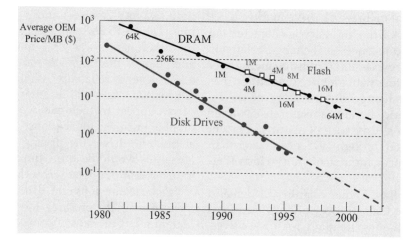

Figure 12.2 Price trends of hard drives vs. semiconductor memory. Source: Dataquest

ment purchases. Long equipment acquisition lead-times often require that capacity decisions be made six months in advance of need. And establishing manufacturing capacity in anticipation of highly volatile market demand is critical to bottom line performance.

The key elements of the Seagate's manufacturing strategy are high-volume, low-cost assembly and test, vertical integration in the manufacture of selected components, and the establishment and maintenance of key vendor relationships.

Manufacturing incurs significant fixed costs, while the industry has a history of declining prices. Thus, the company must continue to produce and sell its disk drives in significant volume, lower manufacturing costs, and carefully monitor inventory levels. Towards these ends, Seagate continually evaluates its components and manufacturing processes. It is paramount that Seagate rapidly achieves high manufacturing yields in new production processes and obtain uninterrupted access to high-quality components in required volumes at competitive prices. Also, it is often desirable to transfer volume production of disk drives and related components between facilities, including overseas to countries where labor costs and other manufacturing costs are significantly lower than in the U.S., principally Singapore, Thailand,

Malaysia, and China.

Manufacturing Processes The manufacturing of disk drives is a complex process, requiring a "clean room" environment, the assembly of precision components within narrow tolerances, and extensive testing to ensure reliability. The first step in the manufacturing of a rigid disk drive is the assembly of the actuator mechanism, heads, disks, and spindle motor in a housing to form the head-disk assembly (the "HDA"). The assembly of the HDA involves a combination of manual and semi-automated processes. After the HDA is assembled, a servo pattern is magnetically recorded on the disk surfaces. Upon completion, circuit boards are attached to the HDA during final assembly and the completed unit is thoroughly tested prior to packaging and shipment. Final assembly and test operations take place primarily at facilities located in Singapore, Thailand, Malaysia, China, Ireland, Minnesota, and Oklahoma. Subassembly and component operations are performed at facilities in Singapore, Malaysia, Thailand, Minnesota, California, Northern Ireland, Indonesia, Mexico, China, and Scotland. In addition, independent entities manufacture or assemble components for Seagate.

Volume production of the two new products,

the *Barracuda 9LP* and the *Cheetah 9LP*, would require investment in new final assembly and test capacity. Given the different technology, each family's HDA and printed circuit board final assembly needed its own product-specific equipment. Both families, however, could be tested in one facility. Disk drive testing involves connecting the drive to intelligent drive testers (IDTs), fast computers that perform a set of read-write tests. IDTs can quickly switch over between testing a *Barracuda* and a *Cheetah* (both take approximately the same amount of tester time).

Product life cycles of disk drives were already short (high volume products introduced in 1995 were sold for about 6 to 7 quarters), but were expected to drop even further. The two new products were planned to be in volume production only for the four quarters of 1998. The capital investment to build production capacity was significant and had two components. First, there were significant fixed costs (estimated at about $40 million) associated with designing, commissioning, and starting up the three new facilities. The second component was that the capital expense (CapEx) of building new capacity increased with the amount of capacity: larger production capacity required larger space requirements and tooling costs, leading to an (approximately) linear increase in the capital expense. These linear components of the CapEx were expressed in terms of a capacity cost for an aggregate, *annual production rate* (APR) of one thousand units[2].

Note that capacity investment costs are incurred during construction and before production. To better understand this, imagine building a house: its construction costs have both fixed and variable components that increase with the square footage of the house. However, the construction costs are incurrent independent of the extent to which the house is later used. The challenge in capacity investment thus is to size facilities relative to expected subsequent usage or production: facilities should be neither too small nor too big. A good estimate of required production rates for each product was thus paramount to a well-sized capacity investment plan. Given the frequency of

Seagate's investments, an extensive *Capacity Requirements Planning* (CRP) process had been developed over time to assist capital investment planning.

Capital Investments and "Sales-plan Driven Planning" To support its growth and frequent new product and technology introductions, Seagate made investments in property and equipment in fiscal 1997 totaling $920 million. This amount included $301 million for manufacturing facilities and equipment related to subassembly and disk drive final assembly and test (FA&T) facilities in the United States, Far East, and Ireland. Capital investments are the result of an extensive Capacity Requirement Planning (CRP) process, which intermeshes with the production planning process as represented by Figure 12.3.

Seagate's monthly "demand-planning" cycle begins when individual marketing and sales product managers use their specialized knowledge of local markets to estimate sales potentials for the following twelve, or even twenty-four, months. These estimates capture both planned purchases by major OEMs as well as possible orders by distributors, resellers, dealers and retailers. Obviously, some of theses estimates are more reliable than others; the accuracy of these forecasts degrades sharply beyond the immediate quarter so that significant uncertainty in total demand remained. The *demand forecast* represents the combined estimates of the monthly worldwide demand for each individual product. Conceptually, the demand forecast captures demand uncertainty by a probability distribution over likely demand scenarios.

Total demand[3] for the two new products was forecasted to be about 600,000 units, as shown in Figure 12.4. Given that the two products were (imperfect) substitutes, total demand was relatively reliable with about plus or minus 100,000 unit error estimate. There was, however, significant uncertainty regarding the adoption of the *Cheetah* and thus the ultimate mix: A pessimistic scenario (with likelihood estimated at 25%) would demand only 150,000 *Cheetah's* and 350,000 *Barracuda's*. The

---

[2]While actual production was planned in terms of a *daily going rate*, capacity planning for investment purposes was done on an aggregate basis.

[3]The following demand, margins, and cost data are all estimated.

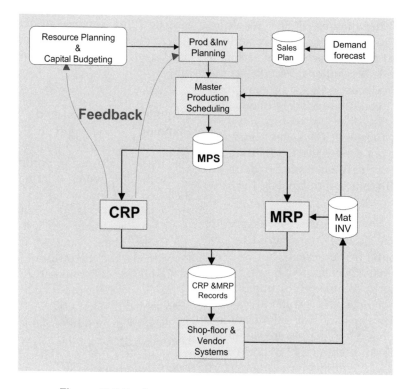

Figure 12.3 Production and capacity planning processes.

optimistic scenario (likelihood of 25%), however, called for 450,000 *Cheetah's* and 250,000 *Barracuda's*.

Through a process of aggregation and negotiation, the marketing and sales division summarizes the demand forecast in a sales plan. The sales plan may adjust the most likely or the average demand scenario to account for additional factors such as end-of-life cycle effects of unannounced products on the sales of the products they supersede. Senior managers may also decide to curtail production of products whose margins have fallen below profitability hurdles or to adjust the mix of capacity or material constrained products.

The sales plan is then passed to the master production schedulers in the materials division, who construct a preliminary Master Production Schedule (MPS). The MPS spells out monthly production quantities ("build proposal") for each product, based on the sales plan and current and future finished goods inventory status. The MPS is then "exploded" to subassembly production schedules for each individual factory location. It forms the basis for their component manufacturing and materials

acquisition decisions.

Before the MPS is finalized, each facility performs a feasibility check of the preliminary MPS. Usually within one day, vice presidents of the various manufacturing plants contact the MPS schedulers to suggest changes to the MPS if needed. After a few iterations, and all within three days, the final version of the MPS is set, signed off by Ron Verdoorn and the senior VPs of Components and Materials. The MPS is then transmitted to each manufacturing facility. Each manufacturing facility thus receives an estimate of required production rates and plant managers can adjust capacity when needed. As such, the sales plan and MPS serve as an efficient coordination tool for corporate-wide capacity planning.

It is rare for a production facility to fail to meet the output levels required by the final MPS. A production facility has several options when a proposed MPS appears to be infeasible. If the infeasibility is detected early enough, the plant manager can inform the MPS schedulers, and production can be shifted to other facilities. Alternatively,

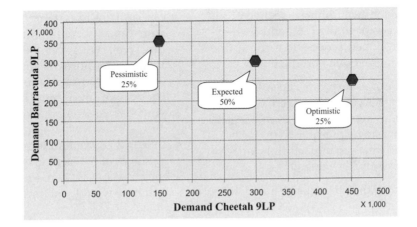

Figure 12.4 Demand forecast for the two new products.

equipment may be flown from one facility to another, which occurs frequently when product lines are shifted among manufacturing locations. Senior managers, who can determine whether the cost of moving the equipment is justified by the profitability of the product, must approve these decisions. Sometimes, however, constraints on equipment and material availability cause some demand to remain unfilled. In 1995, a shortage of media forced Seagate to ration supply among its customers and market segments.

To make longer-term equipment purchases and install new capacity, plant managers must submit a Capital Appropriation Request to senior managers.

The *Barracuda* and *Cheetah* Capacity Investment The "sales-plan driven planning" process for the two new products thus *coordinates* capacity decisions to the single sales plan (and associated master production plan) that marketing, manufacturing, and financial managers have approved. Consistent with cost incentives, the current Capital Appropriation Request on Ron Verdoorn's desk asked for the minimal cost capacity plan to enable the production plan: a *Cheetah* FA facility with an annual production capacity of 300,000 units, a *Barracuda* FA facility also with a 300,000 unit capacity and a testing facility with a corresponding 600,000 unit capacity. A capital appropriation of $103 million was requested. In addition to the fixed $40 million, the CapEx of $103 million in-

cluded the linear capacity sizing costs of $30,000 per one thousand units of annual production rate (APR) in the *Cheetah* final assembly facility. The more cost-efficient *Barracuda* FA facility would require a modest $20,000 per one thousand APR. The testing facility, however, would be more expensive at about $80,000 per thousand APR, reflecting the cost of many expensive IDT's.

New high-end drives such as the *Cheetah* and *Barracuda* are the "bread and butter" of Seagate. Such high-end drives are relatively immune from competition. Throughout the production cycle, the drives were estimated to command average unit contribution margins of about $400 and $300 for the *Cheetah* and *Barracuda*, respectively. Given the high demand uncertainty of the two product families, Ron was wondering whether the current capital appropriation request, which implemented the most likely sales forecast, should be approved or whether he should "adjust" the capacity investment to provide Seagate with a better operational hedge against uncertainty.

DISCUSSION QUESTIONS

1. Describe and evaluate Seagate's operations strategy (using the framework from Chapter 1). Critically evaluate Seagate's product and process development strategy, which

calls for development in its respective product/process center in the U.S., and then exports the developed process to a site in the Far-East for high-volume production.

2. What is the expected profit and ROI of the proposed capacity CAR? (Given the short product life, assume the firm is making its decisions for a single time period of one year, at the end of which manufacturing capacity will have zero salvage value.)

3. The case states that the true demand forecast contains uncertainty. In what sense does your capacity configuration prepare you to deal well with this demand uncertainty? What is the financial impact of uncertainty on your recommendation? (Recall that capacity investment must be performed before you observe actual market demand.)

4. In broad conceptual terms, what are the advantages of "sales-plan driven capacity planning"? What is "wrong" with that practice and how would you improve it?

PEAPOD

[1]The year 2001 brought challenges and changes to Peapod and Webvan, the two pioneers of the vision to "shop online, not inline."

Brothers Andrew and Thomas Parkinson founded Peapod in 1989 in Evanston, Illinois, just outside Chicago. This pioneer of online grocery shopping went public in 1997 at an initial share price of $16. In Fall 1999, at the age of 51, Louis H. Borders, the entrepreneur and man behind bookseller Borders Group Inc. (BGP), the second-largest bookstore chain in the U.S., startled the business world by announcing his approach to on-line shopping. Webvan Group Inc. had been founded in December 1996 to implement Border's idea. On its first day of public trading in 1999, Webvan shares surpassed $20, as Figure 13.1 shows.

In 2001, both companies faced rationalized capital markets and were under intense pressure to perform and become profitable. Both companies had changed their CEO. At a depressed share price of around $1, Peapod was working hard to make its new "bricks-and-clicks" strategy work in cooperation with majority shareholder Royal Ahold, a Netherlands-based international food provider giant. Webvan, on the other hand, continued to believe in Borders' idea of highly automated mass customization, even though its market value was declining exponentially. Will the vision to profitably operate an Internet grocer remain elusive? What are the key performance indicators of mass customization in this industry?

GROCERY INDUSTRY OVERVIEW

In 1999, U.S. consumers spent approximately $458 billion on groceries, with this figure continuing to grow at about 3% annually. While there are many retail outlets that sell groceries, the majority of food (70%) is sold at supermarkets (see Figure 13.2). Other retail outlets include superstores, such as Wal-Mart, convenience stores, and specialty food outlets.

In 1916, Piggly Wiggly, the first self-service store, opened in Memphis, Tennessee. In 1930, King Kullen Grocery Company, the first supermarket, opened in New York.

> "The supermarket revolution thus started when single-store, independent grocery stores invited their customers to take a basket and "serve yourself" in multi-department supermarkets. As their numbers grew, the procurement and selling efficiencies of supermarkets led grocery chain retailers to sell many of their smaller stores. By the 1950's, the chain retailers' transition to supermarkets was complete. Subsequent growth of large supermarket chains was accomplished through building new stores and through mergers and acquisitions."[2]

---

[1]Professor Van Mieghem prepared this case as the basis for class discussion rather than to illustrate either the effective or ineffective handling of a managerial situation. The cooperation of Peapod management is gratefully acknowledged. No part of this case study may be reproduced without permission; direct all inquiries to permissions@vanmieghem.us

[2]Grocery Retailers Demonstrate Urge to Merge, by Phil R. Kaufman, in *Structural Change in US Food Industry*, May-Aug 2000,

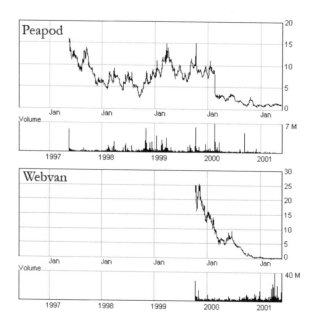

Figure 13.1 Share Price and Daily Volume from 6-24-1996 to 6-23-2001.

Today, this growth is continuing. Among the 10 largest U.S. supermarkets, the average store had weekly revenues of $374,202 in 2000. The average store size was 44,600 square feet. Supermarkets are an archetypical example of "mass production" since they operate at high volumes with razor thin margins of about 1% after tax (Table 13.1). The average customer transaction was $23.03 as stated in *According to the Food Marketing Industry Speaks, 2001* . The average family spends $91 on groceries each week, while average per-person expenditures were $38 each week.

Online Retail The online retail industry experienced triple digit growth in the 1990s with the growing popularity of the Internet. The ability of online retailers to interact directly with customers by tailoring their featured selections, "store" design and pricing made the web an attractive commercial medium. Among the early products sold on the web were computers, travel services, financial services, books, and music.

The total value of goods sold over the Internet in the U.S. in 1999 was $33 billion, compared to $318 million in 1995 (CAGR 219%). Similarly, the

online population was 80 million, up from only 10 million in 1995 (CAGR 68%). Their demographics are attractive: the majority is well educated with high incomes. The online penetration, however, was expected to exceed 10% in only two industries by 2000: computers and software.

On-line grocery sales accounted for only $513 million in 1999, or just 0.1% of the total market; Jupiter Research projected $3.5 billion by 2002. Despite the tremendous growth of Internet online business-to-consumer (B2C) traffic, few companies were profitable in 2000.

Due to increased pressure for profit from investors, consolidation had become the major trend since 2000. Pure-play companies were buying other pure-plays or complementary catalog retailers to build scale in a short time. Traditional retailers were launching online initiatives either internally or by acquiring pure-play startups. After the Nasdaq meltdown in April 2000, e-tailers suffered from an increasingly cautious venture capital market, which became more interested in "business-to-business" (B2B).

The grocery retailing business is extremely competitive. Local, regional, and national food

available at ers.usda.gov

Top 10 U.S. Food Retailers in 2001 (By 2000 Grocery Sales)

		U.S. Sales	Stores	Sales/Store/wk
1. The Kroger Co.	Cincinnati, OH	$ 49,100M	3127	$ 301,961
2. Albertson's, Inc.	Boise, ID	$ 37,110M	2514	$ 283,872
3. Safeway Inc.	Pleasanton, CA	$ 31,977M	1689	$ 364,087
4. Ahold USA, Inc.	Chantilly, VA	$ 22,000M	1229	$ 344,245
5. Costco Companies, Inc.	Issaquah, WA	$ 17,690M	335	$ 1,015,499
6. Wal-Mart Supercenters	Bentonville, AR	$ 17,160M	953	$ 346,275
7. Publix Super Markets, Inc.	Lakeland, FL	$ 14,349M	645	$ 427,818
8. Winn-Dixie Stores, Inc.	Jacksonville, FL	$ 13,697M	1069	$ 246,402
9. Delhaize America 1	Salisbury, NC	$ 12,652M	1486	$ 163,733
10. Great Atlantic & Pacific Tea Co.	Montvale, NJ	$ 10,490M	813	$ 248,131
		Average:		$ 374,202

(Source: Directory of supermarket, grocery & convenience store chains '01. Business Guides, Tampa)

Supermarket Operating Costs (1999)

Sales	100%	
COGS	73.6%	
Gross Margin	26.4%	100%
Expenses		
Payroll	11.2%	39.69%
Employee Benefits	2.9%	11.07%
Utilities	1.2%	4.58%
Property Rentals	1.9%	7.25%
Taxes & Licenses	0.4%	1.91%
Insurance	0.3%	1.15%
Depreciation & Amortization	1.5%	6.11%
Maintenance & Repairs	0.8%	3.05%
Supplies	1.1%	3.82%
Other Operating Costs Allowances NOT included above	3.6%	14.50%
Total Expenses	24.8%	92.37%
Net Operating Profit	1.6%	7.63%
Net Other Income	0.1%	1.15%
Net Income Before Tax & Extraordinary Items	1.7%	6.49%

(Source: Food Marketing Institute Operations Review, Q1 2000–Income Statement Analysis, p. 25.)

Supermarket Chains: Inventory Turns

	1991	1992	1993	1994	1995	1996	1997	1998	1999
Grocery	17.24	16.78	16.55	15.8	18	16.6	17.09	16.1	15.8
Warehouse	14.85	14.8	14.35	16.17	17.65	17.8	18.69	18.36	16.8

(Source: Chains – FMI Operations Review Full Year 1991-1999)

Table 13.1 U.S. supermarket industry, financial and operating information.

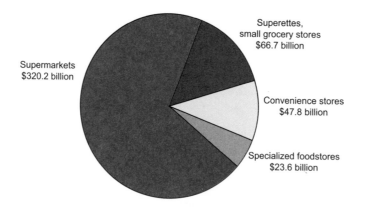

Figure 13.2 Foodstore sales reached $458.3 billion in 1999 (Sources: Bureau of the Census, Monthly Retail Trade Survey, Annual Summary 1990-99, USDA, ERS, U.S. food expenditure tables).

chains, independent food stores, and farmer's markets form the principal competition for online retailers. In addition, convenience stores, liquor retailers, membership warehouse clubs, specialty retailers, supercenters, and drugstore chains fight for the same customers. Several large grocery retailers who entered the "last mile" delivery solution were larger, with more resources than Peapod and Webvan. Yet, at this point, no one seemed to have developed the magic idea to efficiently lock in the customer handshake or the last mile.

With strong competition and weak capital markets, the online grocery industry was experiencing a "shakeout." Several competitors were ceasing operations, such as Streamline, which closed its doors and sold off its assets in November 2000. Others were acquired, such as HomeGrocer, which was bought by Webvan in June 2000. From the initial startups, only Peapod and Webvan remained as e-grocers with national, full-line grocery ambitions. And even they faced restructuring or curtailing of their expansion plans; their ultimate surviving capability was still unclear.

PEAPOD

Peapod's strategy is to "own the handshake" with consumers. With its tagline *"Smart Shopping For Busy People,"* it has provided consumers with a convenient, affordable, high quality home shopping solution.

The Early Days   Peapod began test-marketing in Evanston, Illinois, in July 1990 with about 400 households.[3] The orders were placed online, just not over the Internet. Peapod provided software and even sold the modems customers needed to dial in directly to Peapod. In 1998, Peapod began taking orders over its own website. Years of experience had helped Peapod develop technologies that were central to its business model. Its IT system integrated proprietary and commercial systems that were tailored to the consumer. The website enables consumers to shop at home and view more product and price information than they traditionally have. Peapod's information systems efficiently link its product database with its merchandising systems. Peapod is thus able to provide dynamic pricing and promotions to its customers.

---

[3]Peapod's corporate fact sheet, March 2001.

In-Store Picking During the early days, after receiving a customer order, founders Andrew and Thomas would personally do the picking and packing in an existing local supermarket store, operated by the *Jewel* supermarket chain. They would make deliveries using their own cars! As demand for the service grew, temporary workers were responsible for serving the region within a 2.5-mile radius using their own personal vehicle. The delivery system was thus very similar to a *pizza delivery system*. Once the order was received, the customer order fulfillment process consisted of the following steps:

1. Picking the order in a local supermarket.

2. Driving and delivering the items to the customer living in the service area.

Expansion As the business grew, Peapod expanded operations to include much of the greater Chicago area, which is currently its largest market. By December 1998 it had duplicated its in-store picking fulfillment strategy and opened locations in Boston, Long Island, Houston, Dallas, Austin, and Columbus. Relationships were formed with local supermarkets: Stop & Shop in the Boston metropolitan area, Edwards in the New York area, Kroger in Columbus (2 store pick locations), and Randall's in Texas (10 store pick locations).

Peapod had approximately 240 full-time and 1,125 part-time employees. Most of the part-time employees worked in the grocery picking, packing, and delivery part of the business. Of the full-time employees, approximately 160 were in field operations or member support functions. The remainder worked in information technology, sales and marketing, and general and administrative functions.

Revenues had increased from $27.6 million in fiscal 1997 to $69.3 million in 1998 (Table 13.2). During this same period, however, Peapod's net losses increased from $9.6 million to $21.6 million. This was mainly due to the large investments needed to implement the centralized warehouse model in many cities simultaneously.

Centralized Warehouse Picking And Distribution In January 1999, a new operational strategy

and structure was adopted. No longer would Peapod fill its orders at local supermarkets. Rather, a new 71,000 square foot warehouse was built in Niles, Illinois to serve the greater Chicago area with a series of small trucks that are owned and operated by Peapod. Food suppliers would now deliver to the Peapod-owned warehouse. The San Francisco Bay area was also served by a centralized distribution center in Berkeley.

The centralized distribution model is based on the assumption that its costs are lower than those of operating several local stores. The same argument was used by on-line pioneer Amazon.com and supermarket chain Albertsons.

The customer fulfillment process changed to:

1. Packers at the warehouse collect and pack groceries, while receiving instructions through Palm pilots. Each order is broken into three "picks" corresponding to three zones: chilled temperature zone, dry goods zone, and a fresh, fast-mover zone. A picker downloads a single pick into her Palm, which gives an optimized route to the location of a specific customer's item. A scanner built into the Palm ensures the accuracy of the products selected.

2. Orders in each shift are sorted in reverse order of delivery. The last orders on a delivery route are picked first. Pickers pack items into green totes on a cart (one order per tour, no batching). Chilled and dairy items are put into Styrofoam coolers. The totes for each of the three order picks are then closed and stored in one position in a staging lane in front of a shipping door.

3. Drivers load totes from the lanes into their vans. They also receive a map showing their optimal delivery route obtained from route-optimization software.

4. Drivers traverse petal-shaped routes, similar to *milk runs*, in delivery trucks that have a distinct Peapod logo.

This new delivery system helped Peapod scale up and overcome some limitations in the pizza delivery system. Because goods could be stored in low-rent warehouses, without the display and promotion costs a supermarket bears, Peapod could

	PEAPOD		WEBVAN	
Assets	3-31-2001 (unaudited)	12-31-2000	3-31-2001	12-31-2000
Current assets:				
Cash and cash equivalents	3,703	14,676	85,449	40,293
Marketable Securities			29,125	171,556
Receivables, net of allowance for doubtful accounts	479	397	48	48
Merchandise inventory	1,801	1,662	11,974	13,804
Prepaid expenses	654	677		
Other current assets	2,577	2,549	9,287	9,218
Total current assets	9,214	19,961	135,883	234,919
Property and equipment:		8,212		
Computer equipment and software	11,494			
Service equipment and other	6,418	5,813		
Leasehold improvements	9,102	9007		
Property and equipment, at cost	27,014	23,032		
Less accumulated depreciation and amortization	-11,147	-8,285		
Net property and equipment	15,867	14,747	340,262	370,915
Net goodwill and other intangibles	6,781	7,123	754,398	843,575
Deposits and Other non-current assets	3,468	3,902	56,920	72,127
Total assets	35,330	45,733	1,287,463	1,521,536
Liabilities				
Current liabilities:				
Accounts payable	1,875	2,064	13,901	18,473
Accounts payable to related party	4,076	2,891		
Accrued compensation	1,589	1,926		
Other accrued liabilities	9,982	9,444	67,198	87,906
Borrowings under credit facility	6,000			
Deferred revenue	10	58		
Current obligations under capital lease	1,965	1,965	15,354	13,930
Total current liabilities	25,497	18,348	96,453	120,309
Obligations under capital lease, less current portion	4,226	4,829	39,556	42,210
Total liabilities	29,723	23,177	136,009	0
Stockholders' equity				
Preferred stock	65,395	64,684		
Common stock	184	184	48	48
Additional paid-in capital	74,135	74,832	2,012,272	2,011,041
Deferred Compensation			-31,368	-40,587
Accumulated deficit	-132,234	-115271	-829,674	-612,702
Treasury stock	-1,873	-1873		
Accumulated Other Comprehensive Income			176	1,217
Total stockholders' equity	5,607	22,556	1,151,454	1,359,017
Total liabilities and stockholders' equity	35,330	45,733	1,287,463	1,521,536

Table 13.2 Balance Sheets for Peapod and Webvan

boost profit margins and offer a more affordable service. Peapod's proprietary transportation routing system aims to guarantee on-time delivery and ensure efficient truck and driver utilization. A key metric for delivery performance was *stops per hour* (SPH), or orders delivered per hour. Target values for SPH of 2.5 or higher were believed to represent good truck and driver utilization. With the centralized distribution system, however, actual SPHs were much lower, reflecting less-than-ideal market penetration (the fraction of current to potential customers in a given area) and showing the effect of long distances from the warehouse.

Since December 1998, Peapod had opened centralized distribution centers in San Francisco and Chicago, and a small platform warehouse in Boston. Yet, introducing a direct-fulfillment model has put a strain on the company's financial growth. Peapod revenues for fourth quarter 1998 were $17.2 million, compared with $17.2 million for the same period of 1997. For the year ended December 1998, total revenues were $68.8 million, compared with $56.5 million for the year ended Dec. 1997 (see Table 13.3 on page 426).

According to then-CEO John Walden, "1998 represented a period of tremendous transition for the company. We set out to develop a new service model designed to enhance the company's control over service quality and remove costs from the order fulfillment process. In 1998 we sacrificed short-term growth, but we built the foundation for an exciting and financially attractive long-term business."[4]

The company says the lack of significant growth was due to its efforts to centralize its fulfillment operations, with expenses from investments in facilities, new technologies, and personnel. Peapod also cut back on its marketing spending, which led to a drop in membership. In September 1999, Bill Malloy, executive vice president of AT&T's wireless operations, the largest such operation in the United States, succeeded John Walden as president and CEO.

To accelerate its conversion to the centralized warehouse distribution model, the company implemented state-of-the-art distribution management and systems. The McLane Group, a leading provider of distribution-logistics services and technology to food companies, was responsible for the implementation. To continue its conversion and the expansion of its presence in the metropolitan areas that it served, however, more funds were needed. In February 2000, Peapod announced that it had signed letters of intent under which private equity firms would invest an aggregate of $120 million of equity.

The Partnership With Ahold   On April 14, 2000, after the financing failed to close, international food provider Royal Ahold and Peapod, Inc. announced that they had entered into definitive agreements creating a mutually-beneficial partnership. Under the agreements, Peapod would continue as a stand-alone company. Ahold would supply Peapod with goods, services, and fast pick fulfillment centers.

Ahold initially invested approximately $73 million in a newly issued series of convertible preferred Peapod stock at a price of $3.75 per share, representing 51% of Peapod's outstanding common stock on a converted basis. The founding Parkinson brothers own about 10% of Peapod.

The partnership gives Ahold and Peapod considerable leverage in the rapidly expanding world of food retailing. Peapod brings to the partner-ship its e-commerce and home shopping expertise, web-based software and ordering systems, and web marketing and additional IT skills. Ahold's contributions lie in its considerable buying power, real estate, strong store brand recognition, extensive customer base, and category management expertise. Both companies agreed upon a strategic alignment and on a business review to significantly strengthen Peapod's financial performance.

Bricks And Clicks Strategy   Ahold USA, through its five supermarket companies located along the eastern seaboard, operated 1,063 stores with 1999 sales of $20.3 billion. Peapod had already worked closely with Ahold's operating companies, Stop & Shop in the Boston metropolitan area and Edwards in the New York area. Through improved supply chain processes, former mezzanine storage areas at Ahold's U.S. stores could now be converted into efficient "fast pick" fulfillment centers for Peapod. Adopting this "clicks and mortar" strategy, Peapod would utilize Ahold's real estate assets to open over 50 of these centers in the coming years.

The plan was to change from in-store picking to a dual fulfillment strategy[5] of:

- Leasing two large warehouses, ranging from 70,000 to 100,000 square feet, for its own exclusive use in storing, selecting, packing and delivering orders of the Chicago and the San Francisco bay areas (fulfillment centers hold approximately 6,000-14,000 items).

- Using fast pick centers, ranging from 8,000 to 14,000 square feet, in smaller markets. Ahold and Peapod have entered into a facility licensing agreement for these fast pick centers, which tend to be within existing brick and mortar stores.

While Peapod employees perform all activities in the large warehouses, in fast pick centers, Ahold employees manage and perform all activities.

For these services, Peapod pays either a fixed charge or the actual cost of the services. It also pays certain incentive fees if the volume of revenue generated by Peapod's sale of products supplied by

---

[4]Redherring.com. "Online grocers go hungry."July 28th, 1999.
[5]The following information comes from public SEC fillings by Peapod.

Ahold and the payroll cost incurred by Ahold in rendering such services reach certain levels.

On June 20, 2000, the partners announced a new online shopping and delivery service offering in southern Connecticut. According to Marc van Gelder, Peapod's president and chief executive officer who joined Peapod in May from Ahold's Stop & Shop, this illustrated the benefits from the partnership: "Stop & Shop has strong brand equity among Connecticut residents. In addition, there is a recognized demand for our online shopping service in this area. Finally, the area's customer base truly fits the online shopping profile. All of these factors should enable us to establish a strong presence in this market."[6]

The Peapod by Stop & Shop service offered busy consumers a convenient new way to grocery shop. Orders are filled from a dedicated, fast-pick fulfillment center in Norwalk, Conn., adjoined to a Super Stop & Shop. The fulfillment center offered a wide variety of Stop & Shop and national brands - from fresh produce, cheeses, and seafood to a large selection of baby food, health and beauty products, and pet food. Peapod deployed its state-of-the-art order fulfillment technology and proprietary transportation routing system, which helps it achieve accuracy and efficiency in picking, packing, and delivering grocery orders in its current markets.

"The Connecticut service model leverages the skills and resources of both companies to provide the best possible service to consumers while realizing business efficiencies," van Gelder said. "It is clicks-and-mortar in action."

On September 7, 2000, Peapod announced that it would exit from the Texas and Ohio markets and that it had acquired Internet grocer Streamline.com's operations in Chicago and Washington, D.C.. The Streamline acquisition added two centralized distribution centers to Peapod's assets. Peapod used the Washington distribution center to enter that new market. It also closed its Niles warehouse and transferred its operations to Streamline's distribution center in Lake Zurich, Il. On March 12, 2001, Peapod stopped servicing the San Francisco market.

On March 31, 2001, Peapod was operating nine fulfillment centers across five metropolitan markets (down from 22 centers across eight metropolitan markets the year before) covering 5,031,600 households: Chicago and Washington, D.C. were served from a dedicated warehouse facility; Southern Connecticut was served from the Norwalk fast-pick center; the Boston area used one fast-pick center and four in-store-pick facilities; New York's New Hyde Park area was served from an in-store-pick facility.

These actions accelerated Peapod's exit from an in-store picking model and its conversion to a hybrid distribution model that would serve both larger and smaller markets. The model consisted of freestanding warehouse facilities and smaller fast-pick fulfillment centers. Ahold increased its $20 million credit facility to $50 million.

Peapod's typical customers are females between the ages of 30 and 54, households with children and dual income households. The income levels of Peapod's customer base cover a wide range, with a median income exceeding $60,000 per year. The average Peapod order is $115. As of December 31, 2000, Peapod had approximately 851 full-time and 131 part-time employees. Substantially all of the part-time employees serve in grocery picking, packing, delivery, and customer support positions. Of the full-time employees, approximately 709 are in field operations or customer support functions, with the remainder in information technology, sales and marketing, and general and administrative functions. Employees are non-unionized.

On April 23, 2001, Peapod said it has achieved operating profitability in the Chicago market three months ahead of schedule. The Internet grocer, however, was still not reporting company-wide profitability. Marc van Gelder, Peapod president and chief executive, said "Peapod is "on track" to achieve profitability in 2003. It has $44 million cash on hand," he added. [7]

---

[6]Peapod press release, June 20, 2000.
[7]*Wall Street Journal*, April 23, 2001.

WEBVAN

The Vision Webvan aimed to be the "last mile of e-commerce." Founder Louis Borders' idea was to bring back an improved version of yesterday's milkman providing personable and reliable service to the home. The improvement would be along two dimensions: front-end and back-end. On the front-end, Webvan planned to offer unparalleled customer service with double the variety of a regular grocery store at comparable prices. Shopping categories would extend beyond groceries and include a pet store, consumer electronics, books, CDs, DVDs & videos, a florist, a drugstore, and webvan@work, where business customers could shop for prepared foods for meetings. On the back end, the operational processes would leverage sophisticated infrastructure and technology. Highly automated pick and pack distribution centers would provide scalability and would create the opportunity to expand product offerings.

Earlier in 1971, Borders had founded Borders Books with his brother Tom. From a single store, the company eventually grew into the nation's second-largest book chain behind Barnes & Noble. A good part of Borders' success is credited to a proprietary, computerized inventory tracking system that Louis invented to keep bookstore employees on the floor with customers instead of in back doing paperwork. The system allowed each store to customize its book selection based on the reading tastes of its customers. Borders is said to have invented the inventory system by adapting a computer program he had designed to predict the winners of horse races.[8]

Borders now decided to apply his knowledge of inventory management and customer order assembly to the grocery industry. However, fulfilling a grocery order of dozens of items, including perishables, and promising home delivery during a customer-selected 30-minute window represents an endeavor quite different from packing and shipping books. In addition, the industry's razor thin margins of a mere 1 to 1.5 percent do not allow much room for error, which explains why the big

chains were moving so slowly into the online field. This is an industry that makes its money on volume, not spread.

From the start, Webvan embraced the centralized distribution model. It had the money to directly build warehouses everywhere: half of its initial $120 million seed funding was used to build its first facility in Oakland, California.

The 330,000-square-foot distribution center opened in June 1999, with 4 1/2 miles of conveyor belts along with temperature-controlled rooms to house items such as wine, cigars, and fish. A single worker, standing at "Pod 3" in the midst of the warehouse, is surrounded by motorized rotating carousels that each hold 8,900 grocery items, legions of conveyor belts, a host of electric-eye bar-code scanners, and 16 bins that collect shopper's orders.[9] Apparently, Borders himself proposed various scenarios of his warehouse scheme before deciding on the optimal number of items to put on carousels and on how far apart they should be to minimize the amount of walking a worker would have to do.[10] He designed facilities that at peak would be run by some 700 employees and could handle 8,000 orders per day, the equivalent of 25 traditional grocery stores. In a single hour, a worker should be able to pack 450 grocery items for shoppers—nearly 10 times the productivity of a traditional "shopper" wheeling a cart through a store. The system would be able to pick an average 25-item order out of an eventual 50,000 available products in less than an hour. It would result in a projected doubling of the industry's low operating margins. "If everything goes according to plan," Mr. Borders declared in the Wall Street Journal, "the Oakland facility should be profitable within six to 12 months."

The distribution centers would be supplied by leading regional vendors with the freshest local products, including premium breads, produce, meats, fish, and poultry, many of which were previously only available to restaurants.

Delivery Operations[11] Delivery routes either went directly from the distribution center to the

---

[8]*San Francisco Business Times*, April 9, 1999.
[9]*Wall Street Journal*, April 22, 1999.
[10]*Business Week*, September 27, 1999.
[11]Information comes from public 10K filings.

customer, or otherwise via an intermediate staging, or transfer, station. The latter hub-and-spoke system uses large temperature-controlled trucks to deliver goods from the facility to the transfer (or cross-docking) station. Smaller vans are then used to deliver from the station to the home. The stations are strategically positioned throughout a delivery region within approximately 50 miles of a facility. Each facility serves a geographic zone that typically includes target customer residences within an approximately 25 mile radius from the station. Webvan projected that each of its 70 Oakland drivers could handle about 20 deliveries a day.

In July 1999, Webvan and Bechtel, the world's leading engineering-construction company, announced a $1 billion strategic alliance to develop a distribution and delivery infrastructure in 26 U.S. markets over the following three years. The expansion strategy was accelerated in June 2000 by the acquisition of HomeGrocer.com in a stock-for-stock transaction. The transaction was valued at approximately $1.2 billion, based on Webvan's closing share price of $8.72 that day. On December 4, 2000, the company was serving 10 markets and announced that it would move to a 60-minute delivery window (from the original 30 minutes).

By 2001, however, Webvan's financial performance remained deep in the red and the company was under increasing pressure. As of March 31, 2001, Webvan had an accumulated deficit of $829.7 million (see Table 13.4 on page 427). Webvan incurred net losses of $217.0 million in the three months ended March 31, 2001. This included a restructuring charge of $73.9 million primarily related to the closure of the Dallas facility, and $453.3 million and $144.6 million in the years ended December 31, 2000 and 1999, respectively. Webvan's distribution facilities were operating at less than 40% of their originally designed capacity. In the Bay Area, Webvan averaged a puny 2,160 orders per day in the fourth quarter of 2000, only two-thirds of what the company would require to break even locally.

On February 13, 2001, Louis H. Borders resigned from the company's board of directors for personal reasons. A week later, Webvan announced that it would halt service in Dallas in or-

der to conserve operating capital and focus on the profitability of its nine other markets.

On April 13, 2001, its chairman and chief executive officer, George T. Shaheen, announced his resignation, citing that "the capital markets have altered the timetable and operating approach to the achievement of the model as originally envisioned. A different kind of executive is needed to lead the company at this time." Shaheen, former managing partner and CEO of Andersen Consulting (now Accenture), served as Webvan's chief executive officer since October 1999 and as chairman of the board of directors since February 2001.

As of December 31, 2000, Webvan had approximately 4,476 full-time employees of whom approximately 129 worked in software development, approximately 509 in operations, administration and customer service, approximately 133 in merchandising and marketing, and approximately 3,705 in distribution and transfer facilities.

On June 26, 2001, Bob Swan, who became the company's chief executive officer in April, talked about commanding a company through rough economic conditions and the road ahead:

> "I think the biggest change [in our philosophy during the last year] has been the aspirations to be a big national player. We have dramatically curtailed those plans to focus on the markets we think are closest to profitability, and where we have a loyal customer base, to prove the economics of the model. With our current footprint, it would take us to the second half of (2002) to be self-sufficient. We would need to raise approximately $25 million between now and then. Starting in the second half (of 2002), we believe the company will be able to generate its own capital."[12]

WHAT'S NEXT? TESCO'S ENTRY

Does the Internet grocery model make sense? What are the key performance drivers? What can

---

[12]Following excerpt is from the *Seattle Times*.

be learned from the announcement on June 25, 2001, of a deal between Tesco, Britain's biggest grocer, and Safeway, California's biggest food retailer, to bring its successful Internet shopping service to the birthplace of the Internet? Safeway's Grocery-Works will close its warehouse-based distribution network and replace it with Tesco's store-picking system that will be deployed in some of Safeway's 1,700 stores. After spending about $56 million on getting its system right, Tesco has built up a profitable online food business with annual sales of 300 million pounds, making it the world's biggest Internet grocer.[13]

DISCUSSION QUESTIONS

1. Describe and evaluate Peapod's operations strategy using the framework from Chapter 1.

2. What are the relative strengths and weaknesses of the three different fulfillment strategies: using existing stores, a centralized fulfillment center, or clicks-and-bricks? When is each one more appropriate?

3. Identify the key performance indicators of Peopod's mass-customized service.

4. What is Peapod's "cost-to-serve?" Estimate the cost to fill an average order. (This requires some detective work and estimation, given that not all data is available. The idea is to do your best in estimating financial performance, using case and appendix data where possible, and supplementing it with justified estimates where needed.)

5. What is the "shortest path" to profitability, if one exists? Determine the profitability of an order and break-out its key drivers. (An obvious one is to increase customers; for this case assume conservatively that the customer base will remain fairly constant over time.) Other drivers can be interpreted as productivity measures (e.g., stops per hour SPH). Which specific actions would you recommend to increase the profitability of an order?

---

[13]*The Economist*, June 28, 2001.

	1999				2000				2001
	Q1	Q2	Q3	Q4	Q1	Q2	Q3	Q4	Q1
Net Sales	17,977	16,934	16,351	21,434	24,774	22,632	21,706	23,732	24,937
Cost of Sales	14,366	12,903	12,241	16,075	19,216	17,574	17,293	17,563	16,963
Gross Profit	3,611	4,031	4,110	5,359	5,558	5,058	4,413	6,169	7,974
Operating Expenses									
Fulfillment operations	4,872	5,017	5,571	8,120	8,931	7,796	7,919	12,633	12,443
General and administrative	1,573	1,679	2,155	1,551	2,039	2,150	2,768	4,465	3,757
Marketing and selling	1,207	1,051	1,523	2,949	1,200	987	1,341	4,662	3,019
System development and maintenance	723	787	916	1,117	1,189	1,469	1,490	1,661	951
Depreciation and amortization	474	604	525	619	664	737	942	1,908	1,991
Pre-opening costs	280	360	188	70	—				
Non-recurring expenses			2,830		4,118	1,490		4,510	761
Total operating expenses	9,129	9,498	13,708	14,426	18,141	14,629	14,460	29,839	22,922
Operating loss	(5,518)	(5,467)	(9,598)	(9,067)	(12,583)	(9,571)	(10,047)	(23,670)	(14,948)
Other Income (expense):									
Net investment income (expense)	478	586	288	32	(103)	16	776	390	95
Interest Expense	(29)	(44)	(42)	(72)	(56)	(218)	(94)	(118)	(165)
Non-cash interest expense					—	(616)	(431)	(433)	(434)
Net Loss	(5,069)	(4,925)	(9,352)	(9,107)	(12,742)	(10,389)	(9,796)	(23,831)	(15,452)
OPERATING DATA									
Markets served	8	8	8	8	8	9	6	6	5
# of dedicated fulfillment DC	2	2	2	2	2	2	2	2	2
# of small platform / fast-pick centers	1	1	1	1	1	1	1	2	2
# of in-store-picking fulfillment locations	29	29	19	19	19	20	8	7	5
Total # fulfillment centers	32	32	22	22	22	23	11	11	9
Customers (transacting in last 12 months)	92,600	89,900	92,900	111,900	129,800	135,700	119,300	124,400	120,000
Orders	135,200	128,200	130,200	177,700	205,500	183,700	179,300	203,600	205,500
Households in service area	7,110,000	7,392,100	8,023,500	8,023,500	8,586,100	8,731,000	6,715,800	6,715,800	5,031,600

Table 13.3 Peapod's income statement and operating data.

	1999				2000				2001
	Q1	Q2	Q3	Q4	Q1	Q2	Q3	Q4	Q1
Net Sales	12	383	3,841	9,069	16,269	28,300	52,057	81,830	77,234
Cost of Goods Sold	9	410	3,491	7,379	12,138	20,307	37,509	61,285	55,559
Gross Profit	3	(27)	350	1,690	4,131	7,993	14,548	20,545	21,675
Operating Expenses									
Sales and Marketing Expenses	432	1,907	3,923	5,481	8,359	9,907	13,990	16,864	16,276
Development and Engineering Expenses	3,260	3,048	4,330	4,599	5,523	5,465	8,176	6,352	6,015
General and Administrative Expenses	6,733	16,224	45,157	24,292	38,993	57,890	77,887	117,565	88,168
Amortization of Goodwill and Intangibles							13,962	49,432	47,812
Amortization of Deferred Compensation	1,767	2,186	9,590	22,977	17,720	16,774	13,137	7,602	9,219
Restructuring Charges							40,810		73,859
Total Operating Expenses	12,192	23,365	63,003	57,349	70,595	90,036	167,962	197,815	241,349
Operating Loss:	(12,189)	(23,392)	(62,653)	(55,659)	(66,464)	(82,043)	(153,414)	(177,270)	(219,674)
Other Income (expense):									
Interest Income	873	768	3,017	6,822	8,799	7,824	5,841	5,086	4,105
Interest Expense	(374)	(820)	(801)	(161)	(150)	(146)	(400)	(952)	(1,403)
Net Interest Income	499	(52)	2,216	6,661	8,649	7,678	5,441	4,134	2,702
Net Loss	(11,690)	(23,444)	(60,437)	(48,998)	(57,815)	(74,365)	(147,973)	(173,136)	(216,972)

Other Operating Data (Annual)	1998	1999	2000
Capital Expenditures	32,669	64,253	259,902
Depreciation and Amortization	1,323	44,232	149,545

Table 13.4 Webvan's financial and operational information.

General and administrative expenses include costs related to fulfillment and delivery of products, real estate, technology operations, equipment leases, merchandising, finance, customer service and professional services, as well as non-cash compensation and related expenses. Of its $199.9 million increase in 2000 over 1999, $141.3 million went towards aggregate distribution center operating expenses for the Bay Area, Atlanta, and Chicago locations. Additionally, $35.7 million went for HomeGrocer locations following the merger, compared to only a partial year of the Bay Area operation in the prior year. Such DC operating expenses increased by $30.7 million in 1999 from 1998 due to the opening of the Bay Area DC. At corporate headquarters, payroll and related costs increased to $58.4 million in 2000 from $14.5 million in 1999 and $4.1 million in 1998. Additionally, consulting and professional fees and rent and facility charges increased by $15.0 million in 2000 from the prior year, and by $3.1 million in 1999 from 1998 (source: 10K and 10Q SEC filings).

Appendix 13 | Peapod's Operating Data

Fulfillment data

[14] Number of employees at dedicated fulfillment center: 92. (Source: actual number at SFO DC according to Peapod's March 2001 10K.)

Fixed cost (lease, building maintenance and supervision, etc.) of running a fulfillment center: approximately $150,000 per month.

Delivery data

Capacity limit set per truck (for insurance and truck space purposes) in terms of sales content: $2,500.

Number of truck runs per shift: 1.

Number of delivery shifts per day: 2.

Maximal number of orders per truck: 19 – 23.

Number of drivers in Chicago Niles DC: about 70 (slow season), up to 115 (high season).

Starting wage paid to delivery people: $11.50/hr, which is about $14.50/hr fully loaded, including benefits and tax.

Fixed delivery van cost, including depreciation, maintenance, and insurance: about $100 per day per truck (based on new van price of about $25,000 depreciated straight-line over 4 years, and operating 300 days per year).

---

[14]This section contains the author's estimates unless indicated otherwise.

Part V

Appendices

MAKE-TO-STOCK OPERATIONS (EOQ REVIEW)

Consider a supermarket that regularly replenishes its stock of milk, or a manufacturer that makes several products on a single production process. What models can help them in deciding on the appropriate quantity to order or to make? This appendix reviews two simple yet powerful models of a deterministic batch process.

A simple batch process: the EOQ model

Consider a supermarket's ordering and inventory management of a staple item such as milk. Each replenishment order incurs a fixed order cost S that is independent of the order quantity Q. Placing one big order would minimize the annual fixed order cost, but would maximize the firm's inventory and thus its holding cost. Let H denote the annual inventory holding cost per unit. We seek the economic order quantity Q^* that minimizes the sum of annual holding and order costs. Let R denote the aggregate annual demand or throughput rate, which the model assumes is known for certain and is constant over time.

The process under consideration is the ordering, receiving, and holding of inventory. When a replenishment is received, the inventory increases by the order quantity Q but decreases otherwise at the throughput rate R, as shown in Figure A.1. The average inventory is $Q/2$. Annual demand per product is R, so we place R/Q orders per year. The annual holding and changeover costs are:

$$
\begin{aligned}
TC(Q) &= \text{setup costs} + \text{holding costs} \\
&= \frac{R}{Q}S + \frac{Q}{2}H.
\end{aligned}
$$

This cost is minimized where its first derivative is zero, which yields the familiar *economic order quantity* (EOQ) formula and its associated optimal cost:

$$
Q^* = \sqrt{\frac{2RS}{H}} \quad \text{and} \quad TC(Q^*) = \sqrt{2RSH}.
$$

Thus, the inventory and setup cost per unit is:

$$
\frac{TC(Q^*)}{R} = \sqrt{\frac{2SH}{R}} = c_{\text{HS}}.
$$

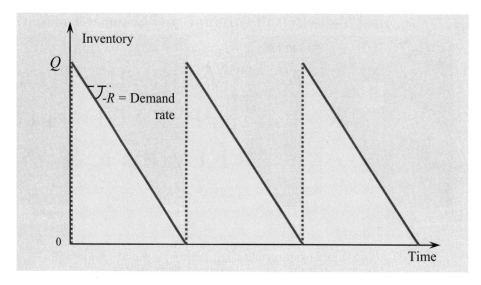

Figure A.1 Inventory build-up diagram for EOQ model.

The conclusion of the EOQ model is that the optimal batch size and cost follow a square-root law of the input parameters. The substantive implications are:

1. When demand doubles, the order size should not be doubled. Rather the order size should be increased only by 41% (a factor $\sqrt{2} - 1$), but the order frequency should also increase by 41%. This is a manifestation of the scale economies in batch processes: the cost per unit decreases in throughput.

2. In order to decrease batch (also known as cycle) inventory, we must decrease the fixed order cost.

A simple batch production process with N products: the ELSP model

To show that the insights of the EOQ model are fairly robust, consider a firm that produces N products to stock on a single process. Assume the simplest setting where products are homogeneous and production capacity equals aggregate demand or throughput R, which again is known for certain and is constant over time. The make-to-stock process is not perfectly flexible and incurs a changeover or setup cost S when switching production from one product to another, while the changeover or setup *time* is 0. Moreover, the changeover cost is independent of the product sequence. In reality, changeovers also take time, and their economic impact then depends on whether we have sufficient excess capacity. If not, then changeovers reduce actual capacity and throughput and can significantly reduce revenues and profits.

It is then optimal to produce according to a *cyclic schedule*: first product 1 is made, then we switch over to product 2 and continue this sequence until we switch back from product N to product 1, then repeating the cycle. Each cycle will produce until its product inventory reaches a level Q for each product (because products are homogeneous). Seeking this Q is known as the economic lot

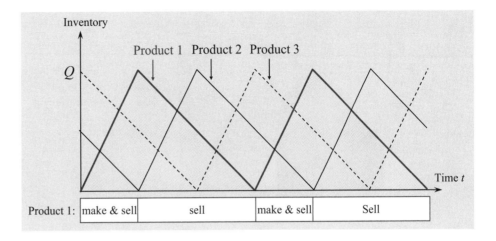

Figure A.2 Inventory build-up diagram when a single make-to-stock process makes 3 homogeneous products.

sizing problem (ELSP).

The process under consideration is the production, storage, and sale of finished goods. The inventory is built up during production and is depleted otherwise through sales, as shown in the Figure A.2 for the case of 3 products. As in the EOQ model above, the average inventory for each product is $Q/2$. Annual demand per product is R/N, so we must produce each product R/NQ times per year. The total number of changeovers per year is thus $N \times R/NQ = R/Q$. The cost structure only differs from that of the EOQ model in that the holding cost is now $N\frac{Q}{2}H$. Mathematically, the ELSP solution is the same as the EOQ, provided we replace H by NH. Thus, the optimal up-to-level Q^* and annual total cost (sum of setup and holding cost) is:

$$Q^* = \sqrt{\frac{2RS}{NH}} \quad \text{and} \quad TC(Q^*) = \sqrt{2RSHN}.$$

The inventory and setup cost per unit thus is:

$$\frac{TC(Q^*)}{R} = \sqrt{\frac{2SHN}{R}} = c_{\text{HS}}\sqrt{N},$$

and the insights of the EOQ model apply again.

Appendix

B | SAFETY CAPACITY AND INVENTORY (NEWSVENDOR REVIEW)

This appendix reviews the simple yet powerful newsvendor model of an operation that faces uncertain demand in a single period. We review how to optimally size the safety level of capacity or inventory, and how to calculate the expected profit, shortfall, and fill rate.

The basic newsvendor model

Every morning, our little boy Max buys K newspapers at a unit cost of c_K in the hope of selling them at the train station at price p. Demand per day is random, but identically and independently distributed as the random demand D. The newsvendor model seeks to find the appropriate quantity K that Max should buy before knowing actual demand.

Max faces a tough trade-off. If he buys too many newspapers, he will have leftovers worth nothing. If he buys too few, he will runs a shortfall and forego profits. After reading Laplace's *Théorie Analytique des Probabilités*, Max realizes that his is a problem of probability. If he buys one more newspaper at cost c_K, his revenues would increase by p only if $D > K$. Then, the change in his expected profit is $p \Pr(D > K) - c_K$. This is decreasing in K, so that his expected profit is concave in K and maximal if $p \Pr(D > K) = c_K$. Assume for simplicity that newspapers are divisible. Then, his venture is profitable if $p > c_K$ and he can maximize value by buying K^* newspapers, where K^* satisfies:

$$\Pr(D > K^*) = \frac{c_K}{p}.$$

This newsvendor solution can be extended to investment problems that seek to minimize the expected underage and overage costs. Recognizing that $\Pr(D \leq K) = 1 - \Pr(D > K)$, the equivalent optimality condition is:

$$\Pr(D \leq K^*) = \frac{C_u}{C_u + C_o}$$

where the underage cost $C_u = p - c_K$ and the overage cost $C_o = c_K$. Thus, Max should compile a demand forecast from past sales history and buy the *critical fractile* $(p - c_K)/p$.

Calculating the newsvendor solution

The newsvendor solution can easily be calculated for any probability distribution $F(x) = \Pr(D \leq x)$ as $K^* = F^{-1}(C_u/(C_u + C_o))$.

If demand is (approximately) normally distributed with mean R (which is mnemonic for demand rate) and standard deviation σ, the newsvendor solution can be easily calculated in terms of the z-statistic:

$$K^* = R + z^*\sigma \text{ where } z^* = \texttt{normsinv}(C_u/(C_u + C_o)).$$

Notice that the optimal safety capacity $K^* - R = z^*\sigma$ is linear in standard deviation and positive if $C_u/(C_u + C_o) \geq 0.5$ and negative otherwise.

Expected profit and shortfall

In contrast to the newsvendor solution, calculating the expected sales, shortfall, and profits typically requires calculus. Remember that

$$\text{sales units} = \begin{cases} \text{demand} & \text{if demand} \leq \text{capacity,} \\ \text{capacity} & \text{otherwise.} \end{cases}$$

Thus, taking expectations we get:

$$\text{expected sales units} = \int_0^K x\,dF(x) + K(1 - F(K)).$$

This can be rewritten as:

$$
\begin{aligned}
\text{expected sales units} &= \int_0^\infty x\,dF(x) - \int_K^\infty x\,dF(x) + K(1 - F(K)) \\
&= \int_0^\infty x\,dF(x) - \int_K^\infty (x - K)\,dF(x) \\
&= \text{mean demand} - \text{mean shortfall.}
\end{aligned}
$$

When capacity shortages result in lost sales and a penalty of c_p, the expected operating profit becomes

$$\Pi(K) = \text{unit margin} \times \mathbb{E}(\text{sales}) - c_p \times \mathbb{E}(\text{shortfall}),$$

so all we have to do is to compute the expected shortfall.

Computing the expected shortfall

Depending on the nature of the demand forecast, different methods can be used:

1. If demand has a known discrete distribution, the expected shortfall can be calculated using Excel, as presented in Table 3.1 on p. 88.

2. If demand is only known via a simulation, then we should simulate n demand points $\{D_i\}$ from the underlying distribution. Then, compute the shortfall $s_i = \max(0, D_i - K)$ for each demand point D_i. The sample mean $\sum_i s_i/n$ is our estimate of the expected capacity shortfall.

3. If demand is (approximately) normally distributed with mean R and standard deviation σ, then the expected shortfall for capacity K is[1]

$$\text{expected capacity shortfall} = \sigma L(z_K) \quad \text{where } z_K = \frac{K - R}{\sigma} \quad \text{(B.1)}$$

and $L(z)$ is the *standard loss function* that is computed in Excel as:

$$L(z) = \texttt{normdist}(z, 0, 1, 0) - z(1 - \texttt{normsdist}(z)) \quad \text{(Excel)}.$$

Or you can simply use Table B.1. Notice that the expected shortfall and expected profits decrease linearly with the standard deviation, in agreement with the volatility principle 6 (p. 86).

Shortfall rate and fill rate

Often we are interested in the expected capacity shortfall as a percentage of expected demand, which is called the expected *shortfall rate*; its counterpart is known as the *fill rate*:

$$\text{Shortfall rate} = \frac{\text{Expected capacity shortfall}}{\text{Expected demand}}$$

$$\text{Fill rate} = \frac{\text{Expected sales}}{\text{Expected demand}} = 1 - \text{shortfall rate}.$$

For normally distributed demand, the shortfall expression (B.1) shows that

$$\text{Shortfall rate} = \underbrace{\frac{\sigma}{R}} \times \underbrace{L(z_K)}$$

$$= \text{COV} \times \text{standard loss},$$

where the *coefficient of variation* (COV) measures the relative amount of volatility. As an example of this calculation, consider our Wolfgang Puck example 3.2 on p. 87. The demand forecast in Table 3.1 has mean $R = 100.12$ and standard deviation $\sigma = 21.6$. The z-statistic of capacity is

$$z_K = \frac{K - \text{mean}}{\text{standard deviation}} = \frac{100 - 100.12}{21.6} = -.0056$$

so that the normal approximation to the forecast yields an expected capacity shortfall of

$$\sigma L(z_K) = 21.6 \times 0.402 = 8.68$$

which indeed is close to 8.50. Using the normal approximation, the shortfall rate is $8.68/100.12 = 8.67\%$ and the fill rate is $100\% - 8.67\% = 91.33\%$.

---

[1] For math fans: The standard normal density ϕ satisfies $\int_z^\infty x\phi(x)dx = \phi(z)$ so that the expected shortfall is $L(z) = \int_z^\infty (x - z)\phi(x)dx = \phi(z) - z(1 - \Phi(z))$.

z-statistic z	Probability $\Phi(z)$	Loss function $L(z)$	z-statistic z	Probability $\Phi(z)$	Loss function $L(z)$
-4.0	0.0000	4.0000	0.0	0.5000	0.3989
-3.9	0.0000	3.9000	0.1	0.5398	0.3509
-3.8	0.0001	3.8000	0.2	0.5793	0.3069
-3.7	0.0001	3.7000	0.3	0.6179	0.2668
-3.6	0.0002	3.6000	0.4	0.6554	0.2304
-3.5	0.0002	3.5001	0.5	0.6915	0.1978
-3.4	0.0003	3.4001	0.6	0.7257	0.1687
-3.3	0.0005	3.3001	0.7	0.7580	0.1429
-3.2	0.0007	3.2002	0.8	0.7881	0.1202
-3.1	0.0010	3.1003	0.9	0.8159	0.1004
-3.0	0.0013	3.0004	1.0	0.8413	0.0833
-2.9	0.0019	2.9005	1.1	0.8643	0.0686
-2.8	0.0026	2.8008	1.2	0.8849	0.0561
-2.7	0.0035	2.7011	1.3	0.9032	0.0455
-2.6	0.0047	2.6015	1.4	0.9192	0.0367
-2.5	0.0062	2.5020	1.5	0.9332	0.0293
-2.4	0.0082	2.4027	1.6	0.9452	0.0232
-2.3	0.0107	2.3037	1.7	0.9554	0.0183
-2.2	0.0139	2.2049	1.8	0.9641	0.0143
-2.1	0.0179	2.1065	1.9	0.9713	0.0111
-2.0	0.0228	2.0085	2.0	0.9772	0.0085
-1.9	0.0287	1.9111	2.1	0.9821	0.0065
-1.8	0.0359	1.8143	2.2	0.9861	0.0049
-1.7	0.0446	1.7183	2.3	0.9893	0.0037
-1.6	0.0548	1.6232	2.4	0.9918	0.0027
-1.5	0.0668	1.5293	2.5	0.9938	0.0020
-1.4	0.0808	1.4367	2.6	0.9953	0.0015
-1.3	0.0968	1.3455	2.7	0.9965	0.0011
-1.2	0.1151	1.2561	2.8	0.9974	0.0008
-1.1	0.1357	1.1686	2.9	0.9981	0.0005
-1.0	0.1587	1.0833	3.0	0.9987	0.0004
-0.9	0.1841	1.0004	3.1	0.9990	0.0003
-0.8	0.2119	0.9202	3.2	0.9993	0.0002
-0.7	0.2420	0.8429	3.3	0.9995	0.0001
-0.6	0.2743	0.7687	3.4	0.9997	0.0001
-0.5	0.3085	0.6978	3.5	0.9998	0.0001
-0.4	0.3446	0.6304	3.6	0.9998	0.0000
-0.3	0.3821	0.5668	3.7	0.9999	0.0000
-0.2	0.4207	0.5069	3.8	0.9999	0.0000
-0.1	0.4602	0.4509	3.9	1.0000	0.0000
0.0	0.5000	0.3989	4.0	1.0000	0.0000

Table B.1 Probabilities and loss function for the normal distribution.

MAKE-TO-ORDER AND SERVICE OPERATIONS (QUEUING REVIEW)

Consider a call center where agents serve customers' calls over time. Or, imagine a European make-to-order manufacturer of customized items, such as windows or cars. These are service and make-to-order (MTO) operations, respectively, where customers may have to wait before being served. How can these firms estimate the quality of service that they offer to customers in terms of the *waiting time W* before a customer is served, or her total *flow time T*, the sum of waiting and service time? This appendix reviews queuing models that help answering these questions.

Data needed for a queuing model

In contrast to a make-to-stock process (as analyzed in Appendix A with the EOQ model), where inventory is held in finished form or output buffers, a make-to-order process holds inventory (orders, customers, etc.) in input buffers, or "queues." While output inventory levels are a key performance indicator of make-to-stock processes, input inventory levels or queue length (equivalently, waiting times[1]) are the key performance indicators of make-to-order processes.

Queuing models require at least two sets of data:

1. Customer arrivals: often one cannot predict exactly when a customer will request service—thus, arrival times may be random variables. Their necessary data is the average inter-arrival time (or its reciprocal, which is the average arrival rate R) and the standard deviation of the inter-arrival times σ_a (or its *coefficient of variation* (COV) $c_a = R\sigma_a$). The coefficient of variation is a relative measure of variability that typically falls between 0 (for predictable or deterministic patterns) and 1 or 2 (for "substantial" variability).

2. Service times may also vary from customer to customer and can be random variables. They are specified by the average service or processing time T_p (or its reciprocal, the average service rate or capacity K $(= 1/T_p$ for a single server)) and the standard deviation of the service times σ_s (or its coefficient of variation $c_s = K\sigma_s$).

While this suffices for the simplest queuing processes, more complex queuing systems may have several servers, a limited input buffer or waiting room,

---

[1]Little's law shows that average queue length = throughput × average waiting time.

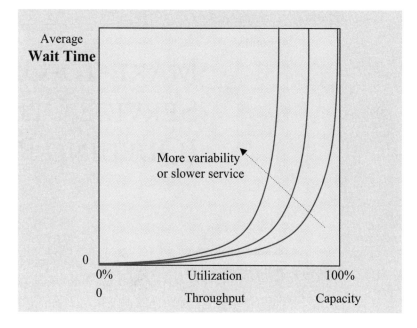

Figure C.1 A key insight to be gained from queuing theory is that the average wait time strongly increases with capacity utilization. More variability in arrival or service times also degrades performance.

several input buffers for different customers types, several stages or even a network of servers.

The average waiting time formula and additional insights

For simple make-to-order processes, queuing theory provides us with analytical expressions that help us predict responsiveness. For a single server, the average *waiting* time w is

$$\text{Average waiting time } w \;\; \cong \;\; T_p \frac{\rho}{1-\rho} \frac{c_a^2 + c_s^2}{2}.$$
$$= \;\; \text{service} \times \text{utilization} \times \text{variability}.$$

While general queuing systems are difficult to analyze, they all share this key insight from queuing theory: waiting and flow time are affected by three drivers, as illustrated by Figure C.1:

1. service effect: longer average service times T_p increase the wait,

2. utilization effect: the wait increases strongly and non-linearly as the average capacity utilization $\rho = R/K$ increases,

3. variability effect: more variability in customer arrivals or service times increases the wait.

Waiting time distribution function

For simple queuing processes, the actual waiting times experienced by customers, i.e. the random variable W, is approximately[2] exponentially distributed, with mean w, meaning that

$$\text{Waiting time distribution } \Pr\left(W > t\right) \cong \rho \exp(-t/w).$$

In addition, if the service times of a single server queue are exponentially distributed, then so are the total *flow* times:

$$\text{Flow time distribution } \Pr\left(T > t\right) \cong e^{-t/(w+T_p)}.$$

---

[2]This so-called Kingman bound is exact for Poisson arrivals ($C_a = 1$) and is a good approximation for highly-utilized processes.

Appendix D

SIMPLE FORECASTING TECHNIQUES

Here we review some simple forecasting techniques worthwhile knowing.

Forecasting a single random variable

Techniques to forecast a single random variable X (e.g., a product's monthly demand) strongly depend on the availability of data. Here are a few possibilities:

1. You have past demand data for that same product. In statistical terms, you have realizations of random variables X_i that are independent and identically distributed like X. This is the easiest case: the histogram of the data directly gives you an empirical distribution. If you compute the mean and standard deviation of the data, which can easily be done in a spreadsheet, you find the mean and standard deviation of the forecast (whether you then use the normal or the empirical distribution).

2. You have an estimate of the product's expected demand (i.e., a *point forecast*) and data on past point forecasts and actual demands of other products. These other products may or may not be similar to the product under consideration as long as you believe that their *relative forecast errors* are similar, meaning that their *A/F ratios*, where

$$A/F \text{ ratio } = \frac{\text{Actual demand}}{\text{Point forecast}},$$

are independent and identically distributed like the A/F ratio of X. Compute the A/F ratio for each product in the data set, and then compute the mean and standard deviation of all the A/F ratios. Then, the best approximating normal forecast has the following mean and standard deviation:

$$
\begin{aligned}
\text{mean} &= (\text{expected A/F ratio}) \times (\text{Point forecast}) \\
\text{st. dev.} &= (\text{st. dev. of A/F ratios}) \times (\text{Point forecast}).
\end{aligned}
$$

3. You have no past demand data. It is then reasonable to estimate a likely range of outcomes by estimating two numbers: a likely minimum and maximum value, such that you believe that X will fall in between them with, for example, 90% probability. In statistical terms, these two numbers

are estimates of the fifth and 95th percentile of X's probability distribution and define a 90% confidence interval. The best approximating normal forecast then has a:

$$\text{mean} = \frac{\text{95th percentile} + \text{5th percentile}}{2},$$

$$\text{standard deviation} = \frac{\text{95th percentile} - \text{5th percentile}}{3.3}.$$

It would be even better to ask every knowledgeable person in relevant functions (e.g., sales, marketing, production, etc.) for their subjective likely minimum and maximum. Then, compute every subjective mean and standard deviation and simply average them to arrive at a reasonable forecast of mean and standard deviation. However, more sophisticated techniques exist.

Forecasting a quantity over time (a stochastic process)

Constructing a forecast of a quantity X_t that evolves over time requires much more work. In practice, a simple yet powerful technique is scenario analysis. Specify a set of specific *scenarios* of the evolution of X over time, also called a set of *sample paths*, with associated probabilities. These scenarios can be manually constructed to represent your approximation of the evolution of the underlying quantity, or can be the result from simulation of the quantity. Scenario analysis and spreadsheets go hand in hand.

GLOSSARY

Principles

Principle 1 (Value Maximization) The goal of strategy is to maximize the net present value of the organization.

Principle 2 (Alignment) Operations strategy should develop resources and configure processes such that the resulting competencies are aligned with the competitive position that a firm seeks over time.

Principle 3 (Trade-offs) Operational competencies are governed by tradeoffs that are defined by the operational system of resources and processes.

Principle 4 (Focus) Operational focus increases operational efficiency.

Principle 5 (Forecasts) Forecasts should contain all available information on the future evolution of demand, supply, technology, competition and environment. At a minimum, each forecast must specify the expected value (mean) and volatility (standard deviation or coefficient of variation) by time bucket. Aggregate forecasts are more precise.

Principle 6 (Volatility) Capacity is a real option whose value typically decreases when volatility increases.

Principle 7 (Flexibility) The value of flexibility exhibits decreasing returns. A little flexibility goes a long way and is often preferred to full flexibility.

Symbols

24-5 vs. 24-7 operations 24 hours a day, 7 days a week production mode.

A

Aggregate planning Acquisition and allocation of limited resources (inventory, workforce, overtime, etc.) to production activities so as to satisfy deterministic customer demands over a short to medium-length time horizon.

Agile automated production Production strategy that relies on highly flexible production facilities making use of automated flexible machinery and cross-trained workers.

Agile worker-based production Production strategy that relies on systems with cross-trained operators and equipment whose operation requires constant human presence.

Agility-flexibility Measure of the speed at which an asset can change from one activity to another.

Alignment Concept of developing resources and configuring processes such that the resulting competencies are fitted or matched with the competitive position that a firm seeks over time.

Alliance Joint venture where two or more firms agree to collaborate on a project or to share information or productive resources.

Annuity A finite sequence of identical cash flows.

Arms length (transaction) A transactional market exchange in which the buyers and sellers of a product act independently and have no relationship to each other, in order to ensure that both parties act in their own interest and are not subject to any pressure from the other party.

Assemble-to-Order (ATO) Strategy where assembly or completion is executed after the customer order is known and never builds in advance of demand.

Asset specificity Characteristic of the supply technology that is specific to one user, causing external suppliers to have little incentive to invest because such investments are susceptible to ex-post expropriation.

Automation Measure of the degree to which a process can operate without human supervision.

B

Backlogging Production and sales strategy that involves putting excess-demand customers on a waiting list.

Backlogging-smoothing capacity strategy Capacity strategy that puts puts excess demand onto a waiting list. Hybrid between leading and lagging, the counterpart of the inventory-smoothing capacity strategy.

Badge engineering The wholesale part-sharing and selling of nearly identical finished products under different names or brands.

Balanced sourcing Strategic sourcing strategy that aims for long-term sourcing relationships that are neither overly trusting nor too adversarial.

Benchmarking Practice of evaluating an organization's practices relative to best available practices.

Booking limit The maximum number of advance orders a company decides to accept.

Bottleneck Any real asset whose resource capacity may constrain the total output of the network.

Bricks and clicks strategy Business model that integrates retail stores and Internet channels.

Brook's law Adding manpower to a late software project makes it later.

Brownfield expansion Strategic capacity expansion that involves adding floor space, employees, and equipment to a current facility.

Brownian motion Mathematical model to explain random events through continuous-time stochastic processes.

Build-to-order *see* Assemble-to-Order (ATO)

C

Capacity The maximal sustainable output rate of a resource.

Capacity controls Techniques designed to influence demand by restricting the availability of supply (while keeping prices fixed).

Capacity frictions Forces that prevent quick, precise, and cheap changes to capacity.

Capacity-inventory-waiting triangle The tradeoff triangle of safety capacity, backlogging, and keeping inventory to mitigate the degrading impact of volatility.

Capacity expansion (contraction) Strategic capacity strategy that includes different ways of adjusting capacity: brownfield expansion, greenfield expansion, outsourcing, subcontracting, and alliances, process improvement and restructuring at current facilities, adding operating shift or days, overtime, inventory buildup, temporary work, etc.).

Capacity location Resource strategy that deals with finding appropriate geographical sites and assigning roles to them.

Capacity portfolio The complete vector of capacity levels of all resources.

Capacity sizing Resource strategy that determines the capacity, in aggregate and per main resource type.

Capacity requirements planning (CRP) Planning model that verifies whether a production plan is feasible given the current capacity i.e., it checks the feasibility of resource allocation rather than planning resource investment or adjustments.

Capacity reservation rule Accept a current request if its revenue (margin) exceeds the displacement cost.

Capacity strategy Operations strategy that involves decisions on the sizing, timing, type, and location of each resource in the processing network.

Capacity timing Resource strategy that determines the availability of capacity and the timing of capacity adjustments.

Capacity type Resource strategy that determines the nature of each resource.

Capacity utilization The level at which a resource is operated at any given time, typically a fraction of the resource capacity.

Capital appropriation request Request plant managers must submit to senior managers in order to make longer-term equipment purchases and install new capacity.

Capital Expenditure (CapEx) Expenditure used by a company to acquire or upgrade real assets (equipment, property, buildings, etc.).

Cash Flow The amounts of cash received or spent over time.

Centralization Consolidating operations in a single location, typically observed when bigger is better.

Central limit theorem Result in probability theory that states that the average of many random variables with finite variance is approximately normally distributed (i.e., follows a Gaussian distribution).

Chaining Allocating resources to products such that all resources and products are connected via one chain of links.

Changeover cost Cost a firm incurs when switching production from one product to another.

Charters Mission statements of an organization for each of its separate operations to maintain focus.

Code sharing Alliance in the airline industry that allows each airline to sell tickets for flights operated by any alliance partner.

Coefficient of risk aversion Measure of a player's risk aversion in the modern portfolio theory model.

Coefficient of variation (COV) Measure of relative volatility or forecast precision, equal to the ratio between the standard deviation and the mean.

Collaboration technology Information technology that allows collaboration in planning and execution.

Commercial risk Any exposure to hazards that originate in marketing and sales and negatively impacts revenues, includes the risk that new products or services are not adopted, cash risks (e.g., sales prices are less than expected), or receivables risks (when customers dont pay).

Commodity business plan A sourcing strategy.

Component commonality Design strategy whereby different products or services share a common component.

Competencies The set of outputs, products, and services that the operation will be particularly good at providing.

Competitive intelligence The action of gathering, analyzing, and applying information about products, domain constituents, customers, and competitors for the short term and long term planning needs of an organization.

Complexity Project or product complexity is roughly estimated as the product of all elements times their interactions.

Complexity cost Additional cost incurred due to the complexity of the operational system.

Compound annual growth rate (CAGR) The growth of revenue over a period of time.

Concurrent design and engineering Simultaneously design of the product and the process to produce it.

Continuation value An estimate of the value of ongoing operations evaluated at a certain time.

Continuous improvement The aggregate result of all the small improvements in how work gets done that people are constantly making throughout the organization.

Contract A set of rules that control the three flows in a processing network: the flow of material, information, and cash. To be effective, the contract should be specified in terms that are verifiable by an independent third party (the judge) and its stipulations should be enforceable.

Contract manufacturer A firm that manufactures components or products for another hiring company.

Coordinating (efficient) contract A contract achieving supply chain-optimal profits.

Coordination & information risk Any uncertainty in coordination and information that may stem from internal miscommunication and often result in internal demand-supply mismatches, including information technology system failures in hardware, software, local and wide area networks, forecasting risks, computer virus risks, and errors during order-taking, receiving, etc.

Coordination and information technology *see* Collaboration technology

Core (activities) Activities that are critical to the business, that differentiate the company from competitors, and that provide a competitive advantage.

Corporate social responsibility (CSR) Concept that organizations have an obligation to consider the interests of customers, employees, shareholders, communities, and ecological considerations in all aspects of their operations.

Corporate strategy Strategy within a corporation that defines the industries in which the organization will be active, configures business units for each industry, and acquires and allocates corporate resources to each business.

Cost-plus contract Contract under which a customer agrees to reimburse the supplier for its total costs and to also pay whatever sum will give the supplier its desired profit margin.

Cost to serve The cost to fill an average order.

Covariance The measure of how much two random variables vary together.

Creative destruction Capitalist free market perspective highlighted by Joseph Schumpeter which states that innovative entry by entrepreneurs is the force that sustains long-term economic growth, even if it destroys the value of established companies that enjoy some degree of monopoly power.

Critical fractile Ratio that gives the solution to the newsvendor problem.

Cross-docking Practice in logistics of unloading materials from an incoming semi-trailer truck or rail car and loading these materials in outbound trailers or rail cars, with little or no storage in between.

Cross-training Training in multiple tasks or ways.

Cube-square rule Mathematical rule which yields that the degree of the scale economies is around 2/3 in the case of a power CapEx function.

Currency risk Risk that arises from the change in price of one currency against another.

Customer surplus Net value a customer enjoys when value exceeds the price of the product or service the customer acquires.

Customer centric view Process view that defines value from the perspective of the customer: a value-added activity is an activity that is valued by the customer.

Customer Relationship Management (CRM) Data-gathering methods to collect information about a firm's customers.

Customer value proposition A clearly articulated set of benefits that the firm offers to its customers.

D

Decision tree A decision support tool that uses a graph or model of decisions and their possible consequences, including chance event outcomes, resource costs, and utility, used to identify the strategy most likely to reach a goal or to calculate conditional probabilities.

Dedicated asset (resource) Asset (resource) that performs a single or very limited range of tasks.

Dedicated network Base-case operational network that employs dedicated resources and processes.

Demand management The set of activities that influence the demand for products and services, including many, if not all, marketing activities, as well as sales and service activities.

Demand planning The function of recognizing all demands for products and services to support the marketplace, by encompassing the activities of forecasting, order entry, order promising, etc.

Demand pooling Operational risk strategy that involves serving diverse markets with one resource (e.g., a centralized warehouse stocking one product to serve multiple areas, or a single facility supplying multiple markets).

Demand risk Any uncertainty in quantities demanded or supplied for a given product or service at a given time.

Demand-chasing strategy Capacity strategy that involves instantaneously adjusting capacity to mirror any demand change, in the absence of capacity adjustment frictions.

Depreciation Accounting practice of spreading the investment cost over several years, in order to deduct it from taxable income.

Design structure matrix (DSM) A practical tool that maps the dependency between components or tasks to estimate the complexity of a design or project.

Discount rate The opportunity cost of capital.

Discounted cash flow (DCF) The present value of a future cash flow.

Discounting The analytic tool that expresses the present value of a future cash flow.

Displacement cost The opportunity cost of reserving assets for current demand.

Disruptions Unlikely hazards with high impact.

Disruptive innovation or technology An initially inferior innovation that ultimately dominates original leaders.

Distributed network Network design strategy involving networks that operate in many locations when the business and market structure is best described by the concept that closer is better.

Diversification The practice of serving multiple risks (e.g., product demands) from one portfolio or network.

Double marginalization Value chain problem that arises as the supplier captures only a part of the total returns and thus has lower incentives for investment and improvement than would be optimal for the value chain as a whole.

Dynamic pricing The sales tactic of varying price over time in response to changes in demand or supply conditions.

E

Economic lot sizing problem (ELSP) Model of homogeneous goods cyclic schedule where each cycle produces until its product inventory reaches a certain level.

Economic order quantity (EOQ) Optimal quantity to order that minimizes the sum of holding and fixed ordering costs.

Economic Value Added (EVA) Net operating profit after taxes minus the opportunity cost of invested capital.

Economies of scale Situation in which an increase in the scale of production causes a decrease in the long run average cost of each produced unit i.e., an equal percentage increase in all inputs results in a greater percentage increase in output.

Economies of scope Situation in which incremental value is obtained from sharing assets over several markets or products.

Efficiency Concept of how well resources are used relative to their optimal use.

Efficient frontier A snapshot that traces the lowest cost in an industry to produce specific competency bundles of variety, quality, and timeliness.

Efficient portfolio Any portfolio that lies on the mean-variance frontier i.e., there is no other portfolio with same expected return but less risk.

Employee involvement Production practice at Harley-Davidson, part of the "Productivity Triad", that involved enlisting the full participation of all employees to solve problems and control quality.

Encroachment strategy Sales strategy that makes a new product encroach on the existing market from either the high-end (high-end encroachment) or low-end (low-end encroachment).

Eurosclerosis Employment problem in Europe frequently attributed to rigid, slow-moving labor markets.

Excess demand Demand that cannot be satisfied given current or planned capacity.

Experience curve The cost formulation of the learning curve: marginal cost decreases by a constant fraction whenever cumulative output is doubled.

F

Facility strategy Strategy that involves decisions on the size, location, and type (or role) of individual facilities.

Fill rate The ratio between expected sales and the expected demand.

Financial assets Claims on a firm's real assets such as stocks, bonds, etc.

Financial hedging Risk mitigation strategy that involves financial instruments such as forwards, options, swaps, etc.

Financial strategy Strategy of a corporation that specifies how capital is raised and invested.

Fixed-price (price-only) contract Contract that specifies a fixed price per transaction unit, or for the entire sourced project or service. (Transfer price arrangements between internal groups in a company also fall into this class.)

Flexible (adaptable) capacity A resource that can produce multiple products or quickly satisfy new requirements.

Flexibility routing Dynamic decision making on routes in network control.

Focus A sharply directed or concentrated activity, attention, or energy.

Focused operation Operation whose required competencies are restricted to a narrow set in the competency space of cost, variety, speed, and quality.

Forecast Prediction about the future.

Forward contract An agreement between two parties to buy or sell an asset (which can be of any kind) at a pre-agreed future point in time.

Franchising Management agreement where a franchisor licenses trademarks and process knowledge to a franchisee in exchange for a recurring payment, and usually a percentage piece of gross sales or gross profits as well as the annual fees.

Future contract A standardized contract, traded on a futures exchange, to buy or sell a certain underlying instrument at a certain date in the future, at a specified price.

G

Gain (profit) sharing contract Contract under which parties agree on the baseline cost of providing a service. If the actual cost exceeds the baseline cost, the provider receives the difference; otherwise, the difference is split between the two parties in an agreed ratio.

Game theory Branch of applied mathematics and economics that studies situations where multiple players make decisions with the goal of maximizing their payoffs.

General-purpose asset (resource) Asset that can perform an endless variety of tasks.

Generalist *see* General-purpose asset (resource)

Global network *see* Global operations

Global operations Operations where process flows cross national boundaries.

Globalization The set of various processes (cultural, social, political, economic, and technological) that lead to increased interaction among disparate locations across the globe.

Greenfield expansion Strategic capacity expansion that involves building a new facility, having the highest flexibility in terms of size and location of adding capacity, but also being the most expensive and incurring the longest leadtimes.

H

Hazard Potential source of danger, where danger is defined as any cause that can have a negative impact on the net present value of the firm.

Hedging The process of mitigating risk, often by taking on one risk to offset an other.

Holding cost Cost to keep a unit in inventory for a unit of time

Holdup problem Situation where two parties (e.g., supplier and manufacturer) could perform better by cooperating but have no incentive of doing so. E.g., if the supply technology is specific to one manufacturer, external suppliers have little incentive to invest because such investments are susceptible to ex-post expropriation.

Horizontal integration Serving different end-markets (locations) from one network.

Hurdle rate The discount rate of a financial project.

Hybrid solution A solution that involves a mixture or compromise of different extreme solutions.

I

Improvement Making something better.

Incomplete contract Contract that does not detail all possible contingencies, typically due to complexity or unforeseeable uncertainty.

Increasing returns to scale *see* Economies of scale

Incremental investing Under the assumption that capacity is endlessly divisble (i.e., continous variable) investment can be performed gradually to match capacity with demand precisely.

Innovation risk Any exposure to hazards that originate during research and development.

Innovation Radical and/or incremental changes to products, processes or services.

Insourcing Sourcing strategy where the supply relationship is internal.

Integrated Device Manufacturer (IDM) A semiconductor company which designs, manufactures, and sells integrated circuit products.

Inventory pooling *see* Pooling

Inventory risk Any exposure of inventory to spoilage, damage, or loss.

Inventory-smoothing strategy Capacity strategy that builds excess capacity into inventory to supply the subsequent under-capacitated period. Hybrid between leading and lagging, the counterpart of the backlogging- smoothing capacity strategy.

Investment Cash flow stemming from capacity expansion and contraction in the expectation of future rewards.

Investment cost One-time cost a firm incurs when acquiring a real asset.

Investment frictions *see* Capacity frictions

Irreversibility State of the capacity adjustment timing where the salvage value from reducing capacity is less than the cost of adding capacity so that a reduction will not make up for a future expansion of equal size.

J

Joint Venture (JV) Entity formed between two or more parties to undertake economic activity together, that share the revenues, expenses, and control of the enterprise, in the form of a specific project partnership or a continuing business relationship.

Just-in-Time (JIT) Operations management to synchronize supply with demand: supplies arrive at the right location, in the right quantity, precisely when needed.

K

Kaizen "Change for the better"–lean operations philosophy promoted by the Toyota Production System that involves making problems or opportunities for improvement visible and relies on a positively-inclined human infrastructure to eliminate those problems.

Key Performance Indicator (KPI) A metrics that is necessary to predict organizational performance.

Knowledge based sourcing Another term for balanced sourcing.

L

Lagging capacity strategy Capacity strategy that expands capacity reactively after there is sufficient demand to use the majority of additional capacity.

Late customization Process design strategy that delays customer-specific activities such as product assembly or service completion, so that earlier activities can be common to all customers.

Leading capacity strategy Capacity strategy that builds capacity in anticipation of demand growth.

Leadtime The lag time between the investment decision epoch and the availability of that new capacity.

Lean operations Operations management philosophy derived from the Toyota Production System that focuses on continuous waste elimination.

Learning-by-doing The process of learning during execution or from experience.

Learning curve The empirical relationship between marginal input requirements (direct labor hours per unit) and cumulative production.

Level production strategy Production strategy that produces equal amounts over a period of time.

Little's Law Average inventory = Average throughput × Average flow time.

Littlewood's rule Optimal capacity segmentation rule that states that it is optimal to keep accepting advance reservations as long as their profit exceeds the expected profit of a regular reservation.

Location strategy A structured approach to deciding where to expand or contract capacity.

Logistics Managing the flow of cash, material, and information from the source of production to the marketplace.

Lost sale Capacity shortage short-term effect that results when a customer no longer wants the service or when she goes to a rival.

M

Make-to-order (MTO) Process that holds inventory (orders, customers, etc.) in input buffers or queues.

Make-to-stock (MTS) Process that holds inventory (orders, customers, etc.) in finished form or output buffers.

Markdown pricing Dynamic pricing tactic that decreases price over time to clear leftover inventory. reflecting decreasing customer valuation near the end of the season.

Marketing and sales strategy Strategy of a corporation that specifies how the market will be segmented and how the product will be positioned, priced, and promoted.

Mass customization Compromise between mass production and full custom work that balances the demand benefits of customization with the supply efficiencies of standardization by limiting customer choice to a pre-set range while increasing the flexibility of a flow process.

Master production schedule (MPS) Plan that details production quantities per period for each product.

Mean-Variance frontier The efficient frontier in Markowitz optimal portfolio selection model, that comprises the best available portfolios in term of expected return for any given risk level of portfolio value.

Mismatch risk Any possible mismatch between supply and demand, excess or shortage.

Moores Law Empirical observation made by Intel co-founder Gordon Moore in 1965 that the transistor density on integrated circuits doubles every 18 months.

N

Natural hedging Currency risk mitigation strategy that involves producing and selling locally.

Natural risk Background risk that reflects exposure to natural hazards such as earthquakes, heavy rains, lightning, hail storms, fires, and tornados, the exposure typically depending on the location of the organization.

Net Present Value (NPV) Present value of its future cash flows minus the investment today that is necessary to generate those future flows.

Network architecture, design, topology Descriptions of the composition of a network.

Newsvendor model (Typically single-period) Model to determine how many assets (newspapers) to acquire at a given unit cost for sale at a given price but recognizing that demand is uncertain.

Normal distribution The Gaussian probability distribution.

O

Offshoring Locating operations abroad.

Operating cost Cost a firm incurs every time a real asset is used.

Operational hedging Risk mitigation strategy that involves operational instruments: reserves and redundancy; diversification and pooling; risk-sharing and transfer; and reducing or eliminating root causes of risk.

Operational effectiveness Relative term to denote how well an operations is achieving strategic objectives. (Measures operational efficiency in the direction of the strategic value proposition and not just in terms of cost.)

Operational efficiency Characteristic of a firm whose competency bundle falls on the efficient frontier, denoting a company that has best-in-class systems, whose challenge is to stay on the frontier by constantly improving and innovating, thereby pushing the frontier outward.

Operations strategy A plan for developing resources and configuring processes such that the resulting competencies maximize net present value.

Operational system The ensemble of resources and processes of an organization.

Option (financial) A contract that gives the holders the right, but not the obligation, to buy or sell a set amount of securities or commodities at a set level.

Option to switch Decision within the capacity strategy that involves switching capacity allocation to the more profitable product, given the capacity flexibility.

Option to wait Decision within the capacity strategy that involves delaying the adjustment of the capacity portfolio for a given period of time.

Option value of waiting The difference between the expected net present value of waiting and the expected net present value of expanding now.

Outsourcing Delegation of non-core operations from internal production to a third party.

Overbooking The practice of selling more reservations than actual available capacity in orderd to improve actual capacity utilization and revenue.

P

Path dependence Characteristic that future dynamics are depended on past actions.

Peak-load pricing Dynamic pricing tactic that increases price during periods of high demand while supply remains constant. It is widely practiced in industries with fixed supply but changing demand over the day, week, or season.

Perpetuity An infinite sequence of identical cash flows.

Planned cost differential Change in cost due to a deviation from planned operating conditions (while keeping strategic positioning unchanged).

Plant within a plant The result of dividing a facility both organizationally and physically.

Platform sharing Originally, the practice of sharing a common wheelbase, powertrain, and other elements among different automobile models; nowadays, one group of engineers who design several vehicles from a common vehicle architecture.

Point forecast A single point prediction that disregards uncertainty.

Political risk Any negative, unexpected change in laws and regulation such as a breach in business contracts without recourse to legal action, unexpected strengthening in environmental or labor laws, unexpected currency devaluations, outbreak of war, etc.

Pooling The practice of aggregation, typically to reduce aggregate risk.

Portfolio A collection (of assets, products, processes, etc.) typically held by one owner.

Postponement Similar to late customization, the practice of delaying customer-specific activities such as product assembly or service completion, so that earlier activities can be common to all customers.

Price controls Techniques designed to influence demand by varying the price.

Price discrimination Practice of selling the same product at different prices to different market segments.

Process Structured, recurrent activities that transform inputs into outputs; network of activities with specific precedence relationships.

Process architecture, design, layout, structure Descriptions of the composition of a process.

Process cost Total cost of operating, including variable and fixed costs.

Process flexibility Operational ability to change inputs, activities, volumes, or outputs.

Process view Operational perspective that considers an organization (or any of its parts) to be an activity network or a collection of processes.

Procurement The simplest and most extreme form of outsourcing, refers to the tactical sourcing of off-the-shelf goods or services using an arms-length relationship.

Product life cycle The succession of stages a product goes through, when its attributes change, and with it the required process competencies i.e., service, timeliness, and flexibility are more important in the introduction and decline phases of the life cycle, while cost and quality are crucial for mature products and services.

Product-process matrix A tool to verify the degree of alignment between the product concept and the process technology.

Product technology Technology that describes the design philosophy, product architecture, and product capabilities (often as perceived by the customer).

Productivity Measure of the efficiency of transforming inputs into outputs over a given time period.

Promotional pricing Dynamic pricing tactic that includes discounting, normally within a limited period.

Protectionism Set of measures adopted to protect domestic economies from foreign competition can induce these competitors to set up local operations.

Purchasing *see* Procurement

Q

Quality The degree of excellence of the process, product, or service, with design-related dimensions such as performance and features, as well as process-related dimensions such as durability and reliability.

Quality of Service (QoS) A set of quality requirements on the collective behavior of a product or service.

Quota Time-measured quantity restriction on imports.

Queuing theory The mathematical study of waiting lines (queues).

R

Ramp time Required time between startup (producing first unit) to reaching full throughput capacity.

Random yield Probability that a unit ordered is of acceptable quality.

Reactive capacity An extreme form of postponement: instead of proactively deciding on capacity, building capacity when demand is known eliminates the need for forecasting.

Real assets All the means an organization needs to coordinate and perform its activities, excluding financial assets.

Real option The ability to have contingent decision making, typically involving the operation of a real asset.

Redundancy Characteristic of a product or process (such as quality) that exceeds the required level.

Reengineering Fundamental rethinking and radical redesign of business processes in order to achieve dramatic improvements in critical contemporary measures of performance such as cost, quality, service and speed.

Reservation price *see* Willingness to pay (WTP)

Resource *see* Real assets

Resource planning *see* Capacity planning

Resource pooling The practice of aggregating all asset capacity in order to prevent asynchronized idleness and to decrease statistical dependence among customers.

Resource sharing Process design which involves that different activities share the same, flexible resources; the counterpart of component sharing.

Resource view Operational perspective that considers any organization (or any of its parts) as a bundle of real assets.

Revenue management The collection of demand management practices that aim to maximize the revenue of available supply.

Risk The exposure to a chance of loss or damage.

Risk (*finance*) The possibility that the actual outcome is likely to diverge (deviate) from the expected value.

Risk (*operational*) Risk that stems from operations (i.e. from activities and assets), meaning any potential source generating a negative impact on the flow of information, goods, and cash in the operations.

Risk assessment Step in any risk management program that analyzes the degree of risk associated with each hazard.

Risk management The broad activity of planning and decision-making designed to deal with the occurrence of hazards or risks.

Risk map A graphical representation of an expert opinions risk assessment for a specific organization that shows the impact versus likelihood of occurrence for each hazard.

Risk pooling Risk management technique of aggregating the volatilities of the elements of a portfolio in order to reduce the total relative volatility of the portfolio.

Risk-reward frontier The best trade-off between risk

and expected return; *see* Mean-Variance frontier

Robustness Term used to denote that performance (e.g., cost efficiency, quality, or responsiveness) does not vary much over the range of activities performed.

Routine An informal process.

Routing flexibility Dynamic decision making on routes within the network design strategies.

S

Safety (excess) capacity The difference between capacity and average demand.

Sales plan Plan put together by the marketing and sales division where the demand forecast is summarized through a process of aggregation and negotiation.

Scenarios A set of sample path that provide a good approximation of the evolution of the underlying quantity.

Scorecard A method of conveying a set of metrics that give managers a (ideally comprehensive) view of the performance of a business.

Seasonality Predictable variation over time.

Selling-up The practice of decreasing shortfall penalties that involves stimulating customers to trade-up for money.

Service customization The tactic of adjusting service (or even the good) to the individual customer, including the use of priority systems and mass customization.

Service guarantee Level of service quality a firm proposes to its customers against a penalty cost incurred in case the promise is not accomplished.

Service level agreement (SLA) Part of a structured contract where the level of service is formally defined.

Service risk Any exposure to hazards during after-sale service interactions, including the lack of procedures to deal with product returns, problems, and service inquiries.

Setup (change-over) cost The cost a make-to-stock process incurs when switching production from one product to another.

Shipping in line sequence (SILS) JIT of different products exactly in the sequence demanded.

Shortfall rate The ratio between expected capacity shortfall and expected demand.

Six-Sigma A continuous improvement philosophy to reduce variability.

Sourcing The process of building interfaces and relationships with suppliers.

Sourcing cost differential Change in cost due to a deviation of the sourcing costs from the planned (standard) costs.

Sourcing risk Any hazards that may result from the interaction with suppliers.

Spot market Market (of commodities, securities, etc.) in which goods are sold for cash and delivered immediately.

Standard loss function Function used to calculate the expected capacity shortfall under normal demand.

Stochastic linear programming Framework for modeling optimization problems that involve uncertainty, available in most spreadsheet optimization tools.

Statistical process control (SPC) Method of monitoring a process through the use of control charts.

Strategic inflection point A moment in the evolution of a business when change is signalled in the strategy of the company, both positively and negatively.

Strategic operational audit Practice of "taking stock" of an organizations operation to assess its degree of fit with competitive strategy and to identify where improvements can be made, by applying the top-down and bottom-up perspectives simultaneously.

Strategic sourcing The process of deciding on appropriate supply relationships for each activity in the value chain.

Strategy cost differential Change in cost due to a change in market positioning.

Structured contract Contract designed to to align business objectives and balance risk as an attempt to produce integrated work flows with greater throughput and profitability.

SWOT (Strengths, Weakness, Opportunities & Threats)

Subcontracting The practice of signing a contract with a third party to provide all or part of the capacity needs of company.

Substitution Situation when a customer chooses another product or service of the same firm.

Supplier relationship management (SRM) Set of practices involved in defining, establishing, and managing the bilateral relationship (often, but not always, involving contracting) to align incentives.

Supply pooling Operational hedging strategy that involves serving one demand from multiple suppliers (e.g., multi-sourcing of a single component).

Supply risk Any uncertainty in quantities supplied for a given product or service at a given time.

Swap Contract between two parties specifying the exchange of a series of payments at specified intervals over a specified period of time.

T

Tactics The execution of plans by deployment of forces.

Tailoring The practice of using the most appropriate asset or activity for the situation.

Tariff (duty) Tax on foreign goods, often collected by custom officers at entry points.

Tax shield The reduction in income taxes that results from taking an allowable deduction from taxable income.

Technical risk The innovation risk of a new technology or product.

Tier 1 supplier Supplier under direct contract with the outsourcing company.

Tiered supply system A hierarchical sourcing strategy.

Total cost of ownership (TCO) Cost that originally accounted for all the costs associated with buying and owning an asset and that nowadays includes the evaluation of the total cost of sourcing and of using any activity provided by a given supplier.

Total factor productivity (TFP) Output growth not accounted for by the growth in inputs.

Total landed cost (TLC) The total end-to-end cost from inputs to outputs at customers.

Total Quality Management (TQM) Management strategy aimed to implant awareness of quality in all organizational processes.

Trade-off A balancing of factors all of which are not attainable at the same time; a giving up of one thing in return for another.

Trading-up The practice of decreasing shortage penalties that involves giving an overbooked customer a substituting, but higher-quality asset.

Transshipment Relocation of assets.

Turn-and-earn Practice employed by firms of controlling the allocation of capacity to various channels when demand exceeds capacity, which gives an additional lever to reward good channels or customers.

U

Unk unks Unknown unknowns–variables that impact a process but that the manager is not aware of.

V

Value chain The process view of an organization that emphasizes the activities through which value is provided to the customer. It starts with inputs and ends with the distribution and sales of goods and services.

Value stream mapping Representation of the process view that emphasizes a customer-centric view and defines value from the perspective of the customer: a value-added activity is an activity that benefits the customer.

Value-at-Risk (VaR) Risk metric that measures the worst expected loss at a given confidence level.

Variance The expected squared deviation around the mean.

Vertical chain *see* Value chain

Vertical disintegration Breaking up the value chain into separate companies, each performing a limited subset of activities required to create a finished product.

Vertical integration Management strategy that involves ownership and control of upstream suppliers and downstream buyers and an extensive performance of activities in the vertical chain.

Volatility Uncertain variability.

W

Waiting penalty Cost a firm incurs per unit time that a customer is waiting.

Waiting time Total time a customer on a waiting list must wait before he or she is served.

Warranty Obligation that a product or service is sold as stated by the company's value proposition and that often provides for a repair or replacement in the event the product or service fails to meet the warranty.

Weighted average cost of capital (WACC) The weighted average between the return on its debt and on its equity.

Willingness to pay (WTP) The highest amount a customer is willing to pay for a product or service.

Work flow Flow through the process.

Working capital Current assets (inventory, cash, etc.) and current liabilities.

Y

Yield Rate of return of a financial instrument or operational project.

Yield management Capacity strategy that uses reservation systems and booking controls to accept and allocate demand to available capacity.

NOTATION

Greek symbols

α = Degree of scale economies, 83

γ = Coefficient of absolute risk aversion, 325

Δc_{OE} = Efficiency cost differential, 49

Δc_{plan} = Planned cost differential, 46

$\Delta c_{plan\ (sourcing)}$ = Sourcing cost differential, 46

$\Delta c_{plan\ (utilization)}$ = Utilization cost differential, 47

Δc_{strat} = Strategy cost differential, 45

$\mathbb{E}X$ = Expected value of X, 324

ε_{X_t} = Forecast error of X_t, 79

λ = Slope of learning curve (in log-log scale), 362

μ = Expected payoff, 325

μ_i = Mean of D_i, 173

$\Pi(K)$ = Operating profit rate, 115

ρ = Average capacity utilization, 98

ρ = Correlation coefficient between D_1 and D_2, 173

σ = Standard deviation, volatility, 87, 324

σ_a = Standard deviation of inter-arrival times, 439

σ_{as} = Total volatility of inter-arrival and service times: $\sigma_{as}^2 = 0.5(C_a^2 + C_s^2)$, 98

σ_i = Standard deviation of D_i, 173

σ_s = Standard deviation of service times, 439

$\phi(x)$ = Probability density function of a standard normal random variable Z, 437

$\Phi(z) = Pr(Z <= z)$ = Cumulative distribution function of standard normal variable Z, 438

A

AC = Average cost per unit, 363

C

c = Unit cost, 40

c_0 = Fixed cost component in CapEx, 82

c_h = Unit holding cost, 96

c_{HS} = Unit inventory and setup cost, 40

c_K = Marginal CapEx, 82

c_p = Shortfall penalty cost, 90

c_S = Setup cost, 66

c_w = Waiting penalty, 98

C_a = Coefficient of variation of inter-arrival times, 98

C_o = Overage cost, 257, 435

C_Q = Marginal value-added Cost of the Q-th produced unit, 362

C_s = Coefficient of variation of service times, 98

C_u = Marginal underage cost, 257, 435

$C(K)$ = Capital expenditure (CapEx) to install capacity K, 82

COV = Coefficient of variation, 79

CS = Consumer surplus, 310

D

D = Demand, 90

E

$\mathbb{E}X$ = Expected value of X, 324

ε_{X_t} = Forecast error of X_t, 79

F

$F(x)$ = Cumulative probability distribution function, 436

G

g = Demand growth rate, 124

GDP = Gross Domestic Product, 51

H

H = Unit holding cost, 39

I

I_t = Inventory at time t, 291

K

K = Capacity, 82

L

L = Learning rate, 362

$L(z)$ = Standard loss function, 92

M

$m =$ Operating profit margin, 90
$MC =$ Marginal Cost, 259
$MR =$ Marginal Revenue, 259
$MV =$ Mean-Variance preference, 325

N

$n =$ Number (e.g., of demand points), 436
$N =$ Number (e.g., of product types, dedicated systems), 39, 171
$NPV =$ Net Present Value, 4

P

$p =$ Price, 281
$p =$ Service probability, 175
$p_H =$ High-fare, 299
$p_L =$ Low-fare, 299
$p_{\text{sell-up}} =$ Sell-up probability, 304
$PV =$ Present Value, 125

Q

$q =$ Quantity, 281
$Q =$ Cumulative units produced, 362

R

$r =$ Discount rate, 99
$r =$ Radius of the linear delivery zone, 214
$R =$ Average throughput or flow rate, 40
$R^2 =$ R-Squared, 336
$R_i =$ Throughput rate in period i, 364

S

$s_i =$ Shortfall, 436
$S =$ Fixed cost per setup or order, 39
$SKU =$ Stock Keeping Unit, 46

T

$t =$ Time (e.g., of order execution, production rate switch), 42, 96
$t_S =$ Setup or changeover time, 66
$T =$ Flow Time, sum of waiting and activity times, 439
$T_p =$ Average processing (service or activity) time, 439
$TFP =$ Total Factor Productivity, 51

U

$U =$ Utility or customer value, 36

V

$v_i =$ Linear contribution margin of activity level x_i, 149

W

$w =$ Average waiting time, 98

$W =$ Actual waiting time (a random variable), 439
$WTP =$ Willingness-To-Pay (Reservation Price), 281

X

$x^* =$ The indifferent customer, 374
$x_i =$ Activity i's level, 149
$X =$ Non-cost competency level, 58
$X =$ Random variable or process, 79, 324
$X_t =$ Random variable at time t, 79
$\overline{X} =$ Mean (expected value) of X, 79, 324
$X^+ = \max(X, 0) =$ Positive part of X, 324

Z

$z =$ Standardized safety level or z-statistic, 90

NAME INDEX

SUBJECT INDEX